Peter Stimpson and Alastair Farquharson

Cambridge International AS and A Level

Business

Coursebook

Third Edition

CAMBRIDGE UNIVERSITY PRESS

CAMBRIDGE
UNIVERSITY PRESS

University Printing House, Cambridge CB2 8BS, United Kingdom

One Liberty Plaza, 20th Floor, New York, NY 10006, USA

477 Williamstown Road, Port Melbourne, VIC 3207, Australia

4843/24, 2nd Floor, Ansari Road, Daryaganj, Delhi – 110002, India

79 Anson Road, #06–04/06, Singapore 079906

Cambridge University Press is part of the University of Cambridge.

It furthers the University's mission by disseminating knowledge in the pursuit of education, learning and research at the highest international levels of excellence.

Information on this title: education.cambridge.org

First published 2002
Second published 2010
Third edition published 2015
20 19 18 17 16 15 14 13 12 11 10 9 8

Printed in Dubai by Oriental Press

A catalogue record for this publication is available from the British Library

ISBN 978-1-107-67736-4 Paperback

The questions, answers and commentary in this title are written by the authors and have not been produced by Cambridge International Examinations.

Contents

Introduction

Who is this book for?

The third edition of this book accurately and comprehensively follows the new Cambridge International AS and A Level Business syllabus (9609).

If you are a student studying this syllabus, or a teacher of the syllabus, you can be confident that the book provides complete coverage of the course to the appropriate level. Other students of Business or Business and Management could also benefit greatly from the subject content, activities and advice that this book contains. Students following the AQA, OCR or EDEXCEL A Levels, the Cambridge Pre-U course or the International Baccalaureate Higher and Standard Diploma Programme will also find this an invaluable resource.

The first and second editions were also used in higher education institutions as an introductory text for Management and Business Studies degree courses. The changes and additions made to this third edition will reinforce its usefulness for this purpose.

What makes this book different?

The key distinctive feature of this book is the international perspective it gives to the study of businesses, strategies and decisions. There are many references to case studies, data and examples from countries all around the world. This is deliberate – very few large businesses operate today in a narrow national marketplace and, as a Business Studies student, you are encouraged to look at business organisations and business decisions from an international viewpoint that accurately mirrors the real world.

The focus on business strategic decision-making in the final unit means that the book also highlights some very important aspects of business management:

- Strategic decision-making is holistic and cannot be undertaken effectively by studying a series of unconnected subject areas.
- There is no one perfect solution to a business problem – a variety of different strategic solutions might exist that reflect the objectives of the business, the external environment and the cultures of both the organisation and the country in which it operates.

Differences between AS and A Level

There are two important differences between the AS and A Level syllabus:

1. More subject content is examined at A Level than at AS.
2. The examination skills are weighted differently – much more emphasis is placed on subject knowledge at AS Level but A Level puts greater emphasis on analysis and evaluation. These differences are reflected in the types of questions contained in this book and in the suggested answers on the Teacher's CD-ROM that accompanies it.

Students who are only taking the AS Level examinations do not need to study the A Level chapters in this book or the associated activities. A Level students and their teachers must remember that the A Level syllabus includes all AS content and, therefore, all sections of this book need to be followed. A Level students should tackle both the AS and the A Level questions in the book.

What are the key features of this book?

- Learning objectives – identifying the content and concepts covered in each chapter.
- 'Introducing the topic' case studies – raising important areas for discussion and giving context to the business applications of the material to be covered in each chapter.
- Clearly laid-out text – with easy-to-follow subsections, many tables of data and 'key advantages and disadvantages'.
- Top tips – helping avoid common errors made by students.
- Key concept links – explaining how the topics are integrated with the key concepts for this subject.
- In-chapter activities – giving practice at applying what is being learned, using evidence and data taken mainly from actual business examples.
- Learning outcomes – reinforcing the issues that should be understood by the end of each chapter.
- Examination-style questions – testing the skills of knowledge and understanding, application, analysis and evaluation, using international business situations.
- Examination-style essay questions – giving practice at writing longer, discursive answers.
- The timings given for each examination-style question are intended as a guide to students to help them practice under timed conditions; please note that they are a guide only.

What is the CD-ROM for?

The CD-ROM attached to this book provides invaluable support to students. It contains:

- a full glossary of all the key definitions in the book
- exemplar marking grids
- revision mind maps for every chapter
- examination and assessment guidance
- worksheets and answers
- hundreds of multiple choice questions and answers
- revision advice and checklists for every chapter
- sample exam papers and marks schemes.
- There is a teachers' CD available too (ISBN 9781107677364, which provides detailed answers to all of the activities, case studies and examination questions in the book along with suggestions for further reading.

Skills needed by students of Business

The key skills you will develop during your course (and will ultimately be tested on in examination) are:

1 Knowledge and critical understanding of the syllabus content.
2 Application of this knowledge and critical understanding of problems and issues that arise from both familiar and unfamiliar situations.
3 Analysis of problems, issues and situations. This skill can be demonstrated by:
   - distinguishing between statements of fact and opinion
   - explaining trends in data and the likely causes of them
   - examining the implications of a suggested idea or strategy.
4 Evaluation and judgement. This skill can be demonstrated by:
   - weighing up the reliability of data
   - discussing and debating issues and arguing points to reach an appropriate decision
   - discriminating between alternative explanations and strategies
   - judging the usefulness of the main concepts and models of Business Studies.

All of these skills will be developed as you progress through this book, especially if you work through the many questions that are presented for your self-assessment. The student CD-ROM gives further details of how the four skills are assessed and how to prepare for examinations.

Key concepts in Business

All Cambridge International AS and A Level syllabuses contain certain key concepts that underpin them and bind the subject together. The key concepts in Business are:

Change – is the only constant in business. New enterprises are often created in response to economic, cultural or technological changes. Existing businesses must adapt to change if they are to survive and grow.

Management – is relevant to every person in a business. Good leadership, strong motivation in workers, effective systems and clear communication are hallmarks of successful businesses.

Customer focus – means a business will design and produce goods and services that people want to buy. Customers provide the revenue that sustains a business. Successful businesses really understand their customers and strive to provide products that their customers love.

Innovation – enables a business to reinvent itself and stay ahead of the competition. The business world is dynamic and companies must seek to innovate through product development, more efficient processes and finding better ways to 'do business'.

Creating value – is the core reason why any business exists. Effective organisations aim to maximise stakeholder value. For many businesses this will be about maximising shareholder value, but social enterprises have other, non-financial aims. Stakeholders also need to measure the value that is being created.

Strategy – is about knowing where you are, where you want to get to and how you are going to get there. Managers need to think about, decide on and put into action major long-term plans – such as buying another business, entering a new market or developing a new technology.

These concepts are the guiding principles on which the subject – at A Level and beyond – is based. A business organisation could not be successful without its leaders being conscious of, and responding to, these important ideas. They are also inter-related and making efforts to link them in answer to questions shows that students understand the complex and integrated nature of successful business operations.

If students are able to develop the ability to see how different strands of the syllabus can be pulled together within one key concept then this a high level skill.

The ways in which these concepts can be used to bind together the subject of Business is referred to at different stages of this book through 'Key concept links'. It is important to make clear that there will no specific assessment of the principle of key concepts – no questions, for example, will use the expression 'key concepts'. However, an awareness of the interconnected nature of Business and successful business decisions will help students to succeed in their course and provide a strong foundation for future study or practical application of skills.

Using the book

Even the keenest student is unlikely to read this textbook from cover to cover in one evening. Instead, it should be used to support and guide your learning as you progress through the syllabus. Make use of the many activities and revision questions to support and assess your learning.

The authors hope that the book, as well as providing essential subject support, will achieve two further objectives. First, that it will encourage students to be observant and curious about all forms of business activity. Second, that, as a consequence, they will be keen to discover what is happening in business organisations, at international, national and local levels, and to bring these

findings into their studies. To this end, there is also the expectation that students will update their knowledge through the frequent use of libraries, newspapers, business-oriented television programmes and the Internet.

Peter Stimpson (coursebook author)

Peter Stimpson is former Head of Business Studies at Hurtwood House School, Surrey. He has more than 35 years' experience in teaching Economics and Business Studies to A Level standard. He is an experienced examiner and he also trains teachers overseas in A Level course development, teaching methods and examination skills.

Alastair Farquharson (CD-ROM author)

Alastair Farquharson is a teacher at Torquay Boys' Grammar School and has taught A Level Economics and Business Studies for more than 20 years. He is an experienced examiner and has provided training for teachers overseas in A Level course development, teaching methods and examination skills.

Unit 1:
Business and its environment

Introduction

This unit focuses on understanding the nature and purpose of business activity. It identifies and analyses the structures, functions and objectives of different business organisations. Central to an understanding of business and its internal and external environments is a recognition that the world in which businesses operate is in a constant state of change. This key concept can also be linked to the creation of value, as the most successful businesses are able to continue to create value despite the impact of political, economic, social, technological and environmental changes.

1 Enterprise

On completing this chapter, you will be able to:

- understand what business activity involves
- recognise that making choices as a result of the 'economic problem' always results in opportunity cost
- analyse the meaning and importance of creating value
- recognise the key characteristics of successful entrepreneurs
- assess the importance of enterprise and entrepreneurs to a country's economy
- understand the meaning of social enterprise and the difference between this and other businesses.

Introducing the topic

DULIP STARTS HIS BUSINESS

Dulip lives in a large country with many natural resources, such as coal and timber. He plans to start a business growing and cutting trees to sell as timber. He wants to buy a forest from a farmer and cut down a fixed number of trees each year. As Dulip is concerned about his environment country's, he will plant two new trees for each one he cuts down. He has been planning this business venture for some time. He has visited a bank to arrange a loan. He has contacted suppliers of saws and other equipment to check on prices. Dulip has also visited several furniture companies to see if they would be interested in buying wood from the forest. In fact, he did a great deal of planning before he was able to start his business.

Dulip is prepared to take risks and will invest his own savings, as well as using the bank loan, to set up the business. He plans to employ three workers to help him to start with. If the business is a success, then he will also try to sell some of the timber abroad. He knows that timber prices are high in some foreign markets. After several months of planning, he was able to purchase the forest.

Points to think about:

- Why do you think Dulip decided to own and run his own business rather than work for another firm?
- Why was it important to Dulip that he should do so much planning before starting his business?
- Do you think Dulip will make a successful entrepreneur?
- Are new businesses such as Dulip's good for a country's economy?

Introduction

Many business managers are paid high salaries to take risks and make decisions that will influence the future success of their business. Much of this book is concerned with how these decisions are made, the information needed to make them and the techniques that can assist managers in this important task. However, no student of Business can hope to make much progress in the study of this subject unless they have a good understanding of the economic environment in which a business operates. Business activity does not take place in isolation from what is going on around it. The very structure and health of the economy will have a great impact on how successful business activity is. The central purpose of this whole unit, 'Business and its environment', is to introduce the inter-relationships between businesses, the world in which they operate and the limits that governments impose on business activity. This first chapter explains the nature of business activity and the role of enterprise in setting up and developing businesses.

The purpose of business activity

A business is any organisation that uses resources to meet the needs of customers by providing a product or service that they demand. There are several stages in the production of finished goods. Business activity at all stages involves creating and adding value to resources, such as raw materials and semi-finished goods, and making them more desirable to – and thus valued by – the final purchaser. Without business activity, we would all still be entirely dependent on the goods that we could make or grow ourselves – as some people in virtually undiscovered native communities still are. Business activity uses the scarce resources of our planet to produce goods and services that allow us all to enjoy a very much higher standard of living than would be possible if we remained entirely self-sufficient.

What do businesses do?

Businesses identify the needs of consumers or other firms. They then purchase resources – or factors of production – in order to produce goods and services that satisfy these needs, usually with the aim of making a profit. Before we go on, it will be useful to explain some important business terms that have either already been used, or will be referred to soon, in this chapter. Business activity exists to produce **consumer goods** or **services** that meet the needs of customers. These goods and services can be classified in several ways.

> **KEY TERMS**
>
> **Consumer goods:** the physical and tangible goods sold to the general public – they include durable consumer goods, such as cars and washing machines, and non-durable consumer goods, such as food, drinks and sweets that can be used only once.
>
> **Consumer services:** the non-tangible products sold to the general public – they include hotel accommodation, insurance services and train journeys.

What do businesses need to produce goods and services?

Factors of production

These are the resources needed by business to produce goods or services. They include:

- **Land** – this general term includes not only land itself but all of the renewable and non-renewable resources of nature, such as coal, crude oil and timber.
- **Labour** – manual and skilled labour make up the workforce of the business.
- **Capital** – this is not just the finance needed to set up a business and pay for its continuing operations, but also all of the man-made resources used in production. These include **capital goods**, such as computers, machines, factories, offices and vehicles.
- **Enterprise** – this is the driving force, provided by risk-taking individuals, that combines the other factors of production into a unit capable of producing goods and services. It provides a managing, decision-making and coordinating role.

> **KEY TERM**
>
> **Capital goods:** the physical goods used by industry to aid in the production of other goods and services, such as machines and commercial vehicles.

Businesses have many other needs before they can successfully produce the goods and services demanded by customers. Figure 1.1 shows the wide range of these needs.

Timber is a natural resource

Capital equipment can be very complex

All businesses need labour

The concept of creating or adding value

All businesses aim to create value by selling goods and services for a higher price than the cost of bought-in materials, this is called '**creating value**'. If a customer is prepared to pay a price that is greater than the cost of materials used in making or providing a good or service, then the business has been successful in creating value. This can also be referred to as 'adding value'. The difference between the selling price of the products sold by a business and the cost of the materials that it bought in is called '**added value**'. Without creating value a business will not be able to survive as other costs have

> **KEY TERMS**
>
> **Creating value:** increasing the difference between the cost of purchasing bough-in materials and the price the finished goods are sold for.
>
> **Added value:** the difference between the cost of purchasing bought-in materials and the price the finished goods are sold for.

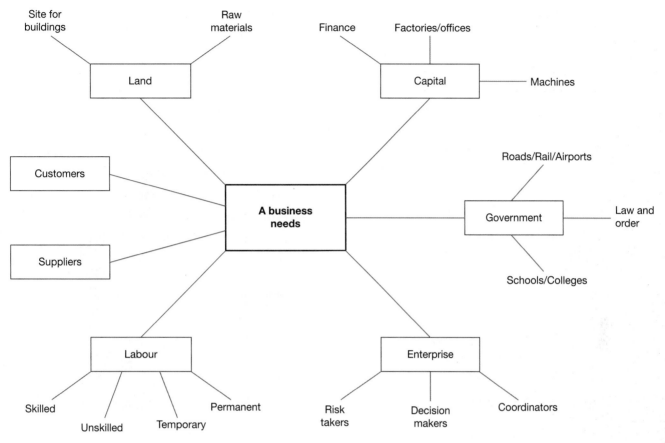

Figure 1.1 What businesses need

to be paid and, usually, a profit must be made to justify staying in operation.

The concept of creating added value can be illustrated by an example taken from the building industry – see Figure 1.2.

From the value created or added by the business, other costs have to be paid, such as labour and rent, so value created by a business is *not* the same as profit. However, if a business can create increased value without increasing its costs, then profit *will* increase.

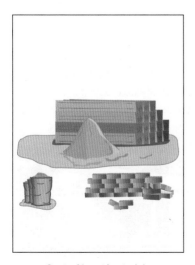

Cost of input/materials

Production process adds value

Value of output of finished goods

Figure 1.2 Creating value by building a house from bought-in materials

Here are two examples of how different businesses could create added value to their products:

1 **Jewellers** – well-designed shop-window display, attractive shop fittings, well-dressed and knowledgeable shop assistants and beautiful boxes offered to customers to put new jewellery in. These features might allow an increase in jewellery prices above the additional costs involved.

2 **Sweet manufacturer** – extensive advertising of the brand of sweets to create an easily recognised name and brand identity, attractive packaging, selling through established confectionery shops and not 'cheap' vending machines. Higher prices as a result of successful branding should create added value.

ACTIVITY 1.1

[12 marks, 25 minutes]

Explain how the following businesses could create added value to the goods they buy in:

a hotel [3]

b car dealer [3]

c clothing manufacturer [3]

d fast-food restaurant. [3]

KEY CONCEPT LINK

Creating value requires effective management of resources. The most successful businesses in terms of creating value tend to be customer-focused. Many customers are prepared to pay relatively high prices for products which exactly meet their needs – creating more value for the business.

Economic activity and the problem of choice

We live in a world of great wealth and great scarcity. Very poor people are unable to obtain the basic requirements of life – food, clean water, shelter – and they have many unsatisfied needs and wants. Even very rich people may not be able to satisfy all of their wants for luxury goods and services. It should be clear to us all that there are insufficient goods to satisfy all of our needs and wants at any one time; this is known as 'the economic problem'. It is the purpose of economic activity to provide for as many of our wants as possible, yet we are still left wanting more. This shortage of products – together with the resources needed to make them – lead to us all having to make choices. As we cannot satisfy all of our wants, then we must choose those which we will satisfy now and those which we will forgo. If we are careful and rational, we will choose those things that give us the greatest benefit,

leaving out those things of less value to us. This need to choose is not exclusive to people as consumers. All economic units have to make choices – governments, businesses, workers, charities and so on.

Opportunity cost

This need to choose leads to the next important principle of our subject – **opportunity cost**. In deciding to purchase or obtain one item, we must give up other goods as they

KEY TERM

Opportunity cost: the benefit of the next most desired option which is given up.

or

If consumers choose to buy the smart phone, then the trainers become the opportunity cost

or

If government chooses to build the fighter plane, then the hospital becomes the opportunity cost

cannot all be purchased. The next most desired product given up becomes the 'lost opportunity' or opportunity cost. This concept exists for all economic decision makers: consumers, businesses and government.

The role of the entrepreneur

New business ventures started by **entrepreneurs** can be based on a totally new idea or a new way of offering a service. They can also be a new location for an existing business idea or an attempt to adapt a good or service in ways that no one else has tried before. In this chapter, we will be looking at several examples of people who have set up their own new business and have shown skills of 'entrepreneurship'. They have:

- had an idea for a new business
- invested some of their own savings and capital
- accepted the responsibility of managing the business
- accepted the possible risks of failure.

KEY TERM

Entrepreneur: someone who takes the financial risk of starting and managing a new venture.

Characteristics of successful entrepreneurs

The personal qualities and skills needed to make a success of a new business venture include:

Innovation: The entrepreneur may not be an inventor in the traditional sense, but they must be able to carve a new niche in the market, attract customers in innovative ways and present their business as being different from others in the same market. This requires original ideas and an ability to do things differently – this is the skill of innovation.

Commitment and self-motivation: It is never an easy option to set up and run your own business. It is hard work and may take up many hours of each day. A willingness to work hard, keen ambition to succeed, energy and focus are all essential qualities of a successful entrepreneur.

Multiskilled: An entrepreneur will have to make the product (or provide the service), promote it, sell it and keep accounts. These different business tasks require a person who has many different qualities, such as being keen to learn technical skills, being able to get on with people and being good at handling money and keeping accounting records.

Leadership skills: The entrepreneur will have to lead by example and must have a personality that encourages people in the business to follow them and be motivated by them.

Self-confidence and an ability to bounce back: Many business start-ups fail, yet this would not discourage a true entrepreneur who would have such belief in themselves and

their business idea that they would bounce back from any setbacks.

Risk taking: Entrepreneurs must be willing to take risks in order to see results. Often the risk they take is by investing their own savings in the new business.

KEY CONCEPT LINK

Innovative entrepreneurs can often **create much value** for their business as long as their new ideas for goods or services are **customer-focused**.

ACTIVITY 1.2

Bangalore enterprise blossoms

Rama Karaturi gained the idea for his rose-growing business when he searched, without success, for a bouquet of roses for his wife in Bangalore. The city was a rose-free zone, so he decided to start growing them himself. Initially, he opened two greenhouses growing just roses. He used his own savings, so took a considerable risk, but his confidence in the growth of flower-giving at times of major festivals encouraged other investors too. He sold the flowers in India, but his business also became one of the first in India to start exporting flowers on a large scale. Rama worked long hours to make his business a success. The business, called Katuri Networks, has grown at a tremendous rate, helped by Rama's all-round business skills. He recently bought out a large rose-grower in Kenya and his business is now the world's largest cultivator of roses – and Rama achieved this in a little over ten years.

[9 marks, 15 minutes]

1. Rama is an example of a 'business entrepreneur'. Explain what is meant by this term. [3]

2. Outline any **three** characteristics of Rama's personality that led to the success of his enterprise. [6]

Major challenges faced by entrepreneurs

Identifying successful business opportunities

Identifying successful business opportunities is one of the most important stages in being an effective entrepreneur. Many people say that they 'want to work for themselves', but they do not make the leap into entrepreneurship successfully because they have not been able to identify a market need that will offer sufficient demand for their product to allow the business to be profitable. The original idea for most new businesses comes from one of several sources including:

- Own skills or hobbies – e.g. dress-making or car bodywork repairing. Very often, these skills will enable an entrepreneur to offer them to friends and relatives and this could be the start of the business.
- Previous employment experience – working for a successful hairdresser, for example, allows a potential entrepreneur to see the working of such a business and judge whether they could set up a similar business themselves.
- Franchising conferences and exhibitions – these offer a wide range of new business start-up ideas, e.g. fast-food restaurants, which also give the potential benefits of the support of a much larger franchiser business.
- Small-budget market research – the Internet allows any user to browse business directories to see how many businesses there are in the local area offering certain goods or services. Such small-scale research might indicate gaps in local markets that could be profitably filled by the entrepreneur.

Sourcing capital (finance)

Once the entrepreneur has decided on the business idea or opportunity, the next task is to raise the necessary capital. In an International Labour Organization survey of new business start-ups, the problem of finance came top of the list of replies from entrepreneurs regarding the main difficulty. So why is obtaining finance such a major problem for entrepreneurs?

- Lack of sufficient own finance – many entrepreneurs have very limited personal savings, especially if they are setting up their own business because they were previously made redundant.
- Lack of awareness of the financial support and grants available.
- Lack of any trading record to present to banks as evidence of past business success – a trading record would tend to give a bank confidence when deciding to lend money or not for a new venture.
- A poorly produced business plan that fails to convince potential investors of the chances of a business's success.

Determining a location

Perhaps the most important consideration when choosing the location for a new business is the need to minimise fixed costs. When finance is limited, it is very important to try to keep the break-even level of output – the output level that earns enough revenue to cover all costs – as low as possible. This will greatly increase the business's chances of survival. Operating from home is the most common way for entrepreneurs to establish their

business. This has the great advantage of keeping costs low, but there are drawbacks:

- It may not be close to the area with the biggest market potential.
- It lacks status – a business with its own prestigious premises tends to generate confidence.
- It may cause family tensions.
- It may be difficult to separate private life from working life.

The cost and position of the location chosen could have a big impact on the business entrepreneur's chance of success.

New businesses that offer a consumer service need to consider location very carefully. Whereas a website designer could operate from home very effectively, as communication with customers will be by electronic means, a hairdresser may need to consider obtaining premises in an area with the biggest number of potential customers. An alternative is to visit customers in their own homes – this way, the entrepreneur may avoid the costs of buying or renting their own premises altogether.

Competition

This is nearly always a problem for new enterprises unless the business idea is so unique that no other business has anything quite like it. A newly created business will often experience competition from older, established businesses, with more resources and more market knowledge. The entrepreneur may have to offer better customer service to overcome the cost and pricing advantages that bigger businesses can usually offer.

Building a customer base

This is linked to the previous point about competition. To survive, a new firm must establish itself in the market and build up customer numbers as quickly as possible. The long-term strength of the business will depend on encouraging customers to return to purchase products again and again. Many small businesses try to encourage this by offering a better service than their larger and better-funded competitors. This better service might include:

- personal customer service
- knowledgeable pre- and after-sales service
- providing for one-off customer requests that larger firms may be reluctant to provide for.

Why do new businesses often fail?

Even if an entrepreneur has all of the qualities listed above, success with a new business can never be guaranteed. In fact, many businesses fail during their first year of operation. The most common reasons for new enterprises failing are:

Lack of record keeping

The lack of accurate records is a big reason for business failure. Many entrepreneurs fail to pay sufficient attention to this need as either they believe that it is less important than meeting their customers' needs, or they think they can remember everything. The latter will be quite impossible after a period of time. How can the owner of a new, busy florist shop remember:

- when the next delivery of fresh flowers is due?
- whether the flowers for last week's big wedding have been paid for?
- if the cheque received from the government department for the display of flowers in its reception area has been paid into the bank yet?
- how many hours the shop assistant worked last week?

There are many other examples that could be given to illustrate the crucial importance of keeping accurate and up-to-date records of business transactions and other matters.

With the falling cost of computing power, most businesses, even newly formed ones, keep records on computer. It is always advisable to keep hold of paper records too – when these exist – for example, receipts from suppliers or details of big deliveries. Not only can these act as a check or back-up system if the computer should fail, but they can also provide evidence to the tax authorities if they dispute the entrepreneur's own tax calculations.

Lack of cash and working capital

Running short of capital to run day-to-day business affairs is the single most common reason for the failure of new businesses to survive the first year of operation.

Capital is needed for day-to-day cash, for the holding of inventories and to allow the giving of trade credit to customers, who then become trade receivables. Without sufficient working capital, the business may be unable to buy more supplies, or pay suppliers offer credit to important customers. All these factors could lead to the business closing down.

Serious working capital deficiencies can usually be avoided if several simple, but important, steps are taken as the business is being established:

- Construct a cash flow forecast so that the liquidity and working capital needs of the business can be assessed month by month. Keep this updated and also show it to the bank manager.
- Inject sufficient capital into the business at start-up to last for the first few months of operation when cash flow from customers may be slow to build up.
- Establish good relations with the bank so that short-term problems may be, at least temporarily, overcome with an overdraft extension.

- Use effective credit control over customers' accounts – do not allow a period of credit that is too long, and regularly chase up late payers.

Poor management skills

Most entrepreneurs have had some form of work experience, but not necessarily at a management level. They may not have developed:

- leadership skills
- cash handling and cash management skills
- planning and coordinating skills
- decision-making skills
- communication skills
- marketing, promotion and selling skills.

They may be very keen, willing to work hard and have undoubted abilities in their chosen field, e.g. an entrepreneur opening a restaurant may be an excellent chef, but may lack management skills. Some learn these skills very quickly once the business is operating, but this is quite a risky strategy. Some organisations exist to provide support for new entrepreneurs in the form of advice and training. Some entrepreneurs 'buy in' experience by employing staff with management experience, but how many newly formed businesses can afford this expensive option?

It is wrong to think, just because a business is new and small, that enthusiasm, a strong personality and hard work will be sufficient to ensure success. This may prove to be the case, but often it is not. So potential entrepreneurs are usually encouraged to attend training courses to gain some of these skills before putting their hard-earned capital at risk, or to first seek management experience through employment.

 KEY CONCEPT LINK

The section above introduces some of the important functions of and skills required by good managers, suggesting why the key concept of **management** is so important.

Changes in the business environment

Setting up a new business is risky because the business environment is dynamic, or constantly changing. In addition to the problems and challenges referred to above, there is also the risk of change, which can make the original business idea much less successful. Change is a key feature of Business syllabuses and, therefore, of this book – indeed there is a whole section on change in Unit 6, Chapter 40. It is enough to observe at this stage that new businesses may fail if any of the following changes occur, which may turn the venture from a successful one to a loss-making enterprise:

- new competitors
- legal changes, e.g. outlawing the product altogether
- economic changes that leave customers with much less money to spend
- technological changes that make the methods used by the new business old-fashioned and expensive.

Farah branches out on her own

Farah was a well-qualified dressmaker. She had worked for two of the biggest dress shops in town. She was always arguing with her shop manager, who was very jealous about Farah's superior dress-making skills. Farah was now determined to set up her own business. She was lucky that her father was prepared to invest $5,000 in it, but she would have to find the rest of the capital needed – about $10,000, she guessed – from her own savings and a bank loan. Her first step was to investigate the prices of shop premises and she was disappointed when she found out how expensive the city-centre locations were. Her father suggested a cheaper but less busy out-of-town location. She contacted an accountant who offered to look after the financial side of the business, but he would charge at least $2,000 per year. Farah wondered if she could learn to keep the accounts herself if she attended classes at the local college in the evening. She wanted to make her shop very different from all of the competitors in the city and she had the idea of offering lessons in dress-making as well as selling finished dresses. She had been asked so many times by customers, 'How did you do that?' when they were pleased with her latest dress designs, that she was sure this was a great business opportunity. What she had not realised was the amount of paperwork she had to complete before her business could even start trading.

[22 marks, 30 minutes]

1 Outline **three** problems that Farah had to deal with in setting up this new business. [6]

2 Which of these problems do you think was the most important one for Farah to find a good solution to? Explain your answer. [6]

3 Do you think Farah had some of the right qualities to be a successful entrepreneur? Justify your answer. [10]

This list of changes could be added to, but even these four factors indicate that the business environment is a dynamic one, and this makes owning and running a business enterprise very risky indeed.

Common types of entrepreneurial businesses

New business start-ups can be found in nearly all industries, yet it is true to say that there are some industries and sectors of industry where there is a much greater likelihood of new entrepreneurs entering. These include:

Primary sector
- fishing – e.g. a small boat owned by an entrepreneur
- market gardening – producing cash crops to sell at local markets.

Secondary sector
- jewellery-making
- dress-making
- craft manufacture, e.g. batik cloth
- building trades.

Tertiary/service sector
- hairdressing
- car repairs
- cafés and restaurants
- child-minding.

It would be most unusual for entrepreneurs to successfully establish themselves in, say, the steel-making industry or in car manufacturing, because of the vast amount of capital equipment and financial investment that would be required.

Impact of enterprise on a country's economy

All governments around the world are following policies that aim to encourage more people to become entrepreneurs. What are the claimed benefits to the economy of business enterprise?

Employment creation: In setting up a new business, an entrepreneur is employing not only themselves (self-employment), but also, very often, employing other people too. Very often these are members of the family or friends, but in creating such employment, the national level of unemployment will fall. If the business survives and expands, then there may be additional jobs created in the businesses that supply them.

Economic growth: Any increase in output of goods or services from a start-up business will increase the gross domestic product of the country. This is called economic growth, and if enough small businesses are created, it will lead to increased living standards for the population. In addition, increased output and consumption will also lead to increased tax revenues for the government.

Firms' survival and growth: Although a high proportion of new firms fail, some survive and a few expand to become really important businesses. These will employ large numbers of workers, add considerably to economic growth and will take the place of declining businesses that may be forced to close due to changing consumer tastes or technology. So, in Trinidad and Tobago, the relative decline of the sugar industry has been balanced out by the growth of the tourist industry, which has itself been boosted by small guesthouse businesses operating as sole traders.

Innovation and technological change: New businesses tend to be innovative and this creativity adds dynamism to an economy. This creativity can rub off on to other businesses and help to make the nation's business sector more competitive. Many new business start-ups are in the technology sector, e.g. website design. The increased use of IT by these firms, and the IT services they provide to other businesses, can help a nation's business sector become more advanced in its applications of IT, and therefore more competitive.

Exports: Most business start-ups tend to offer goods and services that meet the needs of local or regional markets. Some will expand their operations to the export market, however, and this will increase the value of a nation's exports and improve its international competitiveness.

Personal development: Starting and managing a successful business can aid in the development of useful skills and help an individual towards self-actualisation – a real sense of achievement. This can create an excellent example for others to follow and can lead to further successful new enterprises that will boost the economy still further.

Increased social cohesion: Unemployment often leads to serious social problems and these can be much reduced if there is a successful and expanding small business sector. By creating jobs and career opportunities and by setting a good example for others to follow, entrepreneurship can help to achieve social cohesion in the country.

TOP TIP

Some questions may ask you to make references to businesses 'in your own country'. You are advised to take a close interest during the Business course in the activities of businesses – new and well established ones – in your country.

Social enterprise

Social enterprises are not charities, but they do have objectives that are often different from those of an entrepreneur who is only profit motivated.

KEY TERM

Social enterprise: a business with mainly social objectives that reinvests most of its profits into benefiting society rather than maximising returns to owners.

In other words, a social enterprise is a proper business that makes its money in socially responsible ways and uses most of any surplus made to benefit society. Social entrepreneurs are not running a charity, however – they can and often do keep some of any profit they have made. Social enterprises compete with other businesses in the same market or industry. They use business principles to achieve social objectives. Most social enterprises have these common features:

- They directly produce goods or provide services.
- They have social aims and use ethical ways of achieving them.
- They need to make a surplus or profit to survive as they cannot rely on donations as charities do.

Social enterprise – objectives

Social enterprises often have three main aims. These are:

1 **economic** – make a profit to reinvest back into the business and provide some return to owners
2 **social** – provide jobs or support for local, often disadvantaged, communities
3 **environmental** – to protect the environment and to manage the business in an environmentally sustainable way.

These aims are often referred to as the **triple bottom line**. This means that profit is not the sole objective of these enterprises.

KEY TERM

Triple bottom line: the three objectives of social enterprises: economic, social and environmental.

ACTIVITY 1.4

Research a social enterprise business in your own country. Try to find out:

- what its social and environmental objectives are
- how it is different from a charity
- how it is different from a traditional profit only business.

Write a report on your findings.

Example 1: SELCO in India. This social enterprise provides sustainable energy solutions to low-income households and small businesses. In one scheme, solar-powered lighting was provided by SELCO to a silkworm farmer who depended on dangerous and polluting kerosene lamps. The farmer could not afford the upfront cost, so SELCO helped with the finance, too.

Example 2: The KASHF Foundation in Pakistan provides micro-finance (very small loans) and social-support services to women entrepreneurs who traditionally find it very difficult to receive help. This enables the women to set up their own businesses in food production, cloth making and other industries. The loans have to be repaid with interest, but the interest rates are much lower than a profit-maximising international bank would charge.

ACTIVITY 1.5

Caribbean cook tastes success

A Jamaican reggae musician turned businessman has hit the headlines. Levi Roots appeared on a famous BBC TV programme called *Dragons' Den*. On this programme, he persuaded wealthy businessmen to invest $100,000 in his new business idea. He plans to increase production of his Reggae Reggae Sauce, which uses an old family recipe. Levi realised this might be a good business opportunity when he started selling jerk chicken with this sauce on at local carnivals. Such was the demand from his street stall that he believed he could set up his own business making and selling the sauce.

At first, his request for finance was turned down by many banks, but he was not dispirited. He applied to appear on *Dragons' Den* and his business presentation was so effective that he had no problems in getting the $100,000 of start-up capital he asked for. In return, he agreed to give up 25% of his business profits to the businessman who agreed to offer the venture capital.

Levi's popularity after the programme and his great personality convinced one of the largest supermarket companies in Europe, Sainsbury's, to buy enough of Levi's sauce to stock all of its stores. His new financial backer said, 'Levi is a great guy and he has created a great product which he is passionate about. I am sure that this deal with Sainsbury's will be the first of many fantastic milestones on the way to business success and making his dreams a reality.' Levi is now in discussion with an export company that wants to export the sauce back to the Caribbean.

Levi Roots had a bright idea for a new business – and he is now a successful entrepreneur.

[26 marks, 35 minutes]

1 Explain **four** possible benefits to the UK economy from Levi's enterprise. [8]

2 Analyse **two** reasons for the initial success of Levi Roots as an entrepreneur. [8]

3 Do you think that Levi's business will always be successful? Justify your answer. [10]

SUMMARY POINTS

- Business activity uses resources to try to satisfy customers' needs.
- Most businesses are always looking for ways to create value.
- Entrepreneurship is about taking risks to set up new business ventures.
- Successful entrepreneurs tend to have many characteristics in common.
- An economy can obtain many important benefits from entrepreneurship.
- Entrepreneurs face challenges such as a dynamic business environment.
- Social enterprises have three objectives, not just 'to make a profit'.

RESEARCH TASK

Use the internet to find out about three social enterprises in your own country.

Write a brief report on:

- what goods/services they provide
- their main objectives
- the main sources of finance.

AS Level exam practice questions

Short answer questions

[80 marks, 90 minutes]

Knowledge and understanding

1 Explain what 'creating value' means. [3]
2 What do you understand by the term 'entrepreneur'? [3]
3 List **three** characteristics of successful entrepreneurs and explain why they are important. [9]
4 Identify **three** challenges faced by entrepreneurs. [3]
5 Explain the concept of opportunity cost and give **three** examples of it. [9]
6 Explain why a country is likely to benefit from expansion of its business enterprises. [6]
7 What is meant by the term 'social enterprise'? [3]
8 Explain what is meant by the term 'triple bottom line'. [3]
9 Explain the difference between a charity and a social enterprise. [3]

Application

10 List **three** factors of production that a new hairdressing business will require. [3]
11 A new business selling computer software has just opened in your town. Explain **three** needs that this business will have if it is to be successful. [6]
12 Explain how a supermarket could create value added to the food and other goods it buys in. [4]
13 Explain why there are so many new business enterprises in the tertiary sector of industry, such as hairdressing and car servicing. [7]
14 Using an example of a small business/recently established new business, explain how its owners overcame the **three** challenges you identified in Q4. [9]
15 List **three** benefits of entrepreneurship to your country's economy and explain why they are important. [9]

13

Data response

1 Rivelino – entrepreneur, innovator and strategic thinker

'We are a global business,' states Rivelino Simmons, one of the three partners in Integrated Trade Solutions (ITS). This is a fast-growing business that responds to the changing needs of other businesses by developing cutting-edge software to facilitate e-commerce and e-trade transactions within the regional and global marketplace.

This is not Rivelino's first business venture. He has also set up businesses selling herbal teas and arranging boat tours for tourists. He has always been on the lookout for business opportunities. He started by using his hobby of video filming to offer his skills to film companies as a freelance cameraman, quickly developing a large number of important business contacts. He is now one of the best-known freelance cameramen in the Caribbean region. However, ITS is his biggest success by far. He discussed the opportunity to set up a software development company with an old school friend who was trained in software design and development. There have been opportunity costs. Rivelino not only gave his time to the new business venture but he also contributed his savings, marketing skills and business contacts. Rivelino and his friend were also joined by another partner who brought financial skills as well as software design experience.

After much success selling software to the Caribbean market, Rivelino and his fellow entrepreneurs plan to provide advanced customised software on a global scale. Rivelino's vision is fuelled by a drive to succeed and a love for the software development business. He recognises, however, the strength of competing businesses and the changes occurring in the business world, especially in e-commerce.

2 Returned next day, or nothing to pay

Wesley had been really pleased with himself six months ago. His business plan for a new laundry business had been well received by the bank manager. She had agreed to lend him $30,000 – half of the capital he needed for starting the business. Wesley planned to offer a premium laundry service for local hotels and guesthouses that did not have their own sheet and towel washing facilities. His promise was 'returned next day, or nothing to pay'.

The number of customers was small at first, but news of Wesley's service standards and next-day promise soon spread. By the end of month three, the laundry was working to full capacity and Wesley needed more resources. He recruited four workers to help him. At the end of month four, the bank manager asked to see him again. He was shocked by what he was told:

'You have reached your overdraft limit and cash coming in to the business is not enough to ensure survival. I want to see all of your accounting and sales records next week,' she told him. Wesley knew that would be a problem. He had been so busy that his accounting records were three weeks out of date. Customers had not paid during this period – because he had not sent the bills out. Some customers were claiming that they should not pay anyway as their laundry had taken three days to be returned. Another problem concerned the workforce. They were always arguing because there were certain jobs that no one wanted to do, such as handling the chemicals used and cleaning the boiling tanks at the end of each day. Wesley had not allocated jobs clearly enough and the workers could not decide themselves.

After his visit to the bank, he sat down with all of the company's paperwork and wondered why he had not gained some experience in computer-controlled accounting. Wesley's own business skills had mainly been gained in marketing – no wonder the sales of the laundry were doing so well.

[30 marks, 45 minutes]

1 a Define the term 'entrepreneurs'. [2]

  b Briefly explain the term 'opportunity costs'. [3]

2 Explain the qualities Rivelino has that make him a successful entrepreneur. [6]

3 Analyse **two** examples of opportunity cost experienced by Rivelino when setting up ITS. [8]

4 Assess the likely importance of a dynamic business environment to the future success of ITS. [11]

[30 marks, 45 minutes]

1 a Define the term 'capital'. [2]

  b Briefly explain the term 'resources'. [3]

2 Explain **three** problems that Wesley now faces in managing his business. [6]

3 Explain the skills that Wesley should have had from the start of the business that would have reduced the significance of these problems. [8]

4 Recommend to Wesley what steps he should now take to overcome the difficulties his business is experiencing. [11]

AS Level essay questions

[20 marks, 40 minutes each]

1 To what extent do you believe that a successful entrepreneur depends on luck rather than personal qualities and skills? [20]

2 a Outline the main benefits to your country's economy of an increase in the number of new business start-ups made by entrepreneurs. [8]

  b Discuss the challenges that face new business entrepreneurs in your country. [12]

2 Business structure

On completing this chapter, you will be able to:

- classify industries into levels of economic activity – primary, secondary and tertiary
- understand the differences between the private sector and public sector in your country
- identify the different forms of legal organisation of business and evaluate the most appropriate one for different businesses.

Introducing the topic

DULIP'S BUSINESS IS A SUCCESS

Dulip's business had been operating successfully for two years when he decided to expand. He wanted his business to grow so that he could eventually bring his two sons into the venture. 'I need to start using the timber I cut to make furniture and other products. This will allow me to add value to the natural products that I produce,' he explained to his family.

Dulip realised that he would need much more capital to build a furniture-making factory. Although his business was profitable, it was not making enough of a surplus to pay for the extra costs involved. 'Why don't you ask one of your friends to invest in your business?' asked Maria, his wife. 'This would mean that you would not have to borrow so much.'

Dulip thought about this and replied, 'I could do this and also ask them to help me manage the business. I am not sure that I could carry all of the management responsibilities. I may consider making my business a legally recognised business – called a company – because this would be easier to leave to our sons and offers some protection for our savings.'

Points to think about:

- Why is it important to Dulip that he should expand his business?
- Do you think it is a good idea for this business, currently only producing timber for other businesses, to make and sell furniture?
- Would you advise Dulip to involve one of his friends in the business?
- What benefits does Dulip think being a 'company' will offer to him?

Introduction

In the last chapter, we recognised the importance of business activity to an economy. The role of entrepreneurs and the main characteristics of successful entrepreneurs were also studied. Building on this knowledge, this chapter focuses on the different types of business structures that exist and the different ways of classifying business activity. The importance of the legal structure used by a business is examined and these different forms are examined and evaluated. The diminishing role of public-sector enterprises in many countries, through the process of privatisation, is also explained and discussed.

Classification of business activity

Firms produce a vast range of different goods and services, but it is possible to classify these into three broad types of business activity. These broad categories, introduced in Chapter 1, are also the three stages involved in turning natural resources, such as oil and timber, into the finished goods and services demanded by consumers. The stages are the **primary**, **secondary** and **tertiary sectors** of industry.

> **KEY TERMS**
>
> **Primary sector business activity:** firms engaged in farming, fishing, oil extraction and all other industries that extract natural resources so that they can be used and processed by other firms.
>
> **Secondary sector business activity:** firms that manufacture and process products from natural resources, including computers, brewing, baking, clothes-making and construction.
>
> **Tertiary sector business activity:** firms that provide services to consumers and other businesses, such as retailing, transport, insurance, banking, hotels, tourism and telecommunications.

Primary production – dairy farm in France

Secondary production – clothing factory in China

Tertiary sector – the breath-taking Burj Al Arab hotel in Dubai

The balance of these sectors in the economies of different countries varies substantially. It depends on the level of industrialisation in each country. Table 2.1 shows the differences between three countries.

Country	Primary	Secondary	Tertiary
United Kingdom	2	19	79
China	42	26	32
Ghana	54	20	26

Table 2.1 Employment data 2013 – as percentage of total employment

Changes in business activity

It is very important to recognise two features of this classification of business activity:

1 The importance of each sector in an economy changes over time. Industrialisation is the term used to describe the growing importance of the secondary-sector manufacturing industries in developing countries. The relative importance of each sector is measured in terms either of employment levels or of output levels as a proportion of the whole economy. In many countries in Africa and Asia, the relative importance of secondary-sector activity is increasing. This brings many benefits as well as problems.

Benefits

■ Total national output (gross domestic product) increases and this raises average standards of living.
■ Increasing output of goods can result in lower imports and higher exports of such products.
■ Expanding manufacturing businesses will result in more jobs being created.
■ Expanding and profitable firms will pay more tax to the government.
■ Value is added to the countries' output of raw materials, rather than just exporting these as basic, unprocessed products.

Problems

■ The chance of work in manufacturing can encourage a huge movement of people from the countryside to the towns, which leads to housing and social problems.
■ Imports of raw materials and components are often needed, which can increase the country's import costs.
■ Much of the growth of manufacturing industry is due to the expansion of multinational companies. The consequences of this are covered later in this chapter.

2 In developed economies, the situation is reversed. There is a decline in the importance of secondary-sector activity and an increase in the tertiary sector. This process is termed deindustrialisation. In the UK, the proportion of total output accounted for by secondary industry has fallen by 15% to 23% in 25 years. Reasons for this include:

- Rising incomes associated with higher living standards have led consumers to spend much of their extra income on services rather than more goods. There has been substantial growth in tourism, hotels and restaurant services, financial services and so on – yet spending on physical goods is rising more slowly.
- As the rest of the world industrialises, so manufacturing businesses in developed countries face much more competition and these rivals tend to be more efficient and use cheaper labour. Therefore, rising imports of goods are taking the market away from the domestic secondary-sector firms.

3 The importance of each sector varies significantly between different economies. Table 2.1 gives details of the differences that exist between three different countries' economies and the share of total employment accounted for by each sector of industry.

Public and private sectors

Industry may also be classified in other ways, for example by **public** or **private sector** and by type of legal organisation. As we shall see, these two types of classification are interlinked, as some types of legal structure are found only in the private sector. What is the difference between the private sector and public sector of the economy?

KEY TERMS

Public sector: comprises organisations accountable to and controlled by central or local government (the state).

Private sector: comprises businesses owned and controlled by individuals or groups of individuals.

In nearly every country with a **mixed economy**, most business activity is in the private sector. The relative importance of the private sector compared to the public sector is not the same in all countries. Those economies that are closest to a **free-market** system have very small public sectors. Those countries with central planning **command economies** will have very few businesses in the private sector.

KEY TERMS

Mixed economy: economic resources are owned and controlled by both private and public sectors.

Free-market economy: economic resources are owned largely by the private sector with very little state intervention.

KEY TERM

Command economy: economic resources are owned, planned and controlled by the state.

The types and sizes of businesses in the private sector can vary considerably. The legal organisation of firms in the private sector is covered below. In most mixed-economy countries, certain important goods and services are provided by state-run organisations as it is argued that they are too significant to be left to private businesses. These usually include health and education services, defence and public law and order (police force). In some countries, important strategic industries are also owned and controlled by the state, such as energy, telecommunications and public transport. In recent years, there has been a trend towards selling these off to the private sector – privatisation – and the impact of this policy is analysed on page 67.

Another reason for the state or public sector to provide goods or services rather than the private sector is the existence of what economists call 'public goods'. These are goods and services that cannot be charged for, so it is impossible for a private-sector business to make a profit from producing them. A good example is street lighting. It is impossible to exclude people from obtaining the benefit of the streetlights if they have not contributed to paying for them – so why should anyone contribute directly towards paying for them? This means that taxes will have to be used to raise revenue to pay for a street-lighting system and this means that it can be provided only by the public sector.

The legal structure of business organisations – the private sector

Figure 2.1 on the next page shows the main types of private sector business.

Sole trader

This is the most common form of business organisation. Although there is a single owner in this business organisation, it is common for **sole traders** to employ others, but the firm is likely to remain very small. Because of this, although they are great in number, sole traders account for only a small proportion of total business turnover. All sole traders have unlimited

KEY TERM

Sole trader: a business in which one person provides the permanent finance and, in return, has full control of the business and is able to keep all of the profits.

17

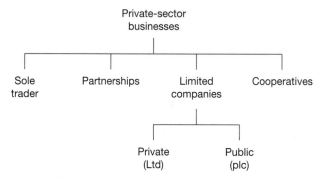

Figure 2.1 The private sector – legal structure

liability. This means that the owner's personal possessions and property can be taken to pay off the debts of the business, should it fail. This can discourage some potential entrepreneurs from starting a business. Another significant problem is finance for expansion. Many sole traders remain small because the owner wishes to remain in control of their own business, but another reason is the limitations that they have in raising additional capital. As soon as partners or shareholders are sought in order to raise finance, then the sole trader becomes another form of organisation altogether. In order to remain a sole trader, the owner is dependent on their own savings, profits and loans for injections of capital.

This type of business organisation is most commonly established in the construction, retailing, hairdressing, car-servicing and catering trades. The advantages and disadvantages of this form of organisation are summarised in Table 2.2.

Partnership

The **partnership** agreement does not create a separate legal unit; a partnership is just a grouping of individuals.

Partnerships are formed in order to overcome some of the drawbacks of being a sole trader. When planning to go into partnership, it is important to choose business partners carefully – the errors and poor decisions of any one partner are considered to be the responsibility of them all. This also applies to business debts incurred by one partner – in most countries there is unlimited liability for all partners should the business venture fail. In the UK, it is possible to set up limited liability partnerships. It is usual, although not a legal requirement, to draw up a formal Deed of Partnership between all partners. This would provide agreement on issues such as voting rights, the distribution of profits, the management role of each partner and who has authority to sign contracts.

 KEY TERM

Partnership: a business formed by two or more people to carry on a business together, with shared capital investment and, usually, shared responsibilities.

ACTIVITY 2.1

Read the 'Introducing the topic' case study on page 15 again.

[15 marks, 20 minutes]

Would you advise Dulip to convert his business into a partnership? Explain all of the potential advantages and disadvantages before giving your recommendation. **[15]**

Partnerships are the most common form of business organisation in some professions, such as law and

Advantages	Disadvantages
■ easy to set up – no legal formalities ■ owner has complete control – not answerable to anybody else ■ owner keeps all profits ■ able to choose times and patterns of working ■ able to establish close personal relationships with staff (if any are employed) and customers ■ business can be based on the interests or skills of the owner – rather than working as an employee for a larger firm	■ unlimited liability – all of owner's assets are potentially at risk ■ often faces intense competition from bigger firms, for example in food retailing ■ owner is unable to specialise in areas of the business that are most interesting – is responsible for all aspects of management ■ difficult to raise additional capital ■ long hours often necessary to make business pay ■ lack of continuity – as the business does not have separate legal status, when the owner dies the business ends too

Table 2.2 Advantages and disadvantages of sole-trader organisations

Advantages	Disadvantages
■ partners may specialise in different areas of business management ■ shared decision-making ■ additional capital injected by each partner ■ business losses shared between the partners ■ greater privacy and fewer legal formalities than corporate organisations (companies)	■ unlimited liability for all partners (with some exceptions) ■ profits are shared ■ as with sole traders, no continuity and the partnership will have to be reformed in the event of the death of one of the partners ■ all partners bound by the decisions of any one of them ■ not possible to raise capital from selling shares ■ a sole trader, taking on partners, will lose independence of decision-making

Table 2.3 Advantages and disadvantages of partnerships

accountancy. Small building firms are often partnerships, too. Many other owners of businesses prefer the company form of organisation and these are considered next.

The advantages and disadvantages of partnerships are summarised in Table 2.3.

Limited companies

There are three distinct and important differences between companies and the two forms of 'unincorporated' business organisation that we have just studied. These are:

1 Limited liability

The ownership of companies is divided into small units called shares. People can buy these and become shareholders – part owners of the business. It is possible to buy just one share, but usually these are owned in blocks, and it is possible for one person or organisation to have complete control by owning more than 50% of the shares. Individuals with large blocks of shares often become directors of the business. All shareholders benefit from the advantage of **limited liability**.

KEY TERM

Limited liability: the only liability – or potential loss – a shareholder has if the company fails is the amount invested in the company, not the total wealth of the shareholder.

Nobody can make any further claim against shareholders, should the company fail. This has two important effects:

■ People are prepared to provide finance to enable companies to expand.
■ The greater risk of the company failing to pay its debts is now transferred from investors to creditors (those suppliers/lenders who have not been paid). Creditors, as a result, are very interested in both checking whether the word 'limited' appears in the business name and

scrutinising the company's accounts for signs of potential future weakness.

2 Legal personality

A company is recognised in law as having a legal identity separate from that of its owners. This means, for example, that if the foods sold by a company are found to be dangerous or contaminated, the company itself can be taken to court – not the owners, as would be the case with either a sole trader or a partnership. A company can be sued and can itself sue through the courts. This does not take all legal responsibilities away from the managers and owners. For example, directors can be legally responsible if they knowingly continue trading when their company is illiquid. They must still act responsibly and in accordance with the stated aims of the business and within the law.

3 Continuity

In a company, the death of an owner or director does not lead to its break-up or dissolution. All that happens is that ownership continues through the inheritance of the shares, and there is no break in ownership at all.

Private limited companies

The protection that comes from forming a company is, therefore, substantial. Small firms can gain this protection when the owner(s) create a **private limited company**.

KEY TERM

Private limited company: a small to medium-sized business that is owned by shareholders who are often members of the same family; this company cannot sell shares to the general public.

Advantages	Disadvantages
■ shareholders have limited liability ■ separate legal personality ■ continuity in the event of the death of a shareholder ■ original owner is still often able to retain control ■ able to raise capital from sale of shares to family, friends and employees ■ greater status than an unincorporated business	■ legal formalities involved in establishing the business ■ capital cannot be raised by sale of shares to the general public ■ quite difficult for shareholders to sell shares ■ end-of-year accounts must be sent to Companies House – available for public inspection there (less secrecy over financial affairs than sole trader or partnership)

Table 2.4 Advantages and disadvantages of private limited companies

The word 'Limited' or 'Ltd' ('Pte' in some countries) tells us that the business has this legal form. Usually the **shares** will be owned by the original sole trader, relatives, friends and employees. The former sole trader often still has a controlling interest. New issues of shares cannot be sold on the open market and existing **shareholders** may sell their shares only with the agreement of the other shareholders. Certain legal formalities must be followed in setting up such a business and these are explained in the section after public limited companies. The advantages and disadvantages of private limited companies are summarised in Table 2.4.

KEY TERMS

Share: a certificate confirming part ownership of a company and entitling the shareholder owner to dividends and certain shareholder rights.

Shareholder: a person or institution owning shares in a limited company.

Public limited companies

These can be recognised by the use of 'plc' or 'inc.' after the company name. It is the most common form of legal organisation for really large businesses, for the very good reason that they have access to very substantial funds for expansion.

A **public limited company** (plc) has all the advantages of private-company status, plus the right to advertise their shares for sale and have them quoted on the stock exchange. This not only means that public

KEY TERM

Public limited company: a limited company, often a large business, with the legal right to sell shares to the general public – share prices are quoted on the national stock exchange.

limited companies can raise potentially very large sums from public issues of shares, but existing shareholders may also quickly sell their shares if they wish to. This flexibility of share buying and selling encourages the public to purchase the shares in the first instance and thus invest in the business. The other main difference between private and public companies concerns the 'divorce between ownership and control'. As was explained above, the original owners of the business are usually still able to retain a majority of shares and continue to exercise management control when it converts to private company status. This is most unlikely with public limited companies, due to the sheer volume of shares issued and number of people and institutions as investors. These shareholders own the company, but they appoint, at the annual general meeting, a board of directors who control the management and decision-making of the business.

This clear distinction between ownership and control can lead to conflicts, for example over the objectives to be set and direction to be taken by the business. The shareholders might prefer measures that aim at short-term profits, whereas the directors may decide to aim for long-term growth of the business, perhaps in order to increase their own power and status. Many private limited companies convert to plc status for the reasons given in Table 2.5 on page 22. It is possible for the directors or the original owners of a business to convert it back from a plc to private limited company status: Richard Branson and the Virgin group is one of the best-known examples. The reasons for doing this are largely to overcome the divorce between ownership and control – in a private limited company, it is normal for the senior executives to be the major, majority shareholders. In addition, the owner of a private limited company can take a long-term planning view of the business. It is often said that the major investors in a plc are only interested in short-term gains. 'Short-termism' can be damaging to the long-term investment plans of a business.

ACTIVITY 2.2

Twitter 'goes public'

Twitter founders – Evan Williams and Jack Dorsey – became multimillionaires overnight when Twitter sold 70 million shares at US$26 each. The decision to convert the business into a public limited company was mainly to allow directors to spend capital on expanding the 'micro-blogging' business with expensive purchases of other Internet businesses.

[16 marks, 20 minutes]

1 Explain what 'going public' means. [4]

2 Analyse **two** potential benefits to the founders of the company from the decision to sell so many shares to the public. [6]

3 Analyse **two** potential drawbacks to Twitter of becoming a public limited company. [6]

A summary of the advantages and disadvantages of public limited companies is given in Table 2.5 on the next page.

Legal formalities in setting up a company

All governments insist that certain legal stages are completed before a company may be established, in order to protect investors and creditors. In the UK, the following steps must be taken:

1 A **Memorandum of Association** must be completed.

 KEY TERM

> **Memorandum of Association:** this states the name of the company, the address of the head office through which it can be contacted, the maximum share capital for which the company seeks authorisation and the declared aims of the business.

The last two points in this definition – the maximum share capital for which the company seeks authorisation and the declared aims of the business – are of great interest

ACTIVITY 2.3

Footie Ltd to stay private after ruling out float

Footie Ltd, the shoemaker and retailer that in 2013 was planning to ballot the owning family on a possible public flotation, is to stay private. The chairman said yesterday that the board had received overwhelming advice against trying to float the company and convert it into a plc. The company has no need of further capital to fund further expansion. The board and the shareholder council, which represents 72% of the shares, had agreed that a ballot would be 'effectively a waste of time'. The company was formed over 100 years ago and has grown into one of the world's largest private limited companies. Recently, it came within five votes of opting for a takeover by Shoeworks plc after a decade of declining fortunes. However, in April it announced annual profits up from £42.7 million to £50.8 million on sales of £825 million. That was its third year of record profits, reflecting its strategy of reducing

its reliance on own manufacture and investing in its brands and shops.

Footie Ltd is now more of a retailer and wholesaler than manufacturer, owning or franchising 650 shops and importing shoes from abroad. Five years ago, 75% of its shoes were manufactured in Footie's European factories. Now it is just 25%, with 40% of the business based in Asia. Jim Parker, chief executive, has claimed that Footie is the largest conventional shoe brand in the world, having sold 48 million pairs last year. Yesterday he said the business was expanding rapidly in nearly all markets. 'I am confident that we can continue to build the business as the benefits of moving to lower-cost countries come through, along with investment in our brand and retailing operations.'

Despite ruling out a float for now, the company said it would continue periodically to examine 'the most appropriate legal structure to meet shareholders' interests in the light of its strategy for future growth and the conditions in the footwear market'.

[30 marks, 35 minutes]

1 Explain **two** differences between a private limited company and a public limited company. [4]

2 Is Footie Ltd in the private or public sector? Explain your answer. [3]

3 Which industrial sector(s) does Footie Ltd operate in? Explain your answer. [5]

4 Examine possible reasons for the directors deciding to keep Footie Ltd a private limited company. [6]

5 Analyse the main benefits to the business and to existing shareholders if the company did 'go public'. [6]

6 Explain what appear to be the main reasons for the recent growth in profits at Footie Ltd. [6]

Advantages	Disadvantages
■ limited liability ■ separate legal identity ■ continuity ■ ease of buying and selling of shares for shareholders – this encourages investment in plcs ■ access to substantial capital sources due to the ability to issue a prospectus to the public and to offer shares for sale (called a flotation)	■ legal formalities in formation ■ cost of business consultants and financial advisers when creating such a company ■ share prices subject to fluctuation – sometimes for reasons beyond business control, for example state of the economy ■ legal requirements concerning disclosure of information to shareholders and the public, for example annual publication of detailed report and accounts ■ risk of takeover due to the availability of the shares on the stock exchange ■ directors influenced by short-term objectives of major investors

Table 2.5 Advantages and disadvantages of public limited companies

to shareholders. Knowing the maximum share capital means that the relative importance of any one share can be determined. Being aware of the company's aims means that shareholders can avoid businesses that may operate in markets and products – such as weapons – that they may not want to be associated with.

2 The other main document is called the **Articles of Association**.

KEY TERM

Articles of Association: this document covers the internal workings and control of the business – for example, the names of directors and the procedures to be followed at meetings will be detailed.

When these documents have been completed satisfactorily, the registrar of companies will issue a certificate of incorporation. Private limited companies may now begin trading. In addition, to gain a listing on the stock exchange, which as explained above will greatly increase the marketability of shares, the accounts and trading record of the business will be carefully scrutinised by the stock exchange.

Other forms of business organisation

Cooperatives

These are a very common form of organisation in some countries, especially in agriculture and retailing. It is common to differentiate between producer or worker cooperatives that are involved with making goods and consumer or retail cooperatives that sell goods and services. Certain features are common to all cooperatives:

■ All members can contribute to the running of the business, sharing the workload, responsibilities and decision-making, although in larger cooperatives some delegation to professional managers takes place.

■ All members have one vote at important meetings.
■ Profits are shared equally among members.

In agricultural cooperatives, the members arrange for the purchase of seeds and materials in bulk so that they may benefit from economies of scale. The cooperative often buys the produce of the members and then sells it collectively in order to obtain a better price.

The advantages of such business units are:

■ buying in bulk
■ working together to solve problems and take decisions
■ good motivation for all members to work hard as they will benefit from shared profits.

The potential drawbacks can include:

■ poor management skills, unless professional managers are employed
■ capital shortages because no sale of shares to the non-member general public is allowed
■ slow decision-making if all members are to be consulted on important issues.

Franchises

A **franchise** is not strictly a form of legal structure for a business, but it is a legal contract between two firms.

KEY TERM

Franchise: a business that uses the name, logo and trading systems of an existing successful business.

This contract allows one of them, the franchisee, to use the name, logo and marketing methods of the other, the franchiser. The franchisee can then, separately, decide which form of legal structure to adopt. Franchises are a rapidly expanding form of business operation. They have allowed certain multinational businesses, which are now household names, to expand much more rapidly than they could otherwise have done, McDonald's and Ben and Jerry's being just two examples. Why would a business entrepreneur want to use the name, style and products of another firm? Consider the case study activity 'Harry goes it alone' on page 25, which includes all of the main features of a typical franchise contract. Table 2.6 below outlines the advantages and disadvantages of franchises.

 **KEY CONCEPT LINK**

If buying a franchise only adds the cost of a business and does not lead to the potential to increase revenue or sell products at a higher prices, then the **value created** by a franchise operation could be lower than a non-franchised one.

Benefits of opening a franchised business	Possible limitations
■ fewer chances of new business failing as an established brand and product are being used ■ advice and training offered by the franchiser ■ national advertising paid for by franchiser ■ supplies obtained from established and quality-checked suppliers ■ franchiser agrees not to open another branch in the local area	■ share of profits or revenue has to be paid to franchiser each year ■ initial franchise licence fee can be expensive ■ local promotions may still have to be paid for by franchisee ■ no choice of supplies or suppliers to be used ■ strict rules over pricing and layout of the outlet reduce owner's control over their own business

Table 2.6 Advantages and disadvantages of franchises

ACTIVITY 2.4

Shah's garage

Salman Shah has been in business as a sole trader for many years, owning a small garage and petrol station. He has two sons and a daughter and they want to be involved in his business. Each of them is married and has a family. The garage supplies petrol and oil to local customers and some passing motorists. However, there is little profit in petrol retailing. The car-repair side of the garage is facing increasing competition from the large franchised operations of the major car manufacturers. Salman wants to expand the business so that his children can become involved – at present, the profits could not support more than one family. He is thinking of three possible ways to expand the business:

■ Ayman, one of his sons, has bus- and taxi-driving licences. There could be the chance of providing a taxi service with a new five-seater taxi.

■ The local bus services are being withdrawn. There is a possibility of running a bus service to local factories and schools. The bus would therefore not be used all day and every day.

■ Local shops have been closing because of competition from supermarkets. Salman could build a small extension to the petrol-station shop and stock it with groceries and everyday household items. His daughter Stella would be keen to manage this shop.

Salman knows that unless he takes some quick decisions his business will not survive. He also wants to keep control of it and to pass it on, as a profitable firm, to his children. He has very little money saved and all of the expansion options will require capital. He is very keen to avoid business risks and he has always been opposed to borrowing money for his firm.

[25 marks, 35 minutes]

1 Assume that Salman's garage is located in the area where you live. He can only afford to choose one of the possible ways of expanding. Which would you suggest and why? [6]

2 For the option you have suggested in Q1, make and justify an assumption about how much capital you think the business will need. [4]

3 Advise Salman on ways in which capital might be obtained, making clear the options open to him if he changed the form of business organisation. [6]

4 Which form of business organisation would you suggest for Salman's business, and why? [9]

Many McDonald's restaurants are franchised outlets – like this one in Malaysia

Joint ventures

These are not the same as a merger, but they can lead to mergers of the businesses if their joint interests coincide and if the joint venture is successful. The reasons for **joint ventures** are:

- Costs and risks of a new business venture are shared – this is a major consideration when the cost of developing new products is rising rapidly.
- Different companies might have different strengths and experiences and they therefore fit well together.
- They might have their major markets in different countries and they could exploit these with the new product more effectively than if they both decided to 'go it alone'.

Such agreements are not without their risks:

- Styles of management and culture might be so different that the two teams do not blend well together.
- Errors and mistakes might lead to one blaming the other for mistakes.
- The business failure of one of the partners would put the whole project at risk.

Holding companies

Holding companies are not a different legal form of business organisation, but they are an increasingly common way for businesses to be owned.

Often, the separate businesses are in completely different markets, and this would mean that the holding company had diversified interests. Keeping the businesses separate means that they are independent of each other for major decisions or policy changes, yet there will always be the possibility of centralised control from the directors of the holding company over really crucial issues, such as major new investments.

Public-sector enterprises – public corporations

The use of the term 'public' in two ways often causes confusion. We have already identified public limited companies as being owned by shareholders in the private sector of the economy. Thus, public limited companies are in the private sector. However, in every country there will be some enterprises that are owned by the state – usually central or local government. These organisations are therefore in the public sector and they are referred to as **public corporations**.

TOP TIP

Public limited companies are in the private sector of industry – but public corporations are not.

Public-sector organisations do not often have profit as a major objective. In many countries, the publicly owned TV channels have the quality of public-service programmes as their main priority. State-owned airlines have safety as a priority. In the section on privatisation, the issues involved in selling off public corporations to the private sector, and the resulting change in objectives that often follows, are considered. A summary of the potential advantages and disadvantages of public corporations is given in Table 2.7.

Advantages	Disadvantages
▪ managed with social objectives rather than solely with profit objectives ▪ loss-making services might still be kept operating if the social benefit is great enough ▪ finance raised mainly from the government	▪ tendency towards inefficiency due to lack of strict profit targets ▪ subsidies from government can also encourage inefficiencies ▪ government may interfere in business decisions for political reasons, for example by opening a new branch in a certain area to gain popularity

Table 2.7 Advantages and disadvantages of public corporations

---

ACTIVITY 2.5

Harry goes it alone

Harry was really bored with his job as second chef in a top-of-the-market hotel. He was also tired of being ordered around by the manager and the head chef. He never liked taking orders and had always hoped to use his talents preparing food for customers in his own restaurant. The main problem was his lack of business experience. Harry had just been to a business conference with a friend of his and had been interested in the franchising exhibition there. One of the businesses offering to sell franchises was Pizza Delight. This firm sold a new type of pizza recipe to franchisees and provided all ingredients, marketing support and help with staff training. They had already opened 100 restaurants in other countries and offered to sell new franchises for a one-off payment of $100,000. If Harry signed one of these franchising contracts, then he would have to agree to:

- ▪ buying materials only from Pizza Delight
- ▪ fitting out the restaurant in exactly the way the franchiser wanted
- ▪ making an annual payment to Pizza Delight of a percentage of total turnover.

In addition, he would have to find and pay for suitable premises and recruit and motivate staff. Pizza Delight claimed that their brand and products were so well known that 'success was guaranteed'. As the product had been tested already, there would be none of the initial problems that small firms often experience and Pizza Delight would pay for national advertising campaigns.

They assured Harry that no other Pizza Delight restaurant could open within five kilometres of one already operating. Harry was almost convinced that this was the business for him. He had inherited money from a relative. However, several things still bothered him, for example, would it give him the independence he wanted so much?

One important function of the franchisee is motivating staff

[25 marks, 35 minutes]

1   Explain **three** potential benefits to Harry of opening a franchised Pizza Delight restaurant. **[6]**

2   Explain **three** potential drawbacks to Harry of agreeing to the terms of the franchise contract. **[6]**

3   If he decided to open his own restaurant, but under his own name, why might the risks of failure be greater than for a Pizza Delight franchise? **[4]**

4   Using all of the evidence, would you advise Harry to take out a franchise with Pizza Delight? Justify your answer. **[9]**

Ford teams up with Chinese auto maker

A joint-venture agreement has been signed between the American auto giant Ford and China's Chang'an Automobile Group. According to the agreement, the construction of a newly launched Chang'an-Ford Motor Company will be completed in two years. Each party holds 50% of the joint venture's shares. The initial investment of the joint venture amounts to $98 million. Sources said that Chang'an-Ford will manufacture and sell Ford-designed cars as well as car parts and components. Ford started cooperation with its Chinese counterparts in manufacturing auto parts and components in 1978. The auto giant considers its latest move a necessary strategy to be a part of China's fast-developing auto market. The market is expected to reach 22 million cars in 2014. Chang'an Automobile Group was established some 45 years ago and produced some 2.7 million automobiles in 2012. It ranked first in China's mini-car production last year.

Nestlé and Fronterra in dairy joint venture in Trinidad

A new joint venture has been announced by Nestlé and Fronterra. It creates a business that will concentrate on milk processing and the marketing of dairy products. This joint venture should strengthen the position of both companies in the Caribbean market. Nestlé concentrates mainly on marketing branded dairy products, but Fronterra is much better known as a milk-product processor. By combining forces in Trinidad and Tobago, the joint venture will gain from Fronterra's production and processing facilities and experience and Nestlé's marketing expertise. The potential for success of the new joint venture, which will make and sell dairy products in Trinidad and Tobago, appears high. Much will depend, however, on milk prices and the ability of the new management team, made up of employees from both companies, to work well together.

[25 marks, 35 minutes]

1   What seem to be the main reasons for the joint venture between Ford and Chang'an? [4]

2   Which business, in your opinion, seems to gain most from this venture? Explain your answer. [5]

3   What problems might these two businesses have in dealing with each other in this venture? [4]

4   Evaluate the likely advantages to both Nestlé and Fronterra of their new joint venture in Trinidad and Tobago. [12]

SUMMARY POINTS

- Different methods of classifying business activity exist; the method used will depend on the nature and purpose of the study being conducted.
- Classification can be based on the level of activity: primary, secondary or tertiary.
- Classification can be based on the legal structure of the organisation.
- Classification can be based on whether the business is in the public or private sector.
- Businesses in the private sector can have different legal structures – the selection of the most appropriate one is an important factor in determining success.

RESEARCH TASK

- Make a list of up to ten businesses that operate in your region or country. Try to select both small and large businesses.
- Research the legal structure of these businesses, e.g. sole trader, public limited company etc.
- Explain for any four of these businesses whether you think their legal structure is appropriate.

AS Level exam practice questions

Short answer questions

[48 marks, 1 hour]

Knowledge and understanding

1   What is the difference between private-sector and public-sector organisations? **[3]**
2   State **three** differences between a sole trader and a private limited company. **[3]**
3   Who (a) owns and (b) controls a public limited company? Explain why this distinction might lead to conflict. **[6]**
4   State **two** benefits and **two** risks for a business of engaging in a joint venture. **[4]**
5   Why might the directors of a public limited company decide to convert the business back into a private limited company by buying a majority of the shares? **[3]**
6   Explain how legal identity and continuity help businesses and companies to operate effectively. **[4]**
7   How does limited liability make it easier for companies to raise finance? **[3]**
8   Using the examples of a sole trader business and a public limited company, explain how the relationship between ownership and control differs in these two types of organisations. **[6]**
9   Using the examples of a partnership and a public limited company, explain how the legal structure of a business affects its ability to raise finance. **[4]**
10 Why might an entrepreneur decide not to take out a franchise agreement, but to establish an independent business? **[4]**

Application

11 List **two** organisations in your own country that are in the public sector. **[2]**
12 Explain **three** advantages to your own country from increased industrialisation. **[3]**
13 Why might an entrepreneur opening a hairdressing business stand a greater chance of success if they bought a franchise licence than if they attempted to establish an independent business? **[3]**

Data response

Joe to expand his business

Joe Sharma owns a small tea and coffee blending and packaging business. He buys in coffee beans and tea leaves and processes them. He sells the finished product to chains of retail stores. His business is facing increasing competition from large processors of tea and coffee based in other countries. Sales of his product to retail stores are falling for another reason. The rapid increase in consumer income is leading to many more people eating and drinking in hotels and restaurants and buying less tea and coffee to consume at home. The situation with his business is becoming so serious that he is thinking of selling his factory and using the capital to purchase some cafés and tea shops. He would then be able to benefit from the changes in consumer spending habits. Joe realises that he will need more capital than the sale of his factory would raise. Therefore, he is considering converting his sole-trader business into either a partnership or a private limited company.

[AS Level – 30 marks, 45 minutes]

1 a Define the term 'sole trader'.   [2]
   b Briefly explain the term 'partnership'.   [3]
2 a In which sector of industry is Joe's business currently operating? Explain your answer.   [3]
   b In which sector of industry is Joe planning to set up his new business? Explain your answer.   [3]
3 Analyse the problems Joe might face in switching from making tea and coffee products to entering the café and tea shop market.   [8]
4 Advise Joe, giving your reasons, on the most suitable form of legal structure for the business, given that extra capital will be required.   [11]

AS Level essay questions

[20 marks, 40 minutes each]

1 a Explain the key features of limited companies.   [8]
   b Evaluate the factors that the owners of a rapidly expanding private limited company should consider before deciding whether to apply for conversion to a public limited company.   [12]
2 a Analyse the potential benefits to an entrepreneur of setting up a franchised business.   [8]
   b Evaluate the use of joint ventures by a food manufacturing business planning to expand sales into other countries.   [12]

3 Size of business

This chapter covers syllabus section AS Level 1.3.

On completing this chapter, you will be able to:

- identify several ways of measuring the size of businesses and evaluate each of them
- analyse the beneficial impact that small firms can have on a country's economy
- analyse advantages and disadvantages of small and large businesses
- explain the difference between internal and external growth.

Introducing the topic

TALE OF TWO INDUSTRIES

The size of the average Indian steel plant compared to the size of the average Indian retail shop could not be more different. Steel plants employ thousands of workers, have millions of dollars of capital invested in advanced equipment and produce annual output valued in the millions too. Tata, one of the largest steel makers in the world, has recently grown by taking over European steel giant Corus. The contrast with typical Indian retail outlets could not be greater. The small shopkeepers and street hawkers that presently account for more than 95% of Indian retail sales often employ just a few workers with little investment in modern technology. However, all this could be about to change. There is a growing trend of mergers and takeovers in the retail sector. Large retail groups, such as Reliance and Walmart, are becoming established. It is claimed that the market share of this organised sector will be 28% by 2017. A pressure group of small retailers, the National Movement for Retail Democracy, is organising demonstrations to demand that big corporations leave the retail industry.

Tata steel plant, India

Points to think about:

- Why do you think the average steel plant is much larger than the average shop?
- How could you compare the sizes of different businesses?
- Do you think consumers of steel, such as car makers, will benefit from a takeover of Corus by Tata?
- Do you think Indian consumers will benefit from increasing numbers of large retail shops owned by just a few large corporations?

Introduction

Businesses vary in size from sole traders with no additional workers to huge multinational corporations employing hundreds of thousands of employees. Measuring the size of businesses is a rather inexact science, but efforts are still made so that comparisons can be made between them, and so that growth or contraction can be assessed over time. This information is of interest not only to the managers of a business, but to investors and governments too. Small firms offer many benefits for the dynamism of an economy and often receive special assistance from governments. Even the world's greatest companies started off as very small firms and the ways in which firms can expand and the impact of these forms of growth on stakeholders are the focus of the last section of this chapter.

Measuring business size

It is common to compare businesses by their size. Who wants to know how large a particular business is? The government might wish to give assistance to 'small' firms, so will need a measure of size. Investors in a firm may wish to compare the size of the business with close competitors – particularly in order to compare the rate of growth. Customers may prefer to deal only with large firms, assuming, perhaps, that they are more stable and less likely to cease production than smaller ones. There are two problems with these and other requirements for a way of measuring business size:

1 There are several different ways of measuring and comparing business size and they often give different comparative results. A firm might appear large by one measure but quite small by another.

2 There is no internationally agreed definition of what a small, medium or large business is, but the number of employees is often used to make this distinction.

Different measures of size

1 Number of employees

This is the simplest measure. It is easy to understand – for example, it is obvious to everyone that a shop run by just the owner or their family is small. It is also clear that a firm employing many staff is likely to be large. However, there are problems. How about a business that needs to employ only a few people – such as a highly automated computer-chip maker with expensive capital equipment?

Example: There are two soft drink firms in the same town. One uses traditional methods of production, using 108 people to make 300,000 litres of drink a week. The other is totally automated and produces one million litres a week with just ten staff.

2 Revenue

Revenue is often used as a measure of size – especially when comparing firms in the same industry. It is less effective when comparing firms in different industries because some might be engaged in 'high-value' production, such as precious jewels, and another might be in 'low-value' production, such as cleaning services. This measure is needed to calculate market share.

KEY TERM

Revenue: total value of sales made by a business in a given time period.

3 Capital employed

Generally, the larger the business enterprise, the greater the value of capital needed for long-term investment, or the greater the amount of **capital employed**. Again, comparisons between firms in different industries may give a rather misleading picture. Two firms employing the same number of staff may have very different capital equipment needs, such as a hairdresser and an optician. The latter will need expensive diagnostic and eyesight-measuring machines.

KEY TERM

Capital employed: the total value of all long-term finance invested in the business.

4 Market capitalisation

Market capitalisation can be used only for businesses that have shares quoted on the stock exchange (public limited companies). It is calculated by this formula:

Market capitalisation = current share price × total number of shares issued

KEY TERM

Market capitalisation: the total value of a company's issued shares.

As share prices tend to change every day, this form of comparison is not a very stable one. For example, a temporary but sharp drop in the share price of a company could appear to make it much 'smaller' than this measure would normally suggest.

5 Market share

Market share is a relative measure. If a firm has a high market share, it must be among the leaders in the industry and *comparatively* large. However, when the size of the total market is small, a high market share will not indicate a very large firm. This is calculated using the following formula:

$$\frac{\text{total sales of business}}{\text{total sales of industry}} \times 100$$

KEY TERM

Market share: sales of the business as a proportion of total market sales.

Other measures that can be used

These will depend very much on the industry. The number of guest beds or guest rooms could be used to compare hotel businesses. The number of shops could be used for retailers. Total floor sales space could also be used to compare retail businesses.

TOP TIP

Profit is not a good measure of business size – but it can be used to assess business performance.

Which form of measurement is best?

There is no 'best' measure. The one used depends on what needs to be established about the firms being compared. This could depend on whether we are interested in absolute size or comparative size within one industry. If an absolute measure of size is required, then it is almost certainly advisable to test a firm on at least two of the above criteria and to make comparisons on the basis of these.

TOP TIP

If asked to comment on data showing the sizes of different businesses, do remember that if another measure were used, the conclusions about relative size might be very different.

The significance of small and micro-businesses

Even though we have not established a universally agreed definition of small firms, it will be easy to identify them within your own economy. They will employ few people and will have a low turnover compared to other firms. The official definition within your own country could be discovered from the trade and industry department. It is now common to make a further distinction for very small businesses known as 'micro-enterprises'. The European Union definitions are shown in Table 3.1.

Small firms (including micro-enterprises) are very important to all economies and to the industry in which they operate. Encouraging the development of small business units can have the following benefits:

- Many jobs are created by small firms and, even though each one may not employ many staff, collectively the small-business sector employs a very significant proportion of the working population in most countries.
- Small businesses are often run by dynamic entrepreneurs, with new ideas for consumer goods and services. This helps to create variety in the market and consumers will benefit from greater choice.
- Small firms can create competition for larger businesses. Without this competition, larger firms could exploit consumers with high prices and poor service. The cost of air travel has been reduced in recent years due to the establishment of many small airlines competing with the large, established companies.
- Small firms often supply specialist goods and services to important industries in a country. For example, the global car industry is dominated by major manufacturers such as Toyota, BMW and Ford. All of these large businesses depend on small specialist suppliers of on-board computers, high-quality audio equipment and headlights. Very often, by being able to adapt quickly to the changing needs of large firms, small businesses actually increase the competitiveness of the larger organisations.
- All great businesses were small at one time. The Body Shop began in one small rented store in 1976. Hewlett-Packard started assembling electrical equipment in Packard's garage! The large firms of the future are the small firms of today – and the more small firms are encouraged to become established and expand, the greater the chances that an economy will benefit from large-scale organisations in the future.
- Small firms may enjoy lower average costs than larger ones and this benefit could be passed on to the consumer too. Costs could be lower because wage rates paid to staff may be less than the salaries paid in large organisations, or the sheer cost of the administration and management structure of bigger enterprises may increase their costs dramatically.

Business category	Employees	Revenue	Capital employed
Medium	51–250	over €10m to €50m	over €10m to €34m
Small	11–50	over €2m to €10m	over €2m to €10m
Micro	10 or fewer	up to €2m	up to €2m

Table 3.1 EU classifications of business size

Problem of defining size

Supermarket	Employees	Capital employed (£m)	Revenue (£m)	Selling space (Sq. metres)	No. of outlets
W	300	150	250	55,000	15
X	800	500	1,200	300,000	20
Y	1,200	700	1,000	400,000	35
Z	1,500	400	400	150,000	40

[25 marks, 35 minutes]

1 Which business is largest, using the following measures of size:
   - employees
   - capital employed
   - revenue
   - selling space
   - number of outlets? [5]

2 What do your results tell you about your attempt to measure business size? [5]

3 Explain which would be the preferred measure of size in the following circumstances:
   - the government wishes to identify the supermarket with the greatest degree of monopoly power
   - a bank wishes to lend money to the business with the largest capital base
   - a shareholder wishes to invest in the business with the greatest sales potential. [9]

4 What can you conclude about the levels of efficiency of these four businesses? [6]

Even huge corporations started out small! The founders of Hewlett-Packard started the business in this garage.

These factors demonstrate the key benefits to a country's economy of a thriving small-business sector. They explain why nearly all governments are keen to encourage and assist business start-ups and existing small businesses.

Government assistance for small businesses

Most governments provide special assistance for small businesses (see also Table 3.2). These include:

1 Reduced rate of profits tax (corporation tax) – this will allow a small company the chance to retain more profits in the business for expansion.

2 Loan guarantee scheme – this is a government-funded scheme that guarantees the repayment of a certain percentage of a bank loan should the business fail. This makes banks much more likely to lend to newly formed businesses. However, the rates of interest are often higher than market rates and the firm must pay an insurance premium to the government.

3 Information, advice and support will be provided through the Small Firms agency of the Department for Business, Innovation and Skills.

4 In very economically deprived areas, such as cities with high unemployment, governments finance the establishment of small workshops, which are rented to small firms at reasonable rents. Other aid is designed to help small firms overcome the particular problems that they frequently experience. These include:
   - Lack of specialist management expertise – often the owner has to undertake all management functions, such as marketing, operations management, keeping accounts and dealing with staff matters, because the business cannot afford to employ specialists in each of these areas.
   - Problems in raising both short- and long-term finance – small firms have little security to offer banks in exchange

for loans and this makes obtaining finance much more difficult than for most larger firms. Also, suppliers may be reluctant to sell goods on credit if the business has been operating for only a short time.

■ Marketing risks from a limited product range – many small firms produce just one type of good or service – or at least a very limited range of them. This exposes them to problems should consumer tastes and demand conditions change.

■ Difficulty in finding suitable and reasonably priced premises.

ACTIVITY 3.2

Use the Internet, libraries or government agencies to research details of government support programmes for small businesses in your own country (if you live in one of the countries below, there is still a lot more to find out).

The potential advantages and disadvantages of small and large business organisations are summarized in Tables 3.3 and 3.4.

KEY CONCEPT LINK

Do you think small or large businesses are likely to be more **innovative**? Most social media innovations have been produced by small-scale entrepreneurs setting up a business – which then becomes hugely successful, e.g. Twitter and Facebook.

TOP TIP

Many business observers focus only on the benefits of small businesses. Do remember that large businesses supply most of the world's consumer goods and they do so with increasing efficiency and, in most cases, improving levels of quality.

India	Trinidad and Tobago	United Kingdom
Small Industries Development Organisation: ■ credit guarantee scheme ■ micro-finance programme ■ capital subsidy scheme for technology upgrading National Small Industries Corporation: ■ marketing support scheme for small firms ■ credit support scheme, e.g. for marketing activities and purchase of raw materials ■ technology support scheme, e.g. application of new technologies in small businesses	Venture Capital Incentive Programme: ■ increase in supply of share capital to new enterprise sector ■ tax credits offered to investors in new businesses National Enterprise Development Company: ■ financial support to small businesses ■ professional advice to entrepreneurs on marketing, business management and business planning Ministry of Social Development: ■ offers financial assistance to underprivileged persons to set up micro-businesses ■ help with writing business plans	■ National Department for Business and Enterprise Grant for Research and Development by Small Businesses ■ Regional Selective Assistance scheme offers grants to small firms that invest capital in areas of high unemployment and create jobs – up to 35% capital grants available ■ England Rural Development Programme offers grants to farmers for conversion of rural buildings for use by small businesses and for farm diversification programmes

Table 3.2 Examples of support for small businesses offered by three governments

Advantages of small businesses	Advantages of large businesses
■ can be managed and controlled by the owner(s) ■ often able to adapt quickly to meet changing customer needs ■ offer personal service to customers ■ find it easier to know each worker, and many staff prefer to work for a smaller, more 'human' business ■ if family-owned, the business culture is often informal, employees well-motivated and family members perform multiple roles	■ can afford to employ specialist professional managers ■ benefit from the cost reductions associated with large-scale production (see Chapter 23) ■ may be able to set low prices that other firms have to follow ■ have access to several different sources of finance ■ may be diversified in several markets and products so that risks are spread ■ are more likely to be able to afford research and development into new products and processes

Table 3.3 Potential advantages of small and large businesses

33

Disadvantages of small businesses	Disadvantages of large businesses
■ may have limited access to sources of finance ■ the owner/s has/have to carry a large burden of responsibility if unable to afford to employ specialist managers ■ may not be diversified, so there are greater risks of negative impact of external change ■ few opportunities for economies of scale	■ may be difficult to manage, especially if geographically spread ■ may have potential cost increases associated with large-scale production ■ may suffer from slow decision-making and poor communication due to the structure of the large organisation ■ may often suffer from a divorce between ownership and control that can lead to conflicting objectives

Table 3.4 Potential disadvantages of small and large businesses

Strengths and weaknesses of family businesses

Family-owned businesses are those that are actively owned and managed by at least two members of the same family. In many cases, the family that founded the business retains complete ownership of it. Family-owned businesses are very important in nearly all economies, especially newly industrialising ones. It is estimated that 80% of all businesses in South Africa are family owned and operated. Many family businesses are small – 65% of all small businesses in Malaysia are family-owned and managed. However, not all family businesses are small. In Asia, family businesses make up 50% of all public limited companies (67% in India) and the founding families still retain a controlling interest (over 50% of shares). Family businesses have several significant strengths and weaknesses – see Table 3.5.

Business growth

The owners of many businesses do not want the firm to remain small – although some do, for reasons of remaining in control, avoiding taking too many risks and preventing workloads from becoming too heavy. Why do other business owners and directors of companies seek growth for their business? There are a number of possible reasons:

- Increased profits – expanding the business and achieving higher sales is one way of becoming more profitable.
- Increased market share – this will give a business a higher market profile and greater bargaining power with both suppliers (e.g. lower prices) and retailers (e.g. best positions in the shop).
- Increased economies of scale – these are fully covered in Chapter 23.

Strengths	Weaknesses
Commitment: The family owners often show dedication in seeing the business grow, prosper and get passed on to future generations. As a result, many family members identify with the company and have the incentive to work harder and reinvest part of their profits into the business to allow it to grow in the long term.	**Succession/continuity problem:** Many family businesses fail to be sustainable in the long term. On average only around 15% continue into the third generation of the descendants of the founder(s). This high rate of failure among family businesses can often be explained by the lack of skills and ability of later generations or the splitting of management responsibilities between several family members to give them all a role in it.
Reliability and pride: Because family businesses have their name and reputation associated with their products, they strive to increase the quality of their output and to maintain a good relationship with their stakeholders.	**Informality:** Because most families run their businesses themselves, there is usually little interest in setting clear and formal business practices and procedures. As the family and its business grow larger, this situation can lead to inefficiencies and internal conflicts.
Knowledge continuity: Families in business make it a priority to pass their accumulated knowledge, experience and skills to the next generation. Many family members become involved in the family business from a very young age. This increases their level of commitment and could provide them with the necessary tools to run their family business.	**Traditional:** There is quite often a reluctance to change systems and procedures, preferring to continue to operate as it was historically run. Lack of innovation could be a consequence. **Conflict:** Problems within the family may reflect on management of the business and make effective decisions less likely.

Table 3.5 Strengths and weaknesses of family businesses

- Increased power and status of the owners and directors – for example, the opportunities to gain publicity or influence government policy will increase if the business controlled by the owners or directors is large and well-known.
- Reduced risk of being a takeover target – a larger business may become too large a target for a potential 'predator' company.

Internal growth

Business growth can be achieved in a number of ways and these forms of growth can lead to differing effects on stakeholder groups, such as customers, workers and competitors. The different forms of growth can be grouped into **internal** and external growth. Figure 3.1 illustrates this.

KEY TERM

Internal growth: expansion of a business by means of opening new branches, shops or factories (also known as organic growth).

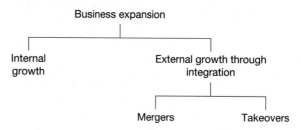

Figure 3.1 Different forms of growth

An example of internal growth would be a retailing business opening more shops in towns and cities where it previously had none. This growth can be quite slow with, perhaps, only a few branches or shops opening each year. However, it can avoid problems of excessively fast growth, which tend to lead to inadequate capital (overtrading), and management problems associated with bringing two businesses together that often have different attitudes and cultures.

35

SUMMARY POINTS

- There are several ways of measuring the size of businesses – there is no 'best' measure.
- Governments offer special assistance to small firms because of their economic benefits.
- Small firms experience particular problems.
- Not all owners of small firms wish to expand their business.
- Business growth can be achieved in a number of ways.
- Different forms of external growth have different impacts on stakeholders.

RESEARCH TASKS

1 Over a period of one month, gather all of the information that you can, from newspapers, the Internet and other media, on business plans to expand by opening new factories, offices or shops. Make a list of these plans and comment on them. Research the business reasons for these expansion plans. Do you think that these expansion plans will be successful? How are they likely to affect customers and employees?

2 Make a list of 20 local 'small' firms – use your own definition of 'small'. Classify them according to:

- primary, secondary or tertiary activity
- type of legal structure.

Comment on your findings.

AS Level exam practice questions
Short answer questions

[38 marks, 40 minutes]

Knowledge and understanding

1 List **three** stakeholder groups that might wish to compare the size of one business with another. [3]

2 For each of the stakeholders in Q1, explain why they might be interested in the size of a business. [3]

3 Why might comparing the size of two businesses by number of employees give a misleading picture? [2]

4 What is meant by the 'market capitalisation' measure of business size and how will it be affected by a stock exchange crash? [3]

Application

5 Explain **one** potential strength and **one** potential weakness for a business if an entrepreneur, who is retiring, encourages their children to continue owning and managing the business. [6]

6 Outline **four** benefits to your country's economy that would result from the growth of the number of small firms. [8]

7 Identify a small business in your own town/area. Explain **two** problems this business experiences because it is small. [5]

8 A computer manufacturer is planning to expand. Explain to its management, with appropriate examples, the difference between internal and external growth. [4]

9 A fast-food business in your country decides to expand by using retained earnings to purchase more small shops that it can convert into restaurants. Explain one advantage and one disadvantage to the business from this form of expansion. [4]

Data response

Small restaurant business expands rapidly

Chai Wei's restaurant business is proving to be a great success. His strategy of charging very low prices and locating in poor areas of town is starting to bring rewards. He has taken advantage of the small-firms loan scheme operated by the government, which offers cheap loans to business people who set up firms in areas of high unemployment. His three restaurants now employ 50 staff and Chai Wei manages all aspects of the business himself. He is a very ambitious entrepreneur and has applied for the prize of the 'Most successful small family business of the year'. The Trade Department, the organisers of the competition, have written back to ask for details of the size of his workforce, as only firms with less than 40 employees can take part in the contest. Chai Wei was very upset when he saw this. His best friend, who ran a design firm based on computerised design software, had also applied and, because he had only ten workers, he was able to enter. Despite this setback, Chai Wei was pleased with the progress of his business.

He wants to ensure that his business continues after he retires. He has three sons, one of whom has worked in the restaurant since leaving school. Chai Wei plans to give management roles to all three sons and to slowly withdraw from operating the business himself.

[AS Level – 30 marks, 35 minutes]

1 a Define the term 'small firms'. [2]

   b Briefly explain the term 'family business'. [3]

2 Outline **three** other measures the Trade Department could have used to assess the size of Chai Wei's business other than number of employees? [6]

3 Analyse the possible advantages and disadvantages to the business if Chai Wei gives his sons management positions. [8]

4 Do you think businesses such as Chai Wei's restaurant should receive government support? Explain your answer. [11]

AS Level essay questions

[20 marks, 40 minutes each]

1 a Examine **three** different ways in which business size may be compared. [8]

   b Evaluate the advantages and disadvantages to a mobile (cell) phone manufacturer of internal growth. [12]

2 a Explain the role of small firms in any industry of your choice. [8]

   b Discuss the likely strengths and weaknesses of family-owned businesses. [12]

4 Business objectives

On completing this chapter, you will be able to:

- understand the importance of setting objectives
- understand the importance of these being SMART
- appreciate the links between mission statements, corporate objectives and business strategy
- understand the relationship between objectives and strategies
- assess the importance of communicating objectives to stakeholders, especially employees
- analyse why objectives might change over time
- critically assess how corporate social responsibility and ethics can influence business objectives and activities.

Introducing the topic

HEALTH AND BEAUTY FOR YOU

June Wong was rather pleased with herself. Since setting up the business called Health and Beauty for You with her brother, Will, they had managed to keep the business going through three very difficult years. When they set the business up, they agreed that their first objective was survival at all costs. Despite the country's economic difficulties and some fierce competition, the business had built up a good customer base and had covered all of its costs for the first three years. Now the pair had decided to plan for the next three years and the first stage of this was to agree on new objectives for the business. June wanted the business to grow and she thought the best way to do this was to buy another beauty salon in another area of the city. 'This will get the business name really well-known and will give us the basis for further sales growth of at least 20% a year,' she told Will. He was not so sure he wanted the staffing and marketing problems associated with another salon. 'I think we should aim to make as much profit as we can

from the existing salon. I think we could aim for a profit of $40,000 per year. We could offer a wider range of services and increase our prices. After all, we went into business with the intention of becoming rich!' he reminded June.

After much argument, the pair agreed that the new business objective should be, in the short term, to open a new salon and to double sales within three years. After this had been achieved, the aim should be to maximise long-term profits from the two locations by improving image and raising prices – Will thought a five-year target of $90,000 per year was realistic.

Points to think about:

- What do you understand by the term 'objective'?
- Do you think it is important that Health and Beauty for You should have clear objectives? Explain your answer with as many reasons as you can.
- Why do you think June and Will are thinking of changing the objectives for their business over time?

Introduction

Businesses of any size can benefit from having clear objectives or targets to work towards. In small sole-trader businesses, these objectives are often not written down or formalised in any way, but the owners will often have a clear idea of what they are trying to achieve. In partnership organisations, it is important for partners to agree on the direction their business should take or future disagreements can cause much time to be wasted that would be better spent on running the business effectively. Limited companies must state the overall

objectives of the business in their Memorandum of Association, but this often lacks strategic detail. This chapter focuses on the importance of business objectives, the different forms that these can take and how they can be used to help direct the work of all staff in an organisation.

The importance of objectives

Almost all aspects of human activity are made clearer and more focused if there is a distinct objective to aim for. A business aim helps to direct, control and review the success of business activity. In addition, for any aim to be successfully achieved, there has to be an appropriate strategy – or detailed plan of action – in place to ensure that resources are correctly directed towards the final goal. This strategy should be constantly reviewed to check whether the business is on target to achieve its objectives. Both the aims of an organisation and the strategies it adopts will often change over time. Indeed, a change of objective will almost certainly require a change of plan too. A poor plan or strategy will lead to failure to reach the target (Unit 6 focuses on how businesses develop strategies to meet their objectives).

The most effective business objectives usually meet the following 'SMART' criteria:

S – Specific: Objectives should focus on what the business does and should apply directly to that business. A hotel may set an objective of 75% bed occupancy over the winter period. This objective is specific to this business.

M – Measurable: Objectives that have a quantitative value are likely to prove to be more effective targets for directors and staff to work towards. For instance, to increase sales in the south-east region by 15% this year.

A – Achievable: Setting objectives that are almost impossible in the time frame given will be pointless. They will demotivate staff who have the task of trying to reach these targets. So objectives should be achievable.

R – Realistic and relevant: Objectives should be realistic when compared with the resources of the company and should be expressed in terms relevant to the people who have to carry them out. So informing a factory cleaner about 'increasing market share' is less relevant than a target of reducing usage of cleaning materials by 20%.

T – Time-specific: A time limit should be set when an objective is established – by when does the business expect to increase profits by 5%? Without a time limit, it will be impossible to assess whether the objective has actually been met.

TOP TIP
Remember the slogan: SMART.

Aims, mission statements, objectives and strategies – what do they all mean?

The links between these concepts can be made clearer by studying this 'hierarchy of objectives' (Figure 4.1), which shows, visually, the balance and dependencies between the different stages in the setting of aims and objectives. Later in this chapter we will consider the importance of these objectives to business strategies.

Figure 4.1 Hierarchy of objectives

Corporate aims

These are the very long-term goals that a business hopes to achieve. The core central purpose of a business's activity is expressed in its corporate aims. Sole traders and partnerships – not just companies – will also commonly develop the same kind of long-term vision for their business.

The case study demonstrates a typical corporate aim. Daimler Mercedes-Benz tells us that it aims to achieve profitable growth by continuing to play a leading role in the automobile industry. Other corporate aims tend to concentrate on customer-based goals – such as 'meeting customers' needs' – or market-based goals – such as 'becoming the world leader'. All corporate aims have certain characteristics in common. They are all-embracing, that is they are designed to provide guidance

39

ACTIVITY 4.1

Daimler Mercedes-Benz

Daimler is one of the world's largest manufacturers of luxury cars. It aims to maximise value for shareholders through a strategy of profitable growth in both existing and new markets and by increasing market share through product innovation.

'We don't only want to get better. We want to beat the competition – on a permanent basis,' stated Dr. Dieter Zetsche, chairman of the board of management of Daimler AG.

[10 marks, 15 minutes]

Explain the benefits to Daimler of the company's aims and objectives.

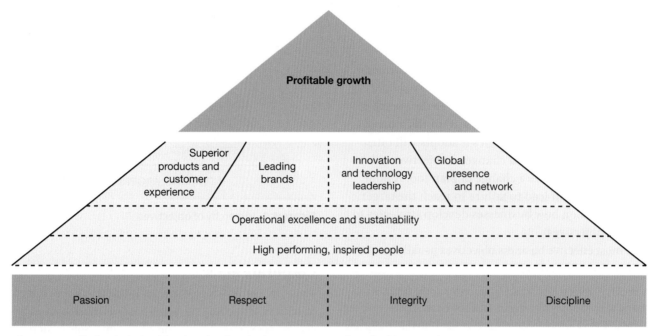

Figure 4.2 All of Daimler's objectives lead to the long-term aim of profitable growth

to the whole organisation and not just a part of it. This is shown by Daimler's target system illustrated in Figure 4.2. So, what benefits flow from establishing corporate aims?

- They become the starting point for the entire set of objectives on which effective management is based. This is shown by their position at the top of the hierarchy of objectives in Figure 4.1. Daimler is pursuing the following specific objectives in order to achieve its aim of profitable growth:
  - selling at least 1.6 million Mercedes-Benz passenger cars each year by 2015 and leading the way in the premium segment in terms of unit sales by 2020
  - consolidating its leading role in the truck sector by selling more than 500,000 units in 2015 and more than 700,000 units in 2020.
- Corporate aims can help develop a sense of purpose and direction for the whole organisation if they are clearly and unambiguously communicated to the workforce.
- They allow an assessment to be made, at a later date, of how successful the business has been in attaining its goals.
- Aims provide the framework within which the strategies or plans of the business can be drawn up. A business without long-term corporate aims is likely to drift from event to event without a clear plan of action for the future. This will quickly become obvious to the workforce and customers, who may respond in adverse ways.

It is becoming increasingly common for businesses to express the corporate aim in one short, sharp 'vision-like' statement to be made known to as many stakeholders as possible, and these are the mission statements that are discussed next.

New car and truck designs are an important strategy to help Daimler achieve its long-term aim

Mission statements

Mission statements are an attempt to condense the central purpose of a business's existence into one statement. They are not concerned with specific, quantifiable goals, but try to sum up – often in rather

 KEY TERM

Mission statement: a statement of the business's core aims, phrased in a way to motivate employees and to stimulate interest by outside groups.

woolly language, it must be said – the aims of the business in a motivating and appealing way.

Here are some examples of mission statements:

A Level college: 'To provide an academic curriculum in a caring and supportive environment.'

British Telecom: 'To be the most successful worldwide telecommunications group.'

Unigate: 'We are committed to consistent profitable growth as the means by which we can provide attractive returns to shareholders, be a responsible employer and support the communities in which we operate.'

Microsoft: 'To enable people and businesses throughout the world to realize their full potential.'

Google: 'To organize the world's information and make it universally accessible and useful.'

Merck: 'Provide society with superior products and services by developing innovations and solutions that improve the quality of life and satisfy customer needs, to provide employees with meaningful work and advancement opportunities and investors with a superior rate of return.'

Evaluation of mission statements

Which of the mission statements above is the most effective, do you think? Do you agree that some of them are interchangeable, that is, some of them could apply to any of the businesses? If you do, then this is one of the potential limitations of such statements. Virtually any organisation of any size will, in recent years, have established a mission statement. Do they perform a useful function or are they just another management fad? Some of the arguments used in favour of mission statements seem to be they:

- quickly inform groups outside the business what the central aim and vision are
- can prove motivating to employees, especially where an organisation is looked upon, as a result of its mission statement, as a caring and environmentally friendly body – employees will then be associated with these positive qualities
- often include moral statements or values to be worked towards, and these can help to guide and direct individual employee behaviour at work
- are not meant to be detailed working objectives, but they help to establish in the eyes of other groups 'what the business is about'.

On the other hand, these statements are often criticised for being:

- too vague and general, so that they end up saying little that is specific about the business or its future plans
- based on a public relations exercise to make stakeholder groups feel good about the organisation

- virtually impossible to really analyse or disagree with
- often rather woolly and general, so it is common for two completely different businesses to have very similar mission statements.

Communicating mission statements is almost as important as establishing them. There is little point in identifying the central vision for a business and then not letting anyone else know about it. Businesses communicate their mission statements in a number of ways. They often feature in the published accounts and in other communications to shareholders. They will appear in the corporate plans of the business – the detailed report on the company's aims and strategies for the future. Internal company newsletters and magazines may draw their title from part of the mission statement. Advertising slogans or posters are frequently based around the themes of the mission statements – The Body Shop is most effective in incorporating its mission into the different eco-friendly campaigns it launches. In summary, mission statements, rather like the corporate aims on which they are based, are insufficient for operational guidelines. They do not tell managers what decisions to take or how to manage the business. They provide a vision and an overall sense of purpose, and, in public relations terms at least, they can prove very worthwhile.

> **ACTIVITY 4.2**
>
> 1 Using either company websites or printed published accounts, discover the 'missions' of three well-known public limited companies.
>
> 2 Analyse how much these mission statements tell you about the vision and operations of these businesses.
>
> 3 Suggest how the statements that you have researched might be communicated to three different stakeholder groups.
>
> 4 Find out if your school or college has a mission statement. By asking staff, students and parents, attempt to establish whether this statement has had any impact on their view of the school.

Corporate objectives

The aim and mission statements of a business share the same problems – they lack specific detail for operational decisions and they are rarely expressed in quantitative terms. They need to be turned into goals or targets quite specific to each business that can themselves be broken down into strategic departmental targets. Corporate objectives are designed to do just this. They are, of course, based upon the central aim or mission of the business, but they are expressed in terms that provide a much clearer guide for management action or strategy.

Common corporate objectives

1 Profit maximisation

All the stakeholders in a business are working for reward. Profits are essential for rewarding investors in a business and for financing further growth. Profits are necessary to persuade business owners – or entrepreneurs – to take risks. But what does 'profit maximisation' really mean? In simple terms, it means producing at that level of output where the greatest positive difference between total revenue and total costs is achieved.

The chief argument in support of this objective is that it seems rational to seek the maximum profit available from a given venture. Not to maximise profit, according to this objective, is seen as a missed opportunity. However, there are serious limitations with this corporate objective:

- The focus on high short-term profits may encourage competitors to enter the market and jeopardise the long-term survival of the business.
- Many businesses seek to maximise sales in order to secure the greatest possible market share, rather than to maximise profits. The business would expect to make a target rate of profit from these sales.
- The owners of smaller businesses may be more concerned with ensuring that leisure time is safeguarded. The issues of independence and retaining control may assume greater significance than making higher profits.
- Most business analysts assess the performance of a business through return on capital employed rather than through total profit figures.
- Profit maximisation may well be the preferred objective of the owners and shareholders, but other stakeholders will give priority to other issues. Business managers cannot ignore these. Hence the growing concern over job security for the workforce or the environmental concerns of local residents may force profitable business decisions to be modified, yielding lower profit levels.
- In practice it is very difficult to assess whether the point of profit maximisation has been reached, and constant changes to prices or output to attempt to achieve it may well lead to negative consumer reactions.

2 Profit satisficing

This means aiming to achieve enough profit to keep the owners happy but not aiming to work flat out to earn as much profit as possible. This objective is often suggested as being common among owners of small businesses who wish to live comfortably but do not want to work longer and longer hours in order to earn even more profit. Once a satisfactory level of profit has been achieved, the owners consider that other aims take priority – such as more leisure time.

3 Growth

The growth of a business – usually measured in terms of sales or value of output – has many potential benefits for the managers and owners. Larger firms will be less likely to be taken over and should be able to benefit from economies of scale. Managers will be motivated by the desire to see the business achieve its full potential, from which they may gain higher salaries and fringe benefits. It is also argued that a business that does not attempt to grow will cease to be competitive and, eventually, will lose its appeal to new investors. Business objectives based on growth do have limitations:

- expansion that is too rapid can lead to cash-flow problems
- sales growth might be achieved at the expense of lower profit margins
- larger businesses can experience diseconomies of scale
- using profits to finance growth – retained earnings – can lead to lower short-term returns to shareholders
- growth into new business areas and activities – away from the firm's core activities – can result in a loss of focus and direction for the whole organisation.

4 Increasing market share

Closely linked to overall growth of a business is the market share it enjoys within its main market. Although the two are usually related, it is possible for an expanding business to suffer market share reductions if the market is growing at a faster rate than the business itself. Increasing market share indicates that the marketing mix of the business is proving to be more successful than that of its competitors. Benefits resulting from having the highest market share – being the brand leader – include:

- retailers will be keen to stock and promote the best-selling brand
- profit margins offered to retailers may be lower than competing brands as the shops are so keen to stock it – this leaves more profit for the producer
- effective promotional campaigns are often based on 'buy our product with confidence – it is the brand leader'.

5 Survival

This is likely to be the key objective of most new business start-ups. The high failure rate of new businesses means that to survive for the first two years of trading is an important aim for entrepreneurs. Once the business has become firmly established, then other longer-term objectives can be established.

6 Corporate social responsibility (CSR)

Should firms have objectives about social, environmental and ethical issues? Increasingly, there is general agreement that firms must adopt a wider perspective when setting their objectives and not just be aiming for profits or expansion. One reason for this is the much greater adverse publicity given to business activity that is perceived as being damaging to stakeholder groups and the wider world. Increasingly, influential pressure groups are forcing businesses to reconsider their approach to decision-making. Also, legal changes – at the local, national and EU level – have forced businesses to refrain from certain practices. Firms can no longer pay staff very low wages or avoid legal responsibility for their products. Managers clearly wish to avoid conflicts with the law or bad publicity.

There are other reasons for these trends in business objectives – increasingly, consumers and other stakeholders are reacting positively to businesses that act in 'green' or socially responsible ways. Examples include:

- Firms that promote organic and vegetarian foods.
- Retailers that advertise the proportion of their products made from recycled materials.
- Businesses that refuse to stock goods that have been tested on animals or foods based on genetically modified ingredients.

In these cases, is the action being taken because trade and reputation might be lost if it is not or because such action is increasingly profitable? Might businesses be criticised for 'jumping on the corporate social responsibility bandwagon' rather than praised for their genuine concern for society and the environment? Conceivably, firms are being ethical or environmentally conscious because they have an objective that Peter Drucker, a famous writer on management, calls 'public responsibility', because they want to behave in these ways. Many consumer groups and pressure groups are still dubious as to whether these objectives are based on genuinely held beliefs or not. Chapter 5 discusses the impact of social and environmental pressures on business and business stakeholders in more detail.

Reuters achieving its aims

Reuters, one of the world's largest news agencies, has returned to profitability after several years of losses. It aims to increase value for shareholders, and the fact that Reuters's shares have risen 7% faster than average share prices suggests that the company is becoming increasingly successful. Profits are being made for two main reasons. Many jobs have been lost in the company in recent years as a result of the chief executive's policy of cutting costs. Secondly, an ambitious growth objective has been established to increase sales and this target is being reached. New products (such as electronic trading) and new markets (such as China, Russia and India) have allowed an increase in sales of over 6% this year. This is above the growth target that was set. Some analysts are predicting a 40% increase in profit for the company next year.

[18 marks, 25 minutes]

1. What evidence is there that Reuters is meeting its objectives? [4]
2. Explain two benefits to the managers and other employees of the company from having clearly stated company aims and objectives. [6]
3. To what extent does the policy of increasing shareholder value conflict with other objectives the business might have? [8]

7 Maximising short-term sales revenue

This could benefit managers and staff when salaries and bonuses are dependent on sales revenue levels. However, if increased sales are achieved by reducing prices, the actual profits of the business might fall.

8 Maximising shareholder value

This could apply to public limited companies and directs management action towards taking decisions that would increase the company share price and dividends paid to shareholders. These targets might be achieved by pursuing the goal of profit maximisation. This shareholder-value objective puts the interests of shareholders above those of other stakeholders. Chapter 5 considers the potential conflict between this objective and the aims of other stakeholder groups.

Relationship between mission, objectives, strategy and tactics

Aims and objectives provide the basis and focus for business strategies – the long-term plans of action of a business that focus on achieving its aims. Without a clear objective, a manager will be unable to make important strategic decisions. For example, should a marketing manager decide to sell products in new markets or attempt to sell more in existing markets? Without a clear corporate objective that is then translated into a marketing objective, decisions of this kind become very arbitrary. These links between objectives and strategies are shown in Figure 4.3

Without clear objectives, decision-making will lack direction and a means of assessing success. Every stage of decision-making – collecting data about options, choosing a strategic option and reviewing success/failure – is made much more meaningful with specific business objectives to refer to.

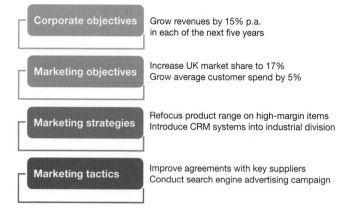

Figure 4.3 Links between objectives and strategies

 KEY CONCEPT LINK

The setting of clear and realistic objectives is one of the primary roles of senior **management**. Before **strategy** for future action can be established, objectives are needed.

ACTIVITY 4.4

Is STS plc successful?

STS plc is a waste-disposal business. It collects waste from houses, offices and factories. Most of the waste is burnt to produce heat and electricity for the company's own use. This saves costs and reduces the impact on the environment by not using fields and valleys in which to bury the rubbish. A recent increase in the number of customers has meant that not all of the waste can be burnt and the company has dumped it in old quarries where it causes smells and gas emissions. Investment in labour-saving equipment has allowed the business to save on wage costs. The company's new mission statement is to 'Become the country's number-one waste business and to protect the environment for our children's benefit'. This has been explained to all shareholders in a recent letter to them, but the company's employees were not involved in helping create the mission statement and they have not been informed of it.

The latest company accounts stated that: 'We aim to maximise returns to shareholders through a strategy of aggressive growth. Our objectives are to expand year on year.' These accounts also contained the following data:

	2010	2011	2012	2013
Sales revenue $m	20	25	35	40
Operating profit $m	3	8	10	20
Total value of country's waste market $m	120	140	160	180
Number of employees	1,000	950	900	800

[20 marks, 30 minutes]

1 How useful is the company's new mission statement? [4]

2 The company's objectives do not appear to be completely SMART. Explain the problems that might result from this. [6]

3 Using the information provided, to what extent is the business achieving success? Justify your answer. [10]

Objectives and decision-making

Effective decision-making requires clear objectives. Business managers cannot decide on future plans of action – strategies – if they are uncertain of which direction they want to take the business in. This essential link between decisions and objectives is illustrated in the decision making framework model shown in Figure 4.4.

The stages in this decision making framework are:

1 Set objectives.
2 Assess the problem or situation.
3 Gather data about the problem and possible solutions.
4 Consider all decision options.
5 Make the strategic decision.
6 Plan and implement the decision.
7 Review its success against the original objectives.

Clearly, without setting relevant objectives at the start of this process, effective decision-making for the future of the business becomes impossible.

How corporate objectives might change

There are many examples of businesses changing their corporate objectives over time. These are some of the reasons for this:

1 A newly formed business may have satisfied the 'survival' objective by operating for several years, and now the owners wish to pursue objectives of growth or increased profit.

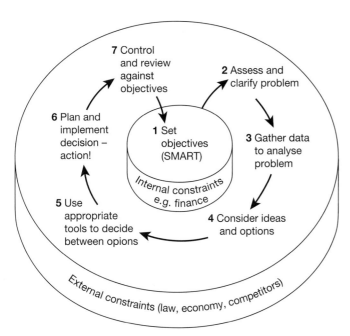

Figure 4.4 A decision-making framework

2 The competitive and economic environment may change, so the entry into the market of a powerful rival or the start of an economic recession may lead a firm to switch from growth to survival as its main aim – or even just to revise its objectives for sales and profits downwards.

3 A short-term objective of growth in sales or market share might be adapted to a longer-term objective of maximising profits from the higher level of sales.

Factors that determine the corporate objectives of a business

Corporate culture

Clearly, not all businesses pursue the same objectives. There are several factors that influence the nature of the objectives established for any business. Chief among these is the culture of the organisation. This can be defined as the code of behaviour and attitudes that influence the decision-making style of the managers and other employees of the business. Culture is a way of doing things that is shared by all those in the organisation. Culture is about people, how they perform and deal with others, how aggressive they are in the pursuit of objectives and how adaptable they are in the face of change. If directors are aggressive in pursuit of their aims, are keen to take over or defeat rival businesses and care little about social or environmental factors, then the objectives of the business will be very different to those of a business owned and controlled by directors with a more people- or social-oriented culture.

The size and legal form of the business

Owners of small businesses may be concerned only with a satisfactory level of profit – called 'satisficing'. Larger businesses, perhaps controlled by directors rather than owners, such as most public limited companies, might be more concerned with rapid business growth in order to increase the status and power of the managers. This is often a result of a development known as the 'divorce between ownership and control', which nearly always exists in large companies with professional directors who do not own it. They may be more concerned about their bonuses, salaries and fringe benefits – which often depend on business size – than on maximising returns to shareholders.

Public-sector or private-sector businesses

State-owned organisations tend not to have profit as a major objective. The aims of these organisations can vary greatly, but when the service they provide is not charged for, such as education and health services, then a financial target would be inappropriate.

45

Figure 4.5 Influences on corporate objectives

Instead, 'quality of service' measures are often used, such as the maximum number of days for a patient to wait for an operation. Even businesses earning revenue in the public sector, such as a country's postal service, may have among their objectives the target of maintaining services in non-profitable locations. Recent branch closures in rural areas by private-sector banks, in order to increase profits, make an interesting contrast.

The number of years the business has been operating

Newly formed businesses are likely to be driven by the desire to survive at all costs – the failure rate of new firms in the first year of operation is very high. Later, once well established, the business may pursue other objectives, such as growth and profit. These factors are summarised in Figure 4.5.

Divisional, departmental and individual objectives

Refer to Figure 4.6. Once corporate objectives have been established they need to be broken down into specific targets for separate divisions, departments and, ultimately, individuals. Corporate objectives relate to the whole organisation. They cannot be used by each division of the business to create strategies for action until they have been broken down into meaningful targets focusing on

divisional goals. These divisional objectives must be set by senior managers to ensure:

■ coordination between all divisions – if they do not work together, the focus of the organisation will appear confused to outsiders and there will be disagreements between departments

■ consistency with corporate objectives

■ that adequate resources are provided to allow for the successful achievement of the objectives.

Once the divisional objectives have been established, then these can be further divided into departmental objectives and budgets and targets for individual workers. This process is called management by objectives (MBO).

Management by objectives (MBO)

If this process is undertaken after discussion and agreement with personnel at each level of the organisation, then it can be a very effective way of delegating authority and motivating staff. This approach would accord with McGregor's Theory Y approach (see Chapter 11). If, however, the targets at each level were merely imposed from above, as with McGregor's Theory X style, then motivation is likely to be low.

 KEY TERM

Management by objectives: a method of coordinating and motivating all staff in an organisation by dividing its overall aim into specific targets for each department, manager and employee.

Figure 4.6 is an example of how the hierarchy of objectives could now look, incorporating the principle of management by objectives. The mission statement has not been included as we have identified that it is of little operational use.

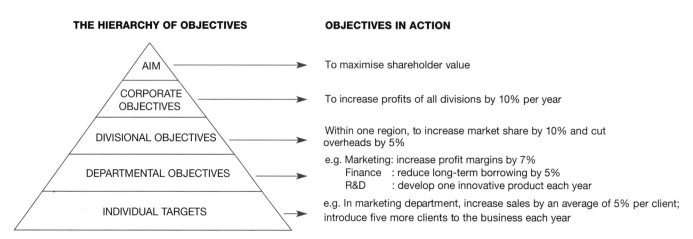

Figure 4.6 Management by objectives – how the corporate aim is divided at every level of the organisation

Oil refinery, Mexico

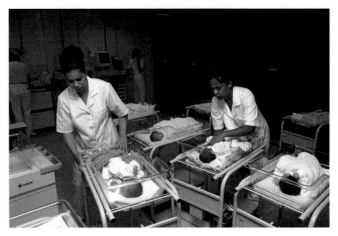
New babies in hospital, Brazil

The corporate culture of organisations may differ between private and public sectors

Communicating objectives

If employees are unaware of the business objectives then how can they contribute to achieving them? Communication of corporate objectives – and translating these into individual targets – is essential for the effective setting of aims and objectives.

If employees are communicated with – and involved in the setting of individual targets – then these benefits should result in:

- **Employees and managers achieving more** – through greater understanding of both individual and company-wide goals.
- **Employees seeing the overall plan** – and understanding how their individual goals fit into the company's business objectives.
- **Creating shared employee responsibility** – by interlinking their goals with others in the company.
- **Managers more easily staying in touch with employees' progress** – regular monitoring of employees' work allows immediate reinforcement or training to keep performance and deadlines on track.

Ethical influences on business objectives and decisions

The growing acceptance of corporate social responsibility has led to businesses adopting an '**ethical code**' to influence the way in which decisions are taken.

KEY TERM

Ethical code (code of conduct): a document detailing a company's rules and guidelines on staff behaviour that must be followed by all employees.

Most decisions have an ethical or moral dimension. For example:

- Should a toy company advertise its products to young children so that they pester their parents into buying them?
- Is it acceptable to take bribes to place an order with another company?
- Should a bank invest in a company that manufactures weapons or tests new chemicals on animals?
- Is it acceptable to feed genetically modified food to cattle?
- Do we accept lower profits in the short term by purchasing less polluting production equipment?
- Should chief executives receive substantial pay rises and bonuses when other workers in the business are being made redundant?
- Is it acceptable to close a factory to save costs and increase profits even though many jobs will be lost and workers may find it hard to get other jobs?
- If legal controls and inspections are weak in a country, is it acceptable to pay very low wages for long hours of work – as this policy will reduce the firm's costs?
- If a business can get away with it, should it employ child labour to reduce costs compared to employing adults? Or should it keep producing potentially dangerous goods as long as no one finds us out?

These are all examples of ethical dilemmas. The way in which employees behave and take decisions in these cases should be covered and explained by a company's ethical code of conduct. To what extent should and do businesses take ethics into consideration when taking decisions? There is now considerable evidence that more and more companies are considering the ethical dimension of their actions – not just the impact they might have on profits.

You are advised to think about the issues involved in all of these decisions. Different people will have different answers to these dilemmas. Some managers will argue that any business decision that reduces costs and increases profits is acceptable as long as it is legal – and some might argue that even illegal actions could be justified. Other managers will operate their business along strict ethical rules and will argue that, even if certain actions are not illegal, they are not *right*. Morally, they cannot be justified even if they might cut costs and increase sales.

Evaluating ethical decisions

Adopting and keeping to a strict ethical code in decision-making can be expensive in the short term:

- Using ethical and Fairtrade suppliers can add to business's costs.
- Not taking bribes to secure business contracts can mean failing to secure significant sales.
- Limiting the advertising of toys and other child-related products to just adults to reduce 'pester power' may result in lost sales.

- Accepting that it is wrong to fix prices with competitors might lead to lower prices and profits.
- Paying fair wages – even in very low-wage economies – raises wage costs and may reduce a firm's competitiveness against businesses that exploit workers.

However, perhaps in the long term there could be substantial benefits from acting ethically:

- Avoiding potentially expensive court cases can reduce costs of fines.
- While bad publicity from being 'caught' acting unethically can lead to lost consumer loyalty and long-term reductions in sales, ethical policies can lead to good publicity and increased sales.
- Ethical businesses attract ethical customers and as world pressure grows for corporate social responsibility, this group of consumers is increasing.
- Ethical businesses are more likely to be awarded government contracts.
- Well-qualified staff may be attracted to work for the companies with the most ethical and socially responsible policies.

ACTIVITY 4.5

Siam Cement Group (SCG)

The SCG has a strict ethical code of conduct. The key features are shown below:

Business ethics	Code of conduct
<ul><li>fairness to all who have business relationships with the company, including society and environment</li><li>making business gains in a proper manner</li><li>no alliances with political parties</li><li>non-discriminatory treatment of all staff and stakeholder groups</li></ul>	<ul><li>upholding the principles of honesty and fairness</li><li>protecting the properties and reputation of SCG</li><li>conducting business in the best interests of SCG and its stakeholders</li><li>behaving appropriately at all times towards others</li></ul>

According to a report by a business analyst, as SCG expanded beyond Thailand, managers came under pressure to compromise on its corporate code of ethics. The company's standards on bribes and other improper payments, for example, made it difficult to compete in places where such unethical payments are a way of life. This example demonstrates the classic problem: should firms conform to the standards of the country they operate in or should they try to export their own high moral principles to other lands?

[24 marks, 35 minutes]

1 Explain the following terms:
   - business ethics
   - code of conduct. [6]

2 Analyse how SCG and its employees might benefit from the clear statement of business ethics and the code of conduct. [8]

3 Should a business such as SCG ever use unethical methods in a country where they are the norm, for example the giving and accepting of bribes to obtain contracts? Justify your answer. [10]

SUMMARY OF CHAPTER 4

- There are important benefits of setting business objectives.
- The most effective objectives are likely to meet the SMART criteria.
- Mission statements are now common for almost every business but their value has been questioned.
- There should be a hierarchy of objectives, starting with the corporate aim.
- Business objectives often need to be adapted to meet changing circumstances.
- Management by objectives sets and communicates objectives to all levels of an organisation and all employees who work within it.
- Ethical policies are now common in large firms and they are contained in an ethical code for all employees to follow.

RESEARCH TASK

- Investigate the mission statement and objectives of any local organisation or company – these can often be researched through the Internet.
- Examine how useful the mission statement is to groups within the business e.g. managers and workforce, and external groups.
- Are the objectives of the organisation SMART?
- Examine the likely importance of the organisation's objectives to its future success.

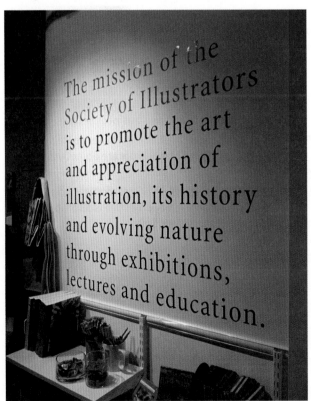

AS Level exam practice questions

Short answer questions

[55 marks, 70 minutes]

Knowledge and understanding

1   What is the purpose of a mission statement?   [3]
2   What are often considered to be the practical limitations of mission statements?   [3]
3   What do you understand by the corporate objective 'increasing shareholder value'?   [4]
4   Why might the objective of 'increasing shareholder value' conflict with corporate social responsibility?   [4]
5   Why should departmental objectives be coordinated?   [2]
6   What is meant by 'management by objectives'?   [3]
7   What do you understand by an 'ethical code of conduct'?   [3]
8   Why might some firms decide not to act ethically in a competitive market?   [6]

Application

9   Give an example of a SMART objective that could be set for your school or college.   [3]
10   Explain, with **two** examples, what corporate objectives a clothing manufacturing business could establish.   [4]
11   Why might short-term profit maximisation not be an appropriate objective for such a business?   [3]
12   Why might the owners/directors of a small private limited company set a 'profit satisficing' objective?   [3]
13   Using a business example from your own country, explain why its key corporate objectives might change over time.   [4]
14   Explain the possible benefits to a clothes retailer of strictly observing an ethical code when choosing and checking on its suppliers.   [6]
15   Explain, with an example from the soft drinks industry, how a company's marketing strategy depends on the company's objectives.   [4]

Data response

1 Peugeot Citroen's road ahead laid out

The chairman of the French car maker Peugeot Citroen has established the company aim of becoming the 'most competitive car maker in Europe by 2015'. This overall aim is supported by more specific and measurable objectives. The profit margin of each car sold is targeted to increase from 2% to 7% by 2017. The overall sales objective is to reach four million car sales a year. One million car sales are aimed for in the emerging markets by 2017. In Europe, one of the most competitive car markets in the world, the target is to increase sales by 300,000 cars a year by the same date.

Departmental operating targets have also been established. For example, the human resources department must prepare for up to 8,000 job losses and operations must aim to cut fixed manufacturing costs by 30% and costs of purchasing car parts by 4–6% a year. Marketing must plan to launch 12 new models in the Chinese market.

The chairman also announced his intention to take both car brands up market and establish them as premium car brands that increasing numbers of customers will want to own.

[AS Level – 30 marks, 45 minutes]

1 a Define the term 'company aim'. [2]

   b Briefly explain the term 'measurable objectives'. [3]

2 Explain whether the objectives outlined by Peugeot Citroen fit the SMART criteria. [6]

3 Analyse the importance of the chairman not only setting an overall aim for the company but also establishing departmental objectives. [8]

4 To what extent might these objectives have to be changed before the 2017 time limit for them is reached? [11]

2 Virgin Atlantic and British Airways to refund passengers

Two famous airlines have admitted a price-fixing agreement over fuel surcharges. They agreed to fix the same surcharges so that there would be no difference between them on the North Atlantic route. This clearly damaged passengers' interests as there was no competition. This action was against US and UK competition law. Both airlines have agreed to contact all passengers who flew over the two-year period of the illegal agreement and arrange a refund for them.

The chairman of British Airways claimed that the price-fixing agreement had been made by managers against the company's strict code of ethics. 'As we have previously said, we absolutely condemn any anti-competitive activity by anybody,' he said.

[AS Level – 20 marks, 30 minutes]

1 Explain what is meant by 'ethics'. [3]

2 What benefits could these two airlines have gained if they had not been caught breaking the law? [6]

3 Discuss whether a business acting ethically is likely to be profitable in the long run. [11]

3 Kenya Reinsurance Corporation (Kenya Re)

Kenya Re is one of the largest 'reinsurance'* businesses in Africa. It operates in a very competitive industry that is growing rapidly as many countries in Africa are experiencing economic growth. Kenya Re has corporate objectives that include:

- Promoting professionalism and ethics in the insurance industry.
- Increasing return on capital.
- Increasing revenue in new and existing markets.

The company also pursues a corporate social responsibility objective. Rather than contributing to many local and national charities, Kenya Re focuses its efforts on the 'Ability Beyond Disability' campaign. This improves the quality of lives of people living with physical disabilities by providing assistance and medical support.

Kenya Re chairman Nelius Karuki said: 'Many of the physically challenged persons do not get adequate care or support as a result of humble backgrounds or financial limitations.'

* Reinsurance: charging premiums for accepting the risk of existing insurance policies

[30 marks, 45 minutes]

1 a Define the term 'corporate objectives'. [2]

   b What is meant by the term 'corporate social responsibility objective'? [3]

2 Explain how operating in a 'very competitive industry' could affect the objectives a business sets. [6]

3 Analyse the benefits to Kenya Re's of any **two** of its corporate objectives, apart from CSR. [8]

4 Discuss whether a corporate social responsibility objective is appropriate for this business. [11]

AS Level essay questions

[20 marks, 40 minutes each]

1 a Explain the possible benefits to a business of having an objective of corporate social responsibility. [8]

   b Discuss whether the owners of a farm with three managers for different departments and 12 workers should adopt a system of 'management by objectives'. [12]

2 a Explain how ethics may influence business objectives and activities. [8]

   b Evaluate the extent to which the success of a large retail business depends upon having a clear mission statement. [12]

5 Stakeholders in a business

On completing this chapter, you will be able to:

- explain what is meant by 'stakeholder'
- analyse and comment on the roles, rights and responsibilities of key business stakeholders
- demonstrate an awareness of how and why a business might consider stakeholder interests in its decision-making – the benefits of being 'socially responsible'
- evaluate ways in which conflicting stakeholder objectives might be recognised and responded to by business.

Introducing the topic

TATA NANO – WHICH STAKEHOLDERS BENEFIT FROM IT?

It is three metres long, seats four, does 100 kilometres an hour and, when launched, aimed to revolutionise travel for millions. The 'People's Car' is also the cheapest in the world at 100,000 Rupees (US$2,600) – about the same price as a DVD player in a Lexus. When Rattan Tata, the company chairman, unveiled the cute, snub-nosed car it was believed that it would allow millions of Asia's emerging middle classes to buy a car for the first time. 'This will change the way people travel in India and Asia. This is a car that will be affordable to millions of consumers for the first time,' he said when the car was launched. However, sales levels are currently way below those forecast – just 554 units in December 2013. Customers are being put off by the car's poor safety record and the title 'the world's cheapest car'. Tata plan to relaunch the car at a higher price with an improved specification under the advertising headline of 'celebrating awesomeness' – hoping to make the car profitable for shareholders once more.

The car is built in a factory in West Bengal, offering relatively well-paid factory employment to many workers for the first time. India gains export revenue when the car is sold abroad. The steel and other materials used in the car are purchased from Asian suppliers, which helps to boost local economies and suppliers.

The idea of millions of cheap cars on the road alarms environmental groups. Rajendra Pachauri, the UN's chief climate scientist, said that he was

What makes the Nano so cheap?

'having nightmares' about the environmental impact. Delhi, where air pollution levels are more than twice the safe limit, is registering 1,000 new cars a day. Average speed of traffic at rush hour is only ten kilometres an hour and the government might be forced to spend much more on building new roads if Nano ownership becomes more widespread. Bus operators also fear increased competition from private car users.

Points to think about:

- List the groups of people who benefit from Nano car production.
- List the groups of people who might be badly affected by the use of large numbers of small, cheap cars.
- Do you think Tata should attempt to reduce the potential conflicts between the interests of these groups?

Introduction

The traditional view of business is often called 'the shareholder concept'. The shareholders are the owners of the company and the firm has a legally binding duty to put their needs first – in other words, to take actions and to make decisions that will increase shareholder value. It is important to remember that directors and managers ultimately owe their position to shareholders – so it is important to keep them satisfied.

In recent times, this limited view of business responsibility has been extended to include the interests not just of the investors/owners, but also the suppliers, employees and customers. This more recent approach to business responsibilities does not end with these four groups, however. The **stakeholder theory** or **stakeholder concept** is that there are many other parties involved and interested in business activity and that the interests of these groups – local communities, the public, government and pressure groups, such as environmental lobbyists – should be considered by business decision-makers.

KEY TERMS

Stakeholders: people or groups of people who can be affected by – and therefore have an interest in – any action by an organisation.

Stakeholder concept: the view that businesses and their managers have responsibilities to a wide range of groups, not just shareholders.

Business stakeholders

The main **stakeholders** of a business – other than owners/shareholders – are therefore:

- customers
- suppliers
- employees and their families
- local communities
- government and government agencies
- special interest groups – for example, pressure groups that want to change a business's policy towards pollution or the testing of chemicals on animals
- lenders.

TOP TIP

Do not confuse the two terms 'stakeholder' and 'shareholder'. Stakeholder is a much broader term that covers many groups, including, of course, shareholders.

Impact of business activities on stakeholders

Business activities and business decisions can have both positive and negative effects on stakeholders. In fact, it might be rare for all stakeholders to be either positively or negatively affected by any one business activity. Also, it is possible for any one stakeholder group to experience both negative and positive effects from the same business decision. Let's look at some typical business decisions and actions to allow an analysis of these effects (see Table 5.1).

What are their roles, rights and responsibilities?

Before we consider a business's responsibility towards stakeholders, it is useful to analyse what role the stakeholder groups play in a business's performance or success, and what, if any, rights they have and the responsibilities they need to fulfil (see Table 5.2 on page 54).

ACTIVITY 5.1

[18 marks, 25 minutes]

1. In the three examples in Table 5.2, analyse the likely positive and negative effects on **two** other stakeholder groups. [6]

2. State **two** other examples of business decisions. Try to use actual, recent examples from your own country. Analyse the impact of these on any three stakeholder groups. [12]

Responsibilities to stakeholders – and impact on business decisions

1 Responsibilities to customers

In a world of increasing free trade and international competition, it is essential to satisfy customers' demands in order to stay in business in the long term. Decisions about quality, design, durability and customer service should consider the customers' objectives for, in most cases, well-made, attractive goods that perform as intended – all at reasonable prices. Businesses also have responsibilities to customers not to break the law concerning consumer protection and accurate advertising. Avoiding taking advantage of vulnerable customers, such as the elderly, and not using high-pressure selling tactics are other policies of responsible businesses.

Benefits of accepting these responsibilities: consumer loyalty; repeat purchases; good publicity when customers give word of mouth recommendations to others; good customer feedback, which helps to improve further goods and services.

Business decision/ activity	Possible impact on employees	Possible impact on local community	Possible impact on customers
Expansion of the business by building a new head office	■ more job and career opportunities ■ disruption during building and more complex lines of communication after expansion	■ more jobs for local residents and increased spending in other local businesses ■ disruption caused by increased traffic and loss of green fields for amenity use	■ better service provided by bigger business with more staff ■ larger business could be less personal and therefore offer inferior customer service
Takeover of a competing firm (horizontal integration)	■ the larger business may be more secure and offer career promotion opportunities ■ rationalisation may occur to avoid waste and cut costs – jobs might be lost	■ if the business expands on the existing site, local job vacancies and incomes might increase ■ rationalisation of duplicated offices or factories might lead to some closures and job losses	■ the larger business may benefit from economies of scale, which could lead to lower prices ■ reduced competition could have the opposite effect – less customer choice might result in higher prices
Significant application of IT into production methods	■ training and promotion opportunities might be offered ■ fewer untrained staff will be required and those unable to learn new skills may be made redundant	■ local businesses providing IT services could benefit from increased orders ■ specialist workers may not be available locally, so more commuting by staff in cars might be necessary	■ more efficient and flexible production methods might improve quality and offer more product variety ■ IT reliability problems could cause supply delays

Table 5.1 Impact of business activity on stakeholders

2 Responsibilities to suppliers

The quality of a firm's good or service is only as good as the supplies it purchases. If these are of poor quality or frequently late, then the same problems will apply when trying to satisfy your own customers. So good, reliable suppliers must be found and given clear guidance on what is required. In return, the purchasing business should pay promptly, place regular orders and offer long-term contracts.

Benefits of accepting these responsibilities: supplier loyalty – prepared to meet deadlines and requests for special orders; reasonable credit terms more likely to be offered.

3 Responsibilities to employees

All countries have some laws that outline business responsibilities to workers – these laws are stricter in some countries than others. Apart from not breaking these laws, do businesses have other responsibilities to employees? Many people think they do. Providing training opportunities, job security, paying more than minimum wages when these are very low, offering good working conditions, involving staff in some decision-making – these are some examples of business decisions that, it is often claimed, should be influenced by business responsibilities to workers.

Benefits of accepting these responsibilities: employee loyalty and low labour turnover; easier to recruit good staff; employee suggestions for improving efficiency and customer service; improved motivation and more effective communication.

4 Responsibilities to local community

Businesses that fail to meet responsibilities to the local community may experience serious problems with opposition to plans to expand or they may not attract local customers. It is argued that businesses should meet the following responsibilities to the local population: offer secure employment so that there is less local fear of job losses, spend as much as possible on local supplies to generate more income, reduce the transport impact of business activity as much as possible and also keep the adverse environmental effects to a minimum.

Benefits of accepting these responsibilities: local councils will be more likely to give planning permission to expand the business; local communities are more likely to accept some of the negative effects caused by business operations if they provide financial support for community groups and projects such as children's playgrounds; local councils often only give contracts to businesses with a record of community involvement.

	Roles	Rights	Responsibilities (not necessarily legally binding)
Customers	■ purchase goods and services ■ provide revenue from sales, which allows the business to function and expand	■ to receive goods and services that meet local laws regarding health and safety, design, performance and so on ■ to be offered replacements, repairs, compensation in the event of failure of the product or service – to at least the minimum levels laid down by law	■ to be honest – to pay for goods bought or services received when requested ■ not to steal ■ not to make false claims about poor service, underperforming goods or failed items
Suppliers	■ supply goods and services to allow the business to offer its products to its own customers	■ to be paid on time – as laid down either by law or by the service agreement agreed between the business and suppliers ■ to be treated fairly by the purchasing business, e.g. not to have lower prices forced on them by a much larger and more powerful customer business	■ to supply goods and services ordered by the business in the time and condition as laid down by the purchase contract or supplier's service agreements
Employees	■ provide manual and other labour services to the business, in accordance with employment contract, to allow goods and services to be provided to customers	■ to be treated within the minimum limits as established by national law, e.g. minimum wage rate ■ to be treated and paid in the ways described in the employment contract ■ in most countries, to be allowed to join a trade union if desired	■ to be honest ■ to meet the conditions and requirements of the employment contract ■ to cooperate with management in all reasonable requests ■ to observe the ethical code of conduct
Local community	■ provide local services and infrastructure to the business to allow it to operate, produce and sell within legal limits	■ to be consulted about major changes that affect it, e.g. expansion plans or changing methods of production ■ not to have the community's lives badly affected by the business's activities	■ to cooperate with the business, where reasonable to do so, on expansion and other plans ■ to meet reasonable requests from business for local services such as public transport (e.g. to allow staff to get to work) and waste disposal
Government	■ pass laws that restrain many aspects of business activity ■ provide law and order to allow legal business activity to take place ■ achieve economic stability to encourage business activity	■ businesses have the duty to government to meet all legal constraints, such as producing only legal goods, and to pay taxes on time	■ to treat businesses equally under the law ■ to prevent unfair competition that could damage business survival chances ■ to establish good trading links with other countries to allow international trade
Lenders	■ provide finance to the business in different forms	■ to be repaid on the agreed date ■ to be paid finance charges, e.g. interest on loan	■ provide agreed amount of finance on agreed date for the agreed time period

Table 5.2 Stakeholders – their roles, rights and responsibilities

Fury at Bangladesh mine scheme

A huge open-cast coal-mining project by a British firm, that would involve moving the homes of up to 130,000 workers in Bangladesh, is at the centre of an international row. The company, GCM, is behind plans to dig up to 570 million tonnes of coal in a project that will displace people from Phulbari in north-west Bangladesh. A river will also have to be diverted and the mangrove forest, which is a World Heritage Site, would be destroyed too.

The project has attracted widespread hostility. In protests against the scheme 18 months ago, three people were killed in an area now said to be controlled by the armed forces. More than 60 international campaign groups have written to the Asian Development Bank demanding that it turns down a US$200 million loan to the project. These groups, including the World Development Movement, are claiming that the social and environmental damage can never be repaired if the scheme receives government approval. A spokesman for GCM, on the other hand, stressed the importance of jobs, incomes and exports to one of the world's poorest countries.

Protests in Dhaka over the mine project

[22 marks, 30 minutes]

1   Explain the benefits to any **two** stakeholder groups resulting from this mine project. **[6]**

2   Explain the disadvantages to any **two** stakeholder groups resulting from this mine project. **[6]**

3   Do you think the conflict of interests between these different stakeholder groups could ever be resolved? Explain your answer. **[10]**

5 Responsibilities to government

Clearly, all businesses should meet their legal responsibilities as defined by government legislation. In addition, business should pay taxes on time, complete government statistical and other forms accurately and, where possible, seek export markets. The foreign currency earned by exports allows a country to pay for important imports of food, materials, new technology and so on.

Benefits of accepting these responsibilities: good relations with government might lead to success with expansion projects receiving planning permission; businesses are more likely to receive valuable government contracts; requests for subsidies to expand businesses are more likely to be approved by government; licences to set up new operations are more likely to be awarded to businesses that meet their responsibilities to the government and the wider society.

TOP TIP

Many questions involve the conflict of stakeholder objectives. Remember that it is difficult for a business to meet all of its responsibilities to all stakeholders at any one time. Compromise might be necessary – meeting as many stakeholder objectives as possible or meeting the needs of the most important group in each situation. See section on page 56 – 'Conflicts arising from different stakeholder objectives'.

KEY CONCEPT LINK

Customer focus is a key concept in business – but other stakeholder groups have to be considered too if a business is to avoid damaging conflicts that could lead to loss of image or even legal action.

No way to treat 'guest workers'

For several years, the construction industry in the UK has benefited greatly from the influx of Polish building workers. UK construction bosses have used the 800,000 building workers from Eastern Europe to fill skill vacancies and to drive down wage costs – they will work for lower wages than UK workers. Many of these workers are not offered permanent contracts, they do not have pension schemes and no national insurance is paid for them by employers – all because they want to save on costs. In addition, working conditions in the industry are still dangerous. In 2012, 148 building workers were killed on UK construction sites.

[16 marks, 20 minutes]

1 Outline **three** ways in which you think UK construction companies are not meeting their responsibilities to migrant building workers. **[6]**

2 Analyse the likely long-term disadvantages construction firms might experience as a result of failing to meet responsibilities towards employees. **[10]**

Corporate social responsibility (CSR) – an evaluation

This is the modern term that is now widely used to sum up the stakeholder concept.

 KEY TERM

Corporate social responsibility: the concept that accepts that businesses should consider the interests of society in their activities and decisions, beyond the legal obligations that they have.

The practice of CSR is subject to much debate and comment. Supporters argue that it is a sign that ethical business leaders accept that there is more to business than just making money. However, there is a strong business case for CSR too. As noted above, businesses can benefit in multiple ways by making decisions and using policies that take into account the objectives of groups other than shareholders and take a broader and longer view than their own short-term profits. In fact, not only will society benefit from CSR schemes, but there could be opportunities for businesses adopting such policies to become more profitable because they are socially responsible.

Critics argue that CSR distracts from the key role of business activity – using economic resources as efficiently as possible in order to make profits for owners. By spending money on CSR projects, it is suggested that businesses have less to invest for expansion and less to pay out to owners, who took the risk to originally invest in them.

In addition, it is suggested that CSR is just a form of 'window dressing' or public relations spin to make unscrupulous businesses appear society-friendly when, in fact, they are really damaging the interests of society by some of their activities. If companies are found to be exploiting their social responsibility for public relations purposes then this might backfire on them badly if it is discovered that the activities of the businesses are not genuinely focused on stakeholders. Other critics state that CSR is an attempt to get governments to impose fewer controls and restrictions on powerful multinational firms.

On balance, it seems that meeting social responsibilities can be expensive and might reduce profits in the short run, for example giving employees better working conditions than other firms, subsidising worthwhile local community activities and paying slightly more for ethically sourced products from suppliers. However, over a longer period of time, the marketing, public relations and employee motivation benefits of CSR policies might pay for themselves and even generate higher profits.

Whatever the arguments, there is no doubt that society's view of business seems to expand each year. We are expecting companies to take a much wider view of their role than they once did. Shell, the oil company, and other multinationals are criticised for dealing with a Nigerian government that has been accused of having a poor human rights record. Should companies be held responsible for the activities of these governments? Nike has had more than one negative report about the employment policy of its suppliers in Asia – evidence suggests that some of them have used child workers. Should Nike be held responsible for the business practices of its suppliers? Increasingly, many groups are saying 'yes' in response to questions such as these.

Conflicts arising from different stakeholder objectives

According to the traditional shareholder concept, any attempts to meet non-legally binding obligations to other stakeholders will conflict with the business's duty to its shareholders. Any non-essential costs reduce profits – so the argument goes. Taking the stakeholder, corporate social responsibility approach, we have seen how the objectives of different groups may be met in ways that result in benefits to shareholders in the long term.

Community-based development projects

The Shell Foundation is a charity set up and financed by the Shell Oil Group. One of its aims is to support entrepreneurs in poor countries. The Flower Valley project is a typical success story. The Shell Foundation decided to support the flower growers of the Agulhas Plain in South Africa. This is a region with some of the world's richest biodiversity, but much of the natural vegetation has been replaced by farming and commercial vineyards. It also has an unemployment rate of 80%. The Flower Valley Conservation Trust (FVCT) aims to protect the fragile natural environment and create more jobs. It does this by encouraging local people to sustainably harvest the fynbos flower that grows naturally. The bouquets of fynbos flowers are all purchased by the UK retailer Marks & Spencer as part of its fair-trading scheme – paying local producers fair prices and cutting out 'middle men' in the distribution chain. Shell Foundation subsidised the FVCT, helped it write a business plan and paid for a professional manager.

The Flower Valley community project is a great success

The scheme now employs 80 workers and 850,000 bouquets of fynbos are sold through Marks & Spencer shops each year. The Shell Foundation also paid for an Early Learning Centre in the valley to help educate local children as well as develop new skills for adults.

[26 marks, 35 minutes]

1 Explain what you understand by the term 'corporate social responsibility'. [3]

2 Explain why the Shell Foundation case above would be described as an example of corporate social responsibility. [5]

3 Analyse how the support to schemes offered by the Shell Foundation are likely to be of benefit to the company. [8]

4 Evaluate the likely impact on Shell's other stakeholders of the company's corporate social responsibility policy. [10]

However, conflicts might still arise between the objectives of these different stakeholder groups. In Activity 5.2, the company plan to open a new coal mine would benefit some stakeholders but not others – in fact they would lose out. Any major business decision is likely to have this effect.

How do businesses deal with these conflicts of stakeholder objectives? A compromise is often the answer. Perhaps a factory will close in stages rather than immediately to allow workers time to find other jobs – but business costs will fall more slowly. Plans to build a new chemical plant may have to be adapted to move the main site away from a housing estate to protect the local community – but the new site might be more expensive. The introduction of 24-hour flights at an airport – to the benefit of the airlines and passengers – may only be accepted if local residents are offered sound insulation in their homes, paid for by the airport and airlines.

Clearly, senior management must establish its priorities in these situations. Which are the most important stakeholders in this case? What will be the extra cost of meeting the needs of each stakeholder group? Will bad publicity resulting from failure to meet the interests of one group lead to lost revenue? Perhaps this will be greater than the costs savings of *not* satisfying this group. Taking such difficult decisions, which are based on weighing up the conflicting interests of these groups, is why managers and directors are often paid more than other employees.

Daily Record: 'Merger results in job losses'

The merger of two of the largest airlines in the country will lead to job losses, reports the *Daily Record*. Special Air and Flights4U have announced a huge merger that will result in a business worth more than US$2 billion. The long-term plans are to offer more routes and cheaper prices to passengers. This will help keep inflation down and boost tourist numbers into our country – so the government is supporting this merger. However, routes to small regional airports are being closed – they were never profitable enough. Also, as only one head office will be needed, Special Air's headquarters in New City will close. These cutbacks will result in 500 jobs being cut, but annual savings of more than $10 million. Trade union leaders are threatening to take industrial action to support workers who will lose their jobs. The local governments in the towns that are losing routes are very worried about the impact on local suppliers of fuel and food to the airlines. The chief executive of Flights4U said: 'Sure, there will be losers from this merger, but there will be many more winners as we expand our operations from the major cities.'

[34 marks, 40 minutes]

1 Do you think these two businesses more focused on profit or stakeholder interests? Explain your answer. **[10]**

2 Why is it difficult in this case for the two merging companies to meet their responsibilities to all stakeholder groups? **[6]**

3 Why might the negative impact on some stakeholders mean that the merger will not turn out to be as profitable as expected? **[6]**

4 Discuss how the newly merged business could attempt to meet some of its responsibilities to the stakeholder groups worst affected by this decision. **[12]**

Impact on stakeholders of changing business objectives

The dynamic business environment often means that directors or senior managers might be forced to change corporate objectives. When this happens, the impact on stakeholders can be significant. Two examples illustrate this:

■ Nokia experienced a collapse in sales of its mobile phones in 2013. Instead of aiming for growth it was forced to fight for survival: 10,000 jobs were cut and it sold a large part of its business to Microsoft.

■ The Body Shop has as one of its major objectives 'social and environmental change' but due to difficult trading conditions, it was forced in 2013 to focus on cost-cutting to achieve profitability and has closed some shops.

Different stakeholder groups will be affected in different ways by these changes in objectives – employees' jobs will be lost and customers will have less choice, for example. However, owners' returns might be safeguarded in the future by the decisions taken above – and lenders might be reassured that action is being taken to stem losses that should mean they are repaid the loans they have given.

SUMMARY POINTS

- Stakeholders are important to a business.
- It is important for a business to take stakeholder responsibilities into account in decision-making.
- Stakeholders may have conflicting interests. These can be evaluated and resolved, but may require compromises and impact on profits in the short-term.

RESEARCH TASK

- Identify a major construction or development project in your region or country, e.g. dam, airport, new power station.
- Identify **eight** stakeholder groups that will be affected by this project.
- Examine the ways in which each stakeholder group could be affected – both positively and negatively.
- Write a report indicating how the conflicts between the stakeholder groups – resulting from the different effects of the project – could be reduced.

AS Level exam practice questions

Short answer questions

[37 marks, 50 minutes]

Knowledge and understanding

1   Distinguish between the shareholder concept and the stakeholder concept. [3]

2   Explain why a business might experience lower profits by meeting stakeholder objectives. [4]

3   Explain why a business might experience higher profits by meeting stakeholder objectives. [4]

4   Explain the difference between a business acting legally and acting socially responsibly. [6]

5   What do you understand by the term 'conflicts between stakeholder interests'? [4]

Application

6   Outline the responsibilities a business in the oil industry might have to **two** stakeholder groups. [4]

7   Outline the responsibilities a business in a tertiary industry might have to **two** stakeholder groups. [4]

8   Explain an example, from your own country, of a business decision that involves a conflict of stakeholder interests. [4]

9   Explain how the business made attempts to resolve this conflict. [4]

Data response

1   Major palm oil companies accused of breaking ethical promises

Palm oil is one of the world's most versatile raw materials. It is estimated that it is an ingredient in 50% of all products sold by a typical supermarket. It is used in a wide range of products from margarine, cereals, crisps, sweets and baked goods, to soaps, washing powders and cosmetics but it is often listed as just 'vegetable oil'. So, its production benefits customers of these products. In addition, an estimated 1.5 million small farmers grow the crop in Indonesia, along with about 500,000 people directly employed in the sector in Malaysia, plus those connected with related industries. The governments of these countries have encouraged production as it is a major export for these economies.

However, the industry has a poor image. Palm oil production has led to deforestation with a resulting negative impact on climate change. There has been substantial loss of wildlife habitat, even endangering the Orang Utan. Palm oil companies have been accused of driving native people off their land which is then used for palm oil production. Socially responsible businesses, such as KL Kepong in Malaysia, have agreed to an ethical code which aims to make palm oil production sustainable, with fair treatment for all local populations affected by it. However, many companies have been accused of breaking the code as there is no strong world body to stop them behaving irresponsibly. In any case, food manufacturers want to maximise profits and final consumers want the cheapest raw materials possible.

Environmental impact of business activity

Sources: Various.

[30 marks, 45 minutes]

1 a Define the term 'maximise profits'. [2]

   b Briefly explain the term 'socially responsible business'. [3]

2 Explain the role and responsibilities of any **two** of KL Kepong's stakeholder groups. [6]

3 Analyse the impact on these **two** stakeholder groups of a decision by KL Kepong to close one of its palm oil plantations. [8]

4 Discuss why an expansion of the palm oil industry in either Malaysia or Indonesia is likely to cause conflicting views between stakeholder groups. [11]

2 Virgin's green idea loses its pulling power

Virgin Atlantic airline sold its new environmental policies to airline passengers as a bold, green initiative that would save thousands of tonnes of carbon dioxide from its flights. But Virgin Atlantic has quietly abandoned its plans to tow the Boeing 747 jumbo to the end of runways instead of powering up the jet engines to do this. It was found that pulling these giant planes weakened the structure of the landing gear by a long way. Other green initiatives by Virgin – part of a claim to make it the most environmentally friendly airline in the world – are not having much effect either. It offered free train tickets to business-class passengers in place of large chauffeur-driven cars to take them to the airport – but only 1% accepted. Also, only 5% of the total fuel used on a normal flight had been replaced by bio-fuel on a recent test flight, which Virgin claimed made it 'the first airline in the world to fly on renewable fuel'.

Jeff Gazard, a member of the Aviation Environment Federation, said: 'Virgin is using bogus green initiatives in an attempt to make passengers feel less guilty about flying and persuade governments to allow the airline industry to continue to grow at its present unsustainable rate.' So, some stakeholders see this type of corporate 'socially responsible' move as just a 'greenwash' or 'window dressing'.

Despite this controversy, Virgin Atlantic has ambitious expansion plans – 1,500 new jobs are to be created, largely to ensure the new routes to Cuba and the Bahamas are launched on time.

[30 marks, 45 minutes]

1 a Define the term 'environmental policies'. [2]

   b Briefly explain the term 'stakeholders'. [3]

2 Explain **two** benefits that Virgin Atlantic might receive from being looked upon as the 'world's greenest airline'. [6]

3 Analyse the impact on stakeholders in Virgin Atlantic of the company's expansion plan. [8]

4 Evaluate the long-term impact on this airline if its environmental initiatives are thought to be 'bogus' or 'greenwash'. [11]

AS Level essay questions

[20 marks, 40 minutes each]

1 Evaluate whether all businesses should accept their social responsibilities to stakeholders. [20]

2 a Explain the responsibilities a business operating a large chain of supermarkets has to its stakeholders. [8]

   b Discuss how this business might overcome the problems resulting from a conflict of stakeholder objectives caused by a decision to open a large new supermarket. [12]

6 Business structure

On completing this chapter, you will be able to:

- analyse the reasons for recent growth in international trade and the development of multinational businesses
- evaluate the impact of multinational businesses on the country in which they become established
- evaluate the arguments for and against privatisation of state-owned industries.

Introducing the topic

FOUR THAI BUSINESSES IN WORLD'S TOP 100 MULTINATIONALS

The rapid expansion of four Thai-based businesses has led to them featuring in the Boston Consulting Group's list of the world's top 100 multinationals. The tins of tuna displayed in the boardroom of Thai Union Frozen (TUF) might not look very big but they have some of the best known brand names in canned fish production: John West (UK), Petit Navire and Parmentier (France) and Chicken of the Sea (USA) are all owned by TUF, which now has total sales in excess of US$3 billion. TUF operates a large fishing fleet and has warehouses in low-cost countries such as Ghana and the Seychelles to maintain a global competitive advantage.

Other Thai businesses in the top 100 are: Charoen Pokphand (poultry), PTT (oil) and Indorama Ventures (plastics). They all have operations in several countries – a sign that globalisation is benefiting the growth of businesses from emerging economies such as Thailand just as much as the big multinationals from USA and Europe.

Points to think about:

- Why do you think that there are a growing number of multinational businesses?
- Explain possible reasons why TUF bought foreign businesses and brands rather than selling its own branded products in other countries.
- Should a country's government welcome the growth of multinational businesses in its economy?

Introduction

Most of the world's largest businesses now operate 'multinationally' – with operations in more than one country. The biggest of them have wealth that exceeds that of some nations. How can the growth of such huge businesses be explained? Is the growth of such businesses beneficial for the countries that they operate in? These are some of the important issues to be covered in this chapter.

Local, national and international businesses

Local businesses operate in a small and well-defined part of the country. They do not have expansion as an objective and make no attempt to expand to obtain customers across the whole country. Typical examples are small building and carpentry firms, single-branch shops, hairdressing businesses and child-minding services.

National businesses have branches or operations across most of the country. They make no attempt to establish operations in other countries. Good examples include large car-retailing firms, retail shops with many branches selling goods in just one country, and national banking firms.

International businesses operate in more than one country. These are often called multinational businesses.

Nature and scope of international trading links

All countries, to a greater or lesser degree, engage in international trade with other countries. This is true no matter which economic system is in place. The growth of world trade in recent years has been very rapid. In addition, the huge expansion in trade between certain countries, for example China with the USA and the EU, has had a great impact on their economic development.

By trading together, countries can build up improved political and social links and this can help to resolve differences between them. Trading internationally can also have drawbacks, however. These need to be considered carefully by governments. Selective assistance may need to be given to those firms and groups most adversely affected. The potential risks from international trade include:

- There may be loss of output and jobs from those domestic firms that cannot compete effectively with imported goods.
- There may be a decline, due to imports, in domestic industries that produce very important strategic goods, for example coal or foodstuffs; this could put the country at risk if there were a conflict between countries or another factor leading to a loss of imports.
- The switch from making goods that cannot compete with imports to those in which the country has a comparative advantage may take a long time. This, again, will cause job losses and factory closures before other production increases.
- Newly established businesses may find it impossible to survive against competition from existing importers. This will prevent 'infant industries' from growing domestically.
- Some importers may 'dump' goods at below cost price in order to eliminate competition from domestic firms.
- If the value of imports exceeds the value of exports (products sold abroad) for several years, then this could lead to a loss of foreign exchange. In 2008, Zimbabwe was unable to finance imports of essential foods to feed its population.

Free trade and globalisation

The most common forms of trade barriers are **tariffs**, **quotas** and **voluntary export** restraints. When any of these are used, this is called **protectionism**.

KEY TERMS

Free trade: no restrictions or trade barriers exist that might prevent or limit trade between countries.

Tariffs: taxes imposed on imported goods to make them more expensive than they would otherwise be.

Quotas: limits on the physical quantity or value of certain goods that may be imported.

Voluntary export limits: an exporting country agrees to limit the quantity of certain goods sold to one country (possibly to discourage the setting of tariffs/quotas).

Protectionism: using barriers to free trade to protect a country's own domestic industries.

What are the benefits of free trade between nations?

- By buying products from other nations (importing), consumers are offered a much wider choice of goods and services. Many of these would not have been available to them at all without international trade because the farming or production facilities might not have existed in their own country, for example bananas in Europe or deep-sea fish in Botswana.

- The same principle applies to raw materials – the UK steel industry depends entirely on imports of foreign iron ore.
- Imports of raw materials can allow a developing economy to increase its rate of industrialisation.
- Importing products creates additional competition for domestic industries and this should encourage them to keep costs and prices down and make their goods as well designed and of as high quality as possible.
- Countries can begin to specialise in those products they are best at making if they import those that they are less efficient at as compared to other countries. This is called comparative advantage.
- Specialisation can lead to economies of scale (Chapter 23) and further cost and price benefits.
- By trading in this way, the living standards of all consumers of all countries trading together should increase as they are able to buy products more cheaply than those that were produced just within their own countries.

In recent years, there have been moves towards free trade by reducing international trade restrictions. These measures have been a major factor driving the **globalisation** process.

KEY TERM

Globalisation: the increasing freedom of movement of goods, capital and people around the world.

This increasing interconnectivity of the world is having a major impact on business activity, especially from multinationals. The free-trade movement and the increasing use of the Internet are reducing the differences that once existed between national markets, reducing the importance of national borders and making it easier for firms to trade with and locate in many countries. This is forcing firms, which were once protected by national governments, to become internationally competitive. The recent moves towards free trade have been driven by:

1 **The World Trade Organization (WTO):** This is made up of countries committed to the principle of freeing world trade from restrictions. It holds regular meetings to discuss reductions in tariffs and quotas and these have to be agreed by all members. When China joined the WTO, other countries were concerned about the effect of such a major producer of goods – with very low labour costs – competing freely with them.

2 **Free-trade blocs:** These are groups of countries, often geographically grouped, that have arranged to trade with each other without restrictions. The best examples are NAFTA (USA, Canada, Mexico in the North American Free Trade Association) and ASEAN (Association of South East Asian Nations). The members of the European Union (EU)

also trade freely among themselves, but the EU is more than a free-trade bloc. This organisation is covered in more detail later in the book. The danger with these blocs is that they may agree to impose trade barriers on other groups of countries in order to attempt to gain competitive advantage against imports from these other groups.

Multinational businesses

These firms have benefited greatly from the freedoms offered by globalisation. They are more than just importers and exporters; they actually produce goods and services in more than one country. The biggest multinationals have annual revenues exceeding the size of many countries' entire economies. This sheer size – and the power and influence it can bring – can lead to many problems for nations that deal with such firms. This point is made more obvious by the fact that many multinationals have their head offices in Western European countries or in the USA, yet have many of their operating bases in less-developed countries with much smaller economies. If the companies need to save costs by reducing the size of their workforces, often the *last* countries to lose jobs will be the ones where the head offices are based.

KEY TERM

Multinational business: business organisation that has its headquarters in one country, but with operating branches, factories and assembly plants in other countries.

TOP TIP

When defining a multinational business, it is not enough to state that such businesses 'sell products in more than one country'.

Why become a multinational?

There are several reasons why businesses start to operate in countries other than their main base.

1 Closer to main markets – this will have a number of advantages, such as:
   - Lower transport costs for the finished goods.
   - Better market information about consumer tastes as a result of operating closer to them.
   - It may be viewed as a local company and gain customer loyalty as a consequence.

2 Lower costs of production – apart from lower transport costs of the completed items, there are likely to be other cost savings, such as:
   - Lower labour rates, e.g. much lower demand for local labour in developing countries compared to developed economies.

   - Cheaper rent and site costs, again resulting from lower demand for commercial property – these cost savings can make the local production very efficient in terms of the market in the rest of the world and can lead to substantial exports.
   - Government grants and tax incentives designed to encourage the industrialisation of such countries.

3 Avoid import restrictions – by producing in the local country there will be no import duties to pay and no other import restrictions.

4 Access to local natural resources – these might not be available in the company's main operating country; see Activity 6.2.

Potential problems for multinationals

Setting up operating plants in foreign countries is not without risks. Communication links with headquarters may be poor. Language, legal and culture differences with local workers and government officials could lead to misunderstandings. Coordination with other plants in the multinational group will need to be carefully monitored to ensure that products that might compete with each other on world markets are not produced or that conflicting policies are not adopted. Finally, it is likely that the skill levels of the local employees will be low and this could require substantial investment in training programmes.

63

ACTIVITY 6.1

Global reach of Coca-Cola

Coca-Cola is a global business that operates in more than 200 countries. It claims to operate on 'a local scale in every community where we do business'. It is able to create global reach with local resources because of the strength of the Coca-Cola system, which comprises the main company and its bottling partners around the world – nearly 300 of them, which are not owned by Coca-Cola.

[22 marks, 30 minutes]

1 Analyse **two** reasons why Coca-Cola operates globally. [6]

2 Analyse **two** potential problems to Coca-Cola of operating in so many different countries. [6]

3 Why do you think Coca-Cola has agreements with many local bottling companies and does not own and operate all of the bottling plants it uses? [10]

ACTIVITY 6.2

South Africa accelerates its car production

Over the past ten years, South Africa has emerged as a profitable production and export base for some of the world's household names in auto manufacture, despite the country's geographical remoteness, its reputation for labour militancy and its political uncertainties. South Africa has also become a key supplier of motor-industry components, providing everything from windscreens to exhaust pipes for some of the most demanding markets in the world. The most impressive success story lies with the production of catalytic converters. With massive platinum and palladium deposits, South Africa has emerged from nowhere to take nearly 10% of the world's production of the anti-pollution components, which is set to increase to 25% by the end of the decade. This did not happen by accident. It is the result of a deliberate strategy by the government to draw the world's best car manufacturers into South Africa, and drag the domestic industry from behind protectionist barriers into the highly competitive global market for cars and components.

'When we started, the South African auto industry was basically in ruins,' said Antony Black, an economist at Cape Town University, and one of the architects of the government's Motor Industry Development Programme (MIDP). 'Domestic production could not even compete with imports, which faced duties in excess of 115%,' he added. Launched in 1995, MIDP sought to kick-start South Africa's ailing motor industry by attracting the world's big car-makers with many financial incentives. The new factories have had the benefit of generating thousands of new jobs, while at the same time forcing hundreds of small and medium-sized local suppliers to improve quality and productivity or face extinction.

The strategy has succeeded in getting some of the world's biggest companies to invest huge sums in South Africa. Exports of fully built cars have increased to some R5 billion, and are expected to double within two years. At the same time, exports of components have trebled to R12 billion. German car manufacturers, traditionally strong in South Africa, have been the first to take advantage of MIDP's export credits and investment allowances, although Italian and French companies such as Fiat and Renault are rapidly following. Daimler-Chrysler has just announced that it is switching its entire production of right-hand-drive C-Class Mercedes-Benz cars from Bremen in Germany to the Eastern Cape in an investment project worth R1.3 billion, which will create 800 new jobs at the plant and 3,000 new jobs in the supply industry. Mercedes's East London – one of South Africa's major cities – factory has recently started exporting C-Class models to the USA, the second biggest car market in the world.

BMW has invested R1 billion upgrading its Rosslyn plant near Pretoria, which will export 75% of the 40,000 3-Series cars produced each year to Britain, Germany, Japan, America, Australia, Hong Kong, Singapore, New Zealand, Taiwan and Iran. Daily output has increased fivefold since 1989 and this has helped create 900 new jobs at the Rosslyn plant and an estimated 18,000 jobs in the car-component industry. The government is determined to keep these investments in the country and to prevent their closure following the recent announcement that IBM was quitting South Africa as it was worried about possible political instability.

Today the Eastern Cape remains one of the poorest regions in the country. Average black disposable income stands at a low R5,000 a year, compared with the white population's R45,000 a year. Little wonder that when Volkswagen were looking for 1,300 workers to replace those who were sacked for participating in the illegal strike, 23,000 turned up outside the factory gates in the hope of being chosen. Port Elizabeth and East London, the province's two main cities, are rapidly emerging as South Africa's new car-making centres. The extra incomes created by the industry help to boost other local industries such as retailing and house construction. The success of MIDP 'has been a huge confidence booster for us,' Black says. 'It has enabled us to bring about big productivity improvements, stabilise employment, reduce the real cost of new vehicles, and give consumers more choice.'

[32 marks, 50 minutes]

1 List **four** examples of multinational companies that have invested in South Africa. [4]

2 Using the information above as well as your own knowledge explain **three** reasons for these manufacturers setting up factories in South Africa. [6]

3 Analyse the benefits South Africa appears to be gaining from such investment. [10]

4 Evaluate whether the government of South Africa should continue to support investment by multinational businesses in its economy. [12]

Evaluation of the impact on 'host' countries of multinational operations

The potential **benefits** are clear:

- The investment will bring in foreign currency and, if output from the plant is exported, further foreign exchange can be earned.
- Employment opportunities will be created and training programmes will improve the quality and efficiency of local people.
- Local firms are likely to benefit from supplying services and components to the new factory and this will generate additional jobs and incomes.
- Local firms will be forced to bring their quality and productivity up to international standards either to compete with the multinational or to supply to it.
- Tax revenues to the government will be boosted from any profits made by the multinational.
- Management expertise in the community will slowly improve when and if the foreign supervisors and managers are replaced by local staff, once they are suitably qualified.
- The total output of the economy will be increased and this will raise gross domestic product.

It will not be all good news, however. The expansion of multinational corporations into a country could lead to these **drawbacks**:

- Exploitation of the local workforce might take place. Due to the absence of strict labour and health and safety rules in some countries, multinationals can employ cheap labour for long hours with few of the benefits that the staff in their home country would demand. Recent poor publicity has forced the Gap and Nike clothing companies to improve their monitoring of the employment of illegal child workers at factories that produce their clothes in Thailand. How many large businesses would not care about these practices, especially as the factories are so far removed from Western media investigation?
- Pollution from plants might be at higher levels than allowed in other countries. Either this could be because of slack rules or because the host government is afraid of driving the multinational away if it insists on environmentally acceptable practices. This is a sign of the great influence multinationals can have.

- Local competing firms may be squeezed out of business due to inferior equipment and much smaller resources than the large multinational.
- Some large Western-based businesses, such as McDonald's and Coca-Cola, have been accused of imposing Western culture on other societies by the power of advertising and promotion. This could lead to a reduction in cultural identity.
- Profits may be sent back to the country where the head office of the company is based, rather than kept for reinvestment in the host nation.
- Extensive depletion of the limited natural resources of some countries has been blamed on some large multinational corporations. The argument is that they have little incentive to conserve these resources, as they are able to relocate quickly to other countries once resources have run out.

 TOP TIP

In case study questions on multinational business activity, you may have the opportunity to use examples from your own country as well as from the case study to support your answers. Keep a file of news reports about multinational business activities in your own country.

Privatisation

The policy of **privatisation** includes other features apart from the outright sale of state assets, for example making state-owned schools, hospitals and local authorities 'contract out' many services to private business. However, the main aspect of privatisation is the transfer of ownership of nationalised (state-owned) industries into the private sector by creating public limited companies. This policy began in the UK in the 1980s, but is now widespread throughout most mixed economies. The list of privatised companies in Europe is very extensive and includes British Airways, Deutsche Telekom and Skoda. The main argument used by supporters of privatisation is that business enterprises will use resources much more efficiently in the private sector, as they will be driven by the profit motive. Those against the policy argue that the state can pursue other objectives apart from just making a profit through public-sector enterprises and that privatisation nearly always leads to job losses in order to cut costs.

 KEY TERM

Privatisation: selling state-owned and controlled business organisations to investors in the private sector.

ACTIVITY 6.3

Privatisation of Pakistan International Airlines (PIA) takes off

Pakistan's state-owned international airline, PIA, is to be privatised, the government has recently announced. The loss-making airline requires subsidies of Rs3 billion a month just to keep operating and it still requires further capital injections to purchase or lease newer aircraft. Industry analysts claim that PIA is overstaffed and poorly managed. The existing management is trying to prevent the privatisation – which will almost certainly lead to a new management team being

appointed – by announcing 16 new international routes to boost revenue.

The Pakistan government is determined to cut its own budget deficit and the huge privatisation programme has been agreed. Ministers hope that private ownership of many of the state-owned businesses in Pakistan will lead to more capital being invested, more incentives for managers and workers and more efficient operations.

State to hang on to chunk of SAA

South African Airways (SAA) has spoken out on its proposed privatisation and stock exchange listing, saying it would like the government to hold a stake of between 30% and 40% in the airline, with the balance floated on the stock market. Andre Viljoen said: 'We have been speaking to a number of merchant banks and the advice they have been giving us is that we should aim for about 30–40% being retained by the stakeholder (the government) and the rest being listed. SAA is among R150 million worth of state assets earmarked by the government for restructuring and partial privatisation in an exercise expected to unlock more than R40 billion.'

[24 marks, 35 minutes]

1 Define the term 'privatisation'. [2]

2 Identify **two** possible advantages of privatisation referred to in the articles. [2]

3 Explain **one** reason why the South African government appears keen to keep a stake in South African Airways after the stock exchange listing. [4]

4 Explain **one** possible problem resulting from the Pakistani government's decision to privatise Pakistan International Airlines. [4]

5 Discuss the impact of **one** of these proposed privatisations on the consumers and the government. [12]

Arguments for and against privatisation

The debate over privatisation is a long and complex one. The sale of state industries continues despite the reservations listed above. Supporters of this policy would argue that there is 'no going back' to nationalisation and state ownership of assets that could be better managed in the private sector (see Table 6.1). This is one of the important issues in Business. You need to weigh up the issues very carefully so that you are able to form your own opinions and make your own judgements. One approach to the problems caused by the rigid dividing lines that exist between the private sector and public sector has been the growing use of partnerships between organisations in both sectors.

Arguments for privatisation	Arguments against privatisation
■ The profit motive of private-sector businesses will lead to much greater efficiency than when a business is supported and subsidised by the state.	■ The state should take decisions about essential industries. These decisions can be based on the needs of society and not just the interests of shareholders. This may involve keeping open business activities that private companies would consider unprofitable.
■ Decision-making in state bodies can be slow and bureaucratic.	■ With competing privately run businesses it will be much more difficult to achieve a coherent and coordinated policy for the benefit of the whole country, for example railway system, electricity grid and bus services.
■ Privatisation puts responsibility for success firmly in the hands of the managers and staff who work in the organisation. This can lead to strong motivation as they have a direct involvement in the work they do. There is a greater sense of empowerment.	■ Through state ownership, an industry can be made accountable to the country. This is by means of a responsible minister and direct accountability to parliament.
■ Market forces will be allowed to operate: failing businesses will be forced to change or die and successful ones will expand, unconstrained by government limits on growth. Profits of most of the privatised businesses have increased following their sell-off.	■ Many strategic industries could be operated as 'private monopolies' if privatised and they could exploit consumers with high prices.
■ There is always a temptation for governments to run state industry for political reasons or as a means of influencing the national economy, for example keeping electricity prices artificially low. Thus, decisions may not be taken for commercial reasons.	■ Breaking up nationalised industries, perhaps into several competing units, will reduce the opportunities for cost saving through economies of scale.
■ Sale of nationalised industries can raise finance for government, which can be spent on other state projects.	
■ Private businesses will have access to the private capital markets and this will lead to increased investment in these industries.	

Table 6.1 Arguments for and against privatisation

SUMMARY POINTS

- There has been a substantial policy shift towards privatisation – this increases the size of the private sector by reducing the number of public corporations in the public sector.
- There has been rapid growth in international trade in recent years and this is mainly the result of free trade agreements.
- Globalisation is leading to the free movement of goods, people and capital, leading to both positive and negative effects on business and economies.
- The growth of multinational businesses is one aspect of globalisation.
- There are arguments for and against a country encouraging the establishment of multinational businesses.

RESEARCH TASK

Select one large multinational operating in your country.

1 Use the Internet or a copy of the company's published accounts to discover its main products and services.

2 Have the business's operations in your country grown, declined or stayed the same in recent years?

3 How do you explain this change or the fact that there has not been one?

4 Explain the possible impact on the community and the national economy if it closed its local operations.

68

A Level exam practice questions
Case study

Waste – a good case for privatisation?

Capital Waste Disposal plc was created several years ago when the capital city's rubbish collection service was privatised. As a public-sector enterprise, the organisation was well-known for being greatly overstaffed and inefficient. However, charges for collecting waste from both homes and businesses were very low and, because of this, the service was popular with local residents. The city subsidised the waste services each year and this helped to keep charges down. The organisation was privatised by the sale of shares to the public and financial companies. Just after privatisation, the directors announced substantial job cuts to save on costs. At the same time, the waste collection service was reduced to once a week, yet charges were increased. The city government also announced that other businesses could set up in competition if they wished to.

The business started to make big profits. The directors said that these would be used to invest in new equipment and to pay dividends to shareholders. Last year, for the first time since privatisation, profits fell. This was due to competition from a newly formed waste disposal business. Many of the shareholders of Capital Waste wanted the directors to be replaced. The biggest shareholders demanded to be on the board of directors. The current chief executive decided to discuss with the bank whether a loan could be obtained to enable him to buy out most of the shares so that he could convert the business into a private limited company. He told the bank manager: 'If I turn the business into a private company, I can run it without any interference from these big shareholders and I can get away with publishing less information about the company.'

[44 marks, 60 minutes]

1 Analyse the likely reasons why the city government decided to privatise this organisation. [10]

2 Evaluate the likely impact of this privatisation, in the short run and the long run, on:
- customers
- shareholders
- workers [12]

4 Assess the importance of changing the long-term objectives of a business that has been privatised. [10]

5 Recommend to the chief executive whether he should maintain the business as a public limited company (plc) or not. Justify your answer. [12]

Multinational to produce in Malaysia

The European Tyre Group (ETG) has announced its plan to open a huge new factory on the outskirts of Kuala Lumpur. The government is delighted that this new investment will bring hundreds of jobs to the area. Other responses to the news were less encouraging. One trade union leader said: 'If the workers are paid the same low wages as those paid to foreign workers in other ETG factories, then our members will be in poverty.' A local resident said: 'In other countries, their factories have got a bad record for pollution – I am worried about the health of my children.' A spokesman for the Malaysian Tyre Group said: 'This multinational could lead to the closure of our own factory – we just do not have the same cost advantages.' ETG, a British-based company, today announced record profits from its operations in 12 countries and the dividends paid to shareholders will increase by 50% this year. Despite this, the company announced it would go ahead with the closure of its loss-making Mexican factory.

[30 marks, 45 minutes]

1   Explain why ETG could be described as a multinational business.   [3]
2   Outline **three** possible disadvantages to Malaysia that might result from the operation of the new ETG factory.   [9]
3   Analyse possible reasons why ETG is expanding its production facilities outside Europe.   [8]
4   Discuss the extent to which a government should control the operations of multinational companies within its own country.   [10]

A Level essay question

[20 marks, 45 minutes]

To what extent should the government of your country positively encourage multinational businesses to establish themselves in your country?   [20]

7 Size of business

On completing this chapter, you will be able to:

- identify different forms of external growth
- evaluate the impact of different forms of external growth on business stakeholders
- assess the ways in which management can deal with the problems associated with rapid growth.

Introducing the topic

CHINESE GIANT TAKES OVER SMITHFIELD FOODS INC.

Shuanghui Holdings Ltd – the largest meat producer in China – has taken over Smithfield Foods Inc., a US-based public limited company. The buyout deal, which is worth US$34 per share – a total of US$4.7 billion – was agreed to by 96% of Smithfield's shareholders. Workers in Smithfield's farms and factories are also pleased with the deal – existing US managers will not be replaced and pay levels are not changing.

Smithfield is one of the largest meat producers and processors in the USA. The takeover will give Shuanghui a huge new source of meat to supply its meat-processing plants in China. The demand for meat is increasing in the world's most populated country as incomes rise with economic growth. The importation of US-produced meat by China will increase the already close trade links between the two countries.

In the past, many Chinese companies have preferred to set up joint ventures or strategic alliances with foreign businesses but now they increasingly have the spare capital that allows them to take over companies outright.

Points to think about:

- Why do you think Smithfield's shareholder agreed to this takeover?
- Explain the benefits to Shuanghui of its takeover of Smithfield.
- Do you think Shuanghui will experience any problems as a result of this form of expansion?

Introduction

Businesses grow in different ways. In Chapter 3, business growth focusing on internal expansion was studied. In this A Level chapter we turn to discuss forms of external expansion and the potential benefits and limitations of these.

External growth

External growth is often referred to as 'integration' as it involves bringing together two or more firms. This form of growth can lead to rapid expansion, which might be vital in a competitive and expanding market. However, it often leads to management problems. These are caused by the need for different management systems to deal with a bigger organisation. There can also be conflict between the two teams of managers – who will get the top jobs? – and conflicts of culture and business ethics.

KEY TERM

External growth: business expansion achieved by means of merging with or taking over another business, from either the same or a different industry.

Table 7.1 provides a reference guide to the different types of integration, their common advantages and disadvantages and the impact they often have on stakeholder groups.

Synergy and integration

When two firms are integrated the argument is that the bigger firm created in this way will be more effective, efficient and profitable than the two separate companies. Why might this be the case?

1 It is argued that the two businesses might be able to share research facilities and pool ideas that will benefit both of the businesses. This is only likely to be the case if the two firms deal with the same kind of technologies.

2 Economies of operating a larger scale of business, such as buying supplies in large quantities, should cut costs.

3 The new business can save on marketing and distribution costs by using the same sales outlets and sales teams.

In practice, many **mergers** and **takeovers** fail to gain true **synergy**, and shareholders are often left wondering what the purpose of the integration really was. Many examples of business integration have not increased shareholder value for the following reasons:

1 The integrated firm is actually too big to manage and control effectively – this is a 'diseconomy of scale'.

 KEY TERMS

Merger: an agreement by shareholders and managers of two businesses to bring both firms together under a common board of directors with shareholders in both businesses owning shares in the newly merged business.

Takeover: when a company buys more than 50% of the shares of another company and becomes the controlling owner of it – often referred to as 'acquisition'.

Synergy: literally means that 'the whole is greater than the sum of parts', so in integration it is often assumed that the new, larger business will be more successful than the two, formerly separate, businesses were.

71

Type of integration	Advantages	Disadvantages	Impact on stakeholders
Horizontal integration – integration with firms in the same industry and at same stage of production	■ eliminates one competitor ■ possible economies of scale ■ scope for rationalising production, for example concentrating all output on one site as opposed to two ■ increased power over suppliers	■ rationalisation may bring bad publicity ■ may lead to monopoly investigation if the combined business exceeds certain market share limits	■ consumers now have less choice ■ workers may lose job security as a result of rationalisation
Vertical integration – forward integration with a business in the same industry but a customer of the existing business	■ business is now able to control the promotion and pricing of its own products ■ secures a secure outlet for the firm's products – may now exclude competitors' products	■ consumers may suspect uncompetitive activity and react negatively ■ lack of experience in this sector of the industry – a successful manufacturer does not necessarily make a good retailer	■ workers may have greater job security because the business has secure outlets ■ there may be more varied career opportunities ■ consumers may resent lack of competition in the retail outlet because of the withdrawal of competitor products
Vertical integration – backward integration with a business in the same industry but a supplier of the existing business	■ gives control over quality, price and delivery times of supplies ■ encourages joint research and development into improved quality of supplies of components ■ business may now control supplies of materials to competitors	■ may lack experience of managing a supplying company – a successful steel producer will not necessarily make a good manager of a coal mine ■ supplying business may become complacent due to having a guaranteed customer	■ possibility of greater career opportunities for workers ■ consumers may obtain improved quality and more innovative products ■ control over supplies to competitors may limit competition and choice for consumers
Conglomerate integration – integration with a business in a different industry	■ diversifies the business away from its original industry and markets ■ this should spread risk and may take the business into a faster-growing market	■ lack of management experience in the acquired-business sector ■ there could be a lack of clear focus and direction now that the business is spread across more than one industry	■ greater career opportunities for workers ■ more job security because risks are spread across more than one industry

Table 7.1 Types of business integration and their impact

2   There may be little mutual benefit from shared research facilities or marketing and distribution systems if the firms have products in different markets.

3   The business and management culture – for example, the approach each company takes to environmental issues – may be so different that the two sets of managers and workers may find it very difficult to work effectively and cooperatively together.

> **TOP TIP**
>
> If a question refers to a merger or takeover, you should start by identifying what type it is. Do not forget that mergers and takeovers often cause businesses as many problems as they solve.

Joint ventures and strategic alliances

These are two forms of external growth that do not involve complete integration or changes in ownership. Joint ventures were analysed on page 24. Strategic alliances are agreements between firms in which each agrees to commit resources to achieve an agreed set of objectives. These alliances can be made with a wide variety of stakeholders, for example:

- with a university – finance provided by the business to allow new specialist training courses that will increase the supply of suitable staff for the firm
- with a supplier – to join forces in order to design and produce components and materials that will be used in a new range of products; this may help to reduce the total development time for getting the new products to market, gaining competitive advantage
- with a competitor – to reduce risks of entering a market that neither firm currently operates in. Care must be taken that, in these cases, the actions are not seen as being 'anti-competitive' and, as a result, against the laws of the country whose market is being entered.

ACTIVITY 7.1

Starbucks confirms rapid-growth strategy

Howard Schultz, the chairman of Starbucks, confirmed growth plans for the world's largest chain of coffee shops. The business will open at least 10,000 new cafés over the next four years by using internal growth. Schultz said at the company's annual meeting that he planned to double the size of the business eventually. At the end of 2013, there were more than 21,000 stores worldwide.

China will be the main focus of this growth strategy. The US giant opened its first Chinese branch in 1999 and has plans to open at least 1,000 outlets there. 'No market potentially has the opportunities for us as China hopefully will,' said Schultz. Like many Western retailers, Starbucks sees China as its key growth area due to its fast-growing economy, lack of strong local competitors and sheer size of population. The business is also expanding its network of branches in Russia and Brazil.

There are plans to increase sales of non-coffee products to reduce its reliance on just hot drinks. It has expanded its sale of audio books and music, and Sir Paul McCartney, the former Beatle, will be the first artist to release an album on Starbucks's Hear Music label.

This rapid internal expansion has not been without problems. *Consumer Reports* magazine recently ranked McDonald's coffee ahead of Starbucks's, saying it tastes better and costs less. The chairman has also criticised the time-saving policy of designing stores uniformly rather than with some local decoration. In 2013 Starbucks were criticised for charging high prices to Chinese consumers but the company responded by stating that operating costs were higher than in some other countries and high investment in China had to be paid for.

[32 marks, 40 minutes]

1   Why would you describe Starbucks's growth strategy as being an example of 'internal growth'?   [3]

2   Suggest **two** reasons why Starbucks has adopted a rapid-expansion strategy.   [6]

3   Analyse the possible advantages of focusing on growth in China.   [8]

4   Explain why Starbucks is planning to reduce its reliance on just selling coffee.   [5]

5   Do you think Starbucks would be advised to continue to expand internally or take over a chain of Chinese cafes? Explain your answer.   [10]

ACTIVITY 7.2

Jet Airways, Air Sahara and Etihad

India's largest private airline, Jet Airways, bought out its smaller rival, Air Sahara, for US$640 million in 2007. The takeover gave the airline a combined market share of about 32%. Jet Airways acquired the aircraft, equipment and landing and take-off rights at the airports Air Sahara had. Jet Airways founder and chairman, Naresh Goyal, believed that the external growth of Jet Airways would benefit shareholders. Some analysts predicted substantial synergy from this takeover. Better discounts from aircraft manufacturers were expected. Streamlining the two head offices into one unit will reduce fixed costs.

The interlinking of the different air routes allowed more passengers to be offered connecting flights with the new enlarged airline.

The takeover had to be approved by the Indian Ministry of Company Affairs. There was some concern that the takeover could lead to a monopolistic position, as Jet Airways now enjoys a dominant position on many domestic air routes. In 2013 Jet Airways sold 24% of its shares to Etihad Airways, which injected US$379 million into the airline to finance new aircraft and more routes. This partial takeover was called a 'strategic alliance'.

Daimler sells Chrysler after failed merger

After nine years of trying to make the merger of two large car makers work successfully, Mercedes-Benz has at last admitted defeat and sold its 80% stake in the US-based operator Chrysler. The merger never increased returns to shareholders and it failed in its original aim of creating a global motor company to compete effectively with General Motors, Ford and Toyota.

Management problems in controlling the merged businesses were huge. Distance between Germany

(Mercedes-Benz) and the USA (Chrysler) made communication difficult. The car ranges of the two companies had very little in common, so there were few shared components and economies of scale were less than expected. Culture clashes between the two management approaches led to top-level director disputes over the direction the merged business should take.

[48 marks, 70 minutes]

1 How would you classify the type of integration used in both of these case studies? Explain your answer. [4]

2 If Jet Airways were now to merge with an aircraft manufacturer:

  a How would this merger be classified? Explain your answer. [2]

  b Analyse **two** potential benefits to Jet Airways of this merger. [6]

3 Assess the likely impact of the Jet Airways takeover of Air Sahara on any two stakeholder groups, other than shareholders. [12]

4 Assess the likely impact on Jet Airways shareholders of the strategic alliance with Etihad Airlines. [12]

5 Using the Daimler-Chrysler case study and any other researched examples, discuss why many mergers and takeovers fail to give shareholders the benefits originally predicted. [12]

Problems resulting from rapid growth

Growth is a common business objective. Failure to expand in a market that is itself growing will lead to shrinking in the relative size of the business and the danger of being increasingly side-tracked by other more dynamic companies. However, rapid business growth is not without its problems – and, when these are not effectively tackled, they can even lead to business failure, or retrenchment (cutting back) of activities. These problems are summarised in Table 7.2, together with some proposed policies to deal with them.

The issue of business growth is one that most teams of managers have to face at one time or another. Managers must evaluate whether growth is a desirable objective for achieving the aim of maximising returns to investors. The cost of growth, especially external integration, can easily outweigh the expected benefits. The pace of growth is also significant. Expanding the company too swiftly can overstretch both management and financial resources. If this problem becomes too serious, then rapid retrenchment may become necessary and this could lead to bad publicity and negative reaction from stakeholders. The pace of growth, the form that it should take and how the consequences of expansion are dealt with are some of the most vital issues for any manager.

Potential problem from rapid growth	How this affects the business	Possible strategies to deal with problem
Financial	<ul><li>business expansion can be expensive</li><li>additional fixed capital and working capital will be required</li><li>takeovers can be particularly expensive</li><li>these factors could lead to negative cash flow and an increase in long-term borrowing</li></ul>	<ul><li>use internal sources of finance when possible, for example retained earnings</li><li>raise finance from share issues – but see 'control' point below</li><li>when proposing a takeover, offer shares in the new business rather than making a cash offer to the shareholders of the target business</li></ul>
Managerial	<ul><li>existing management may be unable to cope with problems of controlling larger operations</li><li>there may be a lack of coordination between the divisions of an expanding business – a real problem for integrating businesses</li><li>the original owner – or boss of the business – may find it difficult to adapt to being leader and manager</li></ul>	<ul><li>new management systems and structures may be required: a policy of delegation and empowerment of staff should reduce pressure on top staff</li><li>decentralisation, for example allowing national divisions reasonable autonomy, could provide motivated managers with a clear local focus</li><li>original owner may need to decide which are the most important areas of the business to remain heavily involved with, and relax control over others</li></ul>
Marketing	<ul><li>the original marketing strategy may no longer be appropriate for a larger organisation with a wider range of products</li><li>growth from national to international markets may not succeed if market strategies are not suitably adapted</li></ul>	<ul><li>adopt focused marketing strategies for each specific product or each country operated in – if this is what the results of market research indicate is essential</li></ul>
Loss of control by original owners	<ul><li>most likely to occur if a sole trader takes on partners or if a private limited company converts to a public one</li></ul>	<ul><li>almost an inevitable consequence of changing legal structure to gain additional capital, but original owners could try to remain as directors</li></ul>

Table 7.2 The problems of rapid growth and possible ways of tackling them

SUMMARY POINTS

- External business growth results from mergers and takeovers (acquisitions)
- External growth can be horizontal, vertical (backwards and forwards) and conglomerate
- These forms of external growth result in different potential benefits and limitations
- Rapid growth can create problems for management
- The synergy from mergers and acquisitions is not always as great as expected.

RESEARCH TASK

- Research the significant business mergers and takeovers over a three-month period – both in your own country and internationally.
- List these examples of external growth and classify them according to whether they are examples of horizontal, vertical or conglomerate integration.
- Analyse the benefits which the businesses are hoping to achieve from these mergers and takeovers.
- Using one of these examples, assess the likely impact on employees, customers and owners of the businesses.

A Level exam practice questions
Case study

Growth strategy in dispute at Traffic Clothing plc

Traffic Clothing plc produces suits and dresses and sells them to major retailers in several countries. Revenue has grown by around 15% each year for the past decade. Low prices have been possible due to the opening of low-cost factories in developing countries. This internal growth strategy was supported by most of the board of directors. They believed that it had been achieved without too much external borrowing. The management team had grown slowly and was now experienced at dealing with the issues involved in building new factories. There were some real causes for concern, however. Although sales revenue was increasing, profits were unchanged for the last three years. This was the result of several factors. Firstly, new competitors were entering the clothing manufacturing market and driving down prices. Secondly, raw material prices for both natural and man-made inputs were rising. Lastly, the number of mergers between large clothing retailers had increased their bargaining power when dealing with producers like Traffic. Major shareholders in Traffic were not happy with the directors' growth strategy. At the last board meeting, the finance director had proposed a policy of rapid external growth. He argued that this could be achieved by aggressive takeovers of either other clothing producers or material suppliers. The marketing director was suggesting buying up a major clothing retailer. 'Our own shops will give us real power in the high street as we will be able to offer just our own products.' The chief executive suggested that both directors prepare a detailed report on these proposals.

[34 marks, 50 minutes]

1   Analyse how the business increased sales revenue, yet gained no increase in profits for the last three years.   [6]

2   Assess the likely advantages and disadvantages of internal growth for this business.   [12]

3   Write a report evaluating the proposed forms of external growth through integration for this business. Your report should contain an assessment of the advantages and disadvantages of each proposal and a final recommendation for the board of directors.   [16]

A Level essay question

[20 marks, 45 minutes]

Discuss the likely impact on a food manufacturing business' stakeholders of a decision to merge with a food manufacturer in another country.   [20]

External influences on business activity

On completing this chapter, you will be able to:

- critically explain how and why the state intervenes through the law in business activities
- examine ways in which legal changes may influence business behaviour and the threats and opportunities this creates
- analyse and evaluate the impact of technology on business decisions
- analyse specific business situations and evaluate the positive and negative impacts of technology upon them
- explain how changes in society can impact on business strategy
- examine ways in which businesses can and should ensure environmental protection
- critically assess the nature, purpose and potential uses of environmental audits
- use understanding of all of these issues as a basis for strategy and strategic considerations in given circumstances.

Introducing the topic

NOKIA SETS A GOOD EXAMPLE – BUT TELEFONICA IS FINED

Businesses operate within a legal environment that constrains their activities. When the Spanish communications business Telefonica engaged in anti-competitive agreements with Portugal Telecom it was fined a massive €67 million fine by the European Competition Commissioner. The EU reported that: 'The EU is committed to a genuine free and single market in telecommunications. Anti-competitive practices that raise prices and limit consumer choice will not be tolerated.'

In contrast, Nokia has always offered workers who are made redundant payments and deals in excess of the legal minimum. When the Finnish company announced the closure of its Bochum factory in Germany with the loss of 2,300 jobs, it reached an agreement with the workers' trade union leaders in which Nokia paid US$314 million in redundancy pay. It also set up a social plan for employees to help them look for other jobs. These arrangements were more than the legal EU requirement. For example, the

EU law states that redundant workers should be paid 1.5 weeks' salary for each year worked. Nokia's policy showed that it was trying to set a good example and attempting to limit the bad publicity in Germany from the factory closure. Several years later, when Nokia closed the Salo factory in Finland, because of falling demand, the Finnish trade unions demanded the same deal as offered to the German workers who lost their jobs. One trade union leader said: '€125,000 per worker is the least that Nokia should pay for all of the decades of work that helped Nokia to flourish.'

Points to think about:

- Why do you think Nokia agreed to pay such large sums in compensation to redundant workers in Germany and set up a plan to help them find other jobs?
- Do you think government laws should control anti-competitive actions and redundancy payments?
- What was Telefonica hoping to gain from a 'no competition' agreement with Portugal Telecom?

Introduction

This chapter assesses the importance of the main external influences on business performance and business decision-making – apart from economic factors, which are considered in the next chapter. All businesses depend for their survival on understanding and responding to

external factors that are beyond their control. Many of the factors are 'constraints' in the sense that they may limit the nature of decisions that business managers can take. The legal requirements imposed by governments are one of the most obvious constraining influences on business activity. However, external influences can also create opportunities and enable a business to become even more successful – applying new technology in advance of rival firms is a good example.

Note: Some UK and EU laws are discussed in this chapter. You do not need to learn the details of these laws – they are simply given as examples.

The impact of the government and law on business activity

Legal constraints on business activity

In most countries – for political and social reasons – governments decide to introduce laws that constrain business decisions and activities. These fall into the following main categories:

- Employment practices and conditions of work.
- Marketing behaviour and consumer rights.
- Business competition.
- Location of businesses.

The law and employment practices

These laws control the relationship between employers and employees. The two main objectives are to:

- prevent exploitation of workers by powerful employers by, for example, laying down minimum levels of health and safety and minimum wage rates
- control excessive use of trade union collective action.

Legal constraints usually cover the following areas of employment practices:

- Recruitment, employment contracts and termination of employment.
- Health and safety at work.
- Minimum wages.
- Trade union rights and responsibilities.

Recruitment, employment contracts and termination of employment

Protecting the rights of workers usually takes the following forms. A written contract of employment must be signed so that the employee is fully aware of the pay, working conditions and disciplinary procedures to be followed. There are minimum ages at which young people can be employed. The length of the maximum working week is controlled in European Union countries by the Working Time Directive. Holiday and pension entitlements are usually guaranteed by legal regulations. Discrimination against people during recruitment and selection or while at work on the grounds of race, colour, gender or religion is illegal. In the EU, it is illegal to discriminate on the basis of an employee's age. The EU has some of the most protective legislation in the world for employees and

includes not only paid maternity leave after the birth of a baby but paternity leave too.

The way in which decisions over termination of employment are made is also often subject to legal constraints. For example, in EU countries, large-scale redundancies – where many workers have their contracts of employment ended – have to be discussed with trade union leaders and with works councils before the courts will accept the legality of the action. In cases where individuals have their contract terminated, and this is considered to be unfair, then the case can be taken to an industrial or employment tribunal where both sides of the argument will be heard by independent lawyers. If the worker wins the case, then compensation will have to be paid by the employer and an offer of reinstatement of employment can be made.

In the UK and other EU countries, unfair dismissal can be claimed if the employment contract is ended because of:

- pregnancy
- refusal to work on a holy day
- refusal to work overtime if this takes the total working hours over 48 hours in one week
- incorrect dismissal procedure having been followed
- being a member of a trade union.

In other countries, compared to EU states:

- maximum weekly working hours can be long – 52 hours in Central African Republic but only 37 hours in Denmark
- there is no minimum wage law – as in Iraq and Namibia
- minimum working age is lower – just 13 years in Burma for example
- health and safety at work requirements are less stringent – Bangladesh has not agreed to adopt some International Labour Organization standards on work health and safety.

These differences have been a major factor driving the location decisions of some European and multinational organisations.

Health and safety laws

These aim to protect workers from discomfort and physical injury at work. Providing a healthy and safe environment in which to work is now a legal requirement in most countries, although the strictness of the laws and the efficiency of inspection systems vary considerably. Health and safety laws usually require businesses to:

- equip factories and offices with safety equipment
- provide adequate washing and toilet facilities
- provide protection from dangerous machinery and materials
- give adequate breaks and maintain certain workplace temperatures.

In the UK and the EU there is a comprehensive inspection system supervised by the Health and Safety Executive. This has the power to inspect any work premises at any time and to start legal proceedings against firms that fail to meet minimum standards.

TOP TIP

You do not need to know about specific laws for A Level Business – but it is a good idea to know what the main employment laws are in your country and what they expect employers to do.

Evaluating the impact on business on employment and health and safety laws

There are both positive and negative effects. On the one hand, these laws are constraints that add to business costs. These costs will include:

- supervisory costs regarding a firm's recruitment, selection and promotion procedures
- higher wage costs if less than the minimum wage was being paid before this law was introduced

---

ACTIVITY 8.1

Employment rights in your country

In China, current employment rights are governed by the PRC Employment Law of 1995. There are 13 sections to this law, which cover almost all aspects of employment relationships. These include: working hours, holidays, health and safety, training, social welfare, disputes and discrimination on the grounds of race, sex, disability or age.

[14 marks, 15 minutes]

1 Why do you think the Chinese government introduced such a wide-ranging law as this, covering all aspects of employer–employee relationships? [4]

2 Do these laws help or damage business interests? Explain your answer. [10]

3 **Research task:** Find out about the main employment laws in your own country and the main rights they offer to workers. Do you think that these laws need changing in any way? If so, how and why?

This construction site in the USA should follow all health and safety laws to protect its workers

- higher costs from giving paid holidays, pension contributions and paid leave for sickness, maternity and paternity leave
- employment of more staff to avoid overlong hours for existing workers
- protective clothing and equipment to meet health and safety laws.

Clearly, multinationals that operate in countries with very few legal constraints will enjoy lower production costs.

On the other hand, there are real benefits to be gained by businesses that meet or even exceed the minimum standards laid down by law. Some businesses offer conditions of employment, pay levels and working conditions that far exceed legal minimum levels. What are the benefits to businesses from meeting – or even exceeding – the minimum legal requirements?

- Workers will feel more secure and more highly valued if they are offered a clear and fair employment contract. This will lead to more satisfied and motivated workers. These workers will be much more likely to work hard to help a business achieve its goals.
- A safe working environment will reduce risks of accidents and time off work for ill health or injury.
- Failing to meet minimum standards may lead to expensive court cases and heavy fines.

- Businesses that make a policy of providing employment conditions and a healthy environment beyond legal requirements can adopt a high-profile campaign to attract the best employees. This will also receive good publicity that might have marketing benefits for the business.
- The culture of the business will be looked upon as one that treats workers as partners in the business, equal in status and importance to managers and shareholders. This will again reflect well on the firm and make it easier to attract and keep the most effective staff. Workers will be keen to ensure quality output as they feel a part of the business.

The law, consumer rights and marketing behaviour

Why do consumers need protection from business actions? Why is the need for consumer protection increasing? What marketing practices are, in most countries, illegal? Here are some reasons why governments around the world take legal action to protect consumers of goods and services from unfair or unscrupulous business activity:

- Individual consumers are relatively weak and powerless against a large business with large marketing and promotion budgets. It is not easy for consumers

79

ACTIVITY 8.2

Employment laws being observed?

Gowri Sivakumaran was delighted to be offered the job of receptionist at Panang Cosmetics Ltd. She had been offered the post after a short interview with the office manager. He had stressed the need for a flexible worker who would put in hours of overtime when needed. Gowri was a little concerned when the manager said: 'You will be on a trial period of two months, so we will not bother with a contract yet. As we are a small company, we cannot pay you the government minimum, but I have spoken with the firm's accountant and we can pay you in cash each week, so there will be no tax to pay.' Several months after her appointment, Gowri had still not received

a contract, but she enjoyed her work. She had even applied for promotion – to junior bookkeeper – but that had been filled by a man who seemed to have inferior qualifications to Gowri and was already having trouble with the work. The finance department was, in fact, all male. Gowri decided to contact a local trade union official about this as she wondered if the firm was acting legally. Unfortunately, when she told the office manager he 'sacked' her on the spot, saying: 'We never wanted union troublemakers here and as you seem so keen on them you can leave now.' Gowri was obviously upset about the way she had been treated and decided to seek legal advice.

[20 marks, 25 minutes]

1   Identify as many examples as possible of how the firm might have broken the employment and other laws of your own country. [6]

2   What action could Gowri now take if the firm was based in your own country? [4]

3   Do you think this business should observe employment laws? Justify the reasons for your answer. [10]

to make good decisions when the power of advertising can be so influential.

■ Products are becoming more scientific and technological and it is difficult for consumers to understand how they operate and to assess the accuracy of the claims being made for them.

■ Selling techniques are becoming more pressurised and are increasingly difficult for some consumers to resist. These include the many offers of apparently cheap loans and consumer credit, which, if not studied very carefully, can commit consumers to paying off debts for many years at high interest rates.

■ The increasingly globalised marketplace is leading to increases in imported goods. Consumers may need protection from producers of goods that adopt different quality and safety standards from those existing in the domestic country.

■ The increasingly competitive nature of most markets leads to some firms trying to take advantage of consumers by reducing quality, service, guarantee periods and so on in order to offer an apparently lower price and better deal.

The following laws are the main UK consumer protection laws. Many countries have similar legislation.

Sale of Goods Acts, 1979 and 1982

There are three main conditions of these acts:

■ that goods and services are fit to sell – they should be safe and have no defects in them that will make them unsafe if they are used in the ways intended

■ that they are suitable for the purpose for which they are bought

■ that they perform in the way described.

Trade Descriptions Act, 1968

The most important condition is that:

■ there should be no misleading descriptions of, or claims made for, goods being sold, so a chair that was claimed to be covered in leather could not, in fact, be covered in plastic.

Consumer Protection Act, 1987

This law updated UK law in line with the requirements of the EU. The two main conditions are:

■ that firms that provide dangerous or defective products are liable for the cost of any damage they cause

■ that it is illegal to quote misleading prices – if it is claimed that 'the price is £50 less than the manufacturer's recommended price' when it is not, then the business has broken the law.

Other laws govern weights and measures, consumer credit regulations and the safety and preparation of food products.

Evaluating the impact of consumer protection laws on business

Clearly, business costs might have to rise to meet the requirements of consumer protection legislation. Redesigning products to meet health and safety laws or redesigning advertisements to give only clear and accurate information can be expensive. Improving quality-control standards and the accuracy of weights and measures in food preparation will be essential to reduce the danger of legal action. Treating consumers fairly and responding to complaints quickly may also reduce the risk of court action. Above all else, consumer protection legislation may require a change of strategy and culture in the organisation. Putting consumer interests at the forefront of company policy may demand a change of heart among very senior managers, but it can also bring substantial rewards for the firm. If it becomes well-known and widely publicised that a business is not only prepared to meet the minimum standards of protection laid down by law but to offer consumers a genuinely improved deal in terms of clarity of advertisements, accuracy of promotional offers, quality of product and good after-sales service, then the sales and marketing benefits – and therefore profit gains – could be real and long-lasting.

TOP TIP

You do not need to give specific details on consumer protection laws, but you may be asked how a business is affected by consumer laws in your country.

The law and business competition

It is usually argued that free and fair competition between businesses has the following benefits for consumers:

■ Wider choice of goods and services than when just one business dominates a market.

■ Businesses have to keep prices as low as possible to be competitive.

■ Businesses compete by improving the quality, design and performance of the product.

■ Competition between businesses within one country will also have external benefits. These firms will be more able to compete effectively with foreign firms and this will help to strengthen the domestic economy.

Governments attempt to encourage and promote competition between businesses by passing laws that:

■ investigate and control monopolies and make it possible to prevent mergers

■ limit or outlaw uncompetitive practices between firms.

ACTIVITY 8.3

Consumer rights in your country

In Malaysia, a very important law protecting the interests of consumers is the 1999 Consumer Protection Act. It has 14 main sections and these include: outlawing all misleading and deceptive conduct by firms, false advertising claims, guarantees in respect of supply of goods, and strict liability for defective and potentially dangerous products.

In India, the 1986 Consumer Protection Act provides for the regulation of all trade and competitive practices, creates national and state-level Consumer Protection Councils and gives a detailed list of unfair and uncompetitive trade practices.

[14 marks, 20 minutes]

1 Why do you think countries' governments, such as Malaysia and India, pass laws to protect consumer rights? **[4]**

2 Do you think that such laws help or damage business interests? Justify your answer. **[10]**

3 **Research task:** Find out the main consumer protection laws in your own country (others do exist in Malaysia and India, too). Can you give examples of how firms try to break these laws? Are the laws strict enough? If not, why not?

ACTIVITY 8.4

Ryanair – adverts are 'misleading'

Ryanair is one of Europe's most successful low-cost airlines. It has been threatened with prosecution and a substantial fine for repeatedly misleading customers about the availability of its cheapest fares. Some customers claim that they are not told when the fares include taxes and charges and when they do not. Also, the cheapest fares have many restrictions placed on them and it is suggested that these are not made clear when a booking is being made. The airline has broken the Advertising Code seven times in the past two years and has failed to heed warnings

by the Advertising Standards Authority (ASA). The company is being referred to the Office of Fair Trading, which has the power to take advertisers who make misleading claims about products or prices to court. Ryanair could face substantial fines. In January, Ryanair refused to withdraw an advert of a woman dressed as a young schoolgirl, despite the ASA's ruling that it breached advertising rules on social responsibility and ethics. Ryanair accused the ASA of censorship, saying it was run by 'unelected, self-appointed dimwits'.

[26 marks, 30 minutes]

1 In what ways might Ryanair gain from 'misleading' customers in the ways described? **[6]**

2 Do you think that advertisers should be controlled over the claims they make and the way they promote their products? Give reasons for your answer. **[10]**

3 If you were the Chief Executive Officer of Ryanair, how would you respond to this bad publicity and the threat of legal action? Justify your answer. **[10]**

Monopolies

As most **monopolies** are created by merger or takeover, government action can also be directed towards investigating and, if necessary, preventing, these forms of integration. In the UK the Competition Commission is able to undertake studies of proposed mergers

 KEY TERM

Monopoly: theoretically a situation in which there is only one supplier, but this is very rare: for government policy purposes this is usually redefined as a business controlling at least 25% of the market.

and takeovers and of alleged abuse of market power by monopoly firms. The aim is to establish whether consumer interests will suffer or are suffering. If the view is that they will or are, then the Commission makes proposals for the Office of Fair Trading (OFT) to take action. For example, the OFT can prevent a merger or takeover from taking place or can insist that unfair monopoly practices are stopped. However, if the Commission does not find significant evidence that the public interest will be harmed, then the merger or monopoly continues without further action being taken. This is unlike the monopoly policy in some countries, such as the USA, where the courts have the legal right to break up a monopoly or to prevent a merger whether or not there is evidence of existing or resulting negative public interest. In the USA this is called 'trust busting'.

How do monopolies develop?

Monopolies are developed by:

- invention of new products or processes that are then legally patented to give the originator a monopoly in production (although this reduces potential competition, patents are designed to encourage inventors and designers to develop original product ideas)
- merging or taking over other firms in the industry
- legal protection – for example, a government may choose to protect its country's postal service by giving it a legal monopoly for the delivery of letters
- the existence of 'barriers to entry' into an industry, such as advanced technical knowledge, huge costs of building facilities or buying equipment, or the need to advertise extensively to get established – these barriers will prevent, or make very difficult, the start-up of new competitors.

How are consumers affected by monopolies?

There can be both positive and negative effects. Possible benefits include:

- lower prices if large-scale production by a monopolist reduces average costs of production
- increased expenditure on new products and technical advances as the monopolist will be able to protect their position and make monopoly profits from the new idea.

However, the drawbacks include:

- higher prices if the monopolist has so little competition that consumers have no option but to buy from this one firm
- limited choice of products
- less investment in new products as a result of complacency and little risk of competition

- no incentive for the firm to lower costs and improve efficiency.

Uncompetitive – or restrictive – practices

These practices are attempts by firms – often acting or colluding together – to interfere with free market forces and so limit choice for customers or drive up prices. When firms act together they operate as if they are one monopoly. Identifying and acting against these practices is an important part of a government's competition policy. Examples of such restrictive practices include:

1 **Refusal to supply a retailer if they do not agree to charge the prices determined by the manufacturer:** Keeping prices high is clearly a disadvantage for the consumer, yet manufacturers can argue that it is an essential part of their branding of the product and helps to pay for extensive advertising and product development.
2 **Full-line forcing:** This is when a major producer forces a retailer to stock the whole range of products from the manufacturer – not just the really popular ones. If the retailer refuses, then even the popular items will not be supplied any longer.
3 **Market sharing agreements and price-fixing agreements:** This form of collusion involves forming a cartel between the firms concerned. They agree to fix prices and divide the market between them and not to compete for new business – they will agree to share new business or new contracts out around the group so that they do not compete with each other to drive prices down.
4 **Predatory pricing:** When a major firm in an industry tries to block new competitors by charging very low prices for certain goods, then this is called predatory pricing. As the new business is unlikely to have the low costs enjoyed by a large, established business, the firm may find it very difficult to survive this extreme form of competition.

In most countries governments have passed competition laws that make all of these anti-competitive practices illegal.

TOP TIP

When evaluating the impact of laws on business decisions and activity, do not forget that they can present opportunities as well as constraints. Meeting all legal obligations – and even exceeding their requirements – can create such a good public image that a business can use this as a major marketing tool.

Benefits	Limitations
■ identifies what social responsibilities the business is meeting – and what still needs to be achieved ■ sets targets for improvement in social performance by comparing these audits with the best-performing firms in the industry ■ improves a company's public image and this will help to act as a useful marketing tool to increase sales	■ if the social audit is not independently checked – as published accounts must be – will it be taken seriously by stakeholders? ■ time and money must be devoted to producing a detailed social audit – is this really necessary if these audits are not legally required? ■ many consumers may just be interested in cheap goods – not whether the businesses they buy them from are socially responsible or not

Table 8.1 The main benefits and limitations of a social audit

Social audits – checking on corporate social responsibility

There is a growing demand that businesses should report annually on how socially responsible they have been. Just as annual accounts report on profits or losses, an annual social report would indicate what the social impact of a business has been over the same period. Have profits been made at the expense of stakeholder interests? Has the firm made real efforts to meet its social responsibilities – but at high expense? Annual social reports are called **social audits** (see Table 8.1). It is not currently a legal requirement for businesses to produce such audits but many do so voluntarily.

KEY TERM

Social audit: a report on the impact a business has on society – this can cover pollution levels, health and safety record, sources of supplies, customer satisfaction and contribution to the community.

The impact of technology on business activity

Technology – what does it mean?

In its simplest form, technology means the use of tools, machines and science in an industrial context. This chapter is not concerned with the business use of 'low-technology' tools and machines, such as drills and lathes. Many of these have been in use for hundreds of years. Instead this chapter will assess the impact on businesses of the introduction of high-technology machines and processes that are based on **information technology** (IT). This is a much more recent development.

KEY TERM

Information technology: the use of electronic technology to gather, store, process and communicate information.

Technological change is affecting all businesses and all departments within business. Table 8.2 explains some of the most common business applications of IT, the departments likely to benefit most from them and the potential advantages to be gained.

Table 8.2 can only provide a summary of the business applications of technology. By the very nature of this external influence, the potential opportunities for technological applications are increasing almost daily. In addition to these uses of technology, advances in technical knowledge are opening up new product markets, such as hydrogen-powered cars and flexible mobile (cell) phones. The use of technology to develop new products is part of the research and development functions of businesses.

83

TOP TIP

It is wrong to assume that a business must always use the latest technology in all circumstances. There are substantial costs and some businesses thrive on apparently 'being backward'. For example, handmade designer furniture will sell because each piece is unique, and computer-controlled robots might be completely impractical.

KEY CONCEPT LINK

Innovation especially, but not exclusively, through new technology is one of the most important ways for businesses to **create value**. Not all inventions turn out to be successful innovations – new product ideas need to be **customer-focused** too.

KEY TERM

Innovation: creating more effective processes, products or ways of doing things in a business.

ACTIVITY 8.5

Vacuum cleaner Dyson victorious in bagless-machine court case

The law protects new inventions by allowing the inventor to take out a 'patent' on the new idea. This is designed to prevent copying of this idea by other businesses.

Hoover European Appliances continued to sell bagless vacuum cleaners, despite losing a High Court case over patent infringement brought by Dyson Appliances. James Dyson, founder and owner of Dyson, and inventor of the bagless machine, said after the hearing: 'I spent 20 years developing the technology and I am very pleased to see Hoover, who made a lot of false claims about their product, now found guilty of copying my patented design.' Hoover, which is owned by Candy of Italy – one of Europe's biggest makers of home appliances – said it had activated contingency

plans to sell a new type of bagless cleaner in Britain. This was developed over several months and Hoover claimed it did not infringe Dyson's patents. Alberto Bertali, managing director of Candy's UK subsidiary, said: 'The court judgment was a setback but not the end of the world. We brought out a new generation of bagless cleaner, which is an improvement on the current one.' At stake was a European market for vacuum cleaners worth some £1 billion a year at retail level. Dyson claims about a fifth of this and Hoover about a tenth. It is one of the most competitive consumer markets in the world. Consumers look for good value, reliable and very efficient machines. The rival companies try to improve on their products and be as competitive as possible.

[22 marks, 25 minutes]

1 A patent in effect creates a monopoly for the inventor. Outline the possible impact on Dyson and similar firms of this legal monopoly. **[4]**

2 Analyse the benefits to consumers of competition between firms in the vacuum-cleaner market. **[8]**

3 If Dyson's product continues to gain market share, should this, in your opinion, be of concern to the Competition Commission authorities in the UK and in the EU? Justify your answer. **[10]**

Information technology system	Common business applications	Advantages
Word processing	■ used in all departments for administrative tasks – typing, printing, storing, amending all forms of written letters and messages for internal and external communication	■ speed ■ accuracy ■ ease of amending documents ■ fewer administrative staff needed – managers can operate the system with some training ■ links with use of email for quick internal/external communications
Pagemaker and publishing programs	■ specialist publishing programs can create magazine and newspaper pages for high-quality printing direct from computer ■ marketing department can produce own promotional material ■ internal business newspaper can be produced to aid internal communications	■ may reduce the need for use of professional publishing firms – reducing costs ■ documents can be amended quickly, e.g. promotional leaflets changed for different countries ■ professional appearance given to company publications
Databases	■ used in all departments where the storing, filing and retrieving of large quantities of data are necessary ■ human resources department for keeping of personnel records ■ marketing department for storing details of all customers, addresses, numbers of products purchased, most frequently purchased products	■ replaces vast quantities of paper records ■ rapid retrieval of information saves time ■ linking two sets of data, e.g. customers and preferred products, allows focused promotional campaigns

(continued)

84

Information technology system	Common business applications	Advantages
	■ operations department for stock handling, electronic ordering of new supplies, application of JIT stock-control process ■ finance department for recording all transactions, including trade receivable payments and for producing up-to-date accounting data to management	■ stock control in retail stores is much more effective with electronic tills that relay information directly to a central stock-holding computer and then to the supplier for automatic reordering ■ credit control more effective with up-to-date trade receivable records
Spreadsheet programs	■ financial and management accounting records can be updated and amended ■ cash-flow forecasts and budgets can be updated in the light of new information ■ changes in expected performance can be input to the spreadsheet and changes in total figures are made automatically ■ income statements and statements of financial position can be drawn up frequently	■ flexibility and speed – changes to accounting records can be made quickly and the impact of these on total figures can be demonstrated instantly ■ 'what if' scenarios in budgeting and sales forecasting can be demonstrated – e.g. what would happen to forecast profits if sales rose by 10% following a 5% cut in price?
Computer-aided design (CAD)	■ nearly all design and architectural firms now use these programs for making and displaying designs – cars, house plans, furniture, garden designs are just a few examples ■ designs can be shown in 3D and turned around to show effect from all angles	■ saves on expensive designer salaries as work is now much quicker ■ more flexibility of design as each customer's special requirements can be easily added ■ can be linked to other programs to obtain product costings and to prepare for ordering of required supplies
Computer-aided manufacturing (CAM)	■ these programs are used to operate robotic equipment that replaces many labour-intensive production systems ■ used in operations management in manufacturing businesses	■ labour costs are reduced as machines replace many workers ■ productivity is increased and variable cost per unit is lower than in non-computerised processes ■ accuracy is improved – less scope for human error ■ flexibility of production is increased – modern computer-controlled machinery can usually be adapted to make a number of different variations of a standard product, and this helps to meet consumers' needs for some individual features ■ all of these benefits can add to a firm's competitive advantage
Internet/Intranet	■ the Internet is the World Wide Web of communication links between computers ■ marketing department – for promoting to a large market and taking orders online (see Chapter 19 for e-commerce discussion) ■ operations management – business to business (B2B) communication via the Internet is used to search the market for the cheapest suppliers ■ human resources uses these programs for communicating within the organisation ■ Intranets allow all staff to be internally connected via computers	■ cost savings from cheap internal and external communications ■ access to a much larger potential market than could be gained through non-IT methods ■ webpages project a worldwide image of the business ■ online ordering is cheaper than paper-based systems ■ B2B communications can obtain supplies at lower costs ■ use of social media and mobile marketing allows access to consumer groups not reached by traditional promotional methods ■ internal communication is quicker than traditional methods

Table 8.2 Common business applications of technology

KEY TERMS

Computer-aided design: using computers and IT when designing products.

Computer-aided manufacturing: the use of computers and computer-controlled machinery to speed up the production process and make it more flexible.

Applying technology to business – potential limitations

1 **Costs:** Capital costs can be substantial, labour training costs will be necessary and will recur regularly with further technological development. Redundancy costs will be incurred if any existing staff are being replaced by the technology.

2 **Labour relations:** These can be damaged if the technological change is not explained and presented to workers in a positive way with the reasons for it fully justified. If many jobs are being lost during the process of change, then remaining workers may suffer from reduced job security and this could damage their motivation levels. Trade unions can oppose technological change if it risks too many of their members' jobs.

3 **Reliability:** Breakdowns in an automated production or stock-handling systems can lead to the whole process being halted. There may be teething problems with new systems and the expected gains in efficiency may take longer to be realised than forecast.

4 **Data protection:** The right to hold data on staff and customers is controlled by national laws and the business must keep up-to-date with these legal constraints on its use of IT.

5 **Management:** Some managers fear change as much as employees do – especially if they are not very computer literate themselves. In addition, recognising the need for change and managing the technological change process require a great deal of management skill.

KEY CONCEPT LINK

The **management** of **change** within a business is one of the major determinants of successful organisations. See Chapter 40 for more details of change management.

IT and business decision-making

The provision of huge amounts of data to management through the use of IT is referred to as 'management information systems'. Computers now provide managers with more data about the operations of their business than was previously thought possible. This has the following benefits:

- Managers can obtain data quickly and frequently from all departments and regional divisions of the business – aiding overall control.
- Computers can be used to analyse and process the data rapidly so that managers can interpret them and take decisions quickly on the basis of them.
- Management information systems accelerate the process of communicating decisions to those in the organisation who need to know.

Information gives managers the opportunity to review and control the operations of the business. IT-based management information systems provide substantial power to centralised managers and, although this could be used for improving the performance of a business, there are possible drawbacks, too.

- The ease of transferring data electronically can lead to so many messages and communications that 'information overload' occurs. This is when the sheer volume of information prevents decision-makers from identifying the most important information and the areas of the business most in need of action.
- The power that information brings to central managers could be abused and could lead to a reduction in the authority and empowerment extended to work teams and middle managers. Information used for central control in an oppressive way could reduce job enrichment and hence motivation levels.

The best managers will apply the detailed information provided by the modern electronic IT systems to improve and speed up their decision-making. They should not allow it to change their style of leadership to a centralised or authoritarian one based on using data to control all aspects of the organisation.

Introducing technology effectively

These are the important stages a business should go through when introducing or updating technology to reduce opposition to change:

- **Analyse** the potential use of IT and the ways in which it can make the business more effective.
- **Involve** managers and other staff in assessing the potential benefits and pitfalls of introducing IT – better ideas often come from those who will use the system than from those responsible for purchasing it.
- **Evaluate** the different systems and programs available – compare the cost and the expected efficiency and productivity gains. Consider the budget available for this system.
- **Plan** for the introduction of the new system, including extensive training for staff and demonstrations to all users.

- **Monitor** the introduction and effectiveness of the system – is it giving the expected benefits and, if not, what can be done to improve performance?

TOP TIP

Be prepared to evaluate a firm's use of IT and how it introduced the system. Using IT is *not* the best solution to all problems – and introducing it badly can create more problems than it solves.

Social and demographic influences on business activity

The structure of society is constantly evolving. The changes occurring in many countries include:

- an ageing population with reduced birth rates and longer life expectancy – although in some nations the average age is falling due to high birth rates
- the changing role of women – not just to bear and look after children but to seek employment and to take posts of responsibility in industry
- better provision of education facilities, which is increasing literacy and leading to more skilled and adaptable workforces
- early retirement in many high-income countries, which is leading to more leisure time for a growing number of relatively wealthy pensioners
- in some countries, rising divorce rates are creating increasing numbers of single-person households
- job insecurity, often created by the forces of globalisation, which is forcing more employees to accept temporary and part-time employment – some workers actually prefer this option.

This list is by no means complete and you could undoubtedly add to it from knowledge of the changes occurring in your own society. How do these changes impact on business strategy and decisions? We will look at the impact of two of the most significant of these changes.

An ageing population

This means that the average age of the population is rising. It is often associated with:

- a larger proportion of the population over the age of retirement
- a smaller proportion of the population in lower age ranges, for example 0–16 years old
- a smaller number of workers in the economy but a larger number of dependants, that is those below working age or retired. This puts a higher tax burden on the working population.

These changes often result from lower birth rates (smaller families, improved contraception), increasing numbers of women in work and longer life expectancy (better health and social care). The impact on business of these changes is most apparent in two ways:

1 Changing patterns of demand as greater numbers of 'grey' consumers demand different types of goods from those sought by, say, teenagers. Therefore, a construction company might switch from building large apartments for families to smaller units with special facilities for the elderly. Market research will be important for a business that considers that the demand for their portfolio of products could change as a consequence of an ageing population.

2 Age structure of the workforce may change. There may be reduced numbers of youthful employees available and it may be necessary for workforce planning to include provision for employing older workers – or for keeping existing workers up to, and perhaps beyond, retirement age. It is often stated that younger employees are more adaptable and easier to train in new technologies. However, older workers are often said to show more loyalty to a business and will have years of experience that could improve customer service.

Patterns of employment

Changing patterns of employment are one of the social constraints on the activities of business. For many businesses, labour is still a crucial factor of production and probably the greatest single expense. This is particularly true in the personal-service industries, such as childcare or homes for the elderly.

The main features of changing patterns in most countries are as follows:

- In many industries, labour is being replaced by capital. This is particularly true of the secondary sector of the economy – see the section above on applications of IT. Output and efficiency can rise due to increasing productivity, yet total employment often falls.
- Transfer of labour from the old, established industries, such as steel, to the new, hi-tech industries, such as computer-games design.
- An increase in the number of women in employment and in the range of occupations in which they are employed.
- An increase in part-time employment. Part of this is due to single part-time jobs and some of it to job sharing. Much of it is second jobs, as people supplement their income.
- An increase in student employment on a part-time basis, among both those who are in, or waiting to go into, higher education and those who are still in secondary education. Some industries are substantially staffed by students and part-timers. McDonald's, most of the other fast-food shops and many supermarkets are largely staffed in this way.

- An increase in temporary and flexible employment contracts. These are often imposed by employers on staff to reduce the fixed costs of full-time and salaried posts and to allow for flexibility when faced with seasonal demand or uncertainties caused by increasing globalisation.
- Flexible hours are more common. This is most likely in large towns and cities, where the problems of being at work for 9am or of getting home at the normal end of the day have produced a more flexible approach. Such an approach is also helpful to working parents.
- An ageing population changes the balance between those in work and those supported, and this puts increasing burdens on the health service, pensions, private pension funds and the care industries. In the UK, the decision to raise the retirement age for receiving the state pension will increase the working population a little, but longevity during retirement will be an increasing problem.
- Women are tending to stay in full-time employment for longer; families are smaller, more women do not have children and there is an increasing tendency to have children later in life.
- More women take maternity leave and then return to work.
- Many countries are increasingly multicultural and this has an effect on the pattern of women at work.
- In the UK, three out of ten women of Pakistani origin and two out of ten women of Bangladeshi origin seek full-time employment. In the UK as a whole, 75% of women seek full-time employment.
- Almost half of all British male employees work more than 48 hours a week, whilst for women the percentage is only 7%. Note that the EU Working Time Directive came into force in October 1998. It requires employers to 'take all reasonable steps to ensure that employees do not work, against their will, more than an average of 48 hours a week'. The directive is not universal, does not apply to the self-employed, and employees can agree to work longer hours if they want to.

Evaluating effects on business of the changes in the pattern of employment

Firms can make these changes work to their own benefit, while accepting some of the cost implications of them. Higher-quality and better-qualified workers should be more efficient – but they will expect improved pay and conditions. Part-time workers can offer a firm much greater flexibility by being available at peak times and this will help to keep down overhead expenses. Yet part-time and temporary staff can be difficult to mould into a team and may not contribute as much as a result. By employing more females, and particularly by removing barriers to their progress and promotion, firms can benefit from a wider choice of staff and improved motivation among women workers. However, there will be the increased costs of maternity leave and of

providing staff cover for this. As with all other external influences on business behaviour, the most successful firms will be those that quickly adapt to changes and attempt to turn them to their own competitive advantage.

TOP TIP

Changing social and employment patterns can create just as many opportunities for businesses as potential risks or threats.

ACTIVITY 8.6

Changing employment patterns

In 2013, there were more than eight million employees in the UK with part-time jobs – an increase of two million in ten years. There has also been an increase in temporary working – almost 12% of all employees now have temporary and not permanent employment contracts. 600,000 workers have zero-hours contracts, which do not guarantee any work some weeks but result in workers being called in by employers when there is a labour shortage.

[25 marks, 30 minutes]

1   Why might employees prefer part-time to full-time employment?   [6]

2   What benefits could a business gain from employing:
    a   more staff on part-time contracts?   [6]
    b   more staff on temporary contracts?   [6]

3   What disadvantages might these trends in employment patterns have for workers?   [7]

Environmental constraints on business activity

The environment and corporate social responsibility

To whom is a business answerable? Should business activity be solely concerned with meeting the objectives of shareholders and investors – by working for maximum profit – or should business decisions also be influenced by the needs of other stakeholders? When a firm does

ACTIVITY 8.7

Changing labour force data and impact on business – country A

	2010	%	2015	%	(Estimated) 2020	%
Total labour force (000)	7,042		9,572		12,939.6	
Age distribution		100.0		100.0		100.0
15–24	2,014.0	28.6	2,498.3	26.1	3,112.2	24.1
25–34	2,204.1	31.3	2,979.2	31.1	4,118.9	31.8
35–54	2,436.5	34.6	3,611.3	37.7	4,995.5	38.6
55–64	387.4	5.5	483.7	5.1	713.1	5.5
Educational structure		100.0		100.0		100.0
Primary education only	2,380.2	33.8	2,604.3	27.2	1,643.3	12.7
Lower & middle secondary	4,042.1	57.4	5,624.5	58.8	6,767.4	52.3
Tertiary (university education)	619.7	8.8	1,343.7	14.0	4,528.9	35.0
Labour force participation rate (%)		65.3		65.5		68.1
Male		85.6		85.4		86.4
Female		44.1		44.5		49.0

[22 marks, 25 minutes]

1 Calculate the forecast percentage increase in the labour force between 2010 and 2020.   [2]

2 Identify **two** changes to the structure of the labour workforce forecast over this period. Explain how each of these changes might have an impact on the employment policy of a business in country A.   [10]

3 Evaluate whether a business should provide more than the basic legal minimum in terms of conditions of employment and health and safety at work.   [10]

accept its legal and moral obligations to stakeholders other than investors, it is said to be accepting 'corporate social responsibility'. One important measure of a firm's attitude to its social responsibility is the way in which it deals with environmental issues.

The environment in which we all live can be greatly affected by business activity. Air and noise pollution from manufacturing processes, road congestion caused by heavy trucks, business expansion into country areas, emissions of gases that can lead to global warming and the use of scarce non-renewable natural resources – these are all environmental issues that are of increasing concern to people and governments all over the world. How should business managers react to these concerns? Should they respond by adopting environmentally safe or 'green' policies, even if these are expensive, or should they always take the cheapest option no matter what the consequences for the environment might be?

Arguments for and against adopting environmentally friendly business strategies

Arguments for adopting environmentally friendly business strategies:

1 Businesses that reduce pollution by using the latest 'green' equipment or use recycled material rather than scarce natural products can have a real marketing and promotional advantage. Consumers are becoming increasingly aware of environmental issues and there is good evidence that

growing numbers of them will support businesses that adopt green policies. The success of The Body Shop worldwide has been built on producing products that do not harm animals in testing or the wider environment through production methods. The reverse is also true. Companies that damage the environment, such as through oil-tanker spills, can suffer an adverse consumer reaction, which can even amount to a boycott of their goods. Much of this adverse reaction will be caused by extensive pressure-group activity (see page 93). Businesses must ensure that their environmental policies are genuine, though – if they are found out to be just a cover-up (sometimes called 'greenwash') for environmentally damaging practices, then the bad publicity could backfire on the firm.

2   Low-polluting production methods and responsible waste disposal will reduce the chances of businesses breaking laws designed to protect the environment. In this way they can avoid very bad publicity and heavy court fines.

3   Businesses that switch to a more environmentally friendly strategy often report an improvement in the number and quality of applications they receive from potential employees. It seems that staff would rather work for a firm that they can have pride in and that adopts policies that reflect their own personal views and standards.

The success of The Body Shop has been built on its concerns for the environment

4   There could be long-term financial benefits too. Generating electricity by using solar panels may involve very heavy capital expenditure. However, if the cost of energy generated by oil and gas increases due to world shortages of these scarce natural commodities, the businesses that had invested in solar power would gain substantial cost savings. A further cost point relates to 'external costs'. These are the costs of production methods that are paid for by the rest of society, not the producing firm. These might include the damaging health effects from air pollution or the cost of clearing rivers or tips with polluted waste. If the government introduced additional penalties on businesses, such as pollution permits or the right for local residents to sue for health risks, then firms would have to pay these costs, which were formerly 'external'. A numerical example will help to illustrate this point:

- An electricity-generating company is planning a new power station, which will be coal-fired. The cost of construction will be $20 million.

- Each tonne of coal costs $100, and the electricity generated from one tonne of coal can be sold for $150.

- However, the government has estimated that the environmental damage of burning one tonne of coal is $20. After the station is built, the government imposes this amount of tax on each tonne of coal. Can you see how this additional cost will reduce the profitability of the new station? This is why some businesses such as Shell are now assuming that this kind of 'carbon' tax will be imposed shortly and have added it to estimates of the total costs of opening and operating new oil refineries and other energy-consuming plants.

Arguments against adopting environmentally friendly business strategies:

1   There might be a marketing advantage from keeping costs as low as possible, even though the environment is damaged as a result. Lower prices may increase sales and consumers will benefit from these low-priced goods – and may be prepared to overlook the environmental consequences.

2   Profits may be reduced if expensive but low-polluting equipment is used or if waste is disposed of in responsible ways rather than just dumping it into rivers. If profits are lower as a result, then this will limit how much firms can invest in the future.

3   In many countries, legal protection of the environment is weak and inspection systems are inadequate. There will, as a result, be little risk of legal action and heavy fines against business activity in these countries even if they use low-cost yet polluting production methods.

4   In developing countries, it is argued that economic development is more important than protecting the environment. Businesses can achieve more good by producing cheaply in these countries than if they are forced to always adopt the 'greenest' production strategy.

Environmental audits

An audit simply means an independent check. It is most commonly known in connection with the accounts of a company, which have to be verified by an external auditor as a true and fair account. Accounts only measure the financial performance of a business. In recent years, some businesses have been using the auditing approach to evaluate their performance in ways other than just profit and loss.

KEY TERM

Environmental audits: assess the impact of a business's activities on the environment.

Environmental factors are often difficult to measure in monetary terms and they do not currently have to be legally included in published accounts. An environmental audit would check the pollution levels, wastage levels, energy use, transport use and recycling rates of the business and compare them with previous years, pre-set targets and possibly other similar businesses. At present, these audits are entirely voluntary. Those firms who undertake them and publish the results nearly always have a very good environmental record – that is why they are published. Firms with a poor reputation or record in this area are unlikely to get involved unless it becomes compulsory.

Those few firms that publish the results of environmental audits expect to gain something from the process. Favourable consumer reaction could lead to increased sales. Positive media coverage will give free publicity. Working towards the common aim of reducing harm to the environment could help to bring workers and managers together as a team. Better-qualified applicants will want to join a company with a good reputation and a fine team spirit.

Social audits

Social audits can include an environmental audit but they give details of other impacts on society too. These include:

- health and safety record, for example number of accidents and fatalities
- contributions to local community events and charities
- proportion of supplies that come from ethical sources, for example Fairtrade Foundation suppliers
- employee benefit schemes
- feedback from customers and suppliers on how they perceive the ethical nature of the business's activities.

KEY TERM

Social audit: a report on the impact a business has on society. This can cover pollution levels, health and safety record, sources of supplies, customer satisfaction and contribution to the community.

91

ACTIVITY 8.8

Virgin's environmental policies – genuinely green or just 'greenwash'?

The Virgin Atlantic jumbo jet that flew between London and Amsterdam using a proportion of bio-fuel was a world first. This fuel was derived from Brazilian babassu nuts and coconuts and is much less polluting than ordinary jet kerosene. The airline boss Sir Richard Branson hailed this as a 'vital breakthrough' for the industry. Other well-publicised fuel-saving measures used by the airline are the towing of aircraft to the runways for take-off and not using their own engines and offering first-class passengers train tickets to travel to the airport not chauffeur-driven cars. Unfortunately, very few passengers have taken up this last offer, and towing of aircraft has been stopped as it causes damage to the undercarriage.

Greenpeace's chief scientist has labelled these efforts to make air travel more environmentally friendly 'high-altitude greenwash' and said that 'less air travel is the only answer to the growing problem of climate changing pollution caused by air travel'. A Friends of the Earth spokesman said that bio-fuels do little to reduce emissions and large-scale production of them leads to higher food prices.

[18 marks, 25 minutes]

1 Analyse why Virgin Atlantic is making efforts to reduce the amount of jet fuel (kerosene) used by its aircraft. **[8]**

2 To what extent will the company lose or benefit from these well-publicised attempts to reduce air pollution? **[10]**

The social audit will also contain annual targets to be reached to improve a firm's degree of social responsibility, and details of the policies to be followed to achieve these aims will also be given. By constructing and publishing these reports, firms are often able to identify potentially anti-social behaviour and take steps to root this out of the company's practices. Publishing detailed and independently verified social audits (this also applies to environmental audits) can improve a firm's public image, increase consumer loyalty and give the business a clear direction for future improvements in its social responsibility aims.

ACTIVITY 8.9

Corporate social responsibility

Corporate social and environmental awareness has become essential for companies as they realise that they must listen to all stakeholders if they are to achieve their objectives.

Judging from his public statements, Bill Ford Jr, former chairman of Ford, has changed his great-grandfather's most quoted statement to reflect a different hue. It might now read: 'Any colour as long as it's green.' Speaking at a Greenpeace conference in London, the head of the world's third-largest car manufacturer said that he would like to see the end of the internal combustion engine and also predicted the decline of car ownership. However, he combined this environmental commitment with an equally strong desire to ensure Ford's continued profitability. Such a combination of environmental responsibility, ethics and profits is one that is attracting increasing attention. The Business Leaders Forum's Human Capitalism campaign disagrees with the idea that the interests of shareholders and those of other stakeholders (i.e. employees, community, customers) must always conflict. The campaign seeks to weld these two seemingly opposite forces so that doing good and doing good business become one and the same thing. Members of the campaign include Andersen Consulting, Coca-Cola, Diageo, *The Financial Times, Time Magazine* and the WPP Group.

Social and environmental responsibility has moved from a 'nice to do' to a 'need to do'. One of the main findings of a recent report by the International Business Leaders Forum is a focus on employees and their views of the companies they work for or may wish to work for. When asked to rank their principal reasons for admiring certain companies, nearly a quarter (24%) of all respondents said respect for employees. That compared to 21% who rated environmental responsibility, 12% financial stability and 4% who thought creativity the most important aspect of an admirable company.

The importance of the employee has been highlighted by the so-called 'war for talent'. Recruiting the brightest and best has become a key concern of corporate strategy. Says Tom Cooper, of PricewaterhouseCoopers: 'There is such a limited number of the right type of graduates right now, and they are choosy about the type of company they will work for. The cost of recruiting and retaining staff is likely to be higher if you are deemed not to be an ethical employer and organisation.' A company's reputation also has significant implications for its financial performance. Some analysts believe it is one of the key factors in valuation of companies. One company could have a higher stock market valuation than another one solely due to its good social and environmental reputation.

Shell, a company with traditionally one of the worst reputations among environmental and social pressure groups, has made enormous efforts to reinvent itself from being the environmentalists' favourite whipping boy to pioneer a socially responsible business. It has stated its aims as nothing less than to become 'the leading multinational in economic, environmental and social responsibility'. Shell's chairman has said that the reason for Shell's conversion to sustainability is commercial: 'We won't achieve our business goals unless we are listening to – and learning from – the full range of our stakeholders in society.'

[30 marks, 40 minutes]

1 a Define the term 'socially responsible business'. [2]

   b Briefly explain the term 'ethics'. [3]

2 Examine **two** factors given in the article that could encourage a business to adopt an ethical and environmentally aware strategy. [8]

3 Why did the chairman of Ford express 'an equally strong desire to ensure Ford's continued profitability'? [6]

4 Discuss the likely costs and benefits for Shell of being seen as 'the leading multinational in economic, environmental and social responsibility'. [11]

Evaluation of environmental and social audits

1 Until they are made compulsory and there is general agreement about what they should include and how the contents will be verified, some observers will not take them seriously.

2 Companies have been accused of using them as a publicity stunt or a 'smokescreen' to hide their true intentions and potentially damaging practices.

3 They can be very time-consuming and expensive to produce and publish and this may make them of limited value to small businesses or those with very limited finance.

Environmental and ethical issues – the role of pressure groups

More and more businesses are accepting the need to incorporate environmental and ethical considerations into their strategic decision-making. One of the main reasons concerns the growing power and influence of **pressure groups** at both national and international levels.

KEY TERM

Pressure groups: organisations created by people with a common interest or aim who put pressure on businesses and governments to change policies so that an objective is reached.

Perhaps the best-known international examples are:

- **Greenpeace** – campaigns for greater environmental protection by both businesses adopting green strategies and governments passing tighter anti-pollution laws.
- **Fairtrade Foundation** – aims to achieve a better deal for agricultural producers in low-income countries.
- **WWF** – aims to improve animal welfare, especially protecting and conserving the habitat of wild animals.
- **Amnesty International** – rigorously opposes anti-human rights policies of governments.
- **Jubilee 2000** – campaigns for Western governments to reduce or eliminate the debt burden on developing countries.

How do they operate? Pressure groups want changes to be made in three important areas:

- governments to change their policies and to pass laws supporting the aims of the group
- businesses to change policies so that, for example, less damage is caused to the environment
- consumers to change their purchasing habits so that businesses that adopt 'appropriate' policies see an increase in sales, but those that continue to pollute or use unsuitable work practices see sales fall.

Pressure groups try to achieve these goals in a number of ways:

1 **Publicity through media coverage:** Effective public relations are crucial to most successful pressure-group campaigns. Frequent press releases giving details of undesirable company activity and coverage of 'direct action' events, such as meetings, demonstrations and consumer boycotts will help to constantly keep the campaign in the public eye. The more bad publicity the group can create for the company concerned, then the greater the chance of it succeeding in changing corporate policy. The pressure group may spend money on its own advertising campaign – as Amnesty International does – and the success of this approach will depend upon the financial resources of the group.

2 **Influencing consumer behaviour:** If the pressure group is so successful that consumers stop buying a certain company's products for long enough, then the commercial case for changing policy becomes much stronger. The highly successful consumer boycott of Shell petrol stations following a decision to dump an old oil platform in the sea led to a change of strategy. Shell is now aiming to become 'the leading multinational for environmental and social responsibility' (see Activity 8.9). Public sympathy for a pressure group campaign can increase its effectiveness significantly.

3 **Lobbying of government:** This means putting the arguments of the pressure group to government members and ministers because they have the power to change the law. If the popularity of the government is likely to be damaged by a pressure-group campaign that requires government action, then the legal changes asked for stand a greater chance of being introduced.

ACTIVITY 8.10

Tibet protesters target BP over PetroChina stake

The oil giant BP Amoco will face action from Tibetan pressure groups to withdraw from PetroChina, the state-run Chinese oil company that is building a gas pipeline through ethnic Tibetan areas. Tibetan activists coordinated a worldwide series of protests while the Free Tibet Campaign tried to disrupt BP's AGM in April. BP is being asked to dispose of its PetroChina stake on the grounds that it contravenes the company's ethical policy on human rights and the environment. The pressure group also attempted to organise a consumer boycott of BP petrol stations. A government minister admitted to reporters in Beijing that BP and PetroChina would face a public relations 'disaster' if BP gave in to the pressure group's demands. Human rights groups view the pipeline project as a main policy of Beijing's 'economic colonisation' of the Tibetan people. A spokesperson for BP, which paid $578 million for its 2.2% stake in PetroChina, said there was nothing it could do about the pipeline. 'Our investment in PetroChina is a passive one. We have no influence with the PetroChina management and no interest in the Tibetan pipeline.'

[22 marks, 30 minutes]

1 Analyse the possible impact of pressure group activity on BP. [10]

2 Evaluate the factors that determine whether a pressure group's campaign against business activity is successful. [12]

SUMMARY POINTS

- Laws have a significant impact on the relationship between employer and employee.
- Consumer protection laws cover issues such as advertising, weights and measures, guarantees and defective products.
- Technology is making an irreversible impact on business activity including communication, product technology, costs of production, marketing techniques, employee relations and consumer tastes.
- The application of technology in business can also have some undesirable effects.
- Social forces and changes, including community action through pressure groups, cannot be overlooked by business.
- Patterns of employment are changing and businesses must adapt to these changes.
- Business impact on the environment is becoming an increasingly important consideration.

RESEARCH TASK

1 Choose a well-known pressure group, such as Greenpeace, that operates in your country, or even internationally.

   - Refer to its webpage on the Internet.
   - Find out some of the cases and actions it is currently involved in.
   - Make notes on which business activities this pressure group is attempting to change and how it is going about it.
   - Write a brief assessment of the group's likely chances of success.

2 Use the Internet to research **one** of the following and write a brief report explaining the potential benefits to any one well-known business in your country: CAD; CAM; RFID.

A Level exam practice questions
Case studies

1 Ethics pays

Ethics pays – this appears to be one of the conclusions from the latest annual list of the 'world's most ethical companies' compiled by Ethisphere. The 2013 list includes some of the world's most profitable businesses suggesting that 'doing the right thing' can also mean 'doing the profitable thing'.

Although some may criticise Google, the company regularly makes good on its motto: 'Don't be evil.' Through its Google Green Program, the company has donated more than US$1 billion to renewable energy projects, and has decreased its own footprint by using energy efficient buildings and public transportation. These improvements were publicised in the company's social audit. The company is also a staunch advocate of free speech, which can be observed from its frequent conflicts with the Chinese government. Google is also an open supporter of workplace equality. Yet all this pales in comparison to Google's status as a paragon for employee benefits. Just to name a few, Google employees have access to free health care and treatment from on-site doctors, free legal advice with discounted legal services, a fully stocked snack pantry and on-site cafeteria (staffed by world-class chefs, no less), and a free on-site nursery. With such a stellar record of social awareness and positive employee relations, Google is claimed to be one of the best examples of 'ethics = profits' in the corporate world today. The company reported profits of US$2.97 billion in just four months – July to September 2013. Shareholders are happy too – the share price rose by 6% to a record US$941!

[36 marks, 50 minutes]

1 Analyse the benefits to Google of its ethical policies. **[10]**

2 Analyse the likely benefits to a company of your choice of publishing a social audit. **[10]**

3 Discuss the view that 'ethics can be made to pay' for all businesses. **[16]**

2 Petrobras bids to clean up dismal safety and environment record

An oil company is having to change its culture over safety and the environment. Petrobras, the Brazilian state-run oil company, has had much to celebrate in recent years. Oil output as well as productivity has increased significantly and profits last year reached an all-time record. Yet a recent devastating explosion on an offshore oil platform, which killed ten people and yesterday caused the $450 million rig to sink to the bottom of the sea, revealed what may be the company's biggest challenge yet: overcoming a dismal safety and environmental record. The fatal explosion brings the death toll for work-related accidents in the oil industry to 91 over three years. There have been 22 recent oil or fuel spills, two of them very large. The chief executive admits that some of the company's installations and equipment are outdated, industrial waste goes untreated and the attitude of many employees towards environment and operational safety is inadequate. Petrobras has now started to tackle the problems seriously. Within a year, the company has put together a global health, safety and environment (HSE) plan with investments of $1.3 billion. The company has also stepped up inspections, overhauled safety regulations and is obtaining international safety certifications for its installations, from refineries to ports. Yet judging by the accidents, the company has a long way to go before reaching its goal of environmental and safety excellence. Critics argue that accidents such as the oil platform explosion may have been the result of Petrobras pushing too hard to meet its production targets.

One oil engineer said the four-month test phase of the oil platform was only half as long as normal. Working and living conditions on several platforms are said to be inadequate. 'We sleep on a chair in the television room because the bedrooms are overcrowded,' said a worker on one platform. Union leaders argue that employees of contracted companies, who account for 54% of a total workforce of 75,000, are under-qualified. 'Some of these companies exist only for the duration of their contract and have no interest in their workers,' says Elio Luiz Seidel, from the Federation of Oil Workers (FUP). Petrobras disagrees that outsourcing is part of the problem, but admits it is difficult to ensure contractors comply with safety and environmental norms. 'There is definitely room for improving the level of training and safety with our contractors,' admits the manager of human resources. Petrobras used to train all personnel, but recently either transferred that responsibility to contractors or is charging them for training. Some contractors, in turn, are now said to be taking the cost of training out of employees' pay checks. Management has reassured investors that the platform was insured and that financial damages were limited to no more than $450 million this year.

[32 marks, 50 minutes]

1   What evidence is there for the claim that Petrobras is putting the interests of investors before those of other stakeholder groups? **[6]**

2   Analyse the likely factors contributing to the recent accidents at Petrobras sites. **[6]**

3   The company is now taking steps to improve its safety and environmental records. Explain the likely reasons for this policy. **[8]**

4   To what extent will the future profitability of companies, such as Petrobras, depend on meeting high ethical and environmental standards? **[12]**

3   More chips, please?

The major European supermarkets have been putting information technology at the front of their drive for lower costs, improved customer service and more information about their customers. Bar codes, check-out scanners, automatic product reordering systems, automated stock-control programs, robot-controlled transport systems in warehouses, chip-and-pin machines for payment, loyalty cards that record each individual shopper's purchases, internet shopping for customers – the list of IT applications employed by the large supermarkets seems almost endless.

Some of these systems have been controversial. For example, centralised ordering and delivery of products reduced the independence and control of individual store managers. The rapid growth of internet shopping left some companies with a shortage of stock and delivery vehicles, which led to poor service. Some smaller suppliers who have been unable to cope with the cost of introducing compatible IT systems to take orders from the huge retailers have been dropped.

And now the latest development is causing further controversy. RFID, or radio-frequency ID tagging, involves putting a small chip and coiled antenna, at the initial point of production, into *every* item sold through the supermarkets. Unlike bar codes that have to be manually scanned, the RFID simply broadcasts its presence and data, such as sell-by date, to electronic receivers or readers. German supermarket chain Metro already uses RFID and claims that food can be easily traced back to the farm where it is produced, queues at tills no longer exist as customers' bills are calculated instantly as they pass by a receiver and all products are tracked at each stage of the supply chain – 'We know where everything is!'

There are some concerns, however. Consumer groups suggest that shoppers will be tracked and traceable too – not just the goods they have bought. Is this an invasion of privacy? Unions are opposed to it as it could lead to many redundancies due to its non-manual operation. Some supermarket managers fear yet another IT initiative that will mean even more central control over them and they fear breakdowns in the system and lack of training in dealing with problems.

[32 marks, 50 minutes]

1   Analyse how any **two** of the IT systems mentioned in the passage are likely to benefit customers. **[10]**

2   Analyse the likely benefits of supermarkets using RFID to trace and collect data from every product they sell. **[10]**

3   Discuss how a supermarket business should effectively introduce the new RFID technology. **[12]**

4 Social audits – measuring corporate social responsibility

There could not be a much bigger contrast between ExxonMobil and the Soft Touch Community arts cooperative.

Exxon has an estimated revenue of $45 million per hour while Soft Touch has an annual turnover of $700,000 – yet they both produce annual social audits (called corporate citizenship reports in the USA). Social auditing is a system of reviewing a company's operations, to examine its social impacts and to compare social performance with any social objectives the organisation might have. This makes the process very useful for social enterprises – such as Soft Touch – and businesses keen to correct a poor reputation – the Exxon Valdez oil tanker disaster in 1989 is the worst the world has seen.

Exxon's social audit contains a huge quantity of evidence concerning the company's social impact. For example, it gives details of the amount of oil the company spilt into the environment in one year, employee fatalities, percentage of all employees who are women, sponsorship of ethnic minority councils and the financial support for a large teacher training programme in the USA. The directors of Exxon are determined to match the best social performance in the oil industry.

Soft Touch depends on many state bodies for its funding. It needs to convince them of the social value of its work. This can only be done by gaining feedback from the young, disadvantaged people it helps. Many local councils were so impressed by the content of the social audit that they increased their funding.

Alan Kay, social audit adviser, admits that the labour and finance resource commitment required in compiling a detailed social audit can be great. Kay says that, on a cost–benefit basis, social auditing is most likely to produce gains for big companies and charities. 'I am not sure that this is of benefit to businesses of perhaps ten staff. Which stakeholders are going to read the social audit of a small local shop?'

[27 marks, 40 minutes]

1 Explain the main purposes of a social audit, using the examples in the case study and any others that you have researched. [12]

2 Discuss the view that social audits might be a more worthwhile investment for large businesses than for very small businesses. [15]

5 Chinese toys recalled

Millions of toys with famous brand names have been withdrawn from sale as it has been discovered that they were painted with potentially dangerous paint. Fisher Price and Mattel have recalled well-known toy characters such as Big Bird, Elmo and Dora the Explorer from shops. The companies had found that, against their strict instructions to the factories, non-approved paint pigment, which contained excessive amounts of lead harmful to children, had been used to decorate the toys. In other products, small magnets could be shaken loose by young children and then swallowed. The chairman of Mattel said: 'The safety of children is our primary concern and we are deeply apologetic to everyone affected.'

This scare has given parents of young children real cause for worry – are all the toys in the shops safe for their children? However, it is not their only worry. According to a recent opinion poll for *The Times* newspaper, 96% of parents surveyed were alarmed about 'pester power' and admitted buying toys that many of them could not really afford, just because of pressure from their children who had seen the toys advertised on television.

[24 marks, 40 minutes]

1 Were Fisher Price and Mattel right to withdraw millions of suspect toys from the shops if consumers had not noticed the dangers? Justify your answer. [10]

2 Do you think that toy companies should be allowed to use persuasive TV and other forms of advertising directly aimed at children? Justify your answer. [14]

A Level essay questions

[25 marks, 45 minutes each]

1 'Technology causes businesses as many problems as it solves.' Discuss. [25]

2 To what extent should managers of public limited companies allow environmental and ethical considerations to influence their business decisions? [25]

9

External economic influences on business behaviour

On completing this chapter, you will be able to:

- understand the economic objectives of governments
- explain the nature and causes of economic growth and its impact on business strategies
- analyse the business cycle and its impact on business strategies
- recognise and analyse the different causes of unemployment
- analyse the different causes of inflation and deflation and assess the impact of the changing value of money on business strategy

- understand the policy measures that may be taken by governments to pursue their economic objectives
- analyse the possible impact on business strategies of changes in tax rates, interest rates and exchange rates
- understand the meaning of market failure and how the state might deal with this
- analyse why governments intervene in industry.

Introducing the topic

ICELAND'S ECONOMY MAKING SOME PROGRESS

Iceland's economy has gained a reputation for wild fluctuations in its growth rate. The annual economic growth rate has varied from –0.3% to +5.6% over the ten years since 2003 – it was 2.9% in 2013. It has suffered from rapid inflation over this period but the annual rate is now 5.2% (2013). However, this is still higher than all developed economies. Partly as a consequence of the global financial crisis and the negative impact on Icelandic banks, the country has huge foreign debts and government borrowing is high.

The exchange rate value of the Icelandic krona has fallen by 50% compared to the euro in recent years. As Iceland has to import most of the goods and materials it needs – its two main resources are fish and geothermal energy – this has made inflation even worse.

Recent economic growth has helped to keep unemployment low by international standards. It is now 4% of the working population. Wage demands from workers could rise as they realise that employers cannot easily find replacement employees.

The Icelandic government is determined to bring down inflation and high interest rates are part of this

policy. These may encourage foreign speculators to leave their money invested in Icelandic banks and stop the krona exchange rate from falling further. As with most economic developments, there is both bad news and good news for Icelandic businesses. High interest rates are bad news for firms like Baugur, which have borrowed very heavily to invest in UK retail companies. A fall in the exchange rate is good news for Iceland's exporters, such as fish processing firms and aluminium producers, attracted to Iceland by its cheap supplies of renewable and environmentally friendly energy.

Points to think about:

- What problems might Icelandic businesses experience with 'wild fluctuations in its growth rate'?
- Is inflation a problem for Icelandic businesses? Explain your answer.
- Explain how some of the data in the passage are 'good news' for some businesses but 'bad news' for others.

Introduction

The state of a country's economy – meaning the rate of economic growth, the rate of price inflation, the unemployment level and the exchange rate – can contribute directly to the success or failure of businesses. If business expansion goes ahead just before a long economic recession, then the additional cost of borrowing can destroy a business as it will probably not be able to increase its sales. However, the ability to spot and exploit a gap in a fast-growing economy can lead to high profits. It is, therefore, misleading to think just of 'economic constraints' on business activity as the country's economic performance can just as easily enable a business to take advantage of great new opportunities. Governments have objectives for the nation's economy. In pursuing these objectives, governments take economic policy decisions that can have a significant impact on the success and profitability of businesses. Understanding these objectives and these policies is important to managers who plan to protect their organisation from negative policy changes and to position their business to take advantage of positive policy changes.

Economic objectives of governments

All governments set targets for the whole economy and these are referred to as 'macro-economic' objectives. These are likely to include:

- economic growth – the annual percentage increase in a country's total level of output (known as gross domestic product or GDP)
- low price inflation – the rate at which consumer prices, on average, increase each year
- low rate of unemployment
- a long-term balance of payments between the value of goods and services bought from other countries (imports) and the value of the goods and services the country sells to other countries (exports)
- exchange rate stability – the government will try to prevent wild swings in the external value of the currency in terms of its price compared with other currencies
- wealth and income transfers to reduce inequalities. Some governments – but not necessarily all – attempt to reduce extreme inequalities of personal income and wealth, usually by using the tax system.

Unfortunately, several of these objectives may conflict with each other. This means that in trying to achieve one of these targets above, the government could actually make it less likely that one or more of the others will be achieved. For example, if it is believed that the rate of inflation is too high, then policies might be followed to reduce spending. This will lead to lower demand – and result in increased unemployment.

We now look in detail at each of these objectives and why they are considered to be desirable. Then we consider the policies governments can use to try to achieve these objectives.

TOP TIP

Start to keep your own file of newspaper articles on economic events and data and how businesses are responding to changes in these.

Economic growth – why it is considered desirable

Economic growth means that a country is becoming richer. It is measured by increases in **gross domestic product (GDP)**.

KEY TERMS

Economic growth: an increase in a country's productive potential measured by an increase in its real GDP.

Gross domestic product (GDP): the total value of goods and services produced in a country in one year – real GDP has been adjusted for inflation.

GDP is measured in monetary terms, and inflation will raise the value of GDP. Such an increase is not true economic growth. Economic growth in the economy occurs when the real level of GDP rises as a result of increases in the physical output of goods and services in an economy. Every economy is striving to achieve consistent economic growth – some with more success than others. For example, annual real GDP growth varied in the USA from 3% to –2% between 2008 and 2013. Over the same period GDP rose by an average of 8% in China and exceeded 10% in 2008. Negative economic growth or a recession is when GDP falls; this occurred in Zimbabwe in 2008 (–13%) and in 2013 the Italian economy was 8% smaller than it had been in 2008.

Economic growth is important to a country for several reasons:

- Higher real GDP increases average living standards if the population increases at a slower rate.
- Higher levels of output often lead to increased employment, which will increase consumer incomes.

- More resources can be devoted to desirable public-sector projects, such as health and education, without reducing resources in other sectors.
- Absolute poverty can be reduced or even eliminated if growth is substantial enough and the benefits are sufficiently widely spread.
- Businesses should experience rising demand for their products, although this will depend on income elasticity of demand for their products.
- Higher GDP makes more resources available for government through greater income from taxes and a decreased burden of social expenditure, e.g. reduced unemployment benefits. These additional government resources can be used to pursue government objectives more effectively or they can be used to reduce the burden of taxation.

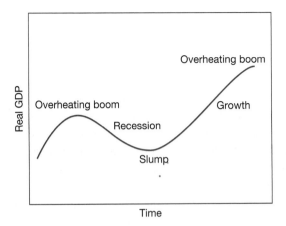

Figure 9.1 The business cycle

TOP TIP

Rapid economic growth is not always beneficial to everyone. For example, rapid industrial growth can make pollution worse and damage health. Some workers may lose their jobs as a result of technological changes that lead to economic growth.

KEY TERM

Business cycle: the regular swings in economic activity, measured by real GDP, that occur in most economies, varying from boom conditions (high demand and rapid growth) to recession when total national output declines.

The factors that lead to economic growth

The main factors that lead to growth are:

1 **Increases in output resulting from technological changes and expansion of industrial capacity:** Governments want to encourage this form of non-inflationary economic growth by encouraging **business investment** and innovation in new industries and products.

2 **Increases in economic resources, such as a higher working population or discovery of new resources of oil and gas:** A country's economy can increase its total output when more economic resources are available.

3 **Increases in productivity:** If existing resources can produce a higher level of output this year than last year, then total output will increase. Higher labour productivity can be achieved with a higher-skilled and better-qualified workforce and a greater willingness by workers to accept and work with new technology.

KEY TERM

Business investment: expenditure by businesses on capital equipment, new technology and research and development.

The business cycle

It is unusual for economic growth to be achieved at a steady, constant rate. Instead, economies tend to grow at very different rates over time. This leads to the **business cycle** (see Figure 9.1).

The four key stages are:

1 **Boom:** A period of very fast economic growth with rising incomes and profits. However, a boom often sows the seeds of its own destruction. Inflation rises due to very high demand for goods and services, and shortages of key skilled workers lead to high wage increases. High inflation makes an economy's goods uncompetitive and business confidence falls as profits are hit by higher costs. The government or central bank often increases interest rates to reduce inflationary pressure. A downturn often results from this.

2 **Downturn or recession:** The effect of falling demand and higher interest rates starts to bite. Real GDP growth slows and may even start to fall. This is technically called a recession. Incomes and consumer demand fall and profits are much reduced – some firms will record losses and some will go out of business.

3 **Slump:** A very serious and prolonged downturn can lead to a slump where real GDP falls substantially and house and asset prices fall. This is much more likely to occur if the government fails to take corrective economic action. Unlike with the great world slump of the 1920s, most governments took the necessary action to prevent the 2009 downturn becoming a serious slump.

4 **Recovery and growth:** All downturns eventually lead to a recovery when real GDP starts to increase again. This is either because corrective government action starts to take effect or the rate of inflation falls so that the country's products become competitive once more and demand for them starts to increase.

Is a recession always bad?

An economic **recession** has serious consequences for most businesses and the whole economy. As output is falling, fewer workers will be needed. Unemployment will increase and as incomes fall, so demand for goods and services declines further. Government tax revenue will also fall as less income tax and sales revenue tax will be received. Firms producing 'normal' and income-elastic goods will experience reduced demand, which will leave them with spare capacity.

> **KEY TERM**
>
> **Recession:** a period of six months or more of declining real GDP.

However, there will also be opportunities that well-managed firms may be able to take advantage of (see Table 9.1).

- Capital assets, such as land and property and even other businesses, may be relatively cheap and firms could invest in expectation of an economic recovery.
- Demand for 'inferior' goods could actually increase.
- The risk of retrenchment and job losses may encourage improved relations between employers and employees, leading to increased efficiency.
- Hard decisions may need to be taken regarding closures of factories and offices – this could make the business 'leaner and fitter' and better able to take advantage of economic growth when this eventually starts again.

> **TOP TIP**
>
> As a Business student you should think about how the stages of the business cycle will affect different businesses in different ways – and how businesses will respond to these stages with different strategies.

Inflation and deflation – changes in the value of money

The spending power of one dollar is the goods that can be bought with that dollar. The spending power of money can change over time. If one dollar buys fewer goods this year than it did last year, then the value of money has fallen and this must have been caused by **inflation**.

> **KEY TERM**
>
> **Inflation:** an increase in the average price level of goods and services – it results in a fall in the value of money.

If one dollar buys more goods this year than it did last year, then the value of money has increased. This must have been caused by **deflation**.

> **KEY TERM**
>
> **Deflation:** a fall in the average price level of goods and services.

101

Type of producer	Period of economic growth	Period of recession
Producers of luxury goods and services – e.g. cars	<ul><li>increase the range of goods and services</li><li>raise prices to increase profit margins</li><li>promote exclusivity and style</li><li>increase output</li></ul>	<ul><li>may not reduce prices for fear of damaging long-term image</li><li>credit terms to improve affordability</li><li>offer promotions</li><li>widen product range with lower-priced models</li></ul>
Producers of normal goods and services – e.g. tinned food	<ul><li>add extra value to product – better ingredients/improved packaging</li><li>brand image may attract exclusive tag</li><li>do nothing – sales not much affected anyway</li></ul>	<ul><li>lower prices</li><li>promotions</li><li>do nothing – sales not much affected anyway</li></ul>
Producers of inferior goods and services – e.g. very cheap clothing	<ul><li>attempt to move product upmarket</li><li>add extra value to the product – e.g. higher quality</li><li>extend the product range to include more exclusive or better-designed products</li></ul>	<ul><li>promote good value and low prices</li><li>free consumer tests</li><li>increase range of distribution outlets</li></ul>

Table 9.1 How business strategy could adapt to either economic growth or recession

ACTIVITY 9.1

De Smit sees recession haven in safari parks

The holiday market changes when world economies fall into recession. Many people still take an annual holiday – but they take cheaper or shorter breaks than they would during times of economic growth. Levels of disposable income have a great impact on both the number of tourists and the type of holiday they take. This is already being seen as the world economies enter a period of rising inflation and slower economic growth.

Phil De Smit, the owner of several holiday companies, believes that the safari-park holiday business in southern Africa is 'recession proof'. He argues that in times of recession, those tourists who would normally stay in expensive hotels change their plans and save money by taking a safari-park holiday. This usually offers much cheaper accommodation together with the bonus of trips into the safari park to see wild animals included in the overall holiday price. In addition, in the last recession he was able to take over another African holiday business cheaply as it was being badly run and was losing money. De Smit has been making further plans to expand his extensive safari-park business in several countries in southern Africa. He has invested US$10 million of his own capital but also borrowed $15 million from banks. He believes that he will make a profit from his business whatever happens to the world economy. 'In times of economic boom, 90% of Africans who never take a holiday can be tempted into trying one of my parks – and think of the millions of non-Africans who I can promote my parks to as well,' he said.

[22 marks, 30 minutes]

1 Explain the terms:
   a recession [2]
   b economic boom. [2]

2 Analyse why the number of tourists and the type of holiday they buy depends on whether economies are in recession or growing rapidly. [8]

3 Evaluate De Smit's strategy of business expansion during a period of 'rising inflation and slower economic growth'. [10]

The UK has experienced inflation for each of the last 60 years – although it fell to very low levels in 2012 as shown in Figure 9.2. The rates of inflation of all countries in the world in 2013 is shown in Figure 9.3. Price rises – or falls – do not occur at the same rate in every country.

Recent inflation data for selected countries:

Zimbabwe inflation passes 100,000%

The official rate of inflation in Zimbabwe has rocketed past the 100,000% barrier, by far the highest in the world, the state statistical office reported. Independent economists

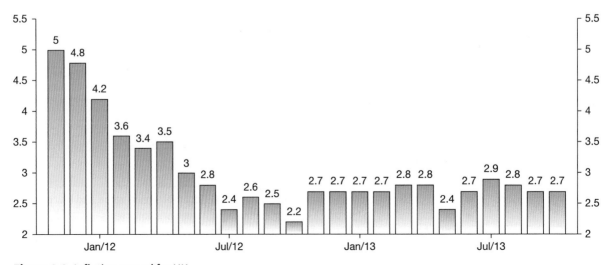

Figure 9.2 Inflation record for UK

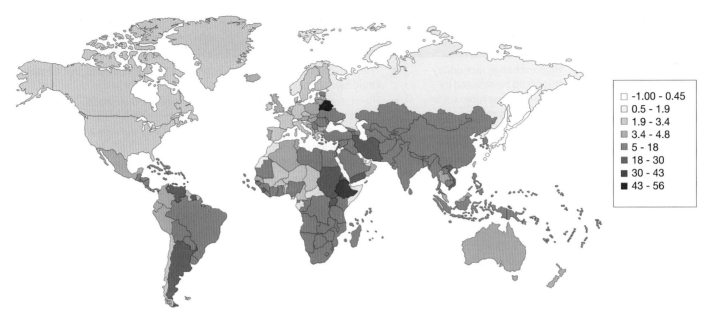

Figure 9.3 Global inflation rates 2013

Legend:
- -1.00 - 0.45
- 0.5 - 1.9
- 1.9 - 3.4
- 3.4 - 4.8
- 5 - 18
- 18 - 30
- 30 - 43
- 43 - 56

have estimated that the price of chicken rose more than 236,000% to 15 million Zimbabwe dollars between January 2007 and January 2008. Zimbabwe is facing acute shortages of food, foreign currency, petrol and most basic goods.

2013 data: Zimbabwe's inflation has been brought down to 2.5%. This was achieved by replacing the domestic currency with a number of international currencies.

Inflation in Malaysia at 2.6% in September 2013

Malaysia's inflation rate jumped to 2.6% in September from 1.9% in August, mainly due to higher petrol prices, and was at the highest level in 20 months. The Central Bank expects inflation to continue to rise this year and into 2014 due to domestic factors, such as subsidy reductions.

Eurozone inflation falls to 0.8% in October 2013

There is now a real fear that average prices could start to fall in the countries that use the euro common currency. Deflation – falling prices – is a sign of economies in recession and the European Central Bank might be forced to cut interest rates from the historically low level of 0.5%.

Why are there different rates of inflation? Does inflation matter and how does it affect business? Is deflation a desirable situation? What causes inflation – or deflation – to occur? We now turn to these issues after considering briefly how inflation is measured in modern economies.

How is inflation measured?

The UK is typical in using a consumer price index (CPI) to measure annual inflation. An index number can be used to record average changes in a large number of items. Each month, government statisticians record the prices of around 6,000 items that commonly feature in an 'average' household's budget. These prices are compared to those of the previous month and the changes are then 'weighted' to reflect the importance of each item in household budgets. It would be unwise to give the same weight or importance to price changes for bread as to changes in package-holiday prices, for example.

All of the weighted price changes are then averaged and given an index number. This index number is easy to compare with past time periods, because the series of index numbers will have started from a base period, given a value of 100. So, in June 2013 the CPI stood at 125.9 using a base period of June 2005, so the weighted average of price inflation over this period was 25.9%. To put it another way, the value of money fell by 25.9% since 2005.

What causes inflation?

Essentially, it is accepted that prices rise either because businesses are forced to increase them, since their costs are rising, or businesses take advantage of high consumer

Cause of inflation	Government and central bank policy	Impact on business strategy of government policy aiming to control inflation
Cost–push	■ High exchange rate policy – this could be assisted by higher interest rates set by the central bank. ■ Discourage high wage settlements – may use public sector workers as an example.	■ The high exchange rate will make exports less competitive. Businesses could switch to concentrating on the domestic market. ■ High interest rates will discourage business borrowing and investment. Businesses may cancel investment projects. ■ Consumer credit will also be discouraged, reducing demand, especially for expensive goods. ■ Businesses are unlikely to be influenced by government views on wage settlements – they will pay what is needed to attract and keep staff, as long as the business remains profitable.
Demand–pull	■ Policies designed to reduce aggregate demand such as higher tax rates and lower government spending. ■ Central bank is likely to raise interest rates.	■ Higher taxes will reduce consumer demand. If progressive taxes are increased, there could be a swing away from luxury goods. Businesses may change their product mix to offer less-expensive goods. ■ Lower government spending could hit certain industries very hard, e.g. defence equipment suppliers or hospital equipment manufacturers. These firms may attempt to enter foreign markets. ■ Interest rate increases – these will have same effects as above.

Table 9.2 Controlling inflation and possible impact on business strategy

demand to make extra profits by raising prices. These two causes can be considered as:

■ cost–push causes of inflation
■ demand–pull causes of inflation.

Cost–push causes of inflation

In certain situations, businesses are faced with higher costs of production. These could result from:

■ a lower exchange rate pushing up prices of imported materials, e.g. the average exchange rate value of pound sterling fell by 15% in 2013
■ world demand for materials raising their prices, e.g. the price of oil rose by over 50% between 2008 and 2012
■ higher wage demands from workers, possibly in response to inflation in the previous year. In order to maintain their real living standards, workers will expect wage rises in line with previous or expected inflation, e.g. in Romania in 2008, Dacia Cars workers were demanding a 40% wage increase to increase their living standards ahead of inflation.

When businesses face higher costs of production, they will attempt to maintain profit margins, and one way of doing this is to raise selling prices. This then becomes cost–push inflation.

Demand–pull causes of inflation

When consumer demand in the economy is rising, usually during an economic boom, producers and retailers will realise that existing stocks can be sold at higher prices. If they do not raise prices, stocks could be sold out, leaving unsatisfied demand. Supply shortages leading to excess demand are the major reason for the Zimbabwean

inflation referred to above. By raising prices, businesses will be earning higher profit margins.

The impact of inflation on business strategy

Inflation can have the following benefits for business if the rate is quite low (see also Table 9.2):

■ Cost increases can be passed on to consumers more easily if there is a general increase in prices.
■ The real value of debts owed by companies will fall. This means that, because the value of money is falling, when a debt is repaid it is repaid with money of less value than the original loan. Thus, companies that are heavily dependent on loan finance see a fall in the real value of their liabilities.
■ Rising prices are also likely to affect assets held by firms, so the value of fixed assets, such as land and buildings, could rise. This will increase the value of a business and, when reflected on the statement of financial position, make the company more financially secure.
■ Since inventories are bought in advance and then sold later, there is an increased profit margin from the effect of inflation.

Therefore, during periods of low inflation, businesses could decide to raise their own prices, borrow more to invest and ensure that increased asset values appear on their statement of financial position. However, high rates of inflation, say above 5–6% per year, can have very serious drawbacks for business:

■ Employees will become much more concerned about the real value of their incomes. Higher wage demands are likely and there could be an increase in industrial disputes.
■ Consumers are likely to become much more price sensitive and look for bargains rather than big brand names.

- Rapid inflation will often lead to higher rates of interest. These higher rates could make it very difficult for highly geared companies to find the cash to make interest payments, despite the fact that the real value of the debts is declining.
- Cash-flow problems may occur for all businesses as they struggle to find more money to pay the higher costs of materials and other costs.

Inflation adds to uncertainty about the future:

- Will prices continue to rise?
- Will the rate of inflation go up again?
- Will the government be forced to take strong corrective action, which could reduce business profitability?

These uncertainties make forecasting for the future much less reliable. This will be the case in particular with sales forecasts and with investment appraisal, which requires estimates about future cash flows.

- If inflation is higher in one country than in other countries, then businesses will lose competitiveness in overseas markets.
- Businesses that sell goods on credit will be reluctant to offer extended credit periods – the repayments by creditors will be with money that is losing value rapidly.
- Consumers may stockpile some items and cut back on non-essential items of spending

Business strategy during a period of rapid inflation might focus on:

- cutting back on investment spending
- cutting profit margins to limit their own price rises to stay as competitive as possible
- reducing borrowing to levels at which the interest payments are manageable
- reducing time period for customers (trade receivables) to pay
- reducing labour costs.

TOP TIP

Don't forget that the impact of inflation on any one business depends very greatly on the rate of inflation – and forecasts for the future rate of price rises.

Does this mean that deflation is beneficial?

It might be thought that, if rapid inflation has so many serious side effects, a period of falling prices – deflation – could be positively desirable. Here are some reasons why most businesses would not actually benefit from deflation:

- Consumers would delay making important purchases, hoping that prices would fall further. This would cause a reduction in demand, which could lead to a recession.
- Businesses with long-term liabilities would find that they were making interest payments and repayments of the debts with money that had gained in value since the original loan was taken out. This will discourage borrowing to invest.
- As prices fall, so the future profitability of new projects appears doubtful. This again will make firms unwilling to commit funds to further investment.
- Holdings of stocks of materials and finished goods will be falling in value. Businesses will hold as few stocks as possible. Although this will reduce their working capital needs, it will also reduce orders for supplies from other businesses. This is another factor that could push the economy into recession because output will decline.

So it seems as if businesses cannot win either way – they are potential losers from both rapid inflation and deflation. There is now a general consensus that the optimum position for most economies is to tolerate low rates of inflation, but to keep a very careful watch to ensure that the rate does not rise above a predetermined target. In the UK and in the Eurozone this target is for the consumer price index to rise by 2.0% per annum.

Unemployment – definition and causes

Table 9.3 shows the percentage of the **working population** registered as unemployed in certain European countries in two separate years. Although the average rate of **unemployment** has risen in the EU and some countries have experienced significant increases, notably Portugal and Spain.

 KEY TERMS

Working population: all those in the population of working age who are willing and able to work.

Unemployment: this exists when members of the working population are willing and able to work, but are unable to find a job.

	2002 %	2014 %
EU average	8.9	10.8
Germany	8.1	5.5
France	9.0	11.7
Netherlands	2.4	5.3
Portugal	4.3	15.9
Slovakia	18.0	14.1
Spain	12.8	25.0
UK	5.1	6.8

Table 9.3 Unemployment rates in the European Union (% of workforce)

ACTIVITY 9.2

China to take action against inflation

The Chinese government is becoming increasingly concerned about higher rates of inflation. Oil and petrol prices have raised costs to industry and firms are being forced to increase their prices to cover these higher costs. In addition, rising demand for food from a wealthier population together with supply problems resulting in excess demand have led to the price of pork rising by 63% and fresh vegetable prices rising by 46%.

The People's Bank of China has just increased interest rates by a further 0.27%. This is the third increase in less than a year. A spokesman from Goldman Sachs, the investment bank, reported that this increase in rates shows that the central bank is now much more prepared to use interest rates to manage the economy and tighten monetary policy at the first signs of the economy 'overheating'. The Chinese GDP increased by 7.8% in 2013 and the prime minister has said that this rate of growth is becoming 'unsustainable'. Chinese leaders face conflicting pressures in balancing the top priority of maintaining high-speed economic growth, to create millions of new jobs each year, with managing increasing environmental problems and rising supply constraints causing higher inflation.

[35 marks, 45 minutes]

1   State **two** reasons for the reported increase in inflation in China. [2]

2   Are these causes of inflation 'cost–push' or 'demand–pull' pressures? Explain your answer. [4]

3   If the Chinese government increased interest rates again, explain what impact this could have on:
    a   consumer spending on luxury goods
    b   spending on new investment projects by Chinese businesses
    c   the value of the Chinese currency exchange rate. [9]

4   Examine the long-term problems for Chinese businesses if inflation is not brought under control. [10]

5   China has experienced rapid economic growth in recent years. Discuss the likely effects of this on Chinese manufacturing businesses. [10]

What factors cause unemployment?

There are three main causes or categories of unemployment:

- cyclical unemployment
- structural unemployment
- frictional unemployment.

Cyclical unemployment

This cause of unemployment is therefore associated with the business cycle. The recession stage of the business cycle results in a fall in the demand for firms' output. Businesses, therefore, need fewer workers as they will be producing fewer goods and services. Workers who are consequently unemployed have lower incomes, as do some of those still employed when overtime opportunities are reduced. They will spend less. This can then cause a deepening of the recession. The four-year long recession (ended in October 2013) in Spain is the major factor for that country's increasing unemployment.

Structural unemployment

This cause of unemployment can exist even when the economy is growing rapidly. It was still a major cause of unemployment in the UK in 2013 even though the job losses caused by the collapse of the mining and shipbuilding industries occurred several years previously – former workers have found it very difficult

 KEY TERM

Cyclical unemployment: unemployment resulting from low demand for goods and services in the economy during a period of slow economic growth or a recession.

 KEY TERM

Structural unemployment: unemployment caused by the decline in important industries, leading to significant job losses in one sector of industry.

to find alternative jobs. This type of unemployment results in certain types of workers being unable to find work, even though other labour markets in expanding industries may be short of labour. How does this occur? It results from structural changes in the economy, which radically change the demand for labour. Here are the most likely causes:

- Changes in consumer tastes and expenditure patterns, possibly resulting from higher incomes.
- Workers in some industries may find the demand for their services declining, e.g. in high-street banking, as consumers switch to online banking with their home computers.
- Deindustrialisation in heavy manufacturing industries, such as steel-making and shipbuilding, have declined in most Western economies. The workers losing their jobs as a result have often found it difficult to transfer their skills to other industries and occupations.
- Improvements in technology in many industries have meant that employers are looking for adaptable and multiskilled workers. Many unskilled workers who performed manual jobs have found it difficult to adapt to these new requirements and have lost out in this new labour market.

Frictional unemployment

Most workers who lose their jobs are able to move quickly into new ones, but others may take longer to find suitable employment. While they are looking for other work, they are said to be 'frictionally' unemployed. This type of unemployment can also occur when cyclical unemployment is not a problem. It is a feature of the changing labour demands in different businesses and industries, which are occurring all the time. If labour turnover rates increase in the economy as a whole, then the level of frictional unemployment will increase.

> **KEY TERM**
>
> **Frictional unemployment:** unemployment resulting from workers losing or leaving jobs and taking a substantial period of time to find alternative employment.

Government policy towards the causes of unemployment

Cyclical

- The government attempts to manage the economy so as to avoid substantial swings in the business cycle, which lead eventually to recessions.
- This includes the objective of keeping inflation low. If inflation rises sharply, the government might be forced to

use anti-inflationary measures, which are most likely to lead to cyclical unemployment.

- The government may also aim to maintain a competitive rate of exchange so that overseas demand for home-produced goods does not fall, leading to cyclical unemployment.

Structural

- The aim of the government is not to prevent the economic changes that lead to structural unemployment. This would be standing against economic change and progress.
- It will provide education and training programmes for workers who do not have the required skills.
- The UK government's 'New Deal' programme has offered training courses to all long-term unemployed – refusal to take up these offers has led to state benefits being reduced.

Frictional

The efficiency of the labour market can be improved and frictional unemployment reduced by the provision of information about job opportunities, both locally and in other regions. Job Centres or employment agencies are given this responsibility. Some economists argue that the government should reduce unemployment benefits for those people who are slow to find alternative employment. This would encourage them to take up offers of work more quickly.

The costs of unemployment

Unemployment is a waste of human resources. The costs of this are significant:

- The economy could be producing more goods and services, which would then be available for consumption.
- The cost of supporting unemployed workers and their families is substantial and is paid for out of general taxation.
- High unemployment may lead to social problems, such as crime, which is a cost to society.
- Unemployment reduces demand for goods and services by reducing the incomes of those looking for work.
- There will be loss of income and lower living standards.
- The longer the period of unemployment, the more difficult it is to find work, as skills become increasingly out of date.

TOP TIP
Unemployment is a cost to society and a personal cost to the individuals affected by it. Businesses may be able to negotiate lower wages or lower wage rises, however, during periods of high inflation. But would this be seen as exploiting the workforce?

Balance of payments (current account)

If a country's economy has a large and persistent deficit on its **balance of payments**, then serious economic problems could result, such as:

■ a fall or depreciation in the value of its currency's **exchange rate**

■ a decline in the country's reserves of foreign currency

■ an unwillingness of foreign investors to put money into the economy.

KEY TERMS

Balance of payments (current account): this account records the value of trade in goods and services between one country and the rest of the world. A deficit means that the value of goods and services imported exceeds the value of goods and services exported.

Exchange rate: the price of one currency in terms of another.

The business importance of these problems is likely to be most serious if:

■ the **exchange rate depreciation** (or frequent fluctuations in the exchange rate) make **importing** and **exporting** too risky (see below on exchange rates)

■ the government takes corrective actions by, for example, limiting foreign exchange transactions and putting substantial controls on imports, such as tariffs and quotas. This policy, used currently by Zimbabwe, might have short-term benefits by reducing imports of competitors' products. However, serious consequences could also result. The policy could lead to retaliation by other countries that will then reduce export demand. Also, import controls are serious for firms that depend on imported supplies.

Exchange rates

As with any price on a free market, exchange rates are determined by the forces of supply and demand. Table 9.4 gives a summary of the factors that make up the demand for and the supply of a currency on the foreign exchange market.

KEY TERMS

Exchange rate depreciation: a fall in the external value of a currency as measured by its exchange rate against other currencies. If $1 falls in value from €2 to €1.5, the value of the dollar has depreciated in value.

Imports: goods and services purchased from other countries.

Exports: goods and services sold to consumers and business in other countries.

Exchange rate appreciation: a rise in the external value of a currency as measured by its exchange rate against other currencies. If $1 rises from €1.5 to €1.8, the value of the dollar has appreciated.

Demand for the currency	Supply of the currency
■ foreign buyers of domestic goods and services	■ domestic businesses buying foreign imports
■ foreign tourists spending money in the country	■ domestic population travelling abroad
■ foreign investors	■ domestic investors abroad

Table 9.4 Factors that determine the demand for and supply of a currency

Exchange rate fluctuations

When demand for a currency exceeds supply, its value will rise. This is called an **exchange rate appreciation** because one unit of the currency will buy more units of other currencies.

Appreciation of the currency – winners and losers

The impacts of exchange rate fluctuations are summarised in Table 9.5. The domestic firms that gain from an appreciation of the country's currency are:

■ Importers of foreign raw materials and components, for whom the domestic currency cost of these imports will be falling – this increases their competitiveness.

■ Importers of foreign manufactured goods, who are able to import the product more cheaply in terms of domestic currency – in 2008, it was claimed that European importers of US-produced cars were profiteering at the expense of consumers. This was because, although the import price of cars was falling due to the appreciation of the euro against the US dollar, they were not selling them more cheaply to European consumers. Hence, they were taking advantage of the appreciation to make much higher profits.

Lower import prices will help to reduce the rate of inflation for the whole economy and all firms are likely to gain from this more stable position.

The domestic firms that lose from an appreciation are:

■ Exporters of goods and services to foreign markets – this will include not just manufactured goods, such as cars, but also own-country holiday resorts will experience a fall in demand from overseas tourists because of the higher costs of products in terms of the foreign currency. Some businesses may decide to locate overseas to avoid the high exchange rate.

■ Businesses that sell goods and services to the domestic market and have foreign competitors – as appreciation makes imports cheaper, it will make domestic producers less competitive in their own market. Consumers will be prepared to switch to imported goods and foreign holidays because of the cost advantages they have over home-produced products. However, firms importing raw materials from other countries should be able to lower prices to combat this.

Importer	Exporter
■ places an order for €86,000 worth of components from French supplier	■ has a contract to supply $50,000 worth of goods to a French customer
■ at the old exchange rate, this would cost $10,000	■ at the old exchange rate these goods would be sold for €430,000
■ at the new exchange rate, this would cost $8,600	■ at the new rate, these would be sold for €500,000
■ the importer's costs have fallen and this makes the domestic business more competitive	■ the exporter's products are now less competitive on the French market – export orders are likely to be lost
■ other businesses that are currently buying domestic components will now be encouraged to buy French ones	■ sales are also likely to be lost in the home market since firms may be able to import more cheaply from the French

Table 9.5 Impact of dollar appreciation from €8.60 for $1 to €10.00 for $1

A depreciation of the currency

The fall in the value of a currency in terms of other currencies will have effects which are the reverse of those already analysed for an appreciation. These effects can be investigated by working through Activity 9.3 below.

Depreciation of the currency – winners and losers

The domestic businesses that gain from a depreciation are:

■ Home-based exporters, who can now reduce their prices in overseas markets – this should increase the value of their exports and lead to an expansion of the business.

■ Businesses that sell in the domestic market will experience less price competition from importers – prices of imported goods and services are likely to rise on the domestic market.

The home-based businesses that are likely to lose from a depreciation are:

■ Manufacturers who depend heavily on imported supplies of materials, components or energy sources – these costs will rise and will reduce competitiveness.

■ Retailers that purchase foreign supplies, especially if there are close domestic substitutes – the prices of these imports will rise and the retailers may be forced to find domestic suppliers of similar quality goods.

109

ACTIVITY 9.3

Tobago City industrial estate

Tobago City industrial estate contains many small to medium-sized trading businesses. Two of the firms on the estate are Renard Traders and Foxbore Engineering. Renard specialises in importing German jewellery and selling this to department stores. Foxbore manufactures precision surgical instruments and has built up a reputation at home and abroad for top-quality products. Regular monthly orders valued at $15,000 are transported to a German trader. The chief executives of both Renard and Foxbore were interested in the dollar–euro exchange rate and have noticed that over the last six months the dollar has depreciated against the euro by 10% – from €3 = $1 to €2.70 = $1.

[20 marks, 20 minutes]

1 If Renard imported €30,000 of jewellery from Germany, what would have been the cost in dollars at the original exchange rate? [2]

2 What would the cost of the same order be at the new exchange rate? [2]

3 State **two** ways in which Renard could respond to this change in the price of its imports. [2]

4 Calculate the euro cost of a typical monthly order from Foxbore at the original exchange rate. [2]

5 What is the new euro price once the value of the dollar has depreciated? [2]

6 Explain why the depreciation could be beneficial to Foxbore. [5]

7 Would the depreciation have been more or less beneficial to Foxbore if many of their raw materials and machinery were imported from Germany? Explain your answer. [5]

TOP TIP
Exchange rates are a very important Business topic. You should be able to analyse, with appropriate calculations if necessary, how rises or falls in an exchange rate might impact on importers and exporters (see Figure 9.4).

International competitiveness – non-price factors

It must not be thought that low prices alone will guarantee success of a business product if they are only slightly less than those of competitors. Consumers consider many non-price factors in making purchasing decisions too. German and Japanese businesses became worldwide successes in the 1970s and 1980s, even though their exchange rates were often said to be high during this period, making their goods relatively expensive abroad. How did they compete so successfully even though other countries may have had a price advantage over them? The following are the factors, other than product prices, that can determine the international success – or competitiveness – of a business:

- **Product design and innovation:** An innovative product, such as the latest Apple iPad, will attract custom, even though it may be sold at premium prices.
- **Quality of construction and reliability:** For several years, Japanese cars have been declared the most reliable on the US market and, even though they are not the cheapest models around, this encourages consumer interest.

- **Effective promotion and extensive distribution:** These two factors go some way to explain the universal success of McDonald's restaurants.
- **After-sales service:** This includes extended guarantee periods.
- **Investment in trained staff and modern technology:** This should allow flexibility of production to meet frequent changes in consumer tastes. Higher labour productivity can overcome drawbacks caused by higher costs of other resources.

Macro-economic policies

These are policies that are designed to impact on the whole economy – or the 'macro-economy'. They mainly operate by influencing the level of total or aggregate demand in the economy. This level of demand then works through to determine the value of output of goods and services (GDP) and, as a consequence, the level of employment.

Fiscal policy

In many countries, the government is responsible for spending (and raising in taxes) up to 40% of the GDP. The major expenditure programmes include social security, health service, education, defence and

KEY TERM

Fiscal policy: concerned with decisions about government expenditure, tax rates and government borrowing – these operate largely through the government's annual budget decisions.

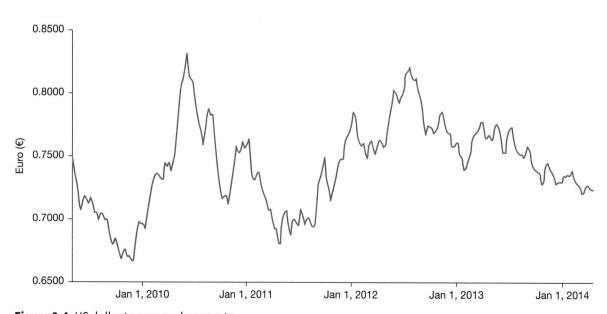

Figure 9.4 US dollar to euro exchange rate

law and order. The government raises finance to pay for these schemes through taxation, and the main tax revenues come from income tax, value added tax, corporation tax and excise duties. Each year, at budget time, the finance minister (or Chancellor of the Exchequer) announces the spending and tax plans of the government for the coming year. The difference between these two totals is called either the **budget deficit** or the **budget surplus**.

Many changes will be relatively minor and will only affect individual product markets – such as an increase in duties on petrol or a reduction in spending on new defence equipment. These changes will have an impact – sometimes of very great importance – on certain businesses, but not on the macro-economy. Only when the finance minister announces an overall change in total tax revenues or total government expenditure plans will there be a macro-economic effect that will be noticed by virtually all businesses. Under what circumstances is the chancellor likely to make these changes? We will consider two major scenarios.

Scenario 1: The economy is in recession and unemployment is rising

This is the result of aggregate demand for domestic goods falling below the potential output of industry.

Two of the major macro-economic targets are not being met. The government is likely to want to increase aggregate demand and this can be done in two ways – or both could be undertaken together. There could be increases in government expenditure plans, such as in hospital or school construction. There could also be decisions to reduce taxes to leave consumers and firms with higher disposable incomes, that is incomes after tax. This should encourage increased spending by these two groups. Using fiscal policy in this way is described as 'expansionary' and will lead to a budget deficit. This policy is summarised in Figure 9.5.

Scenario 2: The economy is booming and is in danger of overheating

This scenario could lead to two other macro-economic targets not being met. A booming economy is likely to lead to both higher inflation and a large balance of payments (current account) deficit. It results from excess aggregate demand in the economy, and the chancellor could respond by reducing government expenditure levels, which will have a direct impact on demand in the economy. Unfortunately, all governments tend to find it easier to cut back on investment spending, such as on road construction or hospital equipment, than on current expenditure, such as social security benefits or numbers of teachers. The chancellor could also decide to increase taxes, which would take spending power out of the economy by leaving consumers and/or businesses with less disposable income. Both of these policies would be termed 'contractionary' or 'deflationary' policies and are summarised in Figure 9.6.

Governments are now using fiscal policy for controlling aggregate demand with much more caution than in previous periods. This is because fiscal policy changes can take time to be effective and it is very difficult to predict the precise effects of these changes. More emphasis is now placed on achieving a 'balanced budget' over a period of some years and using monetary policy to generate changes in the level of demand needed to help achieve the macro-economic objectives.

111

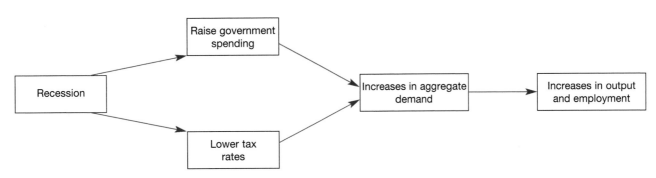

Figure 9.5 Expansionary fiscal policy

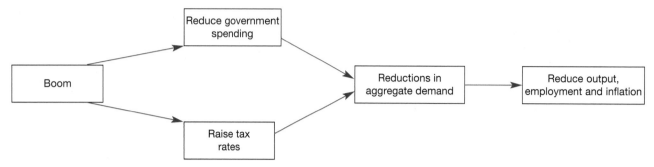

Figure 9.6 Contractionary fiscal policy

Monetary policy

In the UK and in the Eurozone countries the major **monetary policy** weapon is the monthly review of the level of interest rates in the context of current and likely future inflation. Therefore, monetary policy is mainly concerned with changes in interest rates, which are determined by the base interest rate set each month by the central bank. In the UK and the Eurozone, the central banks (the Bank of England and the European Central Bank) are given a clear inflation target to reach and they use interest rates to achieve these targets. When the forecast for inflation is that it will rise above the targets set by government, then the central bank will raise its base rate and all other banks and lending institutions will follow. This situation nearly always occurs when the economy is reaching the overheating stage of the growth phase of the business cycle.

 KEY TERM

Monetary policy: is concerned with decisions about the rate of interest and the supply of money in the economy.

If inflation is low and is forecast to remain below government targets, then the central bank may decide to reduce interest rates – especially if economic growth is slowing down and there is a danger that unemployment might rise. The European Central Bank did this in 2013. Although the central bank is concerned about these other targets of economic policy, its primary objective is the control of inflation. Using higher interest rates will have an impact on businesses in three main ways:

1   Increases interest costs and reduces profits for business that have very high debts.
2   Reduces consumer borrowing and this reduces demand for goods bought on credit, e.g. houses, cars, washing machines.

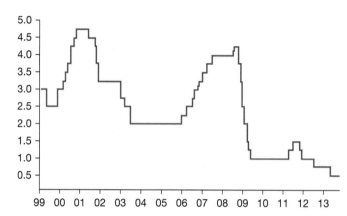

Figure 9.7 Significant changes in Eurozone interest rates since 1999

3   It tends to lead to an appreciation of the country's exchange rate. The effects of this are examined below.

 TOP TIP
It is important to evaluate the possible impact of interest rate changes on any one business. Even small changes in interest rates could be significant for highly indebted firms or for those businesses selling goods on credit.

Figure 9.7 shows the significant changes in Eurozone interest rates that have occurred since 1999.

Fiscal and monetary policy – a summary

Table 9.6 summarises the measures that the government and the central bank can take to control an overheating economy. These measures, and effects, will be reversed if the economy is slipping into recession.

Monetary policy and the exchange rate

There is often a very important link between the level of interest rates and the exchange rate. If domestic interest rates increase – especially if they increase above those

Type of policy	Measures to slow down economic growth and reduce inflation	Likely impact on businesses
Fiscal policy Decisions about government spending, taxes and borrowing.	Raise direct tax rates.	As consumers' disposable incomes fall, the demand for products will fall. The precise impact will depend on income elasticities (see below). If corporation tax rates are increased, then businesses' retained earnings will decline. This will reduce funds available for business investment.
	Raise indirect tax rates.	The retail prices of the goods affected will increase. The impact on demand will depend on price elasticities.
	Reduce government spending. The combined effect of these measures will reduce government borrowing.	Businesses providing goods and services directly to the government will risk experiencing a reduction in demand. Defence suppliers and construction companies could be hit, for example.

Monetary policy
 	
Decisions about interest rates and the supply of money.
	The most likely policy measure will be an increase in interest rates.	The impact of higher rates will be:
		
		■ Highly geared businesses will experience increases in interest payments that may endanger their cash flows.
		■ Businesses will be less likely to borrow to finance further investment as the costs of loans may exceed the expected returns.
		■ Consumers will be affected in two ways:
		  ❏ They will be less likely to buy goods on credit as the interest charges will be higher. This will hit demand for expensive consumer goods, such as cars and household durable goods.
		  ❏ The demand for houses will fall as mortgages are the biggest loan most consumers take out. The interest on existing consumer debts, such as mortgages, will take a higher proportion of incomes. This reduces consumers' discretionary incomes and will impact on consumer demand. The precise effect will depend on income elasticities.
		■ Higher domestic interest rates may encourage overseas capital to flow into the country. This will be likely to lead to an appreciation of the currency exchange rate. This will have implications for the competitiveness of businesses.

Table 9.6 A summary of fiscal and monetary policy in response to an economic boom

in other countries – then the currency's exchange rate is likely to appreciate against other currencies. Why is this? One source of demand for a currency on the foreign exchange market is from international investors who decide to leave their capital on deposit in domestic banks. These investors, because they invest money only for short periods of time, are called speculators. Their funds are more likely to be invested in a country's bank if rates of interest are higher than those in other countries. If domestic interest rates rise, then the speculators will want to convert their own currency deposits into this currency, thus increasing the demand

for it. This increase in demand will cause an appreciation in its exchange rate.

Exchange rate policy

In addition to financial and monetary policies, the government also has to have a view about the exchange rate of the currency. Should it allow this exchange rate to 'float' or try to 'fix' it or even join a common currency such as the euro? The exchange rate level and the degree of exchange rate fluctuations can have significant effects on domestic industry.

Allowing the country's currency to float against other currencies on a day-to-day basis, finding its own exchange rate according to the supply of it and the demand for it can lead to significant advantages and disadvantages. The disadvantages of 'floating exchange rates' is one of the reasons why the euro common currency was adopted by the Eurozone members of the European Union. Other trading blocs are also considering common currencies such as the East African Community (EAC). These common currency schemes also have advantages and disadvantages.

Claimed drawbacks to floating rates – or the benefits of joining a common currency

1   Figure 9.8 shows the depreciation of pound sterling against the euro over a ten-year period. Substantial appreciation and depreciation of a currency against others causes industry many problems. These include:
    - fluctuating prices of imported raw materials and components, making costing of products difficult
    - fluctuations in export prices and overseas competitiveness, which lead to unstable levels of demand
    - uncertainty over profits to be earned from trading abroad or from investing abroad – the value of overseas assets also varies with currency fluctuations.

These factors, when combined, may discourage firms from engaging in international trade because of the increased risk caused by currency movements. A common currency, it is argued, would encourage trade and investment between the participating countries.

2   When firms are planning to purchase goods from abroad it is difficult to make cost comparisons because suppliers from different countries will be using different currencies and these may change from one month to another. This means the cost differences are not clear – there is no 'price transparency' as there would be if all suppliers used the same currency.

3   Having different exchange rates adds considerably to the costs of firms trading overseas in three main ways:
    - currencies have to be converted into the domestic currency and this involves a commission cost to the bank
    - different price lists have to be printed and frequently updated for each separate country
    - attempts to take out the risk of dealing in different currencies by using currency contracts and 'hedging' can be expensive as charges have to be paid to the specialist institutions involved.

4   The world economy has become increasingly dependent on overseas investment, much of it in the form of foreign factories and offices. The danger is that if the currency continues to float and if the common currency is not adopted, much of this foreign investment could be lost to countries with a common currency where there will be fewer exchange rate risks and costs.

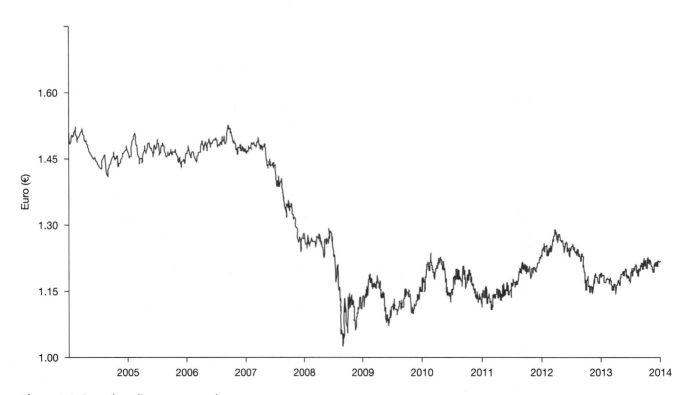

Figure 9.8 Pound sterling to euro exchange rate

5   Business strategy may have to adapt to the country remaining outside the common currency. For example, to avoid the currency costs and risks, UK businesses that trade extensively in Europe may decide to relocate into a Eurozone country.

Claimed advantages of not joining a common currency

1   By not joining the common currency, the central bank could keep its status as the interest-setting authority. If the UK did adopt the euro, then the European Central Bank would determine the interest rates for the UK. Having one rate of interest across the European Union may mean that it is too high for some economies but not high enough for others, such as those experiencing 'overheating'.

2   Replacing the currency with a common currency will eventually lead to common tax policies throughout the currency zone, which reduce the independence of each government to control its own tax rates.

3   Allowing exchange rates to float means that, except in extreme cases, the government and the central bank can allow the exchange rate of the pound to find its own level and will not use economic policies to keep it at one level or another. Interest rates can therefore be adjusted to achieve other economic objectives.

4   Conversion costs from one currency to the common currency could be substantial in terms of dual pricing and the changeover of notes and tills.

Government policies and business competitiveness

Government policies that aim to increase industrial competitiveness are often referred to as supply-side policies because they aim to improve the supply efficiency of the economy. If successful, these policies will make a country's industries more competitive in global markets. Three examples of policies that could have this effect are:

1 Low rates of income tax

If workers and managers are forced to pay high rates of tax on any increase in income, then they could lose motivation to work hard and to gain promotion. Also, high rates of income tax will discourage entrepreneurs from setting up new businesses as they will consider that the rewards after tax do not justify the risks involved. So, *reducing* rates of income tax is a supply-side policy.

2 Low rate of corporation tax

This is a tax on the operating profits of limited companies after interest. High rates of this tax will leave fewer funds for reinvestment in businesses and will discourage new investments and new projects. This lack of investment will reduce the competitiveness of businesses. Many governments have steadily *reduced* the rates of corporation tax in recent years, especially for smaller companies. In the

---

ACTIVITY 9.4

BMW – strategies to deal with economic changes

BMW, the world's largest maker of premium cars, is on course to meet its target of selling 1.8 million cars worldwide in 2012 despite worries about the state of the world economy. Sales of all three brands owned by the German car maker – BMW, Mini and Rolls-Royce – are forecast to rise despite dark clouds on the economic horizon. The company is worried about three main problems:

- A huge depreciation of the US dollar, making German exports to the USA more expensive – currently, the US market is the second-largest buyer of BMW vehicles after the EU.
- Rapid inflation of oil and material prices, raising the cost of making cars.
- Slower rises in consumer spending in the USA and European Union countries due to a general decline in the rate of economic growth.

BMW is not standing still. It has made the following strategic decisions to:

- cut back on its expensive German workforce
- increase production by 60% in its US factory
- buy more supplies from US suppliers
- expand marketing of its products in non-US and non-EU markets such as China.

[22 marks, 30 minutes]

1   Explain why BMW is badly affected by the depreciation of the US dollar.   [4]

2   What advantages does BMW gain from selling many cars to EU countries that use the euro as their common currency?   [6]

3   Evaluate the long-term impact on BMW's profits of any **three** of the strategic decisions that the company has made.   [12]

Republic of Ireland and Poland, for example, it has been reduced to just 10%.

3 Increasing labour market flexibility and labour productivity

Labour is, of course, a key economic resource. Most governments want to use policies that will increase the skills and efficiency of the country's workforce and encourage workers to demonstrate a strong incentive to work.

115

These are some of the policies used by governments to achieve these aims:

- Subsidies for worker training programmes and increasing state provision at colleges for skills training.
- Increased funding of higher education to allow a higher proportion of future workers to enter employment with degrees and other high-level qualifications.
- Low rates of income tax to encourage workers to take the risk of setting up their own businesses and to encourage work incentives, e.g. gaining promotion and working harder to earn more money.
- Encouraging immigration of skilled workers who can fill job vacancies and help to increase total industrial output.
- Restricting welfare benefits to those in genuine need so that healthy and potentially productive workers are not encouraged to stay at home and 'live off the state'.

KEY CONCEPT LINK

External economic events are one of the most important causes of **change** that can result in businesses needing to take **strategic decisions** to try to ensure that its objectives can still be achieved.

116

Further economic issues

Government intervention in industry

Chapter 3 explained why most governments have policies that support small businesses. Chapter 6 examined the use of laws by governments to restrain business activities. It is also common for governments to intervene in industry in ways that will support both small and large businesses. These measures could include:

- subsidies to help keep down prices
- subsidies to stop a loss-making business failing
- grants to locate to particular regions
- financial support for consumers to buy products – e.g. houses – that will increase demand.

Market failure – what it means

The product and market factors that you have studied are where the prices of goods, services and factors of production are determined. These prices act as signals to the allocation of resources. This is a difficult idea, so two examples will help to illustrate it:

1 The world demand for rice rose in 2008 and 2009. This led to a doubling in the world price of rice. Farmers in rice-growing countries were encouraged by this high price to plant more rice and produce less of other crops. More resources were allocated to the product with the increased price.

2 High salaries offered in the Singapore financial sector are attracting staff into the financial industries away from more traditional careers, such as retailing and teaching. Labour resources are being allocated to one industry and away from others as a result of wage differences.

These two examples illustrate how markets should work. Sometimes they do not operate in this way and then **market failure** occurs.

KEY TERM

Market failure: when markets fail to achieve the most efficient allocation of resources and there is under- or overproduction of certain goods or services.

What instances are there of market failure and why should businesses be concerned about it? We will look at three examples to illustrate the concept and then consider the relevance of this to business and government decision-making.

ACTIVITY 9.5

Ford closure despite huge subsidies

Should governments subsidise failing businesses in order to protect jobs? Over a ten-year period the Australian government paid Au$2.5 billion in subsidies to Ford to 'prop up a loss-making enterprise', yet the company has announced it is closing its factories in Victoria, Australia. Many jobs will be lost directly within the factory as well as among many Australian supplier firms. High production costs and an overvalued Australian dollar exchange rate both contributed to the losses made by Ford in Australia – estimated to be £600 million in the past five years.

Some economists suggest that the government subsidy did not encourage Ford to become more efficient. It would have been better spent, they argue, on supporting new business start-ups or even used to reduce corporation tax that would have benefited all companies.

[14 marks, 20 minutes]

Discuss whether it is ever appropriate for a government to subsidise a loss-making business. **[14]**

Market failure 1: External costs

Pollution resulting from manufacturing is a good example. When a business makes a product, it has to pay for the costs of the land, capital, labour and materials. These are called the private costs of production. We are all aware, however, of the consequences of production other than those from the use of these factors. Air pollution, noise pollution and the dumping of waste products are all side effects of most manufacturing processes. Who pays the costs of cleaning up after the production of chemicals or plastics, for example? Unless the business is forced to pay, the costs will be borne by the rest of society; the government or local authority will have to raise taxes to clean the buildings dirtied by smoke, pay for medical provision for those affected by air pollution and make provision for waste disposal.

 KEY TERM

External costs: costs of an economic activity that are not paid for by the producer or consumer, but by the rest of society.

In this example, the market has failed to reflect the true and total cost of production in the price of the product. If the price charged to consumers included all of the costs of production – private as well as external – then less would be demanded and produced. As the price charged does not include the external costs, too much of the product will be demanded and too much produced. There has been market failure.

Market failure 2: Labour training

Will firms pay for the training of staff when there is a real danger that, once qualified, they could be 'poached' by other businesses that have not paid for the training? The answer is that many firms will not make sufficient provision for training. This means that the country has a shortage of skilled workers and professional staff, which will reduce economic growth. In this case there is under-provision of training and this again is a form of market failure.

Market failure 3: Monopoly producers

When a market is dominated by one firm, a monopoly is said to exist. The business will be interested in making profits as high as possible. The easiest way of achieving this will be to restrict output and raise prices. As the monopolist is able to prevent competitors from entering the market, this strategy will lead to under-provision

of goods and services compared with what consumers would really like. This is, therefore, a form of market failure.

Correcting or controlling market failure

Table 9.7 takes the three examples of market failure we have considered and looks at the groups most affected and the corrective action that could be taken.

Income elasticity of demand

Virtually all businesses will have greater opportunities for increased sales, profits and expansion during periods of economic growth. The impact of growth and the rising consumer incomes that accompany it will not be evenly felt, however. Some businesses will experience substantial increases in the demand for their goods and services, while others will notice a more limited rise – and, in certain cases, demand may actually fall for particular product categories. This varied experience resulting from economic growth is most clearly analysed by considering the concept of **income elasticity of demand**. Elasticity measures the responsiveness of the demand for a product following a change in a variable. There are several measures of elasticity and others are explained in Chapter 18.

 KEY TERM

Income elasticity of demand: measures the responsiveness of demand for a product after a change in consumer incomes.

Income elasticity of demand is calculated by the following formula:

Income elasticity of demand =

$$\frac{\% \text{ change in demand for a product}}{\% \text{ change in consumer incomes}}$$

Income elasticity can be described for three classes of goods.

1 **Normal goods:** The income elasticity for normal goods is positive and between 0 and 1. This means that, when consumer incomes rise, the demand for these goods may well also increase, but by a smaller proportion. These tend to be essential or necessity goods, which will be bought in roughly the same quantities by consumers no matter what their incomes. Examples might include basic foods and pharmaceutical goods. Producers of normal goods will not experience sharp increases in demand when incomes are rising during economic growth, but neither will the demand for them fall greatly when consumer incomes decline.

117

Examples of market failure	Stakeholder groups most affected	Corrective policy action
External costs – pollution from manufacturing process	<ul><li>Consumers – as there may be few alternatives, they may be forced to buy environmentally damaging goods.</li><li>Government and local authorities, which will be forced to take the issue seriously by voters and pressure groups.</li><li>Workers, who may be concerned about their own health and job security if bad publicity leads to a decline in sales.</li></ul>	<ul><li>Business may take action to reduce externalities if bad publicity leads to lasting damage to reputation and sales.</li><li>Government can impose fines on polluting businesses or impose strict limits on pollution levels.</li></ul>
Labour training – inadequate provision for training skilled staff	<ul><li>Consumers – scarcity of qualified staff may reduce consumer service or lead to higher prices as output is restricted.</li><li>Government – lack of skilled staff will limit the international competitiveness of industry.</li><li>Shareholders – potential profits will be lost as output will be below potential.</li></ul>	<ul><li>Industry-wide organisations, such as the Engineering Employers Federation, could levy members to pay for industry-wide training, which would benefit all firms in the industry.</li><li>Government could pay for more training courses at colleges funded from general taxation.</li></ul>
Monopoly producers – restrict output of goods to keep prices high	<ul><li>Consumers, who will be concerned about lack of choice, restricted supplies and high prices. There may be a reluctance by monopolies to develop new goods as there is limited competition.</li><li>Government – high prices and lack of competitiveness of important industries.</li></ul>	<ul><li>Consumers who, where at all possible, can purchase from other suppliers. The increasing use of the internet for consumer goods is allowing consumers to choose from a wider range of suppliers and this will break down some monopoly situations.</li><li>Government can use competition policies. Government can also investigate and act against monopoly practices. Privatisation has led to the break-up of many state-run monopolies.</li></ul>

Table 9.7 Government intervention to correct market failure

2 **Luxury goods:** The income elasticity of luxury goods is positive and greater than 1. This means that, when consumer incomes rise, the demand for these goods will rise by an even greater proportion. This is because consumers may already be purchasing sufficient quantities of normal goods. Thus, when their disposable incomes rise, they are able to spend these increases on more unusual non-necessity items, such as holidays, leisure activities and consumer durables. Among these will be the expensive but preferred alternative goods, which cannot be afforded when incomes are low.

3 **Inferior goods:** The income elasticity for these products is negative. This means that demand for these products will

decline following an increase in consumer incomes, but will rise when consumer incomes are reduced. Such products tend to have preferred but more expensive substitutes. Examples of these goods and services could include:

- second-hand goods, such as furniture
- 'economy' own-brand food products
- poorer cuts of meat
- weekend breaks in own country rather than long holidays abroad.

Thus the producers and retailers of these products may actually gain during a recession and experience a decline in sales when the economy is growing. A recession is when output in the economy falls. This will lead to lower consumer incomes as unemployment increases. Once you have grasped this very important concept, it will be easier to identify appropriate strategies that might be taken by different businesses if the economy is either expanding or contracting.

ACTIVITY 9.6

[15 marks, 15 minutes]

Three products A, B and C have very different income elasticities of demand. The income elasticities are: A = 2; B = –1; and C = 0.2.

1 Identify which is a normal good, which is an inferior good and which is a luxury good. [3]

2 If consumer incomes were to rise by 10% on average, calculate the expected change in demand for these three products. [6]

3 The three products are, in no particular order, white sliced bread, personal computers and aspirin tablets. Explain which letter you think best identifies each of these products. [6]

ACTIVITY 9.7

Excel Hi-Fi

Excel Hi-Fi manufactures two types of games console. The standard model has a retail price of $200. The superior model retails for $500. Recent increases in interest rates by the central bank have left consumers cautious about buying expensive items on credit, and disposable incomes have fallen as consumers pay higher mortgage interest. It is estimated that, on average, consumer incomes have fallen by 2%. Last month the sales of the standard model fell by 5%, but the sales of the superior model fell by 20%.

[15 marks, 18 minutes]

1 Calculate the income elasticity associated with both models of console. [4]

2 How would you explain why the income elasticity was greater for the more expensive model? [5]

3 How would you expect Excel's product mix strategy to change during a period when interest rates fell substantially? [6]

SUMMARY POINTS

- Governments have macro-economic objectives.
- Business cycles exist and economies can experience growth and recessions.
- Businesses often respond to changes in the business cycle.
- Economic growth can be caused by several factors.
- There are several causes of inflation and businesses might be affected by rising prices.
- Governments can use macro-economic policies to attempt to achieve economic objectives.
- Businesses can adopt a variety of strategies following changes in interest rates, tax rates and exchange rates.
- Market failure leads to inefficiency and governments can intervene to attempt to correct it.
- Income elasticity of demand is an important consideration of many business decisions.

RESEARCH TASK

1   Find out the current rate of unemployment for your region and that for your country as an average.
2   Research the rate of inflation for your country and how this has changed over the last 12 months.
3   Keep a weekly record of the tourist rate of exchange of your country's currency against one foreign currency of your choosing. Draw a line graph of this rate over a period of six weeks. Assess whether the exchange rate of your currency has appreciated or depreciated against the other currency.
4   Find out the current central bank base rate and how this has changed over the last 12 months.
5   Write a report of these economic changes to the chief executive officer of one of your country's major companies explaining:
    a   the likely impact of the changes on the business
    b   the possible strategies the business could adopt to respond to these changes.

A Level exam practice questions
Case studies

1   Hotels offering big discounts to Jamaicans

Jamaican hotels are cutting their rates to local residents by as much as a half, in a programme aimed at driving occupancy levels up. Several of these hotels have been reporting below normal occupancy as the Americans shy away from spending money during the current recession. Many Americans have taken on too many debts and they now find that they cannot afford expensive foreign holidays. The price reduction by the Jamaica Hotel and Tourist Association members forms part of the initiative by leaders of the tourism industry to reduce the impact of the drastic reduction in visitor arrivals that is now being experienced across the industry and that the sector expects to continue into next year. Global recession is expected to be a major problem in the next few years.

Only last week, the government announced tax reductions for small hotels that are now expanding or refurbishing, in addition to the millions of dollars of additional funding that are being pumped into overseas promotion of Jamaica as a tourist attraction.

[24 marks, 35 minutes]

1   Explain why hotels in Jamaica have announced price reductions for local residents.   [4]
2   Outline **two** measures that the Jamaican government could take to assist Jamaican hotels at this difficult time.   [8]
3   Discuss **two** other strategies that the Jamaican hotels could take to try to increase tourist numbers if there is a global recession in the next few years.   [12]

2 Pakistan economy: a mixture of hope and future problems

Pakistan recorded economic growth of around 3% per year between 2008 and 2013. According to a recent report from the United Nations Economic and Social Commission for Asia (ESCAP): 'Due to economic reforms and sound macro-economic policies in recent years, investment-led growth and expansion of the agricultural sector have contributed to a stronger economy.'

ESCAP states that the prospects for millions of rural poor could be further improved by government policy that aims to increase agricultural productivity and improve transport, allowing food products to be taken to markets and exported. By being able to sell more of their output, the rural poor would see an increase in incomes, helping to reduce the country's substantial income inequalities. ESCAP said that if the government used expansionary fiscal policy and increased development spending both investment growth and poverty reduction would occur.

Problems remain, however. Inflation (8% in 2013) and interest rates (9.5%) are high by international standards. Any attempt to reduce inflation by the government – such as even higher interest rates or higher taxes – might carry the risk of lower economic growth. The large fiscal deficit of 6.2% of GDP will have to be cut back eventually – possibly by further privatisation programmes. A widening current account deficit on the balance of payments is forecast – despite the depreciation of the Rupee by 40% since 2007. Pakistan has increasing import costs of expensive oil and the greater competition from China in export markets for clothing and textiles.

The prime minister recently announced that the government will increase spending on infrastructure projects, such as dam building and irrigation projects. This will help to increase agricultural productivity. He also said the government will intervene to help set up of new industries to generate more employment throughout the country.

[35 marks, 50 minutes]

1 Explain what is meant by the terms:
   a 'expansionary fiscal policy' [3]
   b 'economic growth' [3]
   c 'the balance of payments current account deficit' [3]
2 Discuss whether governments, such as that in Pakistan, should intervene to support agricultural producers and new business start-ups. [10]

3 Evaluate the likely impact on a clothing manufacturer in Pakistan following:
   a economic policies aimed at reducing inflation
   b further deprecation of the country's currency exchange rate. [16]

3 Prospects for the Malaysian economy

The Malaysian economy has experienced a classic 'business cycle' over the past 20 years. In the first quarter of 2001, Malaysian GDP fell by 2.8%. In the second quarter, it shrank by a further 6.8%. Many small and medium-sized businesses were expected to go out of business as a result of the recession. Three major decisions were made to prevent the recession getting worse:

■ Interest rates were cut.
■ Government spending was increased and taxes were cut – increasing the government's budget deficit.
■ The exchange rate of the Malaysian currency, the ringgit, was allowed to depreciate.

By 2008, the country's economic performance was much improved:

■ The GDP grew by 6%
■ The ringgit had appreciated.
■ Unemployment fell.

This 'boom' period did not last long. By 2013, economic growth was down to 4.3% – but still good compared to most economies. The recession in much of the European Union has hit Malaysian exports of hi-tech products, as European consumers spend less. The ringgit depreciated by nearly 6% between May and October 2013. The government is planning to reduce its deficit by cutting fuel subsidies and infrastructure spending and increasing indirect taxes. Low inflation is a real benefit for industry, however, and the current (2013) rate of 2% means that the Malaysian Central Bank is unlikely to increase interest rates soon.

[40 marks, 60 minutes]

1 What data are given in the article to suggest that the Malaysian economy was in recession in 2001? [3]
2 Explain how a recession could lead to the bankruptcy of many Malaysian businesses. [7]
3 Explain how the three decisions taken in 2001 helped to achieve economic growth in Malaysia. [6]

4 Evaluate, using numerical illustrations, the impact of the 2013 ringgit depreciation referred to in the passage on:
   a Malaysian manufacturers of electronic goods [6]
   b Malaysian importers of foreign goods. [6]
5 Discuss **two** possible strategies a Malaysian manufacturing business might decide on in response to the government's fiscal policy changes in 2013. [12]

4   Coaching Inns plc

Coaching Inns plc operates a chain of 23 hotels in Trinidad. It has always adopted a policy of aiming at the premium end of the market and all of its hotels have either a four- or five-star accreditation. As the economy has expanded in recent years, the hotels have all reported increases in room occupancy rates, hotel diners and overall profit margins. Also encouraging has been the increasing proportion of guests from overseas, drawn by the company's reputation for traditional service and historic but modernised hotels. There has been a sustained period of expansion, and unemployment is now very low. The directors have supported a policy of heavy borrowing in order to purchase more suitable properties. The prospects for the company appear to be excellent and the latest meeting of the board of directors even discussed the proposal to open the first hotel overseas, in the USA.

There seem to be just two main problems on the horizon. First, for some months, many hotels have found it increasingly difficult to recruit new staff for the kitchens and in customer support. Coaching Inns does not have an extensive training scheme and always prefers to recruit qualified staff with some experience from other hotels. The second issue concerns the recent meetings of the Trinidad and Tobago Central Bank. Reports have been issued suggesting that if the recent sharp increase in inflation is repeated next month, then there will be significant increases in interest rates over the next few years.

[40 marks, 60 minutes]

1   Analyse the likely reasons for the company's increasing difficulty in recruiting new staff.   [6]

2   Analyse the impact this problem might have for the future expansion strategy of the business.   [6]

3   Evaluate **two** ways the directors could attempt to overcome this problem.   [8]

4   Discuss the impact that higher interest rates could have on the future prospects of Coaching Inns plc.   [10]

5   Assuming that interest rates did rise significantly for a considerable time period, evaluate alternative strategies the business could adopt in response to this change in policy.   [10]

A Level essay questions

[20 marks, 45 minutes each]

1   Evaluate how the following policy measures are likely to affect businesses in your country:

   a   increase in interest rates

   b   expansionary fiscal policy.   [20]

2   Discuss the likely impact on the strategies adopted by manufacturing businesses in your country as a consequence of a substantial:

   a   appreciation of your country's currency exchange rate

   b   depreciation of your country's currency exchange rate.   [20]

End of Unit 1: Exam-style case study questions

African Publishing Company (APC)

APC is a public limited company. It was privatised by the government of country A five years ago. The performance of the company since privatisation in 2009 is summarised below:

	2009	2014
Profit (after tax and interest but before dividends)	$13m	$108m
Average APC book price	$5	$8
Number of APC books in publication	3,250	4,560
Average annual salaries paid	$8350	$7690
% change in annual energy usage	12%	4%
Employee accidents on APC premises	125	64

Table 1 Selected data for APC 2009–2014

APC is a vertically integrated business. Its operations include:

- commissioning authors to write books
- computer typesetting of each book
- printing books
- transport and distribution of books.

APC does not own any book retailers so it does not control the sales promotions of its own publications. The directors of the company are considering two options for growth:

Option A: Taking over DSF – the country's largest chain of book shops. APC could then focus on marketing and promoting its own books at prices decided by the company.

Option B: Merging with a publishing business, PAN, in country Y. This would allow book printing for both businesses to be concentrated in country Y where costs are lower than in country A.

The chief executive told directors at a recent board meeting: 'We can only chose one of these options as the necessary reorganisation of the business will be too disruptive. I prefer Option A as it would make us a more fully integrated business with full control over costs at all levels.'

The marketing director commented: 'With Option A we will be again focusing on printed books whereas current trends are towards digital e-books. Do we need to diversify? Option B would not be easy to control effectively as PAN is managed very differently to our business. For example, cheap paper is used that comes from non-sustainable sources and most workers have short-term contracts that make it easy for the business to make redundancies.'

Dynamic business environment

There have been many recent technological developments that have affected the publishing industry. Some of these changes include using computers to typeset books, computerised inventory control, highly productive automated printing presses and the advances in digital technology prompting a huge growth in the use of tablets and e-readers. Initially, APC was swept along by these changes rather than being an industry leader in introducing them but a new operations director has enthusiastically introduced the latest production methods at considerable cost to the business. The economic environment in which APC operates is also changing. The changes forecast in Table 2 offer opportunities as well as potential threats to the business. The chief executive plans to discuss these economic forecasts with his fellow directors at the next board meeting.

	In 1 year	In 2 years
Annual increase in real GDP	1.5%	– 2%
Annual inflation	4%	6%
Average exchange rate index of country A's currency against other currencies (This year = 100)	95	88
Unemployment %	5.5%	7%

Table 2 Economics forecasts for country A

 KEY CONCEPTS REVIEW

Obviously, both of the growth strategies being proposed are focused on creating further value for the business. Management has to assess which one is likely to create most value with an acceptable degree of risk. Both strategies will involve change – the effective management of this change will be an important factor in the future success of APC. This business is a good example of one that is affected by almost constant changes in the business environment. How do you think managers of businesses such as APC should respond to these changes?

A Level 50 marks 90 minutes

1 Analyse the benefits to any two stakeholder groups resulting from the privatisation of APC. [10]
2 Assess the likely impact on APC's future success of technological change. [12]
3 Recommend to APC's directors which growth option, A or B, APC should choose. [12]
4 Discuss the likely impact on APC of the forecast economic trends shown in Table 2. [16]

123

Unit 2:
People in organisations

Introduction

This section focuses on how businesses can manage and lead employees effectively to allow the achievement of organisational goals. It is concerned with the procedures, structures and approaches to management and leadership that allow the full potential of employees to be developed for the benefit of both the workers themselves and the business. Current management approaches are based on the concept that effective employees can be an important means of helping the business create value and be more customer-focused.

Students will need to understand the distinct theories that underpin business management and leadership. The importance of motivation theories and practices in satisfying human needs will be considered. The contribution to business success made by human resource management through effective workforce planning and the recruitment, selection and training of workers will also be examined. The management of employees through periods of change and innovation is an important theme.

10 Management and leadership

This chapter covers syllabus section AS Level 2.1.

On completing this chapter, you will be able to:

- understand the main functions of managers
- analyse the importance of good management to the success of a business
- analyse the differences between McGregor's Theory X and Theory Y
- recognise the key differences in management styles
- evaluate the appropriateness of these styles to different business situations
- understand the significance of informal leadership
- analyse the four competencies of emotional intelligence.

Introducing the topic

WHAT MAKES A GOOD LEADER?

The question is eternal: what makes a good leader? There is no definitive answer but one thing is certain: as business technologies evolve, new industries come and go and employee demographics change, the best leaders are those who can change with the times. They're the ones with foresight and adaptability, who don't rule from a manual but customise their approach to suit to each company, its mission and the personality of its work force. Here are four quotes from, or about, famous chief executives:

- Ted Devine, Insureon: 'Having a completely open plan office says this about leadership: No walls, no barriers, no hierarchy. Everybody can talk to everybody. Everybody can participate in a decision. We work together, and that's very important in leadership.'
- Shelie Johnson, BET cable network: 'I want every one of my employees to look at me with dignity and respect. I want to be someone they are proud to work for.'
- Jeff Weiner, LinkedIn: As a manager, Weiner takes time to acknowledge relatively small

accomplishments by his employees. He often ends a meeting or speech by asking what he could have done better. His workdays are as long as – or longer than – those of his employees. 'That allows him to be extremely credible as a leader,' says David Hahn, LinkedIn's vice-president

- Tony Hsieh, Zappos: 'Tony's imprint is all over the company,' says Jamie Naughton, a Zappos senior manager. 'Our culture was inspired by how he does business and the people he hires and how we all are as a group.' He takes a hands-off approach to leadership that requires effective delegation. 'He is more of an architect; he designs the big vision and then gets out of the way so that everyone can make the things happen.'

Points to think about:
- What do you think 'leadership' means?
- Do you think that all of the quotes above suggest 'good leadership'? Why?
- Do you think there is a difference between 'leading' people and 'managing' them? Explain your answer.

Introduction

It is not easy to precisely define the role of management. It is easier to recognise a business that is poorly managed than it is to pinpoint the specific features of good management in a successful business. Badly managed businesses will be poorly organised, will often have poor staff motivation and resources will be

wasted or inefficiently used. In addition, the business is unlikely to have long-term plans or objectives and will, as a consequence, lack direction and purpose. By identifying these common problems of failing businesses, perhaps the following definition of management – or effective management – can now be offered.

Management and managers

Managers 'get things done' – not by doing all jobs themselves but by working with and delegating to other people. Managers do not all use the same style of leadership and different managers will approach problems and decisions in very different ways, but the key functions of management are common to all. These are best explained by reference to some of the best-known management writers, such as Fayol and Drucker. By combining the main ideas of these two writers we can arrive at the following list of management tasks and functions.

 KEY TERM

Manager: responsible for setting objectives, organising resources and motivating staff so that the organisation's aims are met.

The functions of management – what managers are responsible for

1 **Setting objectives and planning:** All good managers think ahead. Senior management will establish overall strategic objectives and these will be translated into tactical objectives for the less-senior managerial staff. The planning needed to put these objectives into effect is also important. A new production or marketing objective will require the planning and preparation of sufficient resources.

2 **Organising resources to meet the objectives:** This is not just about giving instructions. People throughout the business need to be recruited carefully and encouraged to take some authority and to accept some accountability via delegation. Senior managers will ensure that the structure of the business allows for a clear division of tasks and that each section or department is organised to allow them to work towards the common objectives.

3 **Directing and motivating staff:** This means guiding, leading and overseeing of employees to ensure that organisational goals are being met. The significance of developing staff so that they are motivated to employ all of their abilities at work is now widely recognised. This will make it more likely that organisational aims are achieved.

4 **Coordinating activities:** As the average size of business units increases – especially true for multinationals – so the need to ensure consistency and coordination between different parts of each firm increases. The goals of each branch, division, region and even all staff must be welded together to achieve a common sense of purpose. At a practical level, this can mean avoiding the situation where two divisions of the same company both spend money on researching into the same new product, resulting in wasteful duplication of effort.

5 **Controlling and measuring performance against targets:** Management by objectives establishes targets for all groups, divisions and individuals. It is management's responsibility to appraise performance against targets and to take action if underperformance occurs. It is just as important to provide positive feedback when things keep going right.

Management roles

To carry out these functions, managers have to undertake many different roles. Henry Mintzberg (*The Nature of Managerial Work*, 1973) identified ten roles common to the work of all managers. These are divided into three groups (see Table 10.1):

- Interpersonal roles – dealing with and motivating staff at all levels of the organisation.
- Informational roles – acting as a source, receiver and transmitter of information.
- Decisional roles – taking decisions and allocating resources to meet the organisation's objectives.

Leadership – the importance of it and qualities needed

Leadership is a key part of being a successful manager. It involves setting a clear direction and vision for an organisation – often a new direction and vision if circumstances demand it – that others will be prepared to follow. Employees will want to follow a good leader and will respond positively to them. A poor leader will often fail to win over staff and will have problems communicating with and organising workers effectively. The best managers are also good leaders of people – but some managers are not. Managers that focus so much on control and allocation of people and resources can fail to provide a sense of purpose or focus that others will understand and be prepared to follow. Without clear and charismatic leadership workers may be very well managed, but will they be inspired to help the leader and the business take a fresh direction and achieve new goals?

 KEY TERM

Leadership: the art of motivating a group of people towards achieving a common objective.

What makes a good leader? Many studies have been conducted on this very point – some argue that leaders are born with natural assets that create an aura or charisma that others will find appealing. Other research is more inclined to support the view that leaders can be trained to adopt the key attributes of good leadership. A number

Role title	Description of role activities	Examples of management action to perform the role
1 Interpersonal roles		
Figurehead	symbolic leader of the organisation undertaking duties of a social or legal nature	opening new factories/offices; hosting receptions; giving important presentations
Leader	motivating subordinates; selecting and training other managers/staff	any management tasks involving subordinate staff
Liaison	linking with managers and leaders of other divisions of the business and other organisations	leading and participating in meetings; business correspondence with other organisations
2 Informational roles		
Monitor (receiver)	collecting data relevant to the business's operations	attending seminars, business conferences, research groups; reading research reports
Disseminator	sending information collected from external and internal sources to the relevant people within the organisation	communicating with staff within the organisation, using appropriate means
Spokesperson	communicating information about the organisation – its current position and achievements – to external groups and people	presenting reports to groups of stakeholders (e.g. annual general meeting) and communicating with the press and TV media
3 Decisional roles		
Entrepreneur	looking for new opportunities to develop the business	encouraging new ideas from within the business and holding meetings aimed at putting new ideas into effect
Disturbance handler	responding to changing situations that may put the business at risk; assuming responsibility when threatening factors develop	taking decisions on how the business should respond to threats, such as new competitors or changes in the economic environment
Resource allocator	deciding on the spending of the organisation's financial resources and the allocation of its physical and human resources	drawing up and approving estimates and budgets; deciding on staffing levels for departments and within departments
Negotiator	representing the organisation in all important negotiations, e.g. with government	conducting negotiations and building up official links between the business and other organisations

Table 10.1 Managerial roles according to Mintzberg

of personal characteristics have been identified as being common among effective leaders:

- They have the desire to succeed and natural self-confidence that they will succeed.
- They possess the ability to think beyond the obvious – to be creative – and to encourage others to do the same.
- They are multitalented, so that they can understand discussions about a wide range of issues affecting their business.
- They have an incisive mind that enables the heart of an issue to be identified rather than unnecessary details.

Clearly, not all managers will have all of these important characteristics. In fact, the particular strengths and weaknesses of managers is one of the factors that determines the style of leadership that they might adopt.

Important leadership positions in business

Directors

These senior managers are elected into office by shareholders in a limited company. They are usually head of a major functional department, such as marketing. They will be responsible for delegating within their department, assisting in the recruitment of senior staff in the department, meeting the objectives for the department set by the board of directors and communicating these to their department.

Allstyles department store

Rebecca Allahiq's working day was busy and varied. She had recently been appointed general manager of the Allstyles department store. This was a large shop in the city centre. It had ten departments selling a wide range of products from clothes to carpets, furniture and electrical goods. A film crew from the local TV company had asked if they could film a typical working day for a programme they were making about different people's working lives. Rebecca agreed and the ten-minute programme used six different clips of film with Rebecca involved in the following activities:

1   Meeting with all departmental managers to explain the store's pricing and promotional strategy for the next end-of-season sale. At this meeting she expected all managers to inform staff of the agreed price reductions and the way in which goods should be presented in the sale so that consumers would have clear messages about the promotion.

2   Attending a planning meeting with senior executives from head office to agree the sales targets for the store for the next 12 months. Rebecca explained that the opening of a competitor's store very close to hers was a factor that should be taken into account.

3   Presenting three shop workers with 'Reach for the stars' badges for outstanding sales records over the last month. She had her picture taken with them for publication in the store's internal newspaper.

4   Reviewing the poor performance of the electrical products division with the manager. Poor staff absence figures had contributed to this problem and Rebecca suggested that the manager should attend additional training sessions on staff motivation and monitoring of staff performance.

5   Meeting with builders, architects and planners to discuss progress on the new store extension. Rebecca was concerned that they were not working together closely enough and the project could fall behind schedule.

6   Settling a dispute between two departmental managers over which department should be able to stock a new electronic exercise bicycle – sports or electrical goods? It was agreed that it could not appear in both because of lack of space, so sports would stock it for six months next to gym equipment. Sales would be monitored closely and if it did not do well, then relocation might be possible.

[28 marks, 40 minutes]

1   Identify and briefly explain all of the different management functions that Rebecca fulfilled during this busy day.   **[10]**

2   Outline the personal qualities that you think Rebecca needed to carry out all of these roles successfully.   **[8]**

3   Discuss the problems that this store might encounter if Rebecca was not an effective manager.   **[10]**

Manager

Any individual responsible for people, resources or decision-making, or often all three, can be termed a manager. They will have some authority over other staff below them in the hierarchy. They will direct, motivate and, if necessary, discipline the staff in their section or department.

Supervisors

These are appointed by management to watch over the work of others. This is usually not a decision-making role, but they will have responsibility for leading a team of people in working towards pre-set goals. The modern role of these members of staff is less of an inspector and much more of a work colleague who is appointed to help staff achieve objectives in a cooperative spirit.

Workers' representatives

These are elected by the workers, either as trade union officials or as representatives on works councils in order to discuss areas of common concern with managers.

Leadership styles

Leadership (or management) style refers to the way in which managers take decisions and communicate with their staff. There are four distinct leadership styles (see also Table 10.2):

■ autocratic (or authoritarian)
■ democratic
■ paternalistic
■ laissez-faire.

Autocratic leadership

Autocratic leaders will take decisions on their own, with no discussion. They set business objectives themselves, issue instructions to workers and check to ensure that they

KEY TERM

Autocratic leadership: a style of leadership that keeps all decision-making at the centre of the organisation.

Style	Main features	Drawbacks	Possible applications
Autocratic	■ leader takes all decisions ■ gives little information to staff ■ supervises workers closely ■ only one-way communication ■ workers only given limited information about the business	■ demotivates staff who want to contribute and accept responsibility ■ decisions do not benefit from staff input	■ defence forces and police where quick decisions are needed and the scope for discussion must be limited ■ times of crisis when decisive action might be needed to limit damage to the business or danger to others
Democratic	■ participation encouraged ■ two-way communication used, which allows feedback from staff ■ workers given information about the business to allow full staff involvement	■ consultation with staff can be time-consuming ■ on occasions, quick decision-making will be required ■ level of involvement – some issues might be too sensitive (e.g. job losses) or too secret (e.g. development of new products)	■ most likely to be useful in businesses that expect workers to contribute fully to the production and decision-making processes, thereby satisfying their higher-order needs ■ an experienced and flexible workforce will be likely to benefit most from this style ■ situations that demand a new way of thinking or a new solution, then staff input can be very valuable
Paternalistic	■ managers do what they think is best for the workers ■ some consultation might take place, but the final decisions are taken by the managers – there is no true participation in decision-making ■ managers want workers to be happy in their jobs	■ some workers will be dissatisfied with the apparent attempts to consult, while not having any real power or influence	■ used by managers who have a genuine concern for workers' interests, but feel that 'managers know best' in the end – when workers are young or inexperienced this might be an appropriate style to employ
Laissez-faire	■ managers delegate virtually all authority and decision-making powers ■ very broad criteria or limits might be established for the staff to work within	■ workers may not appreciate the lack of structure and direction in their work – this could lead to a loss of security ■ the lack of feedback – as managers will not be closely monitoring progress – may be demotivating	■ when managers are too busy (or too lazy) to intervene ■ may be appropriate in research institutions where experts are more likely to arrive at solutions when not constrained by narrow rules or management controls

Table 10.2 Summary of leadership styles

are carried out. Workers can become so accustomed to this style that they are dependent on their leaders for all guidance and will not show any initiative. Motivation levels are likely to be low, so supervision of staff will be essential. Managers using this style are likely to only use one-way communication – that is, they will issue instructions but will not encourage any feedback from the workforce.

This style of management does have some useful applications. Armed forces and the police are likely to adopt this approach, as orders may need to be issued quickly with immediate response. Also, in crises, such as an oil tanker disaster or a railway accident, leaders may have to take full charge and issue orders to reduce the

unfortunate consequences of the incident. It would be inappropriate to discuss these instructions with the staff concerned before they were put into effect.

Democratic leadership

Democratic leaders will engage in discussion with workers before taking decisions. Communication links will be established on the two-way principle, with every

KEY TERM

Democratic leadership: a leadership style that promotes the active participation of workers in taking decisions.

opportunity for staff to respond to and initiate discussion. Managers using this approach need good communication skills themselves to be able to explain issues clearly and to understand responses from the workforce. Full participation in the decision-making process is encouraged. This may lead to better final decisions, as the staff have much to contribute and can offer valuable work experience to new situations. In the light of research by Herzberg, this style of management should improve motivation of staff, as they are being given some responsibility for the objectives and strategy of the business. Workers should feel more committed to ensuring that decisions that they have influenced are put into effect successfully. Employing the democratic approach can be a slow process, however, and this could make it unsuitable in certain situations.

Paternalistic leadership

Paternalistic literally means 'father-like', and **paternalistic leaders** will listen, explain issues and consult with the workforce, but will not allow them to take decisions. The paternalistic manager will decide 'what is best' for the business and the workforce but the delegation of decision-making will be most unlikely. These managers are less concerned with Herzberg's motivators and more directed by the need to satisfy the safety and security needs of the workers (Maslow). Therefore, this approach is not democratic – and, like some fathers, is rather more autocratic than it might at first appear. This style could be suitable in a situation with unskilled, untrained or newly appointed staff, but it may lead to disappointment and disillusionment in more experienced staff that would prefer to be delegated real decision-making and given opportunities for participation.

KEY TERM

Paternalistic leadership: a leadership style based on the approach that the manager is in a better position than the workers to know what is best for an organisation.

Laissez-faire leadership

Laissez-faire leadership literally means 'let them do it' – or allow workers to carry out tasks and take decisions themselves within very broad limits.

KEY TERM

Laissez-faire leadership: a leadership style that leaves much of the business decision-making to the workforce – a 'hands-off' approach and the reverse of the autocratic style.

Disaster at the bakery

The fire at the bakery was a disaster for T&S Provisions Ltd. Eli Tarranto, the chief executive and main shareholder, had been the first one to be called by the fire brigade officer at 3am. 'The whole building is up in flames – we have not been able to save anything,' he had shouted down the phone. The next day, as Eli waited for his staff to turn up for work outside the burnt-out shell of his bakery, a plan was beginning to form in his head. He had already contacted both the owner of a small competing bakery, who was actually a very good friend, and the commercial estate agent from whom he had bought the land for the bakery four years ago. The owner of the bakery agreed to allow Eli to use one of his spare ovens if he sent his own workers to operate it. This would give him about 50% of his normal capacity. The commercial estate agent suggested that Eli rent, for a period of three months, an empty depot on the other side of town. He believed that it would take around two weeks to have this equipped as a temporary bakery. When the staff started to arrive, Eli gave them all clear instructions. They were shocked by the state of the old building but they seemed willing to help in this time of crisis. Six of them were despatched to his friend's bakery to start organising production there. Two were sent to the estate agent to pick up keys for the depot and had instructions to start cleaning the premises. The remaining three workers were to help Eli salvage what he could from the office records of the burnt-out building. Before this could start, Eli telephoned all of his major customers – he did not leave it to his sales manager – to explain the extent of the problem and to promise that some production would be back on stream just as soon as possible. He then contacted suppliers to inform them of the disaster, to reduce order quantities and to give them the new, temporary address for deliveries.

[17 marks, 25 minutes]

1 Identify the management roles that Eli seems to have demonstrated in this case. [4]

2 What leadership style did Eli seem to be employing in the case? Explain your answer. [3]

3 Discuss whether this is the most appropriate style of leadership to apply in all situations. [10]

This is an extreme version of democratic management. There will be very little input from management into the work to be undertaken by subordinates. This style could be particularly effective in the case of research or design teams. Experts in these fields often work best when they are not tightly supervised and when they are given free rein to work on an original project. Many scientific discoveries would have been prevented if the researchers concerned had been restricted in their work by senior management. In other cases, a laissez-faire management style could be a disaster. Leaving workers to their own devices with little direction or supervision might lead to a lack of confidence, poor decisions and poor motivation as they are never sure if what they are doing is right.

KEY CONCEPT LINK

Views differ over the most appropriate leadership style for **creating value** in a business. Some managers believe that an **autocratic** style will encourage the workforce to work efficiently to create value. Other managers consider that a **laissez-faire** or **democratic** style is most appropriate to bring the best out of a workforce.

TOP TIP
Paternalistic leadership is not part of the Cambridge syllabus; it has been included here to act as a good contrast to democratic leadership.

ACTIVITY 10.3

[15 marks, 20 minutes]

Explain briefly which style of leadership might be most appropriate in the following business situations:

a   Business is flooded and important inventory and company records have been damaged.

b   Electronics company plans to establish a group to research into new types of batteries.

c   The quality of output from a pipe manufacturing factory has declined and no one knows why. The production team have been asked to attend a meeting about the problem.   **[15]**

Small research team

Flooded business

Factory workers in a group

131

McGregor's Theory X and Theory Y

What factors determine the style of leadership that managers use? According to Douglas McGregor, as a result of his studies in the 1950s, one of the most important determinants is the attitude of managers towards their workers. He identified two distinct management approaches to the workforce and he called these Theory X and Theory Y. Theory X managers, according to McGregor, view their workers as lazy, disliking work and unprepared to accept responsibility, needing to be controlled and made to work. Clearly, managers with this view will be likely to adopt an autocratic style of leadership.

On the other hand, McGregor believed that the managers who held Theory Y views believed that workers did enjoy work and that they found it as natural as rest or play. They would be prepared to accept responsibility, were creative and they would take an active part in contributing ideas and solutions to work-related problems. A very important point to note about McGregor's work is this – he did not suggest that there were two types of workers, X and Y, but that the attitudes of management to workers could, in extreme cases, be described by these two theories. In practice, of course, most managers will have views somewhere between these two extremes.

What is the significance of McGregor's work? It is a very widely quoted piece of research. The general view is that workers will behave in a particular way as a result of the attitude that management have towards them. For instance, if a manager believes that all workers behave in a Theory X way, there will be control, close supervision and no delegation of authority. The staff, as a result of this approach, will almost certainly not enjoy their work and may indeed try to avoid it and fail to contribute in any meaningful way. Therefore, they will become like Theory X because of the way they are treated. The exact reverse could be the case for workers treated in a more democratic style, based on the Theory Y view (see Table 10.3).

Theory X managers believe that workers	Theory Y managers believe that workers
■ dislike work ■ will avoid responsibility ■ are not creative	■ can derive as much enjoyment from work as from rest and play ■ will accept responsibility ■ are creative

Table 10.3 Summary of Theory X and Theory Y management attitudes

Modern steel-making requires a new approach

Kevin Bai is the type of manager who has one set way of doing a job, and expects everybody to do it his way. He has worked in the steel plant for 25 years – first as an apprentice, then as a skilled steel ladle operator and then progressing to works supervisor. His latest promotion, however, was unexpected, especially by his workmates. Although he was very reliable and had never taken a day off work, his colleagues questioned whether he was the right man for the new position. He is now the manager of the blast-furnace operation – in charge of 30 men and $10 million worth of equipment. He knows that he has a great deal of responsibility. He wants the plant to work efficiently and he believes that this means doing things his way. He deals with the workers in the same way as he was managed in the past – given clear instructions and not to think for himself but to do as he was told. This had worked best when he was young and he believes that the young workers coming into the plant should operate in the same way. Many things have changed since Kevin was an apprentice, however. There is now virtually no manual work involved. The equipment is now computer-operated and controllers need to be well-educated and good with their brains –not their hands. All of the heavy work is now automated. Workers operate a flexible shift system and could be asked to do any of the ten different jobs that the steel-making process involves. They are, therefore, adaptable and multiskilled and are used to solving problems themselves – so Kevin's style has taken them by surprise and they do not approve of it.

[20 marks, 30 minutes]

1 How would you classify Kevin's style of leadership according to McGregor – Theory X or Y? Explain your answer. [4]

2 Outline **three** ways in which methods of working and, with them, the expectations of steel workers may have changed in the 25 years since Kevin started working at the plant. [6]

3 Discuss whether the leadership style used by Kevin is the best one to use in the circumstances described. [10]

The 'best' leadership style – it depends on many factors

There is not one leadership style that is best in all circumstances and for all businesses. The style used will depend on many factors:

- The training and experience of the workforce and the degree of responsibility that they are prepared to take on.
- The amount of time available for consultation and participation.
- The attitude of managers, or management culture – this will be influenced by the personality and business background of the managers, e.g. whether they have always worked in an autocratically run organisation.
- The importance of the issues under consideration – different styles may be used in the same business in different situations. If there is great risk to the business when a poor or slow decision is taken, then it is more likely that management will make the choice in an autocratic way.

Democratic leadership – involving participation and two-way communication – is increasingly common for a number of reasons. Working people are better educated than ever before and have higher expectations of their experience from work – they expect higher-level needs to be partly satisfied at work. Many managers have realised that the rapid pace of changes at work, as a result of technological and other factors, has increased the need to consult and involve workers in the process of change. People find change less threatening and more acceptable if they have been involved in some meaningful way in managing it. Despite these factors, many managers will still avoid consultation and staff participation, perhaps because they find it very difficult to adapt to these ways. Others may so doubt their own ability to discuss and persuade that they would rather issue instructions that do not allow for any feedback from staff. Whichever style of management is used in an organisation – or is referred to in a question – it is important to remember that there is no one right or wrong way of managing people, but there is always an *appropriate* style for any situation.

Informal leadership

So far we have discussed only formal leaders or managers – those appointed by the organisation to exercise authority over others. In any group of people, at work or in a social context, it is very common for **informal leaders** to be established. Many researchers have recognised that the impact of informal groups and leaders could be very important for business performance. Look around you at school or college – would you rather listen to and be led by a supervisor or manager appointed by the principal of the school or college or 'one of your own' who has gained the respect and trust of most students?

These informal leaders are people who have the ability to lead without formal power, perhaps because of their experiences, personality or special knowledge. They may have more influence over workers than formal leaders, especially if the latter are just seen as supervisors of work rather than true leaders and motivators. How should management react to these informal leaders? Appointing them as formal leaders might be a wise move, but in an organisation where employer–employee relationships are not based on trust, the person concerned could quickly lose support if they were seen to be joining the 'other side'. To cut them out or in some way to ignore them could be equally disastrous, as they may gather around them many worker supporters and this could lead to disruption of production or other types of industrial action.

In an ideal business situation, where workers and employers work together in a trusting relationship, managers should attempt to work with the informal leaders to help achieve the aims of the business. This is best done by attempting to ensure that the aims of the informal leader and the group are common with, or fit in with, the aims of the business. It is an unwise manager who ignores the potential influence of an informal leader or who attempts to diminish this influence by switching them to another group or cutting them off from work colleagues.

Emotional intelligence

This is a relatively new area of study. We have all met people who are brilliant at school with very high levels of intelligence yet they cannot handle people well or make social contact easily. Does being super-intelligent make a person a good manager or leader? Not necessarily, according to many recent studies. These put much more emphasis on **emotional intelligence**, which involves:

- understanding yourself, your goals, your behaviour and your responses to people
- understanding others and their feelings.

The more managers can understand these feelings, it is argued, the more effective they become as leaders of people and decision-makers. The more emotionally intelligent a person is,

133

then the higher their measurable EIQ or emotional intelligence quotient would be. Many studies have suggested that business performance can be improved by appointing people with high levels of emotional intelligence – not necessarily the brightest people in traditional academic terms.

ACTIVITY 10.5

Informal leadership and tension in the workplace

'This cannot go on – every time we tell the work group about new production targets or the need for higher-quality products, that troublemaker Zeke Lin talks them out of it.' The frustration of the works supervisor, Keira Malik, was showing in her voice. She had warned Zeke several times about his tactic of always chatting to the group after every new instruction from management and asking them if they were happy to go along with it. When the changes involved higher output or using materials less wastefully, Zeke managed to lead the workers to refuse to accept it or to create obstacles as to why it could not happen. The trouble had started several years back when Zeke had lost his job as team leader after taking a day off when his son was being born. The formal leadership role was now in the hands of Akiko, but he was really only interested in doing his own job, so the workers largely ignored him anyway. Rules had since been changed regarding family reasons for time off, but that did not help Zeke. Keira discussed the problem with her own manager. He was in favour of seeing Zeke to discuss whether he would be interested in taking up a position training new workers. 'He has so much influence over his workmates that we could use this to our advantage – we could ask him to help establish training targets and methods,' he said. 'Alternatively, we could just give him his old job as formal group leader back.' Keira was keen to see the back of Zeke for good: 'We should make an example of him and give him a formal warning which should lead, eventually, to him being asked to go.'

[18 marks, 20 minutes]

1 Outline possible reasons why the members of Zeke's work group were so keen to follow his lead and take his advice rather than that of Akiko and Keira. [8]

2 Discuss all of the options that could be considered by management to deal with the issues raised by Zeke's informal leadership of this work group. Recommend the most appropriate option. [10]

1 **Self-awareness** – knowing what we feel is important and using that to guide decision-making. Having a realistic view of our own abilities and having self-confidence in our abilities.

2 **Self-management** – being able to recover quickly from stress, being trustworthy and conscientious, showing initiative and self-control.

3 **Social awareness** – sensing what others are feeling, being able to take their views into account and being able to get on with a wide range of people.

4 **Social skills** – handling emotions in relationships well and accurately understanding different social situations; using social skills to persuade, negotiate and lead.

Can you imagine working for a manager without these emotional intelligences – or with very low levels of them? Such a manager would:

- attempt projects beyond their abilities but lack self-confidence that targets would be met
- lack the trust and confidence of others and be so stressed out that they would be difficult to approach
- fail to take the views of others into account when taking decisions
- perform poorly in social situations, finding it difficult to talk and negotiate with others, and lacking the ability to build a team.

It would not be much fun would it? What is even more important, it would almost certainly lead to low levels of motivation, achievement and performance. They would, in brief, be poor managers and leaders.

Bus factory, Tanzania – an effectively led workforce will help a business towards achieving its objectives

Daniel Goleman is the best-known researcher into EI. He has suggested that there are four main EI competencies that managers should try to develop and improve on:

SUMMARY POINTS

- Managers perform many important functions within business organisations.
- 'Leadership' is not necessarily the same as 'management'.
- Most effective leaders have particular personal qualities.
- There are significant differences between the main leadership styles (or management styles).
- The most appropriate leadership style depends on many factors such as: type of business organisation, the experience of the manager, the task being undertaken and the attitude of managers towards the workforce.
- McGregor's Theory X and Theory Y is an attempt to classify the extreme views that can be held by managers about workers; these views will have a great influence on the styles of management adopted.
- Formal leaders are those appointed by more senior management.
- Informal leaders can have a great deal of influence on working groups.
- There are four key competencies used to assess emotional intelligence.

RESEARCH TASK

- Identify **four** different situations that could arise in your school or college, such as a fire, a decision about expansion, introducing a new subject to the curriculum and so on.
- Write a short report to your teacher on the leadership styles that could be most appropriate in the four situations you have identified, explaining reasons for your decisions.

AS Level exam practice questions
Short answer questions

[60 marks, 75 minutes]

Knowledge and understanding

1   Explain **three** functions of managers. [3]
2   Outline **two** personality characteristics that you think are important for a successful manager to have. [4]
3   Explain the autocratic style of management. [2]
4   Explain the differences between democratic and laissez-faire leadership styles. [4]
5   Differentiate between McGregor's Theory X and Theory Y approaches to management attitudes. [3]
6   Explain which style of leadership is likely to be used by managers who adopt the Theory X approach to workers. [4]
7   What is the difference between a formal and an informal leader? [2]
8   Why is it important for a management to recognise and, if possible, work with informal leaders? [5]
9   Would it be wise to always appoint informal leaders as formal managers or supervisors? Explain your answer. [5]

Application

10 Under what circumstances might the autocratic style of management be necessary? [3]
11 Explain how the manager of a multinational business operating in your country could demonstrate **four** of Mintzberg's roles of management. [8]
12 Would all workers prefer to operate under democratic management? Explain your answer with examples. [3]
13 Outline **two** of Goleman's emotional intelligence competencies and why they would be important skills for a manager of a hotel to have. [6]
14 Give examples to explain why one manager may need to adopt different styles of management in different circumstances. [5]
15 Under what circumstances would the laissez-faire style **not** be an appropriate style of management? [3]

Data response

1 Leadership styles at McNuggets

As one of the largest take-away food restaurant chains in Asia, McNuggets had established a reputation for cheap meals of consistent quality with rapid customer service. Research surveys had established that the public appreciated that, no matter which town or country they were in, they could always depend on buying exactly the same range of dishes, at similar prices, with the same quality standards. This reputation was built on a very detailed training programme for staff – failure to pass the test at the end of the course or failure to observe the methods and work practices taught would lead to demotion or dismissal. Every single activity of the workers was laid down in company regulations. Here is a list of just some of them:

- All customers to be greeted with the same welcome.
- Chicken nuggets to be cooked for exactly two minutes in oil at 100°C.
- A portion of French fries to contain 150 grams, to be salted with 10 grams of salt and to be kept for no more than five minutes before sale – they would then have to be disposed of.
- Staff to be trained to specialise in undertaking two tasks within the restaurant.

The managers at McNuggets recognised that their leadership style was autocratic but they prided themselves on the fact that they had 'thought of everything' and that workers did not have to use any initiative – all problems had been foreseen and there was a set procedure to deal with all of them. Workers were well looked after. The pay rate per hour was reasonable, there were free uniforms and staff meals, bonuses were paid to staff who, in the managers' view, had given the best customer service each month. Regular meetings were held at which information about branch performance was discussed with the staff. They were encouraged to air their views but they were told that they could not, under any circumstances, change the method of working laid down by McNuggets head office. Despite what the managers considered to be good working conditions, employee motivation seemed to be low with high labour turnover and absences were also a problem.

2 Google – leadership lessons from the billion-dollar brand

By any measure of business performance, Google is a standout company with a value of more than $270 billion in 2013. Perhaps the main reason for its superiority over other search engine businesses is its remarkable style of leadership. The founders, Larry Page and Sergey Brin were research academics when they started Google. Their background in academic work and their own preference for independent thinking have had a considerable impact on their leadership style.

This can be summed up as: empowering employees with laissez-faire leadership and encouraging them to come up with innovative ideas and implement them. Only the most able people are recruited and they expect – and are given – the freedom to be creative. There is a 70-20-10 time split for all Google employees: 70% of their time should be devoted to their core job, 20% to off-shoot projects from the core tasks and 10% free time pursuing any ideas that interest them. There are generous financial incentives for implementing new ideas. Google estimates that 50% of its innovative products are created in the free time that employees are given.

[30 marks, 45 minutes]

1 a Define the term 'autocratic leadership style'. [2]

b Briefly explain the term 'employee motivation'. [3]

2 Using your knowledge of leadership styles, how would you account for the apparent low levels of motivation at McNuggets restaurants? [6]

3 Explain how the leadership style could be adapted in an attempt to improve motivation of staff within these restaurants. [8]

4 To what extent is the style of leadership used at McNuggets appropriate for a business such as this? [11]

[30 marks, 45 minutes]

1 a Define the term 'laissez-faire leadership'. [2]

b Briefly explain the term 'financial incentives'. [3]

2 Explain the main features of two other styles of leadership. [6]

3 Analyse the benefits to Google of the leadership style used within the company. [8]

4 Discuss whether this leadership style would be appropriate for a banking business with many branches. [11]

AS Level essay questions

[20 marks, 45 minutes each]

1 a Outline the main functions of management. [8]

b Examine the view that the appropriate style of leadership varies with business circumstances. [12]

2 a Explain the differences between McGregor's Theory X and Theory Y. [8]

b Discuss the importance of emotional intelligence for a leader to be effective. [12]

11 Motivation

This chapter covers syllabus section AS Level 2.2.

On completing this chapter, you will be able to:

- understand what motivation is and why motivated workers are important to business organisations
- discuss the important contributions of motivational theorists and their relevance to businesses today
- understand the different methods used to motivate workers in practical business situations
- analyse the appropriateness of different payment systems and evaluate their impact on motivation
- assess the role of non-financial methods of motivation and evaluate their impact.

Introducing the topic

HOW IMPORTANT IS PAY FOR MOTIVATING WORKERS?

Many studies have been undertaken to try to explain what motivates workers. There seems to be some agreement that pay and benefits are important in encouraging staff to work well, but these are not necessarily the most important factors. Work enjoyment, work challenges and recognition for work well done – these are the factors most frequently quoted by employees when asked what keeps them with their current employer. Compared to job satisfaction and pay, benefits (financial and non-financial) have a smaller role in terms of recruitment, retention and motivation.

A recent employee survey led to the following response rate in answer to the question: What increases your morale and motivation?

Research carried out by the cell phone company O2 found that 85% of employees would be more loyal to their company if they were praised for their work and 100% suggested that they would stay in their jobs longer if thanked more often and more effectively. Just under 50% of workers had either never been thanked by their companies or could not remember the last time they were. Finally, 71% of workers said they would be willing to work harder if they got more recognition for the work they did.

Increased pay	65%
Increased bonuses	28%
Recognition from managers	22%
Career development through training	20%
Improved career prospects	17%
Option to work flexible hours	17%
Increased benefits, such as holidays/pensions/discounts	15%
Better work environment	11%
Help with childcare	7%
Option to work from home	6%

Points to think about:

- Why do you think a motivated workforce is important to any business?
- Explain why 'loyalty' and 'working harder' are important to a business of your choice.
- Why do you think 'recognition' is important to so many workers? Is it important to you?

Introduction

Motivation of workers has a direct impact on productivity and business efficiency. Managers need to understand what motivates employees to reach peak performance. This is not easy – different workers often respond in different ways to their jobs and the organisation's practices. Managing people has never been easy. In current conditions of rapid change and rising staff expectations of their experience at work, the effective management of people has become a major determining factor in influencing the success of business enterprises. Businesses that manage and motivate staff effectively will gain a loyal and productive workforce – this can be a real competitive advantage. This unit has as its major focus the theory and practice related to the motivation of working people.

What is motivation – and why does it matter?

In business, **motivation** means the desire of workers to see a job done quickly and well. Motivation results from the individual's desire to achieve objectives and to satisfy needs. The best-motivated workers will help an organisation achieve its objectives as cost-effectively as possible. Motivated workers will also be trying to reach their own personal goals. Employers need to be aware of what these are because the greatest motivation levels result from workers feeling that, through working towards the objectives of the organisation, they are achieving their own. Unmotivated staff will be reluctant to perform effectively and quickly and will offer nothing but the absolute minimum of what is expected. Motivation levels have a direct impact on the level of productivity and thus the competitiveness of the business. Highly motivated staff will be keen to stay with the firm, reducing the costs of labour turnover. They will be more likely to offer useful suggestions and to contribute in ways other than their contractual obligations. They will often actively seek promotion and responsibility. All of these benefits have an impact on business efficiency, levels of customer service and unit costs. A summary can be found in Figure 11.1. Some indicators of poor staff motivation are shown in Table 11.1.

> **KEY TERM**
>
> **Motivation:** the internal and external factors that stimulate people to take actions that lead to achieving a goal.

Figure 11.1 Gains from well-motivated staff

Absenteeism	deliberate absence for which there is not a satisfactory explanation; often follows a pattern
Lateness	often becomes habitual
Poor performance	poor-quality work; low levels of work or greater waste of materials
Accidents	poorly motivated workers are often more careless, concentrate less on their work or distract others, and this increases accidents
Labour turnover	people leave for reasons that are not positive; even if they do not get other jobs, they spend time in trying to do so
Grievances	there are more of them within the workforce and there might be more union disputes
Poor response rate	workers do not respond very well to orders or leadership and any response is often slow

Table 11.1 Some indicators of poor staff motivation

Motivation in theory: how can workers be motivated to work well?

There are many theories of motivation, but in this chapter we will concentrate on six of the best-known theorists. You are advised to read about others too and feel free to use the ideas of other theorists in situations you come across during your studies.

Content theories of motivation

These theories focus on the assumption that individuals are motivated by the desire to fulfil their inner needs. These approaches focus on these human needs that energise and direct human behaviour and how managers can create conditions that allow workers to satisfy them.

Taylor (1856–1915) and scientific management

F.W. Taylor made the first serious attempt to analyse worker motivation in order to advise management on the best ways to increase worker performance or productivity. The techniques he used – of establishing an idea or a hypothesis, studying and recording performance at work, altering working methods and rerecording performance – are still used in modern industry. This approach has become known as 'scientific management' due to the detailed recording and analysis of results that it involves.

Taylor's main aim was to reduce the level of inefficiency that existed in US manufacturing industry. Any productivity gains could then, he argued, be shared between business owners and workers. The scope for efficiency gains in early twentieth-century manufacturing plants was huge. The vast mass of workers was untrained and non-specialised. They were poorly led by supervisors and managers with little or no formal training in dealing with people. There was usually no formal selection or appraisal system of staff and many were recruited on a daily or weekly basis with no security of employment.

How to improve output per worker or productivity – Taylor's scientific approach

1　Select workers to perform a task.
2　Observe them performing the task and note the key elements of it.
3　Record the time taken to do each part of the task.
4　Identify the quickest method recorded.
5　Train all workers in this quickest method and do not allow them to make any changes to it.
6　Supervise workers to ensure that this 'best way' is being carried out and time them to check that the set time is not being exceeded.
7　Pay workers on the basis of results – based on the theory of economic man.

The theory of 'economic man' was widely held, and Taylor himself supported this notion. The view was that man was driven or motivated by money alone and the only factor that could stimulate further effort was the chance of earning extra money. This formed the basis of Taylor's main motivational suggestion – wage levels based on output. He always maintained that workers should be paid a 'fair day's pay for a fair day's work' and that the amount should be directly linked to output through a system known as 'piece rate'. This means paying workers a certain amount for each unit produced. To encourage high output, a low rate per unit can be set for the first units produced and then higher rates become payable if output targets are exceeded.

Results of Taylor's work

The results of Taylor's research revolutionised the way work was organised in many industries. The emphasis on increasing efficiency and productivity was greeted by industrial leaders as a route towards greater profits. Workers' leaders were more suspicious as they believed that it would lead to more work but no more pay or benefits. They did not necessarily believe Taylor's view that the fruits of higher efficiency would be shared between workers and business owners.

The Taylor approach was widely taken up by the manufacturers of the early twentieth century, where the first forms of mass production and flow-line techniques were being introduced. Workers specialising in one task, strict management control over work methods and payment by output levels were important features of successful production-line techniques. These principles were the driving forces behind all mass production until the 'Japanese style' of working and people management became more widespread from the 1960s onwards. Even before this, other research had been undertaken on people's behaviour at work and doubt was being cast on the simplistic nature of many of Taylor's assumptions about worker motivation. See Table 11.2 for an assessment of the practical relevance of Taylor's work to today's businesses.

Taylor's approach	Relevance to modern industry
Economic man	Some managers still believe that money is the only way to motivate staff. However, the more general view is that workers have a wide range of needs – not just money – that can be met, in part at least, from work.
Select the right people for each job	Before Taylor there had been few attempts to identify the principles of staff selection. The importance he gave to this is still reflected in the significance given to careful staff selection in nearly all businesses.
Observe and record the performance of staff	This was widely adopted and became known as 'time and motion study'. Regarded with suspicion by workers as a way of making them work harder, it is still employed as a technique but often with the cooperation and involvement of staff.
Establish the best method of doing a job – method study	Again, this is still accepted as being important as efficiency depends on the best ways of working being adopted. However, the Taylor approach of management giving instructions to workers with no discussion or feedback is considered to be undesirable. Worker participation in devising best work practices is now encouraged.
Piece-work payment systems	This is not now a widely used payment system. Quality may be sacrificed in the search for quantity – workers will vary output according to their financial needs at different times of year and it discourages them from accepting changes at work in case they lose some pay. In most of modern industry, especially service industries, it has become very difficult to identify the output of individual workers.

Table 11.2 Evaluating how relevant Taylor's views and methods are today

Ford factory in the 1930s – early mass-production manufacturers adopted Taylor's approach

Mayo (1880–1949) and the human relations theories

Elton Mayo is best known for his 'Hawthorne effect' conclusions. These were based on a series of experiments he and his team conducted over a five-year period at the Hawthorne factory of Western Electric Co. in Chicago. His work was initially based on the assumption that working conditions – lighting, heating, rest periods and so on – had a significant effect on workers' productivity. Experiments were undertaken to establish the optimum working conditions and, as in all good scientific practice, the output of a control group was also recorded and this group experienced no changes in working conditions at all. The results surprised all observers – as lighting and other conditions were changed, both improved and worsened, so productivity rose in *all* groups including the control group. This forced Mayo to accept that:

■ working conditions in themselves were not that important in determining productivity levels
■ other motivational factors needed to be investigated further before conclusions could be drawn.

Subsequent experiments were carried out with a group of assembly-line workers. Changes to rest periods, payment systems, assembly-bench layout and canteen food were made at 12-week intervals. Crucially, before every major change, the researchers discussed the new changes with the work group. At the end of the experiments, the working conditions and hours of work were returned to how they had been before the start of the trial. Output rose far above the original level.

Clearly, other motivational factors were operating to increase productivity completely separately from the conditions of work.

The Hawthorne effect – the conclusions of Mayo's work

Mayo drew the following conclusions from his work:

■ Changes in working conditions and financial rewards have little or no effect on productivity.
■ When management consult with workers and take an interest in their work, then motivation is improved.
■ Working in teams and developing a team spirit can improve productivity.
■ When some control over their own working lives is given to workers, such as deciding when to take breaks, there is a positive motivational effect.
■ Groups can establish their own targets or norms and these can be greatly influenced by the informal leaders of the group.

Evaluation of Mayo's research for today's businesses

Since Mayo's findings were published, there has been a trend towards giving workers more of a role in business decision-making – this is called participation. Personnel departments, which hardly existed in the early years of the twentieth century, were established to try to put the 'Hawthorne effect' into practice.

Team-working and group-working can be applied in many types of modern business organisations and these offer the greatest opportunities for workers and firms to benefit from the Hawthorne effect.

The idea of involving workers, taking an interest in their welfare and finding out their individual goals has opened up new fields of research for industrial psychologists and this area of study is now regarded as an important component of university business courses.

This development of the 'people' side of business has taken industry away from the engineer-focused and purely money-motivated views of Taylor. This trend was sustained by the work of two other famous researchers, Maslow and Herzberg.

Maslow (1908–1970) and the hierarchy of human needs

Abraham Maslow's research was not based solely on people in the work environment and his findings have significance for students of psychology and sociology too. He was concerned with trying to identify and classify the main needs that humans have. The importance of his work to business managers is this: our needs determine our actions – we will always try to satisfy them and we will be motivated to do so. If work can be organised so that we can satisfy some or all of our needs at work, then we will become more productive and satisfied. Maslow summarised these human needs in the form of a hierarchy (see Figure 11.2 and Table 11.3).

This hierarchy was interpreted by Maslow as follows:

- Individuals' needs start on the lowest level.
- Once one level of need has been satisfied, humans will strive to achieve the next level.
- **Self-actualisation**, or self-fulfilment, is not reached by many people, but everyone is capable of reaching their potential.
- Once a need has been satisfied, it will no longer motivate individuals to action – thus, when material needs have been satisfied, the offer of more money will not increase productivity.
- Reversion is possible – it is possible for satisfaction at one level to be withdrawn, for example a loss of job security, and for individuals to move down to the next level.

 KEY TERM

Self-actualisation: a sense of self-fulfilment reached by feeling enriched and developed by what one has learned and achieved.

Limitations of Maslow's approach

Criticisms of Maslow's hierarchy include:

- Not everyone has the same needs as is assumed by the hierarchy.
- In practice it can be very difficult to identify the degree to which each need has been met and which level a worker is on.
- Money is necessary to satisfy physical needs, yet it might also play a role in satisfying the other levels of needs, such as status and esteem.
- Self-actualisation is never permanently achieved – as some observers of the hierarchy have suggested. Jobs must continually offer challenges and opportunities for fulfilment, otherwise regression will occur.

ACTIVITY 11.1

[18 marks, 25 minutes]

1 Analyse the similarities and differences you consider exist between the research findings of Mayo and those of Maslow. **[8]**

2 Discuss how knowledge of the Hawthorne effect **and** Maslow's hierarchy of human needs could be used by the manager of a clothing factory to improve motivation of workers. **[10]**

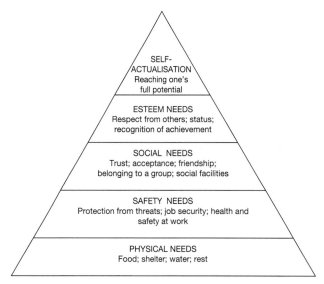

Figure 11.2 Maslow's hierarchy of needs

Level of need	How needs may be satisfied at work
Self-actualisation – fulfilment of potential	challenging work that stretches the individual – this will give a sense of achievement; opportunities to develop and apply new skills will increase potential
Esteem needs	recognition for work done well – status, advancement and responsibility will gain the respect of others
Social needs	working in teams or groups and ensuring good communication to make workers feel involved
Safety needs	a contract of employment with some job security – a structured organisation that gives clear lines of authority to reduce uncertainty; ensuring health and safety conditions are met
Physical needs	income from employment high enough to meet essential needs

Table 11.3 Significance of the hierarchy of needs to today's businesses

Herzberg (1923–2000) and the 'two-factor theory'

Despite basing his research on just 200 professionally qualified workers, Frederick Herzberg's conclusions and famous two-factor theory had the greatest impact on motivational practices since Taylor's work almost 60 years earlier. His research was based around questionnaires and interviews with employees with the intention of discovering:

- those factors that led to them having very good feelings about their jobs
- those factors that led to them having very negative feelings about their jobs.

His conclusions were:

- Job satisfaction resulted from five main factors – achievement, recognition for achievement, the work itself, responsibility and advancement. He called these factors the '**motivators**'. He considered the last three to be the most significant.
- Job dissatisfaction also resulted from five main factors – company policy and administration, supervision, salary, relationships with others and working conditions. He termed these '**hygiene factors**'. These were the factors that surround the job itself (extrinsic factors) rather than the work itself (intrinsic factors). Herzberg considered that the hygiene factors had to be addressed by management to prevent dissatisfaction, but, even if they were in place, they would not, by themselves, create a well-motivated workforce.

KEY TERMS

Motivating factors (motivators): aspects of a worker's job that can lead to positive job satisfaction, such as achievement, recognition, meaningful and interesting work and advancement at work.

Hygiene factors: aspects of a worker's job that have the potential to cause dissatisfaction, such as pay, working conditions, status and over-supervision by managers.

The consequences of Herzberg's two-factor theory for today's businesses

1. Pay and working conditions can be improved and these will help to remove dissatisfaction about work; but they will not, on their own, provide conditions for motivation to exist. Herzberg argued that it is possible to encourage someone to do a job by paying them – he called this movement. However, movement does not mean that someone wants to do the job – that would require motivation. Motivation to do the job, and to do it well, would exist only if the motivators were in place. Herzberg did not claim that pay does not matter, but that it moves people to do a job and does not motivate them to do it well.

2. The motivators need to be in place for workers to be prepared to work willingly and to always do their best. Herzberg suggested that they could be provided by adopting the principles of '**job enrichment**'. There are three main features of job enrichment and, if these were adopted, then the motivators would be available for all workers to benefit from:

   - **Complete units of work:** Typical mass production methods leave workers to assemble one small part of the finished product. This is not rewarding, can be boring and repetitive and prevents the worker from appreciating the importance of what they are doing as part of the overall production system. Herzberg argued that complete and identifiable units of work should be assigned to workers, and that this might involve teams of workers rather than individuals on their own. These complete units of work could be whole sub-assemblies of manufactured goods, such as a complete engine assembly in a car plant. In service industries it could mean that a small team of multiskilled people, such as waiters, chefs and technicians for IT/video equipment, provide all of the conference facilities in a hotel for a business conference rather than many people doing just one small and relatively unimportant task before moving on to another part of the hotel. 'If you want people motivated to do a good job, give them a good job to do,' as Herzberg put it.
   - **Feedback on performance:** This type of communication could give recognition for work well done and could provide incentives to achieve even more.
   - **A range of tasks:** To give challenge and to stretch the individual, a range of tasks should be given, some of which may be, at least initially, beyond the workers' current experience. This, in quite a large measure, ties in with the 'self-actualisation' level in Maslow's hierarchy.

3. A business could offer higher pay, improved working conditions and less heavy-handed supervision of work. These would all help to remove dissatisfaction but they would all be quickly taken for granted. If work is not interesting, rewarding or challenging, then workers will not be satisfied or motivated to offer their full potential whatever the pay level offered to them.

Evaluation of Herzberg's work

Although other researchers who have used Herzberg's methods have failed to arrive at quite such clear-cut conclusions, there is little doubt that the results he drew from his work have had a significant impact on business practices.

Team-working is now much more widespread, with whole units of work being delegated to these groups. Workers tend to be made much more responsible for the quality of their own work rather than being closely supervised by a quality-controlling inspectorate.

Most firms are continually looking for ways to improve effective communication, and group meetings allowing two-way communication are often favoured.

KEY TERM

Job enrichment: aims to use the full capabilities of workers by giving them the opportunity to do more challenging and fulfilling work.

Three workers discuss the work they do in their different businesses

Maria was a self-employed market researcher. She earned a reasonable salary but it was not the same every month as it depended on how much work she had been able to gain. 'I really like my work as it is very interesting and I am very much appreciated by the firms I work for. I do not work with a regular team of people, but that does not bother me. I earn enough for my needs and I would not take a higher-paid job in a large firm as I do not like being told what to do by supervisors.'

Asif's experience was different. He worked in a shop. He enjoyed the group of friends he worked with and really felt part of the team. He thought the money was good too. However, he considered that his work was not appreciated and was not challenging enough. 'I would look for another job that gave me more responsibility and recognition, but for the present I do not want to give up the friends I have made. The interesting jobs, like displaying stock and deciding on which new items should be sold, are all done by the managers.' Imran spoke up too, 'You are both very lucky. My present job is only temporary, and, although the pay is reasonable, I have been told that my contract could end at any time. I am very keen to find a more permanent position.'

[18 marks, 25 minutes]

1 Analyse which level of Maslow's hierarchy each of these workers seems to be on at present. Explain your answer. [8]

2 Discuss Asif's current level of motivation and how it could be increased by referring to Herzberg's 'hygiene factors' and 'motivators'. [10]

It would be wrong to conclude that this is all Herzberg's doing, but there is little doubt that his work and the publicity given to the research conclusions led to a hastening of the trends that may have occurred much more slowly without his intervention.

McClelland (1917–1998) and motivational needs theory

A doctor of psychology, David McClelland pioneered workplace motivational thinking, developed achievement-based motivational theory and promoted improvements in employee assessment methods. He is best known for describing three types of motivational need, which he identified in his book, *The Achieving Society* (1961).

1 **Achievement motivation (n-ach):** A person with the strong motivational need for achievement will seek to reach realistic and challenging goals and job advancement. There is a constant need for feedback regarding progress and achievement and a need for a sense of accomplishment. Research has suggested that this result-driven attitude is almost always a common characteristic of successful business people and entrepreneurs.

2 **Authority/power motivation (n-pow):** A person with this dominant need is 'authority motivated'. The desire to control others is a powerful motivating force – the need to be influential, effective and to make an impact. There is a strong leadership instinct and when authority is gained over others, it brings personal status and prestige.

3 **Affiliation motivation (n-affil):** The person with need for affiliation as the strongest driver or motivator has a need for friendly relationships and is motivated towards interaction with other people. These people tend to be good team members – there is a need to be liked and popular and to be held in high regard.

McClelland stated that these three needs are found to varying degrees in all workers and managers. The mix of motivational needs characterises a person's or manager's behaviour, both in terms of what motivates them and how they believe other people should be motivated. McClelland firmly believed that 'achievement-motivated' people are generally the ones who make things happen and get results. However, they can demand too much of their staff in the achievement of targets and prioritise this above the many and varied needs of their workers.

Process theories

Process theories emphasise how and why people choose certain behaviours in order to meet their personal goals and the thought processes that influence behaviour. Process theories study what people are thinking about when they decide whether or not to put effort into a particular activity. A study of all of the main process theories – expectancy theory, equity theory, goal-setting theory and reinforcement theory – is beyond the scope of the CIE syllabus and therefore of this book. We will

What people want from work

'I was asked by the principal of my university to help form a committee of ten lecturers to discuss holiday dates, student enrolment and ways to check on the quality of lectures. He told us it was a very important committee, we would receive recognition for our time and our views would influence future decisions. We had many meetings, agreed and wrote a report and sent it to the principal. We heard nothing back – no feedback, no thanks and no decisions made on our recommendations. I would not do it again if I was asked.' Can you believe how demotivated these lecturers were? They had been misled about the degree to which the extra effort they put in to attending these meetings would be responded to by the principal.

According to Bob Nelson, a reward and motivation guru, giving people what they want from work is quite easy – even though it depends on the type of work situation and on the individual person. He thinks that people want:

- some control of their work – job enrichment, responsibility for a well-defined task, recognition for achievement
- to receive feedback and to understand how managers take decisions – good communications from management and some participation opportunities
- the opportunity for growth and development – education, career paths, team-working
- leadership – providing clear expectations, structure and appropriate rewards if these expectations are met.

Of course, money is important, but once workers have satisfied their essential needs from money, they look for other things from work. According to Susan Heathfield (humanresources. about.com), 'Most people want involvement in decisions that affect their work. People who contribute ideas should be recognised and rewarded. True employee involvement is based on the expectation that people are competent to make decisions about their work every single day on the job.'

[22 marks, 30 minutes]

1 Analyse how these two sets of views can be applied to the work of Herzberg, Vroom or McClelland. [8]

2 Discuss how the views contained in the extract above could be applied in practice to:

a a restaurant
b a food shop
c teaching staff at a school or college. [14]

consider just one of the best-known process theorists, Victor Vroom.

Vroom (1932–) and expectancy theory

Vroom suggested that individuals choose to behave in ways that they believe will lead to outcomes they value. His expectancy theory states that individuals have different sets of goals and can be motivated if they believe that:

- there is a positive link between effort and performance
- favourable performance will result in a desirable reward
- the reward will satisfy an important need
- the desire to satisfy the need is strong enough to make the work effort worthwhile.

His expectancy theory is based on the following three beliefs:

1 **Valence:** The depth of the want of an employee for an extrinsic reward, such as money, or an intrinsic reward, such as satisfaction.

2 **Expectancy:** The degree to which people believe that putting effort into work will lead to a given level of performance.

3 **Instrumentality:** The confidence of employees that they will actually get what they desire, even if it has been promised by the manager.

Even if just one of these conditions or beliefs is missing, then, Vroom argued, workers will not have the motivation to do the job well. Therefore, according to Vroom, managers should try to ensure that employees believe that increased work effort will improve performance and that this performance will lead to valued rewards.

Motivational theories – how useful are they?

They provide us with a starting point and a framework for analysing and discussing the main motivational issues. The research undertaken has been criticised for its lack of rigour and follow-up work, yet the basic ideas that have been covered in this chapter are still talked about and evaluated many years after the initial findings were published.

It is important not to spend too long describing research methods. It is more important to identify the most appropriate theory to the question set and to explain the relevance of it to managers who have responsibility for motivating staff. It is the application of the motivational theorists' ideas and the potential difficulties in applying them to certain situations that contribute to a successful answer.

TOP TIP

If you are answering a question about motivational theorists, try to do more than just list their main findings – apply their ideas to the business situation given.

KEY CONCEPT LINK

A well-motivated workforce is essential for long-term business success. Motivating workers is an important function of **management** and without this, long-term **value** is unlikely to be created by a business.

ACTIVITY 11.4

[20 marks, 30 minutes]

1   Explain **four** reasons why it is important for your school or college to have well-motivated teachers.   [8]

2   Discuss the importance of the work of any **two** motivational theorists to improving the motivation of employees in a retail store.   [12]

Motivation in practice: introduction

Very few people would be prepared to work without financial reward, although the considerable numbers of charity workers should not be overlooked. Pay is necessary to encourage work effort – all theorists recognise this. The disagreements – particularly between Taylorite views and the others – is over whether pay is *sufficient* to generate motivation and how pay should be calculated. If pay is accepted as being insufficient to ensure that workers are motivated to work to their full potential, then other non-financial methods need to be considered. The attraction of these

is obvious: if they can promote motivation without adding to the pay bill, then unit costs should fall and competitiveness increase. There are many links between how work is organised to boost motivation and the style of management and organisational structure of the business.

Payment or financial reward systems

The most common payment systems are:

- hourly or time-based wage rate
- piece rate
- salary
- commission
- performance-related pay and bonuses
- profit sharing
- fringe benefits.

Time-based wage rate

This is the most common way of paying manual, clerical and 'non-management' workers.

A time-based wage rate or 'time rate' is set for the job – perhaps by comparing with other firms or similar jobs – and the total wage level is determined by multiplying this by the time periods worked. The time period used is usually an hour so it becomes the 'hourly wage rate' and the total wage is often paid weekly. This method offers some security to workers but it is not directly linked to the level of output or effort.

KEY TERM

Time based wage rate: payment to a worker made for each period of time worked, e.g. one hour.

Piece rate

A rate is fixed for the production of each unit, and the workers' wages therefore depend on the quantity of output produced. The piece rate can be adjusted to reflect the difficulty of the job and the 'standard' time needed to complete it. These issues are determined by work study. The level of the rate can be very important. If set too low, it could demotivate the workers, but, if too high, it could reduce the incentives – because workers will be able to meet their target wage level by producing relatively few units (See Table 11.4).

KEY TERM

Piece rate: a payment to a worker for each unit produced.

Advantages	Disadvantages
■ It encourages greater effort and faster working.	■ It requires output to be measurable and standardised – if each product is different, then piece work is inappropriate.
■ The labour cost for each unit is determined in advance and this helps to set a price for the product.	■ It may lead to falling quality and safety levels as workers rush to complete units.
	■ Workers may settle for a certain pay level and will therefore not be motivated to produce more than a certain level.
	■ It provides little security over pay level, for example in the event of a production breakdown.
	■ Workers are discouraged from accepting change at work as this might result in loss of pay.

Table 11.4 Advantages and disadvantages of the piece rate pay system

Job grade	Salary band (per year)
E, e.g. regional heads	$50,000–75,900
D, e.g. departmental heads	$30,000–49,900
C, e.g. office managers	$20,000–29,900
B, e.g. secretaries	$10,000–19,900
A, e.g. junior clerical staff	$5,000–9,900

Table 11.5 Salary bands – typical example

Advantages	Disadvantages
■ It gives security of income. ■ It gives status compared to time-rate or piece-rate payment systems. ■ It aids in costing – the salaries will not vary for one year. ■ It is suitable for jobs where output is not measurable. ■ It is suitable for management positions where staff are expected to put in extra time to complete a task or assignment.	■ Income is not related to effort levels or productivity. ■ It may lead to complacency of the salary earner. ■ Regular appraisal may be needed to assess whether an individual should move up a salary band, although this could be an advantage if this becomes a positive form of worker appraisal.

Table 11.6 Advantages and disadvantages of a salary

Salary

A salary is the most common form of payment for professional, supervisory and management staff. The salary level is fixed each year and it is not dependent on the number of hours worked (time rate) or the number of units produced (piece rate). The fixing of the salary level for each job is a very important process because it helps to determine the status of that post in the whole organisation. Job evaluation techniques may be used to assist in deciding the salary bands and the differences between them (see Table 11.5). In most organisations, all jobs will be put into one of a number of salary bands and the precise income earned within each band will depend upon experience and progress. It is always possible to gain promotion to another job in a higher salary band. Firms that are interested in creating a 'single status' within their organisation are now increasingly putting all staff – manual and managerial – on to annual salaries to give the benefits of security and status to all employees. Table 11.6 outlines the advantages and disadvantages of salary pay systems.

Commission

This is most frequently used in personal selling, where the salesperson is paid a **commission** or a proportion of the sales gained.

KEY TERM

Commission: a payment to a sales person for each sale made.

It can make up 100% of the total income – reducing security as there is no 'basic' or flat-rate payment if nothing is sold during a particular period – or it can be in addition to a base salary. It has the same advantages and disadvantages as piece rates used in production industries except that the potential drawback of 'low quality of production' can be replaced by the risk that sales staff could try too hard to convince a customer to buy and put so much pressure on them that they have a bad view of the whole company. Also, teamwork is not encouraged with

KEY TERM

Salary: annual income that is usually paid on a monthly basis.

commission-based pay – each individual salesperson will be keen to grab each new customer for themselves to earn more commission.

Bonus payments

A **bonus** payment is usually made to employees in addition to their contracted wage or salary. While the base salary usually is a fixed amount per month, bonus payments may be paid in addition based on criteria agreed between managers and workers (or trade unions), such as the increase in output, productivity or annual turnover, or the net number of additional customers acquired.

KEY TERM

Bonus: a payment made in addition to the contracted wage or salary.

Performance-related pay (PRP)

Performance-related pay is usually in the form of a bonus payable in addition to the basic salary. It is widely used for those workers whose output is not measurable in quantitative terms, such as management, supervisory and clerical posts. It requires the following procedure:

- Regular target-setting, establishing specific objectives for the individual.
- Annual appraisals of the worker's performance against the pre-set targets.
- Paying each worker a bonus according to the degree to which the targets have been exceeded.

KEY TERM

Performance-related pay: a bonus scheme to reward staff for above-average work performance.

The main aim is to provide further financial incentives and to encourage staff to meet agreed targets. Bonuses are usually paid on an individual basis but they can also be calculated and awarded on the basis of teams or even whole departments.

There are problems with PRP schemes. The main issue is one that Herzberg would recognise – does the chance of additional pay 'motivate' or just temporarily 'move' a worker to perform better? As there is no change in the nature of the work being undertaken, most of the 'motivators' recognised by Herzberg would not be satisfied by PRP. In addition, the concentration on individual performance can create divisions within teams and groups, and this can work against the findings of the Hawthorne effect. There is also a widely held view that

PRP bonuses are often inadequate, even to achieve short-term productivity gains or improvements in effort. The last problem concerns the style of management that PRP can lead to. By giving senior managers the power to decide which subordinates have achieved performances above target, it can lead to claims of favouritism and the ability to control staff by means of the 'carrot' of extra rewards. Table 11.7 outlines the advantages and disadvantages of performance-related pay.

Profit sharing

This scheme shares some of the company profits not just with the shareholders but also with the workers.

KEY TERM

Profit sharing: a bonus for staff based on the profits of the business – usually paid as a proportion of basic salary.

The essential idea behind profit-sharing arrangements is that staff will feel more committed to the success of the business and will strive to achieve higher performances and cost savings. Some shareholder groups, however, claim that profits should be the return to the owners of the business and are a reward to them for taking risks with their own capital. Some profit-sharing schemes do not offer cash but shares in the business to each worker when the firm declares a profit. This is designed to establish the workers as part owners of the business and reduce the conflict that might exist between 'them' (the owners and managers) and 'us' (the workers). In practice, many of the shares in such schemes are quickly sold by the workers, thus reducing the hoped-for long-term impact on motivation. See Table 11.8 for a summary of the advantages and disadvantages of profit sharing and worker share ownership.

Fringe benefits

These are non-cash forms of reward – and there are many alternatives that can be used. They include company cars, free insurance and pension schemes, private health insurance, discounts on company products and low interest rate loans. They are used by businesses in addition to normal payment systems in order to give status to higher-level employees and to recruit and retain the best staff. Some of these **fringe benefits** are taxed,

KEY TERM

Fringe benefits: benefits given, separate from pay, by an employer to some or all employees.

but others are not and that gives the employees an added benefit, because to purchase these 'perks' from after-tax income would be very expensive. As no cash changes hand between the employer and the employee, these are sometimes classified as non-financial benefits – although they do, obviously, have financial value.

Non-financial methods of motivation

It is now widely recognised that money alone will not create the motivation to complete jobs efficiently that all businesses are looking for in employees. The range of non-financial motivators is very extensive and this section concentrates on the most widely adopted ones. These are:

- job rotation
- job enlargement
- job enrichment
- job redesign
- training
- quality circles
- worker participation
- team-working
- target setting
- delegation
- empowerment.

Job rotation

Job rotation should not be confused with job enrichment. Rotation may relieve the boredom of doing one task and it

KEY TERM

Job rotation: increasing the flexibility of employees and the variety of work they do by switching from one job to another.

Advantages	Disadvantages
■ Staff are motivated to improve performance if they are seeking increases in financial rewards.	■ It can fail to motivate if staff are not driven by the need to earn additional financial rewards.
■ Target-setting can help to give purpose and direction to the work of an individual.	■ Team spirit can be damaged by the rivalry generated by the competitive nature of PRP.
■ Annual appraisal offers the opportunity for feedback on the performance of an individual, but as it tends to occur only once a year this is not usually sufficient to achieve a key feature of job enrichment.	■ Claims of manager favouritism can harm manager–subordinate relationships. ■ It may lead to increased control over staff by managers because of the danger that bonuses may not be awarded if workers do not conform.

Table 11.7 Advantages and disadvantages of performance-related pay

Advantages	Disadvantages
■ Potential conflict between owners and workers is reduced as everyone now has an interest in higher profits.	■ The reward offered is not closely related to individual effort – why should one worker put in greater effort when everyone will be benefiting?
■ They are designed to lead to higher worker effort levels and a greater preparedness to accept cost reduction measures and changes that benefit the business.	■ The schemes can be costly to set up and operate, especially in large firms with many employees.
■ The business is likely to attract better recruits drawn by the chance of sharing profits or owning shares in the firm.	■ Small profit shares paid at the end of the financial year are unlikely to promote motivation throughout the year.
■ As the bonuses are paid out of profits, the scheme does not add to business costs, unlike a normal increase in pay levels.	■ Profit-sharing schemes will reduce profits available to be paid to owners (reducing dividends) and to be reinvested in the business (retained earnings).
■ If successful in increasing motivation, then the schemes could lead to an increase in overall business profitability.	■ Worker share-ownership schemes can increase the total number of shares issued and dilute the value of existing shares.

Table 11.8 Advantages and disadvantages of profit sharing and worker share ownership

can give the worker multiskills, which makes the workforce more flexible, but it does not, by itself, increase empowerment or responsibility for the work being performed. In addition, it does not necessarily give a worker a complete unit of work to perform, but just a series of separate tasks.

ACTIVITY 11.5

Business expansion needs workforce support

Ursula and Jin-Ho had established their retail store selling mobile phones six years earlier. They were now ready to embark on an ambitious expansion programme. This involved opening three new stores a year. They had sufficient capital but they were worried about the staffing needs for these extra stores. How should they attract and keep the best staff? Ursula wanted to make the new store managers fully responsible for the performance of each branch and to reward them with a 'share-option' scheme that would give them the chance to buy company shares at a discount. In addition, she wanted a profit-sharing scheme for all employees. This would involve sharing 20% of annual profits among all the staff in proportion to their annual salaries. Jin-Ho was not keen on either proposal. He suggested a commission-based pay scheme for the shop staff and a performance-related pay bonus system for the managers. The bonus would be paid if the managers reached the annual sales targets that would be set, taking the area and size of each shop into account. He was unhappy about taking profits out of the business. 'As it is still a young company with ambitious growth plans we need to reward our existing shareholders, including ourselves, and put as much back into the firm as possible,' he said. Whichever system they adopted they both agreed that it would have to encourage all staff to contribute fully to the future success of the business.

[30 marks, 45 minutes]

1 Explain the differences between the payment systems mentioned in this case study. [6]

2 Analyse the advantages of each of these two proposed payment schemes. [9]

3 Using all of the information available to you and your knowledge of payment schemes, recommend and justify suitable pay systems for shop workers and managers. [15]

ACTIVITY 11.6

[20 marks, 30 minutes]
For each of the following groups of workers, recommend to management a suitable method of financial payment. Explain your recommendations.

a Shop assistants in a clothing store

b Bank managers

c Teachers

d Car mechanics in a car repair workshop [20]

Job enlargement

Job enlargement can include both job rotation and job enrichment, but it also refers to increasing the 'loading' of tasks on existing workers, perhaps as a result of shortage of staff or redundancies. It is unlikely to lead to long-term job satisfaction, unless the principles of job enrichment are adopted.

 KEY TERM

Job enlargement: attempting to increase the scope of a job by broadening or deepening the tasks undertaken.

Job enrichment

The process often involves a reduction of direct supervision as workers take more responsibility for their own work and are allowed some degree of decision-making authority. Herzberg's findings formed the basis of the job-enrichment principle. The three key features of it are not always easy to apply in practice, but employers are increasingly recognising the benefits to be gained by attempting to implement them:

1 Complete units of work so that the contribution of the worker can be identified and more challenging work offered – for example, cell production.

2 Direct feedback on performance to allow each worker to have an awareness of their own progress – for example, two-way communication.

3 Challenging tasks offered as part of a range of activities, some of which are beyond the worker's recent experience – these tasks will require training and the learning of new skills. Gaining further skills and qualifications is a form of gaining status and recognition – see Maslow's hierarchy of human needs.

Different jobs, different pay systems

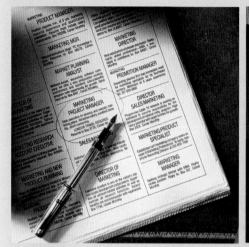 

Job adverts

SIX-FIGURE SALARY (AT LEAST $100,000) +
SUBSTANTIAL FRINGE BENEFITS

CAR, INSURANCE, PENSION, HEALTH CARE

Human Resources Director – Singapore
Diverse Portfolio of International Businesses

Our client is an undisputed leader in the private equity market. It has financed the acquisition of a wide variety of businesses with a presence in more than 50 countries, an annual turnover in excess of £3.5 billion and 50,000 employees. Key to the group's success has been its close financial management and the assistance it has given portfolio companies in areas such as human resources and IT. Due to continuing growth, an HR Director is now sought to add value across the group.

THE POSITION

■ Optimise the deployment of HR to add value within the portfolio businesses and support the group's overall objectives.

■ Provide business and HR support to operating company management teams. Emphasis on management development, leadership teams and compensation.

■ Active involvement in evaluation of potential acquisition targets. Provide critical analysis of management strengths and weaknesses.

QUALIFICATIONS

■ Outstanding HR professional with a minimum of 15 years' experience, a demonstrable record at group and divisional levels in an international business.

■ Practical understanding of business drivers and HR issues within large and small organisations. Highly influential with outstanding business management tool kit.

■ Specific experience in Asia is required, with fluency in an Asian language a distinct advantage.

Please send full CV and current salary details to
S. Amm at the address below.
Alternatively email: samm@partnership.com

THE PACIFIC RECRUITMENT AGENCY
DRIVER WANTED

■ Must have clean driving licence
■ Light removal work
■ $5 per hour
■ Overalls provided
■ Ring: 0837 5108 if interested

[12 marks, 15 minutes]

1 Explain the different pay systems operated by these two businesses for these jobs. [4]

2 Why do you think that these pay systems are different? [4]

3 Why do you think that the higher-paid post also carries a range of other benefits? [4]

Job redesign

Clearly, **job redesign** is closely linked to job enrichment. Journalists now have to be IT experts to communicate through the wide range of technological media. Bank employees are encouraged and trained to sell financial products to customers – not just to serve at tills. Hairdressers may be given opportunities to add beauty therapies as part of their total job skills. All of these are examples of how adding – and sometimes removing – certain tasks and functions can lead to more rewarding work.

> **KEY TERM**
>
> **Job redesign:** involves the restructuring of a job – usually with employees' involvement and agreement – to make work more interesting, satisfying and challenging.

Production lines (see Figure 11.3) have been reorganised in many factories, and team-working introduced in many industries to more easily allow for job redesign and for job enrichment ideas to be introduced (see Figure 11.4). These job changes can lead to improved recognition by management for the work undertaken by workers and can increase workers' chances of gaining promotion as a result of the wider skills gained.

Training

Improving and developing the skills of employees is an important motivator. It increases the status of workers and gives them a better chance of promotion to more challenging – and probably better paid – jobs within the business. It is often an important incentive for employees to stay with a business as they feel that they are being fully developed and appreciated by the company. Training can also, however, lead to employees leaving a business as they are now better qualified to gain employment within other companies.

Quality circles

Quality circles originated in Japan but they have been widely adopted in industry in most countries.

> **KEY TERM**
>
> **Quality circles:** voluntary groups of workers who meet regularly to discuss work-related problems and issues.

They are not just concerned with quality, although improving quality of the product or service can be a major benefit. The meetings are not formally led by managers or supervisors, they are informal and all workers are encouraged to contribute to discussions. As the workers

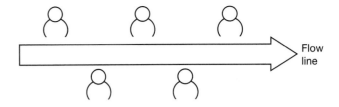

Figure 11.3 Traditional mass production – each worker performs a single task

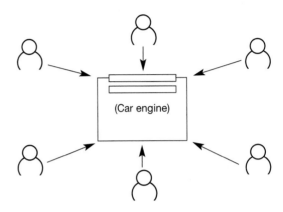

Figure 11.4 Team production allowing for job enrichment – all workers contribute to producing the completed unit

151

have hands-on experience of the issues being discussed, it is often the case that one of the production team will arrive at the best solution to a problem. Results of the quality-circle meetings are presented to management and really successful ideas are often implemented, not just in that factory but also across the whole organisation. Workers are usually paid for attending and the most successful circles may be rewarded with a team prize. Quality circles are a successful method of allowing the participation of all staff and they fit in well with Herzberg's ideas of workers accepting responsibility and being offered challenging tasks.

Worker participation

Worker participation can be introduced at different levels of a business operation. Workers can be encouraged to become involved in decision-making at the team or work group levels. Opportunities for worker participation in a workshop or factory might include involvement in decisions on break times, job allocations to different workers, job redesign, ways to improve quality and ways to cut down wastage and improve productivity.

> **KEY TERM**
>
> **Worker participation:** workers are actively encouraged to become involved in decision-making within the organisation.

At the level of strategic decision-making, workers could be encouraged to participate through electing a 'worker director' to the board of directors or selecting worker representatives to speak for employees at works council meetings. The benefits of participation include job enrichment, improved motivation and greater opportunities for workers to show responsibility. In addition, better decisions could result from worker involvement as they have in-depth knowledge of operations – and some managers lack this.

The limitations of participation are that it may be time-consuming to involve workers in every decision. Autocratic managers would find it hard to adapt to the idea of asking workers for their opinions – they may set up a participation system but have no intention of actually responding to workers' input. This approach could eventually prove to be very demotivating for workers.

Team-working

This approach to work places each member of staff into a small team of employees. Some traditionalists argue that moving away from 'pure division of labour', where one worker performs just one simple task all of the time, will result in lower productivity and time-wasting team meetings. Supporters of job enrichment would respond by claiming that more challenging and interesting work, as allowed by team-working or 'cell' production (see Chapter 26), will lead to:

- lower labour turnover
- more and better ideas from the workforce on improving the product and the manufacturing process
- consistently higher quality, especially when total quality management (TQM, see Chapter 26) is incorporated.

KEY TERM

Team-working: production is organised so that groups of workers undertake complete units of work.

Table 11.9 outlines the advantages and disadvantages of team-working.

TOP TIP
Team-working might not always be a suitable method to organise a workforce. Some very good workers do not make effective team members.

Target setting

This is clearly related to the technique of management by objectives (Chapter 13). As well as making work more interesting and rewarding, the purpose of target setting is to enable direct feedback to workers on how their performance compares with agreed objectives. The basic idea behind this is that people are more likely to do well when they are working towards a goal that they helped to establish and identify.

Delegation and empowerment

These methods of staff motivation are fully examined in Chapter 14. They involve the passing down of authority to perform tasks to workers, although empowerment goes further, by allowing workers some degree of control over how the task should be undertaken.

Advantages	Disadvantages
■ Workers are likely to be better motivated as social and esteem needs (see Maslow) are more likely to be met. By empowering workers within teams, job enrichment can be achieved (see Herzberg). ■ Better-motivated staff should increase productivity and reduce labour turnover – both will help to reduce business costs. ■ Team-working makes fuller use of all of the talents of the workforce. Better solutions to problems will be found as those most closely connected with the work participate in suggesting answers. ■ Team-working can reduce management costs as it is often associated with delayering of the organisation – fewer middle managers will be required. ■ Complete units of work can be given to teams – a key feature of job enrichment.	■ Not everyone is a team player – some individuals are more effective working alone. When teams are formed, this point must be considered and training may need to be offered to team members who are not used to working collaboratively in groups. Some workers may feel left out of the team meetings unless there are good efforts to involve and encourage all team members. ■ Teams can develop a set of values and attitudes which may contrast or conflict with those of the organisation itself, particularly if there is a dominant personality in the group. Teams will need clear goals and assessment procedures to ensure that they are working towards the objectives of the organisation at all times. ■ The introduction of team-working will require training costs to be incurred and there may be some disruption to production as the teams establish themselves.

Table 11.9 Advantages and disadvantages of working in teams

KEY CONCEPT LINK

Many managers believe that non-financial motivational methods will create more **value** than 'just paying workers more'. Why might this be true?

Evaluation of payment systems and non-financial motivational methods

If it is accepted that pay is not the only motivating factor for people to work effectively and to be satisfied in their jobs, then managers need to take a critical look at all of the payment and non-financial methods of motivating staff. What works for some groups of workers will not be effective with others. Managers need to be flexible and adapt the methods and approaches that are available to motivate staff to the particular circumstances of their business and their workforce. The main factors that influence the different degrees of emphasis on pay and non-pay factors include the leadership style of management and the culture of the organisation. If managers have the attitude that workers are naturally lazy and cannot be trusted, then a 'payment by results' system with close supervision will be adopted. If the culture is to view workers as partners or associates in the business, then production will be organised to give workers a chance to accept responsibility and to participate. A monthly salary payment system is likely under these circumstances or possibly a profit-sharing scheme. As with so many important decisions made within a business, so much depends on the attitudes and beliefs of senior managers – and the business culture that they adopt.

TOP TIP

You should be able not just to describe and explain different methods of financial and non-financial motivation but to suggest which ones might be most suitable in different business situations – and why.

153

ACTIVITY 11.8

Quality circles in operation

Most Japanese manufacturers use systems of quality circles to involve all workers and to use their full abilities. The concept spread to other countries, particularly those where Japanese firms had set up manufacturing operations. The data below show that there are certain industries where quality circles are hardly used, such as construction, which is a highly fragmented industry with many part-time and seasonal workers. This is also true of agriculture. Manufacturing firms with large numbers of employees, where the danger of lack of a sense of belonging is greatest, are those most likely to adopt the practice of quality circles.

Sector	Sectorial spread of organisations with quality circles %	Total employees covered
Energy	5	8,000
Mineral extraction/metal manufacture	12	15,375
Engineering, vehicles	48	95,375
Other manufacturing	17	31,500
Construction	–	–
Distribution/hotels	1	750
Transport/communication	2	42,500
Banking/finance/business	8	10,250
Other services	6	9,125
Total		212,875

Quality circles – UK coverage

Benefits	%	Drawbacks	%
Employee involvement	55	Management resistance	33
Communication	24	Lack of interest	9
Problem-solving	21	Time constraint	9
Employee development	12	Inadequate training	7
Job satisfaction	11	Reorganisation/ redundancy	7
Improved quality	10	Bad implementation	7
Management–workforce interaction	9	Union opposition	7
Team building	8	Scepticism	6
Improved morale	8	Other	39
Other	18		
(Many organisations list more than one of each)			

Quality circles – benefits and drawbacks

[20 marks, 25 minutes]

1 What is meant by the term 'quality circle'? [2]

2 Analyse why quality circles are more widely used in some industries than others. [8]

3 Discuss the claimed benefits and drawbacks of quality circles. Use your findings to recommend to a large manufacturing firm in your country whether it should introduce quality circles. [10]

SUMMARY POINTS

- Motivation is the willingness of workers to achieve a good result because they want to do it.
- Organisations that allow workers to achieve personal goals are more likely to achieve their organisational goals.
- Taylor was the first researcher to employ scientific techniques to study workforce efficiency and motivation.
- Taylor accepted the 'economic man' concept and believed that pay was the sole human motivator at work.
- The Hawthorne effect, as explained by Mayo, stresses the importance of factors other than pay and conditions in influencing motivation – such as group spirit and communication with managers.
- Maslow's hierarchy of human needs is an attempt to classify needs in order of achievement.
- The desire to satisfy needs drives human behaviour and when one need is fulfilled it no longer motivates.
- Herzberg's two-factor theory focuses on the nature of the job itself rather than on external factors, such as pay, conditions and supervision.
- No one theorist can claim to have a monopoly on relevant motivational ideas – it is important to recognise that certain ideas may not be applicable to all workers and in all workplace situations.
- There are many different pay systems that can be used to reward and motivate staff.
- Increasing emphasis is being given to non-financial methods of motivation. These recognise that pay is not the main motivational force for many workers.
- The culture of the organisation and the management style adopted often have a considerable influence on the forms of motivation used.

RESEARCH TASK

Cut out ten job advertisements from newspapers. Choose ones that give a great deal of detail about the financial and non-financial rewards of the business.

a   Identify the different salary levels paid for each job. Which jobs carry the highest and lowest pay? Try to explain why this is.

b   What other benefits are offered in each job? Do these benefits seem to increase the higher the salary being offered?

c   Which jobs seem to involve most responsibility and which could give the greatest level of job satisfaction? Do these jobs tend to have the higher or lower salaries?

d   Consider the lowest-paid job from your advertisements. Consider how the business might attempt to motivate the workers using non-financial methods.

AS Level exam practice questions
Short answer questions

[90 marks, 2 hours]

Knowledge and application

1   What do you understand by the term 'motivation'? **[3]**

2   Outline the main findings of Mayo's Hawthorne research. **[4]**

3   Explain why studying human needs is believed to be an important part of motivation theory. **[3]**

4   Give an example of how an individual can revert to a lower level of Maslow's hierarchy of human needs. **[2]**

5   Consider two different levels of Maslow's hierarchy. Explain how these could be satisfied at work. **[4]**

6   Differentiate clearly, using examples, between Herzberg's motivators and hygiene factors. **[6]**

7   Why did Herzberg consider it important to differentiate between 'movement' and 'motivation'? **[3]**

8   Outline the three key features of job enrichment. **[3]**

9   Why did McClelland believe that achievement was so important to motivation? **[3]**

10   Outline the differences between content and process motivation theories. **[4]**

11   Explain how the payment of a fixed monthly salary could help to satisfy some of the needs identified in Maslow's hierarchy. **[3]**

12   Explain to the directors of a private limited company the advantages and disadvantages of introducing a profit-sharing system for the workforce. **[4]**

13   Should performance-related pay should be introduced for the teachers in your school? **[5]**

14   Distinguish between job rotation and job enrichment. **[3]**

15   Explain two benefits to workers from being organised into teams. **[4]**

16   How might business culture influence the motivational methods adopted by managers? **[3]**

Application

17   Explain how a retailing business such as a high-quality clothing shop might be badly affected by low motivation of sales staff. **[4]**

18   State **three** features of Taylor's research that might be relevant to modern manufacturing industries. **[3]**

19   Examine **two** problems of using the piece-rate system for each individual in a business that uses a flow-line production system. **[4]**

20   Explain **two** benefits to a firm that might be gained from adopting teamwork in a factory making computers. **[4]**

21   Give **two** examples of fringe benefits that might be offered to senior managers in a bank. **[2]**

22   Analyse the potential benefits of using worker participation in a busy fast-food restaurant. **[5]**

23   Assume that you are the manager of a computer shop. Which payment system would you use for your staff: commission only, time-based wage rates or a combination of the two? Justify your choice. **[4]**

Data response

1 Unrest at the factory

'The workers on the production line are not happy with these changes. They have been used to working as fast as they can to earn piece-rate bonuses and now you want to put them all on the same salary and to make them join teams. Up until now they have really been competing with each other, now you expect them to cooperate together.' Bik-Kay's reaction to the management proposals was typical among the supervisors at Harvard Electrics. As she had not been consulted about the changes, she was reluctant both to accept them and to explain them to the staff. Min-Chul, the manager with responsibility for organising production, had met with Bik-Kay and the other supervisors to justify the changes after they had been introduced. 'We need to move to a culture of cooperation and team responsibility. By reorganising production into teams, staff will become more skilled, benefit from working in groups and have the opportunity, through quality circles, to contribute to solving work-related problems. The new payment system will take some getting used to but we want to focus on quality, not just output.'

[30 marks, 45 minutes]

1 a Define the term 'piece rate'. [2]

   b Briefly explain the term 'salary'. [3]

2 Outline the problems the business might have experienced from the old production and payment system. [6]

3 Examine the possible benefits to be gained from the changes that managers wish to make to the production and pay system at Harvard Electrics. [8]

4 Discuss why there is reluctance to change in this business and how the managers could overcome this resistance. [11]

2 Staff turnover increases at Telemarketing Ltd

The human resources manager at Telemarketing was under pressure to solve the problem caused by so many staff leaving. Recent data gathered about staff are shown below:

	2011	2012	2013
Labour turnover (% of staff leaving each year)	15	20	45
Staff absence (average % of total staff absent)	5	7	9

The efficiency of the business was being badly affected by these trends. Recruitment and training costs and covering for absent staff were all reducing the profitability of the business. Since it was set up five years ago, Telemarketing has grown rapidly and is now one of the largest telephone direct marketing organisations in the country. It sells insurance and other financial products directly to consumers rather than using banks or insurance brokers as intermediaries. Seventy-five per cent of staff are telephone sales people. They have two ways of selling the products. Either they 'cold call' potential customers from telephone directories or they receive calls from interested members of the public responding to advertisements. All telephonists work at individual work stations. All of their calls are recorded and monitored by supervisors. Rest time is strictly controlled and excess rest periods lead to pay being reduced. Employees are paid a low basic time-based wage, plus a small commission payment. Because of the nature of the job – telephones must be operated 18 hours per day – there is no available time for meetings between all of the staff and workers. The main form of communication is a daily newsletter, which is pinned to all work stations at the start of every shift, giving details of daily sales targets for the whole business.

[30 marks, 45 minutes]

1 a Define the term 'time-based wage'. [2]

   b Briefly describe the term 'commission payment'. [3]

2 Referring to the work of **two** motivational theorists, explain the likely reasons for the employee problems at Telemarketing. [6]

3 Explain how the principles of job enrichment could be introduced into this business to help staff achieve 'self-actualisation'? [8]

4 Recommend a pay system for staff in Telemarketing that will encourage long-term motivation. Justify your recommendation. [11]

3 Why women are happier at work than men

The world of work is a better experience for women than it is for men, according to a survey. Asked to rate their job satisfaction on a scale of one to seven, women scored an average of 5.56, while males scored 5.22. Experts appear divided over the reasons why women appear to get more out of their work than men. Many women work part-time and have job-sharing schemes, which, the survey found, increased job satisfaction as they could pursue other interests too. University graduates are the most dissatisfied of all, according to the survey of 30,000 employees – employees generally enjoyed their first years at work, but then job satisfaction falls between the ages of 30 and 40. But employees over 60 gained the greatest satisfaction from their work. Professor Andrew Oswald of Warwick University, who conducted the survey, said: 'The young are just happy to have a job. As they grow older they realise that ambitions and human needs may not be so easily fulfilled.' It seems that we all begin thinking we will reach the top in our careers but most of us are forced to adjust. 'The older we get, the more settled and content with our role at work we get,' he added. Graduates are often frustrated by the lack of challenging work on offer. They are often forced to take low-skilled jobs for which they are overqualified in order to pay off debts. The survey also revealed that long hours at work did not turn people off their jobs.

Employees of small businesses and non-profit-making organisations, such as charities, were happier at work than those working for big companies.

David Hands, of the Federation of Small Businesses, said: 'There is a greater camaraderie [friendship] and participation in small firms than in big companies.' Workers feel less involved in decision-making and less secure in bigger firms. He added: 'It is more relaxed in small firms and people enjoy it more. Many also get more responsibility, which adds to their satisfaction.'

Female office workers

[30 marks, 45 minutes]

1 **a** Define the term 'human needs'. [2]

   b Briefly explain the term 'participation'. [3]

2 Identify **three** factors that seem to influence job satisfaction and explain them in terms of Maslow's hierarchy of needs. [6]

3 Explain in terms of the features of job enrichment why it might be easier for small firms to motivate staff than big businesses. [8]

4 Discuss the extent to which it might be possible for large firms to use Herzberg's motivators to improve the level of worker motivation. [11]

4 Redundancies fail to hit morale at Technoloc Ltd

Technoloc had grown rapidly during the technology boom of the last few years. The company produces data protection devices for businesses that trade on the Internet. The system protects the credit card numbers and identity of consumers buying products via the internet. Output had doubled in each of the last three years, and jobs too. However, this year, the global economic downturn and the slower-than-expected growth in Internet sales has led to a 20% fall in orders. Swift action has to be taken to cut costs. The business organises production on a team-working system. Each team assembles a significant part of the finished product before passing it on to the next team to add their components. All major decisions concerning production were discussed by management with these teams. In fact, there was no clear worker–management divide, as all employees were called associates and supervisors were only available to assist the manufacturing process, not to observe or give instructions. Workers were always rewarded and recognised for producing outstanding work or for making suggestions that improved quality. Only two people had left the business in the last year, and one of these had moved away from the area for family reasons.

News of the slump in orders was immediately broken to the workers at one of the regular team briefings. Some concerns were expressed about job security. A group of associates was appointed to look into how the workforce could adapt to the new market conditions. It was agreed that the group would report back every week until a final decision had to be made. A month later, the final plan was put to a meeting of all the associates. It was proposed to offer voluntary redundancy to all staff with the offer of generous payments if accepted. An average of one worker from each team would no longer be required, so others in the team would have to be able to do all of the tasks of the group. All remaining workers would be asked to accept a 5% salary cut. The meeting accepted the proposals almost unanimously. Five workers volunteered for redundancy, but it was agreed that they would be offered their jobs back should sales pick up again. The teams coped with the extra workload, and, in the weeks immediately after the changes, productivity actually increased. This helped the business to further increase its international competitiveness in preparation for an upturn in the world economy.

[30 marks, 45 minutes]

1 a Define the term 'team-working'. [2]

  b Briefly explain the term 'salary cut'. [3]

2 Outline the benefits to firms such as Technoloc of having a well-motivated workforce. [6]

3 Explain why the proposals at Technoloc were so willingly accepted by the associates. [8]

4 To what extent does the information given above suggest that Technoloc has adopted the findings of certain motivational theorists? [11]

AS Level essay questions

[20 marks, 45 minutes each]

1 a Outline the major research findings of both Maslow and Herzberg. [8]

  b To what extent are the results of one of these motivational theorists applicable to modern industry? [12]

2 'Money is the most important factor motivating workers today.' Discuss this statement, with reference to motivational theories you are aware of. [20]

3 a Explain the difference between financial reward systems and non-financial forms of motivation. [8]

  b Discuss how it might be possible to effectively motivate a part-time worker in a fast-food restaurant. [12]

4 'If we pay our workers well, then there is no need for any of these new ideas, such as job enrichment and team working.' Discuss the validity of this view expressed by a chief executive of a car manufacturing business. [20]

12 Human resource management

On completing this chapter, you will be able to:

- understand the role and purpose of the human resource managers in an organisation
- analyse the importance of employee recruitment and selection to an organisation
- evaluate the different methods of recruitment and selection

- assess the main features of employment contracts
- discuss the importance of employee training and development in increasing the efficiency and motivation of the workforce
- appreciate the importance of employee morale and welfare.

Introducing the topic

AUSTRALIA AND CHINA – HUMAN RESOURCE MANAGEMENT IN TWO COUNTRIES

Before the 1980s in China, all industry was state-owned and all workers were state employees. Industries were inefficient and overstaffed – jobs were given for life. There was no human resource management (HRM) because firms had no control over staffing or recruitment – these were political decisions. Since privately owned companies have been allowed and many state industries have been bought out by the private sector, the need to improve efficiency and productivity has become very great. Nearly all firms of any size now have professional human resource (HR) managers. They try to recruit and select the best workers for their firms and – unheard of in communist times – they can 'hire and fire' in response to changing demand for their products. Many posts of responsibility are given to internal staff – because it is often said that the cultural links in each firm, or 'guanxi' (interpersonal relationships), are so strong that it is difficult for external recruits to break into the business structure.

Australian businesses have used 'Western-style' HRM for many years. There is widespread belief that good management of people has a direct impact on

a firm's future profitability and success. Advertising in papers and even on TV and radio is common when a firm wants to recruit new workers. Internal promotions are often given – not for cultural reasons, but because firms do not want to lose their training investment in workers by not promoting and retaining them. Interviews are the most widely used selection procedure, but references from past employers are very important too and, for senior management jobs, it is common for the husband or wife to be interviewed too. Unlike China, there is a huge private recruitment industry with more than 300 agencies, which allows people to seek jobs easily in other parts of the country – moving from one region to another in China is still unusual for most workers.

Points to think about:

- From the passage, list as many HRM tasks or responsibilities as you can.
- Do you think there is a close link between managing people and business profitability? Explain your answer.
- What HR problems might an Australian business experience if it tried to open a base in China?

159

Introduction

Human resource management (HRM) aims to recruit capable, flexible and committed people, managing and rewarding their performance and developing their key skills to the benefit of the organisation. This AS-Level chapter and the next one (A Level) explore these specific

 KEY TERM

Human resource management (HRM): the strategic approach to the effective management of an organisation's workers so that they help the business gain a competitive advantage.

roles of the HRM department and the impact it can have on efficiency, flexibility and motivation of the workforce. The change in attitudes to managing people has been great and fundamental since the early years of the twentieth century and the introduction of mass production. There are still firms and factories that hire and fire on an almost daily basis and that offer no training or staff development at all. However, these are now the exception rather than the rule. Modern HRM has been developed not just in response to increasing legal constraints on how workers are treated, but also as a recognition that a truly successful and competitive business depends on the efficiency and motivation of some of its most important assets – the people who work for it.

Human resource management – purpose and role

The central purpose of HRM is to recruit, train and use the workers of an organisation in the most productive manner to assist the organisation in the achievement of its objectives. This management function has developed from, but is different to, the work of traditional personnel departments. These departments were responsible for just the recruiting, training, discipline and welfare of staff. They tended to be:

- bureaucratic in their approach, with an inflexible approach to employee issues
- focused on recruitment, selection and discipline rather than development and training
- reluctant to give any HR roles to any other departmental managers
- not represented at board of directors level and not part of the strategic management team.

HRM is broader and more far-reaching in scope. It focuses on:

- **Workforce planning:** Planning the future workforce needs of the business (see Chapter 13).
- **Recruitment and selection:** Recruiting and selecting appropriate employees and inducting them into the business.
- **Developing employees:** Appraising, training and developing employees at every stage of their careers.
- **Employment contracts:** Preparing contracts of employment for all employees and deciding on how flexible these should be: permanent or temporary, full- or part-time.
- **Ensuring HRM operates across the business:** Involving all managers in the development of their employees – emphasising that this is not just an HR responsibility.
- **Employee morale and welfare:** Monitoring and improving employee morale and welfare including giving advice and guidance.
- **Incentive systems:** Developing appropriate pay systems (and other incentives) for different categories of employees (see Chapter 11).

- **Monitoring:** Measuring and monitoring employee performance (see Chapter 13).

Recruiting and selecting staff

Organisations need to obtain the best workforce available if they are to meet their objectives and compete successfully. As far as possible the workers need to be chosen so that they meet exactly the needs of the organisation in order to reduce the risk of conflict between their personal objectives and those of the business. **Recruitment** and **selection** will be necessary when:

- the business is expanding and needs a bigger workforce
- employees leave and they need to be replaced – this is called labour turnover.

KEY TERMS

Recruitment: the process of identifying the need for a new employee, defining the job to be filled and the type of person needed to fill it and attracting suitable candidates for the job.

Selection: involves the series of steps by which the candidates are interviewed, tested and screened for choosing the most suitable person for vacant post.

The recruitment and selection process involves several steps:

1 Establishing the exact nature of the job vacancy and drawing up a job description

This provides a complete picture of the job and will include:

- job title
- details of the tasks to be performed
- responsibilities involved
- place in the hierarchical structure
- working conditions
- how the job will be assessed and performance measured.

The advantage of the **job description** is that it should attract the right type of people to apply for the job, as potential recruits will have an idea of whether they are suited to the position or not.

KEY TERM

Job description: a detailed list of the key points about the job to be filled – stating all its key tasks and responsibilities.

2 Drawing up a person specification

This is an analysis of the type of qualities and skills being looked for in suitable applicants. It is clearly based on the job description because these skills can only be assessed once the nature and complexity of the job have been identified. The **person specification** is like a 'person profile' and will help in the selection process by eliminating applicants who do not match up to the necessary requirements.

KEY TERM

Person specification: a detailed list of the qualities, skills and qualifications that a successful applicant will need to have.

TOP TIP

Do not confuse the job description and the person specification.

3 Preparing a job advertisement

The job advertisement needs to reflect the requirements of the job and the personal qualities needed. It can be displayed within the business premises – particularly if an internal appointment is looked for – or in government job centres, recruitment agencies and newspapers. Increasingly businesses are using the internet to advertise vacancies and people interested in the job are encouraged to apply online. This saves a great deal of time for both the recruiting business and potential applicants. Some specialist businesses offer online recruitment services – such as Jobtrain and HireServe – and they assist businesses in preparing an effective online advertisement for the vacant positions.

Care must be taken to ensure that there is no element of discrimination implied by the advertisement as nearly all countries outlaw unfair selection on the basis of race, gender or religion. Internal and external recruitment have very different advantages (see Table 12.1).

TOP TIP

The disadvantages of each method of recruitment are the reverse of the advantages of the other method. For example, a drawback in external recruitment is that it *does not* give internal staff a career structure or a chance to progress.

KEY CONCEPT LINK

In any business that requires workers to deal directly with customers it is essential to appoint people who are **customer-focused** and capable of providing good customer service.

Once applications have been received, then the selection process can begin. This can be achieved by using a range of different techniques.

4 Drawing up a shortlist of applicants

A small number of applicants are chosen based on their application forms and personal details, often contained in a CV (curriculum vitae). References may have been obtained in order to check on the character and previous work performance of the applicants. As explained above, much of this information is now obtained online and not in paper format.

5 Selecting between the applicants

Interviews are the most common method of selection. Interviewers question the applicant on their skills, experience and character to see if they will both perform well and fit into the organisation. Some interviewers use a seven-point plan to carry out a methodical interview. Candidates are assessed according to: achievements, intelligence, skills, interests, personal manner, physical appearance and personal circumstances.

Benefits of internal recruitment	Benefits of external recruitment
■ applicants may already be known to the selection team ■ applicants will already know the organisation and its internal methods – no need for induction training ■ culture of the organisation will be well understood by the applicants ■ often quicker than external recruitment ■ likely to be cheaper than using external advertising and recruitment agencies ■ gives internal staff a career structure and a chance to progress ■ staff will not have to get used to new style of management approach if vacancy is a senior post	■ external applicants will bring in new ideas and practices to the business – this helps to keep existing staff focused on the future rather than 'the ways things have always been done' ■ should be a wide choice of potential applicants – not just limited to internal staff ■ avoids resentment sometimes felt by existing staff if one of their colleagues is promoted above them ■ standard of applicants could be higher than if just limited to internal staff applicants

Table 12.1 Advantages of internal and external recruitment

Other selection tests might be conducted, such as aptitude tests and psychometric tests. The former are just designed to test an applicant's ability in a specific task, for example retooling a machine. Psychometric tests are designed to test character, attitudes and personality by using a series of role plays, questions and problem-solving situations. It is claimed that these can be more accurate for selection purposes than an interview where a skilled 'actor' can perform well under stressful conditions, but might not have the personal attributes required.

ACTIVITY 12.1

[40 marks, 55 minutes]

1   Draw up a job description for the head teacher's or principal's post at your school or college.   **[10]**

2   Draw up a detailed person specification for this post.   **[10]**

3   Produce an eye-catching and effective newspaper advertisement for this post (use IT if you can) including key features from the job description and person specification.   **[10]**

4   Discuss the best ways to select the new head teacher or principal from the applicants who have applied for the post.   **[10]**

Employment contracts

Employment contracts are legally binding documents. Care needs to be taken to ensure that they are fair and accord with current employment laws where the worker is employed. A typical employment contract will contain the following features:

- Employee's work responsibilities and the main tasks to be undertaken.
- Whether the contract is permanent or temporary (see Chapter 13).
- Working hours and the level of flexibility expected, e.g. part time or full time, working weekends or not (see Chapter 13), the payment method to be used for the job and the rate for it (e.g. hourly rate).
- Holiday entitlement.
- The number of days' notice that must be given by the worker (if they wish to leave) or the employer (if they want to make the worker redundant).

KEY TERM

Employment contract: a legal document that sets out the terms and conditions governing a worker's job.

The contract imposes responsibilities on both the employer – to provide the conditions of employment laid down – and the employee – to work the hours specified and to the standards expected in the contract.

In most countries, it is illegal for an employer to employ workers without offering the protection of a written employment contract. In some states, for example China, a verbal agreement between worker and employer can also be legally binding, however, if there is some evidence to prove that both sides intended a contract to be formed.

TOP TIP

The precise legal requirements of employment contracts are likely to vary slightly between different countries. It would be useful for you to research what these legal requirements are in your own country – but you are unlikely to be examined directly on them.

Labour turnover

If a business employed, on average, 200 employees last year and 30 left during the year, then the **labour turnover** rate would be 15%. If this result is high and increasing over time, then it is a good indicator of employee discontent, low morale and, possibly, a recruitment policy that leads to the wrong people being employed. High labour turnover is more likely in areas of low unemployment too, as there may be many better-paid and more attractive jobs available in the local area. It is also true that some industries typically have higher labour turnover rates than others. The fact that so many students, looking for part-time and temporary employment, find jobs in fast-food restaurants leads to labour turnover rates that can exceed 100% in one year. In other organisations, labour turnover rates can be very low; this is typical in law practices and in scientific research. Table 12.2 on the next page lists some of the costs and potential benefits of high labour turnover.

KEY TERM

Labour turnover: measures the rate at which employees are leaving an organisation. It is measured by:

$$\frac{\text{number of employees leaving in 1 year}}{\text{average number of people employed}} \times 100$$

Training and developing employees

Having spent a great deal of time and effort on recruiting and selecting the right staff, the HR department must ensure that they are well-equipped to perform the duties

External recruitment for top managers is increasing

Multinational companies Avon Products Inc. and Yahoo! Inc. recruited externally for new chief executive officers (CEOs) in 2012. This was part of a growing trend, as 29% of the USA's biggest companies recruited senior executives externally in 2012, the highest proportion for nearly 20 years.

Avon's hiring of Sherilyn McCoy from Johnson & Johnson and Yahoo's recruiting of Google Inc. executive Marissa Mayer helped cause a 36% jump in outside recruitment for top positions.

External recruitment is rising as companies that may have sought to preserve management continuity during the 2009–2011 recession now want to 'shake things up' with fresh perspectives and more expansion- oriented executives, according to Hugh Shields, co-founder of Chicago-based executive recruiter Shields Meneley Partners. 'During the recession, many of these CEOs were kind of hunkered down in their positions and quite frankly, boards saw termination of their CEO as additional risk to the organization,' Shields said in a telephone interview. 'Now as the market has improved, what they're seeing is the window has opened up' and they're more willing go outside for talent if necessary.

[21 marks, 30 minutes]

1 What is meant by the term 'external recruitment'? [3]

2 Analyse the possible benefits to companies such as Yahoo! and Avon of recruiting new CEOs externally. [8]

3 Discuss whether all businesses should aim to recruit senior managers externally. [10]

Costs of high labour turnover	Potential benefits of high labour turnover
<ul><li>costs of recruiting, selecting and training new staff</li><li>poor output levels and customer service due to staff vacancies before new recruits are appointed</li><li>difficult to establish loyalty and regular, familiar contact with customers</li><li>difficult to establish team spirit</li></ul>	<ul><li>low-skilled and less-productive staff might be leaving – they could be replaced with more carefully selected workers</li><li>new ideas and practices are brought into an organisation by new workers</li><li>a business that plans to reduce staff numbers anyway – due to rationalisation – will find that high labour turnover will do this, as leaving staff will not be replaced</li></ul>

Table 12.2 Costs and potential benefits from high labour turnover

How to cut labour turnover

Online retailer Furniture@Work has cut its labour turnover from 69% to 8.4% in just one year. Two specialist trainers were appointed after employees complained about there being no development or career opportunities at the firm. Workers are now taught how to improve customer service and sales skills. Appraisal has been introduced and this has improved two-way communication between workers and managers. Head of HR, Stephen Jeffers, said: 'There have been massive cost savings in recruitment – the scheme was worth it.'

[21 marks, 25 minutes]

1 What is meant by the term 'labour turnover'? [3]

2 Analyse why the measures taken by Furniture @ Work succeeded in reducing labour turnover. [8]

3 Discuss whether the HR departments of all businesses should aim to achieve the lowest labour turnover rate possible. [10]

KEY TERM

Training: work-related education to increase workforce skills and efficiency.

and undertake the responsibilities expected of them. This will nearly always involve **training** in order to develop the full abilities of the worker.

There are different types of training:

1 **Induction training** is given to all new recruits. It has the objectives of introducing them to the people that they will be working with most closely, explaining the internal organisational structure, outlining the layout of the premises and making clear essential health and safety issues, such as procedures during a fire emergency.

2. **On-the-job training** involves instruction at the place of work. This is often conducted either by the HR managers or departmental training officers. Watching or working closely with existing experienced members of staff is a frequent component of this form of training. It is cheaper than sending recruits on external training courses and the content is controlled by the business itself.

3. **Off-the-job training** entails any course of instruction away from the place of work. This could be a specialist training centre belonging to the firm itself or it could be a course organised by an outside body, such as a university or computer manufacturer, to introduce new ideas that no one in the firm currently has knowledge of. These courses can be expensive yet they may be indispensable if the firm lacks anyone with this degree of technical knowledge.

> **KEY TERMS**
>
> **Induction training:** introductory training programme to familiarise new recruits with the systems used in the business and the layout of the business site.
>
> **On-the-job training:** instruction at the place of work on how a job should be carried out.
>
> **Off-the-job training:** all training undertaken away from the business, e.g. work-related college courses.

Training can be expensive. It can also lead to well-qualified employees leaving for a better-paid job once they have gained qualifications from a business with a good training structure. This is sometimes referred to as 'poaching' of well-trained staff and it can discourage some businesses from setting up an expensive training programme.

The costs of *not* training are also substantial. Untrained employees will be less productive, less able to do a variety of tasks (inflexible) and could give unsatisfactory customer service. Accidents are likely to result from workers untrained on health and safety matters, especially in manufacturing businesses or in the food industry.

Finally, without being pushed to achieve a higher standard or other skills, workers may become bored and demotivated. Training and the sense of achievement that can result from it were identified by both Maslow and Herzberg as important motivators – so there is a very important link between the importance given to the training and development of employees in a business and the levels of motivation that exist.

> **TOP TIP**
>
> One reason commonly given by firms for *not* training their staff is that these well-trained staff will then be 'poached' by other firms. Perhaps they ought to focus on motivating their well-trained staff to stay with appropriate financial and non-financial incentives.

> **KEY CONCEPT LINK**
>
> The **strategy** towards human resources that **management** decides on can have a big impact on the motivation and efficiency of the employees – and this will impact on the **value** they create for the business.

Development and appraisal of employees

This should be a continuous process. Development might take the form of new challenges and opportunities, additional training courses to learn new skills, promotion with additional delegated authority and chances for job enrichment. To enable a worker to continually achieve a sense of self-fulfilment, the HR department should work closely with the worker's functional department to establish a career plan that the individual feels is relevant and realistic. For this process to be a fully strategic one, the HR department should analyse the likely future needs of the business when establishing the development plan for the workforce. In this way, an individual's progress and improvement can also be geared to the needs of the firm.

> **KEY TERM**
>
> **Employee appraisal:** the process of assessing the effectiveness of an employee judged against pre-set objectives.

Appraisal is often undertaken annually. It is an essential component of a staff-development programme. The analysis of performance against pre-set and agreed targets combined with the setting of new targets allows the future performance of the worker to be linked to the objectives of the business. You will recall from Chapter 11 that both appraisal and staff development are important features of Herzberg's motivators – those intrinsic factors that can provide the conditions for effective motivation at work.

Discipline and dismissal of employees

On occasions it will be necessary for an HR manager to discipline an employee for continued failure to meet the obligations laid down by the contract of employment. **Dismissing** a worker is not a matter that should be undertaken lightly. Not only does it withdraw a worker's

> **KEY TERM**
>
> **Dismissal:** being dismissed or sacked from a job due to incompetence or breach of discipline.

How Starbucks develops its employees

For companies that rely on high volume of face-to-face customer interactions, such as Starbucks, it is ultimately the thousands of front-line employees that create the customers' experience and brand image. Starbucks stands for more than just a cup of coffee, it's about the relaxed atmosphere, the excellent locations and the personal nature of the product/customer service. Its baristas (employees who make the coffees) have been the deliverers of this message.

The company's training programme has played a big role in its worldwide success. Here are three features of the training programme:

1 **Starbucks university:** Starbucks has started to offer its own classes, called Barista Basics and Barista 101, which can even earn their students college credits. Several universities in the USA recognise these qualifications as part of management degrees.

2 **Turning a complaint into a latte:** Starbucks' baristas can react fast and serve customers quickly because they have become masters in the art of repeatable routines through extensive on-the-job training. Starbucks employees have dozens of routines that they can

apply when things become hectic or when a customer complains. It is called the 'Latte Method' of responding to difficult customer situations and it involves:

- **Listening** to the customer.
- **Acknowledging** their complaint.
- **Taking action** to resolve the problem.
- **Thanking** the customer for bringing the situation to their attention.
- **Explaining to** the customer why the problem occurred.

3 **Starbucks brews inspiration for its employees:** Recently, Starbucks also invested $35 million in barista loyalty by organising a Leadership Lab conference. The goal of the event was to energise and inspire nearly 10,000 store managers, connecting them with the company's mission statement and motivating them to be enthusiastic about the coffees they serve. By turning the conference centre into a Starbucks theme park, the Leadership Lab provided effective training to its employees in a way that fits Starbucks' corporate culture.

165

The company cares about us.

Starbucks has one of the lowest rates of labour turnover of any large scale catering business. Here is a quote from one of its baristas: 'Starbucks really is a kind company. It gives its employees health insurance, good pay, opportunities for career development and a real sense of belonging. Concern for employee welfare is genuine. All of its baristas are trained to make the customer happy.'

[21 marks, 30 minutes]

1 What is meant by the term 'on-the-job training'? **[3]**

2 Analyse the benefits to Starbucks of extensive employee training. **[8]**

3 Discuss whether an extensive training programme is sufficient to ensure a motivated and loyal workforce. **[10]**

4 **Research task:** Use the following link to discover the tips that Starbucks offers job applicants: www.starbucks.co.uk/careers/interview-tips. Write a short report to Starbucks directors on the importance of effective recruitment and selection of new employees.

immediate means of financial support and some social status, but if the conditions of the dismissal are not fully in accordance with company policy or with the law, then civil court action might result. This can lead to very substantial damages being awarded against the firm. Dismissal could result from the employee being unable to do the job to the standard that the organisation requires. It may also be that the employee has broken one of the crucial conditions of employment. However, before dismissal can happen, the HR department must be seen to have done all that it can to help the employee

reach the required standard or stay within conditions of employment. There should be support and, if necessary, training for the person concerned. It is important from the organisation's point of view that it does not leave itself open to allegations of **unfair dismissal**.

 KEY TERM

Unfair dismissal: ending a worker's employment contract for a reason that the law regards as being unfair.

Sometimes employees become involved in gross misconduct, which may be stealing or some other serious offence. If this happens, the organisation can dismiss with immediate effect, without pay or notice.

However, if an employee is late regularly, then the organisation must give warnings and follow the agreed disciplinary procedure before dismissal can take place. This usually involves verbal warnings followed by written warnings, before dismissal is thought to be fair. Whether or not a dismissal is unfair is a matter of fact to be decided by a tribunal. It is the right of every employee to claim unfair dismissal. To show that a dismissal is fair, employers need to be able to show that one of the following is true and, except in the case of gross misconduct, that the agreed procedures have been followed:

- inability to do the job even after sufficient training has been given
- a continuous negative attitude at work, which has badly affected the employees or their work
- continuous disregard of required health and safety procedures
- deliberate destruction of an employer's property
- bullying of other employees.

There are certain situations in which dismissal can be considered unfair or in breach of employment law. These include:

- pregnancy
- a discriminatory reason, e.g. the race, gender or religion of a worker
- being a member of a union
- a non-relevant criminal record – if the employer has previously been unaware of a criminal record, it is not a reason for dismissal unless it is central to the job, e.g. a cashier convicted of stealing from the till or a schoolteacher convicted of child abuse.

If a worker believes that they have been unfairly dismissed then they can, in most countries, apply for a review of their case at an Employment Tribunal – usually with the support of their trade union if the employee is a member. If the tribunal decides that the worker has been dismissed against the term of the employment contract then compensation can be awarded. A business cannot be required to give someone who has been unfairly dismissed their old job back, but failure to do so or to employ them in another capacity is likely to be reflected in the substantial financial damages awarded to an employee whose case has been successful.

Redundancies

This is not the same as dismissal and the two should not be confused. **Redundancy** occurs when workers' jobs are no longer required, perhaps because of a fall in demand or a change in technology. Often, this is part of a company policy of retrenchment to save on costs to remain competitive. Over the two years to 2013, Nokia Siemens, the mobile (cell) phone manufacturer, made 20,000 workers redundant worldwide in order to cut costs and restore profitability. Directors argued that unless these jobs were cut, the company would continue to make losses that could easily result in further redundancies – or the failure of the entire business.

KEY TERM

Redundancy: when a job is no longer required, the employee doing this job becomes unnecessary through no fault of their own.

The way these announcements are made can have a very serious effect on the staff who remain – loss of job security – and on the wider community. If a firm is seen to be acting in an uncaring or unethical manner, then external stakeholders may react negatively to the business.

Redundancy can happen if a job that someone has been doing is no longer required and there is no possibility of that person being re-employed somewhere else in the organisation. Redundancy may also happen if, due to budget cuts, the firm needs to reduce its workforce. If redundancies are to take place, then set guidelines are normally followed to ensure that the correct person or people are made redundant. Often the principle is 'last in, first out'. Many firms faced with having to lose some members of the workforce will often try to do so by natural wastage, i.e. by not replacing all of those who leave. Where this does not work or is insufficient, they will often pursue a policy of voluntary redundancy. However, an invitation to leave is often a high-risk strategy because workers who are easily employable elsewhere are often the ones a business needs to keep.

Employee morale and welfare

Most HR departments will offer advice, counselling and other services to employees who are in need of support, perhaps because of family or financial problems. These support services can reflect well on the caring attitude of the business towards its workforce. When workers feel that the employer is concerned about their long-term welfare, then this is likely to lead to higher morale and a much stronger sense of loyalty and desire to do well for the business.

Work–life balance

The hours and times people work have always been subject to change but the pace of this change is now more rapid than ever because:

- customers expect to have goods and services available outside traditional working hours

- organisations want to match their business needs with the way their employees work
- globalisation has led to much greater levels of competition, so efficiency and flexibility are important to a business to remain competitive.

KEY TERM

Work–life balance: a situation in which employees are able to give the right amount of time and effort to work and to their personal life outside work, for example to family or other interests.

The demands of working long and often unsociable hours many businesses make on their employees can lead to stress and poor health. Some analysts suggest that HR departments should assist employees to achieve a better **work–life balance** that will reduce stress – but also increase employee efficiency. The following methods have been used by some businesses to allow employees to take more control of their working lives to allow for more leisure and relaxation time, more time for creativity and more time with family:

- Flexible working (see Chapter 13).
- Teleworking – working from home for some of the working week.
- Job sharing – allowing two people to fill one full-time vacancy, although each worker will only receive a proportion of the full-time pay.
- Sabbatical periods – an extended period of leave from work. This can be for up to 12 months. Some businesses do not pay employees during this period but guarantee to keep the job open for them on return, but some businesses do pay employees a proportion of their full time salary.

ACTIVITY 12.5

[20 marks, 30 minutes]

An entrepreneur set up a home decoration business two years ago. The business offers a decorating service to home owners and has established a reputation for quality work. The entrepreneur now needs to increase employee numbers. Explain to her the importance of each of the following:

a   job description
b   person specification
c   training
d   employee welfare.   **[20]**

Policies for diversity and equality

Most organisations have policies which try to ensure **equality** and **diversity** in the workforce. The countries in the European Union have strict laws that govern equality issues – and this is true of many other countries. Businesses that promote equality in the workplace do not base recruitment and dismissal decisions, pay, promotions and other benefits on employees' race, sexuality, gender, age, religion or national origin.

KEY TERMS

Equality policy: practices and processes aimed at achieving a fair organisation where everyone is treated in the same way and has the opportunity to fulfil their potential.

Diversity policy: practices and processes aimed at creating a mixed workforce and placing positive value on diversity in the workplace.

The advantages of promoting equality in the workplace include creating an environment with high employee morale, developing a good reputation and the ability to recruit top talent. Another advantage of equality is that the effectiveness of employees is measured by their contributions, which may motivate them to willingly contribute to the business in a positive way. In contrast, if a company uses discriminatory practices to decide who is promoted, employees who are discriminated against are likely become discouraged and demotivated.

Workplace diversity relates to acknowledging differences among employees and deliberately creating an inclusive environment that values those differences. A workplace that encourages diversity employs individuals from various races, ethnicities, religions and genders. Many businesses implement diversity programs, which educate employees on the definition of diversity and how it helps every member of the workforce.

Businesses can derive significant benefits from implementing diversity policies. Some of the advantages of diversity in the workplace include capturing a greater consumer market as consumers will be attracted to a diverse sales force, employing a more qualified workforce and reducing employee turnover. A diverse workforce also leads to an increase in creativity because individuals from different backgrounds approach problem solving in different ways. Businesses also benefit from diversity in language skills, which allows them to provide products and services internationally.

SUMMARY POINTS

- Human resource management (HRM) has the aim of ensuring the effective use of labour resources to meet the business's objectives.
- HRM performs several main functions.
- Workforce planning enables a firm to forecast future labour needs in terms of both numbers and skills.
- Recruitment and selection of the right staff for each post will enhance organisational efficiency.
- Employment contracts are legal documents with several important features.
- Training of staff is expensive, but not training staff can carry even greater long-term costs.
- Employee development should not end after induction training; continual development can help people achieve their full potential and this has important links with motivational theories.
- Appraisal of staff is a common method of assessing progress, performance and future training needs.
- There is a close relationship between effective HR management, showing concern for employee welfare and the level of worker motivation – this can result in a more successful business.

RESEARCH TASK

Find out how your school of college recruits and selects employees for:

- teaching jobs
- non-teaching jobs.

Prepare a job description and a person specification for a senior management post in your school.

Prepare **six** questions that you would ask the candidates at interview – explain why you would ask each question.

AS Level exam practice questions

Short answer questions

[54 marks, 60 minutes]

Knowledge and understanding

1 List **four** important roles of an HR department. [4]
2 Explain why the recruitment of appropriate employees is so important to a business. [4]
3 Distinguish between a job description and a person specification. [4]
4 Why should the costs of training be weighed against the costs of not training staff? [4]
5 Explain the importance of staff-development programmes for worker motivation. [6]
6 What is meant by the term 'staff appraisal'? [3]
7 Explain why it is important to both the business and the employee to have a contract of employment between them. [6]
8 Explain the difference between 'dismissal' and 'redundancy'. [4]
9 What is meant by the term 'work–life balance'? [3]

Application

10 Explain why a person specification is important to the selection process for a hospital nurse. [4]
11 A bank has a vacancy for a senior executive. Outline **two** reasons for appointing an internal candidate. [6]
12 Differentiate between on-the-job training and off-the-job training for a teacher. [6]

Data response

Recruitment, selection and training at E and B Engineering

'The Job Centre is sending someone round this afternoon,' said Harryo, the operations manager of E and B. 'The new customer order was a bit of a surprise but if I had been kept informed by the marketing people that they were trying for this Trinidad job, then I could have arranged the recruitment of extra workers in good time.' As usual, Harryo was complaining to the chief executive but this time he did have a case. The new order would stretch his existing workforce to the limit and he did not want to drive the existing workers away through overworking them. 'I suppose we have to use the Job Centre,' said the chief executive. 'The trouble is they never really know what we are looking for and we often have to let really unsuitable people start here before we find out what they are really like.'

Harryo agreed but said: 'We cannot afford to be choosy this time. I will give them a quick session on the machines and then I just hope they pick it up after that. The main problem is the new computer-controlled machinery – it takes so long to be trained up on this. My job would be easier if the new supervisor had support from the other workers. I always thought it would be a good idea to recruit someone from outside to break up the informal groups but he seems to have no influence over them at all. To make matters worse, one of the workers we sent on a long college training course last year has taken a better-paid job with another company.'

Harryo left the chief executive's office and wondered what he was going to say to the new workers being sent over by the Job Centre. 'I wish I knew a bit more about them,' he thought to himself. 'If they are no good I will have to think about advertising online, but this always leads to many applications from people who haven't got a clue about machines. It might be best if I just offered them a short-term employment contract to start with.'

[30 marks, 45 minutes]

1 a Define the term 'recruitment.' [2]

   b Explain what is meant by the term 'employment contract.' [3]

2 Analyse **two** HR problems E and B Engineering is facing. [6]

3 Analyse the suitability of recruitment and selection policies used for the new machine operators. [8]

4 Discuss the links that might exist, using this case as a starting point, between effective HR management and employee motivation. [11]

AS Level essay questions

[20 marks, 45 minutes each]

1 a Explain the purpose and roles of human resource management. [8]

   b Discuss the importance of effective recruitment and selection of employees to a business of your choice. [12]

2 a Analyse the benefits of employee training to a business. [8]

   b Discuss whether improving staff morale and welfare is the most important role of the human resource department in a large manufacturing business. [12]

13 Further human resource management

This chapter covers syllabus section A Level 2.3.

On completing this chapter, you will be able to:

- analyse employee performance by using a range of measures
- assess ways in which employee performance might be improved
- recognise the importance of labour legislation
- assess the reasons for and role of workforce planning
- evaluate ways in which cooperation between management and the workforce can benefit both
- assess the role of trade unions in HRM.

Introducing the topic

PRODUCTIVITY GAPS STILL EXIST IN NORTH AMERICAN CAR PRODUCTION

Productivity in the car industry – cars produced per worker per year – is one of the most important measures of efficiency. Obviously, a worker at Rolls-Royce will produce fewer cars per year than a worker in a Hyundai factory, but comparisons between similar manufacturers are very revealing. This is particularly true in the USA where there are North American-owned manufacturers (such as Ford and General Motors), European manufacturers (such as BMW) and Japanese manufacturers (Toyota, Nissan and Honda).

With their widespread use of worker involvement in decision-making and problem-solving, it is little surprise to see Nissan and Toyota at the top of the productivity league table. 'Nissan's labour productivity advantage equates to a $300 to $450 per vehicle cost advantage over less efficient manufacturers,' said Ron Harbour, president of

Harbour Consulting. 'Toyota is also among the best in the industry. It is not just a matter of spending more on the best capital equipment. It also reflects regular kaizen improvement meetings with staff and the flexibility of well-coordinated engineering and manufacturing.' Toyota's engine factory in Buffalo, West Virginia has the highest productivity of any similar factory. It takes a worker just 1.82 hours to produce each new engine.

Points to think about:

- How could productivity be measured in a service industry, such as a hotel?
- Why do you think a high level of productivity gives a business a cost advantage over its rivals?
- Explain why Toyota and Nissan have higher levels of productivity than other car manufacturers.

Introduction

The previous chapter analysed the important role of the HR department in modern business management. This chapter is at A Level standard and studies the work of the HR department in:

- deciding on the most appropriate HR strategy towards employment contracts
- measuring and improving employee performance
- monitoring and applying labour legislation
- managing industrial relations between the workforce and management.

Hard and soft human resource management

Some business analysts use these two terms to define two extreme types of HR management.

KEY TERMS

Hard HRM: an approach to managing staff that focuses on cutting costs, e.g. temporary and part-time employment contracts, offering maximum flexibility but with minimum training costs.

Soft HRM: an approach to managing staff that focuses on developing staff so that they reach self-fulfilment and are motivated to work hard and stay with the business.

It may be viewed as unfair, and possibly unethical, but many businesses now adopt a hard approach to their 'less important' or peripheral workers, but a soft approach to their core workers – those that the business would least be able to cope with losing. It is argued that, as the core workers are key to the business's future success, they should be developed, trained and motivated in ways that will greatly increase the chances of them having high morale and a keen desire to stay with the business. The hard approach might save money on peripheral workers' costs in the short term, but:

- it could increase recruitment and induction training costs in the long term as temporary workers have to be frequently recruited
- demotivated workers with little job security might be unproductive and this could reduce company efficiency and profitability
- bad publicity regarding the treatment of workers – especially the 'them and us' division between core and peripheral staff – might lead to negative consumer and pressure group actions against the company
- hard HRM ignores the research findings of Maslow, Mayo and Herzberg as workers are not offered job security, esteem or job enrichment.

Employment contracts: full- or part-time, temporary or permanent?

One of the most important differences between hard and soft HRM is the type of employment contracts that are offered to employees. The main distinction is between full-time contracts and **part-time** and **temporary contracts**. Assume that, as part of its workforce plan, an insurance company has decided that ten telephone customer service advisers should be employed. Should the firm's future need for these ten additional workers be met by:

- recruiting ten full-time staff on permanent contracts?
- recruiting 20 part-time staff on 'half-time' or 'flexi-time' permanent contracts?
- employing workers on temporary contracts that can be terminated at short notice?

KEY TERMS

Part-time employment contract: employment contract that is for less than the normal full working week of, say, 40 hours, e.g. eight hours per week.

Temporary employment contract: employment contract that lasts for a fixed time period, e.g. six months.

Flexi-time contract: employment contract that allows staff to be called in at times most convenient to employers and employees, e.g. at busy times of day.

- not adding to employed staffing levels at all, but offering '**outsourcing**' contracts to other firms or self-employed people? These will then supply a specific service or product, but will not be directly employed. This is used increasingly by businesses that want to reduce overhead employment costs.

KEY TERM

Outsourcing: not employing staff directly, but using an outside agency or organisation to carry out some business functions.

ACTIVITY 13.1

Business in focus – India wants more flexible labour contracts

The Indian government has approved a proposal that would allow employers to shut down businesses with less than 100 employees without seeking government permission. This change to the law will allow employers to end employment contracts when economic conditions are bad. This greater flexibility will allow employers to save on labour costs when the economy takes a downturn. Trade unions have criticised the decision. However, some economists say the decision will encourage employers to increase jobs when conditions are favourable.

[12 marks, 20 minutes]

Assess the likely impact on employees and employers in your country following the introduction of a law that allows 'more flexible labour contracts'. [12]

Recent trends in labour recruitment have moved towards employing more part-time staff on temporary contracts and increased outsourcing. These developments have certain advantages and disadvantages to both the business and the staff concerned. Part-time employment contracts are those that do not require the worker to work a full week, only a set proportion of it. The claimed advantages of a part-time and flexible employment contract are as follows:

Advantages for the business

- Employees can be required to work at particularly busy periods of the day but not during the slower periods, for example banking staff are needed at lunch times and theatre and cinema staff are required mainly in the evening. This will reduce overhead costs to a business. This flexibility offers firms real competitive advantages, as they can give good customer service without substantial cost increases.

- More staff are available to be called upon should there be sickness or other causes of absenteeism.
- The efficiency of employees can be assessed before they are offered a full-time contract.
- By using **teleworking** from home for some groups of workers, even further savings in overhead costs can be made, such as smaller office buildings.
- **Zero hours contracts** mean that there is no fixed cost element in a worker's pay – no guaranteed work or pay is offered and a wage is only paid if the worker is called in to work for a specified number of hours.

KEY TERMS

Teleworking: staff working from home but keeping contact with the office by means of modern IT communications.

Zero-hours contract: no minimum hours of work are offered and workers are only called in – and paid – when work is available.

Advantages for the workers with part-time and flexible contracts

- This contract could be ideal for certain types of workers, for example parents with young children, students or more elderly people who do not wish to work a full week.
- They may be able to combine jobs with different firms, giving greater variety to their working lives.

There are potential disadvantages too.

Disadvantages for the business

- There will be more employees to manage than if they were all full-time.
- Effective communication will become much more difficult, not just because there will be more staff in total but also because it may be impossible to hold meetings with all the staff at any one time. There could be greater reliance on written communication methods because of this.
- Motivation levels may be adversely affected because part-time staff may feel less involved and committed to the business than full-time workers. It will be much more difficult to establish a teamwork culture if all the staff never actually meet each other because of their different working hours.
- Workers may have more than one zero hours contract with different employers and they may not be available immediately if they are called on to work.

Disadvantages for the workers

- They will be earning less than full-time workers.
- They may be paid at a lower rate than full-time workers.
- The security of employment and other working conditions are often inferior to those of full-time workers. This is now changing in some countries. In all of the states of the European Union for example, the law now gives as many employment rights to part-time as to full-time workers. This is still not the case in other regions of the world.

Temporary contracts

Offering temporary employment contracts is another way firms use to reduce the overhead costs of employing staff when there may be less demand for them. Lower levels of job security can mean that safety needs, as identified by Maslow, may not be satisfied and this will have a negative effect on motivation. Temporary contracts can be either full-time or part-time. They are contracts for fixed periods of time as opposed to permanent contracts. Permanent contracts end only when a worker is sacked (for example for poor discipline), made redundant (for example when demand has fallen) or leaves of their own accord. The advantages and drawbacks of temporary contracts are similar to those of part-time contracts, especially the benefit of flexibility offered to employers. Such flexibility is particularly important to seasonal business activities, such as fruit picking.

The combination of part-time and temporary contracts gives firms the chance to create a small team of full-time staff, called core workers, and combine this with a number of flexible workers, who are employed only as and when necessary. This is further enhanced by the increasing trend towards outsourcing – using outside self-employed contractors to perform specific jobs within the business rather than employing staff directly. The three types of contracts are termed 'peripheral' workers as they are not part of the central core of full-time employees (see Figure 13.1).

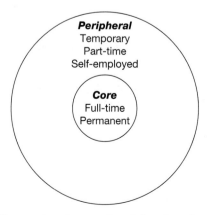

Figure 13.1 Core and peripheral workers

THE SHAMROCK ORGANISATION

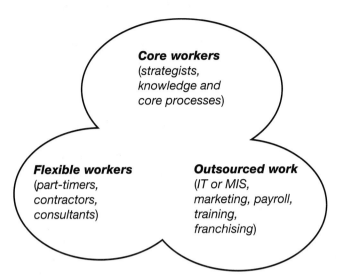

Figure 13.2 Charles Handy's 'Shamrock organisation'

Another way of representing this trend towards fewer core staff on permanent and salaried contracts was devised by the famous business writer, Charles Handy. He first used the term the 'Shamrock organisation' with the three leaves made up of:

- core managerial and technical staff, who must be offered full-time, permanent contracts with competitive salaries and benefits
- outsourced functions by independent providers, who may once have been employed by the company
- flexible workers on temporary and part-time contracts, who are called on when the situation demands their labour (see Figure 13.2).

KEY CONCEPT LINK

Which approach to **management** of employees is likely to create more **value** for a business – hard or soft? Hard management could reduce short-term labour costs but could this be at the expense of lower levels of motivation and higher labour turnover?

Measuring and monitoring employee performance

The consequences of poor workforce performance can be damaging for business prospects. However, improvements in performance should be recognised and fed back to the staff. There are a number of indicators that HR managers can use to assess the level of employee performance.

ACTIVITY 13.2

British Airways (BA) – has outsourcing gone too far?

BA has outsourced more of its operations than any other major world airline. All of its ticketing and Internet operations are designed and managed through Indian IT companies. BA now employs relatively few IT staff directly and these are all employed on key strategic projects. The development of the new shopping basket feature on ba.com is a recent example of BA's tactical use of Indian IT companies. BA's overhead cost per passenger is one of the lowest in the industry.

The strike at Gate Gourmet caused chaos on BA flights a few years ago. The airline could not serve food on thousands of its flights due to the strike at its only outsourced producer of in-flight catering. This was a low-cost, high-risk strategy that backfired – BA employs no catering staff itself and other catering firms were unable to produce the quantity of meals that the airline needed during the lengthy strike.

Sources: www.silicon.com; www.personneltoday.com

[20 marks, 25 minutes]

1 Explain **two** benefits to BA from outsourcing many of its operations. [8]

2 Analyse **three** possible problems for a business of reducing its core staff to an absolute minimum and using flexible workers and outsourced suppliers. [12]

Labour productivity

Labour productivity is often viewed by managers as the key test of employee performance. If output per worker increases over time, then labour productivity or efficiency is increasing. It also means that, given constant wage rates, labour costs per unit of output will be falling. This is, therefore, a major factor influencing the competitiveness of a business. If labour costs per unit are lower than major rivals, there could be an opportunity to set lower prices too.

KEY TERM

Labour productivity: the output per worker in a given time period. It is calculated by:

$$\frac{\text{total output in time period, e.g. one year}}{\text{total workers employed}}$$

Productivity data are usually compared with results from businesses in the same industry, as well as recording changes in labour efficiency over time. There are several reasons why labour productivity might increase over time:

- improved staff motivation and higher levels of effort
- more efficient and reliable capital equipment
- better staff training
- increased worker involvement in problem solving to speed up methods of production, e.g. kaizen and quality circles (see Chapter 26 for discussion of kaizen).
- improved internal efficiency, e.g. no waiting for new supplies of materials to arrive.

Measuring productivity in service industries is usually much more complex than in manufacturing or primary sector industries. Here are some examples:

- Transport industry – kilometres travelled per driver per year.
- Hotels – number of guest nights per employee per year.
- IT and banking/finance service – revenue earned on average per employee per year.

In your answer to question 3 in Activity 13.3 you may have suggested different levels of workforce motivation and performance – and this could well be true. Do not forget that quantitative data can lead to false conclusions, however. Suppose Company A had been affected by a strike at its suppliers, or the capital equipment used at Company C is much more modern. Labour productivity

174

data do have some very important uses but, as with any single measure of performance, the causes of changes need careful analysis.

Business in focus – hotel industry productivity

It is very difficult to increase labour productivity in the hotel industry – especially at the luxury end of the market where top-quality services for guests depend on having staff always on call. This means that prices in the hotel industry have not fallen as they have in, for example, computers or even airline tickets. About the only opportunity for a hotel owner to improve labour productivity is to use IT as much as possible in the support services of booking, billing and ordering supplies.

Absenteeism rates

This can also be worked out for a whole year by knowing the total number of working days lost through **absenteeism** and expressing this as a percentage of the total number of days that could have been worked.

> **KEY TERM**
>
> **Absenteeism:** measures the rate of workforce absence as a proportion of the employee total. It is measured by:
>
>
> $$\text{absenteeism (\%)} = \frac{\text{no. of employees absent}}{\text{total no. of employees}} \times 100$$

ACTIVITY 13.3

Calculating labour productivity and labour costs per unit

In the following table, all three companies operate in the wedding-dress industry. Workers are paid a salary of $20,000 per year.

Company	Total output 2014	Average number of workers employed 2014	Labour productivity	Labour cost per unit
A	1,000	100	10	$2,000
B	1,800	x	12	Z
C	3,000	150	y	$1,000

[13 marks, 15 minutes]

1 Calculate the missing figures in the cells x, y, z. [3]

2 Explain what happens to labour cost per unit as labour productivity increases. [4]

3 How might you explain the different levels of labour productivity in these three companies? [6]

Staff absenteeism is disruptive to any business, especially one providing consumer services. These cannot be held in stock for use during periods of absence. Once a consumer has experienced poor service due to staff absence, that consumer may never return. It is expensive to employ extra staff just to cover for staff away from work or to ask other workers to work overtime. Absenteeism is a commonly used measure of workforce motivation as, it is argued, really well-focused and motivated staff will avoid missing days from work at all costs. It is possible that, apart from Herzberg's motivating factors not being fully present at work, the hygiene factors of the job might be making absenteeism worse. For instance, poor working conditions could lead to illness, or over-supervision could lead to worker stress, and days off work could be a consequence of either problem.

Other measures of workforce performance

There are several other measures of worker efficiency and motivation at work but many of these are not applicable to all types of business activity. They include wastage levels (the number of wasted or damaged products expressed as the proportion of total output), reject rates and consumer complaints as a proportion of total customers served, and the days lost through strikes within a business.

TOP TIP
You will not be asked to calculate these other measures of employee performance for A Level Business, but you should be able to comment on data about these that could be presented to you, e.g. reasons for an increase in wastage rates at a food factory.

Employee performance – strategies to improve it

There is no one solution to a problem of poor employee performance. In fact, the most important first step after calculating the measures explained above is to find out *why* performance is poor. Managers need to analyse why productivity is falling or below that of competitors and why so many staff are taking unexplained absences. There is no point in spending large amounts on more efficient machines to increase efficiency if the main reason for low productivity is a badly trained and poorly motivated team of workers.

However, there is a common thread running through the strategies of those businesses that are most successful in motivating staff and in raising their levels of commitment, loyalty and performance. This common theme is built around the soft approach to HRM. This stresses the need

to consider the worker as a resource to be nurtured and developed so that the full extent and range of his or her abilities can be applied to their work. Most businesses, even those operating in low-wage economies with an apparently plentiful supply of potential workers, now recognise the long-term benefits of improving performance of existing workers using a variety of strategies.

The techniques frequently used to increase employee performance include:

- regular appraisal of performance against agreed pre-set targets (see Chapter 10) – if workers regularly fail to reach these targets for performance, then actions need to be taken by management, which may be of a disciplinary nature or might involve further training
- training to increase efficiency and offering opportunities for educational qualifications to stretch and challenge every worker
- quality circles – small groups of workers encouraged to take responsibility for identifying and suggesting solutions to work-related problems
- cell production and autonomous work groups where teams of workers are given multiskill training and the opportunity to take responsibility for a complete section of work – this could involve them taking decisions on finding the best way to motivate the team in order to achieve predetermined goals
- financial incentives linked to the profits of the business or an offer of a stake in the ownership of the company, such as employee share-option schemes
- investing in more advanced technology to increase labour productivity – this may have implications for employee training and could lead to some redundancies
- adopting a system of management by objectives.

Management by objectives (MBO)

This system is designed to motivate and coordinate a workforce by dividing the organisation's overall aim into specific targets for each division, department and individual. If this process is undertaken after discussion and agreement with personnel at each level of the organisation, then it can be a very effective way of delegating authority and motivating staff. This approach would accord with a Theory Y approach. If, however, the targets at each level were merely imposed by senior management – as with a Theory X style – then motivation is likely to be low. Figure 4.1 (see page 39) is an example of how the hierarchy of objectives would look incorporating the principle of 'management by objectives' (the mission statement has not been included, as we have identified that it is of little operational use).

Individual targets for performance would be established during the annual appraisal process and these should be agreed with each worker for maximum effect – not just established without the worker's agreement.

ACTIVITY 13.4

Improving employee performance at low-cost airline Asian Airlines

	2011	2012	2013
Average number of employees	200	230	275
Employees leaving	15	25	50
Daily average number of staff absent	5	7	15
Productivity index (2010 = 100)	100	105	95
Customer complaints about employee attitude as % of number of customers	5	7	12

[40 marks, 60 minutes]

1 Calculate labour turnover and absenteeism rates for all three years. **[12]**

2 Analyse possible reasons for the trends in the results you have calculated. **[8]**

3 Explain **two** problems to this business of the worsening employee performance. **[8]**

4 Evaluate **two** strategies that the management of Asian Airlines could adopt to attempt to improve employee performance within the business **[12]**

MBO – the possible benefits

For the MBO system to be effective, targets and objectives should be agreed and discussed with the managers and staff at departmental and individual levels. This form of staff involvement is a key feature of job enrichment and should help provide a motivating force.

■ Each manager and subordinate will know exactly what they have to do. This will help them prioritise their time. It will also enable them to see the importance of what they do to the whole organisation and should lead to increased productivity.

■ By using the corporate aim and objectives as the key focus to all departmental and individual objectives, everyone should be working to the same overall target. This will avoid conflict and should ensure a consistent and well-coordinated approach.

■ Objectives act as a control device. By setting targets agreed with the people who have the authority to reach them, managers are able to monitor everyone's performance and measure success or failure.

MBO – the possible problems

■ The process of dividing corporate objectives into divisional, departmental and individual targets can be very time-consuming, especially as this is best performed only after full consultation with those most affected.

■ Objectives can become outdated very quickly and fixing targets and monitoring progress against them can be less than useful if the economic or competitive environment has changed completely.

■ Setting targets does not guarantee success, despite what some managers might believe. Issues such as adequate resources and staff training must also be addressed if the original targets are to have any real meaning or are to act as true motivating goals.

Labour legislation

The need for labour laws and the principles that underlie them were covered in Chapter 8. All governments have passed laws to control working conditions and the relationship between employer and employee. These are collectively called 'labour laws' or 'labour legislation'. Chapter 8 evaluated the impact of some of these laws on businesses, in particular laws relating to health and safety and employment rights, such as protection from discrimination. This section now considers the role of the state in passing labour laws affecting trade unions and industrial relations.

The role of the state in industrial relations

The state intervenes in industrial relations in a number of ways:

■ through industrial-relations laws

■ through agencies set up to improve industrial relations, such as arbitration councils

■ through its own policies as a major employer.

Since 1980, industrial-relations laws in the UK have:

■ removed the right to engage in strike action unless agreed by secret ballot

■ removed the right to 'secondary picketing' where union members used to be able to encourage workers not to attend work at other businesses as well as the one 'in dispute'

■ allowed workers belonging to a union to vote on 'union recognition', which could lead to an employer being forced to recognise a union for collective-bargaining purposes

■ provided greater protection against discrimination in recruitment and at work.

Much of this intervention by the state has been a result of a culture in which most people see union membership as an important right – but also believe that union power

Cause of conflict	Common management view	Common employee view
Business change, e.g. relocation or new technology	Change is necessary to remain competitive and profitable.	Change can lead to job losses, may result in retraining in new skills that causes uncertainty over ability to cope. Demands for increased flexibility from staff may reduce job security.
Rationalisation and organisational change	Business needs to cut overheads and be flexible and adaptable to deal with globalised low-cost competition.	Cost cuts and rationalisation always seem to fall on employees – not the senior managers or owners of the business. Reduced job security will damage employee motivation.

Table 13.1 Common causes of labour–management conflict

should be controlled. There is also common agreement that creating the conditions for improving industrial relations and the protection of the employee is the responsibility of government. Improved industrial relations lead to higher productivity and improved international competitiveness of industry – and higher living standards for the whole country.

In Malaysia, the 1967 Industrial Relations Act (IRA) governs the activities of trade unions. Some of the main features of the act are:

- It protects the right of every worker in Malaysia to join or not join a union.
- It protects workers from being victimised by employers for joining a union.
- Unions may undertake collective bargaining on behalf of members, if they have obtained recognition from the employer.
- A union can request recognition after it has obtained more than 50% of staff as members.
- The IRA allows employers to prohibit management, executives and those who work in a confidential or security capacity from joining a union.
- A Director General of Industrial Relations office was established to arbitrate on industrial-relations disputes.

TOP TIP
You do not need to know the precise details of labour laws in any country – but you are advised to research the industrial relations laws in your own country – how do they differ from those in the UK and Malaysia?

Workforce and management – scope for conflict and cooperation

In any business with employees, that is with employed staff other than the owner/manager, there are always likely to be potential conflicts of opinion and interests. At a simple level, the owner/manager aims to achieve satisfactory profit levels by keeping costs, including labour costs, as low as possible. However, workers – and do not forget that wage costs are often a major part of total business costs – will seek to obtain high pay and shorter working hours. There is clear scope for conflict here, but

it is not the only source of possible clashes of interest between labour and management. Some other common areas of dispute or conflict are shown in Table 13.1.

So, to a certain extent, conflict and differing objectives are inevitable between labour and management within business. How can these be resolved or at least reduced so that the conflict is not so great that it completely prevents all forms of coordination and working together? How can positive cooperation be achieved between these two groups for the benefit of the business and all stakeholders?

In very broad terms, there are three approaches that may be adopted by management and labour to deal with conflict situations. Much will depend on the culture and legal structure of the country in which the firm operates, as well as the culture of the business itself. For example, in some countries, trade unions are still illegal or their operations are strictly controlled. At the other extreme, in the European Union, workers' rights over minimum pay levels, security of employment and working conditions are protected by laws that restrict quite substantially the independence of management in deciding on such issues.

Three broad approaches to labour–management relations are:

1 'Hard' or autocratic management style

Some managers have a 'take it or leave it' attitude to the workforce. Workers might be employed on very short-term contracts – even on a daily basis – offering no security at all. If a worker objects to the conditions of work, then the attitude of management is often to 'sack' the worker and replace them with another person, who might be so desperate for work that they will not raise any objections. This approach to labour–management relations is still quite common in certain countries with weak labour-protection legislation, weak or non-existent trade unions and with high unemployment.

Evaluation: It might lead to very low labour costs, but consider the drawbacks to such an approach:

- No labour security and very low levels of motivation.
- Staff will not have the opportunity to be trained due to frequent job changes.

177

- No common objectives established between labour and management.
- Non-existent job enrichment and no staff involvement or participation – so no contribution from workers to important decisions that can lead to better results.

2 Collective bargaining between trade unions and major employers and their associations

Collective bargaining is when representatives of unions and national employers negotiate wage levels and working conditions for the whole industry or for large sections of it. These collective negotiations made trade union leaders very powerful as they were able to threaten and actually call for strike action from all of their members and this could bring the entire industry to a halt.

Evaluation:

- National agreements were not always suitable, or affordable, for smaller businesses.
- Strikes and other industrial action caused disruption and lost output and sales.
- Powerful unions resisted any changes that might adversely affect their members and this led to a lack of investment in, and development of, key industries.

3 Cooperation between labour and management

This approach is based on the recognition that successful competitive businesses will benefit all parties. Recent management thinking has been not to seek to oppose workers' suggestions and those of their union leaders, but to actively involve them in important decision-making and operational issues. In much of modern industry, therefore, there is much less confrontation, far fewer strikes and a great deal more harmony and working towards common goals than there was in the 1960s and 1970s.

It is a commonly held view, at least in developed economies, that labour–management relations, based on mutual respect, understanding and common aims, are likely to lead to a competitive and productive business that will be able to survive the added strains of a globalised economy. Indeed, participation and employee involvement could become a significant factor determining the long-term success of business in rapidly changing market conditions.

Reasons for and role of a workforce plan

HR departments need to calculate the future staffing needs of the business. Failure to do this can lead to too few or too many staff or staff with the wrong skills. HR departments must work in close harmony with the corporate plan of the business and the objectives this contains. If the overall business plan is to expand production and develop products for foreign markets, then this must be reflected in the

workforce plan – which becomes part of the firm's strategy to meet its long-term goals. So, **workforce planning** means thinking ahead and establishing the number and skills of the workforce required by the business in the future to meet its planned objectives. These two factors need careful thought and the starting point is always a **workforce audit**.

 KEY TERMS

Workforce planning: analysing and forecasting the numbers of workers and the skills of those workers that will be required by the organisation to achieve its objectives.

Workforce audit: a check on the skills and qualifications of all existing workers/managers.

Once this has been conducted, the next stages in workforce planning are to assess how many additional employees and skills might be needed.

1 The number of employees

The number of employees required in the future depends on many factors:

- **Forecast demand for the firm's product:** This will be influenced by market and external conditions, seasonal factors, competitors' actions, trends in consumer tastes and so on. It could be a mistake to replace a worker who decides to leave the firm if consumer demand is falling or if there is likely to be a seasonal downturn in demand. Demand forecasts may be necessary to help establish workforce planning needs, but we know that these are subject to margins of error. For this reason, some firms allow some additional staffing to be built into the plan to allow for unplanned increases in demand. An alternative might be to recruit temporary or part-time staff with flexible hours' contracts – this issue is studied in more detail later.
- **The productivity levels of staff:** If productivity (output per worker) is forecast to increase – perhaps as a result of more efficient machinery – then fewer staff will be needed to produce the same level of output.
- **The objectives of the business:** This could influence future workforce numbers in two main ways. Firstly, if the business plans to expand over the coming years, then staffing numbers will have to rise to accommodate this growth. Secondly, if the firm intends to increase customer-service levels, possibly at the expense of short-term profits, then more workers might need to be recruited. A workforce plan cannot be devised without consideration of business objectives.
- **Changes in the law regarding workers' rights:** If the government of a country decides to pass laws that establish a shorter maximum working week or introduce a minimum wage level, then there will be a considerable impact on the workforce plan. A shorter working week might lead to

a greater demand for staff to ensure that all the available work is completed on time. A minimum wage might encourage firms to employ fewer workers and to replace them with machines where this is possible.

- **The labour turnover and absenteeism rate:** The measurement of these factors is considered later, but their impact is clear. The higher the rate at which staff leave a business, then the greater will be the firm's need to recruit replacement staff. The higher the level of staff absenteeism, then the greater will be the firm's need for higher staffing levels to ensure adequate numbers are available at any one time.

2 The skills of the workers required

The need for better-qualified workers or for workers with different skills is a constantly in the minds of HR managers. The importance of these issues will depend upon two main factors:

- The pace of technological change in the industry, for example production methods and the complexity of the machinery used. The universal application of IT in offices has meant that traditional typists or clerks are now rarely required – skilled computer, photocopier and IT operators are in greater demand than ever.

- The need for flexible or multiskilled staff as businesses try to avoid excessive specialisation. The danger of producing many items of a specialised product or service is that stock levels could build up if demand patterns change. Most businesses therefore need to recruit staff or train them with more than one skill that can be applied in a variety of different ways. This gives the firm much more adaptability to changing market conditions – and can make the workers' jobs more rewarding too.

ACTIVITY 13.5

Planning teacher numbers

[8 marks, 12 minutes]

Explain **four** factors that could influence the number of new teachers your school or college will need to recruit over the next two years. **[8]**

ACTIVITY 13.6

Job losses at Alcatel-Lucent

Alcatel-Lucent factory

Alcatel-Lucent, the telecoms equipment maker, plans to make 14% of its entire global workforce redundant – around 10,000 jobs will be lost. The company made its largest ever loss last year and it needs to cut costs if it is to survive. Fewer workers are needed by Alcatel-Lucent because it faces more competition from other telecoms businesses and the demand in Europe for telecoms equipment has been hit by the economic recession. Most of the job losses will be among production workers but at the same time the company announced an increase in its research and development budget. This will lead to the creation of some more jobs for highly qualified engineers as the company has forecast that demand for the most advanced innovations in new technologies will rise in future.

[21 marks, 25 minutes]

1   Explain what is meant by the term 'redundant'. **[3]**

2   Analyse **two** reasons why Alcatel-Lucent is planning to make 10,000 workers redundant. **[8]**

3   Discuss the importance of effective workforce planning to the success of businesses. **[10]**

TOP TIP
Workforce planning can be effective only if it is linked in closely with the firm's long-term objectives.

ACTIVITY 13.7

Manpower planning at Cameron Sweets Ltd

By accepting the resignation of three key production-line workers, Roman Kauls knew that he would be lucky to meet the staff needs of Cameron Sweets over the next six months. The three workers had been attracted away from the firm by the offer of higher wages and better conditions in a local bakery. As HR manager, Roman had been planning the workforce numbers for the future. He had checked the skills of all current staff and collected data from both the marketing department on estimated sales figures and the production department for details of the new machines being installed next month. Price reductions by Cameron's leading competitor were making accurate forecasting difficult – taking last year's results and adding on 5%, the standard practice in this business, would no longer be accurate enough. The new machinery was fully automated and there would be no more manual packing at the end of the line. The machine would need reprogramming for each new type of sweet and the operations manager had also expressed concern about maintaining such complicated machinery. To add to Roman's resourcing issues, two of the women in the materials preparation department had announced that they would be applying for maternity leave over the next three months. With all of these issues occurring, Roman's plans were thrown into further confusion by a leaked report from the government that suggested a plan to introduce a law making 48-hour working weeks, or longer, illegal.

[35 marks, 45 minutes]

1 Define the term 'workforce planning'. [3]
2 Analyse the possible consequences to firms, such as Cameron Sweets, of not having a workforce plan for the future. [8]
3 Outline **five** factors from the case study that will influence either the number of workers or the skill levels of workers needed by the business over the next year. [10]
4 To what extent will it be possible to accurately predict the workforce needs of Cameron Sweets over the next 12 months? [14]

Trade unions and their role in HRM

Reasons for a worker joining a **trade union**:

- 'Power through solidarity' has been the basis of union influence and this is best illustrated by their ability to engage in collective bargaining. This is when trade unions negotiate on behalf of all of their members in a business. This puts workers in a stronger position than if they negotiated individually to gain higher pay deals and better working conditions.
- Individual industrial action – one worker going on strike, for example, is not likely to be very effective. Collective industrial action could result in much more influence over employers during industrial disputes.
- Unions provide legal support to employees who claim unfair dismissal or poor conditions of work.
- Unions put pressure on employers to ensure that all legal requirements are met, e.g. health and safety rules regarding the use of machinery.

KEY TERM

Trade union: an organisation of working people with the objective of improving the pay and working conditions of their members and providing them with support and legal services.

Union recognition and collective bargaining

In many countries it is not a legal requirement to **recognise** trade unions for purposes of collective bargaining. Many employers prefer to negotiate with individual workers and not to be pressured, through **collective bargaining**, into paying higher wages or making other improvements to **terms of employment**. However, there are claimed benefits to employers and HRM in particular from recognising and working with trade unions:

- Employers would be able to negotiate with one officer from the union collectively rather than with individual workers. This saves time and prevents workers from feeling that one individual has obtained better pay and conditions than others.

KEY TERMS

Trade union recognition: when an employer formally agrees to conduct negotiations on pay and working conditions with a trade union rather than bargain individually with each worker.
Collective bargaining: the process of negotiating the terms of employment between an employer and a group of workers who are usually represented by a trade union official.
Terms of employment: include working conditions, pay, work hours, shift length, holidays, sick leave, retirement benefits and health care benefits.

Trade union? India's BPO workers say 'no'

Opinions in Europe and North America relating to India's offshore workers (business process outsourcing) – call-centre operators, data-entry clerks and telemarketers – often regard them as the sweatshop labourers of the information age, working for long hours with modest pay. However, an international alliance of unions that wants them to become union members is finding it very hard to recruit them. These workers think of themselves as members of a relatively well-paid, respected professional elite in no need of union protection. The back-office outsourcing industry in India employs around 400,000 workers yet the Union Network International (UNI) organisation has recruited only 500 of them so far. 'A union would make sense if we had no job security,' said K.V. Sudhakar, a technical support worker for IMB, 'but there are so many jobs and so few qualified staff that firms are trying all possible means to keep employees happy so they will not leave.'

A similar situation has arisen in the USA where unions have lost many members as traditional manufacturing industries decline. They find it very difficult to recruit white-collar workers and professional workers in the finance and other service industries.

An Indian worker who did join UNI is Raghavan Iyengar, a call-centre supervisor. He said that companies give incentives to those who work beyond contracted time and young workers often ignore health problems, such as insomnia and bad backs, to earn extra money. 'The industry's motto is "Shut your mouth and take your money",' he said, 'and we want to change that.'

[12 marks, 15 minutes]

If you were a call-centre worker in India, would you join UNI? Give advantages and disadvantages before explaining your decision. [12]

Most workers in call centres in India are reluctant to join a trade union

- The union system could provide an additional, useful channel of communication with the workers – two-way communication in the sense that workers' problems could be raised with management by the union and the plans of the employers could be discussed via the union organisation.
- Unions can impose discipline on members who plan to take hasty industrial action that could disrupt a business – this makes such action less likely.
- The growth of responsible, partnership unionism has given employers an invaluable forum for discussing issues of common interest and making new workplace agreements. Very often, these will lead to increased productivity, which should help to secure jobs and raise profits.

Single-union agreement

Single-union deals are a further strategy to reduce conflict at work. Just 50 years ago, the UK still had more than 100 separate trade unions. This Figure has fallen dramatically but it is still possible for the workforce of one business to have members in several different unions. This makes collective bargaining much more difficult and time-consuming. In addition, it can lead to inter-union disputes over which skills or grades of workers should get the highest pay rise. It can also reduce the flexibility of a workforce if members of one union are prevented from doing the work of other workers belonging to another union. This is called a demarcation dispute and reduces total productivity.

 KEY TERM

Single-union agreement: an employer recognises just one union for purposes of collective bargaining.

The 'solution' to these problems has been for employers to insist on signing recognition deals with just one union. Clearly, there has been a great deal of competition among unions for these deals, as total membership depends on them. Two potential consequences of these deals are that, firstly, the newly united workforce and its union representatives may be able to exert greater influence during collective bargaining. Secondly, a single union may not effectively represent the range of skilled staff, and their needs at work, that exist in most businesses. The growth of single-union deals has led to further mergers between unions to prevent smaller unions being gradually excluded from all such industrial deals.

No-strike agreements

At first glance, these seem rather unusual agreements for a union to sign with an employer. Why give up the most effective form of industrial action? There are two main reasons:

1 It improves the image of the union as being a responsible representative body and this could encourage employees to become members.

2 These deals are often agreed to in exchange for greater union involvement in both decision-making and in representing employees in important negotiations. This has led to union–employer agreements to change working methods and increase labour flexibility that lead to higher productivity, higher profits *and* higher pay and worker participation. This is sometimes referred to as a win–win settlement as both employer and employee will gain from this cooperative approach to industrial relations.

 KEY TERM

No-strike agreement: unions agree to sign a no-strike agreement with employers in exchange for greater involvement in decisions that affect the workforce.

Employees/trade unions and employers – what action can they take?

Trade unions

Union leaders can use a number of measures to encourage employers to accept their demands for improvements in pay and conditions:

- **Negotiations** – and, possibly, agreeing to arbitration.
- **Go slow** – a form of **industrial action** in which workers keep working but at the minimum pace as demanded by their contract of employment.
- **Work to rule** – a form of industrial action in which employees refuse to do any work outside the precise terms of the employment contract. Overtime will not be worked and all non-contractual cooperation will be withdrawn.
- **Overtime bans** – industrial action in which workers refuse to work more than the contracted number of hours each week. During busy times of the year, this could lead to much lost output for the employer.
- **Strike action** – the most extreme form of industrial action in which employees totally withdraw their labour for a period of time. This may lead to production stopping completely. Strike action leads to the business shutting down during the industrial action.

 KEY TERM

Industrial action: measures taken by the workforce or trade union to put pressure on management to settle an industrial dispute in favour of employees.

ACTIVITY 13.9

Cathay Pacific avoids damaging strike just before busy holiday season

Cathay Pacific has avoided a threatened strike by cabin crew after it agreed a compromise deal with the flight attendants' union. The union welcomed the deal, which gave it most of what it was asking for, and called off the strike protest. The industrial dispute was over a new money-saving health insurance scheme that Cathay wanted to introduce for its 10,000 workers that would have forced them to pay for visits to the doctor. Cathay has now agreed to drop these charges until May and then to allow ten free visits to the doctor each year. The company refused to say how much the compromise would cost. 'I hope that the management will now improve labour–management relations and continue to work with us,' said Becky Kwan, the chairwoman of the flight attendants' union.

[18 marks, 25 minutes]

1 Outline **two** other forms of industrial action the union could have taken other than a strike. **[6]**

2 Analyse the likely reasons for Cathay Pacific agreeing to the costly compromise to solve this dispute. **[12]**

Employers

Methods employers can use to influence an industrial dispute include:

- **Negotiations** – to reach a compromise solution. If face-to-face negotiations with union leaders fail to reach an agreement, then the dispute may require arbitration.
- **Public relations** – using the media to try to gain public support for the employer's position in the dispute. This may put pressure on the union to settle for a compromise solution.
- **Threats of redundancies** – these threats would put pressure on unions to agree to a settlement of the dispute, but they might inflame opinions on the employees' side and could be looked upon as bullying and lead to poor publicity for the employer.
- **Changes of contract** – if employees are taking advantage of their employment contracts to work to rule or ban overtime, then new contracts could, when the old ones are due for renewal, be issued that insist on higher work rates or some overtime working.
- **Closure** – closure of the business or the factory/office where the industrial dispute takes place would certainly solve the dispute. It would lead to redundancy for all of the workers and no output and profit for the business owners. This is a very extreme measure and would only be threatened or used if the demands of the union would, if agreed to, lead to a serious loss being made by the business or factory anyway.

Figure 13.3 Industrial action by Italian metal workers – businesses may have to shut down while workers are on strike

- **Lock-outs** – short-term closure of the business or factory to prevent employees from working and being paid. Some workers who are not keen on losing pay for long periods may put pressure on their union leaders to agree to a reasonable settlement of the dispute.

Evaluation: which side of an industrial dispute has the greater power and influence?

This depends on a number of factors as outlined in Table 13.2.

Union/employee power will be strong when:	Employer power will be strong when:
<ul><li>most workers belong to one union</li><li>all workers agree to take the industrial action decided on</li><li>the business is very busy, operating close to full capacity, does not want to disappoint customers and profits are high</li><li>industrial action quickly costs the employer large amounts of lost output/revenue/profits</li><li>there is public support for the union case, e.g. for very low-paid workers</li><li>inflation is high, so a high wage increase would seem reasonable to maintain living standards</li><li>labour costs are a low proportion of total costs</li></ul>	<ul><li>unemployment is high – few alternative jobs for workers to take</li><li>action taken by employer, e.g. lock-out, has a very quick impact on workers' wages</li><li>there is public support for employer, e.g. when unions are asking for much higher rises than other workers receive</li><li>profits are low and threats of closure are taken seriously</li><li>threats of relocation to low-cost countries are taken seriously, e.g. the business has already closed other plants and relocated them</li></ul>

Table 13.2 The relative strength of unions and employers

SUMMARY POINTS

- 'Employee performance' has a major impact on business success.
- Employee performance can be measured in several ways.
- Strategies can be adopted by businesses to improve employee performance.
- Workforce planning is an important strategic role of HRM.
- HRM has to make decisions between the type of contract offered to employees: full- or part-time; temporary or permanent; zero-hours.
- Labour law has a major impact on industrial relations in most countries.
- Employees can benefit from joining a trade union and HRM is also affected by trade union membership of the workforce.
- Unions and employers can use various methods to achieve their objectives during industrial disputes.
- Single-union agreements and no-strike deals can be agreed upon.
- Arbitration plays a role in settling industrial disputes.

RESEARCH TASK

- Research the employment laws in your country.
- What rights to do workers have, if any, when managers want to close a business or a factory?
- Is there a minimum wage in your country? If so, what is it? Do you think it should be increased?
- Are part-time and flexible labour contracts often used in your country? You could check this by looking at the working conditions offered in job advertisements in your town or region.

A Level exam practice questions
Case studies

1 Working at Amazon – zero-hours contracts and no collective bargaining

Internet retailer Amazon employs hundreds of staff in the UK on zero-hour contracts. Employees working under the contracts are not guaranteed any income – they are only paid when they are called in to work. One former zero-hour contract employee said: 'You could turn in for work at seven in the morning and be sent home at eight if there was not enough work to do.'

Some employees at Amazon's warehouse in the Midlands region said they were hired for 12 weeks before being sacked and re-employed so that the company did not have to give them the same rights as full-time employees. An investigation found that employees are tracked using GPS tags while inside the warehouse. If staff are found to breach any of the company's rules, such as talking to colleagues, not working fast enough or leaving work early, they can be dismissed on a 'three strikes and you are out' basis. A former supervisor at Amazon said: 'You could log on at any time and see what people were picking, packing and what their productivity was. If their work rate was too slow you'd have to go and give them a bit of a boost or release them.'

An Amazon spokesman said: 'In the Midlands, we have 401 permanent associates, 345 of whom started on temporary assignments. We expect to hire an additional 250 permanent associates in Rugeley in the next year.' Amazon added that it employs more than 4,500 permanent employees in the UK and it expects to expand its operations throughout the European Union, creating even more jobs – often in areas of high unemployment.

Efficient warehouses are central to Amazon's customer service and competitive pricing around the world. However, the priority of keeping labour costs low is causing conflict with some European trade unions. Amazon experienced its first major strike action when the Ver.di union organised industrial action. The union opposes Amazon's refusal to use collective bargaining to set wages and working conditions. It argues that Amazon also refuses to pay the same wage rates agreed by all other firms in the warehousing and logistics industries in Germany. Some industrial relations advisers believe that if Amazon experiences more conflicts with unions in Europe it will just respond by introducing more automation in its factories.

[34 marks, 50 minutes]

1. Analyse the benefits to Amazon of using zero-hours employment contracts [8]

2. Assess whether businesses engaged in warehouse and transport operations should adopt soft HR strategies. [14]

3. Recommend to Amazon whether it should recognise trade unions in its European operations for purposes of collective bargaining. [12]

2 'Single global super union within a decade'

An international trade union could be created within a decade, the leader of one of Europe's biggest trade unions has declared. The UK union Amicus has signed solidarity agreements with IG Metall in Germany and two unions in the USA. It is looking for agreements with other unions in other countries. A spokesman for Amicus said that: 'Our aim is to create a powerful single union that will cross international boundaries to challenge the global forces of capital.'

Trade union leaders are worried by the growth of globalisation that has weakened their power and reduced their membership. Because employers can now easily transfer production to low-cost countries, unions' power to bargain and negotiate higher pay deals has been much weakened. The answer, according to Amicus, is to 'globalise trade unions' too. A single global union would be able to collectively bargain with multinationals on behalf of members throughout the world and this might prevent worker exploitation in very low-wage economies.

'Our aim is to match up to globalised industry. We will force multinational companies to sign deals with one single international union rather than be able to make changes to workers' pay and rights in one country without consulting unions elsewhere.'

[22 marks, 35 minutes]

1 Analyse the potential benefits to both workers and employees of union involvement within a workplace, including collective bargaining. [10]

2 To what extent would any **one** multinational company be likely to be affected by the development of one large global trade union? [12]

185

3 Staff vacancies at Select College

Select College specialises in offering IGCSE and A Level courses for students over 16 years old. The college is expanding rapidly. The deputy principal with responsibility for human resources has been given the job of recruiting three more administration workers and ten more lecturers. The lecturers will be needed to start up the science and geography departments. The office workers are required to cope with the enrolment of the increasing numbers of students. A decision has to be taken on the employment contracts to be offered to these new workers. The principal is keen to see costs kept as low as possible. He is paid a share of the college profits each year. He believes that part-time and temporary contracts should be given to the office workers. The lecturers, he believes, should be offered full-time, but temporary, contracts. This would allow the college to stop employing the teachers at the end of the year if either they were poor performers or student numbers were lower than anticipated. 'I believe that we should pay a specialist recruitment agency to recruit and select all of the college's new staff. We would only need their services for about six weeks each year and we would not have to do any of the interviews,' he told the deputy principal, Judith Huang.

Judith does not believe this proposal will work. She told the principal: 'It would seem unfair to these new office workers and teachers if we offered them shorter-term contracts than our existing staff. Also, there is a national shortage of good science teachers and we need to motivate and keep good staff. We should also have full control over how new teachers are recruited and selected – we have to work with them, after all.'

The two had to agree college policy on these issues soon as the end of term was fast approaching.

[32 marks, 50 minutes]

1 Analyse the benefits to Select College of workforce planning. [8]

2 Discuss the arguments for and against offering full-time and permanent employment contracts to the new office staff and lecturers. [12]

3 Evaluate the best ways for Select College to recruit and select new lecturers. [12]

4 Human resources crisis in the factory

The customer complaints file on Bernardo Alves's desk was bulging with letters received over the last few weeks. He had never known a period like it. Short-staffed for the last three months and with unsuitable recruits being asked to take on quite skilled jobs without training, it was no wonder customers were fed up with late delivery times and poor quality goods.

The Accord Lighting Co. manufactured specialist lighting equipment for theatres and cinemas. Demand has increased in recent years as consumers' incomes have risen and theatre and cinema attendance is increasing. As deputy manager of the factory, Bernardo wondered why the owners had not taken up his suggestion two years ago to create a specialised human resource department. The owners had rejected the proposal, stating that it would cost too much and that it was better for 'such matters to be dealt with by each of the departmental managers'. The trouble was that these managers were not experts at recruiting, training or even retaining staff. They were good at their jobs, whether these were repairing machines, designing new products, ordering raw materials and so on, but Bernardo had never rated their people-management skills very highly. Labour turnover was high in all production departments. Recent output and employment data is shown in the table below:

	2012	2013
Annual output (lighting units)	1400	1100
Total production employees	25	22

The departmental managers did not enjoy recruiting workers and so they used outside agencies to select new recruits. This they did, at a cost, but they often failed to explain to new people what the stresses of working in a busy factory were. Bernardo decided to update his two-year-old report to directors of Accord Lighting, attach the most recent letters of complaint to it and try once again to convince them that specialist management of people was just as important as specialist managers in other areas of the business.

[34 marks, 50 minutes]

1 Outline the HR problems experienced by Accord Lighting Co. [8]

2 a Calculate labour productivity for:
   i 2012
   ii 2013 [4]

b Assess how this manufacturing business could increase labour productivity. [10]

3 To what extent would the profitability of Accord Lighting Co be improved by more effective management of its human resources? [12]

A Level essay questions

[20 marks, 45 minutes each]

1 To what extent does the role of HRM, in any organisation of your choice, impact on the success of that organisation? [20]

2 Evaluate whether 'soft' HRM is the best way to manage employees in an increasingly globalised business environment. [20]

14 Organisation structure

This chapter covers syllabus section A Level 2.4.

On completing this chapter, you will be able to:

- understand why organisations need a structure and why flexibility is important
- analyse the different types of organisational structure that can be adopted and their advantages and drawbacks
- assess the main features of an organisational chart, such as levels of hierarchy, chain of command and span of control
- understand the difference between centralised and decentralised structures
- evaluate the conflict between trust and control with a policy of delegation
- outline the differences between line and staff authority
- examine the appropriateness of centralised and decentralised structures
- understand the difference between authority, accountability and responsibility.

Introducing the topic

WHAT IS HAPPENING TO ORGANISATIONAL STRUCTURES?

There are major changes taking place to the way most businesses organise their internal management structure. Traditionally, head offices housed all key personnel taking all important decisions. Now, more and more firms are using 'flatter' and more decentralised structures where decisions are taken anywhere else but at head office! Instead of all power being focused at the top of an organisation there is now much more involvement and collaboration in decision-making. Why are these changes happening?

- Employees are becoming better qualified and more knowledgeable – they do not want to work in formal hierarchies.
- Multinational organisations find that taking decisions centrally means they are not taking local or regional factors into account.

- Communication systems are becoming more mobile and instantaneous, allowing workers to work in teams much more effectively.
- The old world was one of rigid and formal hierarchies. Today's world needs organisations that encourage and promote leaders who can push, convince and lead people to work in collaborative teams.

Points to think about:

- Has your school or college got an organisational structure? Describe its main features.
- Why would taking all decisions at head office be a 'safe' type of organisation?
- What do you think would be the main benefits of encouraging leaders to work with employees in teams?

Introduction

A sole trader with no employees does not need an organisational structure. The owner does all the work and makes all of the business decisions. But if this sole owner were to take on even just one worker or one partner, a sense of formal structure would become necessary. Who is to do what job? Who is responsible to whom and for which decisions? If the business expanded further, with more workers – including supervisory staff, different departments or divisions – then the need for a structure would be even greater. This would allow the division of tasks and responsibilities to be made clear to all. So what is meant by organisational structure? What would happen if it was confused or misunderstood? How does the structure impact on workers and managers? What are the key principles of designing and analysing an organisation's structure? These are the issues with which this chapter is concerned.

All organisations need structure

A typical business structure is one that is based on departmental lines, and these departments are divided according to function or the type of work carried out. Structures can be illustrated by means of an organisation chart. A traditional one, showing functional structure,

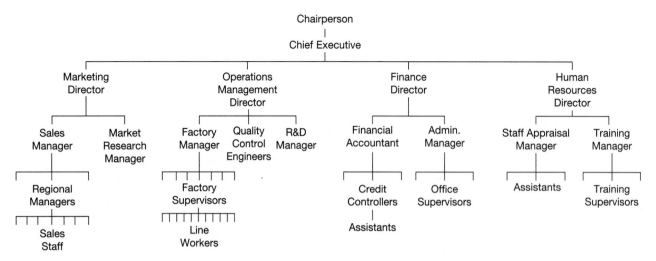

Figure 14.1 An example of an organisation structure

is shown in Figure 14.1. This chart displays a number of important points about the internal organisation of this business. It indicates:

- who has overall responsibility for decision-making
- the formal relationships between different people and departments – individual workers can identify their position in the business and who is their immediate 'line' manager
- the way in which accountability and authority may be passed down the organisation – this is called the chain of command
- the number of subordinates reporting to each more senior manager – this is called the span of control
- formal channels of communication both vertical and horizontal – this will aid the investigation of communication problems if messages are not being received in time by the correct people
- the identity of the supervisor or manager to whom each worker is answerable and should report to is made clear.

 KEY TERM

Organisational structure: the internal, formal framework of a business that shows the way in which management is organised and linked together and how authority is passed through the organisation.

Different types of organisational structure

There are several structural systems that a business might adopt – we will analyse the two most common ones.

The hierarchical (or bureaucratic) structure

This is one where there are different layers of the organisation with fewer and fewer people on each higher level – Figure 14.1 demonstrates this. In general terms it is often presented as a pyramid (see Figure 14.2).

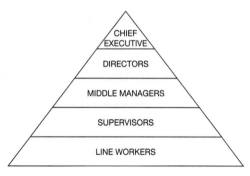

Figure 14.2 A typical hierarchical pyramid

Advantages of hierarchical structure

Many businesses are still organised in this way as decision-making power starts at the top, but may be passed down to lower levels. The vertical divisions do not have to be based on functional departments – they could be based on region or country or product category, for example consumer goods and industrial goods. The rungs on the career ladder for a keen and ambitious employee are illustrated by the different levels of hierarchy. The role of each individual will be clear and well-defined. There is a clearly identifiable chain of command. This traditional hierarchy is most frequently used by organisations based on a 'role culture', where the importance of the role determines the position in the hierarchy.

Disadvantages of hierarchical structure

Such a structure tends to suggest that one-way (top downwards) communication is the norm – this is rarely the most efficient form. There are few horizontal links between the departments or the separate divisions, and this can lead to lack of coordination between them. Managers are often accused of tunnel vision because they are not encouraged to look at problems in any way other than through the eyes of their own department. This type of structure is very inflexible and often leads to change resistance. This is because all managers tend to be defending both their own position in the hierarchy and the importance of their own department.

The matrix structure

This approach to organising businesses aims to eliminate many of the problems associated with the hierarchical structure. This type of structure cuts across the departmental lines of a hierarchical chart and creates project teams made up of people from all departments or divisions. The basic idea is shown in Figure 14.3.

KEY TERM

Matrix structure: an organisational structure that creates project teams that cut across traditional functional departments.

This method of organising a business is task- or project-focused. Instead of highlighting the role or status of individuals it gathers together a team of specialists with the objective of completing a task or a project successfully. Emphasis is placed on an individual's ability to contribute to the team rather than their position in the hierarchy. The use of matrix project teams has been championed by Tom Peters, one of the best-known writers on organisational structure. In his book *In Search of Excellence* (1982) he suggested that:

- organisations need flexible structures that remove as much bureaucracy as possible by getting rid of as many rigid rules and regulations as possible
- the use of project teams should lead to more innovative and creative ideas as staff will be more motivated to contribute.

Advantages of matrix structure

It allows total communication between all members of the team, cutting across traditional boundaries between departments in a hierarchy where only senior managers are designed to link with and talk to each other. There is less chance of people focusing on just what is good for their department. This is replaced with a feeling of what is good for the project and the business as a whole. The crossover of ideas between people with specialist knowledge in different areas tends to create more successful solutions. As new project teams can be created quickly, this system is well-designed to respond to changing markets or technological conditions.

Disadvantages of matrix structure

There is less direct control from the 'top' as the teams may be empowered to undertake and complete a project. This passing down of authority to more junior staff could be difficult for some managers to come to terms with. The benefit of faster reaction to new situations is, therefore, at the expense of reduced bureaucratic control, and this trend may be resisted by some senior managers. Team members may have, in effect, two leaders if the business retains levels of hierarchy for departments but allows cross-departmental teams to be created. This could cause a conflict of interests.

Key principles of organisational structure

Levels of hierarchy

Each **level** in the hierarchy represents a grade or rank of staff. Lower ranks are subordinate to superiors of a higher

KEY TERM

Level of hierarchy: a stage of the organisational structure at which the personnel on it have equal status and authority.

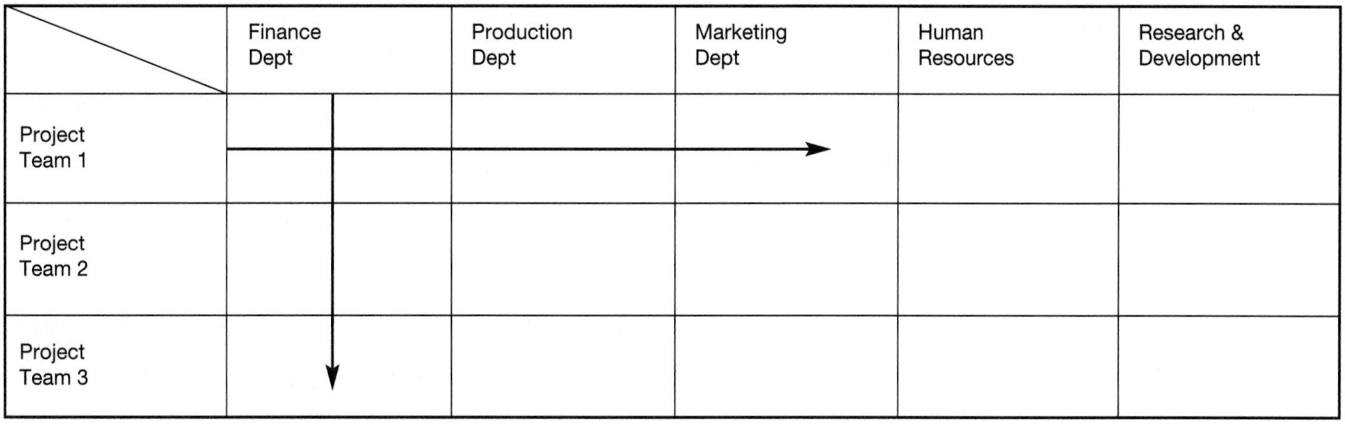

189

	Finance Dept	Production Dept	Marketing Dept	Human Resources	Research & Development
Project Team 1					
Project Team 2					
Project Team 3					

Figure 14.3 A matrix organisational structure

ACTIVITY 14.1

Penang Valley Cars Ltd

Jim Mah founded the Penang Valley car-hire business six years ago. He started out as a sole trader with just three vehicles. His business now employs 33 people and it has a fleet of 2,000 vehicles. Jim is chief executive. He has four fellow directors. They are in charge of finance, vehicle repairs, marketing and administration. The administration role includes dealing with all staffing matters. The finance director has three accounting assistants. The director in charge of vehicle repairs has two supervisors who report to him – one for the day shift and one for the night shift. They each have six mechanics working under them. The marketing department contains four people – one sales manager and three junior sales assistants. Administration has six office staff who take all the bookings and are responsible to an office supervisor who is under the direct control of the director.

This type of structure has served the business well but Jim is concerned about the impact of further expansion on the organisation. In particular, he is planning two developments for the future – one would involve renting trucks to other businesses and the other would be setting up a new office in another country.

Successful garage workshop – such a business could use a matrix structure of organisation

[20 marks, 30 minutes]

1 Sketch the current organisational structure of Penang Valley Cars Ltd. Include all staff on your chart. [6]

2 Do you think the current structure is appropriate for the business? Give reasons for your answer. [6]

3 Discuss how Jim might develop a suitable structure for the two new developments he is planning. [8]

---

rank. The greater the number of levels, the greater the number of different grades or ranks in the organisation. A tall (or narrow) organisational structure has a large number of levels of hierarchy and this creates three main problems:

- Communication though the organisation can become slow with messages becoming distorted or filtered in some way.
- Spans of control are likely to be narrow – see below.
- There is likely to be a greater sense of remoteness, among those on lower levels, from the decision-making power at the top.

In contrast a flat organisational structure will have few levels of hierarchy, but will tend to have wider spans of control – see below.

Chain of command

Typically, instructions are passed down the hierarchy; information, for example about sales or output levels, is sent upwards. The taller the organisational structure, the longer will be the **chain of command** – slowing down communications.

 KEY TERM

Chain of command: this is the route through which authority is passed down an organisation – from the chief executive and the board of directors.

Span of control

Spans of control can be either wide – with a manager directly responsible for many subordinates – or narrow – a

 KEY TERM

Span of control: the number of subordinates reporting directly to a manager.

manager has direct responsibility for a few subordinates. This difference would be illustrated on an organisation chart as shown in Figures 14.4 and 14.5.

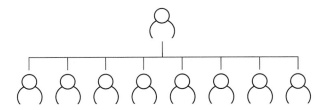

Figure 14.4 Wide span of control of eight – this is likely to encourage delegation. This is a flat organisational structure

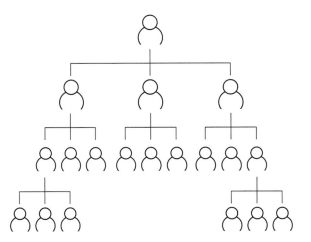

Figure 14.5 Narrow span of control of three – this is likely to lead to close control of subordinates. This is a tall organisational structure

Delegation

This is a very important principle that can have far-reaching effects on both the organisational structure and the motivation levels of subordinate employees. **Delegation** means the passing down of authority to perform tasks and take decisions from higher to lower levels in the organisation. As Herzberg and other researchers pointed out, this process can be very beneficial to motivation. Generally, the wider the span of control, the greater the degree of delegation that is undertaken. Imagine a manager with a span of control of 15 subordinates. It might be impossible to closely control the work of each of these every day – the manager would be allowed no time for more important strategic matters. Thus, the manager will delegate authority to his staff, and he will trust them to perform well. Clearly, they are accountable to the manager for good performance; but the manager

retains ultimate responsibility for the work done in the department whether it was delegated to others or not (see Table 14.1).

KEY TERM

Delegation: passing authority down the organisational hierarchy.

Centralisation and decentralisation

These two principles are linked to delegation. With **centralisation** there will be minimum delegation to managers in other areas, departments or divisions of the business. **Decentralisation**, passing decision-making authority to managers in other areas, departments or divisions in the business, allowing decisions to be taken away from head office, must involve delegation. A centralised organisation would insist on all sections of the business following the same procedures, which gives the business a feeling of uniformity and consistency. Head office will be able to exert considerable control over all operations. Decentralised organisations will allow staff

KEY TERMS

Centralisation: keeping all of the important decision-making powers within head office or the centre of the organisation.

Decentralisation: decision-making powers are passed down the organisation to empower subordinates and regional/product managers.

Advantages of delegation	Disadvantages of delegation
■ gives senior managers more time to focus on important, strategic roles ■ shows trust in subordinates and this can motivate and challenge them ■ develops and trains staff for more senior positions ■ helps staff to achieve fulfilment through their work (self-actualisation)	■ if the task is not well-defined or if inadequate training is given, then delegation is unlikely to succeed ■ delegation will be unsuccessful if insufficient authority (power) is given to the subordinate who is performing the tasks ■ managers may only delegate the boring jobs that they do not want to do – this will not be motivating

Table 14.1 Delegation – advantages and disadvantages

to be empowered and this demonstrates trust in them. Decisions will be taken 'closer to the action' in terms of junior managers being more aware of local factors or closer to the consumers themselves.

Organisational structure – the factors that influence it

The introduction to this chapter referred to the need for structure as a business grows in size. Small firms may manage quite well with an unwritten structure, where the informal links between staff are adequate to allow smooth functioning of the business. This type of arrangement is unlikely to work well in any business other than very small ones with a clear leader. As more employees are appointed, so the need for a formal way of indicating the positions of people and their level of authority becomes greater. Here is an example of a very small garage business with five employees.

This could also be presented in this way:

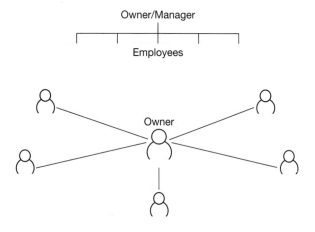

This is called an entrepreneurial structure, and would only be suitable for small firms as it could place too much pressure on the owner or the entrepreneur.

If the business were to grow, another manager or supervisor might be required – it could become too time-consuming for one person to control the work of all

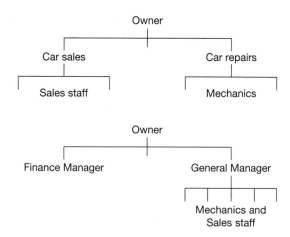

Figure 14.6 Alternative structures for a garage business

the employees, even if delegation were practised. A decision would then need to be made about how the responsibilities were to be divided – by function or by type of operation. Figure 14.6 shows two options for a garage business.

If the business is really successful and further expansion achieved, possibly in another area or region, then further structural changes might become necessary (see Figure 14.7).

This process could continue, but it might be necessary to cut across these divisions if new projects were proposed. If a car-body repair shop were to be opened, then a project team could be established using the matrix system (see Figure 14.8).

The organisational structure will therefore change with the size and the range of activities that the business is involved in. It must be flexible enough to meet the changing needs of a business as it grows and develops.

Here are other factors that could determine the internal structure of a business:

- The style of management, or the culture of the managers. If senior managers adopted a largely Theory X approach, then small spans of control would be adopted in a hierarchical structure. A Theory Y manager would adopt very few levels of hierarchy and may prefer a matrix team-based structure.

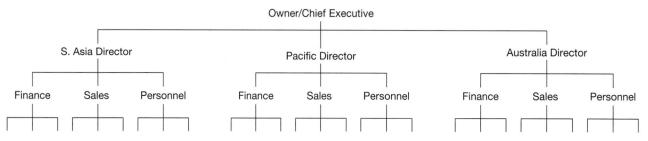

Figure 14.7 Further structural changes will be necessary if the business is really successful and continues to grow and develop

- Retrenchment caused by economic recession or increased competition might lead to delayering to reduce overhead costs – this would again reduce levels of hierarchy and shorten the chain of command.
- Corporate objectives. For example, if one of the long-term objectives of the business is to expand in other countries, then the organisational structure must be adapted to allow a regional market department. Structure must reflect the objectives and needs of the business.
- Adopting new technologies – especially IT – can lead to a reduced need for certain employee types, for example managers sending messages by email rather than letters typed by secretaries. In addition, central control might be made easier by the flow of information through IT and this could make middle management layers less important.

Important links between organisational principles

1 The greater the number of levels of hierarchy, the longer the chain of command

This will have serious consequences for:

- communication effectiveness
- spans of control – these are going to be smaller in tall organisations

- delegation – when spans of control are narrow, managers are more able to control the work of the few people, so delegation is likely to be limited
- motivation levels of junior staff – as they are so far removed from senior management, delegation will be limited
- business costs – ranks of middle managers are expensive to employ and they take up very costly office accommodation.

2 Problems associated with a tall structure – is delayering the answer?

Tall hierarchical structures have communication and employee motivation problems. One conclusion many senior managers have come to is to remove whole layers of management to create shorter structures. This process is known as delayering (see Table 14.2). This

KEY TERM

Delayering: removal of one or more of the levels of hierarchy from an organisational structure.

193

	Marketing	Operations Management	Finance	Personnel
Car Repairs				
Body Repairs				
Car Sales				

Figure 14.8 The use of a matrix structure in a garage business

Advantages of delayering	Disadvantages of delayering
- reduces business costs - shortens the chain of command and should improve communication through the organisation - increases spans of control and opportunities for delegation - may increase workforce motivation due to less remoteness from top management and greater chance of having more responsible work to perform	- could be 'one-off' costs of making managers redundant, for example redundancy payments - increased workloads for managers who remain – this could lead to overwork and stress - fear that redundancies might be used to cut costs could reduce the sense of security of the whole workforce – one of Maslow's needs

Table 14.2 Advantages and disadvantages of delayering

ACTIVITY 14.2

Majestic Cinemas plc

Majestic Cinemas owns one of the largest chains of cinemas in Asia. It operates in more than ten countries. The current organisational structure is shown in Figure 1.

The new chief executive, Paul Lee, is concerned that this structure does not give the business sufficient flexibility. The former head of the corporation was very autocratic in approach and had centralised nearly all major decision-making. There was minimum delegation as he had not believed the staff could be trusted, even with day-to-day decisions. All procedures were clearly laid down from head office, including the opening times of each cinema, the types of films to be shown, the range of drinks and snacks to be sold and so on. He had been reported as saying: 'Our customers know where they are with Majestic – they do not want to see us change the way we do things. In any case, by buying our films centrally we can keep costs down.' Paul did not believe in this approach. He had been educated abroad and had travelled extensively. He recognised the differences in tastes, culture and population trends that existed across the region. He considered that decentralisation was essential in many areas of the business. He wanted to develop and train younger staff to manage cinemas and to stamp their own style and personality on them. The ageing middle management would, he felt, oppose all of these moves. He wondered if the middle managers were really necessary – after all, the cinema managers could send him daily attendance figures over the Internet each day and he could use video conferencing to contact them at any time. Paul realised that he had a job on his hands to change the culture of the organisation – but measures had to be taken to cut costs and to remain competitive.

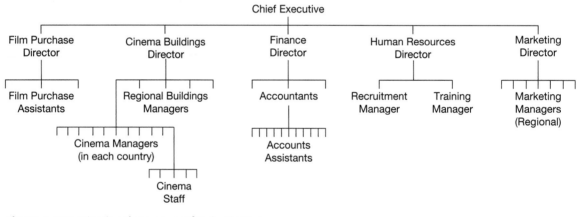

Figure 1 Organisational structure of Majestic Cinemas

[26 marks, 35 minutes]

1 What is the span of control of the film purchase director? [2]

2 How many levels of hierarchy are there in the cinema buildings department? [2]

3 Outline **three** drawbacks of a centralised structure in this business. [6]

4 Explain how Paul might decentralise the decision-making in this business. [6]

5 Discuss the consequences to the business and to the cinema managers of decentralising decision-making authority to them. [10]

development in organisational structures has been assisted by improvements in IT and communication technology, which better enable senior managers to communicate with and monitor the performance of junior staff and widely dispersed departments. This has had the effect of diminishing the importance of the role of middle managers.

3 Delegation: conflicts that can arise and potential benefits

Delegation involves a manager showing trust in a subordinate – to the extent that less control will be exercised over their work. Some managers do not like giving up control. Perhaps they may feel less important if they do so or they may not wish to take any risks at all.

These managers do not make good delegators. There is a conflict between showing trust in a worker and controlling the worker's efforts – effective delegation means slowly releasing management control in order to show more trust. With this trust comes a greater sense of achievement for the worker when the work is done well. A modern development of delegation is called 'empowerment'. This approach not only delegates tasks and authority to individuals and groups but it also allows them to decide on the best method to use to complete the job. This gives even more chance for the subordinates to show initiative and creativity (Herzberg's motivators), but it requires an even greater measure of trust from managers – there is even less direct and immediate control over the work being carried out.

4 Accountability, authority and responsibility

It is important to understand the links and the differences between these concepts. Delegation gives subordinates the authority to perform certain tasks – this means that they have the power to undertake jobs and make decisions necessary for these jobs to be completed. If this job is done poorly, then the worker is accountable to his or her immediate manager – they can be held to account and be disciplined for an inadequate performance. However, the overall responsibility for the work of the department or section – including the performance of each subordinate – rests with the manager. The manager delegates authority, but not responsibility, and the blame for underperformance or mistakes within the department should rest with the manager. The thinking behind this important principle is that it is the manager who chose the subordinate (or delegate) to undertake the task, allocated resources and arranged training – and if any of these were the reasons for poor performance, then the manager should, ultimately, 'carry the can'. Accountability still

exists, however. A subordinate cannot perform a delegated task without considering that they will be held accountable for their actions. This ultimate control over their work is achieved by means of regular appraisal of staff, monitoring of performance against targets (aided by computer links to managers and head office) and by adopting management-by-objectives techniques.

5 Centralisation and decentralisation

Good examples of decentralised businesses are those multinationals that allow regional and cultural differences to be reflected in the products and services they provide. Clothing retailers with operations in several countries often allow local managers to decide on the exact range of clothing to be sold in each country – it could be disastrous for a business to try to sell European winter clothes in Singapore, for example. Centralised businesses will want to maintain exactly the same image and product range in all areas – perhaps because of cost savings or to retain a carefully created business identity in all markets. See Table 14.3 for a summary of advantages and disadvantages.

6 Line and staff relationships

Line managers are those who have authority over others in a hierarchical structure. For example, the sales director will have line authority over the sales managers for each of the different products the firm sells. Line managers have responsibility for achieving specific business objectives.

KEY TERM

Line managers: managers who have direct authority over people, decisions and resources within the hierarchy of an organisation.

195

Advantages of centralisation	Advantages of decentralisation
■ A fixed set of rules and procedures in all areas of the firm should lead to rapid decision-making – there is little scope for discussion.	■ More local decisions can be made that reflect different conditions – the managers who take the decisions will have local knowledge and are likely to have closer contact with consumers.
■ The business has consistent policies throughout the organisation. This prevents any conflicts between the divisions and avoids confusion in the minds of consumers.	■ More junior managers can develop and this prepares them for more challenging roles.
■ Senior managers take decisions in the interest of the whole business – not just one division of it.	■ Delegation and empowerment are made easier and these will have positive effects on motivation.
■ Central buying should allow for greater economies of scale.	■ Decision-making in response to changes, for example in local market conditions, should be quicker and more flexible as head office will not have to be involved every time.
■ Senior managers at central office will be experienced decision-makers.	

Table 14.3 Advantages of centralisation and decentralisation

Staff managers do not have line authority over others. They are specialists who are employed to give advice to senior line managers. They might be economists, specialist market researchers or scientific experts advising on the environmental impact of certain products or processes. They perform a supporting role to the line managers, but do not take decisions. Due to their professional status and experience, they can be very well paid and they are often accused of having less loyalty to the business as their services might be in great demand by a wide range of firms. This could lead to them being attracted by better rewards in other organisations. Finally, the line managers might resent 'experts' coming into the organisation and, as they see it, telling them how to do their jobs.

KEY TERM

Staff managers: managers who, as specialists, provide support, information and assistance to line managers.

ACTIVITY 14.3

New structure needed

A hotel manager is planning to double the size of the company's workforce over the next two years as demand for accommodation and hotel facilities increases. She wants to design an organisation structure for 210 employees working in three divisions: hotel, restaurant, conference centre.

[16 marks, 25 minutes]

1 Explain to the hotel manager the meaning of the following terms:
   a 'span of control'
   b 'levels of hierarchy'
   c 'delegation'   [6]

2 Explain the potential benefits to the hotel manager of a 'flat' hierarchical structure in this case.   [10]

Informal organisations

Within any business there are two types of organisation – the formal structure and the informal structure. So far, this chapter has focused on the formal structure, but informal structures can also have a considerable impact on the success of a business.

KEY TERM

Informal organisation: the network of personal and social relations that develop between people within an organisation.

The main focus of the informal organisation is the employee as an individual person. Power and influence are obtained from membership of informal groups within the business – and these groups may cross over departmental lines. The conduct of individuals within these groups is governed by 'norms' or normal standards of behaviour. If an individual breaks these norms, then the rest of the group imposes sanctions on them. Informal structures can either be beneficial or harmful to the business. People are only human and an individual's effectiveness at work can be greatly affected by the employees around them. A clever manager will try to use informal groups to the benefit of the business, for example by avoiding personality clashes between people in different groups or by basing team-working on informal groups. The problem may arise, however, that the informal group leader has more power and influence over the team than the formal leader – so the managers will have to choose supervisors carefully.

Organisational structure – the future

Over the past 20 years, many large businesses, including most multinationals, have been forced to retrench, rationalise and downsize their organisations. At the same time, the increasing pace of globalisation and technological change means that huge organisational structures with many levels of hierarchy and slow bureaucratic systems have to change. For example, if communication has to go up and down the hierarchy, then business is lost and the organisation gets a bad reputation for being unresponsive to customer needs.

So, in the current environment, businesses need a flexible and fluid organisational structure to allow for growth – or retrenchment – and development. More businesses are moving away from a traditional 'command' structure to one based around team-based problem-solving. This involves removing horizontal boundaries between departments altogether and reducing middle-management 'layers' to the absolute minimum. Future success will depend greatly on being able to respond rapidly to the changing business environment and this almost certainly means that the days of the traditional pyramid 'hierarchy' are numbered.

ACTIVITY 14.4

MAS must change strategy, says new boss

Loss-making Malaysia Airlines System (MAS) must raise labour productivity and double services in the region to become profitable, its new boss said in recent remarks. The national carrier's present business strategy was unsuitable as operational costs were far too high, managing director Mohamad Nor Mohamad Yusoff said in an interview with *The Sun* newspaper. Productivity and customer service were also 'disappointing', he said and had contributed to a decline in overall performance. 'I liken MAS to a house that is supposed to be double-storeyed, but instead has five storeys. In such a situation, the position is untenable,' he added. 'We need to reduce the number of storeys. MAS's operational costs are higher than those of the industry and its competitors… each department does not operate according to expectations.' He said MAS aircraft were stationary too long and were underutilised. He also voiced concern over poor productivity in the catering division.

The airline has now reported losses for four straight years and has borrowings totalling 10.34 billion ringgit.

Kuala Lumpur International Airport, Malaysia

On a suggestion that the airline should decentralise and separate its international and domestic operations, Mohamad Nor said this was being studied, but the management found that 'separation is not the best choice'.

[31 marks, 35 minutes]

1 Analyse **three** possible reasons why labour productivity is lower in MAS than other airlines. **[9]**

2 Evaluate the impact of adapting the organisational structure by reducing the number of 'storeys' from five to two (delayering) on:
   a MAS staff
   b business efficiency. **[12]**

3 Assess the likely impact of a decision to split and operate separately the domestic and international divisions of the airline on:
   a the performance of MAS
   b staff motivation. **[10]**

ACTIVITY 14.5

Business in focus – Tata Steel reorganises structure

India's Tata Steel has reorganised its management structure to realise its corporate goal of becoming a leading player in the global steel industry. The company has formed a centralised body to create common strategies across the whole group, which has steelworks in the UK, Thailand and the Netherlands as well as in India. The functions that will be centralised will be technology, finance, corporate strategy and corporate communications.

[10 marks 15 minutes]

Analyse the benefits to a multinational business such as Tata of having a centralised organisational structure. **[10]**

197

SUMMARY POINTS

- Organisations need a structure to give people an awareness of how they 'fit in' and who their superiors and subordinates are.
- The typical organisation structure is hierarchical in nature but this can be inflexible and may be difficult to adapt to meet changing business needs.
- Matrix systems can be used to reduce some of the disadvantages of a hierarchical system and to create a team ethic.
- Levels of hierarchy, chains of command, spans of control and delegation are important concepts.
- Delegation is increasing in most organisations and there are advantages and disadvantages of this.
- There are significant differences between centralised and decentralised business organisations.
- Potential conflict exists between line management and staff management.
- There are many factors that influence a business's organisational structure.
- There is an increasing need for greater flexibility to meet the needs of the business and to permit growth and development.

RESEARCH TASK

- Investigate the organisational chart or structure of your school of college.
- How many levels of hierarchy are there?
- What is the span of control of some of the senior management?
- Examine ways in which the school or college might be organised on a matrix structure basis. Would this lead to more benefits than drawbacks?

A Level exam practice questions
Case studies

1 Mitsubishi Motors to rejig structure

Mitsubishi Motors (MMC), the Japanese car maker that is 37% owned by Daimler-Chrysler, will reveal significant changes to its senior and middle management structure at the next shareholders' meeting. The changes reflect underlying tensions between the company's new German managers and established Japanese executives who found it difficult adjusting to the new culture. The restructuring will aim to weed out managers whose more traditional mentality could delay the sweeping reforms under way under the new management. Other managers are also likely to be offered early retirement. It is understood that both MMC's chief operating officer and president want to dispense with managers at any level who remain locked into the 'length-of-service' mentality and have acted ahead of this month's meeting to weed them out.

Takashi Sonobe, president, recently demonstrated his commitment to reform when he announced 60 senior staff advisers – who were of an advanced age and made a marginal contribution to the company despite generous remuneration – would be removed in the next three years.

Rolf Eckrodt, the chief operating officer, appointed a 'COO Team' comprising about 25 mainly non-Japanese executives from Daimler-Chrysler. This team, drawn from different departments, is responsible for overseeing the implementation of the company's restructuring plan. It is understood that some long-standing members of MMC's middle and upper management resent the presence and power of the COO Team, all of whom are under 40 years old and who are controlling the strategic direction of the company. The tension between the COO Team and some of MMC's managers has been described as stemming from Japanese managers with a 'job-for-life' attitude. The 'job-for-life' concept is not part of German management culture.

[30 marks, 45 minutes]

1 Outline the 'culture conflict' that seems to exist in this business. **[6]**

2 Analyse the possible benefits to MMC of the decision to delayer the management structure. **[10]**

3 Discuss the possible consequences for the efficiency of the business and employee motivation of the new management structure described in the case. **[14]**

2 Hotels group set for major management shake-up

It is reported that the Empire Hotel group is to undergo an overhaul of its organisational structure. The group has been criticised in the financial press for poor performances in recent years. The blame is put at the door of senior management who have been slow to respond to changing needs for hotel accommodation and the growth of the business conference industry. Rising consumer incomes have made consumers much more demanding about the services they expect. The standard in many Empire hotels leaves a lot to be desired. In addition, they tend to have very old-fashioned conference facilities and need new IT and video equipment to keep up to industry standards. Some staff are reported to be leaving for other hotel chains that offer much more responsibility to hotel and departmental managers.

Excell Hotels, for example, gives its hotel managers much longer training than Empire but also gives them much more freedom when they have qualified. One Excell manager was quoted as saying: 'We are given so much authority early on in our careers and we report directly to senior management, who give immediate feedback.' It is reported that complaints from top managers or requests for new resources from hotels take three weeks before being considered in the Empire organisation because of the number of middle managers who are asked to give their views. Excell hotels also have an excellent reputation for local food dishes and decorations that reflect local culture and traditions. At last, Empire seems to be responding to this criticism. It has appointed several new design and catering experts to advise their own departments, yet the changes being proposed are causing some friction among the existing established line managers.

[50 marks, 75 minutes]

1   Outline the problems that Empire Hotels seem to be experiencing due to a long chain of command. **[8]**

2   Analyse the disadvantages to Empire Hotels resulting from the reluctance of senior managers to delegate. **[10]**

3   Discuss the impact on the performance of this business of adopting extensive delegation. **[10]**

4   Assess the differences between the roles of the newly appointed staff managers at Empire with those of the existing line managers. **[10]**

5   To what extent might the performance of the Empire Hotel group be improved by adopting a different and more flexible organisation structure? **[12]**

A Level essay questions

[20 marks, 45 minutes each]

1   Evaluate the advantages and disadvantages of a traditional hierarchical structure for any large business that operates in your country. **[20]**

2   The chief executive officer of a large multinational computer manufacturing business stated: 'Unless we introduce more flexibility into the rigid and hierarchical structure of our organisation it will fail to meet the needs of the business as it grows and develops.' To what extent do you agree with this view? **[20]**

15 Business communication

This chapter covers syllabus section A Level 2.5.

On completing this chapter, you will be able to:

- understand what is meant by effective communication
- appreciate the importance of feedback, choice of medium and clarity of message in achieving effective communication
- analyse the advantages and disadvantages of the different communication methods or media
- evaluate their application in different situations
- understand the causes of ineffective communication – the barriers to communication and how to overcome them
- analyse the differences between one- and two-way, vertical and horizontal, formal and informal communication
- evaluate the application of different communication networks.

Introducing the topic

TECHNOLOGY AND BUSINESS COMMUNICATION

The impact of new technology on how a business communicates internally – between managers and employees – has been changed forever by the latest technological devices. Mobile (cell) smartphones, iPads and other tablets, networks, Intranets and cloud computing – these are just some of the recent developments that allow people within a business to keep in touch in ways that, even 20 years ago, would have been unimaginable.

Networking allows collaboration between workers on reports, programming and other document production. It forms the core of how most business communication is performed today. Cloud computing allows businesses, such as large multinationals, to operate globally without sacrificing security or limiting user access. Some businesses – such as LinkedIn and Kaplan – give all employees an iPad to allow easier internal communication and easy access to the Intranet/Internet.

Intranets – internal computer networks built on internet technologies – are helping to drastically reduce many administrative jobs. Once online, employees can take training courses, communicate by email with colleagues, find out how much holiday they have left or check out internal job vacancies. As the facilities expand, Intranets are helping to blur the line between work and leisure. For example, BP, the oil company, is developing a 'Virtual Village'; an online shopping mall accessed through the company portal where employees can buy anything from computers to holidays. When British Airways announced the dismantling of its second hub at London's Gatwick airport, the news came out first on the company's intranet.

Are there any drawbacks to IT use in business communication? Initial cost can be significant, some security issues remain and employees may need training. But above all, the tendency to reduce interpersonal contact is not necessarily desirable – either for good communication or for satisfying social needs.

Points to think about:

- Why is it important that there should be effective communication within a business?
- Suggest and explain four benefits to a large business of using the latest technology to communicate with employees
- Do you think technologically advanced methods of communication are always the best ones to use?

Introduction

Communication is effective only if the message has been received and understood by the receiver, and the sender knows that it has been understood. Figure 15.1 shows the key features of **effective communication**:

- sender (or transmitter) of the message
- clear message
- appropriate medium (way in which the message is sent)
- receiver
- feedback to confirm receipt and understanding.

If the message has been sent but there has been no form of feedback, then the effectiveness of the communication cannot be judged. Feedback is defined as the response to a message by the receiver. All businesses communicate. They communicate externally – with suppliers, customers, shareholders and the government, for example. The significance of effective external communication is obvious – a potential customer confused about a product's qualities because of a poor advertisement or suppliers delivering to an incorrect address are just two examples of what can go wrong. Internal communication is between different people or groups within the organisation.

Why is effective communication important?

The quality and effectiveness of internal communication can have an impact on many areas of business:

- Staff motivation – and thus labour productivity. If staff are encouraged to participate through group discussion, for example, then effective communication will aid motivation. Workers feel out of touch and isolated if there is poor communication.
- The number and quality of ideas generated by the staff – if staff are asked for their ideas, then this can assist with problem-solving.
- Speed of decision-making – the more people who have to receive and react to a message, then the slower the decision-making system will be.
- Speed of response to market changes – if changes in consumers' decisions take a long time to be communicated to the decision-makers at the head of an organisation, then the business will be slow to respond with appropriate products.

- Reduces the risk of errors – incorrect understanding of a poorly expressed message will lead to incorrect responses. This could lead to many internal problems, such as the wrong products being made or incorrect prices being set.
- Effective coordination between departments – this will be helped by good communication links between them.

For these reasons it is important for managers to think carefully about how messages are sent and the form they should take. Poor communication will lead to demotivated staff, uncoordinated departments, poor customer service and a lack of overall direction for the organisation.

Communication methods – the media used in communicating

The choice of the method used to communicate a message can have a significant impact on effectiveness. The range of **communication media** available can be classified as follows.

Oral communication

This can be one-to-one conversations, interviews, appraisal sessions, group meetings or team briefings. It allows for two-way communication and feedback and this should

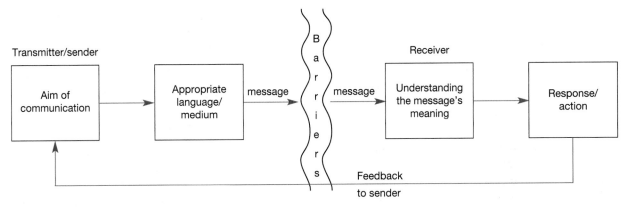

Figure 15.1 Effective communication – barriers must be reduced or eliminated

encourage good motivation. It is instantaneous and evidence of who attended the meeting and, therefore, of who received the message, can be retained. It allows the sender or the transmitter to reinforce the message with appropriate body language. However, some oral communication can be ambiguous, there may be no written record of what was said, it might not be appropriate for complicated and technical matters and it can be costly in terms of time. In addition, body language can also have a negative impact when, for example, the sender appears bored, uninterested or aggressive. All forms of communication that are not oral are sometimes referred to as 'non-verbal' communication.

Written communication

Many managers still like everything to be in writing. They will, therefore, tend to use letters, memos, notices on boards, reports, minutes of meetings and diagrams for technical matters, such as house plans. Written messages can be referred to more than once, they should be an accurate record and they allow for the transmission of detailed data. However, they eliminate supporting body language, do not allow for immediate feedback and there is often no evidence that the message has been received and/or understood.

IT and web-based media (electronic media)

These have the benefit of speed and are often combined with a written record. Internet and email use, Intranets (internal computer links), fax messages, video/web-conferencing and smartphones, including the use of social media, have all revolutionised business communications in recent years. These applications of electronic media do have their drawbacks:

- They may require staff to be trained and the young are usually much more proficient in their use than older employees.
- They reduce social contact and can create a sense of isolation and an important social need may go unsatisfied. Employees may use company time to send personal messages.
- Direct interpersonal contact is lost and most of these media do not allow the use of body language to help convey messages.
- There are security issues with computer technology and hard copies of important messages are often kept too in case of a virus.
- Finally, there is increasing evidence that IT can lead to **information overload** as a result of the speed and low usage cost of these methods. Too many messages can prevent the really important communication from being noticed and acted upon. For example, the sheer volume of email messages can take some workers several hours to reply to each day. Too much information can also cause

stress and a feeling of overwork. The benefits offered by IT and other electronic methods have to be weighed against their actual cost – in terms of equipment and training – and their other potential drawbacks.

The strengths and weaknesses of communication methods are summarised in Table 15.1.

KEY TERM

Information overload: so much information and so many messages are received that the most important ones cannot be easily identified and quickly acted on – most likely to occur with electronic media.

Visual communication

This can be used to accompany and support oral, written or electronic communication. Diagrams, pictures, charts and pages of computer images can be presented by using overhead projection, interactive white boards, data projectors, downloads and other means. The impact is increased if colour and movement are used. This form of communication is particularly useful in training or in marketing.

Factors influencing choice of appropriate media

Managers will consider these factors before deciding on the best communication method:

- The importance of a written record that the message has been sent and received, for example an important new legal contract.
- The advantages to be gained from staff input or two-way communication, for example a new staff shift system proposal could be discussed with workers before implementation.
- Cost – electronic media often require expensive capital resources, but, once these are obtained, emails are cost-effective. Written memos are cheap, but how many people will see them? The cost of management time in meetings should not be overlooked – it would be quicker and cheaper, but much less effective, to email all those at the meeting instead.
- Speed – electronic means can be quick, but is this more important than allowing time for opinions to be discussed at a meeting?
- Quantity of data to be communicated – the longer and more detailed the message, the less likely it is that oral communication will be adequate.
- Whether more than one method should be used for clarity and to be sure that the message has been received – a quick telephone call followed up by an official letter or order form will achieve both speed and accuracy.
- Size and geographical spread of the business – regular and frequent meetings of senior regional managers may be impossible in a multinational business.

Method	Strengths	Weaknesses
Oral	■ direct ■ can be varied to suit needs of receiver ■ easy to understand ■ can be questioned quickly	■ need to listen carefully ■ affected by noise ■ passive ■ no permanent accurate record ■ can be quickly forgotten
Written	■ recorded – permanent record ■ more structured ■ easy to distribute ■ cannot be varied ■ can be referred to again	■ often difficult to read ■ message identical to each receiver ■ no body language ■ feedback slower ■ no immediate response ■ may be misinterpreted ■ costly and time-consuming
Visual	■ more interactive ■ demands attention ■ often easier to remember ■ creates greater interest	■ needs close attention ■ sometimes too fast ■ not always clear ■ interpretations by receivers can vary
IT/web based	■ great speed ■ interactive ■ messages can be sent to many people ■ encourages response ■ overcomes global boundaries ■ good image for external communication	■ cannot always be received, e.g. poor Internet access ■ relies on receiver responding and acknowledging ■ expensive in hardware ■ risk of communication overload, e.g. excessive emails ■ security issues ■ diminishes interpersonal contact

Table 15.1 Strengths and weaknesses of communication methods

Barriers to effective communication

Any factor that prevents a message being received or correctly understood is termed a 'barrier to communication'. These barriers are often much more of a problem for large businesses with operations in more than one location and with several levels of hierarchy.

KEY TERM

Communication barriers: reasons why communication fails.

There are three broad reasons why barriers to communication occur.

1 Failure in one of the stages of the communication process

■ The **medium** chosen might be inappropriate. If the message contained detailed technical language and flow diagrams, trying to explain these over a mobile (cell) phone could lead to incorrect understanding.

■ If a **receiver forgot** part of a long message given to them orally, then a written version would have been more appropriate.

■ A **misleading or an incomplete message** would result in poor understanding – 'send the goods soon' may be interpreted as being tomorrow when in fact the sender meant 'now, or as soon as possible'.

ACTIVITY 15.1

Emails are ruining my day!

Two million emails are sent every minute in the UK alone. Office staff can spend up to half each working day going through their inbox. This makes workers tired, frustrated and unproductive. A recent study found that one-third of office workers suffer from email stress caused by the number they receive, the unnecessary length of some of them and the poor clarity of the language often used.

Now firms are being forced to help staff deal with their avalanche of emails. Some hire email consultants to advise on best email practice, while other firms now insist on an email-free day each week!

[8 marks, 10 minutes]

1 Analyse the reasons why emails might not lead to effective communication. [8]

■ The excessive use of **technical language or jargon** – terms that are understood by a specific group but not by others – may prevent the receiver from being able to comprehend what is required. Messages sent to branches or staff in another country may not be understood unless they are translated into the local language.

- If there is **too much information** – perhaps more than is actually necessary for the receiver to respond in the right way – the threat of information overload leads to 'noise', which is unnecessary data that actually prevent the receiver from grasping the important elements of the message.
- If the **channel of communication is too long** – the channel is the route through which a message is communicated from sender to receiver, as in tall hierarchical organisations – then messages will be slow to reach their intended receiver and they may become distorted or change their meaning on the way. This problem is particularly significant in large organisations.

2 Poor attitudes of either the sender or the receiver

- If the **sender is not trusted** – perhaps because of previous misleading messages or unpopular decisions – then the receiver may be unwilling to listen to or read the message carefully.
- **Unmotivated or alienated workers** make poor receivers. If workers have never been consulted on important issues before, then they may become very suspicious if the management style seems to be changing towards a more participative one. Workers with little interest in their work will not want to take the trouble to ensure that communication is effective.
- **Intermediaries** – those on the communication channel – may decide not to pass on a message, or to change it, if they are poorly motivated. This could occur, for example, if there has been a supplier's query about an order or a customer complaint.
- The sender may have such a **poor opinion or perception** of the receiver that no effort is made to ensure clarity of message or to check on understanding.

3 Physical reasons

- Noisy factories are not the best environment for communication. This indicates that the poor quality of the external environment can limit effective communication.
- Geographical distance can inhibit effective communication – certainly interpersonal communication will be very difficult. Modern electronic methods, such as video-conferencing, are designed to overcome some of these problems.

Reducing communication barriers

There are six steps managers should take in order to minimise the impact of communication barriers:

1 Ensure the message is clear and precise, but adequately detailed.
2 Keep the communication channel as short as possible.
3 Make sure that channels of communication are clear to all involved.
4 Build in feedback to the communication process so that problems with receipt or understanding of the message can be checked quickly.

ACTIVITY 15.2

Which communication method is best?

Here are eight different examples of communication:

- A safety notice on board a cruise ship.
- A sales order from a customer sent to the production department.
- An official warning to a staff member about quality of work.
- Sending of detailed architectural plans from one office to another office abroad.
- The need to solve an IT problem with a team of staff.
- 30 members of staff need to be given essential personnel information – but they are in different regional offices.
- The need to check some details of a product order with the customer.
- A list of emergency telephone numbers in case of accidents in the factory.

[24 marks, 30 minutes]

1 In each case, explain why it is important that communication is effective. [8]

2 Suggest and justify a suitable method of communication to be used in each case. [16]

---

5 Establish trust between senders and receivers – this could be most easily achieved in a business where the culture is to accept all staff as being important and as having useful contributions to make.
6 Ensure that physical conditions are appropriate for messages to be heard or received in other ways.

Formal communication networks

The internal communication structure of a business can be organised in a number of different ways – these systems are called **communication networks**.

KEY TERM

Formal communication networks: the official communication channels and routes used within an organisation.

The chain network

As shown in Figure 15.2, this is typically used in a hierarchical structure, such as the police, army and civil service. One person, at the top, starts off the communication message and this is passed on to the next person on the lower level. This is designed for authoritarian leaders. It reminds us of the weaknesses of both long chains of command and one-way communication. It does not encourage either two-way communication or horizontal communication and individuals at the end of the chain can feel isolated and demotivated. However, this method does give the leader control and allows an overview, from the top of the organisation, of the communication system.

The vertical network

See Figure 15.3. The 'boss', probably the owner, has four subordinates and communicates with them directly but individually – there is no group network here. This method could be used in a small department or any situation with a narrow span of control.

The wheel network

The leader is at the centre – or the person at the centre becomes the leader (see Figure 15.4). There could be two-way communication between the leader and each of the other parts of the wheel, but horizontal communication is poor. The leader is in control and can limit formal contact between the others. This network might represent the

Figure 15.2 The chain network

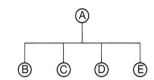

Figure 15.3 The vertical network

situation of a regional manager communicating to each of the branch or site managers.

The circle network

In this network (Figure 15.5), each person or department can communicate with only two others. Although it is a decentralised network – there is no obvious leader – it

205

ACTIVITY 15.3

Palm Nut Oils Ltd

Managers of Palm Nut Oils Ltd want workers to share ideas they may have about working processes, so the following notice is placed on the canteen noticeboard and a suggestion box is placed in the canteen.

> *From January 1st a payment of $25 will be given to anyone making suggestions for improving our computer-aided production processes that we subsequently decide to adopt.*
>
> Sabrina Patel
> ***Managing director***

An incentive is offered and a good response is expected. However, management is not trusted by the workforce, who see this as a worthless gesture, so either they do not make any useful suggestions or they make suggestions that are unprintable.

The message is written in the wrong language. This often happens when the sender is a specialist, e.g. an accountant or engineer. The tone of the language is not right. This can happen in any form of communication, but is most prone to occur when the message is spoken. This is particularly true if body language can also be observed. In its layout, the message is formal and unfriendly. The managing director could not even be bothered to sign it – her name was just printed on the notice.

The wrong medium may have been selected. You don't leave a message you really want to work to its chance reading on a noticeboard. The receivers have negative attitudes to the sender and misinterpret the message. They need to be convinced; a more direct and personally involved approach is needed.

[30 marks, 45 minutes]

1   Outline **four** barriers to effective communication in this case. [8]

2   Analyse the benefits of **three** other communication media that could have been used in this case. [12]

3   Recommend a more suitable method(s) of communication than the noticeboard for Palm Nut Oils Ltd. Justify your answer. [10]

might be difficult for all members of the circle to agree a new strategy between them, because of the slow rate of communicating with the whole group. These methods do not allow the receiver to question the message, to ask for further explanation or to discuss it with the sender. There is no assurance for the sender that the message has been received, understood and acted upon.

The integrated or connected network

This allows full two-way communication between any group members – or with all of them (Figure 15.6). It is typical of team meetings or brainstorming sessions. It allows a participative style of decision-making. It could assist in solving complex problems where input from all group members is needed. These five networks feature in research work undertaken by Bavelas, and his findings are represented in Figure 15.7.

>
> **TOP TIP**
> When discussing suitable communication methods for any business situation, try to assess which formal communication network would be most appropriate.

One-way or two-way communication

Many methods of communication do not allow for or encourage feedback from the receiver of the message. This is called one-way communication. Examples of messages using this approach include safety notices on machinery, messages pinned on noticeboards or written instructions, which need to be acted on immediately.

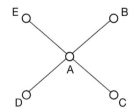

Figure 15.4 The wheel network

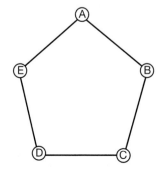

Figure 15.5 The circle network

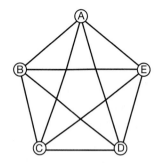

Figure 15.6 The integrated network

	Centralised networks	Decentralised networks
Speed of learning new procedure	FAST	SLOW
Speed of solution with simple problems	FAST	SLOW
Speed of solution with complex problems	SLOW	FAST
Originality of ideas, e.g. brainstorming	LOW	HIGH
Number of messages sent	FEW	MANY
Satisfaction/morale	LOW	HIGH

Figure 15.7 Effectiveness of communication networks

These methods do not allow the receiver to question the message, to ask for further explanation or to discuss it with the sender. There is no assurance for the sender that the message has been received, understood and acted upon.

Two-way communication, obviously, does allow all of these to happen. Meetings – such as works councils – team briefings, one-to-one conversations and using the telephone or intranet links all allow the receiver to contribute to a debate about the message or to question the sender about it. This two-way communication can prove to be much more motivating because it allows for participation. It is essential for democratic leadership styles to operate. It meets some of the conditions for effective staff motivation as explained by Mayo and Herzberg. However, it is time-consuming and is inappropriate for some messages that give clear information that cannot be argued with, for example a list of telephone extension numbers for all staff on a noticeboard.

The above discussion raises a very important issue – the link between staff motivation and effective communication. This link can operate in two ways:

1 **Motivation → effective communication**
   Well-motivated staff → more likely to listen and respond positively to messages → better and more accurate communication.

2 Effective communication → motivation

Effective communication → staff are more likely to feel involved and will receive constant feedback → shorter communication channels reduce remoteness from the 'top' → leads to better motivated staff.

These links are important. They could lead to a virtuous circle in an organisation. The more that staff are involved and given the opportunity to participate through two-way communication and group methods, then the more motivated they should become, and this will raise their ability and willingness to respond positively to communication.

Two-way communication at meetings or video/web conferences can lead to immediate feedback and high motivation levels.

Horizontal communication

Vertical communication is when people from different levels of hierarchy communicate with each other. This is the main direction of communication in formal hierarchies. Horizontal communication occurs along an organisation chart – between people who have approximately the same status but different areas of responsibility. Apart from in team meetings or committees, this type of communication is not as common as might be supposed. This is often because such meetings tend to be about coordinating policy, when most line managers are concerned with their day-to-day responsibilities. There might also be a widespread feeling that meetings with 'equals' will bring either compromise solutions or infighting over the allocation of resources.

The common problems of horizontal communication are:

- Different departments may not understand the culture, ways of working, objectives, problems or technical language of the others.
- The outlook and objectives of different departments could conflict, for example spending money on an advertising campaign that the finance department feels is unnecessary.

The blinkered approach often created by hierarchical and functional organisations means that there is a lack of sympathy with the needs of other sections. The establishment of a matrix structure could help to eliminate these problems. The very fact that this type of structure brings together, in a horizontal fashion, people of similar status from different departments will greatly assist with the communication flows between them.

TOP TIP

Try to link communication effectiveness with organisational structure. Traditional structures will tend to use vertical communication; matrix structures will use horizontal communication.

Informal communication

Have you ever heard about important events in, or decisions about, your school or college through the 'grapevine' before any official announcements? If so, you have been part of an **informal communication** channel. There is unofficial communication in every organisation – it takes place in the rest room or over the lunch table, in the queue next to the photocopier or in meetings before the official agenda begins. It may be no more than gossip but a lot of it can be well-informed information about the organisation too. In fact, much informal communication is not necessarily about work at all – it might just be social interactive chat. Table 15.2 summarises alternative views of informal communication.

KEY TERM

Informal communication: unofficial channels of communication that exist between informal groups within an organisation.

Whatever managers might think about informal communication, they will find it very hard indeed to stop people chatting in groups or with friends at work. Communication is after all, a natural human activity.

Some managers want to reduce informal communication as much as possible:	Some managers think informal communication serves useful purposes:
<ul><li>It wastes valuable working time.</li><li>It spreads gossip and rumours and these can be unsettling and lead to feelings of insecurity.</li><li>It may result in informal groups banding together to resist management decisions – even though they may not have been officially communicated yet.</li></ul>	<ul><li>All informal communication can help create important feelings of belonging and social cohesion.</li><li>Management can use the grapevine to 'test out' new ideas and see what the unofficial reaction might be – if it is too negative, they might never make an official announcement.</li><li>Can help to clarify official messages by talking them over with friends.</li></ul>

Table 15.2 Alternative views of informal communication

207

SUMMARY POINTS

- Effective communication is a key element in successful business management.
- Business managers need to be able to communicate effectively with internal employees and with external stakeholders.
- The choice of the most appropriate communication medium is very significant and it is influenced by many factors.
- There is no one 'right' communication method – different media should be used for different types of messages.
- Potential barriers to communication exist and managers should take action to reduce these.
- IT systems have revolutionised communication in business but they can have their drawbacks and these should be weighed against benefits.
- Communication effectiveness can be reduced as businesses expand – especially the problem of information overload.
- There are several formal communication networks and informal communication will also take place in any organisation.
- There is an important link between effective communication and motivation – employee motivation can both influence and be influenced by communication effectiveness.

RESEARCH TASK

- Undertake research within your school or college to discover the average amount of time each day staff and students spend on reading and sending emails. Present your findings in a report.
- Recommend how the use of IT to send messages at your school/college, could be made more effective in order to save time but maintain effective communication.

A Level exam practice questions

Case studies

1 We all seem to be working in the dark

Metta Viravong was being unusually forthright in his comments. Normally a quiet and patient man, even he had become completely demotivated by the latest problems in trying to communicate with the sales department. As production supervisor at Asian Lights plc, he was in charge of allocating and managing resources to make sure that sufficient output of light bulbs was available to match demand. The last scribbled note from the south-east sales manager had been the latest in a large number of messages regarding the correct product mix to manufacture. 'How am I meant to read this?' he had shouted. 'It is dated three days ago, yet I have only just been handed it by the section head.' Apparently she had just been handed it by the factory manager, who himself was sent it by the production director. 'I needed to know on Tuesday that sales of the standard bulbs are falling in the south-east due to the increased demand for halogen lamps and energy-saving light bulbs,' he complained to his production staff. 'If we end up with huge stocks of unsold bulbs it will not be my fault. If we had known that they were planning a big promotion on energy-saving bulbs we could have switched production in time.'

Problems with communication at Asian Lights had become more serious since the major takeover of Bangkok Brightlights ten months ago. The newly formed business was now twice the size. More managers had been employed. More levels of hierarchy had been created. Important internal messages were still checked by each section head or departmental manager before they passed them on to the next person who needed to know. The autocratic style of management had not changed with the takeover and the importance of 'keeping everything in writing' was still reinforced at every meeting with senior management.

Metta, being technically minded, was well aware of the latest advancements in IT and he was considering writing a report to the directors giving the details of all of the systems available with prices and specifications. 'I think I will give this to one of the directors myself rather than one of the section heads who should see all of my internal notes and letters.'

[50 marks, 75 minutes]

1. Do you consider that writing a report was the best way for Metta to communicate to directors in this case? Explain your answer. [5]

2. Discuss the factors that this business should consider before introducing an internal communication based on IT systems. [12]

3. Analyse **three** causes of communication problems at Asian Lights. [9]

4. Using the case study:

   a. Examine the possible links between the effectiveness of internal communication and staff motivation. [10]

   b. Using your knowledge of communication media and networks, horizontal and vertical communication and barriers to communication, evaluate the internal communication problems within Asian Lights plc and recommend suitable solutions. [14]

2 Switching off is no way to handle job losses – how not to communicate bad news

The voice at the end of the telephone was insistent. There would be no redundancies among the 2,400-strong workforce at the Panasonic factory in Cardiff. The informal rumours on the grapevine in south Wales were without foundation. Two days later, the manager had changed his tune. Yes, there would be job cuts, limited to several hundred. Over the next few days, journalists who left messages at the Panasonic factory were frustrated when nobody returned their calls. Just six days later the company dropped the bombshell many had feared – 1,300 people were to be made redundant.

The company's handling of the affair was a master class in bad management practice. The elusive manager, who had been asked to deal with press enquiries, was head of personnel at the factory. Mike Emmott, adviser on employee relations at the Chartered Institute of Personnel, says: 'A manager from human resources is not the appropriate man to announce big surprises that affect an entire community. You would have thought it was a task for the most senior person on the ground in the area – or possibly in the UK – to handle it.'

Sony, which has also announced job cuts, took a more common-sense approach. Sony's manager of public affairs at the group's corporate headquarters, spent several days at the Welsh factory handling enquiries about the 400 job cuts. 'I would never say to a reporter that we were not laying off people – then on Monday announce a redundancy programme,' he says. 'The idea of staff reading about redundancies in the newspapers before they are told is not an attractive one.'

'I was stunned and angry when we found out,' said a representative from the GMB Union, representing the Panasonic workers. 'Although the cuts were voluntary and nobody is twisting anyone's arm, I would have thought they might have had the decency to get us in and talk to us.' A Cardiff newspaper reporter said that Panasonic mishandled the affair. 'We were receiving calls from workers who felt totally in the dark,' he said. 'People were panicking, asking: "Are we going to lose our jobs? What on earth is going on?" For a long time the company was denying anything was happening.'

Most companies would agree that their workers should find out about impending cuts direct, rather than through the media. 'What people fear most is not knowing. It is common sense to inform employees because rumours and insecurity are much worse,' said a business consultant.

[24 marks, 35 minutes]

1 To what extent does this case demonstrate a failure in effective communication? **[10]**

2 How would you have advised the firm to communicate these redundancies to employees and the newspapers? Give reasons for your answer. Refer to all aspects of effective communication – the appropriate sender and receiver, the clarity of the message, the medium to be used and the opportunity for feedback. **[14]**

A Level essay questions

[20 marks, 45 minutes each]

1 Brunson Ltd is a confectionery and soft drinks manufacturer. It has doubled the number of employees in recent years by opening two factories in other countries to supply local markets there. Discuss how Brunson might ensure that effective internal communication in the firm is achieved. **[20]**

2 Discuss the two-way link between communication methods and employee motivation, drawing on examples of both poor and appropriate communication methods. **[20]**

End of Unit 2: Exam-style case study questions

Soda Cool

Soda Cool is a public limited company that manufactures soft drinks. Its head office is in Asia. The business owns the 'Soda Cool' brand name, logo and distinctive bottle shape. Soda Cool operates its own bottling and canning factories in several countries. The company is profitable but it is losing market share to rivals who are responding more quickly to changes in consumer tastes in the markets Soda Cool operates in.

Soda Cool operates a largely centralised decision-making system. Decisions that affect regional operations are communicated to senior managers within each country in weekly written reports from head office. The basic design of Soda Cool's organisation structure is shown in Figure 1.

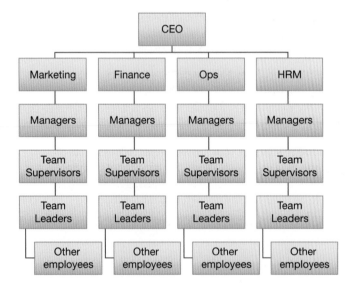

The chief executive officer (CEO) is Leo Zhu. He proposes to redesign Soda Cool's organisation structure to allow for more localised decision-making, increased delegation, more teamwork and fewer levels of hierarchy. He wants more decisions to be taken 'locally' but, at the same time, wants to retain central control over finance and expansion strategies.

Expansion into country X

Soda Cool does not currently operate in country X but is has plans to do so next year. A factory has been built in preparation for the production of Soda Cool drinks. The operations director has decided to equip it with highly automated machinery that needs computer programs to operate it effectively. The marketing director intends to set up a small team in country X to sell and promote Soda Cool drinks through shops and vending machines. The marketing team will have to speak the language used in the country. The size of Soda Cool's overall workforce in country X has not yet been decided but Leo is keen to keep costs as low as possible until the success of the expansion into the country can be determined. 'An effective workforce plan will be important not just to allow us to produce and sell quality drinks but to be able to keep control of labour costs,' he told his fellow directors.

Strike action in country Y factory

Jim Jones, Soda Cool's HR director, reported to the board that Soda Cool's factory workers had taken strike action for one day. 'The workers have recently been asked to sign flexible employment contracts with some of them placed on temporary contracts too. The cost benefits of these new arrangements are huge for us but they have not been well-received. We offered to pay a one-off bonus of $200 per worker but that was rejected. Trade union leaders have told me that the strike is not just about pay but is also a sign that workers are bored with their factory jobs and feel that they have no opportunities for developing new skills or being recognised for the work they do. We have tried to break up some of the work groups so that workers do not talk too much but this has made matters worse.'

Messages not getting through

Leo is proud of the fact that he meets many of his senior managers every week and, in his own words, 'has no need for emails or any IT device'. Directors spend at least two days each week visiting regional and in-country offices and factories. The reasons for these visits is not always clear to the offices and factories they visit – but Leo wants this practice to continue in order to 'allow for feedback from our workers'. In fact the workers in each division are only told about these visits by messages on notice boards and they never actually meet the directors. The marketing department has been disappointed by the customer response to newspaper adverts with a cut off slip for 'comments and suggestions' to be sent to their head office. One leading buyer of soft drinks from a supermarket chain has informed the marketing department by telephone – the Soda Cool website does not provide any other contact details – that the deliveries from Soda Cool are hardly ever on time and that this causes problems at the warehouse.

 KEY CONCEPTS REVIEW

Do you believe that the management of people – human resource management – can have an influence on business success? Most business consultants would say: 'Yes – if management adopt an appropriate strategy towards managing employees then they are likely to be more customer-focused and will be prepared to create more value for the business.' Successful businesses do not just need capital equipment and innovative products – they need a workforce that shares the same objectives and priorities as the management of the business.

A Level *50 marks 90 minutes*

1   Analyse the benefits to Soda Cool of undertaking workforce planning before entering the market in country X.   [10]

2   Assess the likely impact on Soda Cool's success if the changes to its organisational structure proposed by Leo are implemented across the business.   [12]

3   Discuss how the factory workforce in country Y could be motivated effectively without increasing production costs.   [12]

4   Make recommendations to Soda Cool's board of directors as to how they can improve the company's internal and external communications.   [16]

Unit 3:
Marketing

Introduction

Marketing is essentially about 'finding and satisfying' customers. Without customers – either final consumers or business customers – no business can survive as revenue must be earned from the sale of goods and services to pay for the operating costs of the business. This means that management need to be 'customer-focused' if the business is to create value by selling products to customers for more than the 'bought-in' cost.

Marketing objectives, based on the overall objectives of the organisation, focus business managers on achieving key targets such as sales levels, market share and increased competitiveness. These objectives can be met by selling more products to existing customers, entering new markets or developing new products. Marketing managers have certain key 'tools' they can use to analyse markets and adapt the products they are selling – or the price, promotion or method of selling them – to attract more customers and sales away from competitors.

16 What is marketing?

This chapter covers syllabus section AS Level 3.1.

On completing this chapter, you will be able to:

- understand what marketing is and the role of marketing in modern societies
- analyse the relationship between marketing, corporate objectives and other functional departments
- analyse the relationship between demand, supply and price
- recognise the difference between market orientation and product orientation
- assess the main features of markets, such as growth, share and competitors
- understand the distinction between consumer and industrial markets
- evaluate the relative advantages of mass and niche marketing
- assess the significance of market segmentation and how this might be achieved.

Introducing the topic

MCDONALD'S – MARKETING DOES NOT STAND STILL

What food do you think of when you hear 'McDonald's'? Most people would still say 'burger and chips', but the multinational fast-food business is working hard to change its brand image. There are several reasons for this, but two stand out:

- Difficult economic conditions create market opportunities for 'premium products' aimed at consumers who are short of cash and cannot afford a meal in a three-star restaurant.
- Increasing concern about the bad health effects of fast-food – especially the obesity problem of today's youngsters – means that healthier menu options are becoming much more popular.

A McDonald's spokesperson said: 'We are constantly researching consumer wants, and as many people cannot now afford full restaurant meals, we are revising our menu to appeal to them with luxury beef and chicken products in specialist ciabatta bread. The company is also committed to increasing its range of salads and other healthy options.'

At the same time, McDonald's is also aware of the cash limits on its traditional customers and is targeting them with a new 'dollar-saver' menu.

No business can afford to stand still – there are always competitors to worry about. Another giant fast-food outlet, Burger King, is also trying new ingredients, such as Spanish sausages and tiger prawns. It promoted its new upmarket menu with a world record-breaking $95 burger with the most expensive beef in the world. It captured the newspaper headlines, but it will not become a regular product.

Points to think about:

- What do you think marketing managers do? Make a list of as many marketing tasks as you can from this case study.
- Explain why McDonald's is changing its food menu.
- Do you think it will be easy to change the company's 'brand image'? Explain your answer.
- Why are 'researching customer wants' and promotion important to firms such as McDonald's and Burger King?

Introduction

Most people think of **marketing** as just being about advertising and selling of products. This is a very limited view – marketing embraces much more than just telling people about a product and selling it to them. There are thousands of definitions of marketing – each textbook seems to think of a new one. One of the shortest and clearest is from the *Chartered Institute of Marketing*:

> Marketing is the management process responsible for identifying, anticipating and satisfying consumers' requirements profitably.

Marketing: the management task that links the business to the customer by identifying and meeting the needs of customers profitably – it does this by getting the right product at the right price to the right place at the right time.

Another definition comes from *Contemporary Marketing Wired*, by Boone and Kurtz:

> Marketing is the process of planning and undertaking the conception, pricing, promotion and distribution of goods and services to create and maintain relationships that will satisfy individual and organisational objectives.

It seems from this definition that marketing involves a number of related management functions. These include:

- market research
- product design
- pricing
- advertising
- distribution
- customer service
- packaging.

So, marketing is a very important business activity. To sum up, marketing activities are all those associated with identifying the particular wants and needs of target-market customers and then trying to satisfy those customer needs better than your competitors do. This means that market research is needed to identify and analyse customer needs. With this knowledge, strategic decisions must then be taken about product design, pricing, promotion and distribution.

This is the definition of marketing that you should keep in mind during your study of the next few chapters.

Related concepts

Markets

This term is vital to achieve an understanding of marketing. It has two rather different meanings. Perhaps the most obvious meaning is the 'place or mechanism where buyers and sellers meet to engage in exchange'. The weekly fruit and vegetable market would be one example of this. Shopping centres and auctions are other examples of markets. Increasingly, there is no physical place in the sense of a geographical location. The use of the internet as a marketing tool has meant that a market can exist electronically with no physical meeting between buyer and seller.

The term *market* also refers to the group of consumers that is interested in a product, has the resources to purchase the product and is permitted by law to purchase it. It can be broken down into different definitions. For example, the potential market for a product is the total population interested in the product. The target market is the segment of the available market that the business has decided to serve by directing its product towards this group of people.

Human needs and wants

A human need is a basic requirement that an individual wishes to satisfy. Physical needs include food, clothing and shelter. Individual needs include desires for knowledge, recognition, affection, self-esteem and self-expression, e.g. through the clothes people wear.

Wants are broader in their perspective. They are things we do not need for our survival as biological creatures, but they do satisfy certain requirements or individual needs of most human beings. So we need food to physically survive, but, although we may want a juicy steak or fresh crab, we do not need these particular expensive items of food to survive. They may, however, satisfy an individual need, such as being seen in an expensive restaurant. We need shelter to protect us from the elements – but our desire for a house by the beach is a 'want', not an essential requirement for survival.

Wants are often described as being goods and services that fulfil the needs of individual consumers. Many marketing managers believe that it is their aim to convert human needs into wants by very persuasive product imagery through advertising.

Value and satisfaction

Do cheap goods always offer good value? Do expensive goods always provide consumer satisfaction? Clearly, the answer to both of these questions is 'no'. Value is not the same as cheapness. A consumer will consider a product to be of good value if it provides satisfaction at what is thought to be a reasonable price. Customer satisfaction is not always obtained with very expensive products – a good might be so expensive that, although it performs its function well, the consumer believes that 'good value' has not been received.

Two examples will help to support these points:

1 A consumer who is very hungry may be looking to eat in a top-class restaurant. If none is open, and he decides to eat in a pizza café, the meal may be not as good as in a top-class restaurant but because it is much cheaper, it might still provide **value** and, therefore, customer satisfaction.

2 A very expensive car may perform well, but once it is purchased the consumer may have a sense of disappointment if he feels that it is actually too expensive for 'what it offers'. There will be no sense of good value and no long-term consumer satisfaction.

To maintain good long-term customer relations, businesses should aim to offer good value, and hence satisfaction, at all times.

Marketing objectives and corporate objectives

The long-term objectives of the company will have a significant impact on both the **marketing objectives** and **marketing strategy** adopted. A business with clear short-term profit targets will focus on maximising sales at the highest prices possible. In contrast, a business with longer-term objectives, which may include profitability as well as the achievement of goals of social responsibility, may adopt a 'societal marketing' approach. This concept is explained on page 217.

KEY TERMS

Marketing objectives: the goals set for the marketing department to help the business achieve its overall objectives.

Marketing strategy: long-term plan established for achieving marketing objectives.

Examples of marketing objectives include an increase in:

- market share – perhaps to gain market leadership
- total sales (value or volume – or both)
- average number of items purchased per customer visit
- frequency that a loyal customer shops
- percentage of customers who are returning customers
- number of new customers
- customer satisfaction
- brand identity.

To be effective, marketing objectives should:

- fit in with the overall aims and mission of the business – the marketing objectives should reflect the aims of the whole organisation and they should attempt to aid the achievement of these
- be determined by senior management – the key marketing objectives will determine the markets and products a business trades in for years to come and these issues must be dealt with by managers at a very senior level in the company
- be realistic, motivating, achievable, measurable and clearly communicated to all departments in the organisation.

Why are marketing objectives important?

- They provide a sense of direction for the marketing department.
- Progress can be monitored against these targets.
- They can be broken down into regional and product sales targets to allow for management by objectives.

- They form the basis of marketing strategy. These marketing objectives will have a crucial impact on the marketing strategies adopted, as without a clear vision of **what** the business hopes to achieve for its products, it will be pointless discussing **how** it should market them. Examples of marketing strategies, which are explained later in this book, include:

    - Penetrating existing markets more fully – selling more to existing and new customers.
    - Entering new markets – e.g. in other countries.
    - Developing new, or updating existing, products.

Refer to Chapter 4, page 46, for the advantages of setting departmental goals, such as marketing objectives.

Coordination of marketing with other departments

This is vital. The links between the marketing department and other functional departments – such as finance, operations (production) and human resources are an essential component of a successful marketing strategy. As most business decisions will be focused around achieving the central marketing objectives, such as increasing sales and profits, it is inevitable that the marketing department will have a central role in coordinating the work of other departments to help achieve these marketing objectives.

Here are some examples of these links:

Marketing → finance

- The finance department will use the sales forecasts of the marketing department to help construct cash-flow forecasts and operational budgets.
- The finance department will have to ensure that the necessary capital is available to pay for the agreed marketing budget, for example for promotion expenditure.

Marketing → human resources

- The sales forecasts will be used by human resources to help devise a workforce plan for all of the departments likely to be affected by a new marketing strategy, for example additional staff may be needed in sales and production.
- Human resources will also have to ensure that the recruitment and selection of appropriately qualified and experienced staff are undertaken to make sure there are sufficient workers to produce and sell the increase in sales planned for by the marketing department.

Marketing → operations

- Market research data will play a key role in new product development – as explained above.
- The sales forecasts will be used by the operations department to plan for the capacity needed, the purchase of the machines that will be used and the stocks of raw materials required for the new output level.

Market orientation and product orientation

This is an important distinction. Most businesses would today describe themselves as being '**market oriented**' or 'market led'.

KEY TERM

Market orientation: an outward-looking approach basing product decisions on consumer demand, as established by market research.

KEY CONCEPT LINK

Market orientation gives a business **customer focus**.

This approach requires market research and market analysis to indicate present and future consumer demand. The consumer is put first. The business will attempt to produce what consumers want rather than try to sell them a product they may not really want to buy. It has certain important advantages, especially in fast-changing, volatile consumer markets. In these cases, increasing consumer awareness of competitors' products, prices and image can result in significant fluctuations in popularity of goods and services. The benefits of market orientation are:

- The chances of newly developed products failing in the market are much reduced – but not eliminated – if effective market research has been undertaken first. With the huge cost of developing new products, such as cars or computers, this is a convincing argument for most businesses to use the market-oriented approach.
- If consumer needs are being met with appropriate products, then they are likely to survive longer and make higher profits than those that are being sold following a product-led approach.
- Constant feedback from consumers – market research never actually ends – will allow the product and how it is marketed to be adapted to changing tastes before it is too late and before competitors 'get there first'. Compare the market-orientation concept with that of **product orientation** (or product-led businesses).

KEY TERM

Product orientation: an inward-looking approach that focuses on making products that can be made – or have been made for a long time – and then trying to sell them.

The days of traditional product-oriented businesses, which assume there will always be a market for the products they make, are fast disappearing. However, product-led marketing still exists to an extent and the following instances help to explain why:

- Product-oriented businesses invent and develop products in the belief that they will find consumers to purchase them. The development of the WAP mobile phone was driven more by technical innovation than by consumer needs – consumers were not aware that such versatile products were likely to be made available until the basic concept had been invented and developed into an innovative new product. Pure research in this form is rare but still exists, for example in the pharmaceutical and electronic industries. Here there is still the belief that if businesses produce an innovative product of a good-enough quality, then it will be purchased.
- Product-oriented businesses concentrate their efforts on efficiently producing high-quality goods. They believe quality will be valued above market fashion. Such quality-driven firms do still exist, especially in product areas where quality or safety is of great importance, such as bottled-water plants or the manufacture of crash helmets.

Evaluation of these two approaches

The trend then is towards market orientation, but there are limitations. If a business attempts to respond to every passing consumer trend or market fashion, then it may well over-stretch its resources and end up not doing anything particularly well. Trying to offer choice and range so that every consumer need is met can be expensive. In contrast, researching and developing an innovative product can be successful, even if there has been no formal market research – consider Dyson's hugely profitable cyclone vacuum cleaner, for example.

A third way – between market and product orientation – is called **asset-led marketing**.

KEY TERM

Asset-led marketing: an approach to marketing that bases strategy on the firm's existing strengths and assets instead of purely on what the customer wants.

This is based on market research too, but does not attempt to satisfy all consumers in all markets. Instead, the firm will consider its own strengths (or 'competencies') in terms of people, assets and brand image and will make only those products that use and take advantage of those strengths. Using this approach, Levi Strauss restricts its product to clothing and accessories – but it does offer a wider range of clothing than ever before with the addition of its Dockers brand. Similarly, BMW does not enter the commercial-vehicle or motor-caravan markets – but it does use its brand strength to market sports and luxurious 4×4 SUVs (sports utility vehicles). These, and many other firms, focus on their existing strengths, assets and products rather than entering entirely new markets trying to meet every new consumer taste and fashion.

It is very important to realise that not all market-oriented businesses will succeed. Market research and identifying consumer needs are not a guarantee of business success – the new products developed in this way may come to market too late or fail to impress consumers compared to rivals' products. Success and survival in the competitive and globalised markets of the twenty-first century depend upon the whole marketing process. This includes market research but cannot end there – the aim of the rest of this chapter and the next four is to examine the other factors that determine marketing success.

Societal marketing

This approach to marketing adopts a wider perspective than the previous forms of orientation. It focuses on other stakeholders as well as the business and its consumers. Social responsibility is becoming increasingly popular among organisations and can be regarded as an important strategic marketing tool. This raises the question of what the central purpose of marketing should be. Is it 'a management tool to help maximise profits' or should it be 'a means of satisfying consumer needs profitably, but with minimum damage and costs to society'? Managers who believe in '**societal marketing**' claim the latter concept of marketing is the correct one to adopt. The term 'societal marketing' was first coined by Kotler in 1972.

> **KEY TERM**
>
> **Societal marketing:** this approach considers not only the demands of consumers but also the effects on all members of the public (society) involved in some way when firms meet these demands.

These other members of the public or stakeholders include employees, shareholders, suppliers, competitors, government, the community and the natural environment. Examples of societal marketing include The Body Shop, which promises not to support animal testing of its products and purchases its supplies from sustainable sources produced in non-environmentally damaging ways. These products are not the cheapest – but they do meet society's

Tins of dolphin-safe tuna – an example of societal marketing

217

long-term interests. Another example is the sale of dolphin-safe tuna fish, which has been caught by rod and line rather than nets that can trap dolphins. This tuna is more expensive – but it is more appealing to society's concerns.

The societal-marketing concept has the following implications:

- It is an attempt to balance three concerns: company profits, customer wants and society's interests.
- There may be a difference between short-term consumer wants (low prices) and long-term consumer and social welfare (protecting the environment or paying workers reasonable wages). Societal marketing considers long-term welfare.
- Businesses should still aim to identify consumer needs and wants and to satisfy these more efficiently than competitors do – but in a way that enhances consumers' and society's welfare.
- Using this concept could give a business a significant competitive advantage. Many consumers prefer to purchase products from businesses that are seen to be socially responsible.
- A societal-marketing strategy, if successful, could lead to the firm being able to charge higher prices for its products as benefiting society becomes a 'unique selling point'.

Fairtrade products

The Fairtrade Foundation is a non-profit-making body. It promotes products that have been produced using sustainable and environmentally friendly methods and for which fair prices have been paid to farmers and producers – many of whom live in poor developing countries. All Fairtrade products must pass strict tests for sustainable production methods that are then purchased from growers and producers at prices often substantially above world prices for non-Fairtrade goods. The Fairtrade symbol is looked for by many consumers when buying chocolate, coffee, beauty products and many other goods.

Fairtrade logo

[8 marks, 12 minutes]

1 Explain why many consumers will only purchase products which carry the Fairtrade symbol. **[8]**

2 **Research task:** Look out for the Fairtrade symbol when you go shopping – especially for food. Make a list of the products that carry the symbol. Are prices higher for Fairtrade products than non-Fairtrade products?

Demand, supply and price relationship

Meeting consumer wants profitably – the central aim of marketing – means that marketing managers need to know how free markets work to determine prices. If the business can produce the product at this market price, it should be profitable. In free markets the equilibrium price is determined when demand equals supply. '**Demand** and **supply** analysis' helps us understand this relationship.

 KEY TERMS

Demand: the quantity of a product that consumers are willing and able to buy at a given price in a time period.

Supply: the quantity of a product that firms are prepared to supply at a given price in a time period.

The Classic Watch Company

The Classic Watch Company was in trouble. Sales had fallen for each of the last three years. The founder of the company, Harry Brainch, could not understand the reasons behind this crisis. His business had been making the Classic Ladies' wristwatch for the last 20 years and only recently had sales failed to climb every year. The current model had been updated, but was still essentially the same design as the original watch. Consumers had been attracted to its simple, robust design and good value. These were very important qualities during the economic crisis that the country had suffered from for much of the last few years. More recently, consumer incomes had started to rise. Old manufacturing industry had been replaced by service-sector businesses that offered many supervisory and managerial jobs. Youth unemployment, in particular, had fallen and young consumers had much more money to spend than previously. Both men and women were becoming much more fashion-conscious as their consumer tastes changed with higher incomes. Harry knew his business had to change, but he did not know which new styles of watches to introduce. He almost wished for a return to the good old days when shoppers were happy to buy a recognised design at a reasonable price.

[30 marks, 40 minutes]

1 Would you describe the Classic Watch Company as being product-oriented or market-orientated? Explain your answer. **[4]**

2 Analyse why Harry's original marketing strategy is no longer succeeding in increasing sales. **[7]**

3 Explain **three** ways in which Harry could attempt to increase demand for his watches **apart from** reducing prices. **[9]**

4 Evaluate the benefits to the Classic Watch Company of pursuing a policy of market segmentation. **[10]**

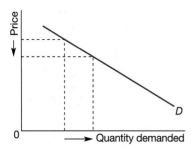

Figure 16.1 A normal relationship between price and demand for a product

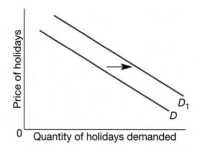

Figure 16.2 New demand curve, D_1, caused by changes in the determinants of demand

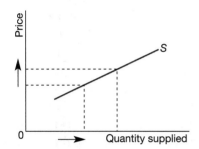

Figure 16.3 Supply increases when the price rises

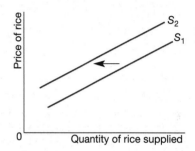

Figure 16.4 Supply of rice falls after a bad harvest

Demand

1 This varies with price – for all normal goods the quantity bought rises with a price fall and the quantity bought falls with a price increase. This is shown by a demand curve (see Figure 16.1).
2 Apart from price changes – which cause a new position on the demand curve as shown in Figure 16.1 – the level of demand for a product can vary due to a change in any of these determinants of demand:
   - changes in consumers' incomes
   - changes in the prices of substitute goods and complementary goods
   - changes in population size and structure
   - fashion and taste changes
   - advertising and promotion spending.
3 All of these changes above lead to a new demand curve (see Figure 16.2). So, for example, the demand for holidays will increase to D_1 after an increase in consumer incomes.

Supply

1 This varies with price – firms will be more willing to supply a product if the price rises and will supply less as the price falls. This is shown in Figure 16.3.
2 Apart from changes in price – which cause a new position on the supply curve as shown above – the level of supply of a product can vary due to a change in any of these determinants of supply:
   - costs of production, e.g. change in labour or raw material costs

- taxes imposed on the suppliers by government, which raise their costs
- subsidies paid by government to suppliers, which reduce their costs
- weather conditions and other natural factors
- advances in technology to make cost of production lower.
3 All of these changes above lead to a new supply curve (see Figure 16.4). So, for example, the supply of rice will be reduced after very poor weather in the major growing areas. This leads to S_2.

219

ACTIVITY 16.3

Demand and supply changes

[4 marks, 5 minutes]

For each of the following changes, identify whether they affect supply or demand and whether they cause supply or demand to increase or fall.

- Bad harvest affecting coffee crop. **[1]**
- Rolls-Royce cars affected by higher consumer incomes. **[1]**
- Fall in price of steel affects shipbuilders. **[1]**
- Fall in price of movie downloads affects DVD market. **[1]**

Determining the equilibrium price

When demand and supply are combined, the **equilibrium price** will be determined. This will be at the point where demand = supply. This is shown in Figure 16.5.

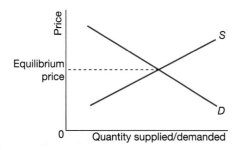

Figure 16.5 Equilibrium price is at the level that equates demand with supply

If the price were higher than this, there would be unsold stocks – excess supply. Suppliers do not want this, so will lower the price. If the price is lower than the equilibrium, then stocks will run out – leaving excess demand. Suppliers could make a higher profit by raising the price – to the equilibrium level.

ACTIVITY 16.4

Rice prices to keep rising

Rice prices are likely to continue rising as demand for this necessity food outstrips supply. The price of rice has risen by 70% over 12 months. There are several factors behind the rise in price:

- Land for rice growing has been lost to town development.
- Demand is rising as consumer incomes in Asia's middle classes rise.
- Flooding in Bangladesh and Indonesia and cold weather in Vietnam – all major rice-growing areas – has cut production.
- The prices of alternative foods have also been rising rapidly.

[8 marks, 10 minutes]

1 Identify **two** supply factors and **two** demand factors that have led to the recent increase in the price of rice. [4]

2 Illustrate the impact of these factors on the equilibrium price of rice on a supply-and-demand diagram. [4]

Features of markets: location, size, growth, share and competitors

Successful marketing requires firms to understand which market they are operating in, who their consumers are and where they are located, whether the market is growing or shrinking, what the business's share of that market is and the major competitors.

Market location

Some businesses just operate locally – they sell products to consumers in the area where the business is located. Firms that usually just sell in these local markets include laundries, florist shops, hairdressers and bicycle-repair shops.

Regional markets obviously cover a larger geographical area and businesses that have been successful locally often expand into the region or county so that they can increase sales. Local markets obviously have limited sales potential. This process might then extend to national markets. Relatively few firms – compared to the thousands that operate just in local markets – will expand to try to sell to the whole national market. Common examples include: banking firms, supermarket chains and large clothing retailers.

International markets offer the greatest sales potential, of course. The rapid rise of multinationals that operate and sell in many different national markets illustrates the sales potential from exploiting international markets. Expanding into foreign markets is a very big strategic step as many aspects of marketing will have to change in order to respond to differences in tastes, cultures and laws between different countries. This idea is more fully developed in Chapter 21.

Market size

This can be measured in two ways: volume of sales (units sold) or value of goods sold (revenue).

The size of a market is important for three reasons:

1 A marketing manager can assess whether a market is worth entering or not.
2 Firms can calculate their own market share.
3 Growth or decline of the market can be identified.

Market growth

Some markets are obviously growing faster than others; some, such as desk top personal computers, are declining rapidly. Is it always better to be operating in a rapidly growing market? In many cases, yes, but not always – there might be many competitors entering the market at the same time so profits might not be high. The pace of growth will depend on several factors, such as general economic growth, changes in consumer incomes and development of new markets and products that take sales away from existing ones, changes in consumer tastes and factors, such as technological change, which can boost market sales when an innovation becomes available. The rate of growth will also depend on whether the market is 'saturated' or not. In most Western countries, sales of washing machines do not rise each year as most households already have one – most purchases are, therefore, replacement models. Sales of laptop computers are still rising in India and China as most potential consumers have yet to purchase one.

> **KEY TERM**
>
> **Market growth:** the percentage change in the total size of a market (volume or value) over a period of time.

> **TOP TIP**
>
> You may need to do some simple calculations about market growth and market share – it is a good idea to use a calculator to help you do this.

Market share

'Firm's sales' and 'total market sales' can be measured in either units (volume) or sales value in this market. **Market share**, and increases in it, is often the most

221

ACTIVITY 16.5

China's auto market growing rapidly

At 23, Chang Lingxi bought his first car. He considered a Ford Focus, but last week he negotiated a huge discount of 35,000 Yuan off a brand new Volkswagen (VW) Lavida. Like millions of other new motorists in China, he does not plan to use it much – it's too hard to find a parking space – but he looks forward to the freedom the car brings.

China's auto industry is now growing by around one million extra vehicles a year – a rate of 12% in 2013 to reach 20 million units. It is now the largest car market in the world having overtaken that of the USA in 2009. No wonder 100 global and Chinese vehicle manufacturers are now competing in this market. The best sellers are the Ford Focus followed by the VW Lavida – VW has a 21% market share. The luxury car segment is growing fastest – both BMW and Mercedes have announced annual sales increases in China of 21%. Many Western car makers – including VW and GM – have joint ventures with Chinese manufacturers such as SAIC.

[15 marks, 20 minutes]

1. Using examples from the article, explain the differences between: Market size, market growth and market share. **[9]**

2. Explain two benefits to VW of having:
   a. a large market share in China **[3]**
   b. one of the best-selling models. **[3]**

ACTIVITY 16.6

A tale of two markets

- Total sales in market A in 2013 were 54,000 units. The average selling price was $3.

- Total sales of market B in 2013 were 10,000 units. The average selling price was $15.

- In 2014, sales volume of market A increased by 5% and the selling price increased by 10%.

- In 2014, total sales value of market B was $180,000, despite the average price falling to $12.

[9 marks, 12 minutes]

1. Calculate the percentage increase in the total value of sales for market A between 2013 and 2014. **[6]**

2. Calculate the percentage increase in total sales volume in market B between 2013 and 2014. **[3]**

effective way to measure the relative success of one business's marketing strategy against that of its competitors. If a firm's market share is increasing, then the marketing of its products has been relatively more successful than most of its competitors. The product with the highest market share is called the 'brand leader'. Why might it be important for a brand or a manufacturer to have market leadership in this way?

> ### KEY TERM
>
> **Market share:** the percentage of sales in the total market sold by one business. This is calculated by the following formula:
>
> $$\frac{\text{firm's sales in time period}}{\text{total market sales in time period}} \times 100$$

The benefits of a high market share – especially of being the brand leader – are:

- Sales are higher than those of any competing business in the same market and this could lead to higher profits too.
- Retailers will be keen to stock and promote the best-selling brands. They may be given the most prominent position in shops.
- As shops are keen to stock the product, it might be sold to them with a lower discount rate – say 10% instead of 15%, which has to be offered by the smaller, competing brands. The combination of this factor and the higher sales level should lead to higher profitability for the producer of the leading brand.
- The fact that an item or brand is the 'market leader' can be used in advertising and other promotional material. Consumers are often keen to buy 'the most popular' brands.

A word of warning: it is not always easy to measure market growth or market share in an unambiguous way. Different results may be obtained depending on whether the growth

ACTIVITY 16.7

Tesco is market leader in Thailand

Tesco Lotus – the brand name used by the European supermarket in Thailand – had 15% of the supermarket grocery (food) market in 2013. Total sales in this sector amounted to £25 billion. Two French-owned companies operating in Thailand were second and third on the list of firms' market shares – Big C had 7% and Carrefour 4%. If non-food item are included then Tesco Lotus has 43% market share. Being market leader gives Tesco Lotus a huge advantage – and it is not standing still. It has plans to open new stores and enter new markets. Recently, Tesco Lotus entered the fast-growing school-uniform market, worth $140 million a year, with prices 20–30% lower than traditional shops.

This expansion is not without its critics and the new Thai government has taken action to protect locally owned shops and to ensure good consumer choice is maintained. A new law is proposed that would severely restrict the opening of all new foreign-owned stores.

A Tesco Lotus store in Bangkok

Consumer groups are split on the new law – they want to keep the variety offered by local stores, but they enjoy the big stores and low prices too.

[25 marks, 35 minutes]

1. Calculate Tesco Lotus's sales in the Thai supermarket grocery market in 2013. [3]

2. If Tesco Lotus's grocery sales increase by $2 billion in 2014, but the total size of the Thai supermarket grocery market increases by $10 billion, calculate Tesco Lotus's 2014 market share. [4]

3. Explain **two** advantages Tesco Lotus might gain from being 'market leader' in Thailand. [8]

4. Do you think the Thai government should place restrictions on Tesco Lotus's future growth? Explain your answer. [10]

and share rates are measured in volume or value terms. For example, if total sales in the market for jeans rose from 24 million pairs at an average price of $32 to 26 million pairs at an average price of $36, then market growth can be measured in two ways:

■ By volume – the market has risen from 24 to 26 million units, an increase of 8.33%.
■ By value – the revenue has risen from $768 million to $936 million, an increase of 21.88%.

Which of these two methods – value or volume – should be used to calculate the changing market share for any one jeans manufacturer? The manufacturer will use the measure that reflects best on their own position. It may, therefore, be difficult to compare firms' changing market shares. A cosmetic company that specialises in selling low volumes of expensive products is likely to have a higher market share in value terms than when measured by volume.

TOP TIP

It is very important to understand that a firm's market share can fall even though its sales are rising. This will happen if the total market sales are increasing at a faster rate than one firm's sales.

Competitors

Businesses operate in a competitive environment. For example, mobile (cell) phone providers are in fierce competition with each other to provide the best possible value for money phones, and to offer the most suitable range of phone services for their customers. Businesses compete in many ways. One of the most obvious ways is over price. For example, sports shoe sellers on the Internet compete to supply the same shoe brand at the cheapest price to customers. Businesses can compete in many other ways, however. These are called forms of non-price competition, e.g. customer service – giving the best personal attention to the needs of customers; location – being at the most convenient place for customers to buy the product.

Most businesses are faced by **direct competitors**. Stall holders in a large open market selling materials or tourist gifts will face competition from many similar stalls. However, most products are differentiated in some way. For example, although soap powders may look highly similar each will offer some form of special ingredient that sets them apart from their competitors. In recent years differentiation in this market has increased by the

development of dissolvable sachets of liquid, solid tablets and other forms of detergent.

In addition to **direct competition**, businesses also face indirect competition. For example, in the bus transport industry, a bus operator experiences indirect competition from other providers of public transport such as taxi firms and rail companies, although they might be in different sectors of the same market, or in apparently different markets.

Important marketing concepts

1 Creating/adding value

In Chapter 1, the important concept of creating or adding value was explained. Literally, 'added value' means the difference between the selling price of a product and the cost of the materials and components bought in to make it. For example, a tub of luxury ice cream sells for $4. The cost of the milk, cream, sugar and flavourings is $1. Value added = $3.

This is not the same as profit – clearly the producer will have to pay wages, rent and other costs – but profit will also be included in this added value. If the business is able to increase this added value, then the potential for greater profits is clear. Effective marketing makes this possible. What will encourage consumers to pay a price that far exceeds the cost of the basic materials needed to produce the good or service? Here are some examples of marketing strategies that are likely to add value:

■ Create an exclusive and luxurious retail environment to make consumers feel that they are being treated as important. This will make them feel more prepared to pay higher prices and may have the psychological effect of convincing them that the product is of higher quality too. This approach is used by perfume and cosmetic retailers, expensive hairdressers and Mercedes car showrooms.
■ Use high-quality packaging to differentiate the product from other brands – again, widely used in cosmetics and confectionery (luxury boxes of chocolates).
■ Promote and brand the product so that it becomes a 'must-have' brand name that consumers will pay a premium price for, even if they may realise that the actual ingredients are little different from those used for other brands. Coca-Cola and Levi jeans are two classic examples of this.

- Create a '**unique selling point**' (USP) that clearly differentiates a product from that of other manufacturers. **Product differentiation** can lend to sales success. Apple's iPad mini is a good example.

Developing a USP can be an expensive strategy, but very rewarding if successful. It is most likely to be achieved either by heavy and effective promotion – for example, Häagen-Dazs ice cream – or by technical innovation that is patented – for example, Microsoft Windows 8 software. These and other features of marketing strategy are discussed in more detail in later chapters. The key point about adding value is that, as consumers generally become wealthier and more selective in their purchasing habits, the producer or retailer who is able to develop something different from other firms is most likely to both capture consumers' attention and gain higher profits.

2 Mass marketing and niche marketing

This market segment in **niche marketing** can be a very small section of the whole market and may be one that has not yet been identified and filled by competitors. Examples of firms employing niche marketing include Versace designs and Clinique perfumes. Both these businesses sell only expensive, high-status products. Other niche markets exist for non-luxury products too such as 'extreme sports'

clothing and '$-stretcher' retail shops that sell only very cheap items, attracting a low-income segment of the market.

Mass marketing is the exact opposite. 'One product for the whole market' is now becoming quite an unusual concept for firms to adopt – yet is still seen in, for example, the toothpaste and fizzy drinks markets. Hoover, the vacuum-cleaner manufacturer, used to sell a very limited range of products as most consumers wanted just a simple and effective cleaner. Now, with increased consumer choice and more competitors operating the market, Hoover offer a much wider range of models of different sizes, power output and prices to appeal to different segments of the mass market. So, although not true niche marketing, the company is recognising the limits of pure mass marketing. The next section looks at market segmentation in detail. Both of these strategies have their advantages (see Table 16.1).

Advantages of niche marketing	Advantages of mass marketing
- Small firms may be able to survive and thrive in markets that are dominated by larger firms. - If the market is currently unexploited by competitors, then filling a niche can offer the chance to sell at high prices and high profit margins – until the competitors react by entering too. Consumers will often pay more for an exclusive product. - Niche market products can also be used by large firms to create status and image – their mass-market products may lack these qualities.	**Note:** these can also be viewed as the disadvantages of niche marketing. - Small market niches do not allow economies of scale to be achieved. Therefore, mass-market businesses are likely to enjoy substantially lower average costs of production. - Mass-market strategies run fewer risks than niche strategies. As niche markets contain relatively small numbers of consumers, any change in consumer buying habits could lead to a rapid decline in sales. This is a particular problem for small firms operating in only one niche market with one product.

Table 16.1 Advantages of niche marketing and of mass marketing

TI to peddle premium cycles for niche market

Tube Investments of India is planning to enter the ultra-premium cycle segment – with price ranges from $300 to $4,000. 'Though the market size is small, we cannot afford to be absent from this segment,' TI Cycles' vice-president, Arun Alagappan, said. Last year TI Cycles sold 2.8 million units and the marketing objective for the current year is 3.1 million units. The company started making electric scooters last year and has already launched BSA WorkOuts exercise equipment. The ultra-premium bicycles will not add greatly to total sales revenue – but they will help to take the brand upmarket as Indian consumers' incomes increase.

[10 marks, 12 minutes]

Explain why businesses such as TI produce and sell products in different market segments. **[10]**

3 Market segmentation

This is a very widely practised marketing strategy. It is customer-focused so it is consistent with the concept of market orientation discussed above. Sometimes segmentation is referred to as 'differentiated marketing' because, instead of trying to sell just one product to the whole market, different products are targeted at different segments. To be effective, firms must research and analyse the total market carefully to identify the specific consumer groups that exist within it. Examples of **market segmentation** are:

- Computer manufacturers, such as Hewlett-Packard, produce PCs for office and home use, including games, but also make laptop models for business people who travel.
- Coca-Cola not only makes the standard cola drink but also Diet Coke for weight-conscious consumers, and flavoured drinks for consumers with particular tastes.

KEY TERMS

Market segment: a sub-group of a whole market in which consumers have similar characteristics.

Market segmentation: identifying different segments within a market and targeting different products or services to them.

- Renault, the car maker, produces several versions of its Mégane model, such as a coupé, saloon, convertible and 'people carrier' – all appealing to different groups of consumers.

Sometimes firms only market their goods or services to one segment and deliberately do not aim to satisfy other segments. Abercrombie & Fitch is a clothing retailer that aims only at the youth market, Nike shoes are only for sports and leisure use and Coutts & Co. only offers banking services to the very wealthy. These businesses make a virtue out of concentrating on one segment and developing an image and brand that suit that segment.

Market segmentation – identifying different consumer groups

Successful segmentation requires a business to have a very clear picture of the consumers in the target market it is aiming to sell in. A 'picture' of the typical consumer needs to be built up to help with market research sampling, designing the product, pricing and promoting the product. This is called the **consumer profile**. The main characteristics of consumers contained in a consumer profile are income levels, age, gender, social class and region.

KEY TERM

Consumer profile: a quantified picture of consumers of a firm's products, showing proportions of age groups, income levels, location, gender and social class.

Total markets may be segmented in a number of different ways. The three commonly used bases for segmentation are:

1 Geographic differences

Consumer tastes may vary between different geographic areas and so it may be appropriate to offer different products and market them in 'location-specific' ways. This approach would be the opposite of adopting one marketing strategy for the whole area or region. This is sometimes referred to as 'pan-Asian' or 'pan-European' marketing. This will not be effective if the geographical differences are so considerable that consumers demand products geared towards their specific needs. These geographical differences might result from cultural differences – for example alcohol cannot be promoted in Arab Muslim countries. A heating and refrigeration business will need to market different products to Malaysia compared with Finland. This issue is not just about products. The way in which products are promoted may have to be adjusted too. Competitions or lottery-type promotions are illegal in some countries.

Advertising jeans or ice cream with pictures of semi-naked models would not be tolerated in some communities. Even product names have to be changed to suit the language of the country. Clearly, as in so many other aspects of marketing, accurate and detailed market research information would be essential before expanding the geographical spread of the markets in which goods are sold.

2 Demographic differences

These are the most commonly used basis for segmentation. Demography is the study of population data and trends, and demographic factors – such as age, gender, family size and ethnic background – can all be used to separate markets. A house-construction firm will use information on these factors to help determine which segment of the market a new block of apartments should be aimed at. Should they be retirement flats with a resident caretaker? Should they be small studio flats for young, single people? Should they offer interconnecting doors and walkways to encourage certain ethnic groups that live in extended families to be attracted to the apartments? It is unlikely that the construction firm will attempt to attract all market segments – but having decided on the most appropriate one, it will be essential to gear the price and promotion strategies towards this segment.

Income and social class are two very important factors leading to market segmentation. An individual's occupation tends to determine their social class and will also have a great impact on their income level.

The main socio-economic groups used in the UK are:

A – upper middle class – higher managerial, administrative and professional, for example directors of big companies and successful lawyers

B – middle class – managerial staff, including professions such as teachers

C1 – lower middle class – supervisory, clerical or junior managerial

C2 – skilled manual workers

D – working class – semi- and unskilled manual workers

E – casual, part-time workers and unemployed

An individual's social class may have a great impact on their expenditure patterns. This will be largely due to income differences between different classes of employment. The wealthy will have very different consumption patterns from the working class. The jobs people do is one of the main factors influencing people's income levels. Other forces apart from income levels could operate, however. For instance, top professional groups would be expected to spend more money on, say, power boating and golfing, as these tend to be class-related activities.

Many marketing acronyms have been created to act as abbreviations for different demographic groups of consumers. Here are just a few:

DINKY – double income no kids yet

NILK – no income lots of kids

WOOF – well-off older folk

SINBAD –

GLAM –

See if you can guess these last two!

3 Psychographic factors

These are to do with differences between people's lifestyles, personalities, values and attitudes. Many of these can be influenced by an individual's social class too – so the middle class tend to have a very different attitude towards private education than most of the working class, which is why some are prepared to spend large amounts of money on it for their children.

Attitudes towards ethical business practices are very strong among some consumers – hence the growth of societal marketing towards these groups. Similarly, the increasing interest in organic foods shows how common values and opinions held by consumers can also be used to group them in a useful way.

Lifestyle is a very broad term that often relates to activities undertaken, interests and opinions rather than personality. The huge increase in TV channels and TV viewing in many countries has contributed to the growth of 'TV meals', which are pre-prepared meals ready to eat without missing any of your favourite programmes.

Personality characteristics are difficult to measure or define, but they do influence consumption decisions. One would expect an aggressive person to have different purchasing patterns from a timid person. The same could be said for impulsive people as opposed to very cautious people. Many firms, particularly in their advertising, attempt to appeal to consumers who share certain personality characteristics. We see, therefore, products such as activity holidays aimed at outgoing people who wish to pursue relatively dangerous sports, for example bungee jumping or white-water rafting.

ACTIVITY 16.9

[12 marks, 15 minutes]

Explain **four** ways in which a food manufacturer could segment the market for ready-made meals. **[12]**

The potential advantages and limitations of market segmentation are explained in Table 16.2.

Advantages	Limitations
■ Businesses can define their target market precisely and design and produce goods that are specifically aimed at these groups, leading to increased sales. ■ It enables identification of gaps in the market – groups of consumers that are not currently being targeted – and these might then be successfully exploited. ■ Differentiated marketing strategies can be focused on target market groups. This avoids wasting money on trying to sell products to the whole market – some consumer groups will have no intention of buying the product. ■ Small firms unable to compete in the whole market are able to specialise in one or two market segments. ■ Price discrimination can be used to increase revenue and profits – see Chapter 18.	■ Research and development and production costs might be high as a result of marketing several different product variations. ■ Promotional costs might be high as different advertisements and promotions might be needed for different segments – marketing economies of scale may not be fully exploited. ■ Production and stock-holding costs might be higher than for the option of just producing and stocking one undifferentiated product. ■ By focusing on one or two limited market segments there is a danger that excessive specialisation could lead to problems if consumers in those segments change their purchasing habits significantly. ■ Extensive market research is needed.

Table 16.2 Advantages and limitations of market segmentation

ACTIVITY 16.10

'Understanding market segmentation key to repeat visits by tourists'

According to a study by Cathy Hsu of the School of Tourism at Hong Kong University, the key to boosting the number of tourists revisiting the region is for companies to understand market segmentation. In a survey of 1,300 tourists passing through Hong Kong International Airport, Professor Hsu identified six distinct groups of tourists who, she claimed, needed to be treated differently by marketing activities. The six groups were:

- leisure travellers aged 55 years or younger
- first-time mature travellers aged 55 years or older
- repeat mature travellers
- business travellers with incomes over US$50,000 per year
- business travellers with incomes under US$50,000 per year
- travellers visiting friends or family in Hong Kong.

Clearly, these groups needed a different marketing focus to encourage repeat visits. Young, single, leisure travellers might be attracted by 'bring a friend' promotions. High-income business travellers could be more influenced by promotions about the wide range of leisure and shopping facilities in the region. Mature repeat travellers made up just 4.5% of the total sample, suggesting that this was a market

Tour group in Hong Kong – the tourist market can be segmented in many ways to allow differentiated marketing at different consumer groups

segment that needed to be much more fully developed. The segment that needed little additional marketing focus was made up of those visiting family and friends – they would be likely to visit Hong Kong again anyway.

[26 marks, 35 minutes]

1 Explain, with examples, what is meant by the term 'market segmentation'. [4]

2 Why does successful market segmentation need to be supported by market research? Use this case as an example in your answer. [6]

3 Explain **two** of the ways that this research has allowed the total tourist market of Hong Kong to be segmented. [6]

4 Discuss the benefits to a travel company in Hong Kong of using the information in this case to target different segments of the tourism market with different marketing activities. [10]

RESEARCH TASK

Research the market size for cars in your country.

1 Is the total size of the market rising or falling?
2 Which **four** companies have the highest market share and which are the best selling models?
3 Write a brief report on the current state of the car market in your country.

AS Level exam practice questions
Short answer questions

[72 marks, 90 minutes]

Knowledge

1 Why is 'marketing' not just 'selling and advertising'? [4]
2 Using examples, differentiate between market orientation and product orientation. [4]
3 Why is it usually better for a firm to be market-oriented? [4]
4 Why would a business that had the second-largest market share be keen to become market leader? [3]
5 List **three** factors that could lead to an overall decline in the size of a market. [3]
6 Outline **two** factors that could lead to a business experiencing declining market share in a growing market. [4]
7 Explain **two** benefits to a business of using mass marketing. [4]

Application

8 Company A is a manufacturer of smartphones. Measure company A's market share and the growth rate of the market it operates in from the following data. Comment on your results. [8]

	2012	2013
Total market sales (units)	36,000	48,000
Total market value ($m)	5.0	6.5
Company A's sales (units)	3,600	5,000
Company A's sales value ($m)	0.5	0.6

9 Outline **four** possible examples of marketing objectives that Coca Cola might set. [4]
10 Explain one strategy that Coca Cola could use to help the business achieve **one** of these objectives. [4]
11 How might a manufacturer of small cars segment the market for them? [4]
12 What would be the advantages to a jewellery retailer from segmenting the market it operates in? [4]
13 Using numerical examples, explain the difference between market share and market size. [6]
14 Explain **three** examples of problems that might result from an e-commerce business of failing to link marketing decisions with other departments of the business. [6]
15 Outline **three** ways a manufacturer of jeans could use to try to increase market share. [6]
16 Explain **two** ways in which a retailer of sports clothing could attempt to 'add or create value' to the products. [4]

Data response

1 Furniture Metallica

Bill Yang is a qualified engineer. He started his own business in Malaysia – Furniture Metallica Ltd – in order to take advantage of his metal-working skills after losing his job at a steelworks. He set up a small workshop 18 years ago and quickly built up a reputation for quality metal furniture goods which he sold in business (producer) markets. He was lucky – during this period the market for office and business metal furniture was growing and Furniture Metallica's share of this market increased rapidly – 10% of sales were also exported to Brunei in 2009.

In 2011, this optimistic picture began to change. Business office styles and fashion were changing and new plastic technologies were transforming the furniture industry. Metal furniture seemed old-fashioned. Bill had no knowledge of other materials and his metal furniture designs had not changed at all. Sales fell but, of even more concern, so did market share.

Bill decided to revise his original business plan and he set three new marketing objectives:

- Increase sales in markets other than Malaysia and Brunei.
- Maintain market share in Malaysia.
- Test consumer market for metal furniture.

Bill looked for markets in other parts of Asia apart from Malaysia. This was quite a success as by 2013 these other markets accounted for 25% of total sales. He also, in 2014, started selling online to consumer markets by extending his product range. He adapted his office desks into coffee tables, student work units and even workbenches. Another idea was to make a range of office desks trimmed in leather that would appeal to a market segment of high income, fashion-conscious consumers wanting stylish metal furniture with a luxury factor built in.

A friend who had recently returned from a European business trip encouraged him to think about exporting to this huge market too. He told Bill that the cost advantages enjoyed by Malaysian factories would be to his advantage, even if metal furniture was not the 'height of fashion'.

[30 marks, 45 minutes]

1 a Define the term 'business (producer) markets'. **[2]**
   b Briefly explain the term 'market segment'. **[3]**
2 a Calculate, using data in the table, Furniture Metallica's Malaysian market share in 2013. **[3]**
   b Using your result from question 2a and other information, comment on the trend in Furniture Metallica's market share. **[3]**

	Total market sales in Malaysia ($m) Office furniture	Furniture Metallica – market share %	Furniture Metallica sales in Malaysia ($m)
2011	200	29	58
2012	180	25	45
2013	150	See Question 2a	33

3 As Bill starts to widen his range of products and enter consumer markets, analyse how he will need to adapt his marketing to be successful. **[8]**

4 Evaluate the benefits to Furniture Metalica of Bill's decision to use market segmentation of the furniture market. **[11]**

2 Niche and mass marketing – sports shoes

Adidas is using mass marketing of cheap sports shoes to sell to rural poor populations of India and Bangladesh. This is in contrast to its niche marketing strategy of designing and selling Adidas Performance shoes to middle-income consumers who want both style and excellent sporting performance from their shows. Rapha – a small UK brand with sales less than 1/800th of big businesses such as Nike and Adidas – sells exclusive premium styles of sports shoes to specialist groups including professional cyclists. The demand from this market segment is growing faster than the total market for 'athletic footwear'. The global footwear market was valued at $50 billion in 2013 and is forecast to grow by 1.75% per year for two years. Sports shoe manufacturers have many direct competitors so differentiating their products is important.

1 a Define the term 'mass marketing'. [2]

   b Briefly explain the term 'direct competitors'. [3]

2 a Calculate the forecast size of the global athletic footwear market by 2015. [3]

   b Explain the importance to Adidas of this forecast growth in the global athletic footwear market if the company forecasts that its own sales will increase by 2% per year over this period. [3]

3 Using examples from the case **and** your own examples, differentiate clearly between niche marketing and mass marketing. [8]

4 Evaluate the decision by a business such as Rapha to only sell premium products to small groups of consumers. [11]

AS Level essay questions

[20 marks, 40 minutes each]

1 a Analyse the benefits to a retailing business of setting marketing objectives. [8]

   b The managing director of a small boat-building business told the other directors: 'There is no need for us to spend money on market research. We have clearly designed the best product on the market and consumers will be certain to buy.'
Discuss whether the managing director is likely to be proven correct. [12]

2 a Analyse ways in which a soft drink manufacturer might segment the market for its products. [8]

   b Evaluate whether a business should always try to become market leader with the highest market share. [12]

17 Market research

On completing this chapter, you will be able to:

- understand what market research is and why it is important
- explain the main stages of the market research process
- recognise the importance of identifying the research problem and objectives
- differentiate between the main sources of data and evaluate the benefits and drawbacks of primary and secondary research
- explain the differences between the main sampling techniques
- present market research results in ways that aid the users' understanding
- assess the cost-effectiveness of market research data
- analyse statistical research results to aid with management decision-making, including averages and measures of spread.

Introducing the topic

PROCTOR AND GAMBLE BELIEVES SOCIAL MEDIA WILL REVOLUTIONISE MARKET RESEARCH

Proctor and Gamble (P&G) is a multinational business operating in the beauty, grooming and home car markets. With sales of more than $85 billion per year, its marketing research budget of $350 million is bigger than most companies' total sales! So when Joan Lewis, the head of P&G consumer and market knowledge says that Facebook, Twitter and other social media will cause actual market research surveys to decline in importance, people listen. The two-way engagement with businesses offered by social media means that people will become a lot less willing to take part in traditional market surveys. She said: 'If I have something to say to a company, now there are lots of ways to say it.'

Market research can be costly. Many businesses are turning to social media as a relatively cheap way of gaining insight into their customers, market and brand appeal. Most platforms such as Facebook and Twitter allow simple searching of the latest posts and popular terms so a researcher can gain insight into emerging trends and see what customers are talking about in real time. By setting up a few searches on Twitter using hashtags related to a brand, industry or product, a business can receive instant notice when customers or competitors use key terms.

Points to think about:

- Why do you think P&G spends so much on gaining customer and market information?
- Explain **four** pieces of information P&G would find useful when planning to introduce a new home cleaning product.
- What are the potential benefits of businesses using information gained through social media sites?
- Are there likely to be any problems with **only** depending on these sources for consumer information?

Introduction

In the previous chapter, the distinction between 'product orientation' and 'market or customer orientation' was explained. At the heart of market orientation is market research and being focused on what customers are willing and able to buy. Finding out important information about customers, their tastes and preferences, market condition and competitors' actions is considered, by most business managers, to be an essential starting point to a successful product or service.

Market Research

Market research is a broad and far-reaching process. It is concerned not just with finding out whether consumers will buy a particular product or not, but also with trying to establish the characteristics of customers – consumer profiles – and their wants and needs. More specifically, research will help a business analyse customer reaction to, among other things:

- different price levels
- alternative forms of promotion
- new types of packaging
- preferred means of distribution.

KEY TERMS

Market research: this is the process of collecting, recording and analysing data about customers, competitors and the market.

The results of market research can, therefore, have a great impact on decisions made in all areas of the marketing process. Market research is itself a growth industry as most research is undertaken by specialist agencies working for other businesses. Why are firms prepared to spend so much on market research? What are the uses to which market research data can be put? Where can the data be obtained from? How should the results be presented? These are the important questions to be answered in this chapter.

The need for market research

1 To reduce the risks associated with new product launches

By investigating potential demand for a new product or service, the business should be able to assess with some degree of accuracy the likelihood of a new product achieving satisfactory sales. No research can guarantee success, however. Later in the chapter, we consider all of the reasons why market research may give a misleading message about the new product's chances of success. However, market research is still a key part of new product development (NPD) and most firms would aim to check market conditions before planning the launch of a new product. Table 17.1 summarises how NPD is supported by market research.

2 To predict future demand changes

A travel firm may wish to investigate social and other changes to see how these might affect the demand for holidays in the future. For instance, the growth in the

The NPD process	The market research process
identify consumer needs and tastes	primary and secondary research into consumer needs and competitors
product idea and packaging design	testing of product and packaging with consumer groups
brand positioning and advertising testing	pre-testing of the product image and advertisements
product launch and after launch period	monitoring of sales and consumer response

Table 17.1 Summary of how market research supports NPD

number of single-person households may suggest that there could be a rising demand for 'singles'-type holidays.

3 To explain patterns in sales of existing products and market trends

Market research is not just undertaken for new or planned products; it needs to be conducted for existing products too. Sales at the fashion retailer Gap had, by the end of 2013, increased by 8% compared to a year earlier, after several years of falling sales. Gap managers were able to analyse the sales data, conduct market research and take effective action to reverse the worrying decline in sales.

4 To assess the most favoured designs, flavours, styles, promotions and packages for a product

Consumer tests of different versions of a product or of the proposed adverts to promote it will enable a business to focus on the aspects of design and performance that consumers rate most highly. These can then be incorporated into the final product.

Market research can, therefore, be used to discover information about:

- market size and consumer tastes and trends
- the product and its perceived strengths and weaknesses
- the promotion used and its effectiveness
- competitors and their claimed unique selling propositions
- distribution methods most preferred by consumers
- consumers' preferences for packaging of the product.

ACTIVITY 17.1

We know who our customers are

IKEA is now one of the world's best-known furniture retailers. It now has 301 stores in 37 countries serving more than 700 million customers annually. Peter Hogsted, one of its senior managers, has researched its consumer base very carefully:

- It is largely middle class and the middle class in most countries is increasing.
- Its core customers are between 25 and 50 years old.
- They are fashion conscious but want good-value products.
- Eighty per cent are female.
- The majority have children.

[12 marks, 15 minutes]

Explain **four** benefits to IKEA's managers of having detailed research information about their customers. [12]

The market research process

1 Management problem identification

This is the single most important step in the whole research process. A business could spend many thousands of dollars on undertaking market research, but if it had no clear idea of the purpose of this research or the problem that needed investigating, then the money would be wasted. Here are some examples of problems that might be investigated by market research:

- What size is the potential market for this business?
- Why are our sales falling?
- How can we break into the market in another country?
- How can we most effectively meet the challenge of new competitors?
- What customer groups buy our products and what groups tend not to buy them?

By setting the problem out accurately, the rest of the market research process can then be directed accurately towards solving it. Without setting out the problem, much unnecessary data would be gathered, which might prevent the real issues or problems from being investigated at all.

2 Research objectives

These objectives must obviously tie in with the original problem. They must be set in such a way that, when they have been achieved, they provide all of the information needed to solve the problem. Here are some examples of market research objectives, expressed in the form of questions that need to be answered through research:

- How many people are likely to buy our products in country X?
- If the price of good Y is reduced, how much will this increase sales volume?
- If we advertise this product on television, what will be the likely impact on sales volume and market share?
- Which new product idea, A or B, is likely to generate more sales?
- What would be the impact of new packaging on sales of our product?
- Why are consumer complaints about our products increasing?

3 Sources of data – primary and secondary research

Primary research collects first-hand data as they are being collected by the organisation for the first time for its own needs. In contrast, **secondary research** is the use and analysis of data that already exist. These data were originally collected by another organisation, often for a different purpose, and are often referred to as second-hand data.

KEY TERMS

Primary research: the collection of first-hand data that is directly related to a firm's needs.

Secondary research: collection of data from second-hand sources.

Which one of these research methods should be used first by a business undertaking market research for the first time, for example data-gathering for a new product launch? Surprisingly, perhaps, it is secondary research that should be undertaken first – but only if the data exist, which they may not if the planned product is so different that no second-hand data exist. Why undertake secondary research first? It is because of the benefits that secondary research offers over primary methods (see Activity 17.2).

Exporting to Trinidad and Tobago

A US-owned food exporting business plans to enter the market in Trinidad and Tobago for the first time. The directors have yet to decide whether to sell high- or low-priced products and what type of shops they should sell through. The marketing manager obtained the following data from secondary sources, without the manager leaving his desk – which is why it is sometimes called desk research.

■ The two-island republic has one of the highest per capita GDPs in the Caribbean – over US$20,000 in 2013.
■ GDP grew by 2% in 2013.
■ The retail market is made up of more than 500 stores (supermarkets, grocery stores and petrol stations), with sales estimated of just over US$1 billion for 2013.

■ Aiming for a 'one-stop' shopping experience, many supermarket chains have begun to renovate and remodel their stores.
■ The market leader is Hi-Lo Food Stores.
■ In-house bakeries and delis are becoming more common.
■ Retail food sales rose by nearly 50% between 2000 and 2013.
■ Supermarkets are increasing the number of premium priced low-fat and health-food products on offer.

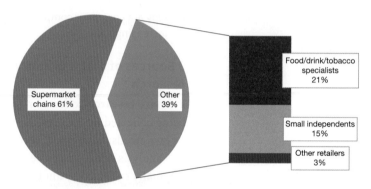

Trinidad and Tobago: distribution of retail grocery sales, 2011

[24 marks, 30 minutes]

1 Explain **four** benefits to the US food exporter of the data researched from secondary sources. [8]

2 Explain whether the two graphs used above (pie graph and bar chart) helped you to interpret the information they contain. [6]

3 Discuss the possible limitations of these data researched from secondary sources. [10]

Having completed Activity 17.2 you probably realise that more detailed information about the food market in Trinidad and Tobago will be needed before final decisions are taken by the US food exporter. But the secondary data has outlined the key features of the market and its structure – other data collection methods will now have to be used.

Sources of secondary data

The data referred to above were all obtained from several of the following well-known sources of secondary data:

1 Government publications

In most countries, sources such as the following from the UK could be referred to:

■ population census
■ social trends
■ economic trends
■ annual abstract of statistics
■ family expenditure survey.

Therefore, if a furniture manufacturer was undecided whether to produce new designs for teenagers' bedrooms or electric reclining armchairs for the elderly, reference to government publications for the forecasted age distribution of the country's population over the next ten years would be a useful starting point.

2 Local libraries and local government offices

If the research data needed were only for a small area – investigating the viability of a new café, for example – then local, not national, data would be necessary, such as:

- local population census returns with details of total numbers and age and occupation distributions
- numbers of households in the area
- the proportions of the local population from different ethnic and cultural groups.

3 Trade organisations

Trade organisations produce regular reports on the state of the markets their members operate in. Examples of such organisations are:

- Society of Motor Manufacturers and Traders
- Furniture Retailers Association
- Engineering Employers Federation.

If a garage owner wanted to start stocking new cars for sale, then details of the type and size of car that is most popular with consumers could be obtained from the first source listed above. Clearly, further research might then be needed to see if, locally, these national data were reflected in consumer demand in the garage's own area.

4 Market intelligence reports

These are very detailed reports on individual markets and industries produced by specialist market research agencies. They are very expensive, but they are usually available at local business libraries. Examples are:

- Mintel reports
- Key Note reports
- Euromonitor.

If the owner of a small hotel planned to expand the business by opening a hotel in the capital city, one of these reports on the hotel and catering market would provide huge amounts of detail on market and consumer trends, eating and holiday habits of consumers, the number of tourists, and so on.

5 Newspaper reports and specialist publications

- *Marketing* – this journal provides weekly advertising spend data and consumer 'recall of adverts' results.
- *The Grocer*.
- *Motor Trader*.

- *The Financial Times* – features regular articles on key industries such as IT and detailed country reports; essential for potential exporters.

6 Internal company records

If the business has been trading for some time, a great quantity of secondary data will already be available for further analysis from:

- customer sales records
- guarantee claims
- daily, weekly and monthly sales trends
- feedback from customers on product, service, delivery and quality.

7 The Internet

The Internet has transformed secondary-data collection – but it only has access to data that have already been gathered from the sources listed above. Whenever research is conducted just from the Internet, the accuracy and relevance of the source should always be checked.

235

ACTIVITY 17.3

What do you want to know about Malaysia?

If you are prepared to pay for it, the range of secondary market research data available for businesses operating in Malaysia is extensive. Four examples, from the many thousands of reports available, are:

- Clothing and footwear in Malaysia (Euromonitor).
- Pet food in Malaysia (Euromonitor).
- Gardening in Malaysia (Euromonitor).
- Malaysian desktop and notebook demand 2009–2013 (IDC).

Research a market for a product or service in your own country. Find out as much as you can about the size of the market, any segments that exist within it and the features of typical consumers for this product.

It is clear that there is a great range of secondary data available both to existing businesses planning a new market development and to newly formed businesses. Secondary research should always be the starting point of any market analysis. It will nearly always indicate the focus that subsequent primary research should have. However, on its own, it is rarely sufficient, which is why

Advantages	Disadvantages
■ often obtainable very cheaply – apart from the purchase of market intelligence reports ■ identifies the nature of the market and assists with the planning of primary research ■ obtainable quickly without the need to devise complicated data-gathering methods ■ allows comparison of data from different sources	■ may not be updated frequently and may therefore be out-of-date ■ as it was originally collected for another purpose, it may not be entirely suitable or presented in the most effective way for the business using it ■ data-collection methods and accuracy of these may be unknown ■ might not be available for completely new product developments

Table 17.2 Advantages and disadvantages of secondary research

Advantages	Disadvantages
■ up-to-date and therefore more useful than most secondary data ■ relevant – collected for a specific purpose – directly addresses the questions the business wants answers to ■ confidential – no other business has access to this data	■ costly – market research agencies can charge thousands of dollars for detailed customer surveys and other market research reports ■ time-consuming – secondary data could be obtained from the internet much more quickly ■ doubts over accuracy and validity – largely because of the need to use sampling and the risk that the samples used may not be fully representative of the population

Table 17.3 Advantages and disadvantages of primary research

primary research is also usually undertaken. Table 17.2 summarises the advantages and disadvantages of secondary research. Secondary research gathers background data, but only primary research can provide detailed, up-to-date information from consumers within the firm's target market.

Methods of primary research

Primary – or field – research can itself be divided into **quantitative** and **qualitative research**. Table 17.3 summarises the advantages and disadvantages of primary research.

KEY TERMS

Qualitative research: research into the in-depth motivations behind consumer buying behaviour or opinions.
Quantitative research: research that leads to numerical results that can be statistically analysed.

Qualitative research

Finding out about the quantities that consumers might purchase is clearly important information but what is often even more revealing is why consumers will or will not buy a particular product. Qualitative research should discover the motivational factors behind consumer buying habits. For example, quantitative research might establish the size of the potential market for a new luxury ice cream. But will consumers buy it for its taste and the quality of its ingredients or because it will be promoted as a life style-branded product that will reflect well on the consumers' image of themselves? Only qualitative research can establish the answer to the last question – and it is important because it will help the business in its pricing and promotional decisions for the new product.

Focus groups

In these discussion groups, questions are asked and participants are encouraged to actively discuss their responses – all members of the group are free to talk with other group members. These discussions are often filmed for use by the market research department as a source of data. **Focus groups** are a widely used method of obtaining feedback about new products, new brand names, new advertisements and so on, before these are launched on to the market. This information is often believed to be more accurate and realistic than the responses to individual interviews or questionnaires, where respondents do not have the discussion opportunity

KEY TERM

Focus groups: a group of people who are asked about their attitude towards a product, service, advertisement or new style of packaging.

presented by focus groups. The information collected from the groups can have a big impact on the business's final product or advertising decisions. Researchers are present in the focus group and they take part in the discussion as well, but only to stimulate it – not to lead the group to a particular conclusion. In one such focus group used by a car manufacturer, all distinguishing name signs on a new model of car were removed and consumers were asked for their reaction to the design, shape and performance of the car. Initial results were very positive – until the consumers were told that it was a Skoda model, a manufacturer with a previously poor reputation. The company knew that consumers would, therefore, be prepared to purchase the product if they could successfully change the image of the company and its brand name.

Possible drawbacks to focus groups include time-wasting, as some members of the group may discuss issues not directly related to the research. The researchers present will have to keep them 'on target' at all times. The data collected, being qualitative in nature, can be difficult to analyse and present to senior managers. Finally, no matter how careful the researchers are who are present during the focus groups discussion, there might be the risk of researchers leading or influencing the discussion too much, leading to biased conclusions.

Quantitative research techniques

1 Observation and recording

Using this approach, market researchers observe and record how consumers behave. They can count the number of people or cars that pass a particular location in order to assess the best site for a new business. Researchers can also observe people in shops to see how many look at a new display or take a product from the shelves. A simple inventory check can also be used to record sales over a period of time. Results can be distorted, however, if people are aware of being watched and behave differently because of this. Also, observation does not give researchers the opportunity to ask for explanations of behaviour – it records only what actually happens.

2 Test marketing

This can take place after a decision has been made to produce a limited quantity of a new product but before a full-scale, national launch is made. It involves promoting and selling the product in a limited geographical area and then recording consumer reactions and sales figures. To be reasonably accurate, the region selected must reflect as closely as possible the social and consumer profiles of the rest of the country. In many countries with regional TV stations, one of these regions is chosen as TV advertising can then be focused on just this one area. Test marketing reduces the risks of a new product launch failing completely, but the evidence is not always completely accurate if the total population does not share the same characteristics and preferences as the region selected.

ACTIVITY 17.4

Carlos plans a new restaurant

Carlos Sanchez is a chef who specialises in Spanish cuisine. He has just given up his job in a large hotel in the capital city. He has always wanted to work for himself, and with his savings he has decided to open his own small restaurant. Property prices are too high in the city, so he has moved to a small coastal resort about 100 km from the capital. He has many important decisions to make before he starts trading. He is not sure whether Spanish cooking will be popular with the locals and the tourists. He is able to prepare many other types of dishes too. He could open just a restaurant or a takeaway as well. If he offers takeaway meals, he could either serve these in plastic containers suitable for microwave heating, which are expensive, or in paper trays, which are cheaper. Carlos has noticed that there are few other restaurants in the area and no takeaways, although one well-known fast-food chain has recently closed down. There are no other Spanish-based restaurants. After finding a suitable shop site, Carlos then has to decide whether to decorate it for younger people's tastes with loud pop music or in a more sober style with old-style Spanish music. Carlos begins to plan seriously for his new venture – he had not realised that so many decisions would need to be taken before he could start cooking!

[24 marks, 35 minutes]

1 Would you advise Carlos to do some market research before he opens his new business? Explain the reasons for your answer. **[6]**

2 List **four** questions Carlos needs answers to from market research. **[4]**

3 Assuming Carlos lives in your country, list **four** sources of secondary research that he could refer to. **[4]**

4 Assess the likely usefulness of secondary research to Carlos. **[10]**

3 Consumer surveys

These involve directly asking consumers or potential consumers for their opinions and preferences. They can be used to obtain both qualitative and quantitative research. For example, here are two questions asked in a recent survey of shoppers:

1   How many foreign holidays did you take last year?
2   What do you look for in an ideal foreign holiday?

The first question is designed to obtain quantitative data, which can be presented graphically and analysed statistically. The second question is designed to find out the key qualitative features of a holiday that would influence consumer choice. There are four important issues for market researchers to be aware of when conducting consumer surveys:

1   **Who to ask?** Given that in most cases it is impossible or too expensive to survey all potential members of a target market (called the survey population), it is necessary to select a '**sample**' from this population. The more closely this sample reflects the characteristics of the survey population, then the more accurate the survey is likely to be.
2   **What to ask?** The construction of an unbiased and unambiguous questionnaire is essential if the survey is to obtain useful results.
3   **How to ask?** Should the questionnaire be self-completed and returned by post or filled in by an interviewer in a face-to-face session with the respondent? Could a telephone survey be conducted instead?
4   **How accurate is it?** Assessing the likely accuracy and validity of the results is a crucial element of market research surveys.

KEY TERM

Sample: the group of people taking part in a market research survey selected to be representative of the overall target market.

Sample size

In nearly all market research situations it is impossible to seek evidence from the total 'population', i.e. the total potential market that the firm is aiming at. This is either because that market is so extensive that contacting everyone in it would be too expensive or time-consuming or it is impossible to identify everyone in that market.

So a sample of the total potential market will need to be chosen. Generally speaking, the larger the sample, the more representative of the total population it is likely to be and greater confidence can be placed in the final results.

In surveying consumer reaction to a new advertising campaign for a major brand of chocolate, a sample of ten people is unlikely to be sufficient. Try to work out why. The first ten people chosen might show a positive reaction to the new advertisement. Yet another ten might show a majority with negative reactions. A sample of ten is too small to be confident about the result, as chance variations could easily occur because of the limited number of respondents chosen. A sample of 100 or even 1,000 will produce results that will reflect much more accurately the total preferences of the whole survey population. There will be much less risk of pure chance distorting the results. Obviously, a sample of 1,000 is more useful than one of 100, especially if the questions are being focused on particular age or income groups. Once a sample of 100 is broken down into, say, ten different age groups, then there will only be ten respondents from each age band. This could be too few.

What prevents all primary research being based on a sample size of 1,000? Cost and time are the two major constraints here – the cost of research increases greatly with the sample size, especially when a specialist firm of market research analysts is used. The results of a survey might be needed quickly to assist managers in making rapid decisions – a sample size of 1,000 will take much longer to organise.

Sampling methods

Probability sampling

This involves the selection of a sample from a population based on the principle of random chance. It is more complex, more time-consuming and usually more costly than non-probability sampling. However, because the sample is selected randomly and the probability of each unit's inclusion in the sample can be calculated, very reliable estimates can be made about both the whole target market (the 'statistical population') and about the chances of errors occurring. These are the most common probability sampling methods:

- **Simple random sampling:** Each member of the target population has an equal chance of being included in the sample. To select a random sample the following are needed:
  - a list of all of the people in the target population
  - sequential numbers given to each member of this population
  - a list of random numbers generated by computer.
  If a sample of 100 is required, then the first 100 numbers on the random number list are taken and the people who had these numbers allocated to them will form the sample.

- **Systematic sampling:** In this method, the sample is selected by taking every nth item from the target population until the desired size of sample is reached. For example, suppose a supermarket wants to study the buying habits of its customers. The sample could be chosen by asking every tenth customer entering the supermarket until the required sample size had been reached. The researcher must ensure that the chosen sample does not hide a regular pattern, and a random starting point must be selected.
- **Stratified sampling:** This method recognises that the target population may be made up of many different groups with many different opinions. These groups are called strata or layers of the population and for a sample to be accurate it should contain members of all of these strata – hence the term, stratified sampling. For example, if you were asked to sample 100 fellow students in your school about soft drink preferences for the school shop, it would be more accurate if, instead of asking 100 friends, you split the school up into certain strata, such as class groups, ages or gender. So if the whole school contains 1,000 students of whom 50 are girls in Year 8, an accurate sample of 100 would contain five girls from Year 8 (50/1,000 × 100). This process would be repeated with all year groups until the total required sample of 100 was reached. The people to be surveyed in each stratum should be selected randomly. Stratified sampling may also be used when a product is designed to appeal to just one segment of the market. So if a computer game is aimed at 16–24-year-olds, only people from this stratum of the population will be included in the market research sample.
- **Quota sampling:** This is similar to stratified sampling. By this method, interviewees are selected according to the different proportions that certain consumer groups make up of the whole target population. For instance, if it is already known that out of all consumers of denim jeans:
  - 65% are male
  - 35% are female
  - 35% are aged 14–20
  - 35% are aged 21–30
  - 20% are aged 31–40
  - 41 10% are aged over 41

  then the sample selected would conform to the same proportions. Therefore, if there were a sample of 200 people, 130 would be male, 70 female, 70 between 14 and 20 years old and so on. The interviewer could then choose the quotas by questioning the right number of people in the high street. However, the interviewer might be biased in their selection of people in each quota – preferring to ask only very attractive people, for example. This makes quota sampling less probability-based than the other methods and more open to individual bias.
- **Cluster sampling:** When a full sampling frame list is not available or the target population is too geographically dispersed, then cluster sampling will take a sample from just one or a few groups – not the whole population. This might be just one town or region and this will help to reduce costs – but it may not be fully representative of the whole population. Random methods can then be used to select the sample from this group. A multinational company wanting to research global attitudes towards its product would save time and money by concentrating on just a few areas for its research.

TOP TIP

Each method of sampling has its own advantages and limitations – so which is best? This depends on the size and financial resources of the business and how different consumers are in their tastes between different age groups and so on. Cost-effectiveness is important in all market research decisions.

KEY TERMS

Random sampling: every member of the target population has an equal chance of being selected.

Systematic sampling: every nth item in the target population is selected.

Stratified sampling: this draws a sample from a specified sub-group or segment of the population and uses random sampling to select an appropriate number from each stratum.

Quota sampling: when the population has been stratified and the interviewer selects an appropriate number of respondents from each stratum.

Cluster sampling: using one or a number of specific groups to draw samples from and not selecting from the whole population, e.g. using one town or region.

Non-probability sampling

This approach to sampling cannot be used to calculate the probability of any particular sample being selected. Non-probability sample results cannot be used to make inferences or judgements about the total population. Any general statements that are made as a result of this method of sampling must be analysed very carefully and filtered by the researcher knowledge of the topic being researched.

These are the most common methods of non-probability sampling:

- **Convenience sampling:** Members of the population are chosen based on their relative ease of access. Sampling friends, fellow workers or shoppers in just one location are all examples of convenience sampling.
- **Snowball sampling:** The first respondent refers a friend who then refers another friend… and so the process continues. This is a cheap method of sampling and is often

used by companies in the financial services sector, such as health- and motor-insurance companies. It is likely to lead to a biased sample, as each respondent's friends are likely to have a similar lifestyle and opinions.

- **Judgemental sampling:** The researcher chooses the sample based on who they think would be appropriate to study. This could be used by an experienced researcher who may be short of time as they have been asked to produce a report quickly.
- **Ad hoc quotas:** A quota is established (say 55% women) and researchers are told to choose any respondent they wish up to the pre-set quota.

All of these samples are likely to lead to less accurate results – which are less representative of the whole population – than probability sampling techniques.

TOP TIP

Students studying the Cambridge syllabus will only be asked questions about random, stratified and quota sampling – the other methods are included for comparison purposes and to show the range of possible alternatives.

240

What to ask – questionnaire design

It is not easy to write an effective questionnaire. The temptation is often to ask too many questions in the hope of gaining every last scrap of information. Yet people may become suspicious or bored with so many questions. Unless it is absolutely essential to know the names and precise ages or income levels of respondents, these questions are best avoided, as there will be reluctance to answer them. One way around this is to group income levels together, such as:

Please indicate which of the following income levels you are in:

$10,000–$20,000
$20,001–$30,000

and so on.

KEY TERMS

Open questions: those that invite a wide-ranging or imaginative response – the results will be difficult to collate and present numerically.

Closed questions: questions to which a limited number of pre-set answers is offered.

Asking all 'open' questions is not a good idea, although questionnaires usually end with one. They allow respondents to give their opinion. For example: 'What do you really think of Jupiter perfume?' – the answers to this will be so varied in length and content that the results will be very difficult to put together and to present statistically. A better option might be: 'What most attracted you to buying Jupiter perfume?' followed by a list of options for the respondents to tick or rate, such as:

- price
- image
- packaging
- widely available
- smell.

As the design of the questionnaire will greatly influence the accuracy and usefulness of the results, it is advisable to undertake an initial pilot survey to test the quality of the questions. Other principles to follow include:

- making the objectives of the research clear so that questions can be focused on these
- writing clear and unambiguous questions
- trying to make sure that the questions follow each other in a logical sequence
- avoiding questions that seem to point to one particular answer
- using language that will be readily understood
- including some questions that will allow a classification of results by gender, area lived in, occupation and so on.

How to ask? Self-completed questionnaire or direct interview?

Self-completed questionnaires are either sent through the post or filled in by the respondent themselves 'on the spot', for example in a shop. Postal surveys are relatively cheap to send out, a wide geographical area can be covered and there is no chance of bias creeping in from the interviewer to distort results. However, the response rate to both these and other forms of self-completed questionnaires is nearly always very poor, questions could easily be misunderstood and the sample returned could be biased in favour of those respondents with the most spare time, for example retired people. Direct interviews are conducted by an interviewer, usually either in the street or in the respondent's home. Skilled interviewers will avoid bias in the way in which they ask questions, and detailed questions can be explained to the interviewee. Follow-up questions can be asked if required. This can be an expensive method, but the interviewer will continue their work until the pre-set sample size has been reached – whereas the response to postal questionnaires is always uncertain.

How accurate is primary research?

Unfortunately, the reliability of primary data can often be called into question. There are three main reasons why primary data may not be as reliable as hoped for.

1 **Sampling bias:** The only really accurate method of primary research is to ask the entire target population – we have already identified the time and cost constraints on this. Results from a sample may be different from those that would have been obtained if the entire target population had been questioned. This is called sampling bias. The less care that is taken in selecting a sample, then the greater the degree of statistical bias that will exist. Therefore, no one can be 100% confident that sample results are really accurate. Statisticians often aim to achieve a '95% confidence level' in their results, which means that the results can be relied upon in 19 cases out of 20. Generally, the larger the sample, the greater the chance that this 95% confidence level will be met.

2 **Questionnaire bias:** This may occur when questions tend to lead respondents towards one particular answer. Because of this, the results are not a completely accurate reflection of how people act or of what they believe. An example of a 'leading question' could be: 'Which of the following factors best explains why you prefer Chocko bars to other manufacturers' chocolate bars?'

3 **Other forms of bias:** These might include the respondent not answering in a very truthful way, perhaps because they do not want to admit to spending so much on music downloads or clothes!

Market research developments

Increasingly, businesses are turning to electronic means to gather the data their marketing strategies require.

ACTIVITY 17.5

Metro Petroleum questionnaire

Read the following questionnaire that was prepared by Metro Petroleum. The company wanted to research motorists' petrol-buying decisions. They hope that the results will help them to improve their marketing strategies. It was distributed at Metro's petrol stations. Customers were asked to return it, fully completed, during their next visit.

Questionnaire for all petrol customers
Please help us by answering the following questions:

1 Name ....

2 Address ....

3 Make and model of car ....

4 Do you buy petrol often? ....

5 Who buys the petrol, you or your wife? ....

6 How much petrol do you buy? ....

7 Do you always buy petrol at Metro stations? Yes/No ....

8 Where else do you buy petrol? ....

9 Why do you choose Metro? ....

10 If you drive a company car, do you keep the free gifts and special offers for yourself?

Thank you for your cooperation – please put the completed questionnaire in the box provided.

[26 marks, 40 minutes]

1 How effective do you think this questionnaire is? Give reasons for your answer. Include comments on the suitability of each question and the use of a self-completed questionnaire. **[10]**

2 Assume that you have been asked by Metro to prepare an improved questionnaire.

a Ask 8–10 questions that you believe will give the type of data that Metro are looking for. **[8]**

b Briefly justify why you have asked each question in the form you have. **[4]**

c Advise Metro on how the questionnaire should be distributed and collected. **[4]**

Not only can questionnaires be sent out, answered and returned over the Internet, but firms can also access the vast quantity of information that electronic data retrieval methods offer them. This is particularly true of retailers such as supermarkets that operate 'loyalty card' schemes. By scanning in the total number and type of goods bought by each consumer, the firms have a complete picture of what each consumer purchases, how often, their age, gender and possibly their income (they would have to provide these details to obtain the loyalty card initially). This allows retailers to target each consumer with advertisements and special offers about just the goods they are most interested in. This form of targeted marketing is cost-effective because money is not wasted on promoting, for example, cat food to people who do not have a cat.

Social media platforms are also transforming market research – reread the 'Introducing the topic' case study on page 231.

Cost-effectiveness of market research

This is an important consideration. Market research is not free – even gathering secondary data takes some time and buying market research reports or undertaking primary research can be very expensive. However, the Internet and mobile (cell) phones have made it much easier to contact a very wide range of potential consumers than the older methods of street surveys or home visits to interview people directly. Even small and medium-sized businesses can use electronic means of contacting large numbers of customers in a short time period. For example:

- Online marketing allows firms to conduct research projects for just a few thousand dollars, taking advantage of pre-screened access panels with the results coming in within a few days. Giving people the opportunity to respond conveniently by using their mobile (cell) phones increases the chance that they will respond to a survey request – especially if it is on a freephone number.
- The mobile (cell) phone method of surveys can use pre-recorded messages and questions to which people respond by using numbers on the keypad or speaking the answers. These results are then automatically presented and analysed electronically.

So although some forms of market research are becoming cheaper and more accessible to firms of all sizes, questions still have to be asked: Is it worth it? Is it cost-effective? These can really only be fully answered after the research has been gathered, analysed and used in management decisions, but the evidence is – from the first case study in this chapter to the last – that well-designed and focused market research pays for itself in higher sales and profits. International business managers think so too – in 2012,

global spending on market research increased by 3.8% to US$33.5 billion (*Source*: ESOMAR World Research).

What happens to the results?

Market research will produce vast amounts of data in both a numerate and descriptive form. This data is said to be 'raw' and unprocessed because it has not yet been presented or analysed in ways that will assist business decision-making. Once these stages have been undertaken, the raw data becomes information that can be used.

Interpretation of data

Numerate data might be presented in many forms including:

- **Tables** – these allow ease of reference can be used to present a mass of data in a precise way.
- **Pie graphs** (or pie charts) – used to display data that need to be presented in such a way that the proportions of the total are clearly shown. Each section of the 'pie' shows how relatively significant that part of the data is of the whole. They allow easy comparison between two sets of results to see if proportions have changed. The size of each section is determined by the angle at the centre of the circle. This is calculated in the following way:

$$\frac{\text{value of one section}}{\text{total value of all sections}} \times 360 \text{ degrees}$$

- **Line graphs** – most commonly used for showing changes in a variable, such as sales over time in time-series graphs. The line graph allows easy reference to trends in the data and shows up seasonal or other fluctuations clearly.
- **Bar charts** – these use bands of equal width but of varying length or height to represent relative values. They allow easy comparison over time or between different items.
- **Histograms** – frequently confused with bar charts but there is one very important distinction, it is not the height of each bar that represents relative values, but the area of each bar.

TOP TIP

At AS/A Level you will not be asked to construct these forms of data presentation – but you will be expected to understand data presented in these forms.

Statistical analysis of results

Interpreting and analysing statistical data can start with an attempt to identify key trends or key features of the data. For example, Table 17.4 contains the results of two small market research surveys. These were conducted to find out more about the number of hours radio listeners

Interpreting research results at Health Spa Ltd (HSL)

HSL operates a specialist health spa. It has limited parking space and is planning to offer incentives to its most loyal existing customers to encourage them to use other forms of transport. This would take the form of money-off vouchers if they switched from using their cars. The results of some primary research undertaken by HSL are shown in Figures 1–3.

[13 marks, 20 minutes]

1 **a** Refer to Figure 1. What is the most common number of annual visits by customers? [1]

   b If HSL decided to award money-off vouchers to all customers who visited three times or more per year, what proportion of the sample of 174 would be included in this scheme? [3]

2 Refer to Figure 2. How many customers arrived:

   a by taxi [1]

   b by bus [1]

   c If HSL's new scheme reduced the number of customers driving to the spa by half, how many customers, out of a sample of 200, would arrive by car? [2]

3 **a** Refer to Figure 3. If HSL operated the money-off scheme for just one day per week, which day would prove to the cheapest? Explain your answer. [2]

   b HSL decides to operate the scheme on Mondays only by offering people who switch from cars, a voucher worth $10. If Figure 3 is an average week, and the proportions in Figure 2 are accurate, how much would this cost HSL in vouchers? [3]

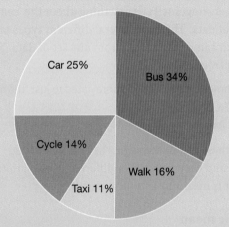

Figure 2 Methods of transport used by a sample of 200 customers

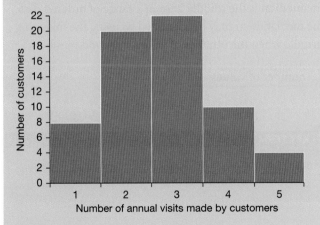

Figure 1 Annual visits made per customer

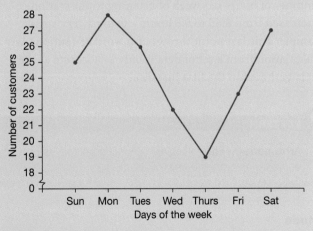

Figure 3 Numbers of customers in one week

tuned into one particular radio station per day. One survey was taken last year and one this year.

These data are currently in their raw form. They have not been ordered, presented or analysed in any way to aid their interpretation by the user. In this raw form, the data make little sense and are of no value. This section will show how numerical data might be summarised using quite basic statistical techniques. The data will then be in a form that will allow for further analysis and can aid decision-making.

	Number of hours per week
Last year	1, 5, 10, 15, 3, 6.5, 6, 4, 7.5, 16, 12, 4, 0, 2, 20, 18, 12, 10, 11, 10
This year	15, 12, 4, 5, 12, 6, 0, 2, 3, 10, 7, 8, 3, 12, 22, 18, 20, 14, 11, 8

Table 17.4 Number of hours respondents listened to radio station

	Number of hours per week
Last year	0, 1, 2, 3, 4, 4, 5, 6, 6.5, 7.5, **10, 10, 10**, 11, 12, 12, 15, 16, 18, 20
This year	0, 2, 3, 3, 4, 5, 6, 7, 8, 8, 10, 11, **12, 12, 12**, 14, 15, 18, 20, 22

Table 17.5 Research data in ascending order

Averages

An average is a typical or representative measure of a set of data. Averages tell us something about the 'central tendency' of data. There are several different types of average that can be calculated from any set of data. The three most frequently used are:

1 the arithmetic mean – often abbreviated to just 'the mean'
2 the mode
3 the median.

Although these are all averages, they are calculated differently and they give rather different information about what is meant by a 'typical' result.

Arithmetic mean

The **mean** of the 'Last year' results in Table 17.4 is 173/20 = 8.65 hours, while the mean of the 'This year' results in the table is 192/20 = 9.6 hours. The mean number of hours per week of listening to the station increased from 8.65 to 9.6 hours – using a very small sample. This last point throws up a word of caution. Any calculation from a set of data is only as accurate as the data gathered in the first instance.

KEY TERM

Arithmetic mean: calculated by totalling all the results and dividing by the number of results.

Mode

To identify the **mode**, it is wise to put the data into ascending or descending order; then values that recur will be immediately obvious. Table 17.5 shows the data

KEY TERM

Mode: the value that occurs most frequently in a set of data.

from Table 17.4 put into ascending order. The mode in each case is clearly visible (and is given in bold type):

- 10 hours was the most frequently occurring length of listening time last year.
- 12 hours was the most frequently occurring response this year.

The mode is of limited value and it would be wrong to assume from these results that 'the average listening time had increased by two hours'. It is meaningless where the data contain results that only occur once, that is there is no most frequently occurring item. In other cases, when analysed together with the mean, it can give a clear picture of the overall central tendency, or average, of the results. It is of use in some instances. For example, where colour or size is the basis of choice, the frequency of occurrence is likely to influence stock-holding choices.

Median

The **median** is the middle item in a range of ordered data. The median item may be identified by using the following formula when the number of values is an odd number:

$$\frac{\text{number of values} + 1}{2}$$

KEY TERM

Median: the value of the middle item when data have been ordered or ranked. It divides the data into two equal parts.

If the number of values is 15, then 15 + 1 divided by 2 gives the eighth value as the median item. When there is an even number of values, the mean of the middle two results will give the most accurate measure of the median. It is more usual, when the number of results gathered is large enough, to approximate the median by using the formula:

$$\frac{\text{number of values}}{2}$$

In the 'Last year' data above, the median will be the tenth result, given by 20/2. This gives the median as 7.5 hours.

ACTIVITY 17.7

Using the data in Table 17.5 prove to yourself that the median for 'This year' data is 8. Explain why this is the median. [4]

Frequency data

When data are presented in a table, it is common to show them in a frequency form, rather than showing each result individually. Table 17.6 shows the sizes of the shoes sold by a shop during one day. Alongside these data another column has been added, which is used in the calculation of the mean. The mathematical notation used is:

- x refers to each individual value
- f means frequency for one individual value
- $\Sigma f(x)$ denotes the sum of all the values.

The three averages can still be calculated from data presented in this form. The mean is:

$$\frac{\sum f(x)}{f} \quad \frac{\text{Column 3 total}}{\text{Column 2 total}}$$

$$= \frac{638}{100} = 6.38$$

This shows that the arithmetic mean shoe size is 6.38. You might like to judge whether this would be very useful for the managers of the shoe shop. The mode is 6, as this is the most frequently sold shoe size. This will be useful and the manager can also work out how much more common size 6 is compared with the others. For example, the data suggest that the sale of size 6 is five times more likely than the sale of size 3. However, the same warning is necessary here; sale of shoes in one day is no real evidence on which to base conclusions about stock-holding levels for the whole year.

The median will be the 50th item. To calculate which item this is, it is necessary to present the information above in a cumulative frequency form. This means adding each frequency to the total of the preceding frequencies, as shown in Table 17.7. This is necessary because the median will be the middle item of an ordered set of data. As you can see, this is within the size 6 group.

Grouped frequency data

Data are presented in this form when what is being measured is not a whole number, but a range of possible responses. For example: 'Which age range are you in?' 12–18 years, 19–26 years, and so on. Table 17.8 shows wage levels within an office.

The three averages are calculated as follows:

$$\text{mean} = \frac{\$39,975}{135} = \$296.11$$

It is complicated to estimate the mode because it lies somewhere within the modal group. The modal group is $300–350 with 58 wage earners in it. For most purposes, it is sufficient to identify the group.

The median worker:

$$\frac{135+1}{2} \text{ worker} = \text{68th worker.}$$

To find out the median wage earned by this worker the cumulative frequency needs to be calculated again. These results are then plotted on a cumulative frequency curve (Figure 17.1). The median can be estimated by observing that the 68th worker will earn just over $300 as 68 is just beyond the upper limit of $300, for which the cumulative

Shoe size (x)	Number sold (frequency, f)	Frequency × shoe size
3	4	12
4	13	52
5	18	90
6	20	120
7	17	119
8	12	96
9	11	99
10	5	50
	f = 100	Σf(x) = 638

Table 17.6 Frequency of shoes sold in a day: by size

Shoe size	Cumulative frequency
3	4
4	17
5	35
6	55
7	72
8	84
9	95
10	100

Table 17.7 Cumulative frequencies of shoe size

Wage x ($)	Number of workers (f)	Midpoint (x)	f(x)	Cumulative frequency
200 to less than 250	25	225	5,625	25
250 to less than 300	40	275	11,000	65
300 to less than 350	58	325	18,850	123
350 to less than 400	12	375	4,500	135
	$\Sigma f = 135$		$\Sigma f(x) = 39,975$	

Table 17.8 Weekly wages grouped data

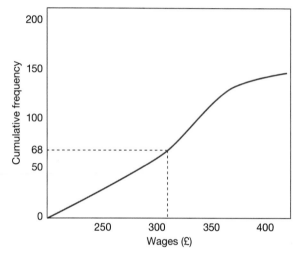

Figure 17.1 A cumulative frequency graph showing wages paid to workers and the median result

total is 65. The value in dollars of the wage earned by the median worker can then be obtained from the graph. In this case, the median is around $303.

Averages – how useful are they?

Table 17.9 suggests the most likely uses of these three averages, as well as evaluating their application in business contexts.

Measures of dispersion or spread of data

Two sets of examination results gave similar arithmetic mean results. Paper 1 had a mean of 52% and Paper 2 had a mean of 54%. One candidate, Joe, gained identical results, 45%, on the two papers. Yet he was much more pleased with his result on Paper 1 than on Paper 2. Why might this be?

Consider the following distribution:

Paper 1: Top mark 83%, lowest mark 14%

Paper 2: Top mark 60%, lowest mark 43%

By knowing the spread of results, Joe was able to conclude that he had been much nearer to the lowest mark in Paper 2 than in Paper 1.

To see the significance of this we have to examine the spread (dispersion) of data. This can be done in a number of ways. Two will be considered, the range and the inter-quartile range.

The range

This is the easiest and most widely used measure of data dispersion. The formula used is: highest result – lowest result = range. In Paper 1 the **range** was 83% – 14% = 69%, while in Paper 2 the range was 60% – 43% = 17%. The main problem with this measure is that it can be distorted by extreme results. A particularly brilliant student may have gained 83% on Paper 1, significantly higher than the other results, and this would give a much higher range than if that student's results were not included. In ranges of this kind, it is sometimes useful to use the 'Butler Range', where the highest and the lowest result are excluded.

 KEY TERM

Range: the difference between the highest and lowest value.

The inter-quartile range

To overcome the problem of one result giving a misleading picture when the range is used, the **inter-quartile range** is often calculated. This measures the range of the 'middle half' of the data and therefore ignores the lowest 25% of results and highest 25% of results. This is calculated by dividing the data into quartiles – or quarter sections. The median divided the data into two halves; quartiles divide each half again. Figure 17.2 helps to illustrate this.

Average measure	Uses	Advantages	Disadvantages
Mean	■ When the range of results is small, the mean can be a useful indicator of likely sales levels per period of time. This could be used to help determine reorder levels. ■ Often used for making comparisons between sets of data, e.g. attendance at football clubs.	■ The mean includes all of the data in its calculation. ■ It is well recognised as *the* average as it is so widely used – and therefore easily understood. ■ It can be used to analyse data further in other ways that assist in understanding the significance of the results collected.	■ The main problem is that the mean is affected by one or two extreme results. For instance, if in the wages example on page 245, the income of the managing director had been included (say, $50,000 per year), then the mean result would increase substantially. This would make it less of a meaningful average for all of the other 135 workers. ■ It is commonly not a whole number. Is it really useful for stock-ordering purposes to know that the mean shoe size sold was 6.38?
Mode	■ As the most frequently occurring, the result could be used for stock-ordering purposes. For instance, the shoe shop in our example above would need to hold more pairs of size 6 shoes than any other size.	■ It is easily observed and no calculation is necessary. The result is a whole number. Easily understood.	■ For grouped distributions, the result is estimated from the modal group – a fairly complex calculation could be made if this estimate was not accurate enough. ■ The mode does not consider all of the data. As a consequence, it cannot be used for further statistical analysis. ■ There may be more than one modal result, which could cause confusion.
Median	■ Could be used in wage negotiations, e.g. 'Half of our union members earn less than $xx per week.' ■ Often used in advertising, e.g. 'The reliability records show that our products are always in the best-performing 50% of all brands.'	■ It is less influenced by extreme results than the mean is. This makes it more representative than the mean when there are a few significantly high or low results.	■ Calculation from grouped data is not straightforward and there is an element of inaccuracy when doing this. ■ When there is an even number of items in the results, its value is approximated. ■ It cannot be used for further statistical analysis.

Table 17.9 Evaluation of the three averages

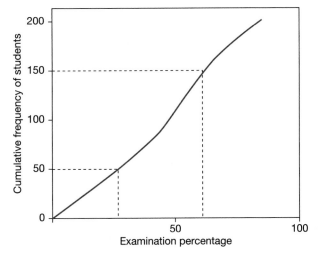

Figure 17.2 Inter-quartile range (200 students)

 KEY TERM

Inter-quartile range: the range of the middle 50% of the data.

The inter-quartile range is calculated by subtracting the value at the third quartile from the value at the first quartile.

■ The value at the third quartile is found by the formula: $3 \times$ number of results $\div 4$.

■ The value at the first quartile is found by the formula: number of results $\div 4$.

[47 marks, 1 hour]

1 A market research agency had been instructed to research into the buying patterns of petrol consumers. One of the questions on a questionnaire, which had been distributed by post, was 'In a typical month, how many times do you visit a petrol station?'

The results from 20 returned questionnaires were:

3, 1, 8, 4, 6, 10, 3, 5, 7, 4, 7, 2, 4, 8, 9, 7, 1, 2, 10, 9.

The oil company paying for the research was planning a new promotion campaign, which would offer promotions for each visit made to a station. It wanted to assess the possible future cost of this promotion and instructed the research agency to analyse the results.

a What was the mean number of visits made by the respondents to the survey? [3]

b What was the modal number of visits? [3]

c Calculate the median of these data. [4]

d Discuss the usefulness of each of these average measures to the oil company. [8]

e Calculate the range and the inter-quartile range. [6]

f Which of these would be likely to be more useful to the oil company? [4]

2 Another question on the survey concerned the typical number of litres of petrol purchased on each visit to a station. The results had been grouped and presented as follows:

Litres of petrol (x)	Number of customers (f)
$1 \leq x < 10$	2
$10 \leq x < 20$	5
$20 \leq x < 30$	10
$30 \leq x < 40$	2

a Calculate the mean number of litres purchased on each visit. [4]

b What is the modal group? [2]

c Estimate the median result. [4]

d Explain how these results could assist the oil company when planning a promotion campaign based on petrol purchases. [9]

248

RESEARCH TASK

A business is considering opening a sweet and soft drink shop near to your school or college. The success of the shop will depend on the number of students who will buy goods from it regularly. The owner has asked you to help research the potential demand from students for the products to be sold from the shop. He asks to you to collect data concerning current buying habits, amount spent on confectionery items, the number of times students would visit the shop and so on. He will use the data to forecast future sales.

1. You decide to conduct a survey of your fellow students. You must decide:
   - the questions to ask
   - whether to use a face-to-face interview or a postal questionnaire
   - how many students to be in the sample and which sampling method to use
   - how to present the results of your survey.
2. Explain and justify the decisions you make about the first and last items above.
3. Undertake this survey. Include just six questions in your questionnaire.
4. On the basis of your results, would you advise the business to go ahead with opening the shop or not? Consider what other information you would find useful.

AS Level exam practice questions

Short answer questions

[70 marks, 90 minutes]

Knowledge

1. Distinguish between primary and secondary market research data. [2]
2. Why is it important to use secondary data, when available, before investing in expensive primary market research? [2]
3. List **two** reasons why secondary data might prove to be inaccurate for a firm's specific purposes. [2]
4. What advantages does primary research have over secondary research? [3]
5. Outline **two** reasons why primary research data might prove to be inaccurate. [4]
6. Explain why it is important to consider the type of market that a new product is aimed at before starting primary research. [3]
7. Why is sampling so frequently used in consumer surveys? [2]
8. Explain the difference between a quota and a stratified sample. [3]
9. Outline the advantages and disadvantages of using a small sample. [4]
10. Explain **three** features of effective questionnaire design. [6]
11. What are the differences between qualitative and quantitative research? [3]
12. Explain why both types of data are necessary for a firm to analyse the sales performance of an existing product. [4]
13. Explain why sample size influences the reliability of research results. [3]
14. How might a business try to assess whether expenditure on market research had been cost-effective? [4]

Application

15. Explain **three** pieces of information a sports-shoe retailer might need to gain from market research before opening a new store. [4]
16. The sports shoe retailer in question 15 decides to conduct primary research from existing customers. Explain **three** ways in which this might be done. [6]

17 The pie chart below shows results from a survey of cinema customers. The sample size was 40. How many customers preferred:

   a action movies   [1]

   b drama movies?   [1]

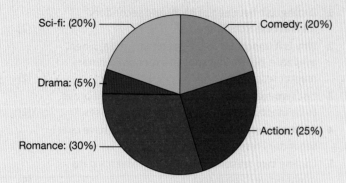

- Sci-fi: (20%)
- Comedy: (20%)
- Drama: (5%)
- Action: (25%)
- Romance: (30%)

18 A manager of a dress shop is studying past sales figures. She wants to know what the most common dress size is so that she can order more of this size than any other. Explain which measure of central tendency she should use.   [3]

19 Details of salaries paid to 50 employees in a business are contained in the table below:

- Calculate the mean and modal classes and the class that contains the median salary.   [4]
- Comment on your results from the point of view of both workers and the senior managers of the firm.   [3]

Salary	No. of employees (frequency)
$6,000 to below $8,000	10
$8,000 to below $10,000	20
$10,000 to below $12,000	10
$12,000 to below $14,000	5
$14,000 to below $20,000	5

20 Explain one business situation when the range would be a useful measure.   [3]

Data response

1 Low market share at Cosmos

The Cosmos Soft Drink Co. Ltd was concerned about its low market share. Despite extensive advertising in newspapers and magazines and colourful displays in most large retailers, sales remained disappointingly low compared to the well-known brands in the market. The image for its drinks that the company was trying to create was a sporty and youthful one. One of the reasons for this was because the directors had found out that the proportion of the population under 18 was expected to increase in the next ten years and the sports-participation rates of most age groups were increasing. The directors were in agreement that the image was the correct one to have and that other factors were to blame for the poor sales performance. They decided to use primary research and conduct a survey of the general public. This was to be a telephone survey as they believed that quick results were essential to allow them to take the right measures to boost sales. A questionnaire of 30 questions was drawn up asking for details of soft drinks bought and the reasons for purchase decisions, names and addresses of the respondents so that vouchers could be sent, income levels to identify consumer profiles and many other details that the directors thought might be useful. A total of 120 people were to be contacted by picking names using random sampling from the telephone directory.

The results of the survey proved to be very disappointing because many calls were not answered, some people refused to answer some of the questions and some of the elderly respondents said that all soft drinks were too sweet and fizzy for them anyway. In total, there were 35 completed questionnaires. The directors were no clearer after the survey than before as to what could be done to increase sales of Cosmos soft drinks.

[30 marks, 40 minutes]

1 **a** Define the term 'primary research'.   [2]

   b Briefly explain the term 'random sampling'.   [3]

2 **a** Calculate the proportion of the sample that completed the questionnaire.   [2]

   b Analyse **two** possible reasons why the results of the telephone survey were so disappointing.   [8]

3 Explain **two** secondary research sources that Cosmos could use if based in your own country.   [4]

4 Recommend an alternative primary research technique that Cosmos could have used to achieve more useful results.   [11]

2 Market research dilemma at GCB Ltd

The highly competitive world of garden machinery is characterised by a large number of quite small manufacturers. One of these firms is called GCB Ltd. This business has a good reputation for producing high-quality lawnmowers for small to medium-sized gardens. A recent survey conducted by consumers completing a 'Guarantee card' immediately after purchase had indicated that 90% of sales were to private households and not commercial gardeners. Social media users were commenting favourably on the reliability of GCB's machines. Other information regarding existing sales and the sizes of consumers' gardens is given in Figures 1 and 2 and Table 1.

The research and development director, James, has been given the task of coming up with a new design of lawnmower that would appeal to a different market segment. 'The demand from local government, schools with large playing fields and other commercial users is huge,' the sales director told him. 'We have no products large enough to enter this market segment. We need a new type of mower to break into this sector.' James thought that he had come up with the ideal machine, called the Robomow. 'It is a large motor mower that, with the latest electronic controls, can be programmed to work robotically – without any driver at all,' he told his fellow directors. 'It can be programmed to mow an entire field without any labour costs at all. It is then taken to the next field and reprogrammed, and so on. We can sell it easily to companies and organisations with large fields of grass to cut. Their workers can get on with other jobs, while our machine does all the hard work.'

The problem was that the largest annual trade fair for garden equipment was coming up in just two months' time. 'There is no time to do any market research,' said James. 'If we can show the new machine at the fair and promise early delivery for the summer months, then I am sure that it will be a great success.' The other directors shared his enthusiasm, but were concerned about the lack of qualitative and quantitative market research. One director commented: 'We know our existing consumer profile well but moving into this sector of the market has too many unknowns.'

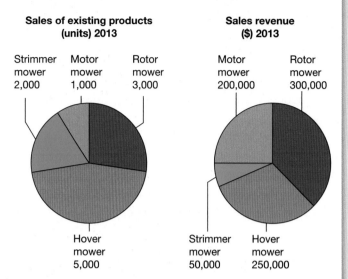

Figures 1 and **2** Pie charts to show sales volume and revenue of GCB products

Garden size (sq. metres)	Number of consumers (2012)
10–100	1,500
101–200	2,000
200–400	1,000

Table 1 Number of customers and the size of their gardens

[30 marks, 45 minutes]

1 a Define the term 'qualitative market research'. [2]

   b Briefly explain the term 'consumer profile'. [3]

2 a Using data from the charts above, calculate for the rotor mower in 2013 the:

   i proportion of total sales accounted for by this product. [2]

   ii proportion of total sales **revenue** accounted for by this product. [2]

   b Comment on your results to question 2a. [2]

3 Analyse the potential problems GCB might face as a result of launching the new product before market research has been fully undertaken. [8]

4 If there had been time, recommend ways in which GCB Ltd could have researched the market for Robomow before starting to produce it. [11]

AS Level essay questions

[20 marks, 40 minutes each]

1 a Explain the essential differences between primary and secondary market research. [8]

   b Examine why some new products fail even if they have been subject to extensive market research. [12]

2 An entrepreneur is planning to open a franchised fast-food café in your area. Discuss the methods of market research that you would recommend the entrepreneur to use before taking this decision. [20]

18 The marketing mix – product and price

This chapter covers syllabus section AS Level 3.3.

On completing this chapter, you will be able to:

- explain what the marketing mix means and what its key components are
- analyse the importance of the customer and customer relationship marketing
- understand and evaluate the importance of product decisions to a successful marketing mix
- analyse the stages of a typical product life cycle and evaluate the usefulness of the concept
- explain what the price elasticity of demand measures, calculate price elasticity of demand and understand the results
- understand and analyse different pricing methods and techniques and evaluate their relevance in different business situations
- understand and evaluate the importance of pricing decisions to a successful marketing mix.

Introducing the topic

MARKETING AN ELEPHANT CAMP TOURIST ATTRACTION IN THAILAND

The success of the fabulous Anantara Resort and Spa in Thailand is due to its effective marketing mix. Firstly, the product they offer is unique. The location, in Thailand's Golden Triangle, allows visitors to see three countries in one day and is easily accessible. The resort offers five-star accommodation, a cookery school and imaginative educational excursions, mahout training (learning to ride an Asian elephant) and exciting treks through unspoiled forests.

Prices are set to cover the costs of running the resort, including keeping the elephants in the best conditions, and to make enough profit to meet the overall targets of the resort. Some of the profits are donated to elephant conservation projects. In addition, pricing decisions are influenced by comparative prices in other resorts, although Anantara claims to offer so much more than the typical resort location.

Promotion and advertising include publicity gained through travel companies' brochures and some paid-for advertising in quality newspapers and magazines aimed at high-income travellers. In addition, free publicity has been gained as the mahout training has attracted the attention of TV companies and daily papers. The impressive website is another important form of promotion as it is both informative and persuasive by generating a quality image. Selling of the Anantara holidays is mainly achieved through two main channels. Firstly, block or 'wholesale' bookings are sold to tour-company operators and, secondly, the resort's own website is used for direct selling to

tourists – avoiding the need to pay commission to other agents or companies. All parts of the marketing mix fit together well to present a coherent unique image to potential tourists.

Points to think about:

- List what you consider to be the key marketing decisions referred to in this case study.
- Why is it important for all of these decisions to give tourists the same unique quality image of this business?
- Why do you the think the resort's website is so important to successful marketing of the resort?

Elephant ride at Anantara resort, Thailand

Introduction

The **marketing mix** is a range of tactical marketing decisions for a product. Deciding on the appropriate marketing mix is a major factor in influencing whether a business can sell its products profitably – the aim of most marketing departments.

Marketing mix

The marketing mix is made up of four inter-related decisions – the 4Ps. These are product design and performance, price, promotion including advertising and place, where and how a product will be sold to consumers:

- Consumers require the right **product**. This might be an existing product, an adaptation of an existing product or a newly developed one.
- The right **price** is important too. If set too low, then consumers might lose confidence in the product's quality; if too high, then many will be unable or unwilling to afford it.
- **Promotion** must be effective – telling consumers about the product's availability and convincing them, if possible, that your brand is the one to choose.
- **Place** refers to how the product is distributed to the consumer. If it is not available at the right time in the right place, then even the best product in the world will not be bought in the quantities expected.

> **KEY TERM**
>
> **Marketing mix:** the four key decisions that must be taken in the effective marketing of a product.

Not all of these 4Ps have the same degree of significance in every case. It is vital that these elements fit together into a coherent and integrated plan. The remainder of this chapter and the next one will analyse in detail the individual significance of these four marketing elements and consider the options available to marketing managers.

In some texts, the number of Ps is increased to five, six or even seven. For example, it is argued that in the marketing of services rather than tangible goods, people (skilled and motivated staff) and process (the way in which the customer accesses the service) are as important as the original 4Ps.

The key issue that must always be remembered about the marketing mix – no matter how many Ps you care to give it – is that these marketing decisions are inter-related and, because of this, they must be carefully coordinated to make sure that customers are not confused by conflicting messages being given about the good or service being sold. This point is returned to in the next chapter.

The role of the customer – the 4Cs

Some business analysts consider that the 4Ps approach is rather old-fashioned and too much centred on the firm and its product rather than the ultimate user – the consumer. The '4Cs' has been proposed as an alternative view of the key elements of successful marketing. These can be summarised as:

- **Customer solution** – what the firm needs to provide to meet the customer's needs and wants.
- **Cost to customer** – the total cost of the product including extended guarantees, delivery charges and financing costs.
- **Communication with customer** – providing up-to-date and easily accessible two-way communication links with customers to both promote the product and gain back important consumer market research information.
- **Convenience to customer** – providing easily accessible pre-sales information and demonstrations and convenient locations for buying the product.

These can be linked to the 4Ps, as shown in Table 18.1

Unfortunately, the 4Cs are not as easy to remember as the 4Ps and they do not so clearly relate to specific marketing decisions, so most textbooks still tend to use the 4Ps. The 4Cs are important, however, in putting the customer first in marketing decisions and this is the key feature of **customer relationship management**.

> **KEY TERM**
>
> **Customer relationship management (CRM):** using marketing activities to establish successful customer relationships so that existing customer loyalty can be maintained.

The key aim of CRM is not necessarily to **win** new customers but to **keep** existing ones. Studies have shown that it can cost between four and ten times as much to gain new customers (with expensive promotions) as it does to keep existing ones. This makes sense – for

4Ps	4Cs
Product	Customer solution
Price	Cost to customer
Promotion	Communication with customer
Place	Convenience to customer

Table 18.1 Linking the 4Ps and the 4Cs

every customer whose loyalty is gained, that is one less customer for competitors.

At the root of CRM is customer information. Gain as much information as possible about each existing customer – income, product preferences, buying habits and so on – and adapt the 4Ps to meet these needs as closely as possible. This is virtually segmenting each customer and is, of course, the opposite of mass marketing. However, now that technology has made customer data collection so much easier and cheaper, it is becoming a widely adopted marketing strategy. Developing effective long-term relationships can be achieved by:

- **targeted marketing** – giving each customer the products and services they have indicated – from past purchases – they most need
- **customer service and support** – essential to building customer loyalty, call centres have been criticised for letting existing customers down and many businesses are now focusing on improving these
- **providing as much information to customers as possible** – about product materials/quality/features and service levels
- **using social media** – some CRM systems integrate social media sites like Twitter, LinkedIn and Facebook to track and communicate with customers. Enterprise Feedback Management software platforms such as Confirmit and Satmetrix combine a company's internal survey data with trends identified through social media to allow businesses to make more accurate decisions regarding which products to supply to satisfy customers

 KEY CONCEPT LINK

Clearly, customer relationship **management** is at the heart of the **customer-focus** concept

Why is product a key part of the marketing mix?

It is sometimes said that 'You can sell any product to consumers once, but to establish loyalty and good customer relationships, the product must be right.' If the product does not meet customer expectations, as discovered by market research, regarding:

- quality,
- durability,
- performance and
- appearance,

then no matter how low the price or how expensive the adverts for it, it will not sell successfully in the long term.

What is meant by the term 'product'?

The term 'product' includes consumer and industrial goods and services. Goods have a physical existence, such as washing machines and chocolate bars. Services have no physical existence, but satisfy consumer needs in other ways – hairdressing, car repairs, child-minding and banking are examples of services. New product development (NPD) is crucial to the success of some businesses, such as the rapidly changing world of computer games. In other markets, it is possible to sell the same product for many years or to adjust and adapt it slightly to meet changing tastes and to enter new segments, such as Pepsi with Pepsi Next, which is a new low-calorie soft drink.

New product development is usually based on attempting to satisfy consumer needs that have been identified through research. It is expensive and not always successful. It involves 'research and development' costs and many of the products initially developed will never reach the final market. It is important to realise that developing new products cannot just be left to the scientists or the engineers. Input from the marketing department is vital to ensure that the new idea is developed into a product that the market will accept and buy.

Unique selling point

The most successful new products are those that are differentiated from competitors' products and offer something 'special'. Product differentiation can be an effective way of distancing a business from its rivals – the best form of product differentiation is one that creates a unique selling point (USP).

Examples of effective USPs include:

- Domino's Pizza deliveries: 'It arrives in 30 minutes or it's free.'
- Dyson vacuum cleaners: '100% suction, 100% of the time from bagless technology.'
- Mast Brothers Chocolate: 'Every bar of chocolate is hand-made from purchasing the cacao beans directly from growers.'

Benefits of an effective USP include:

- Effective promotion that focuses on the differentiating feature of the **product** or service.
- Opportunities to charge higher prices due to exclusive design/service.
- Free publicity from business media reporting on the USP.
- Higher sales than undifferentiated products.
- Customers more willing to be identified with the **brand** because 'it's different'.

Dyson vacuum cleaners

Tangible and intangible attributes

Why do consumers pay more for a well-known **brand** of aspirin than a generic, non-branded, cheaper alternative? What do advertisers mean when they state: 'This model of car is the most luxurious in its class'? Consumer decisions are not always easy to weigh up or explain – which makes market research less accurate. However, marketing managers should try to understand what '**intangible features or attributes**' customers are looking for when making their purchasing decisions, as well as, for example, 'what colour of car and which size of engine' they are likely to prefer. Meeting customers 'intangible expectations' for a **product** is most commonly achieved by effective branding.

 KEY TERMS

Brand: an identifying symbol, name, image or trademark that distinguishes a product from its competitors.

Intangible attributes of a product: subjective opinions of customers about a product that cannot be measured or compared easily.

Tangible attributes of a product: measurable features of a product that can be easily compared with other products.

Product: the end result of the production process sold on the market to satisfy a customer need.

Products and brands

Mobile (cell) phones are an example of a product, but Vodafone is an example of a brand. What is the difference? The product is the general term used to describe the nature of what is being sold. The brand is the distinguishing name or symbol that is used to differentiate one manufacturer's products from another. Branding can have real influence on marketing. It can create a powerful image or perception in the minds of consumers – either negative or positive – and it can give one firm's products a unique identity.

Product positioning

Before deciding on which product to develop and launch, it is common for firms to analyse how the new brand will relate to the other brands in the market, in the minds of consumers. This is called positioning the product by using techniques such as market mapping. The first stage is to identify the features of this type of product considered to be important to consumers – as established by market research. These key features might be price, quality of materials used, perceived image, level of comfort offered (hotels) and so on. They will be different for each product category.

Figures 18.1 and 18.2 illustrate the main cola products of the Coca-Cola Company and PepsiCo and their brand perceptions. The **product positioning** graph uses the two criteria:

- Male/female consumers.
- High/no calories.

It suggests that there might be a market gap for a soft drink with high calories aimed at female consumers. Neither company is aiming new products at this sector however. Can you think why not?

PepsiCo's newest soft drink Pepsi Next is looking to break into the market for people who want to drink 'real tasting' cola but prefer mid-calories instead

of zero-calories. Coca Cola's C2 is operating in the similar area with 'half the carbohydrates, sugars and calories' compared to standard Coke. Both Pepsi and Coke introduced mid-calorie colas back in 2001, Pepsi Edge was the original brand. However, due to slow sales, the product was taken off the market after five years. According to John Sicher, editor of *Beverage Digest*, 'Pepsi seems to believe that times are different now and consumers might want to try this kind of beverage.'

Coca Cola product line		Pepsi product line	
Coca Cola		Pepsi	
Coca Cola c2		Pepsi Max	
Diet Coke		Diet Pepsi	
Coca Cola Zero		Pepsi one	

Figure 18.1 Coca-Cola and Pepsi brand comparison chart

Figure 18.2 Coca-Cola and Pepsi sugar/calories comparison chart

Product life cycle

Knowing when to launch a new product or update an existing one can give a business a crucial advantage. **Product portfolio analysis** helps make these decisions. Allowing existing models of cars or computers to 'soldier on' in the market when other firms are introducing attractive new or revamped ones is a classic business error that has led to many failures. An awareness of the **product life-cycle** principle can assist greatly in dealing with this problem and is one of the main forms of product portfolio analysis. The life cycle of a product records the sales of that product over time. There are several stages in this life cycle and these are shown in Figure 18.3.

Points to note on each stage:

- **Introduction:** This is when the product has just been launched after development and testing. Sales are often quite low to begin with and may increase only quite slowly – but there are exceptions, such as a newly launched DVD by a major global rock star.
- **Growth:** If the product is effectively promoted and well received by the market, then sales should grow significantly. This stage cannot last for ever, although all firms wish that it would. Eventually, and this may take days, weeks or even years, sales growth will begin to slow and might stop altogether, which leads the product into the next stage.

The reasons for growth dying down include increasing competition, technological changes making the product less appealing, changes in consumer tastes and saturation of the market.

- **Maturity or saturation:** At this stage, sales fail to grow, but they do not decline significantly either. This stage can last for years, for example Coca-Cola. The saturation of **consumer durables** markets is caused by most consumers who want a certain product having already bought one. The best recent example is mobile (cell) phones. Although the world market has grown phenomenally in recent years, in 2010 sales growth ended altogether. This was put down to the vast number of consumers who already possessed a phone. It is only when their phone breaks down or is replaced by newer technology that a further spurt to sales growth will be received. This is why all phone companies are working so hard on the next generation of phones – 4G and beyond – to make existing models obsolete.

- **Decline:** During this phase, sales will decline steadily. Either no extension strategy has been tried or it has not worked, or the product is so obsolete that the only option is replacement. Newer competitors' products are the most likely cause of declining sales and profits – and when the product becomes unprofitable or when its replacement is ready for the market, it will be withdrawn.

KEY TERM

Consumer durable: manufactured product that can be reused and is expected to have a reasonably long life, such as a car or washing machine.

Extension strategies

These strategies aim to lengthen the life of an existing product before the market demands a completely new product. Examples of extension strategies include selling in new markets (export markets for example), repackaging and relaunching the product and finding new uses for the

KEY TERM

Extension strategies: these are marketing plans to extend the maturity stage of the product before a brand new one is needed.

product. The MINI Countryman car was relaunched in 2014 with new colours and new interior trim – extending the life of this model before it is replaced in 2016 (see Figure 18.4).

Uses of the product life cycle

The life-cycle concept has three main uses:

- Assisting with planning marketing-mix decisions, such as new product launches and price or promotion changes.
- Identifying how cash flow might depend on the cycle.
- Recognising the need for a balanced product portfolio.

Assisting with the planning of marketing-mix decisions

- When would you advise a firm to lower the price of its product – at the growth or at the decline stage?
- In which phase is advertising likely to be most important – during introduction or at maturity?
- When should variations be made to the product – during introduction or at maturity?

By thinking about these questions you can begin to see how significant an awareness of the product life cycle can be to marketing managers. Although there are no definite and unchangeable answers to the questions above, there are likely to be common links between the phases of the life cycle and the nature of the price, product, promotion and place decisions taken by a firm. Table 18.2 gives some suggestions of what needs to be considered. However, the final decisions will also depend on competitors' actions, the state of the economy and the marketing objectives of the business.

257

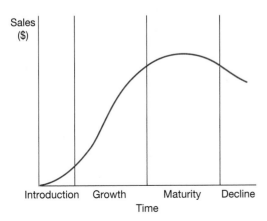

Figure 18.3 Product life cycle – the length of each stage will vary from product to product

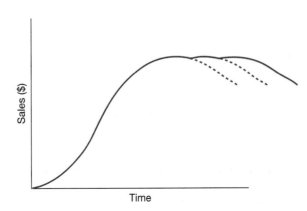

Figure 18.4 Product life cycle – showing the effect of extension strategies

Phase of the product life cycle	Price	Promotion	Place (distribution outlets)	Product
Introduction	■ may be high compared to competitors (skimming) or low (penetration)	■ high levels of informative advertising to make consumers aware of the product's arrival on the market	■ restricted outlets – possibly high-class outlets if a skimming strategy is adopted	■ basic model
Growth	■ if successful, an initial penetration pricing strategy could now lead to rising prices	■ consumers need to be convinced to make repeat purchases – brand identification will help to establish consumer loyalty	■ growing numbers of outlets in areas indicated by strength of consumer demand	■ planning of product improvements and developments to maintain consumer appeal
Maturity	■ competitors likely to be entering market – there will be a need to keep prices at competitive levels	■ brand imaging continues – growing need to stress the positive differences with competitors' products	■ highest geographical range of outlets possible – developing new types of outlets where possible	■ new models, colours, accessories, etc. as part of extension strategies
Decline	■ lower prices to sell off stock – or if the product has a small 'cult' following, prices could even rise	■ advertising likely to be very limited – may just be used to inform of lower prices	■ eliminate unprofitable outlets for the product	■ prepare to replace with other products – slowly withdraw from certain markets

Table 18.2 The marketing mix and phases of the product life cycle

Identifying how cash flow might depend on the product life cycle

- Cash flow is vital to business survival and ignoring the link between cash flow and product life cycles could be very serious. Figure 18.5 shows this typical relationship.
- Cash flow is negative during the development of the product as costs are high, but nothing has yet been produced or sold.
- At introduction, the development costs might have ended but heavy promotional expenses are likely to be incurred – and these could continue into the growth phase. In addition, there is likely to be much unused factory capacity at this stage, which will place a further strain on costs. As sales increase, then cash flow should improve – precisely when this will happen will depend on the length of consumer credit being offered.
- The maturity phase is likely to see the most positive cash flows, because sales are high, promotion costs might be limited and spare factory capacity should be low.
- As the product passes into decline, so price reductions and falling sales are likely to combine to reduce cash flows. Clearly, if a business had too many of its products either at the decline or the introduction phase, then the consequences for cash flow could be serious. This introduces the next concept.

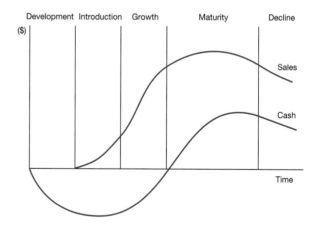

Figure 18.5 The link between cash flow and product life cycle

Identifying the need for a balanced product portfolio

Look at Figure 18.6. This shows an 'ideal' position for a business to be in. As one product declines, so other products are being developed and introduced to take its place. Cash flow should be reasonably balanced, so there are products at every stage and the positive cash flows of the successful ones can be used to finance the cash deficits of others. Factory capacity should be kept at roughly constant levels as declining output of some

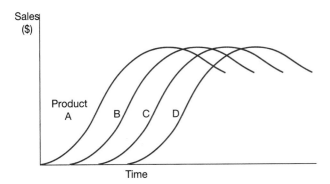

Figure 18.6 A balanced product portfolio

goods is replaced by increasing demand for the recently introduced products. This is known as a balanced portfolio of products. Sony is a good example of a business with this balanced product range.

Product life cycle – evaluation

This is an important tool for assessing the performance of the firm's current product range. It is an important part of a marketing audit – a regular check on the performance of a firm's marketing strategy.

However, the product life cycle is based on past or current data – it cannot be used to predict the future. Just because a product's sales have grown over the past few months does not mean that they will continue to grow until a long period of maturity is reached – sales could crash very quickly with no chance of an extension strategy being employed. Think of all the fashions that died out – such as platform shoes or flared jeans – and then made a comeback. In contrast, sales of other products can, against all predictions, grow and grow.

To be really useful, a product life-cycle analysis needs to be used together with sales forecasts and management experience to assist with effective product planning.

ACTIVITY 18.2

Nokia handset sales, by region

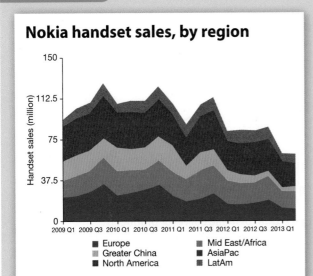

Figure 1 Nokia handset sales by region, in millions. (All handsets, including feature phones, Asha, Symbian and Lumia. Symbian was discontinued in Q2 2013).

	Q3 2013 Unit sales	Market share%	Q2 2013 unit sales	Market share
Apple	30,330.0	12.1	24,620.3	14.3

Apple's sales of smartphones (000 of units and global market share)

[28 marks, 40 minutes]

1 a Define the term 'unit sales'. [2]
   b Briefly explain the term 'market share'. [3]

2 Explain how Apple's sales of smartphones have increased but the market share has fallen. [4]

3 Explain the trends shown in Figure 1 (Nokia) in terms of product life cycle. [8]

4 Discuss how Apple might use extension strategies with the aim of increasing sales and market share. [11]

ACTIVITY 18.3

[14 marks, 20 minutes]

1 Suggest **one** product that you consider to be approaching the decline stage of its product life cycle. Suggest **four** ways in which its life cycle might be extended. [4]

2 Consider **one** of your suggestions to question 1 and discuss how effective this method is likely to be in extending the life cycle. [10]

When do you think this photograph was taken?

Product portfolio analysis – an evaluation

Managing product portfolios effectively can help a business achieve its marketing objectives. Products cannot just be 'launched and forgotten' but must be developed, marketed and managed to help the business increase sales profitably. The product is often considered to be the most important element of the marketing mix, if it fails to work, is poorly designed and looks ugly, will low prices and extensive advertising help sales much?

However, product is just one part of the overall strategy needed to win and keep customers. Price, promotion and place are also key factors in making products successful – and a balanced and integrated marketing mix is essential. But without a well managed product portfolio that offers customer real and distinctive benefits, marketing objectives are unlikely ever to be achieved.

Why is price a key part of the marketing mix?

Price is the amount paid by customers for a product. Determining an appropriate price for a good or service is a vital component of the marketing mix. Price can have a great impact on the consumer demand for the product – see Chapter 16 for a discussion of a typical demand curve.

The pricing level set for a product will also:

- determine the degree of value added by the business to bought-in components
- influence the revenue and profit made by a business due to the impact on demand
- reflect on the marketing objectives of the business and help establish the psychological image and identity of a product.

Get the pricing decision wrong and much hard work in market research and product development can be put at risk. For all these reasons, pricing decisions are some of the most significant issues that marketing managers are faced with.

Price elasticity of demand

Look at the two demand curves in Figures 18.7 and 18.8, $D_2 D_2$ has a steeper gradient than $D_1 D_1$. What impact does the slope or gradient of the curves have on the demand levels for these two products when prices are changed? You will notice that, when the price of both products is increased by the same amount, the reduction in demand is greater for product B than it is for product A. This could be very important information for the marketing manager

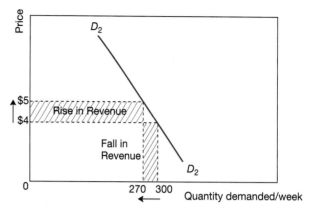

Figure 18.7 Demand curve for product A

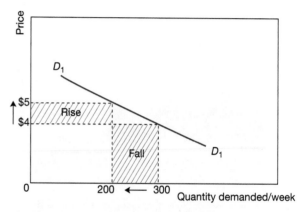

Figure 18.8 Demand curve for product B

because the total revenue for product A has actually increased, but for B it has fallen, as can be seen by the size of the shaded areas.

This relationship between price changes and the size of the resulting change in demand is known as **price elasticity of demand**.

KEY TERM

Price elasticity of demand: measures the responsiveness of demand following a change in price.

This concept can be demonstrated on demand curves as shown above – product A's demand is less elastic or responsive to a price change than product B's. This idea can also be measured mathematically.

The formula for price elasticity of demand (PED) is:

$$\frac{\text{percentage change in quantity demanded}}{\text{percentage change in price}}$$

Value of PED (ignoring minus sign)	Classification	Explanation
Zero	Perfectly inelastic demand	■ The same amount is demanded, no matter what the price. In reality, there is no product that would have this PED.
Between 0 and 1	Inelastic demand	■ The percentage change in demand is less than the percentage change in price. If a firm faces this elasticity of demand, it can raise the price, not lose much demand and increase sales revenue. However, this cannot keep happening. As the price continues to rise, demand will become more elastic.
Unitary	Unit elasticity	■ The percentage change in demand is equal and opposite to the percentage change in price, so any price change will lead to an equal change in demand and the total sales revenue will remain constant. When PED = 1, sales revenue will be maximised.
Between 1 and infinity (∞)	Elastic demand	■ The percentage change in demand is greater than the percentage change in price. If a firm faces this elasticity of demand, then it can lower the price, pick up a lot more demand and increase sales revenue.
Infinity (∞)	Perfectly elastic demand	■ An infinitely large amount is demanded at one price and then demand falls to zero if the price is raised, even by the smallest amount. In reality, there is no product that would have this PED.

Table 18.3 The potential range of elasticity and its effects (negative signs are not shown)

The value of PED is normally negative because a fall in price (–ve) usually results in a rise in demand (+ve). This is called an inverse relationship. It is quite common to ignore the negative sign of the PED result, as it is the extent of the change that is important.

Example: In Figure 18.7, the price increased from $4 to $5 and demand fell from 300 units per week to 270 units. What is the PED?

Step 1: Calculate the percentage change in price.
Step 2: Calculate the percentage change in demand.
Step 3: Use the PED formula:
% change in demand = 10
% change in price = 25

$$PED = \frac{10}{25} = 0.4$$

It is now important to explain this result. A PED of 0.4 (do not forget that we are overlooking the minus sign) means that demand changes by 0.4% for every 1.0% change in price. As this is less than one, it is described as being inelastic. Consumers do not respond greatly to a change in the price in this product: an increase in price will raise a firm's revenue, while a price reduction, because demand will change little, will reduce revenue.

ACTIVITY 18.4

[6 marks, 8 minutes]

1 Using the information in Figure 18.8 calculate the PED following the rise in price of product B. [2]

2 Comment on your result – explain what it means. [4]

Table 18.3 shows how different possible results for PED may be classified.

Factors that determine price elasticity

There are a number of factors that will determine the PED of a product:

1 **How necessary the product is:** The more necessary consumers consider a product to be, the less they will react to price changes. This will tend to make the demand inelastic, for example salt and oil.

2 **How many similar competing products or brands there are:** If there are many competitors, then there are a large number of substitutes, and consumers will quickly switch to another brand if the price of one manufacturer's product increases – for example fruit being sold by one seller in a large street market. Any move by a business to reduce

the number of competing products, such as a merger or takeover, will probably make demand for its own products less elastic.

3 **The level of consumer loyalty:** If a firm has successfully branded its product to create a high degree of loyalty among consumers, like Coca-Cola, then the consumers will be likely to continue to purchase the product following a price rise. Another example of this is designer clothes that have a strong following, despite price increases, among well-off consumers. All businesses attempt to increase brand loyalty with influential advertising and promotional campaigns and by making their products more distinct – this is called product differentiation.

4 **The price of the product as a proportion of consumers' incomes:** A cheap product that takes up a small proportion of consumers' incomes, such as matches or batteries, is likely to have inelastic demand, as consumers will not care too much about a 10% or 15% price increase.

Applications of price elasticity of demand

There are two main business uses of PED:

1 **Making more accurate sales forecasts:** If a business is considering a price increase, perhaps to cover rises in production costs, then an awareness of PED should allow forecast demand to be calculated. For instance, if PED is believed to be –0.8 and the price is increased by 10%, what will be the new weekly sales level if it is currently 10,000 per week? Demand will fall by 8% (check this out using the PED formula) and this will give a forecast sales level of 9,200 per week.

2 **Assisting in pricing decisions:** If an operator of bus services is considering changing its pricing structure, then, if it is aware of the PED of different routes, it could raise prices on routes with low PED (inelastic) and lower them on routes with high PED. This kind of analysis also underpins the strategy known as price discrimination – this is covered later in this chapter.

ACTIVITY 18.5

A firm sells three products. The price elasticity of demand is estimated to be (including the negative signs):

A –3, B –0.5, C –1

[12 marks, 12 minutes]

1 Explain what these results mean.   [6]

2 Explain what the effect on sales will be for each product if all prices rise by 10%.   [6]

ACTIVITY 18.6

The Daily Times

The owner of the *Daily Times* newspaper was concerned about falling circulation (sales). He believed that newspaper readers are mainly influenced by price when making their decisions over which papers to buy. He therefore decided to cut the price of his paper from $1.50 to $1.20. In the following week, circulation increased by 150,000 copies to 1,650,000. After four weeks, however, sales had fallen back to their original level. The owner was confused about the possible reasons for this and wondered whether he should cut the price again to $1.

[25 marks, 35 minutes]

1 From the information given, calculate the PED in the first week after the price reduction.   [4]

2 Comment on your result in terms of the apparent price elasticity of this product.   [2]

3 Calculate the newspaper's daily revenue just before and just after the price cut. Comment on your results.   [5]

4 Explain two possible reasons why demand fell back to the original level some weeks after the price reduction.   [6]

5 What action would you advise the newspaper's owner take now to increase sales – would a further price cut be advisable?   [8]

Evaluation of price elasticity of demand

PED has its uses as we have seen, but the concept and the results gained from it must be used with caution. It has three main limitations:

1 PED assumes that nothing else has changed. If Firm A reduces the price for a product by 10%, it will expect sales to rise because of this – but if, at about the same time, a competitor leaves the industry and consumer incomes rise, the resulting increase in sales of Firm A's product may be very substantial, *but* not solely caused by the fall in price. Calculating PED accurately in these and similar situations will be almost impossible.

2 A PED calculation, even when calculated when nothing but price changes, will become outdated quickly and may need to be often recalculated because over time consumer tastes change and new competitors may bring in new products – so last year's PED calculation

may be very different to one calculated today if market conditions have changed.

3   It is not always easy, or indeed possible, to calculate PED. The data needed for working it out might come from past sales results following previous price changes. These data could be quite old and market conditions might have changed. In the case of new products, market research will have to be relied upon to estimate PED – by trying to identify the quantities that a sample of potential customers would purchase at different prices. This will be subject to the same kind of inaccuracy as other forms of market research.

The pricing decision – how do managers determine the appropriate price?

There are many determinants of the pricing decision for any product. Here are the main ones:

■ **Costs of production:** If the business is to make a profit on the sale of a product, then, at least in the long term, the price must cover all of the costs of producing it and of bringing it to the market. These costs include the variable costs and the fixed costs. Variable costs vary with the number of units produced, such as material costs. Fixed costs can be very substantial, such as rents and advertising and promotion costs. These do not vary directly with the number of units produced and sold.

■ **Competitive conditions in the market:** If the firm is a monopolist, it is likely to have more freedom in price setting than if it is one of many firms making the same type of product. A firm with a high market share may be referred to as a dominant firm and it is likely to be a price-setter – setting prices for other smaller firms in the market to follow. The more competition there is, the more likely it is that prices will be fixed similar to those fixed by other rival businesses.

■ **Competitors' prices:** Related to the previous point, it may be difficult to set a price very different from that of the market leader, unless true product differentiation (see above) can be established.

■ **Business and marketing objectives:** If the aim is to become market leader through mass marketing (see Chapter 16), then this will require a different price level to that set by a business aiming at select niche marketing. If the marketing objective is to establish a premium branded product, then this will not be achieved with rock-bottom prices. The key point is that the price must reflect the other components of the marketing mix that must all be based upon the marketing objectives of the business.

■ **Price elasticity of demand:** The significance of this has already been discussed above.

■ **Whether it is a new or an existing product:** If new, a decision will have to be made as to whether a 'skimming' or a 'penetration' strategy is to be adopted.

Car prices to rise in China?

Although Volkswagen (VW) has denied the rumour of 'general price hikes in April' for its cars in China, business analysts are still predicting substantial car price rises. Due to rising costs of production – steel and other raw materials and higher labour costs – the cost of making each car in China increased on average by $400 last year. Can manufacturers resist these cost pressures? By how much are they prepared to cut their profit margins to stay competitive?

However, the fierce competition in China's car market has deterred many manufacturers from putting up prices. In recent years, due to increased numbers of cars being made in China and more manufacturers exporting to China, competitive pressures have put car prices on a downward trend but that could change now that costs are rising so fast.

To avoid consumer resistance to obvious price increases, manufacturers are increasing their profit margins in other ways. Dealers are promising quick delivery of cars to customers if they order expensive accessories and luxury items such as leather seats. The profit margin on these decorative accessories can be as high as 30–40%, which helps to make up for very low margins on the cars themselves. So indirect price increases could be the solution to the very small profit margins on selling basic car models.

[16 marks, 25 minutes]

1   Explain why increasing costs usually lead manufacturers to raise prices to consumers. **[4]**

2   Why, in this case, are car manufacturers reluctant to raise prices? **[4]**

3   In such a competitive market, how might car manufacturers such as BMW or Mercedes still sell cars profitably? **[8]**

Pricing methods

There are several different pricing methods that can be used and these are broadly categorised into cost-based methods and market/competition-based methods (see Table 18.4).

Cost-based pricing

The basic idea is that firms will assess their costs of producing or supplying each unit, and then add an amount on top of the calculated cost. There are a number of different methods of cost-based pricing that may be adopted:

Mark-up pricing

This method is often used by retailers, who take the price that they pay the producer or wholesaler for the product in question, and then just add a percentage mark-up. The size of the mark-up usually depends upon a combination of the strength of demand for the product, the number of other suppliers and the age and stage of life of the product. Sometimes it also depends on traditional practice in the industry.

Example 1:
Total cost of brought-in materials = $40
50% mark-up on cost = $20
Selling price = $60

Target pricing

This is best explained by an example. If a company has costs of $400,000 when making 10,000 units of output and has an expected rate of return of 20%, then it will set its price by working out its total cost and expected return and then dividing the amount by the output.

Methods	Advantages	Disadvantages
Full-cost pricing	■ price set will cover all costs of production ■ easy to calculate for single-product firms where there is no doubt about fixed cost allocation ■ suitable for firms that are 'price-makers' due to market dominance	■ inaccurate for businesses with several products where there is doubt over the allocation of fixed costs ■ does not take market/competitive conditions into account ■ tends to be inflexible, e.g. there might be opportunities to increase price even higher ■ if sales fall, average costs often rise – this could lead to the price being raised using this method
Contribution pricing	■ all variable costs will be covered by the price – and a contribution made to fixed costs ■ suitable for firms producing several products – fixed costs do not have to be allocated ■ flexible – price can be adapted to suit market conditions or to accept special orders	■ fixed costs may not be covered ■ if prices vary too much – due to the flexibility advantage – then regular customers might be annoyed
Competitor pricing	■ almost essential for firms with little market power – price-takers ■ flexible to market and competitive conditions	■ price set may not cover all of the costs of production ■ may have to vary price frequently due to changing market and competitive conditions
Price discrimination	■ uses price elasticity knowledge to charge different prices in order to increase total revenue	■ administrative costs of having different pricing levels ■ customers may switch to lower-priced market ■ consumers paying higher prices may object and look for alternatives

Table 18.4 Summary of pricing methods

Example 2:
Total output costs for 10,000 units = $400,000
Required return of 20% on sales = $80,000
Total revenue needed = $480,000
Price per unit 480,000/10,000 = $48

Full-cost (or absorption-cost) pricing

However, it is not always easy to allocate or divide all of the costs of a firm to a specific product, especially if the firm makes a range of products. It is especially difficult to allocate the fixed costs. The method differs from mark-up pricing only to the extent that a method of allocating fixed costs among the various products being sold has to be found. See Chapter 29 for more detailed coverage of this issue.

KEY TERM

Full-cost pricing: setting a price by calculating a unit cost for the product (allocated fixed and variable costs) and then adding a fixed profit margin.

Example 3: A business makes industrial training DVDs and the annual overheads or fixed costs are $10,000. The variable cost of producing each DVD is $5. The business is currently producing 5,000 units per year. The total costs of this product each year are:

$10,000 + [5,000 × $5] = $35,000

The average or unit cost of making each DVD:

$35,000/5,000 = $7

The business will have to charge at least $7 each in order to break even on each unit. If the firm now adds a 300% profit margin then the total selling price becomes $28.

Contribution-cost (or marginal-cost) pricing

This method does not try to allocate the fixed costs to specific products. Instead of this, the firm calculates a unit variable cost for the product in question and then adds an extra amount that is known as a 'contribution' to fixed costs. If enough units are sold, the total contribution will be enough to cover the fixed costs and to return a profit.

KEY TERM

Contribution-cost pricing: setting prices based on the variable costs of making a product in order to make a contribution towards fixed costs and profit.

Example 4: a firm produces a single product that has direct costs of $2 per unit and the total fixed costs of the firm are

$40,000 per year. The firm sets a contribution of $1 per unit and so sells the product at $3. Every unit sold makes a contribution towards the fixed costs of $1. If the firm sells 40,000 units in the year, then the fixed costs will be covered. Every unit sold over 40,000 will return a profit. Thus, if the firm sells 60,000 units, then the fixed costs will be covered and there will be $20,000 profit made.

Obviously, it would be good for a firm if it produced a range of products that all made a positive contribution to the fixed costs. Then each product is 'doing its bit'. As a general rule of thumb, a product that makes a positive contribution to fixed costs should continue to be produced so long as there is spare capacity in the firm, it does not take the place of a product with a higher contribution and there is not another option that has a higher contribution. There are many firms that have excess capacity and hence use contribution-cost pricing to attract extra business that will absorb the excess capacity.

Examples are train companies, for which there is substantial excess capacity except in the morning and evening rush hours. Even then, trains tend to run almost empty in one of the two directions. Electricity and telephone companies face the same sort of situation. When this problem arises, some businesses are able to use price discrimination to increase demand during the low-use periods – see below.

Example 5: A firm produces a single product that has a variable cost per unit of $4. The annual fixed costs or overheads are $80,000. The firm decides on a contribution of $2 per unit sold. Therefore, selling price is $6. If the business sells 50,000 units in one year, the total contribution to fixed costs becomes 50,000 × $2 = $100,000. This exceeds the fixed costs by $20,000 and so a profit of this amount has been made. This firm would have to sell at least 40,000 units per year in order to break even.

Competition-based pricing

KEY TERM

Competition-based pricing: a firm will base its price upon the price set by its competitors.

There are a number of different possible scenarios in which this approach can be used:

- Price leadership often exists in markets where there is one dominant firm and other firms simply charge a price based upon that set by the market leader.
- Some markets have a number of firms the same size, but prices are still similar in order to avoid a price war. An example of this would be the large petrol companies.

- Destroyer pricing exists when firms note the price of competitors' products and then deliberately undercut them in order to try to force them out of the market.
- Market pricing is where the price charged is based upon a study of the conditions that prevail in a certain market. This is sometimes also called consumer-based pricing, because, when the market is studied, it is in many ways the actions of consumers in that market that are actually being looked at. However, a study of the market is, in fact, more detailed than just looking at the responses of the consumers. A number of different pricing strategies come under the heading of market-orientated pricing:
  - ❏ **Perceived-value pricing** (customer-value pricing) is used in markets where demand is known to be inelastic and a price is placed upon the product that reflects its value, as perceived by the consumers in the market. The more prestigious the brand name, for example Rolex watches, the higher the perceived value, and so the higher the price that can be set.
  - ❏ **Price discrimination** takes place in markets where it is possible to charge different groups of consumer's different prices for the same product. An example of this would be airline operators who charge many different rates for the same journey. Firms can price discriminate if there are different groups of consumers, with different elasticities of demand for the product, where the firm is able to avoid resale between the groups and when it does not cost too much to keep the groups of consumers separate. Other examples of price discrimination include selling train and bus tickets more cheaply to children or the elderly and setting different prices for products in different export markets.
  - ❏ **Dynamic pricing:** The increasing use of constantly changing prices when selling goods to different customers – especially online through e-commerce. E-commerce has become a 'hot spot' for dynamic pricing models due to the way consumers can be 'separated by and communicated with' over the internet. Consumers cannot tell what other buyers are paying and businesses can vary the price according to demand patterns or knowledge that they have about a particular consumer and their ability to pay.

 KEY TERM

Dynamic pricing: offering goods at a price that changes according to the level of demand and the customer's ability to pay.

Pricing strategies for new products

These are normally split into two different approaches depending on the marketing objectives of the business.

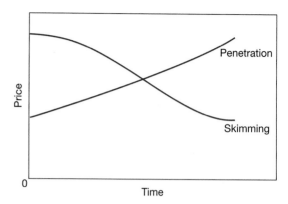

Figure 18.9 Market-skimming and penetration pricing strategies

1 Penetration pricing

Firms tend to adopt **penetration pricing** because they are attempting to use mass marketing and gain a large market share. If the product gains a large market share, then the price could slowly be increased. See Figure 18.9.

 KEY TERM

Penetration pricing: setting a relatively low price often supported by strong promotion in order to achieve a high volume of sales.

2 Market skimming

The aims of this pricing strategy are to maximise short-run profits before competitors enter the market with a similar product and to project an exclusive image for the product. If rivals do launch similar products, it may be necessary for the price of the original product to be reduced over a period of time. An example of this is pharmaceutical firms, who are often given a legal monopoly for a certain number of years for new drugs. They are able to charge high prices in order to recoup their considerable investments in research and to make high profits. It is not uncommon for them to lower their prices in the last year of their legal monopoly in order to hold their market share when other companies enter. This is a typical example of market-skimming price strategy.

KEY TERM

Market skimming: setting a high price for a new product when a firm has a unique or highly differentiated product with low price elasticity of demand.

Does the price fit?

Hartwood Hats manufactures caps for sportswear companies. The caps cost $3 each for materials and labour – the only variable costs. Last year, a total of 400,000 caps was produced and sold to two big sports firms. The fixed costs of the business amount to $200,000 per year. The marketing manager has to decide on pricing levels for the coming year and is uncertain whether to use full-cost or contribution pricing. Last year a price of $6 was set. The firm was left with spare capacity of around 100,000 caps.

[15 marks, 20 minutes]

1 Calculate the profit made by Hartwood last year. **[3]**

2 What was the contribution per cap last year? **[1]**

3 What price would be charged if full-cost pricing was used and 100% mark-up added to unit cost? **[3]**

4 Refer to your answer to question 3. Advise the firm on what factors it should consider before fixing the price at this level. **[4]**

5 If there were a 50% increase in variable costs and the contribution was lowered to $2, what profit would be made if sales remained unchanged? **[4]**

Pricing decisions – some additional issues

Level of competition

The easier it is for new firms to join an industry, the more competitive market conditions are likely to be. It is not technically difficult to become a clothing retailer or a window cleaner – so there are many competing firms in these markets. The firms in these sectors of industry are more likely to have to adopt competition-based pricing than firms in an industry such as electricity generation or aircraft manufacturing. The most extreme form of competition is called perfect competition. Economists suggest that there are four conditions for this to exist:

1 Perfect consumer knowledge about prices and products.

2 Firms' products are of equal quality or homogeneous.

3 There is freedom of entry into and exit from the industry.

4 There are many consumers and producers, and none of the latter is big enough to influence prices on its own.

In this type of market, all firms become price takers, where the market price is the one that all firms must charge. If they try to set a price higher than this, then they will sell nothing – this is true competition-based pricing. The conditions for perfect competition are so strict that very few, if any, industries come close to it. Small-scale farmers come closest: they must accept world market prices for their crops, for example tobacco or coffee; it is relatively easy to join this industry; and they grow crops that are virtually indistinguishable from those of other farmers.

At the other extreme, monopolists are single sellers of a good or service. These firms do not have to take the market price, because they set it. They are said to be price-makers. It is difficult, if not impossible, for other firms to join the industry due to barriers to entry. These barriers might be the huge costs of becoming established, for example nuclear power plants; legal controls, for example patents; and services that would support only one provider, such as water-supply companies. As we saw in Chapter 8, the activities of these firms are often limited by government controls. In between these two extremes, many industries are dominated by just a few large firms – such as oil and petrol retailing, tyre production, detergents – and this type of competition is known as oligopoly. It is quite common in industries that require massive amounts of investment in either research and development or advertising, or capital investment in equipment. As only a few firms are able to afford these expenses, they are able to dominate the market.

How do these firms compete with each other? In nearly all oligopolistic industries, firms compete in one of the following ways:

- **Price wars to gain market share:** These can be very damaging to profits and can, in extreme cases, lead to some weaker firms being forced out of the industry. This might reduce long-run competition in the industry. This reduced competition might lead to higher prices eventually and could reduce the pressure on firms to innovate with new products.

- **Non-price competition:** Due to the potentially unprofitable effect of price wars, oligopolists often engage in fierce and competitive promotional campaigns that are designed to establish brand identity and dominance.

■ **Collusion:** As both of the forms of competition referred to above are expensive and may reduce profits, the few firms in an oligopolistic industry would find it relatively easy to collude, as in the formation of a cartel. These practices, when discovered, are nearly always declared illegal and are then subject to court action and heavy fines.

Loss leaders

This is a common tactic used by retailers. It involves the setting of very low prices for some products – possibly even below variable costs – in the expectation that consumers will buy other goods too. The firms hope that the profits earned by these other goods will exceed the loss made on the low-priced ones. Often, the purpose of loss leaders is to encourage the purchase of closely related complementary goods – cheap razors could lead to additional sales of razor blades, for example.

Psychological pricing

This has two aspects. Firstly, it is very common for manufacturers and retailers to set prices just below key price levels in order to make the price appear much lower than it is. Therefore, $999 is used instead of $1,001, and $1.99 instead of $2.01. In addition, psychological pricing also refers to the use of market research to avoid setting prices that consumers consider to be inappropriate for the style and quality of the product. A very low price for cosmetics or perfume, even though the costs of production may not be high, will not create the status and exclusive image that the firm is trying to portray. Potential consumers may be put off by the fact that too many people can now afford the product and the quality may not be as high as they originally believed. This is similar to perceived-value pricing. Similarly, price can be so high that it exceeds consumer perceptions of the quality and image of the good, and sales will be damaged as a result.

 KEY CONCEPT LINK

Charging the lowest price is rarely the best marketing strategy for **management** to adopt. It may not even be **customer-focused** if the customer expects high quality products with a good brand image.

ACTIVITY 18.9

Prices rise – but for different reasons

Case 1: Florida's theme parks increase prices

Universal Orlando is raising its one-day, one-park adult ticket prices from US$63 to US$67 just days after Disney World also raised their prices. A Universal spokesman refused to comment on whether the price rise was in response to Disney's announcement. Disney has raised its ticket prices twice this year. The latest increase takes an adult ticket to US$67 – Universal has set exactly the same price.

Case 2: Caribbean Cement price adjustment

Caribbean Cement Company Limited announced that from July the price of cement products will be increased by an average of 15%. The company blamed significant increases in input costs, such as electricity and oil prices.

A spokesperson said that: 'The price rises were inevitable as when costs rise, our profits will decline unless prices are increased too.' The company claims that its prices are still among the lowest in the region.

Case 3: Growing demand allows ethanol producers to increase prices

Growing demand in the USA for the corn-based fuel, ethanol, has boosted prices for this 'environmentally friendly' alternative to petrol. The supply of ethanol is limited due to no spare capacity in the industry, but 33 new plants are being planned for the USA. Currently, ethanol fuel is no cheaper than ordinary petrol.

[18 marks, 25 minutes]

1 Identify the different pricing methods used in Case 1 and Case 2. [2]

2 In Case 1, explain two potential benefits to Universal of the company **not** increasing its prices following the decision by Disney World to increase its entry fee. [6]

3 Under what circumstances might you recommend to the managing director of Caribbean Cement that the company should **not** increase its prices, despite higher costs? Explain your answer. [6]

4 Explain what might happen to the price of ethanol in the USA when the 33 new plants start producing it. [4]

Pricing decisions – an evaluation

■ It would be incorrect to assume that one firm will use the same pricing method for all of its products. This would be unwise as the market conditions for the different products could vary greatly. It would, therefore, be important for the business to apply different methods to its portfolio of products, depending on costs of production and competitive conditions within the market.

■ Level of price can have such a powerful influence on consumer purchasing behaviour that marketing managers should ensure that market research is used to test the impact of different levels of price on potential demand.

■ In the world of fast-moving consumer goods, there is often surprisingly little to be gained by adopting a low-price strategy at all times – consumers expect good value, not necessarily low prices. 'Good value' means that all aspects of the marketing mix are combined and integrated together so that consumers accept the overall position of the product and agree that its image justifies the price charged for it.

■ In assessing whether a product offers good value, price is only one factor. The complete brand image or lifestyle offered by the good is increasingly important in a world where many consumers have so much choice and their incomes are rising. A low price for a prestige lifestyle product could easily destroy the image that the rest of the marketing mix is attempting to establish.

ACTIVITY 18.10

Levi claims Tesco cut-price jeans bad for brand image

The maker of Levi's jeans has asked the European Court of Justice to prevent Tesco and another retailer, Costco, from selling their jeans at knock-down prices. The manufacturer fears that its brand image and reputation will be damaged if its jeans are sold in supermarkets. Luxembourg's judges are being asked to decide if Tesco has infringed Levi's trademark rights by importing and selling branded jeans from outside Europe without its consent.

The jeans come from the United States, Canada and Mexico. Some were bought to order by 'accumulators' – people who buy small quantities from authorised outlets and sell them on to wholesalers. Levi tells shops not to sell each customer more than a limited number of pairs, generally six. It stopped supplying Mexican wholesalers when it discovered that its jeans were being sold for export. Several years ago, Levi started legal action against Tesco in the High Court. The retailer argued that it was entitled to buy jeans from abroad and sell them freely. Levi's vice-president of public affairs said that Tesco had undermined Levi's ability to control its own brand. He said: 'Tesco is trying to use our investment in our brand to build its own reputation, and it is doing so illegitimately. For a company that makes as much money as Tesco does, that is simply unacceptable.' Levis public affairs department denied that Tesco was providing a service to consumers by making branded products available at a cheaper price. 'We have retail criteria that describe the conditions under which we want our products to be sold. Tesco does not meet those criteria because it does not specialise in retailing clothing,' a press release stated. 'People want to experience a premium brand like Levi's in the right environment.'

Levi fears that its reputation will be damaged if major British supermarkets such as Tesco sell their branded jeans at knock-down prices.

[12 marks, 15 minutes]

Do you think Levi's is right to try to limit the sale of its clothing products at 'knock-down' prices? Justify your answer.

[12]

SUMMARY POINTS

- There are four main features of the marketing mix.
- The 4Cs are also now considered important as well as the 4Ps.
- Product decisions are vital to business success and new product development has many benefits.
- Differences exist between a product and a brand.
- The stages of a typical product life cycle (PLC) can be analysed.
- Awareness of these stages can be useful when taking marketing decisions.
- It is important to analyse and compare different pricing methods and techniques.
- Price elasticity of demand measures the responsiveness of demand following a price change.
- Price elasticity of demand results are important to marketing managers.
- The usefulness and limitations of price elasticity of demand need to be considered.
- Both product and price decisions need to be integrated with the overall marketing mix.

270

RESEARCH TASK

Choose one of the following products:

- Cola drinks
- Sports shoes
- Tablet computers
- Perfume

1 Find out (approximately) how many different brands there are being sold in your town/city, e.g. by visiting well-known retailers.
2 Make a note of the differences in prices charged for different brands (try to select packets/containers of the same size).
3 Investigate one of the brands you have identified in more detail. What was the last product introduced? Have any changes been made to other products in the range?
4 Write a brief report on your findings and your explanations for them, suitable for consideration by managers of the brand chosen in question 3.

AS Level exam practice questions

Short answer questions

[80 marks, 90 minutes]

Knowledge and understanding

1 List **four** decisions that will be part of the marketing mix for a new product. [4]
2 Explain what is meant by the 4Cs. [4]
3 Explain the links between the 4Ps and the 4Cs. [8]
4 What do you understand by customer relationship marketing? [4]
5 State **two** reasons why the pricing decision is such an important one. [2]
6 State the formula for price elasticity of demand. [2]
7 A manager is reviewing the pricing levels of two products and, from past data, the PED for product X is 0.5 and for product Y is 1.6 (ignoring –ve signs). In which case would you advise the manager to consider increasing price and in which case would a price reduction seem to be more appropriate. Explain your answer with diagrams. [6]
8 Why should pricing decisions not be taken in isolation from other marketing-mix decisions? [4]
9 Define full-cost pricing. [2]
10 What do you understand by 'psychological pricing'? [2]
11 How could variations in the price of a product be used to extend its life cycle? [3]
12 Using your knowledge of price elasticity of demand explain why many businesses use a policy of price discrimination. [4]
13 Would consumers benefit from a policy of destroyer pricing? Explain your answer. [3]
14 Explain **two** reasons why price elasticity results cannot always be relied upon for future pricing decisions. [6]

Application

15 Explain **two** ways in which a supermarket business could improve customer relations to increase customer loyalty. [4]
16 Why is it important that the product and price decisions are integrated, i.e. that they give a consistent image of the product? Explain your answer by referring to at least one product example. [8]
17 Explain **one** business situation in which contribution-cost pricing would seem to be more appropriate than full-cost pricing. [3]
18 Explain why airlines use dynamic/discrimination pricing, especially when selling tickets to online customers. [4]
19 Explain, using business examples, the difference between a skimming pricing strategy and a penetration pricing strategy. [3]
20 Explain an example of when a business is likely to gain from using a loss-leader strategy towards pricing. [4]

Data response

1 Dell to continue price cuts despite falling profits

'It's only a price war if you are losing money and losing market share.' Dell Inc. reported a dramatic drop in quarterly profits, as the PC maker admitted to cutting prices in an effort to maintain sales and market share. This is bad news for other computer manufacturers in a highly competitive market. As sales of PCs continue to fall, Dell is focusing more on providing data services and IT services to companies – markets where it can charge higher prices and make a higher mark-up.

There are two more parts of Dell's plan to become more profitable. One is to cut production costs. The other is to sell more computer 'add-ons' such as data storage and networking, on which it makes higher profit margins. Some industry analysts suggest that, although a desktop might only have a 20% profit margin, add-ons could earn as much as 50%.

Dell's focus is now clear – reduce prices of desktops, increase sales and revenue as a result – even if profit per unit is less – but then make more profit from the sale of add-ons. This is almost a 'loss-leader' strategy.

[30 marks 45 minutes]

1 a Define the term 'mark-up'. [2]

   b Briefly explain the term 'loss leader'. [3]

2 a If a Dell computer costs $200 to manufacture and the company wants to add on a mark-up of 25%, what should the retail price be? [2]

   b Analyse one factor that Dell should consider when making a pricing decision. [4]

3 Analyse two possible benefits to Dell of its decision to reduce prices of desktop computers. [8]

4 Evaluate ways in which one of Dell's competitors – Lenovo, for example – could react to these price cuts. [11]

2 Pricing decision for new computer game

'The price we set for this new interactive computer game will be crucial to its success,' said Stella Sharma, marketing manager for Horizon Software. 'We are under pressure from the finance department to ensure that we cover all of the costs of production, but we also know that new competitors are entering the market virtually every month.' Stella had been in charge of the *Time Traveller* computer game since the idea was first created. She knew that the product life cycle of new games tends to be very short due to the pace of change in the industry – a lower price might need to be offered at its maturity stage. So should she adopt a skimming price strategy for the launch of this new game? Alternatively, was it more important to carve out a substantial market share to begin with and then develop improved versions to maintain consumer interest? There were many factors to take into account. Stella understood that the decision had to be taken quickly – the promotional material was being developed – and that there would only be the one chance to get it right. To help her make the decision, she had the following data:

■ annual fixed costs = $400,000
■ variable costs per unit = $4
■ expected annual output level = 50,000
■ competitors' prices = vary from $10 to $30 per game (although most are of inferior software design).

[30 marks, 45 minutes]

1 a Define the term 'product life cycle'. [2]

   b Briefly explain the term 'skimming price strategy'. [3]

2 a If Stella used full-cost pricing, using a mark-up of 50% on total unit costs, calculate the price that she would charge for *Time Traveller*. [3]

   b The latest market research suggests that 40,000 units might be sold each year at a price of $26 but that 50,000 units could be sold at a price of $22. Calculate the price elasticity of demand if this research is assumed to be accurate. [3]

   c Comment on your result to part question 2b. [2]

3 Once this product has been launched, analyse the impact that knowledge of its life cycle could have on the price charged for it. [6]

4 Recommend to Stella whether an even higher price than this should be charged by adopting a skimming strategy for this new product. Justify your recommendation. [11]

3 Chocolate wars lead to meltdown

Jupiter Confectionery Ltd manufactures four brands of chocolate bar. It is an old, established business and relies heavily on the traditional qualities of rich-tasting chocolate and prestige packaging to sell its products. It rarely introduces new brands – its last launch was three years ago, but the other three brands are each more than ten years old. No extension strategies have been used. The products are:

- **Orion** – the newest brand, designed to appeal to teenagers with *Star Wars* wrappers and a competitive price. Sales are increasing at a steady rate.
- **Venus** – the original product of the company, a dark, rich chocolate bar with a black-and-gold wrapper. The same size as most bars, but slightly more expensive – to suit its image. Sales and cash flow from this product have helped to finance the launch of the other three.
- **Sun** – the firm's only attempt at boxes of chocolates. There is intense competition in this high-value and high-profit-margin market sector. Sales figures are given below.

- **Mercury** – this is a very sweet soft-centred bar that has been very popular with older consumers. Sales have declined in recent years because of imports of healthier low-fat chocolates. Old stocks are being returned by retailers.

The marketing manager is concerned both about sales of Mercury bars and the sales record of Sun boxes. Should they both be dropped or could sales be revived? The manager decides to analyse the current sales of the range of products by using product portfolio analysis.

Sales of Sun boxes of chocolates (units)

Year	Units
2009	120,000
2010	125,000
2011	115,000
2012	123,000
2013	124,000

[30 marks, 45 minutes]

1. a Define the term 'extension strategies'. [2]
   b Briefly explain the term 'product portfolio analysis'. [3]
2. a What stage of its product life cycle does the Sun box of chocolates appear to be in? Explain your answer. [4]
   b Outline the options available to the marketing manager for the Sun box of chocolates product. [4]
3. Outline two problems this business could face as a consequence of launching very few new products. [6]
4. The business has decided to try to extend the life of the Sun box of chocolates product. Evaluate **two** extension strategies that it could use in your country. [11]

4 Body Shop held back by product errors

Mistakes with new products and a failure to control stock properly caused underlying profits to drop by a fifth last year at Body Shop International. 'I take responsibility for the performance of the company,' said Patrick Gournay, chief executive of the retailer of beauty products, best known for its USP of a green and ethical stance. 'We have been going through a huge change process, and some of the things we did have not gone so well. We tried to do too many things, too fast. For instance, we changed the packaging on a new hair care range and discontinued some existing lines. The customers didn't like it very much,' he admitted. Business analysts believe that insufficient market research is being undertaken.

Improvements are already under way, Gournay said, including launching fewer products and making sure that those introduced were closer to the brand's ethical traditions that customers identified with. He also wants to keep better control of costs, so that new products do not sell at lower mark-up than the goods they are replacing. Body Shop has been working hard in recent years to build stronger customer relations. It would benefit the company if consumer loyalty was even higher than currently.

[30 marks, 45 minutes]

1. a Define the term 'USP (unique selling point)'. [2]
   b Briefly explain the term 'consumer loyalty'. [3]
2. Explain the problems faced by a business such as The Body Shop of not undertaking sufficient market research before making product changes. [6]
3. Analyse how The Body Shop could strengthen its relations with customers [8]
4. Evaluate the importance for the future sales success and profitability of Body Shop for it to keep closer to the brand's traditions and exercise 'better control of costs'. [11]

AS Level essay questions

[20 marks, 40 minutes each]

1. a Explain why price decisions are an important part of the marketing mix. [8]
   b Assess the factors a mobile (cell) phone maker should consider before setting the retail price for a new range of smartphones. [12]
2. a Explain why product decisions are an important part of the marketing mix. [8]
   b Evaluate the usefulness of the product life-cycle concept to a car manufacturer. [12]

The marketing mix – promotion and place

This chapter covers syllabus AS Level 3.3 (promotion and place).

On completing this chapter, you will be able to:

- identify the differences between sales promotion and advertising, above- and below-the-line promotion
- understand the different objectives that may be established for a promotion campaign
- analyse the factors a business should consider when making promotion-mix decisions for its products
- evaluate the methods that can be used to measure the effectiveness of promotional spending

- recognise the importance of packaging in the marketing of a product
- understand the importance of place in the marketing mix
- discuss the different distribution channels that can be used and assess their appropriateness in different circumstances.

Introducing the topic

NIKON COOLPIX PROMOTION EXCEEDS TARGETS

The global digital-camera market is saturated with many well-recognised brands. Six manufacturers offer very similar products in terms of quality, features and range. Nikon's new Coolpix camera had to be promoted in exciting new ways so that it would become the number-one choice for retailers to stock and for consumers to buy. The three main objectives of Nikon's promotional campaign were to:

1. encourage consumers to visit camera retailers to try out the Coolpix range
2. give incentives to shop staff to actively demonstrate and recommend this camera
3. meet or exceed sales targets based on a 10% increase over last year.

Promotions were focused on a target group of consumers: digital-camera users, of which 58% were men concentrated in the 35–44 age group, 81% were married with children and with household incomes greater than $70,000 a year.

The three key features of the promotion campaign were:

1. 500,000 leaflets were dropped through letter boxes of target group consumers, each containing a photo memory card.
2. People receiving the leaflet and card were invited to a camera retailer to test the card in a Nikon Coolpix camera – if the LCD screen showed a prize image, then the consumer could claim the prize – such as a holiday to Australia.

3. Retail shop staff were motivated to demonstrate the cameras by being given the opportunity to win the same prize as the consumers.

The campaign was a huge success. Sales increased by 30% during the promotion and consumer recognition of the Coolpix brand increased even after the campaign ended. The budget of $2 million for the prizes was not exceeded and the campaign increased sales by much more than this figure anyway.

Points to think about:

- Why do you think it was so important for Nikon to choose a promotion campaign that was so different?
- Explain the importance of aiming a promotion campaign at a clearly defined target audience.
- Do you think that it was important to have both clear objectives and a budget limit for this campaign?
- Suggest an appropriate promotion campaign for Nikon's Coolpix camera, aimed at young consumers (14–18 years old). Activity 19.2 will help you.

Coolpix cameras

Introduction

The two components of the marketing mix considered so far have been product and price. No matter how good the product or how attractive the prices to consumers, businesses have to communicate with customers – or potential customers – to persuade them to purchase the good or service. This is the role of 'promotion'. 'Place' refers to how the product is sold to the customer – the channel of distribution used from producer to consumer. Both of these key elements of the marketing mix are being transformed by technological change.

Why is promotion an important part of the marketing mix?

Promotion is about communicating with actual or potential customers. Effective promotion not only increases awareness of products, but can create images and product 'personalities' that consumers can identify with. Advertising is only one form of promotion and other techniques include direct selling and sales-promotion offers. The combination of all forms of promotion used by a business for any product is known as the 'promotion mix'. The amount firms spend on promotion – the promotion budget – is often a key decision but successful communication is not just about the total amount spent. It is also about how the budget is allocated between the competing forms of promotion available – this is called the promotions mix. The packaging of products is often considered as a separate 'P' in the marketing mix, but it is very closely tied to promotion and product imagery. This chapter also takes a closer look at the role of packaging in complementing promotional strategies.

KEY TERM

Promotion: the use of advertising, sales promotion, personal selling, direct mail, trade fairs, sponsorship and public relations to inform consumers and persuade them to buy.

Promotion objectives

Promotion campaigns can be planned to achieve several objectives. These are all about communicating with the target consumers. These aims can either be focused on the short term – such as an increase in sales next month – or on the longer term – such as to change the image of the business. These aims should be linked to the overall objectives of the business.

Promotional objectives aim to:

- increase sales by raising consumer awareness of a product – especially important for newly launched ones
- remind consumers of an existing product and its distinctive qualities
- increase purchases by existing consumers or to attract new consumers to the brand
- demonstrate the superior specification or qualities of a product compared with those of competitors – often used when the product has been updated or adapted in some way
- create or reinforce the brand image or 'personality' of the product – this is becoming increasingly important in consumer markets, where it is often claimed that 'all products look the same'
- correct misleading reports about the product or the business and to reassure the consuming public after a 'scare' or an accident involving the product
- develop the public image of the business – rather than the product – through corporate advertising
- encourage retailers to stock and actively promote products to the final consumer.

TOP TIP

When writing about promotion of a product, try to consider the marketing objectives of the business. Is the promotion being used likely to help achieve these objectives?

Promotion decisions – key issues

The promotion mix

It is most unlikely that just one method of promotion will be sufficient to achieve promotional objectives. There are several elements of the **promotion mix**. They include all of the marketing tools that can be used to communicate with consumers.

KEY TERM

Promotion mix: the combination of promotional techniques that a firm uses to sell a product.

Advertising

This form of promotion is sometimes referred to as '**above-the-line promotion**'.

So **advertising** is communicating information about a product or business through the media, such as radio,

274

275

KEY TERMS

Above-the-line promotion: a form of promotion that is undertaken by a business by paying for communication with consumers.

Advertising: paid-for communication with consumers to inform and persuade, e.g. TV and cinema advertising.

TV and newspapers. These advertisements are usually directed towards the appropriate target market by selecting the right media – but it is possible that many people who are unlikely to purchase the product may see the advertisements too. Successful advertising campaigns have led to substantial increases in consumer awareness and sales, and this effect can last for a considerable length of time if brand loyalty can be established.

Advertisements are often classified into two types, but in practice this distinction is often quite blurred.

1 **Informative advertising** – adverts that give information to potential purchasers of a product, rather than just trying to create a brand image. This information could include price, technical specifications or main features and places where the product can be purchased. This style of advertising could be particularly effective when promoting a new product that consumers are unlikely to be aware of or when communicating a substantial change in price, design or specification.

2 **Persuasive advertising** – adverts trying to create a distinct image or brand identity for the product. They may not contain any details at all about materials or ingredients used, prices or places to buy the product. This form of advertising is very common, especially in those markets where there might be little differentiation between products and where advertisers are trying to create a perceived difference in the minds of consumers. Perhaps, in reality, there is little difference between these two styles of advertising: 'The more informative your advertising, the more persuasive it will be' (David Ogilvy, *Confessions of an Advertising Man*, New York: Ballantine Books, 1971).

Not all advertising is aimed at the final consumer. Trade advertising is aimed at encouraging retailers to stock and sell products to consumers and, if possible, to promote them in preference to rival products. This type of advertising is most likely to take place in trade journals and magazines not available to consumers.

Advertising agencies

These are firms who advise businesses on the most effective way to promote products. Although expensive, these specialists can offer a complete promotional strategy and this can be invaluable to a business that does not

have its own marketing experts or to one that might be entering a new market for the first time. These agencies will – for substantial fees – undertake the following stages in devising a promotional plan:

- Research the market, establish consumer tastes and preferences and identify the typical consumer profile.
- Advise on the most cost-effective forms of media to be used to attract these potential consumers.
- Use their own creative designers to devise adverts appropriate to the media to be used.
- Film or print the adverts to be used in the campaign.
- Monitor public reaction to the campaign and feed this back to the client to improve the effectiveness of future advice on promotion.

Advertising decisions – which media to use?

Communication with the public needs a message and a medium to transmit the message. The bigger the advertising budget, the more media choice there is. Limited resources will restrict options to the cheaper media. However, the most expensive forms of communication are not always the most effective. The choice of media requires consideration of the following factors:

1 **Cost:** TV, radio and cinema advertising can be very expensive per minute of advert. The actual cost will depend on the time of day that the advertisements are to be transmitted and the size of the potential audience. National newspapers will be more expensive than local ones. Other media include posters and magazines. Marketing managers are able to compare the cost of these media and assess whether they fall within the marketing budget. It must not be forgotten that buying media time or space is not the only cost. The advert still has to be written and produced and the use of celebrities in TV, radio or cinema adverts can greatly increase the total cost. In contrast, viral marketing through social media can be virtually cost-free.

2 **Size of audience:** This will allow the cost per person to be calculated. Media managers will provide details of overall audience numbers at different times of day or in different regions. Total numbers are of less importance than the 'profile' of the audience, as the advertisements need to be directed towards potential customers only and not 'wasted' on groups that are unlikely to ever buy the product.

3 **The profile of the target audience in terms of age, income levels, interests and so on:** This should reflect as closely as possible the target consumer profile of the market being aimed for. For instance, there is likely to be little point in advertising a new children's toy after 10pm at night. Using a mass-market, low-priced daily newspaper to advertise a new range of exclusive clothing would be aiming at the wrong target. Younger consumers are likely to be most accessible via social media.

ACTIVITY 19.1

Does advertising increase sales?

The Cadbury 'Gorilla' advert was one of the most famous and effective advertisement campaigns of recent years. The aims of the campaign were to:

- improve the public image of Cadbury and the Diary Milk chocolate brand
- increase sales of Dairy Milk, which seemed to be in the maturity stage of its life cycle.

The TV advert featured an actor in a gorilla costume enthusiastically playing a well-known drum solo from the Phil Collins hit record 'In the Air Tonight'. The 90-second performance faded to a computer-generated shot of a Dairy Milk bar over the slogan 'A glass and a half full of joy' (Cadbury has always claimed that each bar contains a glass and a half of fresh milk). Producing the advert and paying for the TV time slots cost US$12 million. One TV advert during the Rugby World Cup cost $1.4 million alone. The campaign was very successful. The advert was uploaded on to YouTube and was viewed more than 500,000 times in the first week. Market research reported that the public's view of Cadbury and Dairy Milk had improved and sales rose by 9% in one year – higher than the original target.

Evian's 'Roller Babies' video holds the official Guinness World Record for the most viral video ad of all time. It has already racked up more than 50 million views on YouTube. But viral success is not the same as sales success. After the 'Roller Babies' ad was released in 2009, sales of the water brand, owned by the Danone Group, actually declined, according to Jonah Berger, a professor of marketing at the University of Pennsylvania. Forbes, a business news agency, reported: 'In the year the Evian 'Roller Babies' video went viral and attracted 50 million views, the brand lost market share and sales dropped 25%.' The Evian brand continued to lose market share in the UK in 2013, but overall the Danone Group's water business is growing.

[32 marks, 50 minutes]

1 Was the Cadbury's 'Gorilla' advert an informative or a persuasive advertisement? Explain your answer. **[4]**

2 Can the expenditure of $12 million on advertising a chocolate bar be justified? Explain your answer. **[10]**

3 Explain **two** possible reasons why sales of Evian water declined despite the apparent success of its online advertising. **[8]**

4 Discuss the importance for businesses of checking and monitoring the effectiveness of a promotional campaign. **[10]**

---

4 **Message to be communicated:** Written forms of communication are likely to be most effective for giving detailed information about a product that needs to be referred to more than once by potential consumers. However, if an image-creating advert is planned, perhaps for a new range of clothes or sports equipment, then a dynamic and colourful TV advert or YouTube video could be more effective.

5 **Other aspects of the marketing mix:** The need for integration of the mix is examined later in this chapter, but the link between the other parts of the mix and the media chosen for adverts could be crucial to success. The use of exclusive and glossy women's magazines to advertise a new 'budget' range of ready-cooked meals could be counterproductive.

6 **Legal and other constraints:** A widespread ban on tobacco advertising in Formula One grand prix racing has forced many sponsors to use other media for presenting their cigarette advertising. In some countries, there are restrictions on the use of TV advertising aimed at children, claiming that it exercises too much influence over young minds. In addition to legal controls, there are, in most countries, other constraints on what advertisements can contain. In the UK, the Advertising Standards Authority (ASA) acts to ensure that advertisements are 'legal, decent and honest'. It can put pressure on advertisers to withdraw or change campaigns that do not meet these standards.

 KEY CONCEPT LINK

Effective communication with customers is an important part of being **customer-focused**.

Advertising expenditure and the trade cycle

The evidence from the advertising industry is that, in most countries, firms tend to spend more when the economy is booming than when it is in recession.

Is spending less on promotion during a recession the right strategy to adopt? It could be argued that advertising is needed most when sales are beginning to slow down or even decline due to economic forces. Perhaps consumers could still be encouraged to buy if they were exposed to really influential adverts or promotions, even if household incomes are quite restricted.

Global ad spending US$503billion in 2013

Share of global ad spend by medium (%)

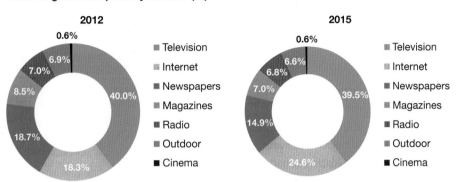

Figure 1 Share of global ad spend by medium (%)

Global expenditure on advertising increased by 3.5% in 2013 to reach US$503 billion with an increasing proportion spent on Internet (digital) advertising. In the US, digital advertising accounted for 21.8% of all ad spend in 2013, up from 19% in 2012. Meanwhile, mobile ads (cell phone advertising) in the US accounted for 3.7%.

Mobile advertising is growing more rapidly than any other media, growing by 81% in 2013 in the US market. Compare that to Internet advertising – which is growing by around 16% – and it will account for 27.8% of all US ad spend by 2015. Globally, mobile advertising is worth $8.3 billion, 1.7% of advertising across all media. 'By 2015 we forecast this total to rise to $33.1 billion, which will be 25.2% of Internet expenditure and 6.0% of all expenditure,' the analysts write.

The rapid adoption of smartphones and tablets is driving the growth in mobile advertising. On top of the fact that sales of tablets have overtaken those of PCs, for many consumers smartphones are becoming the primary way that they go online.

[22 marks, 30 minutes]

1 Use the data to identify:

  a the two advertising media with the fastest forecast growth rates

  b two advertising media that are forecast to become relatively less important. [4]

2 Analyse reasons for the trends in advertising across different media. [8]

3 Evaluate the impact on the CRM strategy of a hotel chain of the 'rapid adoption of smartphones and tablets'. [10]

Whatever the appropriateness of cutting back on promotional spending during an economic downturn, there are many in business who maintain that advertising is a 'luxury' that can be afforded only when sales and profits are booming. This raises questions about how marketing/promotional budgets should be established, and this issue is covered more fully later in the chapter.

Sales promotion

This form of promotion is also known as '**below-the-line' promotion**.

Sales promotion is generally aiming to achieve short-term increases in sales but advertising often aims to achieve returns in the long run through building customer

KEY TERMS

Below-the-line promotion: promotion that is not a directly paid-for means of communication, but based on short-term incentives to purchase.

Sales promotion: incentives such as special offers or special deals directed at consumers or retailers to achieve short-term sales increases and repeat purchases by consumers.

awareness of and confidence in the product. There is a huge range of incentives and activities that come under the umbrella term 'sales promotion'. They include:

■ price deals – a temporary reduction in price, such as '10% reduction for one week only'

- loyalty reward programmes – consumers collect points, air miles or credits for purchases and redeem them for rewards
- money-off coupons – redeemed when the consumer buys the product
- point-of-sale displays in shops – e.g. an 'aisle interrupter' is a sign that juts into the supermarket aisle from a shelf, a 'dump bin' is a free-standing bin centrally placed full of products 'dumped' inside to attract attention
- BOGOF – 'buy one, get one free'
- games and competitions – e.g. on cereal packets.

These examples suggest that sales promotion is very much an active approach to marketing – it is not just about informing consumers. In many cases of sales promotion, consumers already know about a product's existence and any promotion campaign is all about stimulating consumers to buy it. Sales promotion can be directed either at:

- the final consumer, to encourage purchase (pull strategy), or
- the distribution channel, e.g. the retailer, to encourage stocking and display of the product (push strategy).

The types and possible limitations of methods of sales promotion are shown in Table 19.1.

Personal selling

Employing a salesperson to sell to each individual customer is a very expensive form of promotion. It tends only to be used for quite expensive items with a high profit margin, such as furniture, cars or home improvements. Sales success rates are often high with skilled direct-sales staff – but customers often complain about being pressured into buying. This might particularly be the case if the sales staff are paid a high bonus for each sale made. Firms must be careful to ensure that sales staff are well trained and do not make a sale to a reluctant consumer who later regrets the decision and tells friends to avoid this business in future. **Personal selling** is often used for expensive industrial products – and this is often one of the key differences between consumer marketing and business marketing.

KEY TERM

Personal selling: a member of the sales staff communicates with one consumer with the aim of selling the product and establishing a long-term relationship between company and consumer.

Direct mail

This directs information to potential customers, identified by market research, who have a potential interest in this type of product. These 'mailshots' can contain a great deal of detailed information, e.g. about bank saving accounts, or they can just provide simple information, such as 'Sale next week at Hammonds bookshop'. They are well focused on potential consumers, using databases that filter out non-target consumer groups. These campaigns can, therefore, be very cost-effective (see the Coolpix case study on page 273). Direct mailing involving mailshots can suffer from a poor image and can lead to resentment at 'junk mail' that has not been specifically requested. Increasingly, postal mail shots are being replaced by text message and messages communicated via social media.

ACTIVITY 19.3

Does sales promotion work?

A survey of more than 200 supermarket shoppers in Hong Kong found that some sales promotions worked better than others. Price discounts and buy-one-get-one-free offers (BOGOF) were felt by consumers to be the most effective promotional tool for encouraging consumers to bring purchases forward (buying this week rather than next week), stockpiling and spending more. In-store displays and demonstrations were felt to be effective in encouraging consumers to try a product for the first time. Loyalty cards and rewards for spending more were effective in encouraging consumers to buy just from one store. Competitions and games, in contrast, were felt to be ineffective in terms of generating all types of consumer response. A supermarket manager said: 'We have to be careful with the cost of sales promotions – if they reduce our profits through the cost of them, but fail to lead to longer-term increases in sales or brand switching, are they really worthwhile?'

[20 marks, 30 minutes]

1   Explain why it is important for shop managers to compare the cost and effectiveness of sales promotions. [8]

2   Assume you are a supermarket manager. You have been asked by head office to promote **one** very profitable brand of breakfast cereal. Which sales promotions would you use for this product? Explain and justify your answer.   [12]

Method	Method explained	Possible limitations
	Price promotions – these are temporary reductions in price, also known as price discounting. They are aimed at encouraging existing customers to buy more and to attract new customers as the product now appears more competitive.	■ Increased sales gained from price reductions will affect gross profit on each item sold. ■ There might be a negative impact on the brand's reputation from the discounted price.
	Money-off coupons – these are a more versatile and better-focused way of offering a price discount. Coupons can appear on the back of receipts, in newspaper adverts or on an existing pack of the product.	■ They may simply encourage consumers to buy what they would have bought anyway. ■ Retailers may be surprised by the increase in demand and not hold enough stocks, leading to consumer disappointment. ■ The proportion of consumers using the coupon might be low if the reduction it offers is too small.
	Customer loyalty schemes, such as air miles or customer loyalty cards – these are focused on encouraging repeat purchases and discouraging consumers from shopping with competitors. The information stored through these loyalty cards provides a great deal of information about consumers' buying preferences.	■ The discount offered by such schemes cuts the gross profit on each purchase. ■ There are administration costs to inform consumers of loyalty points earned and these may outweigh the benefits from increased consumer loyalty. ■ Most consumers now have many loyalty cards from different retailers, so their loyalty impact is reduced.
	Money refunds – these are offered when the receipt is returned to the manufacturer.	■ These involve the consumer filling in and posting off a form, and this might be a disincentive. ■ Delay before a refund is received may act as a disincentive.
	BOGOF – 'buy one, get one free' – this encourages multiple purchases, which reduces demand for competitors' products too.	■ There could be substantial reduction in gross profit margin. ■ Consumers may consider that if this scheme is able to operate, are they paying a 'normal' price that is too high? ■ Is the scheme being used to sell off stock that cannot be sold at normal prices – impact on reputation? ■ Current sales might increase, but future sales could fall as consumers have stocked up on the product.
	Point-of-sale displays – maximum impact on consumer behaviour is achieved by attractive, informative and well-positioned displays in stores.	■ The best display points are usually offered to the market leaders – products with high market share. ■ New products may struggle for best positions in stores – unless big discounts are offered to retailers.

Table 19.1 Common methods of sales promotion

Trade fairs and exhibitions

These are used in marketing to other businesses to sell products to the 'trade', i.e. retailers and wholesalers. These firms, if they stock the product after a trade fair, will then increase the chances of it gaining increased sales to consumers. Companies seldom sell much directly at trade fairs, but contacts are made and awareness of products is increased.

Sponsorship

The 2016 Olympics in Rio de Janeiro has attracted much **sponsorship** from companies that wish to be associated with this event, which will be watched on TV and the internet by more people than any previous event in history. Sponsorship is now a big and rapidly growing part of the total promotion industry. Global television coverage and the internet have increased the potential marketing impact of major sporting and cultural events. Expenditure on this form of promotion can lead to dramatic results. A study by Repucom and cycling news calculated that for each US$1 spent on sponsoring a team in the Tour de France cycle race, US$5.4 of free publicity is received as the event is covered by TV stations globally. It can cost US$10 million to sponsor one team for this single event!

KEY TERM

Sponsorship: payment by a company to the organisers of an event or team/individuals so that the company name becomes associated with the event/team/individual.

Figure 19.1 Sponsoring a team in the Tour de France is not cheap – but the benefits can be huge

Public relations (PR)

PR is designed to gain free publicity provided by the media as opposed to advertising that is paid for. All large businesses have PR departments that try to arrange as much positive press and TV coverage of their business as possible. The launch of a new product might include a press conference where journalists will be provided with details about the product and its performance – with the hope that this will later appear in an article or TV news programme. Journalists might be encouraged to test drive a car for a week or be offered a week's free holiday in a new hotel – all of these enticements are usually likely to lead to positive media coverage. Sponsorship of major sports and cultural events often leads to free publicity too – when these events are reported in the media, the name of the sponsoring company is nearly always mentioned too. The PR department will also have the task of putting forward the company's view on incidents that might be damaging to image or reputation. If there is a quick and detailed response in public to an event, such as an aircraft accident or a faulty batch of products, then the negative impact of the incident may be reduced.

KEY TERM

Public relations: the deliberate use of free publicity provided by newspapers, TV and other media to communicate with and achieve understanding by the public.

TOP TIP

Do not confuse advertising and sales promotion – they are both forms of promotion, but they are not the same.

Branding

A brand is the name given by a firm to a product or a range of products. The aims of **branding** products include:

- aiding consumer recognition
- making the product distinctive from competitors
- giving the product an identity or personality that consumers can relate to.

KEY TERM

Branding: the strategy of differentiating products from those of competitors by creating an identifiable image and clear expectations about a product.

The choice of brand name is an important part of the overall marketing strategy and there are specialist agencies who will advise firms on name suitability. These agencies will check to see that the proposed name has not been registered by another company and that it does not have an unfortunate translation in other languages. Finally, a survey of consumers will be undertaken to gauge their reaction to the proposed brand name. It is claimed that an effective brand identity will have the following benefits for businesses:

■ Increase the chances of brand recall by consumers, e.g. when shopping in a supermarket and there are several product options available.
■ Clearly differentiate the product from others.
■ Allow for the establishment of a 'family' of closely associated products with the same brand name.

■ Reduce price elasticity of demand as consumers have been shown to have preferences for well-known brands.
■ Increase consumer loyalty to brands, which is a major marketing benefit.

A very important recent development has been the growth of 'own-label brands'. These are ranges of goods that have been launched by retailers under their own store name. It is very rare for the retailers to actually produce the goods – they buy them in with their own labels and brand names on. Often, the goods are made by leading manufacturers who have their own well-known brands on the market that compete with the own-label brands. This clearly has the disadvantage of creating a more competitive environment for the well-known brands – but it can be a way of using up spare manufacturing capacity. For the retail stores, this strategy gives them a reasonable quality product, bought with bulk discounts, over which they have full marketing control.

ACTIVITY 19.4

Gap wins back lost customers

Gap Inc. sells clothes under the Gap, Banana Republic and Old Navy brand names. Consumers and investors are once again becoming excited about the bright and lively store designs, the simple, classic fashion look and the unusual style of advertising. This renewed interest in the company comes after several years of falling sales. In 2008 and 2009 the brand failed to attract younger shoppers. Some analysts believe that Gap's shops look dated and their fashions less appealing than those of main rivals Zara and Uniqlo. In fact, in 2008, Zara overtook Gap to become the world's biggest clothing retailer. It was therefore quite surprising that Gap decided to reduce spending on both design teams and marketing promotions during this period.

However, the good times seem to be back. The table shows how Gap's sales fell in 2009 but increased in 2012/2013.

	% change in sales in July 2009 compared to July 2008	% sales in Jan 2013 compared to Jan 2012
Total Gap Inc sales	−9	+8
Gap-branded stores	−10	+9
Gap stores North America	−10	+8
Banana Republic North America	−20	+8
Old Navy North America	−7	+12
International sales	−5	+1

[22 marks, 25 minutes]

1 Explain why Gap's managers should be worried about the loss of market leadership to Zara. **[8]**

2 Recommend a new promotional strategy for Gap in your own country that could help increase 'international sales'. Consider advertising and social media campaigns, displays in shops, special offers and the image that you think the business should try to create for its products in your country. **[14]**

An example of informative advertising

An example of persuasive advertising

Brand extension

A strong brand identity can be used as a means of supporting the introduction of new or modified products. For example, Mars extended its brand to ice cream, Caterpillar to shoes and watches, Adidas and Puma to personal hygiene and Dunlop from tyres to sports equipment. Using the same name in this way helps to create a family of products and the advertising of one supports sales of the other products, too.

Marketing or promotion expenditure budgets

These spending limits can be set by using a number of different approaches:

- **A percentage of sales:** Using this approach, the marketing budget for expenditure will vary with the level of sales. Thus, if sales increase, the department will have additional funds allocated to it for promotional activities. This method has a major flaw – if sales are declining, perhaps due to inadequate promotional activity, then the amount to be spent declines too.

- **Objective-based budgeting:** This approach starts out by analysing what sales level is required to meet objectives and then assesses how much supporting expenditure is required to reach such targets. This then becomes the promotion budget.

> **KEY TERM**
>
> **Marketing or promotion budget:** the financial amount made available by a business for spending on marketing/promotion during a certain time period.

- **Competitor-based budget:** When two or more firms are of roughly the same size in terms of sales, it is possible that they will attempt to match each other in terms of marketing spending. This can lead to spiralling promotion costs as each tries to outdo the other's advertisements and below-the-line spending. Also, just because the same approximate amount is being spent does not mean that it is equally effective. One firm might have a particularly creative and attractive promotional mix that is not easily matched, even though other firms spend as much.

- **What the business can afford:** Finance is often very limited in smaller businesses and it is quite common for managers to adopt the attitude that marketing is a luxury that can only be afforded after all other expenses have been met. In these cases, marketing budgets will be set on the basis of what can be afforded after all other forecast expenses have been paid for. This method will, therefore, fail to take either market conditions or marketing objectives into consideration.

- **Incremental budgeting:** By taking last year's budget and adding on a percentage to reflect inflation or different sales targets, a new figure is set – and this is called incremental budgeting. One criticism of this approach is that it does not require marketing managers to justify the total size of the budget each year – just the 'increment' that is being asked for.

> **TOP TIP**
> Spending huge amounts on promotion will never guarantee the success of a product – the promotion has to match the marketing objectives and integrate well with the rest of the marketing mix.

Is the marketing budget well spent?

From the viewpoint of society and the consumer

Billions of dollars are spent worldwide each year on all forms of promotion, including advertising. There are many observers who argue that this is a waste of resources and this money would be more effectively spent, in the interests of the consumers, in other ways. This view is also supported by those who believe that society itself has to bear an unreasonable burden from excessive advertising and promotional activity. Table 19.2 summarises some of the arguments.

From the viewpoint of the business

The main test of promotional campaigns is whether or not they have achieved their aims cost-effectively. The main aim of advertising and sales promotion is not always to increase sales in the short term – it could be part of a longer-term 'brand building' exercise, where the benefits will be spread over many years. Whatever the original aim of a campaign, it is vital for the business to assess the degree of success – and this is not always an easy thing to

do. There is a very famous quote from Lord Leverhulme, a British businessman, who said: 'I know half of the money I spend on advertising is wasted, but I can never find out which half' (*The Ultimate Book of Business Quotations*, Capstone Publishing, 1997). By this he meant that it was difficult or impossible to measure the true effectiveness of an advertising campaign. Modern marketing experts would now dispute that view, as new techniques and technology have enabled the effectiveness of all promotion campaigns to be assessed with some accuracy. How can this be done?

1. **Sales performance before and after the promotion campaign:** By comparing the sales of the product before the campaign was launched with the daily and weekly sales during and after the campaign, some conclusions could be drawn. The results of this comparison could then be used to calculate the promotional elasticity of demand – this is an Advanced-level topic covered in the next chapter.

2. **Consumer awareness data:** Each week market research agencies publish results of consumer 'recall' or awareness tests based on answers to a series of questions concerning the advertisements they have seen and responded too. This gives the advertising agencies and their clients rapid feedback on the progress of a campaign, whether the advertisements or sales promotions have been seen and remembered.

3. **Consumer panels:** These were discussed in the market research chapter (17)– they are useful for giving qualitative feedback on the impact of promotions and the effectiveness of advertisements.

4. **Response rates to advertisements:** This is more than just checking on sales levels. Newspaper and magazine adverts often have tear-off slips to request more details and even TV adverts can ask for consumers to ring in, perhaps with the chance of winning a competition. Websites can record the number of hits and video-sharing sites the number of times an uploaded advert has been viewed.

Drawbacks to society from promotional expenditure	Benefits to society from promotional expenditure
Waste of resources – money spent on promotion could be used to lower prices instead.	It informs people about new products and this helps to increase competition between firms.
Promotion is such a powerful business tool that it can encourage consumers to buy goods that they do not need.	By helping to create mass markets, promotion can assist in reducing average costs of production through economies of large-scale production.
It promotes consumerism – a situation where people are judged by the quantity of goods they own.	It generates income for TV, radio and newspaper businesses, which helps to keep the prices of these lower than they would otherwise be.
It encourages consumption, and environmentalists argue this is against the need to conserve limited resources.	

Table 19.2 Arguments for and against promotional expenditure from the viewpoint of society

How much should we spend on promotion?

'If our major competitor spent $3 million on promotion including advertising last year, how can you justify that our company should spend only $1.5 million this year. We will never be able to gain more market share than Shoeflight.'

This was the comment made by the marketing director, Jim Singh, of Panther Sports Shoes Ltd at the recent board meeting. He continued: 'Unless we base our promotion budget on what our competitors are spending, we will always have lower sales. I am asking for a budget of at least $3 million this year.'

The finance director, Imran Farouk, disagreed: 'It isn't just a question of how much we spend – it also depends on what it is spent on. I still believe that the $300,000 we spent on children's TV advertising last year was largely wasted. I still think that a promotion budget of 10% of expected revenue is the right amount to spend.'

The managing director disagreed with both of his directors. 'I think you are both wrong. We should spend more on new designs of shoes that become really well-known and recognised – with distinctive colours and features. These new products would almost sell themselves. The cost of the new designs would mean that we would only be able to afford a promotion budget of around $0.5 million. This should not be a problem.'

[25 marks, 30 minutes]

1   Identify the method of setting the promotional budget suggested by each manager.   [3]

2   Should the promotion budget for Panther Sports Shoes be spent just on advertising or on other forms of promotion too? Explain your answer.   [10]

3   Which manager do you agree with? Recommend which method of promotion budget setting should be used by this company, explaining your answer fully.   [12]

However, the relative significance of the methods used is likely to vary substantially between these two types of markets. Trade- or industry-focused promotional campaigns are unlikely to use commercial TV, radio or national-newspaper advertising. The intended purchaser of industrial goods is much more likely to refer to specialist magazines or journals, and advertising in these is going to be clearly targeted. Trade fairs are often used to display and explain the range of products on offer, and this replaces the point-of-sale displays in shops for consumer goods. Trade promotions will be used instead of consumer sales promotions, and these could take the form of financing deals to aid firms with the purchase of expensive equipment.

Controls on advertising

The UK Advertising Standards Authority has taken a huge multinational pharmaceutical company to court over some of its allegedly misleading advertising claims. Ribena Toothkind is a kids' drink that was claimed 'does not encourage tooth decay'. A pressure group called Action and Information against Sugars tried to force GlaxoSmithKline, owner of Ribena, to change the name of the product after the court ruling found in favour of the ASA. However, the company refused to do this and instead launched an expensive new TV advertising campaign aimed at children and parents, with the slogan 'scientifically proven to minimise tooth decay'. The company believes that this claim is not misleading or untruthful.

[16 marks, 25 marks]

1   Find out which authority in your country judges the honesty and decency of advertisements. Make notes on its main powers.   [6]

2   In this case, do you think the company is right to advertise on television a soft drink that some people consider damaging to children's teeth? Explain your answer by assessing the arguments for and against advertising.   [10]

Consumer markets and industrial markets

Most of the references made so far concern promotion of consumer products. Industrial products – goods and services sold to industry – also need promoting.

Promotion and the product life cycle

Table 19.3 summarises some of the promotion-mix options at different stages of a product's life cycle.

Stage of life cycle	Promotional options
Introduction	■ informative advertising to make consumers aware of the product's existence, price and main features ■ sales promotion offering free samples or trial periods to encourage consumers to test the product – incentives may need to be offered to the trade to stock the product
Growth	■ to continue some informative advertising, but the focus may now move to brand building and persuasive advertising ■ sales promotion to encourage repeat purchase ■ attempt to develop brand loyalty
Maturity	■ advertising to emphasise the differences between this product and competitors – may be needed to remind consumers of the existence of the product ■ sales-promotion incentives to encourage brand switching and continued loyalty
Decline – assuming no extension strategy	■ minimal advertising, apart from informing consumers of special offers ■ sales promotion – there may be little additional support for the product if the intention is to withdraw it

Table 19.3 How promotional strategies may vary over the life cycle of a product

ACTIVITY 19.7

Nescafé's Hot When You Want

Nestlé invested at least $10 million in its Nescafé Original Hot When You Want self-heating coffee brand when it was launched. Nestlé believed this was the biggest technological innovation in the sector since the development of instant coffee more than 60 years ago. Nescafé's advertising agency was responsible for a $7 million campaign that included launching Hot When You Want on TV. It also promoted the brand below the line and on the Internet. Hot When You Want, which costs $1.19 for a 210 ml can was test marketed in one region before a national launch.

The packaging of the product was crucial. It had to be attractive and appealing to consumers and give details of contents and how the heating system worked. A button on the can's base is pressed and the can turned upside down. After the can is shaken, drinking temperature is reached in three minutes. 'Nescafé aims to deliver great-quality coffee, accessible to consumers, whenever and wherever they want it,' said the Nestlé beverage division managing director. 'Consumer reaction to Hot When You Want has been phenomenally positive and stockists are delighted to see a refreshing new category being developed by a brand leader.' The launch of Hot When You Want follows the recent introduction of Nescafé Ice, which targeted 16- to 24-year-olds.

Hot When You Want – the biggest innovation since instant coffee?

[20 marks, 30 minutes]

1 Suggest another name for this product that you think would be popular in your country. [2]

2 Outline **two** ways in which below-the-line activities might be used to support the launch of this product. [4]

3 Explain why the packaging of this product is likely to be an important factor determining its success. [6]

4 Evaluate the most important factors, apart from packaging, that might determine the sales success of this product. [8]

Packaging

The quality, design and colour of materials used in packaging of products can have a very supportive role to play in the promotion of a product. Packaging can perform the following functions:

- protect and contain the product
- give information, depending on the product, to consumers about contents, ingredients, cooking instructions, assembly instructions and so on
- support the image of the product created by other aspects of promotion
- aid the recognition of the product by the consumer.

Cheap and nasty packaging of goods such as clothes or chocolates will destroy any quality and status image that the firm is attempting to establish. Distinctive packaging can help to form the basis of a promotional theme, which will endure as long as the product – the bright red of Coca-Cola cans is a feature of advertisements for the product, while Pepsi is instantly recognisable with blue cans.

In contrast, expensive and wasteful packaging may add unnecessarily to costs that could reduce a product's competitiveness. In addition, with increasing environmental pressures, packaging that is seen to be too ostentatious or wasteful may spark off a negative consumer reaction. For this reason, the use of recycled and recyclable materials in packaging is increasing. Some packaging advances can revolutionise the sale and promotion of products. Wine is now sold in cans and plastic-coated boxes in addition to bottles. Tetra Brik (a registered trademark) boxes have given milk and fruit-juice manufacturers many new marketing and sales opportunities. As with all other aspects of marketing, packaging decisions need to be blended in with the overall objectives of the business for the product in question.

Why are 'place' decisions an important part of the marketing mix?

'Place' decisions are concerned with how products should pass from manufacturer to the final customer. Several different '**channels of distribution**' are available for firms to use.

KEY TERM

Channel of distribution: this refers to the chain of intermediaries a product passes through from producer to final consumer.

Here are some reasons why the distribution channel choice is important:

- Consumers may need easy access to a firm's products to allow them to try them and see them before they buy, to make purchasing easy and to allow, if necessary, for the return of goods.
- Manufacturers need outlets for their products that give as wide market coverage as possible, but with the desired image of the product appropriately promoted.
- Retailers – firms that sell goods to the final consumer – will sell producers' goods but will demand a mark-up to cover their costs and make a profit, so, if price is very important, using few or no intermediaries would be an advantage.

Concept of distribution

'Getting the right product to the right consumer at the right time in a way that is most convenient to the consumer' is a good definition of distribution. Any business, whether it produces goods or provides services, needs to establish a distribution strategy that will define how it is going to move products from the point of creation to points of consumption in an efficient and low-cost manner so that it is convenient for the consumer to buy. The term 'supply chain' is often used to refer to all businesses involved in getting products to the final consumer – the producer and manufacturer, wholesalers, transporters and retailers.

Customer service as objective of distribution

The main purpose of distribution is not necessarily to aim for lowest cost. A farmer could decide to sell his products only to consumers who visit his farm and not to transport goods to retail outlets. This would be cheapest for the farmer – but would it be convenient for many potential consumers? Probably not, as many busy consumers expect home delivery or access to food products through local shops. A computer manufacturer may decide to only sell its products via the Internet and not to shops or other outlets. Again, this might be cheapest for the manufacturer, but how good is the service being offered to customers – especially those without a computer to access the Internet?

Cost must be a factor in the distribution strategy used by any business, but it should not be the primary one. Customer service is the key objective of distribution. Goods and services should be available to customers as and when they choose to purchase them – not at the convenience of the producer. Later in this chapter, the different distribution channels will be analysed for their potential to provide good customer service.

Today's customers are starting to shop very differently from how they did in the past. They increasingly have access to high-quality information via the Internet and this has given them more information about competitors, has increased their price sensitivity and – crucially for the distribution strategy – has given them the ability to purchase online. This trend is not confined to consumer markets. More business-to-business transactions (B2B, as it is sometime referred to) are now being conducted via the Internet, bypassing the traditional distribution channels.

Channel strategy

In deciding on an appropriate channel strategy, a business must answer questions such as:

- Should the product be sold directly to consumers?
- Should the product be sold through retailers?
- How long should the channel be (how many intermediaries)?
- Where should the product be made available?
- Should the Internet be the main channel?
- How much will it cost to keep the stock of products on store shelves and in warehouses?
- How much control does the business want to have over the marketing mix?
- How will the distribution channel selected support the other components of the marketing mix?

The channel strategy must be integrated with the marketing objectives of the business. For example, if the aim is to secure a niche market with a high-quality image product (e.g. branded cosmetics), then selling it through street vendors will not achieve this objective. If, however, the marketing aim is to achieve maximum sales and distribution coverage (e.g. sweets), then selling through a few carefully selected and exclusive food retailers will not be successful.

As with all components of the marketing mix, distribution channel strategy must be clearly linked to marketing objectives and to the other components of the mix for an effective and convincing overall marketing strategy to be developed.

TOP TIP

Do not confuse 'place' or 'distribution' decisions with transportation methods. Place is about how and where the product is to be sold to a customer – transportation is about how the product is to be physically delivered.

Channels of distribution

The most commonly used channels of distribution are shown in Figures 19.2 to 19.4 and the advantages and disadvantages summarised in Table 19.4. Figure 19.2 shows the direct route, sometimes known as direct selling or direct marketing. The growth of the internet has led to a rapid rise in the popularity of this channel of distribution. When the manufacturer wishes to keep complete control over the marketing strategy, then direct routes are more likely to be used – or the producer may even establish their own retail stores. Direct routes are also more likely to be used when the goods are bought infrequently but in large quantity, when they are bulky and expensive to transport or when they have been purpose-built for a particular customer.

With the increasing size of many modern retailers, the 'single intermediary channel' depicted in Figure 19.3 is becoming more common. These huge retailers have great purchasing power. They are able to arrange their own storage and distribution systems to individual stores.

In Figure 19.4 the traditional two-intermediary channel is shown. Until recent developments in retailing and the internet, it was the most common of all channels of distribution.

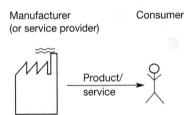

Figure 19.2 Direct selling to consumer

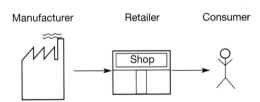

Figure 19.3 Single-intermediary channel

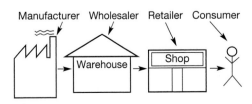

Figure 19.4 Two-intermediaries channel

Type and main features	Examples of products or services	Possible benefits	Possible drawbacks
1 Direct selling: no intermediaries. Can be referred to as 'zero-intermediary' channel.	■ mail order from manufacturer ■ airline tickets and hotel accommodation sold over the internet by the service providers ■ farmers' markets – selling produce directly to consumers	■ no intermediaries, so no mark-up or profit margin taken by other businesses ■ producer has complete control over the marketing mix – how the product is sold, promoted and priced to consumers ■ quicker than other channels ■ may lead to fresher food products ■ direct contact with consumers offers useful market research	■ all storage and stock costs have to be paid for by producer ■ no retail outlets limits the chances for consumers to see and try before they buy ■ may not be convenient for consumer ■ no advertising or promotion paid for by intermediaries and no after-sales service offered by shops ■ can be expensive to deliver each item sold to consumers
2 One-intermediary channel. Usually used for consumer goods but could also be an agent for selling industrial products to businesses.	■ holiday companies selling holidays via travel agents ■ large supermarkets that hold their own stocks rather than using wholesalers ■ where the whole country can be reached using the one-level route, e.g. a small country	■ retailer holds stocks and pays for cost of this ■ retailer has product displays and offers after-sales service ■ retailers often in locations that are convenient to consumers ■ producers can focus on production – not on selling the products to consumers	■ intermediary takes a profit mark-up and this could make the product more expensive to final consumers ■ producers lose some control over marketing mix ■ retailers may sell products from competitors too, so there is no exclusive outlet ■ producer has delivery costs to retailer
3 Two-intermediaries channel. Wholesaler buys goods from producer and sells to retailer.	■ in a large country with great distances to each retailer – many consumer goods are distributed this way, e.g. soft drinks, electrical goods and books	■ wholesaler holds goods and buys in bulk from producer ■ reduces stock-holding costs of producer ■ wholesaler pays for transport costs to retailer ■ wholesaler 'breaks bulk' by buying in large quantities and selling to retailers in small quantities ■ may be the best way to enter foreign markets where producer has no direct contact with retailers	■ another intermediary takes a profit mark-up – may make final good more expensive to consumer ■ producer loses further control over marketing mix ■ slows down the distribution chain

Table 19.4 The main benefits and potential limitations of distribution channels

Factors influencing choice of distribution channel include:

■ Industrial products tend to be sold more directly, with fewer intermediaries than consumer goods.
■ Geographical dispersion of the target market. If the target market is large but widely dispersed throughout the country, then the use of intermediaries is more likely.

■ Level of service expected by consumers, e.g. after-sales servicing of a car, means that internet selling is not appropriate for most manufacturers.
■ Technical complexity of the product, e.g. business computers are sold directly as they require a great deal of technical know-how among the sales staff and a supporting service team.
■ Unit value of the product – it may be worth employing sales staff to sell directly to individual customers if the unit

cost of, for example, a luxury yacht is $5 million, but not worthwhile if items of jewellery are being sold for $5.

- Number of potential customers. If the number of potential customers is few, as with commercial aircraft, direct selling might be used, but Nike or Reebok – with their millions of customers for sports shoes worldwide – would use intermediate channels to distribute their products.

Recent trends in distribution channels in recent years include:

- Increased use of the Internet – often via mobiles and tablets – for direct selling of goods and services. In the service sector this can be seen with internet banking and direct selling of insurance policies online.
- Large supermarket chains perform the function of wholesalers as well as retailers, holding stocks in their own warehouses. By owning another link in the distribution chain, the business is engaging in 'vertical marketing'. Another example of this form of integration is Sony owning its own shops. The use of franchises to sell the producers' goods (e.g. McDonald's hamburgers and Benetton clothes) is another example of vertical marketing.
- Some businesses are increasingly using a variety of different channels, e.g. an ice cream manufacturer may have their own ice cream vans to sell directly as well as supplying retailers. Hotels may sell room accommodation directly as well as through travel agents and holiday companies.
- Increasing integration of services where a complete package is sold to consumers, e.g. air flights, car hire and hotel accommodation all sold or distributed to consumers at the same time.

The Internet and the 4Cs

It is not an exaggeration to state that the Internet is transforming the ways in which businesses market their products and manage relationships with customers.

KEY TERMS

Internet (online) marketing: refers to advertising and marketing activities that use the Internet, email and mobile communications to encourage direct sales via electronic commerce.

E-commerce: the buying and selling of goods and services by businesses and consumers through an electronic medium.

Marketing over the Internet can involve several different marketing functions which impact on the 4Cs:

- Selling of goods directly to consumers (B2C) or other businesses (B2B) as orders are placed online through the company website or through an online retailer such as Amazon. This is known as **e-commerce** (convenience).
- Online and mobile advertising by using the company's own website, by placing a banner advert or 'pop-up' on another firm's website and by using social media. Adverts can

be targeted at potential consumers and can lead to viral marketing – see below (communication).

- Sales contacts are established by visitors to a site leaving their details and then the company emails them or calls on them to attempt to make a sale (communication).
- Collecting market research data by encouraging visitors to the website to answer questions that can provide important consumer data to aid the development of new products (customer solution).
- Dynamic pricing – using online data about consumers to charge different prices to different consumers over the internet, often these prices are much lower than those charged by traditional retailers (cost to customer).

ACTIVITY 19.8

A Coca-Cola tap in every house?

Coca-Cola has considered channelling Coke through taps in customers' homes. The business created a system, fitted inside a customer's house, to mix carbonated water with Coke's secret syrup and pipe it around houses. The company does not see Pepsi as its only main competitor and a former chief executive stated that he would only be happy if customers turned on taps in their homes to drink Coke rather than water. The syrup could be sold directly by Coca-Cola over the Internet as a concentrate in sealed containers.

'You would have water mixing automatically with the concentrate and then when you turn on your tap you have Coke at home. There's a lot more to it than that to ensure quality and it has to be a sealed unit so people can't alter the syrup formula to destroy the value of the brand,' the company said. Cafés and branches of McDonald's have stored the Coca Cola syrup and produced Coke on the spot for years. This idea could be taken a step further when the time is right. 'There's not a market yet,' the former chief executive said. 'People still like to physically go and buy things, but one day, yes, this will be a reality.'

[25 marks, 35 minutes]

1. Explain the importance of the Coca-Cola brand name to the company. [6]
2. This is an example of direct selling from the manufacturer to the consumer. Discuss the advantages and disadvantages of this channel of distributing Coca-Cola from the point of view of both the company and consumers. [10]
3. Outline **three** other methods Coca-Cola could use to 'place' or distribute their product to more consumers more often. [9]

Viral marketing

This is a recent marketing phenomenon that facilitates and encourages people to pass on a marketing message to others. Viral promotions can be in the form of video clips, interactive flash games, e-books and text messages. It is claimed that a customer will tell an average of three people about a product or service they liked and 11 people about a product or service that they did not like. **Viral marketing** is based on this form of communication. Marketing managers try to identify individuals with high social-networking potential – called 'influencers' – and create viral messages that appeal to them and have a high chance of being passed on to many people who may be impressed that the 'influencer' has contacted them about the product.

KEY TERM

Viral marketing: the use of social media sites or text messages to increase brand awareness or sell products.

KEY CONCEPT LINK

Increasingly customers are expecting businesses to communicate with them via social media. By responding to their expectations, **management** would be 'customer-focused'.

Business impact of Internet marketing

Internet marketing has had a huge impact on several industries that used to be entirely focused on retail stores to sell their products. These include music, film, banking, insurance, travel and tourism. The relative decline of the importance of traditional retail stores has been rapid. Apple's iTunes online store is now the largest seller of music in the USA. Of individuals who have a bank account in the UK, more than 40% use only the internet for their transactions. Internet auctions have grown in popularity. Specialised e-stores sell items ranging from antiques to old movie posters. Increasingly, potential consumers are using eBay and other sites to make price comparisons before making a purchase (see Table 19.5). It is certain that online developments will continue to transfer customer relationship management.

Evaluation of promotion and place decisions

The importance of the final two ingredients of the marketing mix should not be underestimated. Promotion supports and helps to create the image of the product intended by its design and specification. It informs and persuades consumers. The rapid growth of promotion spending in all market-driven economies in recent years suggests that successful campaigns can make a difference to sales and market share. Promotion may be closely linked to place too. The increasing use of electronic means of communication and direct marketing is allowing firms to both promote and sell products online. Ease of access to products is essential if consumers are to be attracted to buying them – especially items that are bought regularly and in small quantities. The constant search for cost savings has made many manufacturers question the wisdom of using intermediaries in distribution. The fact

Benefits	Limitations
■ It is relatively inexpensive when compared to the ratio of cost and the number of potential consumers reached. ■ Companies can reach a worldwide audience for a small proportion of traditional promotion budgets. ■ Consumers interact with the websites and make purchases and leave important data about themselves. ■ The Internet is convenient for consumers to use – if they have access to a computer. ■ Accurate records can be kept on the number of clicks or visitors and the success rate of different web promotions can be quickly measured. ■ Computer ownership and usage are increasing in all countries of the world. ■ Selling products on the Internet involves lower fixed costs than traditional retail stores. ■ Dynamic pricing – charging different prices to different consumers – is easier.	■ Some countries have low-speed Internet connections and in poorer countries, computer ownership is not widespread. ■ Consumers cannot touch, smell, feel or try on tangible goods before buying – this may limit their willingness to buy certain products online. ■ Product returns may increase if consumers are dissatisfied with their purchases once they have been received. ■ The cost and unreliability of postal services in some countries may reduce the cost advantage of Internet selling. ■ The website must be kept up-to-date and user-friendly – good websites can be expensive to develop. ■ Worries about Internet security – e.g. consumers may wonder who will use information about them or their credit card details – may reduce future growth potential.

Table 19.5 Benefits and limitations of internet marketing and e-commerce

Marketing Nikon

Nikon wanted to do something a little different during Warner Music Group's SXSW Music Festival in 2013. So rather than just record all of the great musical performances, the company put the camera into the hands of their fans. Selected fans – potential influencers – were given Wi-Fi-enabled cameras to record and take photos of the big three-day musical extravaganza, and instantly share them via social media. Music lovers who attend SXSW tend to be ahead of the curve when it comes to music and tech, so they were the perfect influencers to spread awareness of Nikon's great new camera. The live streams of the concerts that Nikon uploaded as part of the campaign were watched for 11 minutes on average – far surpassing the industry average of just two minutes.

The campaign resulted in more than 166 million social impressions, thanks in large part to the tweeted photos and videos from concert-goers. Part of the social media goodwill generated for Nikon during SXSW was no doubt because they took a risk and put their new cameras – and their brand's reputation – in the hands of their fans.

The 'I AM Nikon' ad campaign was launched in 2010 in order to achieve the marketing objective of improving market positioning in the compact segment for Nikon. This brand is often associated with professional photographers. In order to convey a more accessible, more attractive image, instead of the brand talking about itself, this ad campaign was launched with the concept of Nikon camera customers speaking from their perspective. Through this campaign, brand awareness in 12 European countries increased dramatically with a 37% rise in Germany alone.

The marketing strategy was based around the idea that the photos you take tell a powerful story about the character that you want to project; to make this more powerful, the strategy tapped into youth's obsession with celebrity.

Supermarket distribution and point of sale displays were essential to achieving a successful sales increase, so Nikon's marketing agency created a partnership between *Hollyoaks* characters (a popular TV show in the UK), the supermarket chain Asda and Nikon. Buyers of *Hollyoaks*-branded cameras distributed in Asda could win an acting part in the Channel 4 show. Sales of the cameras through Asda increased by 332% over the course of the campaign.

Nikon camera – promotion through social media is increasingly important

[34 marks, 50 minutes]

1 Analyse the benefits to Nikon of using social media to promote its products. **[10]**

2 Evaluate the likely importance of supermarkets as channels of distribution for Nikon's products. **[12]**

3 Assume that a new Nikon camera, aimed at young consumers, is launched in your own country. Recommend to Nikon how the Internet should be used to market and sell this product. **[12]**

that traditional shopping will continue in its present form for many years for most products will ensure that these intermediaries continue to perform essential functions – particularly for those consumers who lack mobility or IT facilities.

An integrated marketing mix

- If an expensive, well-known brand of perfume was for sale on a *market stall*, would you be suspicious?
- If the most exclusive shop in your town sold expensive gifts and *wrapped them in newspaper*, would you be surprised?
- If a cheap range of children's clothing was advertised in a *glossy colour magazine aimed at professional women*, would this advert lead to many sales?

KEY TERM

Integrated marketing mix: the key marketing decisions complement each other and work together to give customers a consistent message about the product.

These are all examples of poorly integrated marketing decisions. Hopefully, you agree that the part of the marketing strategy in italics stands out as being inappropriate and lacks integration with the rest of the marketing mix. Why does this matter? The impact a product has on consumers is explained by human psychology – as complex beings we are influenced by a

ACTIVITY 19.10

E-commerce on the increase

Online retailing in the UK increased by 22% in 2013 compared with high-street sales growth of 1.8% according to industry analyst Verdict Research. 'E-tailing' now accounts for almost 10% of total retail spending. Verdict forecasts that by 2016 this share will increase to 14%. Consumers were surveyed and 74% of them believed the Internet meant cheaper goods, and 67% agreed that it is better for comparing prices. The decisions of Dixons, a major retailer of electrical products in the UK under the Dixons and Currys brand names, are typical of the changes that e-commerce are forcing on many businesses.

Dixons decided to:

- close many of its high-street stores
- rebrand those remaining into 'Currys.digital'
- move the Dixons brand completely online.

The strategy cost £7 million, but was expected to increase sales as well as reduce annual costs by £3 million. 'I am very excited about the prospects for the Dixons brand as a pure e-tailer,' said the chief executive of Dixons. 'Consumer buying behaviours are developing with the growth in broadband and tablet usage.'

E-commerce is now an indispensable part of the fashion industry too. Online retailer www.asos.com receives more than 1.7 million searches on its site each month and is the most visible fashion retailer online. Another site, Net-a-Porter, has partnered with fashion label Halston. It displayed one particular dress that sold out in 45 minutes after its launch. Burberry uses digital and mobile technology to live stream its new collections via Twitter and Facebook allows users to make instant purchases from its website. There is also potential for young new designers keen to enter the industry to show off their styles to a huge online audience. However, when consumer spending started to fall during the recession in 2009/2010, online traders reported lower 'conversion rates' (online shoppers actually buying). Tesco withdrew its clothing ranges from Tesco Direct after its initial claim of 'selling online will enable us to reach a greater number of customers eager to buy items from our collections' seemed not to be supported by sales figures.

There are also familiar customer complaints about difficult-to-use sites, delays in postal deliveries and 'it was not as it seemed on screen', so perhaps high-street shops are not doomed after all. 'The high-street will not die,' said a director of Verdict Research. 'Internet retailing is certainly set to become more significant, but shopping is a tactile process and for many people it is a leisure activity – e-tailing does not provide those two things.'

[29 marks, 45 minutes]

1 Outline **three** reasons for the recent growth in online retailing. [9]

2 Evaluate the potential advantages and disadvantages to an electrical and computer retailer such as Dixons of going exclusively online. [10]

3 Do you agree that 'the high street will never die' or do you believe that e-commerce will eventually replace all traditional shopping? Explain your answer. [10]

range of different messages before we decide on taking an action, such as buying a product.

- If the messages we are receiving about a product appear to be confused or lacking in focus, then we often fail to identify the true identity or 'personality' of the product.
- If the product looks cheap but is highly priced, are we being ripped off – or is quality more than skin deep?
- If the product looks expensive but is priced cheaply, are we about to buy the bargain of a lifetime – or are appearances deceptive and the product is actually of very low quality?

Confused consumers will steer clear of the product and this will result in lower long-term sales than if a clear and unambiguous message about the product is relayed through all aspects of the mix – although everyone can be misled once.

The best-laid marketing plans can be destroyed by just one part of the marketing mix not being consistent or working with the rest. The most effective marketing-mix decisions will, therefore, be:

- based on marketing objectives and affordable within the marketing budget
- integrated and consistent with each other and targeted at the appropriate consumers.

TOP TIP

You may be asked to recommend and evaluate a marketing strategy for a product. As with actual businesses, the best results come to those who suggest a fully integrated marketing mix, clearly aimed at achieving a set marketing objective.

ACTIVITY 19.11

What went wrong?

Here are examples of four marketing-mix decisions:

	Product	Price	Place	Promotion
Mix A	fast sports car	high – based on top-range competitors' prices	exclusive dealers in impressive city showrooms	advertised on radio only
Mix B	range of furniture for families with low incomes	low – low costs allow prices to be set below those of competitors	sold only over the Internet	advertised on posters and in free local newspapers
Mix C	ladies' fashion hairdressing salon with cutting by well-known hairstylists	low-price offers to large family groups	salon located in one of the richest parts of the city	colour fashion and beauty magazines
Mix D	fast-food restaurant	skimming price strategy	expensive business-district location with many top-class restaurants	advertised in business magazines, loyalty card scheme operated together with quality retail department stores

[20 marks, 25 minutes]

1 In each case, identify which marketing mix decision seems to be 'out of place' and not integrated with the other decisions. **[4]**

2 In each case, recommend a change to **one** of the marketing decisions to create an integrated mix. Explain and justify your recommendations. **[16]**

SUMMARY POINTS

- Communication with consumers is the key role of promotion.
- There are different forms of promotion – advertising and sales promotion are two of the most widely used types.
- Promotional objectives should be clear before a campaign starts – increasing sales of existing products is only one of these.
- Advertising has both an informative and a persuasive role, but the distinction between the two is often blurred.
- The value of promotional spending should be assessed – this expenditure needs to be constantly monitored for effectiveness in terms of meeting the original targets set for it.
- Packaging is a very important aspect of the product's image generated by promotion.
- It is important to integrate the promotional mix with the overall marketing strategy or confusing signals will be communicated to consumers.
- 'Place' is about how consumers gain access to a firm's products – direct selling has increased with the internet.
- Wholesalers and retailers can perform important functions but e-commerce is having an impact on both of these 'intermediaries'.
- Internet marketing – e-commerce – is growing rapidly and it is likely to continue to transform the management of customer relations for most businesses.

RESEARCH TASK

Collect **six** newspaper or magazine advertisements for one type of product that interests you, for example sports clothing, cars, perfume, chocolate.

- Classify them according to whether you consider them to be either mainly informative or persuasive adverts – you might need a category for ones that you are unsure of because they seem to do both things.
- Explain in a brief report which of the adverts had the most positive effect on you and which had the least positive effect. Try to analyse why – in a way that would help a marketing manager to plan future adverts.
- Compare the promotional mix of **two** large stores in your area. Consider advertising, sales promotion, own-branded goods and public relations. Analyse the differences between the two promotional mixes and suggest how effective they might be in attracting customers to the stores.

AS Level exam practice questions
Short answer questions

[70 marks, 80 minutes]

Knowledge and understanding

1 Explain the differences between advertising and sales promotion. [2]
2 State **three** reasons why a business might advertise an existing product. [3]
3 Why is it important to measure the impact on sales following an advertising campaign? [3]
4 Outline **three** reasons why spending more money on advertising might fail to increase sales to the expected level. [6]
5 Why is it that branded goods are often sold at higher prices than similar non-branded goods? [3]
6 Explain why it is important to assess whether a promotional campaign has achieved its objectives or not. [4]
7 State **three** methods, other than an increase in sales, that a business might use to assess the effectiveness of a promotional campaign. [3]
8 How can promotion be used to extend a product's life cycle? [3]
9 For which products might point-of-sale displays be a useful form of promotion? [3]
10 Why is packaging an important aspect of promotion for many consumer products? [3]
11 What is meant by public relations and why is this important to a business? [3]
12 Explain the term 'direct marketing'. [2]
13 Outline two functions performed by wholesalers in a traditional channel of communication. [4]

Application

14 Explain **two** reasons why a small specialist clothing manufacturer might decide not to market online. [4]
15 In 2013 VW had to recall more than two million cars owing to a fault in manufacture. Explain **two** ways in which VW could attempt to restore its brand image of quality. [6]
16 Explain **two** ways in which the Internet has changed the marketing of recorded music. [6]
17 State **two** channels of distribution that could be used by a manufacturer of mountain bikes. Compare the advantages to the business and consumers of these two channels. [6]
18 Explain how a sports-shoe manufacturer might use both above- and below-the-line promotion to support the launch of a new product. [6]

Data response

1 Promoting golf equipment

Penang Golf Kit Ltd (PGK) produces golfing equipment. The product range includes clubs, bags, golfing shoes and clothing. Sales have grown steadily in recent years, but market share has remained constant. PGK's products are well-known for their quality and relatively high prices. Promotion is based around sponsorship of one major championship each year, which is widely televised. A limited amount of advertising is paid for in the country's best-known golfing magazine. PGK has recently started designing a new range of golfing equipment and clothing aimed at the youth market (under 21 years). The numbers of young people playing golf has increased by 50% over the past ten years compared to an overall growth of 20% in the total number of players. PGK's directors have yet to decide how this new range of goods should be promoted. A total marketing budget of $1 million has been allocated for this purpose. The aim is to maintain the image of the brand name with these new products. The following data have been gathered – use them to advise the firm on an appropriate promotional strategy.

- **TV advertising** – $0.5 million is the minimum promotion budget required for buying TV time. This purchases five minutes of TV time in 10–30-second slots. Two times are suggested:
  - During the interval of the Saturday evening football match on TV. The audience is forecast to be five million – 25% of whom are likely to be under 21. The average income of viewers is around $10,000 per year.
  - Friday evenings after a popular sports quiz show. Audience figure suggest an average number of six million viewers, 25% under 21. The average income of viewers is around $8,000.

The cost of producing the advertisement for TV will be a further $400,000.

- **National newspaper advertising** – A popular paper will give ten full-page adverts for $0.5 million. This paper has a circulation of two million and, on average, three people read each edition. Another paper, usually bought by high-income groups, offers six pages for the same price. The readership is one million but four people on average read each copy of this paper. The cost of producing a newspaper advert will be $20,000, but a colour magazine advert will cost $50,000.

- **Sponsorship** – Sponsoring one of the country's best young golfers, Tim Lui. He is very popular with young golfers. Tim's agent is looking for $300,000 of sponsorship for each of the next three years. He claims that this would give PGK much additional publicity on TV, social media and newspapers.

[30 marks, 45 minutes]

1 a Define the term 'promotion'. [2]

 b Briefly explain the term 'sponsorship'. [3]

2 Explain **two** ways in which PGK's directors could have decided on the size of the total marketing budget of $1 million. [6]

3 Analyse why increased promotion might not lead to increased market share for PGK. [8]

4 Using all of the data and any other information you have, prepare a fully supported recommendation to the marketing manager concerning the promotional mix that could be adopted for this range of products. [11]

2 Apple opens more of its own stores

Apple has announced plans to open more of its own branded stores in the USA and China. Just a few years ago, the Silicon Valley company, famous for the first popular personal computer in the 1970s and more recently the iPad, always relied on other retailers and its website as channels of communication to sell its ever-growing range of products. The new retail stores are likely to be well-received by consumers if recent reports from London and New York are any guide. The recent launch of the new iPad 4 led to huge queues forming outside these stores as the craze for this company's state-of-the-art products seems to show no signs of weakening.

Some business analysts believe that Apple runs a real risk of coming into conflict with its existing retail partners – including the US chain CompUSA. 'Why should other retail stores bother to sell and promote Apple products if the company is going to compete directly with them on the high street?' said one investment specialist. There are also fears that Apple could fall into the same trap as Gateway, another computer maker focused on the consumer market.

Gateway had to close about 40% of its North American stores, saying it had overextended itself at a time of slowing sales of PCs. Most of its sales are now over the Internet. Apple is investing heavily in property and there is always the risk of inventory build-up at a time of slower world economic growth.

Apple plans to open its two new stores in high-profile shopping centres near Las Vegas in the USA and in the Chaoyang district of China. The company believes that the new retail operations would break even in the run-up to Christmas and would break even next year. Apart from selling the usual Apple products, the main draw in the shops will be the Genius Bar – a counter where shoppers will find several highly trained Mac 'Geniuses' ready to advise on any technical questions. There will be a hands-on Apple Retail Store Experience giving consumers the chance to test-drive Apple's entire product line-up. The stores will also run a series of daily creative workshops to teach customers how to make the most of the programs available.

[30 marks, 45 minutes]

1 a Define the terms 'channels of distribution'. [2]
   b Briefly explain the term 'consumer market'. [3]
2 Explain **two** benefits to consumers of electronic products of being able to purchase these over the internet. [6]
3 Analyse ways in which Apple might promote the opening of its new stores. [8]

4 Evaluate the decision by Apple to open more of its own retail stores – analysing the advantages and disadvantages of a manufacturer operating its own shops. [11]

3 A promotion budget for T and T Clothing

The new marketing strategy had finally been agreed at T and T Clothing, but there was now an argument over the level of the marketing budget. Joe, the owner, said: 'We spent $15,000 last year, inflation is 10%, so I propose that we increase the budget at the same rate.' Imran, the finance director, was not keen to see an increase such as this without it being explained or justified. He wanted to see the annual budget set at 5% of sales revenue achieved in the previous year. Last year sales had totalled $250,000. Raquel, the marketing director, was concerned that neither of these figures made any attempt to relate the

budget to the new marketing objective – breaking into a new market segment with a market share of around 3% by the end of the first year. 'I have estimated that our two closest competitors in this segment spent $30,000 and $38,500 respectively last year. They probably plan a 5% increase this year. We ought to aim to spend at least an average of these two sums if we are to be competitive.' Joe was beginning to regret the marketing changes that were now in place in his business. He had never been one for spending much on marketing, always preferring to, as he put it, 'let the products do the talking for us'.

[30 marks, 45 minutes]

1 a Define the term 'marketing budget'. [2]
   b Briefly explain the term 'marketing objective'. [3]
2 Calculate this year's marketing expenditure budget based on all three proposed methods. [6]
3 Analyse how a business such as T and T Clothing can try to assess the value of its promotion expenditure. [8]

4 Considering all of the evidence in this activity and this chapter, make a justified recommendation to the board of T and T Clothing regarding the budget-setting method that you consider to be most appropriate in this case. [11]

AS Level essay questions

[20 marks, 40 minutes each]

1 a Explain the differences between advertising and sales promotion. [8]
   b Discuss how a marketing department could determine whether 'half of our promotional spending is wasted'. [12]
2 a Analyse the benefits to a large retail store selling fashion clothing of using e-commerce. [8]
   b 'The "promotion" decision is the most important part of the marketing mix for a car manufacturer.' To what extent do you agree with this statement? [12]

20 Marketing planning

This chapter covers syllabus A Level 3.5.

On completing this chapter, you will be able to:

- analyse the content of a marketing plan
- assess the usefulness of marketing planning
- link the marketing plan to a coordinated marketing mix
- evaluate the importance of new product development and research and development
- assess the usefulness of sales forecasting and analyse sales data by the moving-average method.

Introducing the topic

PLANNING FOR THE IPHONE PAYS OFF

Apple's mission is to lead the industry in innovative products. Its constant search for USPs paid off with the original iPhone. It was the first mobile device to have a touchscreen. Not only did it offer more than any other mobile (cell) phone, the marketing of the iPhone was so well planned that it met all of its marketing objectives.

After assessing market trends and rival products in 2007, Apple's senior management told the research department to develop the most advanced mobile phone on the market. Once the iPhone was successfully created and produced with a range of advanced features, clear marketing objectives were set for it:

- 2% market share in USA and UK in first year after launch (445,000 sales)
- 10% market share in second year after launch
- 50% market share three years after launch.

The overall marketing strategy was to differentiate the iPhone from other mobile phones and aim at the primary target market of the upper-middle-class professional. Pricing was premium penetration for the first few months – and then lowered to establish quick market dominance. Promotion was extensive – the Apple website, Apple shop displays and product demonstrations all concentrated on attracting consumers to the product's key features. A multimillion-dollar advertising budget was used to pay for TV and upmarket printed media. Constant market research was undertaken to make sure the strategy was getting through to the target market. All marketing objectives were met – Apple had succeeded in establishing itself as the world's leading maker of smartphones.

It did not stop there, of course. Constant product improvements have been announced – in late 2013 the iPhone 5 and 5C were released to an eager market. The cheaper version – the 5C – was aimed at the expanding markets in developing countries and among younger customers.

Apple revealed that revenue jumped 4% to US$37.5 billion in the three months to September 2013 spurred by sales of almost 34 million iPhone 5s, a new record for the smartphone range. Apple's iPad sales in the same period totalled 14.1 million. The company unveiled new tablets in 2013 including the latest version of the iPad Mini as it looks to maintain its share of the growing tablet category amid mounting competition from cheaper alternatives. The tech giant said the updates to its product line-up would make it an 'iPad Year'.

Points to think about:

- Explain how careful planning helped the original iPhone to meet all of its marketing objectives.
- How important is it for Apple to develop new products regularly?
- To what extent is the marketing mix for Apple products, such as the iPad and iPhone 5, fully 'integrated'?

iPhone 5

Introduction

It should be clear by now that marketing is not about taking separate and unplanned decisions on product, price, promotion and place. Each of these must fit together with:

- marketing objectives
- marketing budget
- each other to create an integrated marketing mix.

In addition, market research should have been undertaken and a time limit for objectives to be met clearly communicated to the marketing department. This complete process is referred to as marketing planning.

Marketing plan

The key contents of a typical marketing plan are:

- purpose of the plan and the 'mission' of the business
- where the firm is now – situational analysis
- where it aims to get to, in marketing terms – marketing objectives and how it plans to achieve these targets – marketing strategy
- turning the strategy into the appropriate marketing tactics to be followed – the marketing mix
- the budget required to implement the plan effectively
- executive summary and a time frame for implementation of the plan.

KEY TERM

Marketing plan: a detailed, fully researched written report on marketing objectives and the marketing strategy to be used to achieve them.

Purpose and mission

The first part of the plan is to provide the reader with the necessary information to understand the purpose of it – is it part of a new business proposal or is it to prepare the business for the launch of a new product?

Background information about the business – including its mission statement – will be particularly important if the audience for the plan is not familiar with the company, for example potential financial investors.

Situational analysis

Essentially, this part of the plan answers the question 'Where are we now?' Look at it like this. Assume you are driving a car in a city and you are looking for a particular address (your objective). You have a map to help you (your plan), but unless you know where you are at present on the map (situational analysis), you will not be able to direct yourself towards your goal. So it is with marketing plans. To take a business forward with new marketing strategies, it is important to know its current strengths, existing product range and market shares, existing and potential competitors, consumer tastes and trends, the state of the market the business operates in and the external problems and opportunities.

This part of the marketing plan is very important and can be time-consuming. It will require extensive market research and detailed analysis of quantitative data. If the business is being established or if it is entering new markets, then the data might be quite difficult to obtain.

If situational analysis is not undertaken, then the rest of the plan can be completely misdirected, either by aiming to reach inappropriate objectives or by using outdated strategies. For example, if Apple did not recognise the potential entry of new competitors in the music-download market, then the company could fail to continuously update and relaunch different versions of its iPod player.

Situational analysis should cover five main areas:

1 Current product analysis – clearly, not needed for new businesses.
2 Target market analysis – important features of consumer profiles, establishing whether it is a mass or segmented market, finding out consumers' perceptions to the company's existing products.
3 Competitor analysis – identifying the main competitors, the strengths and weaknesses of their marketing mix and who the likely future competitors are likely to be.
4 Economic and political environment – a PEST analysis (see Chapter 38) would be the most common way of achieving this.
5 A SWOT analysis (see Chapter 38) of the internal attributes of the business – e.g. management skills or financial strength and potential internal weaknesses – and the external environment and the opportunities and threats that it presents to the business.

Marketing objectives and strategy

Marketing objectives

This section looks at 'Where do we want to be?' All plans need targets to focus attention and to direct effort. Marketing plans are no exception to this and marketing objectives will form a key part of the plan. These targets should, ideally, be specific, measurable and time limited. For example:

- Car manufacturer: 'To take advantage of the expanding customer demand for fuel-efficient cars and to obtain 5% of the small-car market by 2015.'

Sweet manufacturer: 'To capitalise on the trend away from non-healthy food items and to capture 10% of the Asian market for health snacks and drinks by 2016.'

Marketing objectives can be expressed in terms of total sales, by value or in units, market share or sales growth rates and can also be expressed in financial terms, e.g. profitability targets of a new product range. These overall marketing objectives can then be broken down into more specific targets for each section within the marketing department. For instance, taking the sweet manufacturer's objective above, this could then be used to establish targets for:

- number of new customers attracted to the firm's products
- level of brand and advertising awareness to be achieved
- total number of new retailers signed up to sell the products
- the proportion of each market segment that the company hopes to capture.

Another important advantage of setting these clear and measurable objectives – apart from giving a sense of direction to the entire marketing department – is that final review of the company's marketing strategy can be conducted more easily. So, if by 2016, the sweet manufacturer has *not* gained 10% of the Asian market for healthy snacks and drinks, then a full review and analysis of the reasons why will have to be undertaken.

Marketing strategy

This section outlines how the company intends to achieve its marketing objectives. It does not give details of the tactical pricing and promotional decisions that will be taken – these will be in the next section. Instead, it considers the overall approach to be taken by the business. Some significant strategic decisions include:

- Should we pursue a mass-marketing approach with high market penetration, or a niche marketing strategy with more limited penetration, but higher profit margins?
- Should we sell more to the same market or find markets that the business is not currently targeting?
- Should we develop new products for existing customers or new products for new customers?

The final strategy decided upon will depend greatly on:

- the company's mission and objectives
- situational analysis, e.g. where and what competitors are doing and what the market conditions are
- the resources of the business.

Once determined, the strategic direction will then have a great impact on the tactical marketing decisions. Figure 20.1 summarises the constraints on marketing strategy.

Figure 20.1 Constraints on marketing strategy

Marketing-mix tactics

Having explained the marketing strategy, the marketing plan can now focus on the product, price, promotion and place tactics.

1 **Product:** There should be a brief summary of the existing products, and the planned changes or additions to the product range should be identified. Assuming it is a new product – such as the sweet manufacturer producing a no-sugar cereal bar – the development of the new product should be explained and the research behind it outlined. The key features and distinguishing features (perhaps a USP?) should be explained together with the branding, packaging and labelling details.

2 **Price:** The pricing decision is a complex one – and, indeed, there could be more than one pricing decision if the product is to be sold in different markets. Much information must be weighed up before taking a price decision: costs, price elasticity, competitors' prices, market conditions – these are just four issues to be considered. The plan should outline the most significant factors behind the pricing decision, which are likely to be the marketing objectives and marketing strategy. Table 20.1 shows two examples.

3 **Promotion:** The plan should explain the decisions taken on how the product will be promoted. Promotion decisions will cover four major areas: advertising, sales promotion, public relations and personal selling. Timescales for promotion activities are important as some promotions, e.g. magazine adverts, require long lead times and may need to be repeated at different stages of the product launch. The scale and type of the advertising campaign will depend on the image being created for the product, the market being targeted, the price being charged and the marketing budget available. If the sweet manufacturer plans to achieve high market share, then the cereal bar will need to be promoted in different ways from those used for an exclusive and expensive ice cream aimed at high-income consumers.

4 **Place or distribution decisions:** This tactical area lays out the distribution plan for the product. Distribution is a broad concept that includes all activities responsible for getting the product to the consumer. The plan should give details of the channels to be used, the range and number of outlets that will sell the product and how these are linked to the market segment being targeted.

299

Marketing objective	Marketing strategy	Price tactic
■ increase market share by 15%	■ mass marketing to a wide market in several countries	■ low, penetration pricing
■ maintain current prestige image with new product, but increase profit margin to 35%	■ niche marketing to carefully selected target markets	■ high, skimming pricing

Table 20.1 Linking objectives, strategy and tactics

ACTIVITY 20.1

New direction for Asian Airways

The finance director looked long and hard at the latest profit data from Asian Airways. He had to admit to his fellow directors that they did not make happy reading. The reduction in sales revenue, despite the increase in passenger numbers, was the most worrying feature. The battle being fought out between the airline and new low-cost budget airlines for economy-class passengers was resulting in declining revenue and profits. The price-cutting and extensive advertising, designed to attract back customers lost to the new operators, was leading to a serious problem for the company. The marketing director, David Da Rosa, said: 'We have always prided ourselves on being the market leader in this region for air travel. Our desire to maintain market share is now starting to cost us dearly. We could continue to cut ticket prices and run expensive promotions in the daily press – but will the extra passengers we attract actually make us any profits? I believe it is time for a change in marketing strategy – based on a new marketing objective. It is time

we targeted the profitable business customers with a clearly focused niche objective – not just try to fill seats at virtually any cost.'

'Do you mean we pull out of the economy segment altogether? That would lead to job losses and poor publicity,' remarked the operations director. 'Why not reduce prices once more to see if we can get rid of one of these new operators?'

'My new marketing plan,' said David, ' will cut back capacity by removing many economy seats from each plane and fitting new reclining seats, computer terminals and other facilities for the business traveller. With the Asian economies booming at present, there will be a steady demand for this prestige service. We will need to look at a completely new marketing strategy to target this type of traveller, though.' The other directors agreed to allow David time to develop the idea further and to come back to the board with more definite proposals and figures for projected passenger numbers.

[35 marks, 50 minutes]

1 How can Asian Airways' sales revenue be declining when passenger numbers are increasing? [2]

2 Outline what the main sections of the marketing plan proposed by David should be. [8]

3 Explain why a change is being suggested for the business's marketing objective. [4]

4 Analyse why this new objective will require changes in the marketing strategy of the business. [9]

5 Assess the factors most likely to influence the success of the marketing plan proposed by David. [12]

Overall, the marketing mix should be fully integrated to be most effective. The marketing plan will explain how the 4Ps are related and linked to each other so that consumers are not confused by the use of, for example, low prices for a high-image product promoted in exclusive magazines. The 4Ps tactics must be determined consistently and linked in with the overall marketing objective.

Marketing budget

A marketing plan without a budget is unworkable. All marketing decisions have financial implications and the plan must give details of:

■ how much is required to put the marketing strategy and tactics into effect

■ the expected sales performance of the plan, to allow a comparison between marketing expenditure and expected sales.

The plan will, therefore, lay out the spending requirements necessary to meet the plan's overall objectives. The amount to be spent on each type of advertising, market research, promotional technique and so on must be detailed with a clear month-by-month timetable.

The different approaches to arriving at an appropriate marketing budget were explained in Chapter 19 and they include:

- spending as much as competitors
- using correlation of past marketing expenditure and sales to calculate what level would be appropriate to reach new objectives.

Executive summary and timescale

This section gives a short overall summary of the plan and the timescale over which it will be introduced.

Reviewing the plan – and the marketing strategy

How successful was it? This will be the crucial test of the effectiveness of the marketing plan and the strategy it contains. Just because a plan was drawn up and strategic decisions taken and implemented does not mean that the management task is complete. The results of the marketing plan and any new strategy need to be collected and checked against the original objectives, and this should be an ongoing process and not just 'at the end'. If the strategy appears not to be reaching the targets set for it, then an analysis of consumer reactions could be undertaken. Changes to the overall plan might be possible in response to initial negative reactions. At the end of the planning period under review, overall success must also be judged so that information can be used to assist in forming the strategy for the next time period. Setting and monitoring marketing strategies is never a static operation. The entire 'strategic planning cycle' can now be summarised in Figure 20.2.

Figure 20.2 The marketing strategy cycle

Marketing planning – an evaluation

There are three main benefits:

1 A marketing plan is an essential part of an overall business plan, such as a new business proposal. Potential entrepreneurs will need to convince potential financial investors that their business proposal is both sound and potentially profitable. A marketing plan is just one key component of a complete business plan. Unless there is evidence that a market exists, that it could be profitable to exploit it and that the marketing tactics are in place to enter it successfully, then no backer will put money into a new venture.

2 Specific marketing plans might also be needed to help introduce a new strategy that could determine a business's future success. Such new strategies include new product planning or entering completely different markets (either geographically or different market segments). Marketing plans would greatly reduce the risk of failure if such new business directions were taken.

3 Planning is an essential management function that forces marketing personnel to look at the current position of the business, its products and the markets it operates in to allow the setting of achievable goals. These then provide direction and purpose to future marketing decisions that everyone in the department and the organisation as a whole can understand and support. Effective marketing plans are not constructed in isolation from other departments. Finance should be involved – the marketing budget has to be paid for. Human resources will be involved – sales staff may need to be recruited and motivated. Production should be involved – the new product has to be developed and produced in time to meet the marketing timescale. This all requires cooperation and integration if the plan is to work – and this integration of departments will have substantial benefits for the whole business. Marketing plans then become an important part of the annual overall business planning process.

Potential limitations

Firstly, detailed marketing plans, as has been indicated above, are complex, costly and time-consuming. A very small business may not have either the money or the skilled management know-how to produce a professional-looking plan. In a fast-changing market, the plan could become out-of-date even before it is published. In these two cases, the style and complexity of marketing plans may have to be adapted to meet these problems, but the risk of *not* planning marketing activities at all is likely to be far greater than the risk of these two problems rendering the plans unsuitable.

Secondly, marketing managers may become wedded to the plan that they have devoted so much time and energy to. Their attachment to the plan may prevent them from seeing that unseen changes in the external environment – such as an economic downturn – could require substantial revisions to the plan before it has run its course. Inflexibility can be damaging to a business's prospects and marketing plans need to be adaptable enough to cope with changing circumstances.

KEY CONCEPT LINK

Management cannot expect to reach important objectives such as **creating/adding value** unless it adopts new **strategies** that have been well planned.

Elasticity

At AS Level, the concept of price elasticity of demand was explained. It measured the responsiveness of demand for a product following a change in its price. The demand for a product can be influenced by other factors apart from price, such as:

- consumer incomes
- promotional spending
- prices of related goods.

The elasticity concept can also be used to measure the responsiveness of demand for a product following these changes.

Income elasticity of demand

KEY TERM

Income elasticity of demand: measures the responsiveness of demand for a product following a change in consumer incomes.

Income elasticity of demand =

$$\frac{\% \text{ change in demand for the product}}{\% \text{ change in consumer incomes}}$$

Example 1: Following a reduction in consumer incomes of 5%, the demand for a supermarket's own-label breakfast cereal increased by 10%, but the demand for an expensive well-known branded cereal fell by 10%. The demand for salt hardly changed at all – just a small reduction of 1%. Check these income-elasticity results for yourself:

	Own-label cereal	Branded cereal	Salt
Income-elasticity result	−2	2	0.2

What do these results mean?

- The own-label cereal is called an inferior good because it has a 'superior' branded alternative and because quantity demand rises as income falls – and falls when incomes rise. In the case of products like these, income elasticity is negative.
- The expensive branded good is referred to as a normal good because we would expect that the demand for most products would fall if consumers had less income to spend – and would rise when incomes increase. In the case of products like these, income elasticity is positive.
- Salt is a necessity and has very low positive income elasticity.

Promotional elasticity of demand

KEY TERM

Promotional elasticity of demand: measures the responsiveness of demand for a product following a change in the amount spent on promoting it.

Promotional elasticity of demand =

$$\frac{\% \text{ change in demand for the product}}{\% \text{ change in promotional spending}}$$

If the result is greater than 1, then, as with the other forms of elasticity already considered, demand is said to be elastic or responsive following a change in spending on promotion. If the result is less than 1, then demand is inelastic and there might be little point in increasing promotional expenditure.

Generally, it would be more effective for a business to increase spending on those products with a high promotional elasticity of demand and to cut back promotional spending on those with a low elasticity. Much depends on the effectiveness of the promotional campaign, however. Just because last year's advertising campaign was so successful does not guarantee success with higher sales this year if the style of the advert and the media used have changed.

Example 2: A business increases its advertising spending on two of its products by 10%. Product A has a 2% increase in sales but product B's sales record a 12% increase. The promotional elasticities of demand are:

product A = 0.2 and product B = 1.2

Cross elasticity of demand

KEY TERM

Cross elasticity of demand: measures the responsiveness of demand for a product following a change in the price of another product.

Cross elasticity of demand for good A following a change in the price of good B =

$$\frac{\% \text{ change in demand for good A}}{\% \text{ change in price of good B}}$$

If this result is negative, it means that the two goods are 'complements' to each other – in other words, they are often bought together. For example, purchasing a laptop computer (not Apple) will often lead to the purchase of a Microsoft operating system.

If this result is positive, it means that the two goods are 'substitutes' and are competing for consumer spending – when the price of Sony TVs rises, the demand for Toshiba TVs will increase.

Evaluating these measures of elasticity

Chapter 18 explained that price-elasticity results should be analysed and acted on with caution. The same applies to the three measures of elasticity we have just considered. For example, the promotional-elasticity result will not be entirely reliable, as the change in sales may have been due to other factors that might have changed. These could have influenced sales during the same period that the promotion campaign was in place – this is a weakness of the elasticity concept. So if competitors launched an even more appealing promotion or if any of the external economic constraints were changed, the results of a sales comparison with data before the campaign might be misleading. It is possible that an increase in sales after a campaign would have occurred anyway due to favourable

economic conditions. However, especially if a similar elasticity result is obtained on more than one occasion, then the marketing manager should have some useful data on which to base future promotional spending decisions.

TOP TIP

Never assume that just because an elasticity result has been calculated, it will still be accurate for future changes in price, income, advertising or prices of other goods – it would be unwise to base major marketing decisions on elasticity results alone.

Marketing strategies and marketing objectives – getting the focus right

In Chapter 17, the importance of an integrated and consistent marketing mix was discussed. The need for focus and integration in marketing decisions should now be even clearer. A marketing strategy needs to be clearly directed towards the marketing objectives set for the company or it will hopelessly miss the target. Inappropriate strategies will fail to achieve the aims set for them. Here is an example:

A soft drink manufacturer aims to win 10% of the market segment for healthy fruit drinks for children within two years. The strategy is to launch a range of new fruit drinks with eye-catching, colourful packaging. The promotion campaign will use newspaper adverts only – aimed at parents. Only one-litre bottles of the drinks will be produced. They will be distributed through chemists/pharmacists shops only – not supermarkets. This will stress the health-giving qualities of the drink.

- **Result:** 2% market share in two years after launch.
- **Reason:** Some parts of the strategy failed to integrate with the original aim and the other mix decisions.
- **Action:** The company reviewed the sales performance of the product. It was decided not to drop the drinks but to relaunch them with TV advertising aimed at children, and in smaller bottles suitable for lunchboxes and distributed through supermarkets.
- **Success:** Within six months, the drink's sales made up 12% of the market segment for children's health drinks.

TOP TIP

If asked to evaluate or recommend a marketing strategy, remember to link the strategy with the objectives of the business and to integrate the different parts of the strategy with each other.

303

ACTIVITY 20.2

Cross elasticity

Assume that Microsoft reduces the price of the Xbox games console by 10%. This results in an increase in demand of 20% for games designed for this console model but reduces the demand for Sony's PlayStation by 10%.

[16 marks, 25 minutes]

1 Calculate the cross elasticity of demand for both Xbox games and Sony PlayStations following the change in price of the Microsoft Xbox. **[6]**

2 Comment on the significance of your results for Microsoft's marketing department. **[10]**

The importance of an integrated marketing strategy

This has two meanings:

1 Integrating with other departments of the business. Marketing strategies cannot be devised or planned without essential input from all other functional departments. A marketing team that attempts to sell products in export markets with the objective of market development will be almost certain to fail unless it has communicated with and integrated plans with:

- finance – to obtain the necessary resources
- operations – to discuss the viability of locations abroad and to adapt the product for foreign markets
- human resources – to ensure adequate staffing is available.

And so on. All major strategic decisions taken within the marketing department must be discussed and agreed with senior managers of other departments to ensure integration and cooperation between them.

2 The four elements of the marketing mix must be mutually supportive and integrated with each other. This was explained in Chapter 17.

New product development

In many fast-changing markets, there is a constant need to develop new products. If this is not successfully undertaken, then a business may find itself trying to

KEY TERM

New product development (NPD): the design, creation and marketing of new goods and services.

ACTIVITY 20.3

T and T Clothing – does the strategy fit the objectives?

'It has always been my objective to make T and T one of the biggest and most fashionable clothing businesses in the country. I have always used mail order for our clothing range – we built our reputation on a reliable and speedy delivery of our low-priced clothing through the post. With the increasing use of Internet shopping, this still seems the best distribution strategy. It helps us keep our prices competitive and cheaper than the foreign brands,' said Joe Sadik, the owner of T and T Clothing.

'Just because we have extended our range to include business suits, wedding dresses and unique designs does not mean we should change our entire strategy,' he said to Raquel Xavier, head of marketing. Joe did not approve of her decision to contact upmarket clothing retailers to see if they would be interested in stocking T and T Clothing products. Joe had seen his business grow rapidly during recent years of slow economic growth. As average incomes were still quite low in the country and car ownership below levels seen in most Western nations, the mail-order method of distribution and low prices had worked well.

'Times are changing, Joe,' said Raquel. 'Our consumers are now more mobile and they have higher expectations than before. They don't link top-class fashion with low prices and parcels through the post! That is why we are changing our product range and adding more expensive items. You cannot expect consumers to unwrap these brown paper parcels and try on smart, expensive clothes in their own homes.'

'I never wanted you to raise the prices that high anyway – are we forgetting our original consumer base by putting prices up in the way you suggest? What would happen if we did sell through shops? We would have to raise the retail price even more,' complained Joe. 'If we get rid of the mail-order catalogue, then what promotion will we have left?'

'I've thought of that,' said Raquel. 'I have arranged a fashion show for our latest clothes and invited all the top magazines and papers along. Shop-window displays could also be used to demonstrate our new image.' Joe looked at the sketches for the design of these displays and he agreed that they looked impressive, but he thought that these could easily be uploaded to the company's website.

[34 marks, 35 minutes]

1 Analyse the benefits to T and T clothing of using 'mail order' as the only distribution channel. [8]

2 Evaluate whether the marketing strategy proposed by Raquel for the new range of clothing lacks focus on Joe's objective for the business. [10]

3 Discuss a marketing strategy that you consider to be appropriate for the sale of the new clothing ranges in your own country. Justify the strategy chosen. [16]

market products that are perceived as being out-of-date, incorporating technology that has been overtaken by other firms' developments. This is true for the consumer electronics market, cars and cameras. New product development is also very important in the pharmaceuticals industry, where the opportunities to make huge profits from new drugs are considerable, and also in industrial product markets such as machinery, where robots and microchips have revolutionised production methods and machines.

For a new product to succeed it must:

- have desirable features that consumers are prepared to pay for
- be sufficiently different from other products to make it stand out and to offer a 'unique selling point'
- be marketed effectively to consumers – they need to be informed about it.

There are several general categories of new products. These include completely novel ideas that create new products (e.g. the original MP3 players), some products that are new for the company launching them (e.g. Sony's decision to enter the games console market) and some are new to a particular market (e.g. laptop computers from business to domestic market).

There are seven stages in the process of new product development:

1 Generating new ideas

All new product innovations must start with an initial idea. Ideas for new products can come from a variety of sources:

- **Company's own research and development (R&D) department:** This is a very expensive process and not all businesses will have a R&D department. The significance of R&D is discussed in the next section.
- **Adaptation of competitors' ideas:** It is important to be careful not to infringe copyright/patent laws.
- **Market research, such as focus groups:** These can be used to stimulate discussion about new products that consumers would like to see on the market.
- **Employees:** By encouraging workers to become involved in generating new product ideas, the business could benefit twice. Firstly, workers – because of their contact with the existing products – and possibly customers may have excellent ideas for new developments. Secondly, staff may be more motivated by being made to feel important by their participation.
- **Sales people:** They have close contact with the final consumers and they may suggest improvements to existing products or even completely new ones.
- **Brainstorming in groups:** This generates new ideas by members of the group developing and extending ideas

beyond the level that would be achieved by individuals working separately.

2 Idea screening

The purpose of this stage is to eliminate those ideas that stand the least chance of being commercially successful. It can be very expensive to develop and market new products, so care should be taken to try to ensure that only those ideas with a reasonable chance of success are proceeded with. Those doing the screening should ask:

- How will the consumers in our target markets benefit from this product?
- Is it technically feasible to manufacture this product?
- Will the product be profitable enough at the price we are likely to be able to charge the customer for it?

3 Concept development and testing

This stage takes the idea a step further by asking key questions about what features the product should have, the likely cost of these to manufacture and who the consumers are likely to be. These questions need to be asked against the background of how much the final consumer is be likely to be prepared to pay for the product. So the following points are discussed:

- Who are the most likely consumers of the product?
- What product features should be incorporated?
- What specific benefits will this product provide?
- How will consumers react to it? This might be tested by using market research and asking a sample of prospective customers what they think of the product idea and whether they would be likely to buy it and replace their current brand with it.
- What are the most cost-effective methods of manufacture?
- What will it cost to produce?

4 Business analysis

This is the stage that considers the likely impact of the new product on the company's costs, sales and profits. This will need an estimated price to be set for the product based on customer feedback from concept testing and competitors' data. The expected sales volume and market share can be estimated, as can the expected break-even level of production. Other issues to be researched include:

- Is finance available to develop the product?
- Can it be patented? This would offer monopoly rights of manufacture and sale for a certain number of years.
- Will it fit in with the existing product mix?
- How will changes in the economic environment be likely to affect sales in the future?

305

5 Product testing

This is concerned with the technical performance of the product and whether it is likely to meet consumers' expectations, and should include:

- developing a prototype of the product or working model of it
- testing the product in typical use conditions, e.g. a car will be tested in hot and cold countries to test performance under different conditions
- using focus groups to gather opinions about the product
- adapting the product as required after testing or focus-group feedback – the final version should take into account the views of potential customers at this stage.

6 Test marketing

This small market should be as representative as possible of the main market in terms of consumer profiles. Test marketing has certain benefits over a full-scale launch to the entire market:

- actual consumer behaviour can be observed and measured
- feedback from consumers will enable a final decision to be made about investing capital in a full-scale launch
- risks associated with a product failing after a full-scale launch are reduced – and the associated poor publicity
- any weaknesses in the product identified by consumer feedback could be incorporated into the final version of the product.

> **KEY TERM**
>
> **Test marketing:** the launch of the product on a small-scale market to test consumers' reactions to it.

There are some limitations of test marketing as well:

- It can be expensive.
- Competitors are able to observe a firm's intentions and react – perhaps rushing out a copy – before a full-scale launch of the product is put into effect.

Some new products are withdrawn at this stage if the sales results of the test market are disappointing (See Figure 20.3). There are cheaper alternatives to test marketing, such as a free-sample strategy, where small numbers of free samples are distributed to potential consumers who agree to be questioned later about their thoughts on the product.

7 Commercialisation

This refers to the full-scale launch of the product and corresponds to the introduction phase of the product life cycle. A promotional strategy will be put into place with advertisements to inform the market of the new product's arrival. The distribution channel will be 'filled up' with stocks of the product to make sure it is available when consumers want to buy it. This will be the most crucial few weeks or months in the life of the new product, and marketing managers will await the newest sales-results data with keen interest.

Research and development

Effective **research and development** (R&D) is essential in some industries if a business is to keep at the forefront of its market and is to retain or recapture a competitive advantage. Examples of firms that have improved their performance with R&D include Apple, Hewlett-Packard, Toyota and Honda.

> **KEY TERM**
>
> **Research and development:** the scientific research and technical development of new products and processes.

The significance of R&D and possible business strategies

Inventions generate new product possibilities. Some of these are converted into successful and profitable product innovations. New product innovations allow businesses to survive and grow in rapidly changing marketplaces.

They may have a considerable unique selling point or proposition over rivals so that the business can charge premium prices – earning higher profit margins. Expenditure on R&D can be a risky investment, as the success of such scientific enquiry can never be foreseen with great accuracy. The cost of R&D programmes can run into millions of pounds and success cannot be guaranteed. For example, in 2013 the top three UK-based pharmaceutical companies spent between them more than £6 billion on R&D. Much of this was spent on research into new drugs that might not be ready for sale to the public for another ten years.

Some businesses, as a consequence, deliberately adopt the strategy of 'no R&D'. They are then forced to license other businesses' new ideas or to adapt existing products into 'me too' lookalikes. This may be a safer strategy to

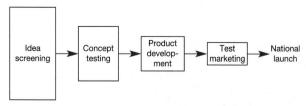

Figure 20.3 Not all new ideas are turned into successful products

ACTIVITY 20.4

Nestlé drops smoothie drinks after four months

Boosted Smoothies entered a market enjoying the biggest growth in the entire drinks sector. Nestlé spent $10 million on promoting its new product. Total sales of smoothie soft drinks grew by 31% last year – so why was Nestlé's new product not successful? The giant food multinational employs around 5,000 scientists worldwide, developing and creating new food processes and products. The company's aim is to become world leader in nutrition and healthy products. Boosted Smoothies became part of the company's strategy – the drinks were claimed to 'aid concentration and memory' and 'strengthen the body's defences' – so why did they fail? Here are some suggestions made by business analysts:

- Wrong bottle sizes of 250 ml and 750 ml – competitors are available in small trial-size bottles and in one-litre family bottles.

- Global economic shocks, such as higher energy costs, rising fruit prices and lower consumer incomes.

- Many competitors – such as global giant PepsiCo's Tropicana, and small entrepreneurial brands, such as Green and Black's and Innocent smoothies.

- Nestlé's size, which means that senior managers and researchers may be far removed from the current market trends towards natural, organic products.

Nestlé's really big world-sellers were all created a long time ago. For example, it sells a quarter of the world's instant coffee – a mature market being overtaken by the trend for freshly ground coffee – while powdered baby milk, invented by company founder Henri Nestlé in 1866, is subject to increasing marketing restrictions in some countries. Nestlé is also strong in dairy and confectionery products, but it fails to give these products a natural healthy image in keeping with modern consumer trends.

The company is not standing still, however. It has set up small 'innovation units', independent of the rest of the organisation, which will try to keep in close touch with the latest market trends. 'These will give scientists and researchers space where they can free themselves from the constraints of a big organisation and start to think entrepreneurially about new products,' said one innovation expert.

[40 marks, 1 hour]

1 Explain why, despite considerable research spending and promotional spending, the Boosted Smoothie product was not a success. [8]

2 Recommend a suitable and detailed marketing strategy for this product in your own country. You should consider carefully Nestlé's objectives and the wider environment within which it will operate in your country. [12]

3 Would you advise Nestlé, and other global food businesses, to continue to spend money on new product developments? Explain your answer. [12]

4 Analyse why small teams of researchers are more likely to develop successful innovative products than when part of a much larger organisation. [8]

307

adopt, but one that can lead to legal battles if the copy is too close to the original concept. It will, generally, fail to capture consumers' imaginations and gives initial market leadership to the initiating business. It is often referred to as a 'follow-the-leader' strategy.

Other possible business strategies regarding R&D include 'offensive' and 'defensive' approaches. An offensive R&D strategy will be to lead the rest of the industry with innovative products. The aim of these businesses is to gain market share and, possibly, market dominance. Success

breeds success as the profits made on a lucrative new product can be reinvested into yet further R&D – Apple provides us with a classic example of an offensive strategy towards R&D. In contrast, a defensive strategy will be to attempt to learn from the initial innovators' mistakes and weaknesses. This approach does not lead the field, but it suggests that the business does not want to be left behind. The defensive strategy will aim to improve on the original products or develop slightly different types of goods, which might appeal to other market segments.

Government encouragement for research and development

Governments can provide a favourable environment for R&D in two main ways.

1 Providing some legal security to inventors and designers by allowing them to 'patent' or 'register' a design. This provides protection to the inventor from unauthorised copying of the new idea or design. If the idea proves to be very popular with consumers, this means that the original inventor will be able to secure the profits from the product without fear of illegal copying.

2 They can provide financial assistance to businesses engaging in R&D. This is usually done either by providing tax-reduction incentives, or by offering grants to firms or university departments with close links to industry, to be spent on specific projects.

TOP TIP

Do not assume that a firm's success will be guaranteed by spending more and more on R&D – some inventions will simply not be commercially successful.

International comparisons of R&D spending

UK businesses spend less than their major competitors on R&D as a proportion of total sales. This is evident from Table 20.2.

This suggests that the international competitiveness of UK industry might fall in future due to fewer inventions and innovations in new products and manufacturing processes – the high figure (relative to GDP) for the Japanese market reflects the very large IT-based industry in that country.

Factors that influence the level of R&D expenditure by a business

- **The nature of the industry:** Rapidly changing technologies – and consumer expectations – in pharmaceutical products, defence, computer and software products and motor vehicles lead to the need for substantial investment by leading firms into R&D. Other businesses, such as hotels and hairdressing, would need to spend much less.

- **The R&D spending plans of competitors:** In most markets, it is essential to spend as much as or more than competitors if market share and technical leadership are to be maintained.

- **Business expectations:** If business managers are optimistic about the future state of the economy and the rate of economic growth and consumer demand, then they are more likely to agree to substantial budgets for R&D.

- **The risk profile or culture of the business:** The attitude of the management to risk and whether shareholders are prepared to invest for the long term will have a significant effect on the sums that businesses can inject into R&D programmes. 'Short-termism' is an accusation made towards many major UK financial institutions, and the need to satisfy these investors could discourage managers from investing in R&D.

- **Government policy towards grants to businesses and universities for R&D:** Programmes and the range and scope of tax allowances for such expenditure will influence decisions by businesses.

	UK	France	Germany	Japan	USA
% of total business sales spent on R&D	1.7	1.9	2.3	3.7	2.9

Table 20.2 Percentage of total business sales spent by five countries on R&D in 2012

ACTIVITY 20.5

Aircraft maker invests $200 million in new wings

Airbus is spending $200 million at its Welsh factory to develop new materials for very light aircraft wings for the planes of the future. Aircraft wings of these new materials will save fuel and allow planes to carry more passengers. It is hoped that some of the new materials or wing designs might be patented, which would give Airbus a clear competitive advantage over rival aircraft makers. The R&D spending will help to maintain the jobs of scientists and engineers in Wales. The Welsh government has contributed $15 million of the total R&D costs. A spokesperson for the government said: 'This will keep the factory in the forefront of world aircraft wing design and put the company in a competitive position to win new contracts.'

[20 marks, 30 minutes]

1 Explain **two** ways in which the government has assisted this R&D project. [4]

2 Explain why the government decided to offer financial support for this R&D project. [6]

3 Is this research guaranteed to produce profitable innovative new products? Explain your answer. [10]

Research and development – an evaluation

Not all R&D leads to scientific or engineering breakthroughs – despite spending billions of dollars, the drugs industry has failed to come up with a remedy for the common cold. Even if the scientists and researchers are successful, not all inventions become innovative products that can be marketed successfully. New ideas often fail to reach the market because of defects in design or manufacture, competitors' products leaping ahead in terms of technology and higher-than-expected costs. Even when they are launched, they may still fail. Products can fail to progress at all stages of the product development process. Here are some of the reasons why a fully researched and developed product may reach the wider market and then fail:

- Inadequate market research.
- Poor marketing support or inappropriate pricing.
- Changes in technology leave the product dated.
- Competitors release a product that the consumers prefer.

Despite these risks, many firms continue to invest in R&D. These firms are taking the long-term view. They believe that the costs and inevitable short-term failures will be compensated for by the occasional outstanding success. Much depends on whether the business is driven by short-termism – the perceived need to satisfy shareholders with high dividends in the short term.

> **KEY CONCEPT LINK**
>
> Successful research and development will lead to **innovation** in both new products and new processes (ways of making products). Both of these can **create value** for a business.

Sales forecasting – potential benefits

If marketing managers were able to predict the future accurately, the risks of business operations would be much reduced. If a precise forecast of monthly sales over the next two years could be made, the benefits to the whole organisation would be immense:

- The production department would know how many units to produce and how many materials to order, distribution would hold just the correct level of stocks.

> **KEY TERM**
>
> **Sales forecasting:** predicting future sales levels and sales trends.

- The marketing department would be aware of how many products to distribute.
- Human resources workforce plan would be more accurate, leading to the appropriate level of staffing.
- Finance could plan cash flows with much greater accuracy.

In reality, of course, such precision in forecasting is impossible to achieve, because of all the external factors that can greatly influence sales performance. Consider, for example, the difficulties in forecasting, even for a short-term period, the sales of DVDs from music shops. Apart from changes in musical and film tastes, new developments in recording, download and playback technology will impact on DVD sales; the growth of Internet shopping, rather than buying from shops, and the general economic climate will also have a great effect on future sales levels. Despite these problems, most firms make sales forecasts in order to reduce to an acceptable minimum the unforeseen nature of future changes.

Market forecasts form an essential part of the market-planning process and of the screening process before new products are launched onto the market. These forecasts will be based on market research data, gained from both primary and secondary sources. For existing products, there are two broad approaches towards sales forecasting. The first approach is to ask the opinions of experts and customers and the second approach is to analyse past sales results to try to use these to predict the future.

Sales-force composite

Sales-force representatives have the task of keeping in contact with customers – usually not the final consumers, but the retail businesses that purchase and stock the product for sale to consumers. Frequent contact with customers means sales representatives are able to develop a real insight into market trends and potential demand for the future. By asking all sales staff for their estimates of future sales to the customers they have contact with and then adding these estimates together, a total sales forecast can be arrived at.

> **KEY TERM**
>
> **Sales-force composite:** a method of sales forecasting that adds together all of the individual predictions of future sales of all of the sales representatives working for a business.

This method has the advantage of being quick and cheap to administer. However, sales representatives may not be aware of macro-economic developments or competitors' actions that could have a substantial impact on future sales. Customers may overestimate the number of products that they hope to sell in the future in the hope of gaining a more favourable arrangement with the supplying business.

Delphi method

KEY TERM

Delphi method: a long-range qualitative forecasting technique that obtains forecasts from a panel of experts.

The experts do not meet and they are anonymous to each other. The 'facilitator' collects and coordinates the opinions from experts who are sent detailed questionnaires asking for their judgement about possible future events – such as demand levels or technology changes that could affect consumer taste and demand levels. After each round of questionnaire results have been collected, they are summarised and sent to all of the experts on the panel. A further questionnaire is then sent out to see if the experts have changed their minds after reading the results of the first round of questionnaires.

In this way, the 'extreme' responses from the experts are often amended and moderated so that, eventually, a consensus is reached that represents the most likely 'correct' forecast. This may take several rounds of questionnaires to achieve. Tests have proven that this Delphi technique – named after the all-knowing Oracle of Delphi – is more accurate than unstructured group experts giving their opinions and forecasts.

Consumer surveys

These are a form of market research and the questions may either be quantitative in nature (e.g. asking for likely future levels of demand) or qualitative (e.g. asking for reasons behind future demand choices). For greater accuracy, the sample of consumers selected must be large enough to be as fully representative of the total number of consumers for a product as possible. Such surveys may be conducted by the business itself, but this takes up management time and requires a detailed awareness of research techniques, questionnaire construction and statistical analysis of results. The other option is to hire a specialist market research agency to undertake the surveys. This can be expensive, although it is likely to lead to a more accurate demand forecast than many in-house surveys.

Jury of experts

The Delphi technique uses experts not directly employed by the business. The **jury of experts** uses senior managers within the business, who meet and develop forecasts based on their knowledge of their specific areas of responsibility. This is quicker and cheaper than the Delphi technique, but it lacks the external view of market conditions and consumer trends that the Delphi approach offers. It is sometimes referred to as 'the jury of executive opinion'.

KEY TERM

Jury of experts: uses the specialists within a business to make forecasts for the future.

The next section is concerned with using quantitative techniques to forecast sales for existing products based on past sales performance data.

Quantitative sales forecasting methods

Correlation – establishing causal relationships

This method attempts to explain the most important factors causing changes in sales data. If a marketing manager considered that the level of advertising expenditure had led, in the past, to significant changes in sales, then a causal relationship might be established. Future planned changes in advertising expenditure could then be used to make predictions about likely changes in sales. Similar causal links might exist between sales and:

- prices
- competitors' promotional activity
- changes in commission payments to sales staff
- levels of disposable income
- the weather.

There are many more factors, depending on the product or service. Establishing such a linked pattern is termed 'correlation'. Figure 20.4 shows two sets of sales data plotted against promotional expenditure.

In Figure 20.4(a), there seems to be strong positive correlation between sales and promotion while, in Figure 20.4(b), sales are rising and falling in an unconnected manner compared with promotional expenditure, which suggests that no correlation exists. In Figure 20.4(a), a 'line of best fit' has been added, which can be extended into the future to make a simple sales forecast based on planned promotion spending alone.

Such a technique has major limitations:

- Establishing correlation does not prove that there is a cause and an effect. Sales could have been rising for other factors entirely.
- It fails to consider other factors, such as sales changes due to seasonal and other variations.
- Mathematical methods of correlation analysis can be undertaken that do not rely on the graphical approach.

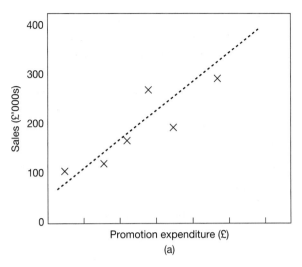
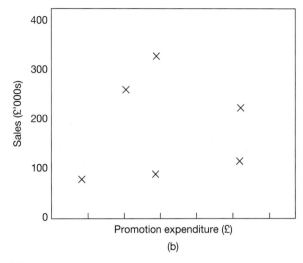

Figure 20.4 Two sets of sales figures – (a) with correlation and (b) without

Time-series analysis

This method of sales forecasting is based entirely on past sales data. Sales records are kept over time and, when they are presented in date order, they are referred to as a 'time series'.

Extrapolation

The most basic method of predicting sales based on past results is termed extrapolation. Extrapolation means basing future predictions on past results. When actual results are plotted on a time-series graph, the line can be extended, or extrapolated, into the future along the trend of the past data; see Figure 20.5. This simple method assumes that sales patterns are stable and will remain so in the future. It is ineffective when this condition does not hold true.

Moving averages

This method is more complex than simple graphical extrapolation. It allows the identification of underlying factors that are expected to influence future sales. These are:

- **the trend**
- **seasonal fluctuations**
- **cyclical fluctuations**
- **random fluctuations**.

Most questions you encounter on this topic will be concerned with the identification of the trend and seasonal variations. The moving-average method is used to analyse these in Table 20.4 on ice-cream sales. Once they have been identified, then short-term sales forecasts can be made.

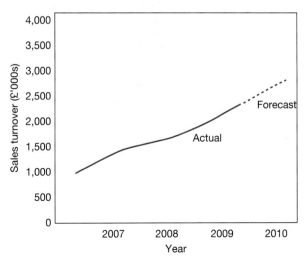

Figure 20.5 Extrapolating a trend

> **KEY TERMS**
>
> **The trend:** the underlying movement in a time series.
>
> **Seasonal fluctuations:** the regular and repeated variations that occur in sales data within a period of 12 months.
>
> **Cyclical fluctuations:** these variations in sales occur over periods of time of much more than a year and are due to the business cycle.
>
> **Random fluctuations:** these can occur at any time and will cause unusual and unpredictable sales figures – examples include exceptionally poor weather or negative public image following a high-profile product failure.

Points to note are:

- The moving-average method involves calculating moving totals from a number of sales figures. Each total in column 4 of Table 20.4 is made up of four results. This is why the total is called a four-period moving total. A four-period moving total was used because the data clearly vary consistently over this length of time. For example, sales are always highest in the summer quarter. If other data were used, perhaps daily sales figures, then a seven-period total would have been used, because the regular variation in sales would have been over seven days. Monthly sales data may require the use of a 12-period moving total.

- If this four-quarter moving total was divided by four in order to calculate the average, this result would not lie alongside any one quarter. This would not make sense – to have a result which does not belong to any one time period (see Table 20.3). The problem is overcome by 'centring' the average so that it lies alongside one actual quarter. This is done by adding two four-quarter moving totals together. This gives an eight-period moving total (column 5 in Table 20.4). This is divided by eight to give the moving average.

The moving average is known as the trend of the data. The underlying movement of the data has been identified by averaging out the regular seasonal fluctuations.

The difference between the actual sales and this trend must have been largely due to seasonal fluctuations. These can then be calculated as shown in Table 20.3.

Seasonal variation (col. 7) = actual result (col. 3) – moving average (trend)(col. 6)

Make sure you obtain the correct plus or minus sign for your results. If the result is negative, it means that in that quarter sales are usually below the trend or average for seasonal reasons.

- The average seasonal variation smoothes out the actual seasonal variations. This is obtained by adding up all of the seasonal variations for each separate quarter and then dividing by the number of results. For example, quarter 3 seasonal variations are:

    $$43.75 + 52.5 + 58.75 = 155/3 = 51.67.$$

Forecasting using the moving-average method

The results from Table 20.4 can now be used for short-term forecasting. You will need to:

1. Plot the trend (moving average) results on a time-series graph (Figure 20.6).
2. Extrapolate this into the future – short-term extrapolations are likely to be the most accurate.
3. Read off the forecast trend result from the graph for the period under review, e.g. quarter 2 in year 2015.
4. Adjust this by the average seasonal variation for quarter 2.

Quarter	Sales	Four-quarter total	Four-quarter average
1	20		
2	30		
			27.5
3	50		
4	10	110/4	

Table 20.3 Four-period moving total and average

1	2	3	4	5	6	7	8
Year	Quarter	Sales revenue	Four-quarter moving total	Eight-quarter moving total	Quarterly moving average (Trend)	Seasonal variation	Average seasonal variation
2011	1	120					
	2	140					
	3	190			146.25	43.75	51.67
	4	130	580		150.00	−20	−15.4
2012	1	130	590	1170 ÷ 8	156.25	−26.25	−33.3
	2	160	610	1200 ÷ 8	163.75	−3.75	−4.6
	3	220	640	1250	167.5	52.5	51.67
	4	160	670	1310	168.75	−8.75	−15.4
2013	1	130	670	1340	172.5	−42.5	−33.3
	2	170	680	1350	176.25	−6.25	−4.6
	3	240	700	1380	181.25	58.75	51.67
	4	170	710	1410	187.5	−17.5	−15.4
2014	1	160	740	1450	191.25	−31.25	−33.3
	2	190	760	1500	193.75	−3.75	−4.6
	3	250	770	1530			
	4	180	780	1550			

Table 20.4 Moving averages for ice-cream sales ($000s)

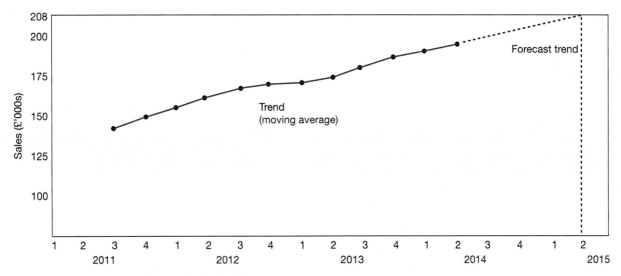

Figure 20.6 Forecasting future trend sales figures

Thus, for quarter 2 in the year 2015: the actual forecast will be the extrapolated trend forecast for this quarter, $208,000, plus the average seasonal variation of – $4,600 = $203,400.

Moving-average sales forecasting method – an evaluation

The advantages are:

- It is useful for identifying and applying the seasonal variation to predictions.
- It can be reasonably accurate for short-term forecasts in reasonably stable economic conditions.
- It identifies the average seasonal variations for each time period and this can assist in planning for each quarter in future.

On the other hand, the disadvantages are:

- It is a fairly complex calculation.
- Forecasts further into the future become less accurate as the projections made are entirely based on past data. External environmental factors can change.
- Forecasting for the longer term may require the use of more qualitative methods that are less dependent on past results.

 TOP TIP
You should be prepared to discuss the limitations of all sales forecasting techniques as well as the potential benefits of predicting future sales.

313

ACTIVITY 20.6

Sodhi's sales forecast

The sales of Sodhi's convenience store were recorded over a four-week period. The shop is open only five days per week. The owner of the store has started to undertake a short-term forecasting exercise and has asked you to help.

		Sales	Moving total (5 period)	Moving average	Daily variation
Week 1	Tues	32			
	Weds	38			
	Thurs	40		43	−3
	Fri	50		44	6
	Sat	55	215		
Week 2	Tues	37	220		
	Weds	40	222		
	Thurs	42	224		
	Fri	53	227		
	Sat	55			
Week 3	Tues	40			
	Weds	44			
	Thurs	50			
	Fri	60			
	Sat	70			
Week 4	Tues	44			
	Weds	48			
	Thurs	52			
	Fri	65			
	Sat	72			

[30 marks, 45 minutes]

1 Why has the shop owner used a five-period moving total? Is he right to do so? [4]

2 Copy out the table above and complete the columns for the moving total, moving average and daily variation. [8]

3 Plot the moving-average (trend) line on a graph and extrapolate this to the fifth week. [6]

4 For each day that the shop is open, calculate the average daily variation in sales. [2]

5 Use your graph, the extrapolation of the trend and the average daily variation in sales to forecast sales for each day of the fifth week. [2]

6 Evaluate the usefulness of this method for forecasting the store's sales in ten months' time. [8]

SUMMARY POINTS

- Detailed marketing planning can be an important factor in the success of a business.
- Income, advertising and cross elasticities of demand can assist marketing managers when making important decisions.
- New product development and R&D is vital for many businesses that operate in markets in which product differentiation is essential.
- Sales forecasts are important for many functional decisions such as workforce planning and operations capacity. Short-term sales forecasts can be obtained using the moving-average method.
- The accuracy and usefulness of sales forecasting methods should be evaluated.

RESEARCH TASK

Your own country's R&D spending

- Use the Internet to research government statistics on research and development spending in your own country. Compare with the figures contained in Figure 20.1.
- Identify **one** completely new product that has been launched in your country this year.
- Assess the likely costs and benefits to the business concerned of commercialising this new product.

A Level exam practice questions
Case studies

1 How Unilever developed Culinesse

Culinesse is the name given to a new type of cooking 'oil' developed over a three-year period by Unilever, the giant food and washing-products multinational. Culinesse is meant to combine the attributes of traditional cooking oil, butter and margarine – it tastes good, 'browns' food attractively and performs well at high temperatures. In addition, it is claimed to have the advantage of not 'spitting' while being used at high temperatures – a unique point compared with ordinary oils.

The product was developed by a multidisciplinary project team of people – scientists, accountants and marketing experts. This was thought to be very important for the success of this new product. All new ideas and suggestions were considered by a range of experts with different experiences. They were able to increase the chances of the product being produced and sold at a profit. The name and the packaging were thought to be crucial to the success of the product. The name did not have to be changed for different countries' markets and the 'squeeze-assisted' bottle was a real innovation for this sort of product. Constant market research was employed at every stage of research and development. Each minor change to the product and its packaging was researched among new consumer panels. A senior product development manager at Unilever said: 'After the extensive research that went into its development, we have great confidence in Culinesse. The only way to get success is to make products that connect with consumers and make a real difference.' He believes that the product could 'go global'.

[34 marks, 50 minutes]

1. Unilever already had a wide range of cooking oils, butters and margarines. Explain why you think it was considered necessary to develop Culinesse. **[6]**

2. Explain the importance of using a 'multidisciplinary project team' for developing this new product. **[6]**

3. Assess the importance of market planning to the success of new products such as Culinesse. **[10]**

4. Do you believe that the product development manager is right to be so confident about the future success of Culinesse? Explain your answer. **[12]**

315

2 Mauritius Hotel Company

The Mauritius Hotel Company operates in the very competitive hotel and restaurant markets in Mauritius. The company has recently greatly increased its promotional expenditure with the objective of increasing both foreign tourists to the hotels and local residents to the restaurants within the group. Magazine advertising had been selected in certain exclusive foreign publications. A radio campaign had been chosen to promote the restaurants to local residents.

The sales and future booking results for the year after both campaigns ended were as follows:

All figures $ million	2013 Promotion spend	2013 Sales	2014 Promotion spend	2014 Sales
Hotels	1.5	50	3.0	60
Restaurants	0.8	10	1.0	15

[34 marks, 45 minutes]

1 Calculate the promotional elasticities of demand from the data above – for hotels and for restaurants. [6]

2 On the basis of these results, do you think the company should change how it spends its promotional budget next year? Explain your answer. [8]

3 Analyse **two** factors that might explain why the promotional elasticities are so different. [8]

4 Evaluate the extent to which this elasticity data is sufficient to allow the management of the hotel to take promotional decisions. [12]

3 GlaxoSmithKline (GSK) – one of the world's big researchers

The profits earned from successful new pharmaceutical products (drugs) can be huge, but they are matched by the risks of the industry. Ten medicines account for 65% of GSK's sales. The world's number-two drugs firm has annual sales of more than $50 billion and profits of around $10 billion – but its sales and profits are under pressure for several reasons:

■ The ending of patents on a number of medicines leading to cheaper generic drugs being produced by other companies.

■ One of its main medicines – Avandia – has been linked to increased risk of heart attacks in patients. The value of GSK's shares fell by $18 billion when this was announced.

■ Uncertain demand from poorer countries – if economic growth is not consistent, then demand for medicines will fall.

■ Competition from rival companies such as Pfizer – this company spends even more on R&D than GSK.

GSK spends almost 15% of its total sales on R&D into new medicines. It is researching into new 'blockbuster' drugs that will cure or treat major diseases that can be patented and then sold at high prices to the medical services of rich countries. Increasingly though, research is being focused on a new approach. Instead of one large research department, scientists have been split into groups of around 80 in seven centres. These groups will have to compete for central funds for research. It is hoped that more drugs that earn modest amounts for the company will be developed by these teams – drugs that will not be worth copying by other companies.

The Top 20 R&D Spenders

The top 20 companies were responsible for about 25 percent of the Global Innovation 1000's total R&D spending in 2013. As in past years, this group was dominated by companies in the computing and electronics, healthcare, and auto industries. Google made its first appearance in the top 20 this year at number 12, joining Microsoft in the software and Internet segment.

Rank 2013	Rank 2012	Company	R&D Spending 2013 US$ Billions	R&D Spending Change from 2012	R&D Spending As a % of Revenue	Headquarters Location	Industry
1	11	Volkswagen	$11.4	22.4%	4.6%	Europe	Auto
2	6	Samsung	$10.4	15.6%	5.8%	South Korea	Computing and Electronics
3	3	Roche Holding	$10.2	14.7%	21.0%	Europe	Healthcare
4	8	Intel	$10.1	21.5%	19.0%	North America	Computing and Electronics
5	5	Microsoft	$9.8	8.5%	13.3%	North America	Software and Internet
6	1	Toyota	$9.8	3.5%	3.7%	Japan	Auto
7	2	Novartis	$9.3	−2.6%	16.5%	Europe	Healthcare
8	7	Merck	$8.2	−3.5%	17.3%	North America	Healthcare
9	4	Pfizer	$7.9	−13.3%	13.3%	North America	Healthcare
10	12	Johnson & Johson	$7.7	1.6%	11.4%	North America	Healthcare
11	9	General motors	$7.4	−9.3%	4.8%	North America	Auto
12	26	Google	$6.8	31.6%	13.5%	North America	Software and Internet
13	15	Honda	$6.8	7.8%	5.7%	Japan	Auto
14	19	Daimler	$6.6	3.2%	4.5%	Europe	Auto
15	13	Sanofi	$6.3	2.3%	14.1%	Europe	Healthcare
16	17	IBM	$6.3	0.7%	6.0%	North America	Computing and Electronics
17	16	GlaxoSmithKline	$6.3	−1.0%	15.0%	Europe	Healthcare
18	10	Nokia	$6.1	−14.4%	15.8%	Europe	Computing and Electronics
19	14	Panasonic	$6.1	−3.5%	6.9%	Japan	Computing and Electronics
20	21	Sony	$5.7	9.3%	7.0%	Japan	Computing and Electronics
		TOP 20 TOTAL:	$159.2	4.6%	8.1%		

317

[32 marks, 45 minutes]

1 a Identify the company which spent most on R&D as a % of sales revenue. [1]

   b Calculate the sales revenue of this company in 2013. [3]

2 Evaluate the benefits to GSK from increased R&D spending. [16]

3 Assess the potential benefits and problems for a company such as GSK of attempting to make accurate sales forecasts. [12]

A Level essay questions

[20 marks, 45 minutes each]

1 'Research and development is so expensive it will be more profitable for us to copy good ideas from our competitors.' To what extent do you agree with this statement from the chief executive of a mobile (cell) phone manufacturer? [20]

2 Discuss whether a computer manufacturer should rely on sales forecasts obtained from the moving average method for making decision about future resources required by the company. [20]

3 Evaluate the importance of marketing planning to the success of a decision by a food-producing business to enter the soft drinks market for the first time. [20]

21 Globalisation and international marketing

This chapter covers syllabus section A Level 3.5.

On completing this chapter, you will be able to:

- understand the implications for marketing of increased globalisation
- analyse different strategies for international marketing
- assess the importance of international marketing for different businesses
- evaluate appropriate international marketing strategies, e.g. pan-global marketing or reflecting regional differences with global localisation
- assess and select appropriate strategies to enter international markets.

Introducing the topic

COCA-COLA'S GLOBAL MARKETING – INDIA DOESN'T BUY IT

Despite spending $1 billion on promotion in India, Coca-Cola sales in this country account for less than 1% of its total global sales. The world's best and most valuable brand – according to Brand Republic – has failed to make any inroads into the Indian market. Per capita consumption of soft drinks is among the lowest in the world, even though both of the USA's giant cola groups – Pepsi and Coca-Cola – have invested millions of dollars in breaking into this market.

What is wrong? Coca-Cola has a serious image problem in many parts of the country. It was thrown out of India in the 1970s for failing to release details of its secret formula and it has been fighting court cases recently against claims that it is causing droughts in some regions due to heavy water use and that its soft drinks contain 25 times the permitted level of pesticides. Perhaps the real problem though, is cultural. Traditionalists in India fear the erosion of long-standing culture by the importation of Western products, advertisements and methods of selling. In addition, tea is still widely drunk in India and Coca-Cola's failure to adapt its global products to

local tastes is another major factor. Finally, most Indian retailing is still through informal unorganised street and market traders – and Coca-Cola is reluctant to see its products sold in this way. Perhaps this is one reason why it has recently set up a branded university in India to teach modern retailing techniques to millions of small shop and stall owners. Even this has met with opposition from traditional sellers, who fear the growing dominance of foreign products and retailers in India. In 2009, Walmart – another US company, the world's largest retailer – launched its Indian chain of shops in partnership with Bharti Enterprises.

Points to think about:
- What advantages might Coca-Cola have from using the same marketing strategy in all countries it operates in?
- Assess the potential problems any multinational business might experience when trying to use the same methods of marketing as in its 'home' or 'base' country.
- Examine how Coca-Cola might achieve more sales success in India than it does at present.

Introduction

Globalisation is not a new process but it has accelerated in recent years with the rapid growth of **multinational companies** and the expansion of **free international trade**

KEY TERM

Globalisation: the growing trend towards worldwide markets in products, capital and labour, unrestricted by barriers.

with fewer **tariffs** and **quotas** on imports. The key features of globalisation that have an impact on business strategy are:

- increased international trade as barriers to trade are reduced
- growth of multinational businesses in all countries as there is greater freedom for capital to be invested from one country to another
- freer movement of workers between countries.

As with many major economic developments, globalisation creates both potential opportunities and limitations to businesses (see Table 21.1 on page 320). This chapter

KEY TERMS

Multinational companies: businesses that have operations in more than one country.

Free international trade: international trade that is allowed to take place without restrictions such as 'protectionist' tariffs and quotas.

Tariff: tax imposed on an imported product.

Quota: a physical limit placed on the quantity of imports of certain products.

focuses on the impact globalisation is having on marketing strategies. Firstly, however, we consider the sheer scale of recent globalisation and the wider impact that globalisation is having on business strategies.

Globalisation and the growth in international trade

World trade – international trade between countries – has grown in recent years. This has been a sign of increased globalisation resulting from:

- the work of the World Trade Organization and its free-trade agreements
- the growth of regional free trade areas that allow no trade barriers between member states, such as ASEAN, NAFTA and the EU.

Averaging 7% growth per year in the decade to 2007, the rate of growth of world trade fell considerably after 2008 as a consequence of the global financial crisis and only reached 2.5% in 2013. Since 2001, Asian economies, led

by China and India, have contributed 40% of total world trade expansion. China's membership of the WTO – the World Trade Organization that negotiates regular reductions in world trade barriers – was one of the major factors behind this rapid growth. Exports accounted for around 30% of China's GDP in 2013. Figures 21.1 and 21.2 show the rapid growth of world trade compared with world GDP and the major exporting nations of the world.

TOP TIP

Globalisation is not just about trade and multinational companies. Increased migration to and from most countries is occurring. Many economists argue that increased migration of young workers from Eastern Europe is a benefit to the UK economy and that the USA benefits from immigration from South America.

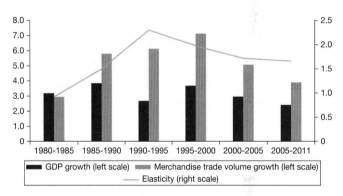

Note: Merchandise trade refers to the average of exports and imports.

Figure 21.1 World merchandise trade and GDP 1980–2011

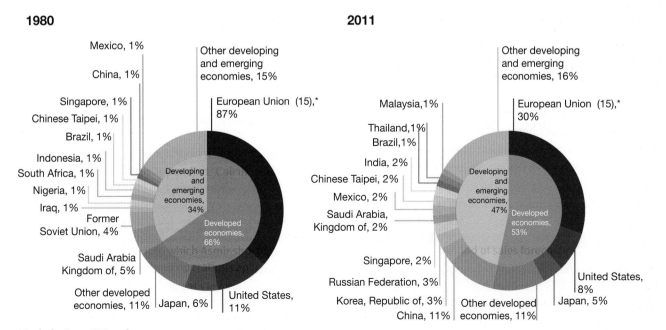

*Includes intra-EU trade.

Figure 21.2 World merchandise trade volume and real GDP (inner circle), 1980–2011

Potential benefits and strategic opportunities	Potential limitations and threats
■ There is greater opportunity for selling goods in other countries. Opening up new markets, which may not have reached saturation as the domestic market may have done, gives the chance of higher sales, economies of scale and improved profitability. ■ Increased competition gives firms the incentives to become more internationally competitive. Hiding behind trade barriers breeds inefficiency and this will no longer be possible. ■ Pan-European or pan-global marketing strategies can be used to create a global brand identity. This saves on the costs of 'different markets – different products'. ■ There is a wider choice of locations – the opportunity to set up operations in other countries and become a multinational. These locations offer, usually, lower costs and direct access to local markets. Working within each country should lead to better market information. ■ Greater freedom to arrange mergers and takeovers with firms from other nations as restrictions on foreign acquisitions are reduced.	■ Businesses from other countries now have freer access to the domestic market, so there will be increased competition. Wider consumer choices will drive firms that are not internationally competitive out of business. ■ The drive for international competitiveness will also be forcing other firms to become more efficient. ■ Pan-European/global strategies can fail to consider the cultural and taste differences between consumers of different nations. Firms may need to 'think global, but act local' – often called global localisation. ■ International locations can lead to significant transport and communication problems. The risk of unethical practices by managers with delegated authority thousands of miles from head office can lead to problems. ■ Businesses are now increasingly at risk of foreign takeovers, e.g. Land Rover and Jaguar by Tata (India), BAA by Ferrovial (Spain). ■ Increasing activity from anti-globalisation pressure groups may result in bad publicity for multinationals in particular and for those firms found guilty of environmental damage in foreign countries. There is growing concern about the environmental impact of globalisation – especially in emerging economies. Coca-Cola is under pressure to limit production in some Indian states due to shortage of water supplies. ■ Governments will have much less influence on business decisions, e.g. preventing closure of factories to relocate in low-cost countries.

Table 21.1 Globalisation – the potential business benefits and limitations

International marketing

Selling in foreign markets was once too risky and expensive for most firms, so only large businesses – growing too large for their national markets – used to commit to this form of marketing. Improved communications, better transport links and freer international trade – all key features of globalisation – have changed all this. For many firms, international marketing is now an opportunity to profitably expand their sales and, indeed, for some firms it is no longer an option to remain based in just one country. This is the case for members of the European Union, where the growth of membership has led to increased competition from other countries and improved chances of successfully selling abroad. The rapid development of major developing countries – the **BRICS** – is leading to huge marketing opportunities for businesses prepared to sell their products and services in these international markets.

KEY TERMS

International marketing: selling products in markets other than the original domestic market.

BRICS: the acronym for five rapidly developing economies with great market opportunities – Brazil, Russia, India, China and South Africa.

Why sell products in other countries?

■ Saturated home markets – one country can have only so many fast-food restaurants. When the market stops growing and competition is severe, a move to another country, with few large competitors, can offer rapid sales increases.

■ Profits – rapid sales growth may be combined with low costs of operation and create high profitability. If the foreign country has low labour and property costs and low tax levels, then selling from there to a high-cost country can offer higher profit margins. In contrast, the great wealth of some Arab oil states gives the opportunity to some luxury goods producers to sell at higher prices than 'back home'.

■ Spreading risks – international marketing means that the sales and profits of a business are much less dependent on economic and legal constraints in the home country.

■ Poor trading conditions in the home market – in 2013, sales of luxury cars in Spain fell due to the Eurozone economic crisis, but sales in China continued to increase.

■ Legal differences creating opportunities abroad – strict legal controls on the selling and advertising of tobacco products in the USA and EU have encouraged most large cigarette manufacturers to target selling in emerging market economies with fewer restrictions. Profitable, yes – but how ethical is this?

KEY CONCEPT LINK

Marketing goods and services in foreign countries opens up new opportunities for **creating value** – especially if the 'home' market is saturated or the economy is in recession. There are substantial costs and risks, however, and **management** will need to be aware of these and respond to them.

Why international marketing is different

Political differences

Changes of governments can cause instability in some countries and this can increase the risk of doing business there. Acts of terrorism or threats of civil violence, which might lead to destruction of a company's assets, will all add to the problems of marketing abroad.

Economic and social differences

Average living standards vary greatly across the globe. The country with the highest GDP per head of population is Luxembourg (US$107,476), and the lowest is Burundi (US $251) (source: World Bank, 2013). Location decisions about a firm's marketing activities will need to take this into account as well as differences in tax rates, interest rates and the age structure of the population. The role of women and the importance of marriage in society vary substantially too and these and other social factors may have a considerable impact on the products to be sold and the marketing strategies used to sell them.

Legal differences

There are many of these and they will impact on international marketing in key ways. For example:

- Some goods, such as guns, can be sold in the USA, but are illegal in other countries.
- It is illegal to advertise directly to children below the age of 12 on Swedish TV – and there are other restrictions in other countries.
- Product safety and product labelling controls are much stricter in the EU than in some African states.

Cultural differences

This is a key factor to consider in international marketing, yet it is often difficult to define and measure. Cultural differences are not written down as laws are, yet they can exercise as powerful an impact on people's behaviour. Failure to recognise cultural differences – including language differences – can have a disastrous effect on a firm's marketing strategy. Some words have unfortunate meanings when translated into another language. The use of male and female models in advertisements would not be acceptable in some countries with strong religious traditions. Colours can

have different significances too – in the Far East, white rather than black is associated with mourning.

Differences in business practices

Accounting standards and rules can vary in different parts of the world. The ease of setting up a limited company varies widely – it can take a few days in the UK, yet the formalities and form-filling can take more than a year in Sierra Leone!

TOP TIP

You need to keep up-to-date with business practices and legal changes in your own country – you may be asked to evaluate a business strategy used by a business operating in your country. Specific references to differences between your country and others could be useful.

International markets – different methods of entry

A decision to market products internationally is just one step in a long and detailed planning process. The next major decision must be the method of entering the markets.

Exporting

Exporting can be undertaken either by selling the product directly to a foreign customer – perhaps the order has been placed via the company website – or indirectly through an export intermediary, such as an agent or trading company based in the country. Some of the benefits and limitations of exporting directly and indirectly are shown in Tables 21.2 and 21.3.

International franchising

Franchising was defined and explained in Chapter 2. International franchising means that foreign franchisees are used to operate a firm's activities abroad. This can either take the form of one foreign company being used as a franchisee for *all* the branches in their own country or individual franchisees are appointed to operate each outlet. McDonald's uses just one franchisee business to operate its branches in Argentina, for example. The benefits and limitations of appointing franchisees are the same as explained in Table 2.6 with the additional benefit that the foreign franchisee(s) will have important local market knowledge.

Joint ventures

These were analysed in Chapter 2 and the same benefits and limitations apply as were explained on page 24. An example of this method to enter an international market is the 50-50 joint venture between McDonald's and two Indian restaurant chains, Hardcastle Restaurants and Connaught Plaza restaurants.

Benefits	Limitations
■ Exporting directly means that the company has complete control over the international marketing of its product. ■ Agents and traders may represent several other companies exporting goods, so may not give priority to a new exporting business and its products. ■ No commission is taken by intermediaries, so profit margins are not reduced.	■ Exporting directly means that the business will have to have dedicated sales personnel dealing with foreign buyers and company management may have to travel abroad to meet customers if the size of contracts justifies this. ■ The business does not have a local agent or trader supporting them, so may lack important local knowledge, e.g. about import controls into that country. ■ The exporting business has to handle the logistics of transporting and storing the product and dealing with all paperwork.

Table 21.2 Benefits and limitations of exporting directly

Benefits	Limitations
■ The overseas agent or trading company will have local market knowledge and contacts with potential customers and this should aid the marketing of the product. ■ Transport and administrative procedures become the responsibility of the agent. ■ It may be cheaper for the exporting firm as fewer staff involved in selling abroad will need to be employed and fewer visits from senior managers will be needed.	■ A commission or payment will have to be paid to the agent or trading company and this will reduce the exporting firm's profit margin. ■ The intermediary will have other firms' products to sell as well – how much focus and effort will be given to selling any one product?

Table 21.3 Benefits and limitations of exporting indirectly

Licensing

Licensing involves the business allowing another firm in the country being entered to produce its branded goods or patented products 'under licence', which will involve strictly controlled terms over quality. This means that goods do not have to be physically exported, saving on time and transport cost – and making food products fresher too. The 'parent' firm avoids the capital cost of setting up its own operating bases abroad. The limitations of this approach include possible lapses in quality, unethical production methods used by the licensee to cut costs – reflecting badly on the main business – and business failure of the licensee causing a hold-up in supplies of the product.

Direct investment in subsidiaries

Studies have shown that setting up company-owned subsidiaries in foreign countries can achieve higher success rates than taking over or merging with locally based companies.

The business cultures, organisational structures and technology differences between the company and the locally acquired business can often present obstacles too great to be overcome. Subsidiaries can be factories set up in foreign countries, as with Toyota in the EU and South America, or retailing operations, as with Tesco in Thailand and China. They may be almost completely decentralised – where local managers take most key decisions – or organised with centralised control from head office in the home country. Table 21.4 shows some of the benefits and limitations of direct investment in foreign subsidiaries.

International marketing – alternative strategies

Globalisation is having a great impact on the marketing strategies adopted by businesses that trade internationally. One feature of globalisation is that national and regional differences in tastes, culture, fashion and wants are becoming less obvious. According to some analysts (e.g. Levitt) the world is becoming more standardised in the goods and services that it is demanding. If this is true, then the opportunities for companies to use technology to gain massive economies of scale by selling the same product across the globe are huge.

Other writers (e.g. Douglas and Wind) suggest that substantial differences still exist in consumer needs in different countries' markets. Standardisation is only one option for entering these markets, and this will sometimes fail. The alternative is for businesses to adapt a global marketing mix to local needs and conditions – this is called localisation.

There are, then, two broad approaches to selling goods and services internationally. These are known as **'pan-global marketing'** and **'global localisation'**.

Benefits	Limitations
■ Head office has control of operations and may decide to decentralise this control to allow local managers to take decisions that reflect local conditions – there is no agent or joint venture partner to consult with or take joint decisions with. ■ All profits after tax belong to the company – no commission is paid and no sharing of profits with partner business. ■ Foreign governments may be willing to offer some financial support to encourage such inward investment.	■ It is expensive to set up operations in foreign countries – senior staff will need to visit and may need to be based in the country. Much higher capital cost required than exporting directly or indirectly. ■ Foreign operations may be subject to changes in government policy – e.g. nationalisation of assets or, as with Coca-Cola in the 1980s, being asked to leave certain states in India. ■ Decentralised foreign subsidiaries might take decisions that could damage the reputation of the whole business – such as unethical labour practices.

Table 21.4 Benefits and limitations of foreign subsidiaries

KEY TERMS

Pan-global marketing: adopting a standardised product across the globe as if the entire world were a single market – selling the same goods in the same way everywhere.

Global localisation: adapting the marketing mix, including differentiated products, to meet national and regional tastes and cultures.

Pan-regional or pan-global marketing strategies

The global corporation operates with considerable constancy at relatively low costs as if the entire world or major parts of it were a single country. The political and cultural backlash experienced by the multinational giants of McDonald's, Coca-Cola and Starbucks in some countries indicates the danger of trying to use a 'one-strategy-suits-all policy'. Slowly, these and other multinationals are

323

ACTIVITY 21.1

Three companies use the franchising path to international marketing

Dunkin' Donuts, a US-based coffee and baked-goods franchise, has opened its 50th United Arab Emirates store. Continental Foods is the UAE-based business that owns the master franchise for Dunkin' Donuts in this country. Michale Cortelletti, Dunkin' Donuts international director for the Middle East, said: 'UAE is an important growth market for the brand and has seen groundbreaking innovation, such as the opening of the first drive-through.'

Cartridge World, the ink cartridge filling business is set to continue its Asian expansion. It already has franchised outlets in India and is aiming to launch stores in Nepal, Sri Lanka, Bangladesh and Bhutan through international franchising. Without the quick growth offered by franchising and the local market expertise offered by local franchisees, the business would not have been able to grow to more than 1,300 branches in 36 countries so rapidly.

Yogen Fruz, a Canada-based frozen yoghurt chain, has signed franchise deals for Argentina and Peru with Fruzco Chile SA. This company already owns and operates Yogen Fruz franchises in Chile. Argentina has one of the fastest-growing economies in South America and has a high GDP per head. The president of Yogen Fruz said: 'We needed a locally based company with experience of the region to introduce our brands in these other countries.' Yogen Fruz does not have to pay the high capital costs of setting up its own subsidiaries in these other countries.

[32 marks, 50 minutes]

1   Explain **two** likely reasons why these companies are all operating in international markets.   [8]

2   Analyse **three** differences one of these franchiser companies might experience from selling goods in international markets compared with their home market.   [12]

3   Assess the reasons why all three companies have decided to enter international markets through franchising.   [12]

Advantages	Disadvantages
■ A common identity for the product can be established. This aids consumer recognition, especially in a world of increasing international travel by consumers and the widespread use of satellite TV channels with 'international' advertising. ■ Cost reduction can be substantial. The same product can be produced for all markets, allowing substantial economies of scale. This is particularly important for firms that have to spend huge sums on developing new products that may have only a short product life cycle. The same marketing mix can be used. This allows just one marketing agency and advertising strategy to be used for the whole world or region rather than different ones for each country. ■ It recognises that differences between consumers in different countries are reducing – it is often said that teenagers in different countries have more in common with each other than they have with their parents. Therefore, a pan-global strategy for a product aimed at teenagers could be developed.	■ Despite growing similarity between consumer tastes in different countries, it might still be necessary to develop different products to suit cultural or religious variations. Market opportunities could be lost by trying to sell basically the same product everywhere. ■ Legal restrictions can vary substantially between countries and this does not apply just to product restrictions. It is illegal to use promotions involving games or gambling in certain countries, and restrictions on what can be shown in advertisements vary too. ■ Brand names do not always translate effectively into other languages. They might even cause offence or unplanned embarrassment for the company if the selection of the brand name to be used in all markets is not made with care. ■ Setting the same price in all countries will fail to take into account different average income levels.

Table 21.5 Advantages and disadvantages of a pan-global and pan-regional marketing strategy

A Dunkin' Donuts franchise in China

realising the importance of developing slightly different strategies and products to suit diverse communities around the world. The more changes that are made to a marketing mix to reflect local and regional differences, then the closer this comes to 'global localisation'.

A 'pan-global marketing strategy' is one that adopts common products, brand messages and promotional campaigns across the whole world. More limited developments of this concept include pan-European or pan-Asian strategies, where the geographical area for such common approaches is more restricted. This strategy of not adopting different marketing strategies for different countries can have a number of advantages and disadvantages for firms (see Table 21.5).

Global marketing may continue to be important for two groups of products in particular. The first is upmarket brands with international appeal for their exclusivity – such as Rolex watches, Rolls-Royce cars and Versace dresses. The opportunity to buy the same product as famous pop stars and film actors is the key promise made by these brands. Consumers do not want them adapted to their markets. The second is mass-appeal brands such as Levi's, Apple and Nike, that have substantial opportunities for global campaigns and standardised products – and the economies of scale that result from these.

However, with growing concern about 'cultural imperialism' from US and European businesses and an expanding anti-globalisation movement, there will be increasing scope for other businesses to benefit from adapting and selling products that are geared directly towards the particular cultural, religious and consumer requirements of each country.

Global localisation

'Thinking global – acting local' is sometimes how this approach to international marketing is summed up (see Table 21.6). YUM, the world's largest fast-food organisation, with top brands such as KFC and Pizza Hut, has adopted this approach to great success. It offers all of its franchisees and branches around the globe the benefits and security offered by a giant multinational corporation. However, it differentiates most aspects of its marketing mix between different countries and markets. For example:

■ In China, it sells products that are not available in other countries to suit local consumers' tastes. So, although it was the first company to introduce the Chinese to pizzas in 1990, its best-selling lines today include 'KFC Dragon Twister'.

- Price levels are varied between different countries to reflect different average incomes.
- Advertisements always contain local 'ethnic' people.

Its distribution and place decisions are being tested for local markets too – In China, it has tried out 14 new Chinese quick-service restaurants offering authentic Chinese food in surroundings designed in a local style.

A summary of the difference between the two marketing approaches

Global marketing:

Single-product marketing mix → Global market

Localised marketing:

Product A → Region A

Product B → Region B

Product C → Region C.

Benefits	Limitations
<ul><li>Local needs, tastes and cultures are reflected in the marketing mix of the business and this could lead to higher sales and profits.</li><li>There is no attempt to impose foreign brands/products/ advertisements on regional markets.</li><li>The products are more likely to meet local national legal requirements than if they are standardised products.</li><li>There will be less local opposition to multinational business activity.</li></ul>	<ul><li>The scope for economies of scale is reduced.</li><li>The international brand could lose its power and identity if locally adapted products become more popular than the 'international' product.</li><li>There will be additional costs of adapting products, adverts, store layouts, etc. to specific local needs – these costs might lead to higher prices than a global marketing strategy would result in.</li></ul>

Table 21.6 Benefits and limitations of global localisation

325

ACTIVITY 21.2

Zumo, the energy drink

Launched in the mid-1980s, this energy product is aimed at fitness-conscious men and women aged between 20 and 45. Zumo is offered in four flavours and is distributed through supermarkets and sports clubs. Advertising is based on TV and radio media, using endorsements from well-known European sports stars. It is currently sold only in Europe, where average incomes are quite high. It is priced above an equivalent non-energy soft drink, such as Coca-Cola, but is not as expensive as some energy drinks. Zumposa is the food and drinks company based in Valencia, Spain, that produces Zumo. The managers want to make Zumo a global brand. They know that Zumo is seen as a Spanish drink and this might not be suitable when developing a global image. The board of directors has decided to focus first on South America and Asia to launch their global campaign – they aim for a 10% market share in the first year. They have to take decisions on:

- Price – should this vary to reflect different average income levels in different countries?
- Flavours – do they keep the same flavours across the globe or adapt existing products to different markets?
- Packaging – should the same style and colours of the drinks can be the same everywhere?
- Advertising – should different adverts be used in each country or could a global advert be made with different languages added for different countries?
- Name and brand image – should these be changed or should a global image and name be established?

[20 marks, 35 minutes]

As a business analyst, write a report to Zumposa's board of directors recommending an appropriate marketing strategy for this product in your country. It should contain: explanations of global marketing and localisation; advantages and disadvantages of **both** strategies for this product in your country; details of the changes you would recommend for the marketing strategy in your country. Don't forget that your marketing strategy should be integrated.

[20]

SUMMARY POINTS

- International marketing is of increasing significance as the world increasingly becomes 'one large market'.
- Globalisation is having a significant impact on business decision-making and on international trade.
- There can be important differences between domestic and international marketing.
- There are different methods of entering international markets.
- The two alternative approaches of global marketing and global localised marketing mean that businesses have to make a major strategic decision when marketing internationally.

RESEARCH TASK

- Find **three** goods (e.g. mobile/cell phone) and three services (e.g. banking services) that are sold in your country by foreign owned businesses (multinationals).
- Study **one** of these products by researching into how it is marketed in your country and whether this is different to how the product is marketed in its 'home country'. (Product/packaging design/pricing/promotion methods/adverts used/channel of distribution.)
- Assess the reasons for the extent of the marketing success of the product chosen.

A Level exam practice questions

Case study

McDonald's – pan-global strategy or global localisation?

The world's best-known fast-food restaurant has always prided itself on high standards for hygiene and levels of service in its outlets, no matter which country it is operating in. It also aims to achieve uniform product standards throughout the world. The principle of a common world approach is also extended to the marketing mix used by the business – same products, same décor, same promotions, same pricing levels. When the company first expanded internationally in the 1970s, it was selling the 'American dream' but that is no longer acceptable in many countries. The emphasis has now changed to 'global brand but local marketing'.

The need to be aware of cultural and religious factors when designing a global marketing strategy was made clear to the business when it was confronted with a lawsuit from Indian Hindus. McDonald's had to apologise to all religious and secular vegetarians for failing to make clear that beef flavouring is added to its fries in the USA. It is claimed that there are at least 16 million vegetarians in the USA, who may have eaten these fries and that they could be suffering from emotional distress as a result. In India, restaurant windows were smashed and dirt was smeared on statues of Ronald McDonald. Hindu leaders called for the food chain to be expelled from the country.

There are benefits to standardisation, however – the McDonald's double-arch logo is now the best-recognised in the world, for example, and internationally standardised adverts as used by Coca-Cola offer economies of scale as well as reïnforcing the global nature of the brand.

However, McDonald's is not alone in increasingly adopting the 'think globally, act locally' concept. Products that are too heavily focused on American culture, tastes and consumer needs are much less well received in some countries than they used to be. Adapting well-known brands to meet the cultural and social demands of countries that are becoming more independent in their approach to business and marketing is now a priority for companies like McDonald's. In India, McDonald's had to move away from reliance on beef and now has an Indian menu with local flavours, such as McCurry Pan and Chicken Maharaja Mac. In France, the changes have been even more substantial. Red and yellow colours are replaced with more 'adult' colour schemes. External restaurant signs are discreet and blend in with the neighbourhood. There are real leather seats, gas fireplaces and hardwood floors. Organic ingredients are used and healthy-eating messages are displayed on every wall. French desserts are offered instead of the standard options and a big seller is *le p'tit moutarde* – a small hamburger with a French mustard sauce. McDonald's sales in France rose by 8% in one year after some years of much slower growth – perhaps meeting local needs and responding to national consumer tastes is the way forward.

McDonald's annual percentage sales revenue growth:

	2011 %	2012 %
USA	2	5
Europe	6	8
Asia, Middle East, Africa	5	11

Sources: www.moneymorning.com and www.mcdonalds.com/corp/news

[32 marks, 50 minutes]

1   Explain the likely reasons why McDonald's decided to enter international markets.   [8]

2   Discuss the advantages and disadvantages to McDonald's of initially using a pan-global marketing strategy for its restaurants.   [10]

3   Assume that a new McDonald's restaurant is planning to open in your town. Evaluate how and why you might adapt the company's marketing strategy to suit local market conditions.   [14]

A Level essay questions

[20 marks, 45 minutes each]

1   Recommend to a marketing director of one of your country's largest manufacturers of consumer goods the best way to sell its products in another country's market that it has not yet entered.   [20]

2   'Pan-global marketing is the only way forward – we must establish a global identity and sell in all markets using the same mix.' Discuss whether this approach is likely to be successful for a manufacturer of quality ice creams.   [20]

End of Unit 3: Exam-style case study questions

General Engineering Group (GEG)

GEG manufactures a wide range of equipment used by the construction industry. The range includes diggers and cranes. GEG currently sells only to customers in country X. Sales rose rapidly during the 'boom' years of economic growth despite competition from imported equipment. However, the recession last year resulted in GEG's sales falling by 20%. This economic downturn had not been predicted by GEG's directors – only 12 months ago they had been planning an extension to the factory and the recruitment of additional employees. The recent loss of 100 jobs at the company shows how much the economic environment has changed. The marketing director admitted at the most recent board meeting: 'We forecast seasonal sales changes with some accuracy – see the data for the last four years I used as a basis for my forecast (Appendix 1) – but we did not see this recession coming.'

New product research – time to cut back?

In recent years, GEG has invested, on average, 10% of its revenue into researching and developing (R&D) new products and updating existing ones. This is one of the highest levels of R&D spending in the industry. Its R&D department is responsible for one of the biggest developments in construction equipment over the past ten years – the Robodigger. This unique computerised digger now generates 35% of GEG's sales and 50% of its operating profits. Since then, the department has been less effective but it is in the final stages of developing a prototype Ezelift crane. A modular construction, it allows different sizes to be made. GEG hope that this prototype will open up the consumer market of those requiring a small crane for small and medium projects around the home. GEG's R&D department stated in a recent report to the board that 'GEG's R&D spending has been falling behind that of our competitors. Despite this we could be on the verge of a major breakthrough with the Ezelift if we increase investment next year.' The finance director of GEG suggested to other directors recently: 'We need to reduce costs: cutting R&D spending is the quickest way to do it. Any benefits from the Ezelift will not be received for several years.'

HiLo crane needs new marketing strategy

GEG's oldest product design – the HiLo crane – still sells around 50 units per year. Marketing director Asmir is planning a market extension strategy for the product using data (Appendix 2) to help plan the most effective changes to the product's current strategy.

Country Y – GEG planning to export for first time

GEG's board has decided to start selling products to customers in country Y. This is a large developing country with a rapidly expanding construction industry. Most major construction equipment manufacturers export to country Y – GEG being the main exception. Phil has to decide on the best marketing strategy to enter the market for country Y. He has outlined two potential strategies to be discussed at the next board meeting (Appendix 3).

Appendix 1: Past GEG sales data analysed by the marketing department

Year	Quarter	Sales $m	Moving average trend $m	Seasonal variation $m
2011	1	23		
	2	27		
	3	35	27.5	7.5
	4	24	28	-4
2012	1	25	28.625	-3.625
	2	29	29.375	-0.375
	3	38	30.125	7.875
	4	27	31	-4
2013	1	28	31.875	-3.875
	2	33	32.5	x
	3	41	32.75	8.25
	4	29	32.625	y
2014	1	28		
	2	32		

Quarter	1	2v	3	4
Average seasonal variation $m	-3.75	0.0625	z	-3.875

Appendix 2: Marketing data for HiLo crane

Current price	$50,000
Price of main competitor's crane	$45,000
Estimated price elasticity of demand for HiLo crane	-1.2
Cost of product redesign for HiLo crane	$2 million
Forecast additional sales of HiLo crane following redesign	10 units per year
Existing annual promotion budget for HiLo crane	$0.25 million
Estimated promotion elasticity of demand for HiLo crane	0.9

Appendix 3: Alternative marketing strategies for country Y

	Strategy A	Strategy B
Prices	Same as in country X to maintain quality image	20% lower than country X
Promotion	Using same advertisements as in country X	Spend additional $3 million on specific promotion material for country X
Product	Same models as sold in country X	Develop cheaper models of existing designs
Distribution channel	Employ direct sales team in country X	Arrange joint venture with existing construction equipment agent
Marketing objective	5% market share within two years	15% market share within two years

 KEY CONCEPT REVIEW

Marketing is an important department or function of all businesses. The growing trend is for businesses to become more 'customer-focused' as the increased competition resulting from **globalisation** has meant that customers have more choice of supplier than ever before. **E-commerce** is an innovation that many businesses have adopted and it can help to reduce costs and create more value. Websites need to be continuously updated, however, and the increased use of social media is an important change that can bring both benefits and risks to businesses.

329

A Level *50 marks* *90 minutes*

1 Analyse the potential benefits to GEG of investing in research and development. [10]

2 **a** Refer to the data in Appendix 1. Calculate the following missing values:

   i x [1]

   ii y [1]

   iii z [2]

   b Evaluate the extent to which Asmir should rely only on this moving average method of sales forecasting when making decisions about operating capacity and staffing levels. [10]

3 Assess the usefulness of the data in Appendix 2 to Asmir when considering changes to the marketing strategy for the HiLo crane. [10]

4 Using the data in Appendix 3 and other information, recommend to GEG's board of directors whether the company should adopt Strategy A or Strategy B to market the company's products in country Y. [16]

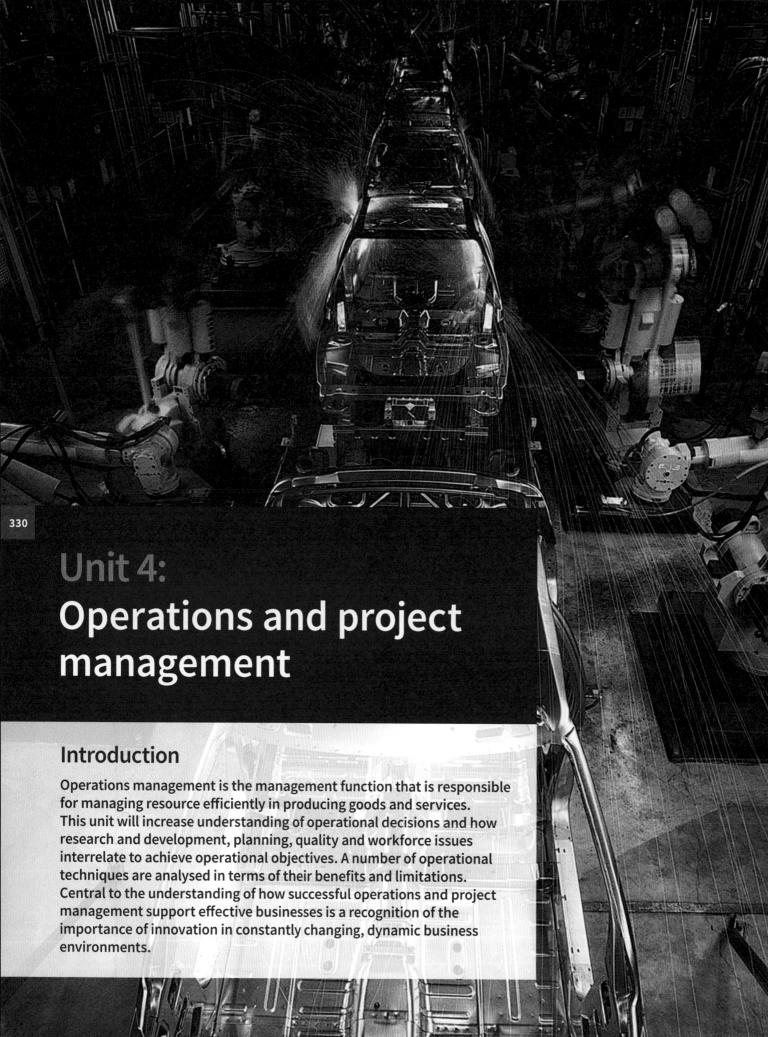

Unit 4:
Operations and project management

Introduction

Operations management is the management function that is responsible for managing resource efficiently in producing goods and services. This unit will increase understanding of operational decisions and how research and development, planning, quality and workforce issues interrelate to achieve operational objectives. A number of operational techniques are analysed in terms of their benefits and limitations. Central to the understanding of how successful operations and project management support effective businesses is a recognition of the importance of innovation in constantly changing, dynamic business environments.

22 The nature of operations

On completing this chapter, you will be able to:

- understand what is meant by operations management
- appreciate the nature of the production process and how value can be added
- understand the difference between production and productivity, efficiency and effectiveness
- evaluate the different advantages and limitations of labour intensity and capital intensity.

Introducing the topic

FURNWARE'S PRODUCTIVITY RISES TO MEET IMPORT CHALLENGE

Furnware, a New Zealand (NZ) company, is a world leader in the design and manufacture of school furniture. When the NZ government adopted the policy that all schools could choose to purchase their own desks, chairs and other furniture, Furnware had to compete and innovate to become schools' first choice for high-quality and affordable products. Cheap imports threatened to flood the market and destroy the company, but the managing director, Hamish Whyte, had other plans. His strategy included:

- researching the market – information gathered suggested 96% of students had furniture that was unsuitable for their size and weight: 19,000 students were measured to assess the right sizes of chairs to make
- using research results to design a unique range of school chairs and desks to suit students of different ages – these are scientifically designed for comfort
- increasing workforce productivity – the units of furniture produced per worker – to keep unit costs

as low as possible. This was achieved with the latest production machinery, staff training and organising work better.

The strategy has proved to be very successful. 'Schools cannot get enough of our furniture,' says Hamish. Even though it is more expensive than cheaper imports, schools get exactly the size and style of furniture they demand. 'And productivity in the factory has risen 100%,' concluded Hamish.

Points to think about:

- Do you think it is important to link the design and manufacture of products with market research results? Explain your answer.
- Why is it important for this business to increase productivity – the number of units made per worker?
- Explain how this business achieved such a substantial increase in productivity.

Introduction

'Operations' or 'operations management' is concerned with the use of resources called inputs – land, labour and capital – to provide outputs in the form of goods and services. In doing this, operations managers must be concerned with:

- **efficiency of production** – keeping costs as low as possible will help to give competitive advantage
- **quality** – the good or service must be suitable for the purpose intended
- **flexibility and innovation** – the need to develop and adapt to new processes and new products is increasingly important in today's dynamic business environment.

Essentially, operations managers are aiming to produce goods and services of the required quality, in the required quantity, at the time needed, in the most cost-effective way.

The production – or transformation – process

In all businesses at all stages of production, the production process is basically the same. 'Inputs' are converted or transformed into 'outputs' and this is sometimes called the 'transformation' process. This can be simply illustrated (see Figure 22.1).

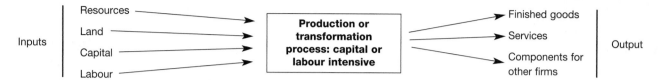

Figure 22.1 The transformation process

This process applies to both manufacturing and service industries. By 'production', we mean the making of tangible goods, such as computers, and the provision of intangible services, such as banking. The aim in all cases is to **add value** to the inputs that are bought in by the business so that the resulting output can be sold at a profit. This concept was covered in Chapter 1 but it is important to revisit it here.

KEY TERM

Added value: the difference between the cost of purchasing raw materials and the price the finished goods are sold for – this is the same as creating value.

The degree of value created and added to the inputs will depend on a number of factors – not all of them operations management issues:

- **The design of the product:** Does this allow for economic manufacture, while appearing to have quality features that will enable a high price to be charged? The Furnware case study on page 331 suggested that customers were prepared to pay higher prices for products that offered a better quality than cheaper substitutes.

- **The efficiency with which the input resources are combined and managed:** For example, by reducing waste, the operations management department will increase the value added by the production process. Increasing productivity will reduce costs per unit and this will increase added value if the customer prices remain unchanged. So efficient operations processes and operations decisions are closely linked to value added.

- **Being able to convince consumers to pay more for the product than the cost of the inputs:** A good example is the market for luxury ice creams, where the marketing campaigns increase the willingness of consumers to pay far in excess of input costs for the product.

The operations process can involve many stages before physically selling the good or service. These include:

- converting a consumer need into a product that can be produced efficiently
- organising operations so that production is carried out efficiently – for example, ordering stocks to arrive on time
- deciding on suitable production methods
- setting quality standards and checking they are maintained.

TOP TIP

Do not think that operations management is only for manufacturing businesses. Businesses providing services, such as banks and bicycle-repair shops, must also plan to use resources productively and effectively.

Resources

All business operations require resources – these are the production inputs.

- **Land:** All businesses need somewhere to operate from, even if it is the bedroom of a sole trader operating an internet-based website design service. Some businesses, of course, require large sites for the extraction of minerals or the manufacture of finished products. Chapter 23 analyses the importance of business location and the site chosen for a business's operations on the success of firms.

- **Labour:** All business activity requires some labour input. This can be the manual labour of a gardener or the mental skills of a research scientist. The quality of the labour input will have a significant impact on the operational success of a business. The effectiveness of labour can usually be improved by training in specific skills – but trained workers will become sought after by other businesses and may leave.

- **Capital:** This refers to the tools, machinery, computers and other equipment that businesses use to produce the goods and services they sell. **Intellectual capital** is becoming increasingly important too in knowledge-based economies. Efficient operations often depend on capital equipment and, in competitive markets, the more productive and advanced the capital, the greater the chance of business success.

KEY TERM

Intellectual capital: intangible capital of a business that includes human capital (well trained and knowledgeable employees), structural capital (databases and information systems) and relational captial (good links with supplier and customers).

Production and productivity

Productivity is not the same as the **level of production** and the two should not be confused. **Production** is an absolute measure of the quantity of output that a firm

These are both examples of capital inputs to the production process

	Number of furniture units produced	Number of workers employed	Labour productivity = output/workers	Annual pay per worker	Labour cost per unit = annual pay/labour productivity
Company A	5,000	10	500	$2,000	$4
Company B	12,000	20	600	$2,000	$3.33

Table 22.1 The higher the level of labour productivity, the lower the labour cost per unit produced – assuming the pay per worker is the same

333

produces in a given period of time. Productivity is a relative measure – and is concerned with how efficiently inputs are converted into outputs. The most common measures of productivity are:

labour productivity (number of units per worker) =

$$\frac{\text{total output in a given time period}}{\text{total workers employed}}$$

$$\text{capital productivity} = \frac{\text{output}}{\text{capital employed}}$$

KEY TERMS

Production: converting inputs into outputs.

Level of production: the number of units produced during a time period.

Productivity: the ratio of outputs to inputs during production, e.g. output per worker per time period.

Nearly all firms are trying at all times to increase productivity, even if total production is not increasing. A business can do this by employing fewer but better-skilled workers and by using fewer but more technologically advanced machines. Improvements in productivity usually lead to a reduction in the unit costs of production. If the costs of labour and capital inputs do not change, then any increase in output per worker or output per machine will lead to a fall in unit costs. In competitive markets, this could give firms a crucial advantage.

Example: Table 22.1 shows the annual output and employment levels in two companies producing kitchen cupboards.

Raising productivity levels

There are four main ways in which productivity levels could be increased:

1 **Improve the training of staff to raise skill levels:** Staff with higher and more flexible skill levels should be more productive. As well as being able to perform tasks more efficiently, they could become more interested in work due to their ability to do different jobs. However, training can be expensive and time-consuming and highly qualified staff could leave to join another, perhaps rival, business.

2 **Improve worker motivation:** Many different views on the most appropriate ways to do this exist. Increasing pay, as identified by Herzberg, is unlikely to have a permanent

impact on productivity. There may be little point in raising pay by 10% if labour productivity only rises by 5%. After all, it is unit costs that firms want to drive down. Most businesses now put the emphasis on non-financial methods of motivation. These include involvement in decision-making, kaizen groups, delegation and quality circles. If these increase productivity without an increase in labour pay then unit costs will fall.

3 **Purchase more technologically advanced equipment:** Modern machinery – from office computers to robot-controlled production machines – should allow increased output with fewer staff. Such expensive investment will only be worthwhile, however, if high output levels can be maintained. In addition to the capital cost, staff may need to be retrained and there may be genuine fear among the workers about lost jobs and reduced security of employment.

4 **More efficient management:** There are many ways in which ineffective management can reduce the overall productivity of a business. Failure to purchase the correct materials, poor maintenance schedules for machines or heavy-handed management of staff are just some of these. More efficient operations and people management could go a long way to improve productivity levels.

> **TOP TIP**
>
> It is possible for a business to achieve an increase in labour productivity but to reduce total output too. If demand for the product is falling, it might be necessary to reduce the size of the workforce – but by a smaller proportion than the reduction in output.

 KEY CONCEPT LINK

Management – and the quality and effectiveness of management – is an important determinant of operational efficiency. It is not all about 'machines' and 'making people work harder' – the management of resources, processes and people are just as important.

Is raising productivity always the answer?

- Increasing productivity does not guarantee business success. If the product is unpopular with consumers, it may not sell profitably no matter how efficiently it is made.

- Greater effort and contributions from workers to increase productivity could lead to much higher wage demands. If these actually lead to increasing unit costs, then the productivity gains have not achieved their goal.

- Finally, workers and their unions are becoming fearful of dramatic improvements in labour productivity. If a firm manages to raise labour productivity by 20% but sales remain at the same level, 20% of the workforce may find themselves without a job.

- In the end, as with most business decisions, it is the quality of the management that will determine the overall success of a policy that aims to increase productivity. If the culture of management is to involve the workforce at every step of the strategy, to seek their views and welcome their contributions, then the productivity improvements are likely to be more significant and accepted by all staff.

- There is a difference between efficiency – as measured by productivity – and effectiveness.

ACTIVITY 22.1

Why productivity is important

In one town there are three take-away pizza stores. Rapid Pizza is losing sales to the other two businesses because its prices are higher. 'We must charge these prices to cover our costs,' said the manager at Rapid Pizza. He asked for advice from a business consultant who was able to obtain the following information:

	Number of pizzas produced each week	Number of workers employed	Weekly pay per worker
Rapid Pizza	3,000	15	$60
Pizza to Go	3,960	18	$60
Pizza4U	6,600	25	$66

[18 marks, 25 minutes]

1 Calculate the labour productivity in all three businesses. [6]

2 Outline **three** reasons for the different levels of labour productivity. [6]

3 Explain the importance of labour productivity to the manager of Rapid Pizza. [6]

Westlife Jeans Ltd

The operations manager at Westlife Jeans Ltd is concerned about the declining rate of productivity in the factory. He has collected the following data from factory records. Each worker is paid $3,000 per year and this has not changed for three years. New staff have been employed and put into the production department with little training. The additional machines were purchased second-hand and some of them have proven to be unreliable. The operations manager has been told to increase productivity within six months, as it is believed that the major competitor to Westlife Jeans has labour costs that are 20% lower. Although the marketing department admits that the higher quality of Westlife's jeans allows higher prices to be charged, the lack of cost competitiveness is cutting into profits. Falling profitability may make it difficult to raise the capital needed for any technological improvements in the factory – but, without these, profits could fall even further.

	2011	2012	2013
Total output of jeans (pairs)	50,000	55,000	60,000
Workers employed	20	24	30
Number of machines used	10	12	15

[34 marks, 45 minutes]

1 For each year, calculate in the Westlife factory:
   a labour productivity
   b capital productivity. [6]

2 Analyse the likely reasons for the trends in productivity that your results indicate. [12]

3 By calculating unit labour cost for each year, explain why declining productivity could be a major problem for this company. [6]

4 Suggest and evaluate **two** methods that the operations manager could use to improve productivity over the next six months. [10]

Efficiency and effectiveness

An important distinction needs to be made between these two terms. **Efficiency** is measured by productivity, but **effectiveness** is rather different. Effectiveness is achieved only if the customer's needs are met. Perhaps an example will help. A business might have recently achieved the highest level of productivity it has ever gained in producing an old model of bicycle it has been making for 25 years. Unfortunately, the sales of this model are falling and stocks of unsold bicycles are building up in the factory. Would you describe the operations of this business as being effective?

Hopefully you would not. Effectiveness means meeting objectives other than just being efficient in operations. It means meeting customers' needs profitably – and being efficient in production is only one part of this. For the long-term future of any business, satisfying customers' needs profitably is much more important than just producing 'at the lowest-possible unit cost'. Obviously, effectiveness is not about wasting inputs – it is about putting them to productive use to achieve the objectives of the business.

 KEY TERMS

Efficiency: producing output at the highest ratio of output to input.

Effectiveness: meeting the objectives of the enterprise by using inputs productively to meet customers' needs.

Labour intensity and capital intensity

Operations managers must decide what combination of factors of production they will use. There are two main approaches. Firms can be described as either being **labour intensive** or **capital intensive**.

Labour-intensive methods of production might be most appropriate, for example, for a furniture company that specialises in making reproduction furniture by hand. Some machines will be used for sawing and shaping the wood, but the assembly and finishing may be done by manual labour. If firms insist on maintaining a high degree of labour

Hand-carved furniture – an example of labour-intensive production

intensity – perhaps because of the marketing advantages of a 'hand-built' image or due to lack of finance – then the opportunities to increase labour productivity are likely to be quite limited.

In contrast, many industries that supply mass-produced goods are capital intensive due to the nature of the production process involved. For instance, electricity generation or aluminium smelting can only be economically undertaken by using vast and very expensive capital-intensive plants. Other businesses may choose to be capital intensive even though labour-intensive production is still possible. An example would be in the baking of bread. All over the world, craft bakers still exist who bake bread in traditional ways, using simple and relatively inexpensive capital tools. However, on a large scale, it is possible to bake thousands of loaves a day in highly automated factories with an absolute minimum of staff. The advantages should be obvious by now – the substantial opportunities for scale economies and unit-cost reductions offered by large-scale capital utilisation make this the first choice for many business managers. In general terms, job production tends to be labour intensive and flow production is nearly always capital intensive (see pages 343–344).

Capital intensity brings its own problems. Fixed costs tend to be high and the cost of financing the purchase of equipment can be beyond some businesses. Maintenance costs are often high too and skilled engineers and computer programmers might be needed to monitor and adjust the performance of the capital plant. The pace of technological change can quickly render the latest production equipment and computer systems obsolete and relatively inefficient. These potential drawbacks are unlikely to slow the trend towards capital-intensive production in most industries. However, for as long as consumers are prepared to pay for traditional craft-made goods that create a sense of distinction, then labour-intensive methods will remain profitable for firms in certain industries.

In conclusion, which approach is chosen depends on:

- the nature of the product and the product image that the firm wishes to establish
- the relative prices of the two inputs – if labour costs are high and rising, then using more capital equipment might be justifiable
- the size of the firm and its ability to afford expensive capital equipment.

SUMMARY POINTS

- Operations management is about transforming input resources into outputs. It is important to all businesses – not just firms engaged in manufacturing.
- Input resources are needed for all businesses.
- Production and productivity are not the same.
- Productivity can be measured by labour productivity and capital productivity.
- There are several ways in which a business might increase productivity.
- Efficiency and effectiveness in operations management are not the same.
- The benefits and limitations of labour-intensive and capital-intensive production can be assessed and the factors that influence business decisions on the type of production used can be analysed.

RESEARCH TASK

- Identify **four** businesses in your area and explain the 'transformation' process in each case.
- Investigate the resources used by these four businesses. You may be able to arrange a visit to one or some of these businesses, through your teachers.
- Explain how productivity could be measured within these businesses.

AS Level exam practice questions

Short answer questions

[48 marks, 60 minutes]

Knowledge and understanding

1 What do you understand by the expression 'transformation process of inputs into output'? **[4]**

2 Explain how it is possible for a business to reduce its level of production but increase its labour productivity. **[6]**

3 Explain the link between levels of productivity and unit costs (average cost per unit). **[4]**

4 Explain how value added depends on both marketing and the operations process. **[4]**

Application

5 Explain the resources that will be needed by a farmer to produce wheat. **[4]**

6 Outline **two** ways in which a factory producing cakes and biscuits could increase its labour productivity. **[6]**

7 Explain the difference between efficiency and effectiveness for a private dentist's business. **[6]**

8 A dress- and suit-maker decides to switch from labour-intensive methods of production to capital-intensive methods. Explain **two** possible reasons for this change. **[4]**

9 Outline **two** effects on workers of the change to production methods in question 8. **[4]**

10 Explain to the owner of a jewellery-making business **two** ways in which operations decisions could increase value added. **[6]**

Data response

Operational issues at KL Juice Bar

Raj and Ameer's first fresh juice bar opened last year with a lot of free publicity. Raj knew a famous actor and he had agreed to 'cut the ribbon' to open the bar in the city centre. Production inputs included juicing machines, fresh fruit and a trained café manager. The drinks and snacks sold in the bar were very popular – they were all handmade on the premises. In fact they were almost too popular, as the two owners soon found it very hard to keep up with demand. Long queues started building up and customers complained about drinks and snacks that were not fresh and were of poor quality. The daily number of customers served fell from 600 during the first week of opening to 500 after two months – even though the same number of workers were employed. This fall in labour productivity worried the owners. They believed this problem resulted from some new part-time employees lacking training, the failure of one of the juice-making machines and a poor attitude among the workers.

[30 marks, 45 minutes]

1 a Define the term 'production inputs'. [2]

   b Briefly explain the term 'labour productivity'. [3]

2 Explain the transformation process that operates in the KL Juice Bar. [6]

3 Analyse ways in which the KL Juice Bar could be made efficient and effective. [8]

4 Currently KL Juice Bar is labour intensive. Evaluate whether Raj and Ameer should make the production process as capital intensive as possible. [11]

AS Level essay questions

[20 marks, 40 minutes each]

1 'Operations management is only important to secondary manufacturing businesses.' To what extent do you agree with this statement? [20]

2 a Analyse **two** ways in which a car repair business could increase labour productivity. [8]

   b Evaluate the factors that a business making bricks should take into account before taking a decision to switch from labour-intensive production to capital-intensive production. [12]

23 Operations planning

This chapter covers syllabus sections AS Level 4.2 and A Level 4.2.

On completion of this chapter, you will be able to:

- understand the need for operations planning
- analyse the influence of marketing, resources and information technology on operations planning
- understand the need for flexibility and process innovation
- differentiate between different production methods: job, batch, flow, mass customisation
- evaluate the factors that determine the production methods used in different situations and understand the problems in changing method
- assess the importance of location decisions to the success of a business and evaluate the factors that influence location and relocation decisions
- understand why businesses may want to increase scale of production
- analyse the importance of economies and diseconomies of scale and the impact on unit costs
- understand enterprise resource planning (ERP) [A Level only].

Introducing the topic

LOCATING IN TRINIDAD AND TOBAGO

Two multinational food companies have located in Trinidad for similar reasons. PR Trinidad Ltd is a subsidiary of a French food and drinks multinational. The 100-employee company extracts anise oil, which is used as flavouring, from the leaves of anise bushes planted on land leased at a reasonable rent from the government. Before deciding on Trinidad as the best location, the company 'looked first at the economic and political stability of the country', reported the operations manager. 'Trinidad also enjoys the right climate for anise production and we found a large area of flat land suitable for its production,' he added. Other reasons given by the company for its location decision were the well-trained workforce with a good supply of qualified technicians from the local university. The company is planning some joint ventures with other local businesses – so the existence of other businesses in the drinks industry was an important factor in moving to Trinidad too.

Coca-Cola recently opened a bottling plant in Trinidad and employs 350 staff there. The flow production method is used with much automated machinery. The demand for soft drinks in the Caribbean is high all year round. The general manager of the bottling plant believes that 'the government is in favour of private-sector industry and supports

it. Many of the qualified young professionals in the Caribbean come from the University of West Indies and this was important to us.' Trinidad is viewed as the key island for manufacturing within the regional free-trade area known as CARICOM. Being a member of this organisation allows free trade between members for goods manufactured on the island. Many of the other countries in the region are too small to have the resources needed for a large operation such as Coca-Cola. 'I believe that in the long term the decision will prove to be an even better one as the CARICOM area opens up more and more and Trinidad is well located to supply all of its members,' added the general manager.

Points to think about:

- List and explain **six** reasons for these companies locating in Trinidad.
- Do you think that the location decision is a very important one for all businesses? Explain your answer by referring to soft drink manufacturers, hotels and hairdressing businesses.
- Flow production is continuous production of large quantities of a product – why do you think this is appropriate for Coca-Cola production?

Introduction

Production decisions cannot be made independently of the rest of the business. If an operations manager announced one day that his department would 'increase output by 50% over the next six months', without coordinating this with other departments, these are some of the problems that would probably occur:

- not enough capital to pay for stocks, machines and labour – because no one had told the finance department
- too few workers – the HR department had not been asked to add this output increase into the workforce plan
- not enough customers – what is the point in increasing output unless there is good evidence from the marketing department that the extra products can be sold profitably?

This rather extreme example helps to demonstrate the need for planning for future production with all departments of the business. Perhaps the most important link is between marketing and operations management.

Operations decisions

The decisions taken by operations managers can have a significant impact on the success of businesses. These decisions are often influenced by:

- marketing factors
- availability of resources
- technology.

KEY TERM

Operations planning: preparing input resources to supply products to meet expected demand.

1 The link with marketing

Perhaps the key information needed by an operations manager when planning future production levels is the estimated or forecast market demand. This is a crucial link – trying to match supply to potential demand. This process is called sales and **operations planning**. If the sales forecasts are reasonably accurate, then operations managers should be able to:

- match output closely to the demand levels – this may require the holding of inventories
- keep inventory levels to a minimum efficient level
- reduce wastage of production, e.g. by perishable products being rejected due to being too old
- employ and keep busy a stable, appropriate number of staff
- produce the right product mix, i.e. the range of products that are forecast to be demanded.

TOP TIP

This is another example of how important it is for departments within a business to communicate effectively together and coordinate their decisions.

2 The availability of resources

The production of all goods and services requires resources – land, raw materials, labour, capital equipment. The availability of these resources – or a lack of them – can influence a number of important operations decisions. Some examples include:

- **Location:** A business might locate in a country or a region that has an abundant supply of necessary raw materials.
- **Nature of production method:** If the supply of suitable employees is good and wage costs are low then a business might decide to operate a labour intensive production method.
- **Automation:** If the cost of automated/robotic computer controlled equipment is falling then a business could decide to change production methods in favour of IT-based systems.

3 Technology

Production methods in both service provision and goods manufacturing have changed dramatically in recent decades as cheap digital technology has made possible the application of IT throughout a typical operations department. Perhaps the two most important technological innovations have been **CAD** and **CAM**.

KEY TERMS

CAD – computer aided design: the use of computer programs to create two- or three-dimensional (2D or 3D) graphical representations of physical objects.

CAM – computer aided manufacturing: the use of computer software to control machine tools and related machinery in the manufacturing of components or complete products.

CAD software may be specialized for specific applications, e.g. architectural designs. It is widely used for computer animation and special effects in movies, advertising and other applications where the graphic design itself is the finished product. CAD is also used to design physical products in a wide range of industries such as furniture-making, where the software performs calculations for determining an optimum shape and size for a variety of product and industrial design applications.

In product and industrial design, CAD is used mainly for the creation of detailed 3D models. CAD is also used throughout the engineering process from design of products, through analysis of component assemblies to the structure of manufacturing methods. This allows an engineer to both interactively and automatically analyse design variations, to find the best design for manufacturing while minimizing the use of costly physical versions of the product. The benefits of CAD include:

- lower product development costs
- increased productivity
- improved product quality
- faster time-to-market
- good visualization of the final product and its constituent parts
- great accuracy, so errors are reduced
- easy re-use of design data for other product applications.

The limitations of CAD include:

- complexity of the programs
- need for extensive employee training
- large amounts of amount of computer processing power required and this is can be expensive.

Through the use of CAM, a factory can become highly automated. A CAM system usually seeks to control the production process through automation. These processes are carried out by various robotic tools, such as lathes, milling machines and welding machines. Each of the many manufacturing processes in a CAM system is controlled by computers, so a high degree of precision and consistency can be achieved that is not possible with machinery that must be controlled by people. The benefits of CAM include:

- precise manufacturing and reduced quality problems – compared to production methods controlled by people
- faster production and increased labour productivity
- more flexible production allowing quick changeover from one product to another
- integrating with CAD, CAM allows more design variants of a product to be produced, which means that niche products can be produced as well as mainstream mass market products. This increased customisation increases the competitiveness of businesses in both small and large market segments.

The limitations of CAM include:

- cost of hardware, programs and employee training – these costs may mean that smaller businesses cannot access the benefits of CAM – although technology is becoming cheaper
- hardware failure – breakdowns can and do occur and they can be complex and time-consuming to solve

Computer screen showing 3D CAD modelling

Computer-controlled machines

- quality assurance is still needed – errors in programs can produce faults that have to be spotted and rectified before being passed on to the next stage of production.

The need for flexibility and innovation

Future demand patterns are not easy to predict accurately. If actual demand turns out to be either higher or lower than forecast, there is a great need for '**operational flexibility**'.

KEY TERM

Operational flexibility: the ability of a business to vary both the level of production and the range of products following changes in customer demand.

This flexibility can be achieved in a number of ways. These will be analysed in more detail in other chapters. A brief outline of these methods is to:

- increase capacity by extending buildings and buying more equipment – this is an expensive option
- hold high stocks – but these can be damaged and there is an opportunity cost to the capital tied up
- have a flexible and adaptable labour force – using temporary, part-time contracts reduces fixed salary costs but may reduce worker motivation
- have flexible flow-line production equipment – see mass customisation below.

Process innovation

Some recent examples will help to show the extent and importance of some of these new methods:

- Robots in manufacturing.
- Faster machines to manufacture microchips for computers.
- Computer tracking of inventories, e.g. by using bar codes and scanners, to reduce the chances of customers finding businesses out of stock.
- Using the Internet to track the exact location of parcels being delivered worldwide and improve the speed of delivery.

KEY TERM

Process innovation: the use of a new or much improved production method or service delivery method.

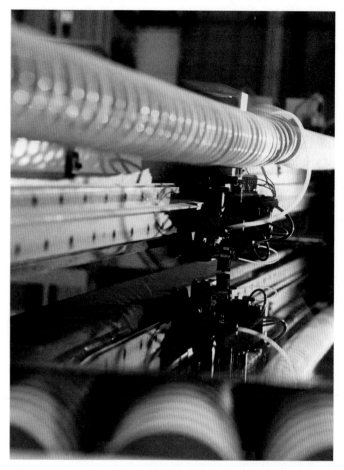

Pilkington's process innovation contributed to the company's international success

Example 1: The float-glass production process revolutionised the manufacture of sheet glass. The UK-based business, Pilkington, patented this process and gained a competitive advantage as it is both cheaper than traditional processes and produces the very highest quality of glass. The company has developed an unrivalled reputation for innovation and research in this industry.

Example 2: Amazon is testing unmanned flying drones to deliver parcels to customers to improve workflow and speed of delivery. According to CEO Jeff Bezos the drones, to be called Octocopters, could deliver parcels weighing up to 2.3kg to customers within 30 minutes of the placing of an order.

The main benefit of process innovation is cheaper production methods, making the business more competitive. It is also possible that if the innovation involves patents of new techniques, that these could be sold or licensed to other businesses.

KEY CONCEPT LINK

Innovation can be one of the most important factors that determines the competitiveness of a business. Product innovation can create new market opportunities; process innovation can transform the efficiency of a manufacturing system. Innovation, if successful, aids a business in creating added **value**.

Production methods

There are several different ways in which goods and services can be produced. They are usually classified into:

- **job production**
- **batch production**
- **flow production**
- **mass customisation**.

KEY TERMS

Job production: producing a one-off item specially designed for the customer.

Batch production: producing a limited number of identical products – each item in the batch passes through one stage of production before passing on to the next stage.

Flow production: producing items in a continually moving process.

Mass customisation: the use of flexible computer-aided production systems to produce items to meet individual customers' requirements at mass-production cost levels.

Job production

This is normally used for the production of single, one-off products. These products may be small or large and are often unique. Thus, good examples of job production would be a specially designed wedding ring, made-to-measure suits or the Yangtze dam in China. In order to be called job production, each individual product has to be completed before the next product is started. Thus, at any one time, there is only one product being made. New, small, firms often use labour-intensive job production before they get the chance to expand and purchase advanced equipment. Job production enables specialised products to be produced and tends to be motivating for workers, because they produce the whole product and can take pride in it.

However, this sort of production tends to be expensive, often takes a long time to complete, and is usually labour

Job production – every Aston Martin engine is built by hand

intensive. The labour force also needs to be highly skilled and this is not always easy to achieve. Aston Martin is an example of a very expensive car that is individually produced for the needs of each customer. Each engine is hand-built and carries a plate with the engineer's name on it. Job production can be slow but rewarding for the workers involved.

Batch production

Batch production involves the production of products in separate groups, where the products in the batch go through the whole production process together. The production process involves a number of distinct stages and the defining feature of batch production is that every unit in the batch must go through an individual production stage before the batch as a whole moves on to the next stage.

A good example of this form of production is a baker making batches of rolls. First, the dough is mixed and kneaded. Then, after being left for a time, the dough is separated into individual amounts, the right size for rolls. After this, the rolls are baked together and then they are left to cool. When they have cooled, they are put on display in the shop while another batch is prepared. Each roll has gone through the process with the other rolls in the batch and all the rolls have undergone each stage of the batch before going on to the next stage.

Batch production allows firms to use division of labour in their production process and it enables some gain from economies of scale if the batch is large enough. It is usually employed in industries where demand is for batches of identical products – such as 500 school uniforms for the students at one school. It also allows

Batch production of identical bread rolls, Germany

Flow production at the Coca-Cola plant in Ho Chi Minh City, Vietnam

each individual batch to be specifically matched to the demand, and the design and composition of batches can be easily altered.

However, there are drawbacks. Batch production tends to have high levels of work-in-progress stocks at each stage of the production process and the work may well be boring and demotivating for the workers. If batches are small, then unit costs are likely to remain high. There is often a need to clean and adjust machinery after each batch has passed through.

Batch production should not be confused with flow production. Some firms produce batches of products using a flow production system, for example a soft drinks firm may bottle a batch of 20,000 cans of orange drink before resetting the line and producing a batch of another drink. This is not, however, batch production. The individual items are free to move through the process without having to wait for others, so it must be flow production.

Flow production

The process of flow production is used where individual products move from stage to stage of the production process as soon as they are ready, without having to wait for any other products. Flow production systems are capable of producing large quantities of output in a relatively short time and so it suits industries where the demand for the product in question is high and consistent. It also suits the production of large numbers of a standardised item that only requires minimal alterations. This is why it is often referred to as mass production.

An example would be a Coca-Cola production plant like the one in Ho Chi Minh City, Vietnam. Here, the product is standardised in that it is a can of soft drink of a standard size. The system is flow production because the cans move through the various stages independently. However, the firm can make changes to the contents of the cans and the labelling on them without having to alter the flow production system. They are capable of producing Coke, Sprite and Schweppes Soda Water on the same production line. It is essential that the flow production process be very carefully planned, so that there are no disruptions in the system. In a perfect system, the production process would be broken down so that all of the stages were of equal duration and producing equal output levels.

Flow production has a number of advantages over other types of production. Labour costs tend to be relatively low, because much of the process is mechanised and there is little physical handling of the products. The constant output rate should make the planning of inputs relatively simple and this can lead to the minimisation of input stocks through the use of just-in-time (JIT) stock control. Quality tends to be consistent and high and it is easy to check the quality of products at various points throughout the process. The main disadvantage is the high initial set-up cost. By definition, capital-intensive, high-technology production lines are going to cost a great deal of money. In addition, the work involved tends to be boring, demotivating and repetitive.

TOP TIP

It is important to weigh up the advantages and disadvantages of each production method if a question asks you to suggest an appropriate production method.

Mass customisation

This process combines the latest technology with multiskilled labour forces to use production lines to make a range of varied products. This allows the business to move away from the mass-marketing approach with high output of identical products. Instead, focused or differentiated marketing can be used, which allows for higher added value – an essential objective of all operations managers. So Dell computers can make a customised computer to suit your specific needs in a matter of hours. By changing just a few of the key components – but keeping the rest the same – low unit costs are maintained with greater product choice.

Recent innovations in production methods

The search for production methods that could combine the advantages of job production – flexibility and worker satisfaction – with the gains from flow production – low unit costs – have led to some important recent developments. CAD and CAM have allowed much quicker developments of new products, designs that feature many common components and robotic machinery that can be switched to making a range of parts – not just one. In addition, developments in the organisation of the production flow line have reduced the alienating effects of typical mass production. The emphasis on repetitive, boring tasks had been a major factor in poor worker motivation.

Production methods – making the choice

Table 23.1 summarises the main features, advantages and disadvantages of the four methods of production considered above – that is job, batch, flow or mass customisation.

The following factors will influence whether a business adopts one of these four production methods:

- **Size of the market:** If the market is very small, such as for designer clothes, then job production is likely to be used. Flow production is most efficiently adopted when the market for similar or identical products is very large and consistent throughout the year. If mass production is used in this way, then mass-marketing methods will also have to be adopted to sell the high output levels that can be manufactured. Even in a market for mass-produced items, such as cars, there may be market niches that will allow smaller manufacturers to survive by making one-off products or batches of identical goods before changing the design or style for another model. If the market demands a large number of units, but at different times of the year, for example textbooks at the start of the academic year, then batch production might be most appropriate.

- **The amount of capital available:** A purpose-built flow production line is difficult and expensive to construct. Small firms are unlikely to be able to afford this type of investment and are more likely to use job or batch production.

- **Availability of other resources:** Large-scale flow production often requires a supply of relatively unskilled workers and a large, flat land area. Job production needs skilled craftspeople. If any of these resources are unavailable, or very limited in supply, then the production method may have to be adapted to suit available resources, given the market constraint referred to above.

- **Market demand exists for products adapted to specific customer requirements:** If firms want the cost advantages of high volumes combined with the ability to make slightly different products for different markets, then mass customisation would be most appropriate. As was seen above, technology is giving firms the flexibility to produce a variety of models from the one basic design and production process.

In search of quality in quantity

The spread of mass-customisation techniques across industries is starting to spell an end to the old production line. Mass production using flow production, based on standardised parts and processes, was introduced by Henry Ford in his car plants early in the twentieth century. It greatly cut the costs of making each unit, but the main drawback was that all goods coming off a single production line were identical. In mass customisation the line can be varied to make different products, either individually or in small batches.

Caterpillar, the US supplier of construction and power equipment, says that virtually all of the 11,000 engines it makes each year are different. The variation comes from changes to 10–20% of the 1,000 parts that go into each product. Software for the engine controls can also be varied.

Cessna makes a wide range of general aviation aircraft from the single engine piston to business jets on several different production lines. The company produces and delivers more than 1,200 planes, based on 17 basic models, to customers.

By producing such a variety of models, Cessna is able to market its products to a much wider range of customers, meeting their individual requirements and adding higher value to the components used.

Mass customisation needs:

- advanced and flexible capital equipment – for example, there are now car-paint robots that can paint vehicles in 'one-off' colours in-between lines of cars in standard colours
- skilled and well-trained workers to operate this machinery and to be able to adapt it to make different products
- product designs that contain as many standardised parts as possible in different versions
- reliable suppliers able to supply slight variations in standard parts or components.

The consultancy Strategic Horizons says examples of mass customisation have increased greatly in the last few years. 'Some time this century mass customisation will be the main form of manufacturing.'

[22 marks, 35 minutes]

1 Explain the difference between traditional flow or mass production and mass-customisation methods of production. [5]

2 Analyse the benefits of mass customisation to either a computer manufacturer or a dress-making business. [8]

3 List **three** of the factors that are necessary for mass customisation to be successful. For each one, explain why you consider it is an important condition for mass customisation to work effectively. [9]

	Job	Batch	Flow	Mass customisation
Main feature	■ single one-off items	■ group of identical products pass through each stage together	■ mass production of standardised products	■ flow production of products with many standardised components but customised differences too
Essential requirements	■ highly skilled workforce	■ labour and machines must be flexible to switch to making batches of other designs	■ specialised, often expensive, capital equipment – but can be very efficient ■ high steady demand for standardised products	■ many common components ■ flexible and multiskilled workers ■ flexible equipment – often computer-controlled to allow for variations in the product

(continued)

	Job	Batch	Flow	Mass customisation
Main advantages	■ able to undertake specialist projects or jobs, often with high value added ■ high levels of worker motivation	■ some economies of scale ■ faster production with lower unit costs than job production ■ some flexibility in design of product in each batch	■ low unit costs due to constant working of machines, high labour productivity and economies of scale	■ combines low unit costs with flexibility to meet customers' individual requirements
Main disadvantages	■ high unit production costs ■ time-consuming ■ wide range of tools and equipment needed	■ high levels of stocks at each production stage ■ unit costs likely to be higher than with flow production	■ inflexible – often very difficult and time-consuming to switch from one type of product to another ■ expensive to set up flow-line machinery	■ expensive product redesign may be needed to allow key components to be switched to allow variety ■ expensive flexible capital equipment needed

Table 23.1 Summary of main production methods

Problems of changing production methods

Job to batch:

■ Cost of equipment needed to handle large numbers in each batch.

■ Additional working capital needed to finance stocks and work in progress.

■ Staff demotivation – less emphasis placed on an individual's craft skills.

Job or batch to flow:

■ Cost of capital equipment needed for flow production.

■ Staff training to be flexible and multiskilled – if this approach is not adopted, then workers may end up on one boring repetitive task, which could be demotivating.

■ Accurate estimates of future demand to ensure that output matches demand.

Final evaluation

The traditional differences between the three basic production methods are becoming much less obvious. Many complex products, such as computers and industrial engines, can be adapted to meet different consumers' different requirements. The flexibility offered by technology to large businesses could put at risk the survival of small firms that used to exploit small market niches with hand-built or batch-produced products. However, there is always likely to be a demand from increasingly wealthy consumers for original and specialist products – small firms with non-mass-production methods will still thrive in these market segments.

Location decisions

Deciding on the best location for a new business – or relocating/expanding an existing one – is often crucial to its success. It is clearly an operations management decision as it is concerned with input decisions – notably land and labour supply – and how these will affect the productive efficiency of the business.

The benefits of an optimal location

Location decisions for existing firms – choosing new sites for expansion or relocation of the business – are some of the most important decisions made by management teams. Selecting the best site will have a significant effect on many departments of the business and, ultimately, on the profitability and chances of success of the whole firm. Location decisions have three key characteristics. They are:

■ strategic in nature – as they are long-term and have an impact on the whole business

■ difficult to reverse if an error of judgement is made – due to the costs of relocation

■ taken at the highest management levels – they are not delegated to subordinates.

An **optimal location** decision is one that selects the best site for expansion of the business or for its relocation, given current information. This best site should maximise the long-term profits of the business. This is not as easy to achieve in practice as it sounds, because the optimal site is nearly always a compromise between conflicting benefits and drawbacks.

Example 1: A well-positioned high-street shop will have the potential for high sales, but will have higher rental charges than a similar-sized shop out of town.

Example 2: A factory location that is relatively cheap to purchase due to its distance from major towns might have problems recruiting staff due to lack of a suitably large and trained working population.

So an optimal location is likely to be a compromise that:

- balances high fixed costs of the site and buildings with convenience for customers and potential sales revenue
- balances the low costs of a remote site with limited supply of suitably qualified labour
- balances quantitative factors with qualitative ones (see below)
- balances the opportunities of receiving government grants in areas of high unemployment with the risks of low sales as average incomes in the area may be low.

A high-street location will have high rents – but many potential shoppers too

 TOP TIP

Do not assume that the 'best' location for a business will *always* be competitive – cost and other factors can change over a period of time and this accounts for many firms relocating to new sites – but this can be expensive.

 KEY TERM

Optimal location: a business location that gives the best combination of quantitative and qualitative factors.

Some of the potential drawbacks of poor, non-optimal location decisions are shown in Table 23.2.

Factors influencing location decisions: quantitative factors

Site and other capital costs such as building or shop-fitting costs

These vary greatly from region to region within a country and between countries too. The best office and retail sites may be so expensive that the cost of them is

Problem	Disadvantages to business
High fixed site costs	■ high break-even level of production ■ low profits – or even losses ■ if operating at low capacity utilisation, unit fixed costs will be high
High variable costs, e.g. labour	■ low contribution per unit produced or sold ■ low profits – or even losses ■ high unit variable costs reduce competitiveness
Low unemployment rate	■ problems with recruiting suitable staff ■ staff turnover likely to be a problem ■ pay levels may have to be raised to attract and retain staff
High unemployment rate	■ average consumer disposable incomes may be low – leading to relatively low demand for income-elastic products
Poor transport infrastructure	■ raises transport costs for both materials and finished products ■ relatively inaccessible to customers ■ difficult to operate a JIT stock-management system due to unreliable deliveries

Table 23.2 Disadvantages to a business of non-optimal location decisions

beyond the resources of all but the largest companies. The cost of building on a 'greenfield' site – one that has never previously been developed – must be compared with the costs of adapting existing buildings on a developed site.

 KEY TERM

> **Quantitative factors:** these are measurable in financial terms and will have a direct impact on either the costs of a site or the revenues from it and its profitability.

Labour costs

The relative importance of these as a locational factor depends on whether the business is capital or labour intensive. An insurance company call centre will need many staff, but the labour costs of a nuclear power station will be a very small proportion of its total costs. The attraction of much lower wage rates overseas has encouraged many European businesses to set up operations in other countries – for example, bank and insurance company call centres.

Transport costs

Businesses that use heavy and bulky raw materials – such as steel-making – will incur high transport costs if suppliers are at a great distance from the steel plant. Goods that increase in bulk during production will, traditionally, reduce transport costs by locating close to the market. Service industries, such as hotels and retailing, need to be conveniently located for customers, and transport costs will be of less significance.

Sales revenue potential

The level of sales made by a business can depend directly on location. Confectionery shops and convenience stores have to be just that – convenient to potential customers. In addition to this, certain locations can add status and image to a business and this may allow value to be added to the product in the eyes of the consumers. This is true for high-class retailers situated in London's Bond Street or Ngee Ann City in Singapore, but also for financial specialists operating from an address in New York's Wall Street.

Government grants

Governments across the world are very keen to attract new businesses to locate in their country. Grants may be offered to act as an incentive. Existing businesses operating in a country can also be provided with financial assistance to retain existing jobs or attract new employment to deprived areas of high unemployment.

349

ACTIVITY 23.4

Government support

Senior management at Nissan were initially reluctant to build the new Qashqai at their Sunderland factory. However, a UK government grant of £3.26 million helped to clinch the decision to invest a total of £95 million in the new production facilities at this factory in the north of the UK. It secured 250 jobs in this area of high unemployment.

[16 marks, 20 minutes]

1 Explain the benefits the regional economy would gain as a result of this new investment. **[6]**

2 Discuss whether the location that offered the highest government grant would always be the best site for a new car factory. **[10]**

Once these **quantitative factors** have been identified and costs and revenues estimated, the following techniques can be used to assist in the location decision.

1 Profit estimates

By comparing the estimated revenues and costs of each location, the site with the highest annual potential profit may be identified.

Limitation: Annual profit forecasts alone are of limited use – they need to be compared with the capital cost of buying and developing the site. A site offering 10% higher annual profits than an alternative location is unlikely to be chosen if the capital cost is 50% higher.

2 Investment appraisal

Location decisions often involve a substantial capital investment. Investment appraisal methods can be used to identify locations with the highest potential returns over a number of years. These techniques are examined in detail in Chapter 36. The simplest of these, the payback method, can be used to estimate the location most likely to return the original investment quickest. This could be of particular benefit to a business with a capital shortage or in times of economic uncertainty. Calculating the annual profit as a percentage of the original cost of each location is another useful measure.

Limitation: These methods require estimates of costs and revenues for several years for each potential location.

This introduces a considerable degree of inaccuracy and uncertainty into this form of quantitative decision-making.

ACTIVITY 23.5

Profits in different locations

	Site A – city-centre location	Site B – shopping arcade out of the city
Estimated annual costs (including rent and labour costs)	£975,000	£498,000
Expected annual sales (units)	25,000	17,000
Forecast selling price per unit	£50	£45

[12 marks, 18 minutes]

1 Calculate the estimated annual profit from these two possible locations for a mobile-phone shop. **[6]**

2 In future years, why might the annual profits made from each location change? **[6]**

3 Break-even analysis

This is explained fully in Chapter 29. It is a relatively straightforward method of comparing two or more possible locations. It calculates the level of production that must be sold from each site for revenue to just equal total costs. The lower this break-even level of output, the better that site is, other things being equal. This information might be particularly important for businesses that face high levels of fixed costs and that may benefit from a location with lower overheads.

Limitations: Break-even analysis should be used with caution and the normal limitations of this technique apply when using it to help make location decisions.

Qualitative factors

Clearly potential profit is a major consideration when choosing an optimal location but there are other important factors that cannot be measured in financial terms. These are called **qualitative factors**.

ACTIVITY 23.6

Which site is the best investment?

TLC Cosmetics is planning to open a new branch of its shops selling upmarket cosmetics. The company has expanded rapidly and it has substantial loans. Some economists are predicting an increase in interest rates by the Bank of England.

	Site X – capital cost £2 million	Site Y – capital cost £3 million
Length of time to repay initial capital cost (payback period)	2.5 years	3.8 years
Annual profit made as % of initial cost	12%	14%

[8 marks, 12 minutes]

Using the investment appraisal results in the table and any other information, which of these two sites would you recommend for the new shop? **[8]**

KEY TERM

Qualitative factors: non-measurable factors that may influence business decisions.

Safety

To avoid potential risk to the public and damage to the company's reputation as a consequence of an accident that risks public safety, some industrial plants will be located in remote areas, even though this may increase transport and other costs.

Room for further expansion

It is expensive to relocate if a site proves to be too small to accommodate an expanding business. If a location has room for further expansion of the business, then this might be an important long-term consideration.

Managers' preferences

In small businesses, managers' personal preferences regarding desirable work and home environments could influence location decisions of the business. In larger

ACTIVITY 23.7

Which site covers its costs at a lower output level?

ICT Chemicals Ltd plans to open a new paint factory with a maximum capacity of 10 million litres per year. It has narrowed the choice of sites down to Site C in the UK, located five miles away from a large city, and Site D in a less economically developed country with very low labour-wage rates and few health and safety controls. The figures exclude transport costs.

	Site C	Site D
Level of output needed to cover all costs (break-even output)	4 million litres	2 million litres

[10 marks, 15 minutes]

1 Suggest to the business which location should be selected by using the data shown in the table. The expected annual production level is 6 million litres. Briefly explain your answer. **[6]**

2 What other factors do you think the business should consider before taking the final location decision? **[4]**

organisations, such as a plc, this is unlikely to be a factor, as earning profits and increasing returns to shareholders will be key objectives that will take priority in location decisions.

Ethical considerations

A business deciding to relocate from the UK is likely to make workers redundant. This will cause bad publicity and could also be contrary to the ethical code of the business and may be viewed by stakeholders as being immoral. In addition, if the relocation is to a country with much weaker controls over worker welfare and the environment, there could be further claims that the business is acting unethically.

Environmental concerns

A business might be reluctant to set up in an area that is particularly sensitive from an environmental viewpoint, as this could lead to poor public relations and action from pressure groups.

Infrastructure

The quality of the local infrastructure, especially transport and communication links, will influence the choice of location. Singapore's huge port facilities have encouraged

many of the world's largest shipping firms to set up bases there. The quality of IT infrastructure varies considerably around the world and this is an important consideration for companies that need quick communication with their different sites or customers, e.g. call centres or selling via the Internet. The growing popularity of online shopping in developed countries may lead to some retailers opening fewer high-street stores and more warehouse operations to supply consumers.

ACTIVITY 23.8

Rolls-Royce goes for a quality location

Choosing the lowest-cost location for the Rolls-Royce factory was not a priority. When BMW moved production from the industrial northern town of Crewe, it chose one of the most crowded and expensive parts of the country – the southeast of England. The Goodwood factory has many advantages but low cost is not one of them. One of its main benefits is its proximity to a small airport where the helicopters and executive jets of intending purchasers of Rolls-Royce cars can arrive in style. Potential buyers are identified by the company and invited to visit the factory and attend events held at the nearby exclusive marina and horse-race and motor-race courses. The area has been termed a 'playground for the wealthy' and future customers often spend a day or two at the races or a morning at the marina before browsing the cars – and more often than not, signing an order form.

[8 marks, 12 minutes]

Explain why qualitative factors were considered to be so important in this case when Rolls-Royce could find much cheaper locations to produce its cars. **[8]**

Other locational issues

The pull of the market

This is less important with the development of transport and communication industries and with the world becoming a single market for so many goods. The Internet can achieve a massive amount in terms of making location of a retailing business less important, but the market is still very important for the service industries, and the power of the car has taken many of these out of the convenient centres of towns and on to the ring roads. The cinema is a good example. Once the centrepiece of a town, it is now found on the ring roads. Superstores and other retail stores have relocated in a similar fashion.

Planning restrictions

Local authorities have a duty to serve the interests of their populations. On the one hand, they want business and industry because they provide employment. On the other hand, they want to protect the environment of the towns and villages. In some areas, large development corporations have been set up to develop a town or city into a much more successful combination of dwellings and industrial activity. In most countries, local or central government has set up industrial estates and business parks that both businesses and consumers find very attractive.

External economies of scale

These are cost reductions that can benefit a business as the industry grows in one region. It is common for firms in the same industry to be clustered in the same region – Silicon Valley in the USA and Bangalore in India have a very high concentration of IT-focused businesses. All IT firms in these regions will benefit from the attraction of a pool of qualified labour to the area, local college courses focused on IT and a network of suppliers whose own scale economies should offer lower component costs. In addition, it will be easier to arrange cooperation and joint ventures when the businesses are located closely to each other.

Advantages and disadvantages of multi-site locations

Most relatively large businesses operate on more than one site. This is clearly true of the major retailing companies that expand mainly by opening new sites in new locations. It would be pointless trying to serve the whole of a country from one shop – unless of course the business sold only over the Internet, such as Amazon, and one giant warehouse was adequate to provide supplies to consumers throughout the country.

KEY TERM

Multi-site location: a business that operates from more than one location.

Banks, building societies, hotels, hairdressers and other tertiary service providers *must* operate from more than one site if they wish to expand beyond a certain size by offering convenient customer services in several locations. Primary producers, such as oil-exploration companies and

---

ACTIVITY 23.9

One company, many factories

Toyota is one of the best examples of a multi-site business with 52 manufacturing facilities in 26 different countries. In a typical recent 12-month period, it opened its first factory in Mexico and opened its 13th manufacturing facility in the USA – in Mississippi. Concerns are now being expressed by the company that its production capacity in the USA is starting to outstrip demand for vehicles, so this could be the last new factory the company builds there for some time.

[10 marks, 15 minutes]

Discuss the advantages and disadvantages to Toyota of operating factories in so many different countries. **[10]**

mining businesses, will operate in more than one location to avoid the risks of exhaustion of supplies from just one site. Very large secondary manufacturing businesses also operate from more than one location – despite the potential gains from technical economies of scale on one site. See Table 23.3 for a summary of **multi-site locations**.

TOP TIP

Do not confuse offshoring with outsourcing, although they may be linked. Outsourcing is transferring a business function, such as HR, to another company. It is only offshoring if this company is based in another country.

By opening more branches, Starbucks has greater market reach as well as economies of scale

352

Advantages of multi-site locations	Disadvantages of multi-site locations
■ greater convenience for consumers, e.g. McDonald's restaurants in every town ■ lower transport costs, e.g. breweries can supply large cities from regional breweries rather than transport from one national brewery ■ production-based companies reduce the risk of supply disruption if there are technical or industrial-relations problems in one factory ■ opportunities for delegation of authority to regional managers from head office – helps to develop staff skills and improves motivation ■ cost advantages of multi-sites in different countries	■ coordination problems between the locations – excellent two-way communication systems will be essential ■ potential lack of control and direction from senior management based at head office ■ different cultural standards and legal systems in different countries – the business must adapt to these differences ■ if sites are too close to each other, there may be a danger of 'cannibalism' where one restaurant or store takes sales away from another owned by the same business

Table 23.3 Advantages and disadvantages of multi-site locations

International location decisions

The issues considered so far could apply to any location decision – new business start-up, relocation of existing business or expansion of existing business. These issues are all relevant whether the location decision is a regional, national or international one. However, there are some additional factors that need to be weighed up when a firm is considering locating in another country.

One of the main features of globalisation is the growing trend for businesses to relocate completely to another country or to set up new operating bases abroad. This process is often referred to as '**offshoring**'. The world's largest corporations are now virtually all **multinationals**.

> **KEY TERMS**
>
> **Offshoring:** the relocation of a business process done in one country to the same or another company in another country.
>
> **Multinational:** a business with operations or production bases in more than one country.

Reasons for international location decisions

1 To reduce costs

This is undoubtedly the major reason explaining most company moves abroad. With labour-wage rates in India, Malaysia, China and Eastern Europe being a fraction of those in Western Europe and the USA, it is not surprising that businesses that wish to remain competitive have to seriously consider relocation to low-wage economies. Examples include:

■ Panasonic TV production → Czech Republic
■ Hornby Toy Trains → China
■ Dyson vacuum cleaners → Malaysia.

Country	Average hourly pay in euro [2013]	Compared with United Kingdom (=100)
India	0.83	4
China	1.73	8
Bulgaria	3.7	17
Hungary	7.8	35
Sweden	39	180

Table 23.4 Average hourly wage rates in different countries compared with UK

Look at the data in Table 23.4 for average hourly wages in different countries compared with UK hourly wages, which are some of the highest in the world. It is now easy to see what cost advantages multinational companies have when they operate in countries such as Bulgaria, Hungary, India and China.

2 To access global (world) markets

Rapid economic growth in less-developed countries has created huge market potential for most consumer products. Access to these markets is often best achieved by direct operation in the countries concerned. Markets for some products in Western Europe have reached saturation point and further sales growth can only be achieved by expanding abroad. Some businesses have reached the limit of their internal domestic expansion, as there are threats from government regulatory bodies about increasing monopoly power. All of these reasons help explain Tesco's recent international expansion. Tesco shops are now common sights in Thailand and Eastern Europe and it also became another major UK-based retail business to expand into the USA. Carrefour's expansion in China has helped to compensate for slow growth in supermarket sales in its home country of France

3 To avoid protectionist trade barriers

Barriers to free international trade are rapidly being reduced, but some still exist – notably between the large trading blocs, such as the EU, North American Free Trade Association (NAFTA) and Association of South East Asian Nations (ASEAN). To avoid tariff barriers on imported goods into most countries or trading blocs, it is necessary to set up operations within the country or trading bloc concerned. Examples include Honda's factory in Swindon that produces cars for the EU market and Toyota's new factory in Mexico that gives tariff-free access to this country's car market.

KEY TERM

Trade barriers: taxes (tariffs) or other limitations on the free international movement of goods and services.

4 Other reasons

These include substantial government financial support to relocating businesses, good educational standards (as in India and China) and highly qualified staff and avoidance of problems resulting from exchange rate fluctuations. This last point makes pricing decisions very difficult with products that are not made within the country, but are imported, when its currency fluctuates considerably. One way around this problem is to locate production in this country.

TOP TIP

Do your own research during the Business Studies course on major location decisions, both at home and abroad, of businesses based in your country.

Issues and potential problems with international location

International locations have potential for success but they also add to the number of drawbacks that might result from an inappropriate location decision. Here are some

ACTIVITY 23.10

TRG's excellent experience in Pakistan

TRG is a company listed on the Karachi Stock Exchange. The business takes controlling stakes in firms offering services to other businesses – such as web- and phone-based customer-service centres – and prepares them for rapid expansion. It has operations in Lahore, Karachi, the Philippines and Morocco. The company's decision to base its head office in Lahore, Pakistan was based on a number of factors:

- large pool of English-proficient graduates
- well-organised capital market giving opportunities to raise the finance needed
- land costs 30% less than in India or the Philippines
- wages 60% less than in the USA

- government willing to offer incentives, a 15-year tax 'holiday' and willing to invest in IT infrastructure.

There were some initial problems:

- cultural differences – workers did not expect to work US business hours
- lack of general management experience among the graduates – they had to be trained in this
- lack of support organisations, such as specialist personnel recruitment firms or training institutes, as TRG were one of the first businesses in this industry in the country.

[18 marks, 25 minutes]

1 Using knowledge of your own country, do you think TRG would be advised to move its head office to your country or remain in Pakistan? Give reasons for your answer.

Students in Pakistan: Evaluate the main reasons for TRG's decision to base the company in Pakistan. [12]

2 Explain why another business-services firm setting up in Lahore might benefit from TRG's presence there. [6]

of the major additional issues that need to be weighed up carefully before going offshore.

1 Language and other communication barriers

Distance is often a problem for effective communication – for example, direct face-to-face contact is less likely. This problem is made worse when some operations are abroad and when company employees, suppliers or customers use a different language altogether. This is one of the reasons for India's success in attracting offshoring companies – English is one of the official languages.

2 Cultural differences

These are important for the marketing department if products are being sold in the country concerned – consumer tastes and religious factors will play a significant role in determining what goods should be stocked. Cultural differences also exist in the workplace. Toyota found that the typical Mexican worker is self-reliant and independent, yet the Toyota manufacturing system depends greatly on teamwork and cooperation. Effective staff training may be necessary to ensure that cultural differences do not prevent successful overseas expansion.

Example: Oscar Rodriguez was only 20 when he was employed by Toyota's new Tijuana factory. 'I was self-reliant and I would conceal production problems and try and fix them myself,' he said. 'But I was taught how to communicate and I have learned that there is never a stupid question. The company supervisors teach us well and they are patient'.

3 Level-of-service concerns

This applies particularly to the offshoring of call centres, technical support centres and functions such as accounting. Some consumer groups argue that offshoring of these services has led to inferior customer service due to time-difference problems, time delays in phone messages, language barriers and different practices and conventions, e.g. with accounting systems.

4 Supply-chain concerns

There may be some loss of control over quality and reliability of delivery with overseas manufacturing plants. This reason is always cited by Zara, the clothing company, for their decision not to offshore clothing production to cheaper countries, as 'fast fashion' requires very close contact with suppliers. Using 'just-in-time' manufacturing may become much riskier if important supplies have to be shipped thousands of miles to an assembly plant.

Is it right to sell clothing in European shops that has been made by low-wage labour in Asian countries?

5 Ethical considerations

There may be a loss of jobs when a company locates all or some of its operations abroad and this may, as in the case of Burberry clothing, lead to a consumer boycott as there were claims that the company's decision to close its Welsh factory was not 'the right thing to do'. In addition, there are several reports of high-street clothing retailers sourcing supplies from Asian factories that use child labour and very low-wage labour. Could this negative publicity cancel out the competitive advantage of low-cost supplies? This important consideration is just another reason why the important location decisions should be taken at the highest management level.

> **TOP TIP**
>
> Remember that the lowest-cost location may not always be the optimal location – if quality suffers or if there is negative public reaction to products being made by low-paid workers then low costs may be outweighed by even lower revenue.

Scale of operation

There is a huge difference between the **scale of operations** of a small business – perhaps operated by just one person – and the largest companies in the world. Some of the latter have total annual sales exceeding the GDP of small countries. In 2013, ExxonMobil recorded sales of more than US$482 billion, yet the GDP of Thailand, for example, was US$365 billion.

Factors that influence the scale of operation of a business include:

- owners' objectives – they may wish to keep the business small and easy to manage
- capital available – if this is limited, growth will be less likely
- size of the market the firm operates in – a very small market will not require large-scale production
- number of competitors – the market share of each firm may be small if there are many rivals
- scope for scale economies – if these are substantial, as in water supply, each business is likely to operate on a large scale.

Increasing the scale of operations

The decision to expand the scale of operations of a business cannot be taken lightly. There are likely to be considerable costs involved – purchasing land, buildings, equipment, employing more staff – and the capital needed for this will always have alternative uses. Business expansion by employing more of all factors of production is referred to as an increase in the 'scale of production'. Firms expand to increase capacity to avoid turning business away but they also benefit from the advantages of large-scale production – these are called **economies of scale**.

TOP TIP

Do not confuse 'producing more' with increasing the scale of operation. More can be produced from existing resources by increasing capacity utilisation. Changing the scale of operation means using more (or less) of all resources, e.g. opening a new factory with additional machines and workers.

Economies of scale

These cost benefits can be so substantial in some industries that smaller firms will be unlikely to survive due to lack of competitiveness, such as in oil refining or soft drink production. The cost benefits arise for five main reasons.

1 Purchasing economies

These economies are often known as bulk-buying economies. Suppliers will often offer substantial discounts for large orders. This is because it is cheaper for them to process and deliver one large order rather than several smaller ones. In addition, they will obviously be keener to keep a very large customer happy due to the profits made on the large quantities sold. Big firms employ specialist 'buyers' who may travel the globe to strike the best possible deals at the lowest possible prices for materials and components. Recently there has been a growing trend towards firms buying supplies over the Internet, and this process – whether using the Internet or other methods – is known as B2B (business-to-business) trading. Cheaper deals are offered for greater quantities ordered.

2 Technical economies

There are two main sources of technical economies. Large firms are more likely to be able to justify the cost of flow production lines. If these are worked at a high-capacity level, then they offer lower unit costs than other production methods. The latest and most advanced technical equipment – such as computer systems – is often expensive and can usually only be afforded by big firms. Such expense can only be justified when output is high so that fixed costs can be spread 'thinly' – a small firm, even if it could afford the equipment, would be unlikely to keep it operating for very long each week and this would raise the unit fixed costs. It is often the case that such equipment is 'indivisible' – this means that it cannot be purchased in smaller models with a lower total capacity.

3 Financial economies

Large organisations have two distinct cost advantages when it comes to raising finance. Firstly, banks and other lending institutions often show preference for lending to a big business with a proven track record and a diversified range of products. Interest rates charged to these firms are often lower than the rates charged to small, especially newly formed, businesses. Secondly, raising finance by 'going public' or by further public issues of shares for existing public limited companies is very expensive. Professional advisers' fees, prospectus publishing costs and advertising charges will not vary greatly whether it is a

Cooking pots

Ben Rishi is operations manager for a factory making cooking pots. He has calculated that the maximum capacity of the factory is 3,000 units per week. The main limit on capacity is the old-fashioned machine for stamping out the metal pans from sheet metal. Purchasing another machine would be expensive – and would require an extension to the building to accommodate it. Workers are currently working very long shifts. Ben has also been working long days to ensure that all resources are fully employed at all times. For the past three months, demand has been high and last week there were orders for 3,100 pots. Ben is under pressure from his managing director to see that this number is made to meet the orders. Ben is unsure whether to recommend purchasing the new machine or to buy in components from another firm in the city that has spare capacity.

[24 marks, 35 minutes]

1   Outline the problems facing Ben because his factory is operating at full capacity.   [6]

2   Analyse the advantages and disadvantages of the two methods he is considering for solving the problem.   [12]

3   Outline **three** additional pieces of information Ben would find useful before making a decision about how to solve the capacity problems.   [6]

large or a small issue of shares. Therefore, the average cost of raising the finance will be lower for larger firms selling many millions of dollars' worth of shares.

4 Marketing economies

Marketing costs obviously rise with the size of a business, but not at the same rate. Even small firms will need a sales force to cover the whole of the sales area. They may employ an advertising agency to design adverts and arrange a promotional campaign. These costs can be spread over a higher level of sales for a big firm and this offers a substantial economy of scale.

5 Managerial economies

Small firms often employ general managers who have a range of management functions to perform. As a firm expands, it should be able to afford to attract specialist

functional managers who should operate more efficiently than general managers. The extreme case of a small firm not benefiting from this economy would be a sole trader managed by just the owner. The skills of specialist managers and the chance of them making fewer mistakes because of their training is a potential economy for larger organisations.

TOP TIP

When answering questions about economies of scale, make sure your answer is applied to the business specified in the question.

Diseconomies of scale – big can be inefficient too

If there were no disadvantages to large-scale operations, nearly all industries and markets would be dominated by huge corporations. Some are, of course, as with oil exploration, refining and retailing – the benefits of large-scale production are so substantial that smaller firms find it increasingly difficult to operate profitably. In many other industries, the impact of '**diseconomies of scale**' prevents one or just a few firms from being able to completely dominate. Diseconomies of scale are those factors that increase unit costs as a firm's scale of operation increases beyond a certain size. These diseconomies are all related to the management problems associated with trying to control and direct an organisation with many thousands of workers, in many separate divisions, often operating in several different countries. There are three main causes of these management problem.

KEY TERM

Diseconomies of scale: factors that cause average costs of production to rise when the scale of operation is increased.

1 Communication problems

Large-scale operations will often lead to poor feedback to workers, excessive use of non-personal communication media, communication overload with the sheer volume of messages being sent, and distortion of messages caused by the long chain of command. These communication inefficiencies may lead to poor decisions being made, due to inadequate or delayed information. Poor feedback reduces worker incentives. Communication overload is 'noise' that may prevent the really important messages being acted upon first. All of these factors will reduce management efficiency.

2 Alienation of the workforce

The bigger the organisation, the more difficult it becomes to directly involve every worker and to give them a sense of purpose and achievement in their work. They may feel so insignificant to the overall business plan that they become demotivated and fail to give of their best. As was identified above, larger manufacturing firms are the ones most likely to adopt flow-line production and workforce alienation is a real problem if new ways of organising this method are not employed. The use of cell-working, team-working and other job-enrichment methods has gone a considerable way to minimise this problem, but the danger of staff alienation is ever-present in large businesses.

3 Poor coordination

Business expansion is often associated with a growing number of departments, divisions and products. The number of countries a firm operates in often increases too. A major problem for senior management is to coordinate and control all of these operations. Coordination really means that all divisions of the business are aiming to achieve the same objectives by adopting similar ethical standards and by producing goods that are consistent with each other. So if one division of an oil company in one country adopts a weaker ethical stance on issues such as pollution than the divisions in other countries, then poor publicity for the whole operation could be the result. Another problem could be the existence of more than one research department, with wasteful duplication of research into similar products. These are all issues that result from poor coordination. They could lead to substantially higher production costs than for a smaller business with much tighter control over operations.

Large-scale production – unit costs of production

The combined effect of economies of scale and diseconomies of scale on unit (average) costs of production is shown in Figure 23.1. It is important to point out that there is not a particular point of operation at which economies of scale cease and diseconomies begin. The process is much more difficult to measure than this, as certain economies of scale may continue to be received because scale increases, but the growing significance of diseconomies gradually begins to take over and average costs may rise. In practice, it is often impossible to state

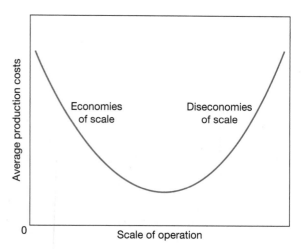

Figure 23.1 The impact of economies and diseconomies of scale on average costs

at what level of output this process occurs, which is why many managers may continue to expand their business unaware that the forces causing diseconomies are building up to a significant degree.

Are diseconomies avoidable?

Nearly all managers recognise the problems inherent in operating large-scale operations. Can these problems be reduced and diseconomies avoided? Three approaches could be used to overcome the impact of potential diseconomies:

1. **Management by objectives:** This will assist in avoiding coordination problems by giving each division and department agreed objectives to work towards that are components of the long-term aims of the whole business.
2. **Decentralisation:** This gives divisions a considerable degree of autonomy and independence. They will now be operated more like smaller business units, as control will be exercised by managers 'closer to the action'. Only really significant strategic issues might need to be communicated to the centre, and such issues might be the only ones requiring decisions from the centre.
3. **Reduce diversification:** The recent movement towards less-diversified businesses that concentrate on 'core' activities may help to reduce coordination problems and some communication problems.

Enterprise resource planning (ERP) [A Level only]

Enterprise resource planning did not exist 25 years ago – it has only become possible with increased computerisation and the use of a single database program in all departments of business. By using this database program, it is possible

Economies of scale: supertankers hold much more oil than smaller tankers for a lower unit cost per tonne

to coordinate and link together all of the support systems of a business – stock control and ordering, invoicing to customers, human resource planning, production planning and so on.

Two examples will help to show the scope of this approach to operations management:

Example 1 – Bicycle shop: A bicycle is ordered by a customer (credit sale); the order is recorded on the ERP programme, which updates the stock of bicycles; a replacement is automatically ordered from the manufacturer; the customer is sent an invoice; when payment is made, the accounting records are updated. The ERP programme could also handle bicycle-repair orders, manage spare-parts stock and provide forecasts of future sales to plan staffing needs over the next few months.

Example 2 – Water supply company: Customer requests repair; a date is scheduled in by the ERP system; the job is allocated to a team of staff and correct spare parts are ordered; the job is done and entered on the system; the customer is sent an invoice for the job – all done with one database program.

Supply chain management (SCM) is becoming an increasingly significant application of ERP software. Operations managers can use SCM programs to improve customer service and gain competitive advantage.

 KEY TERMS

Enterprise resource planning: the use of a single computer application to plan the purchase and use of resources in an organisation to improve the efficiency of operations.

Supply chain: all of the stages in the production process from obtaining raw materials to selling to the consumer – from point of origin to point of consumption.

The five main stages of SCM for one customer's large order can all be made more effective by using ERP:

1 **Plan:** Deciding which resources – workers and machines – are needed for this order and how many.

2 **Suppliers:** Choosing the best and most cost-effective suppliers of the components needed and order them to arrive just in time.

3 **Costs:** At each stage costs can be recorded and the appropriate price to the customer calculated.

4 Manufacture: Check the quality and monitor the rate of progress of the customer's order

5 Deliver: Pick transport systems that can deliver goods on time, safely and cost-effectively.

6 Returns: If there is a problem with the product, it will have to be taken back from customers and other items made or the cost reimbursed.

ERP software will monitor all of these stages and, by using the Internet, allows the supply chain of a business to be linked into the supply chains of customers and suppliers in a single overall network. This is often referred to as B2B – business-to-business – communication.

The following benefits can be gained from ERP software:

- Supply only according to demand – lean production that avoids waste and helps move the business towards achieving **sustainability** in its operations.
- Just-in-time ordering of inventories – see Chapter 24.
- Reduces costs at all stages of the supply chain – materials and products are electronically tracked at all stages.
- Improved delivery times and better customer service.
- Departments linked more closely together by the single database – this results in better coordination between them and less waste.
- Management information increased – data from all stages of the production process and all of the supporting departments will be available to senior management via the computer system. This may help future decision-making, e.g. changing suppliers if lower-priced supplies of consistent quality are offered.

ACTIVITY 23.12

Expansion plans at Bookworm Ltd

Bookworm started seven years ago as a single shop selling books and magazines. It was owned by just one person with a passion for books – Aymen Gasim. He employed three assistant staff to help him in the shop, but he undertook all management tasks himself. He selected and ordered all stock, negotiated prices and delivery dates with suppliers, recruited and selected his assistants, kept accounting records and decided selling prices and promotional strategies, such as window displays. All stock was manually recorded in a stock book and this was adjusted on each delivery and with sales data at the end of each week. The business did not have its own transport and Aymen delivered large orders once a week using a hire van. Finance for the business had been obtained from his own savings and a bank overdraft on which a high interest rate was charged. Advertising was rarely undertaken, as Aymen found that the charges expected by a radio or newspaper company for just designing and preparing an advert were too high.

That was seven years ago. Aymen is still surprised by the speed at which his business has grown. He now has 20 shops. He has taken his two brothers into the business – initially as partners, but now as fellow directors in a private limited company. One is an accountant who manages the financial affairs of the business so well that the overdraft limit is never reached. The other has a degree in marketing and has introduced many new promotional ideas. Aymen is convinced that there are still areas of his country, away from city regions, that offer great demand opportunities and he wants to expand the business even further. Additional capital will be required to finance additional premises, stock and to purchase larger vans to replace the three that the company now owns.

A new stock-management computer system will also be needed. This will allow for computerised cash tills to automatically record each sale. Staff numbers will have to increase again – possibly up to around 300 – and a new level of middle management would be introduced to take some of the burdens off the three brothers. The directors have discussed the merits of seeking a stock-exchange listing to allow for a public issue of shares. The good economic news being released by the government has convinced the brothers that now is the right time to expand the business's scale of operation.

[33 marks, 45 minutes]

1 Using this case as an example, outline the cost and efficiency disadvantages often experienced by small firms. [6]

2 a What is meant by 'economies of scale'? [3]

  b Explain how the expansion of the Bookworm business might result in lower average costs of selling each book. [15]

3 Examine the potential diseconomies of scale that could result from continued expansion of the business. [9]

Sustainability: production systems that prevent waste by using the minimum of non-renewable resources so that levels of production can be sustained in the future.

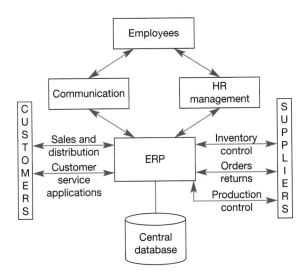

Figure 23.2 Enterprise resource planning uses a company-wide computer software system to manage resources

There are potential limitations too:

- The costs of the database and computer systems have to be considered – although these costs are falling with technological advances in computing power.
- The multiple ways of operating in different departments now have to be reduced to one common system – this may cause resentment as departments are forced to give up tried-and-tested ways of operating.
- It is estimated that in most businesses the full implementation of ERP can take one to three years and a lot can happen in business during this time – technological advances could make the chosen software obsolete, management could change and increased competition might force the company to change course.

Final evaluation

ERP is by no means some sort of management short-term fad. It is proven to be an effective way of saving costs and increasing competitiveness, despite its potential limitations. Most of the world's largest companies now use ERP software routinely, despite the cost and time involved in putting it into practice, and increasingly many of the smaller ones are adopting it too. Since the late 1990s, there has been an irreversible trend towards conducting B2B and B2C (business-to-customer) operations online and this cannot be accomplished without an ERP program in operation.

SUMMARY POINTS

- Operations planning is essential to help ensure the efficient use of resources.
- Different production methods are appropriate in varying situations and they have significant advantages and disadvantages.
- Location decisions are important to the competitiveness of a business.
- There are key quantitative and qualitative factors involved in every business location decision.
- Quantitative techniques can be applied to location decisions, such as break-even analysis and investment appraisal.
- There are advantages and disadvantages of multi-site locations.
- There is a growing trend towards international locations resulting in advantages and potential drawbacks.
- The significance of economies and diseconomies of scale needs to be assessed as a business grows.
- Enterprise resource planning can improve operational efficiency.

RESEARCH TASK

- Identify businesses that have recently located in your town or region.
- Classify them according to primary, secondary and tertiary activity.
- Analyse possible reasons why **one** of these business located in your town/region.
- Do you think that this is a suitable location for this business? Justify your answer.

AS Level exam practice questions

Short answer questions

[114 marks, 2 hours]

Knowledge and understanding

1 What is meant by 'operations planning'? [4]
2 Why are market demand forecasts important when making operational plans? [4]
3 What do you understand by 'flexibility' in operations management? [4]
4 Distinguish between job and batch production. [3]
5 Analyse **one** advantage and **one** disadvantage associated with flow production. [6]
6 Explain how mass customisation differs from traditional flow production. [4]
7 Explain the impact that economies of scale have on unit costs of production. [2]
8 If diseconomies of scale exist, why do many managers still consider business expansion to be important? [5]

Application

9 Why might a high-technology business decide to locate in the UK, despite the huge labour-cost advantages that some developing countries have? [6]
10 What is meant by 'clustering' of similar firms in an industry and why might this be of significance in the location decision for a new car factory? [5]
11 Why do governments often award grants to firms setting up in certain areas of the country? [3]
12 Explain why the location of a new clothes retailer is of strategic importance to the business. [4]
13 Outline **two** examples of qualitative factors that might be considered by an insurance company planning to relocate its offices to a cheaper region, far away from its existing operations. [4]
14 Outline possible reasons why Tesco chose the USA as a country in which to expand. [8]
15 Analyse **two** possible reasons why the expansion referred to in question 15 failed. [6]
16 Explain **two** problems to a small furniture manufacturer of switching from job-production to flow-production. [6]
17 Analyse **two** ways in which the location of a retail shop could affect its competitiveness. [6]
18 Examine the quantitative factors that a hairdressing business might take into account when deciding whether to relocate. [8]
19 How might the increasing use of internet shopping have an impact on the location decisions of businesses that sell to final consumers? [5]
20 A business that started as a sole trader building firm is now a multinational construction public limited company (plc). Explain how it is likely to have benefited from economies of scale. [10]
21 Explain the **three** main causes of diseconomies of scale that the business in question 20 may be experiencing. [6]

Data response

1 Business location in the UK

Indo European Foods to manufacture ethnic foods in the UK

'There is a huge potential market for our authentic Indian spices, sauces, pastes and chutneys in the UK and the rest of Europe,' said the operations director of Indo European Foods. By locating a factory in eastern England, the company will be able to supply this market more quickly, efficiently and profitably than importing directly from India. Felixstowe offers the business a suitable site of more than 9,000 square metres, close proximity to ports, excellent rail links and east–west road connections via the A14. 'This area also gives us a good base for finding a suitably skilled multicultural workforce,' added the director.

Electrolux factory closed in Durham with loss of 500 jobs

An Electrolux cooker factory in Durham has closed with the loss of 500 jobs. It had been making increased losses. Until recently, the company believed this was still the best location for manufacturing cookers and invested £7 million in the plant with the aid of a government grant of £1.6 million. Now the company believes that the sterling exchange rate and wage and other cost pressures make it uncompetitive and have decided to switch production to a factory in Poland. It has been estimated that the break-even level of production at this new plant will be less than half that of the UK factory.

[30 marks, 45 minutes]

1   a   Define the term 'suitably skilled workforce'.   [2]
     b   Briefly explain the term 'government grant'.   [3]
2   Explain why a good location is important to any **one** of these businesses.   [6]

3   Analyse **four** factors referred to in the cases that influenced these two location decisions.   [8]
4   Discuss the problems and benefits that Electrolux might experience following the decision to relocate to Poland.   [11]

2 Is offshoring the best option for HiSonic Ltd?

HiSonic manufacture some of the highest-quality hi-fi systems in the world. They are not cheap – some systems cost up to £50,000 – but the company's products have an excellent reputation for both sound quality and reliability. Currently, all systems are assembled to specific customer requirements from components in the company's factory in Western Europe. The workforce is loyal and skilled. The components are not made 'in house' but are imported from the best suppliers all over the world.

The company is experiencing increasing demand and the factory has reached capacity. One option being considered is to establish a flow-line assembly plant in Malaysia. Rents and wage rates are only 25% of the levels in the current location. The chief executive has asked an external consulting firm to undertake an appraisal of this project, based on sales forecasts for the next five years. These quantitative results could then be compared with those estimated from expanding the existing European factory. One of the potential benefits of a Malaysian site, according to the chief executive, is the access to the expanding Asian markets and the opportunity in the future to transfer all production to this site, if quality proves to be up to standard.

363

	Malaysian site	Expansion of European site
Capital cost	$5 million	$3 million
Payback of capital cost	2 years	1.5 years
Annual profit	$1 million	$450,000
% of expected output that must be sold to cover all costs	40% of expected output	60% of expected output

Comparison of Malaysian site with expansion of existing European site

[34 marks, 45 minutes]

1   a   Define the term 'flow-line assembly'.   [2]
     b   Briefly explain the term 'capital cost'.   [3]
2   Differentiate between quantitative and qualitative factors involved in location decisions.   [6]
3   What is the current production method used by HiSonic? Explain your answer.   [4]

4   Analyse the potential advantages and disadvantages to this business of changing its current production method to flow production.   [8]
5   Using the information provided, make a justified recommendation to the chief executive as to whether the business should expand its European factory or open a new operating plant in Malaysia.   [11]

3 German efficiency

Two large banners hanging from the ceiling – 'Zero defects is perfection' and '0.01 of a millimetre makes a difference' – remind the staff of their employer's quality standards. Welcome to the Egyptian German Automotive company, an oasis of German efficiency 30 kilometres south-west of the busy streets of Cairo. Almost every one of the 1,600 Mercedes sold in Egypt comes from this plant, a joint venture between Mercedes and a group of Egyptian entrepreneurs. Roland Sabais, managing director of Mercedes Egypt, which produces Mercedes E- and C-class cars, says the company is in the country for two reasons. 'Egypt is a very important strategic market because it is the largest automotive market in the Middle East and Africa region,' he says.

The company had no choice other than to set up its own operations in order to serve this market, where some 65,000 cars are sold a year. Very high import duties, imposed by the government to safeguard local industries and jobs, force manufacturers to charge exorbitant prices for imported cars. 'Egypt is a local-assembly market because the average import duty on a car is 230%. If you want to sell in this market, you have to be there,' says Roland.

On arrival you have to deal with many rules and regulations designed to help local producers. A recent example was the government's decision to increase the required percentage of local parts in the car from 40% to 45% virtually overnight. Despite these hurdles, the operations are profitable and have met the targets set by head office. One of the reasons why the company is profitable, despite the non-tariff trade barriers, is that labour is cheap and productivity is high. The 400 workers in the Cairo Mercedes plant are paid on average 80% less than their counterparts in Germany, even though they are trained and perform to similar standards. Infrastructure costs are also low. The factory cost Daimler-Benz E£150 million (US$38.5 million) but its revenues are tax-free for ten years because it is located in one of the government-sponsored industrial zones.

Roland believes the high productivity and the low labour costs can still be used to the company's advantage. The Egyptian factory has started making Mercedes parts that can be exported to the rest of the Mercedes empire at competitive prices. These parts are supplied on demand by the operations of the company's comprehensive ERP system. When a customer orders a new car with certain options, such as satellite navigation, the ERP program stores the details in the computer database. As the car is being assembled, the necessary components and extras have already been ordered by the computer system to arrive just in time. Each worker on the production line has a computer printout of which parts must be added at each stage. Once the car is completed, the customer is invited to the factory to pick the car up themselves or it can be delivered. The payment for the car is recorded, via the computer system, in the firm's accounts.

[30 marks, 45 minutes]

1 a Define the term 'joint venture'. [2]
   b Briefly explain the term 'productivity is high'. [3]
2 Explain **two** benefits to Mercedes from manufacturing cars in Egypt. [6]
3 Analyse the importance of the following factors in Mercedes's decision to locate a factory in Egypt:
   ■ the size of the Egyptian car market
   ■ low unit labour costs due to high productivity and low wages
   ■ high Egyptian import tariffs imposed on foreign-built cars. [8]
4 To what extent might qualitative factors have influenced this location decision? [11]

[14 marks, 20 minutes] [A Level only]

5 Evaluate the significance of the enterprise resource planning system to the profitability of Mercedes's operations in Egypt. [14]

4 Wicklow Fine Foods to increase scale of operation

Wicklow Fine Foods has developed a reputation for being one of Ireland's best producers of luxury handmade chocolates and biscuits. The business prides itself on the excellent quality and taste of its products – all with a high level of handwork with small production batches to ensure the best-possible consistency. The owners now want to double revenue by increasing the scale of operation. Export markets – in Europe and beyond – will be targeted even though the world recession is a real threat. This will mean moving to larger premises but the business does not want to lose its quality craft image.

Finding the right balance between craft or job production and the cost advantages of large-scale production will be a real challenge. Efficient machinery will reduce costs per box of chocolates – but will the unique selling point of the business be lost? Wicklow Fine Foods will not use total automation and it wants to avoid large-scale batch production. This would lead to larger stocks, longer lead times (time between order and delivery) and more quality problems.

Perhaps the answer lies in just-in-time (JIT) production. This is the opposite of batch production – it uses minimum inventories, materials, equipment time and space. It produces products with shorter lead times and meets the varied needs of customers while delivering goods on time.

A management consultant recommended: 'The owners of Wicklow's should plan for the long term. It is expensive to increase the scale of production and to move to larger premises – they should make sure that the new facilities have the capacity to increase output and sales not just two times but up to five times current levels.'

[30 marks, 45 minutes]

1 a Define the term 'large scale production'. [2]
   b Briefly explain the term 'batch production'. [3]
2 Explain **two** possible reasons why the owners of this business want to double production capacity. [6]
3 Analyse why it might be cheaper to produce each box of chocolates or biscuits after the increase in scale of production. [8]
4 Evaluate whether the business might experience diseconomies of scale following the expansion. [11]

AS Level essay questions

[20 marks, 40 minutes each]

1 a Analyse the possible reasons why a manufacturer of toys might relocate from the USA to China. [8]
   b Assess the view that a good location guarantees business success. [12]
2 a Explain the benefits of operations planning to any business of your choice. [8]
   b Discuss the factors that a manufacturing firm should consider when deciding on the most appropriate method of production. [12]

24 Inventory management

This chapter covers syllabus section AS Level 4.3.

On completion of this chapter, you will be able to:

- understand why businesses hold **stocks (inventories)** and the costs of stock holding
- analyse the advantages and disadvantages of traditional stock-management systems
- discuss the just-in-time (JIT) stock-management system.

KEY TERM

Inventory (stock): materials and goods required to allow for the production and supply of products to the customer.

Introducing the topic

THE SHOCKING COST OF HOLDING INVENTORIES

It is commonly accepted that the cost to a business of holding inventories is between 4% and 10% of the value of the inventory goods. So, if an average inventory level is $1 million, the annual cost of actually keeping and looking after the goods could be up to $100,000. However, recent research has shown that the figure could be as high as 40%. These costs include:

- storage costs – the rent on the warehouse, for example
- inventory-handling costs – moving goods around the warehouse or factory, requiring a forklift truck and driver
- loss and damage – making products and not finding them in a large warehouse, or damaged goods that have to be sold off cheaply
- obsolescence – many businesses hold inventories of goods that are out-of-date and would be difficult to sell for the full price
- opportunity cost of capital tied up in inventories – using precious capital held in stock items means that this money could not be used to invest in more capacity to increase output and sales.

All of a sudden the figure of 30–40% as the total cost of holding inventories does not seem so outrageous after all.

But how to cut down on these costs? Could businesses manage their operations with lower inventories – or even none at all? The experience of a large Scottish supermarket group suggests that it is possible to move away from holding large inventories 'just in case' there is a demand for the products. In place of this approach, the managers of Scotmid decided on an IT-driven inventory-ordering system that reordered goods from suppliers automatically as remaining goods on the shelves were purchased by customers. 'We now have much tighter control of inventory, wastage and improved cash flow. Inventory-holding has reduced dramatically with huge benefits throughout the supermarket group,' said the IT manager of Scotmid.

Points to think about:

- Give some examples of inventories held by: (a) a supermarket, (b) a house builder and (c) an insurance company.
- Give as many reasons as you can for why businesses hold inventories.
- Could a business manage with 'zero' inventories? Explain your answer.
- Examine the usefulness of IT in managing inventories effectively.

Introduction

All businesses hold inventories of some kind. Banks and insurance companies will hold supplies of stationery and retailers have goods on display and in their warehouses.

Manufacturing businesses will hold inventories in three distinct forms:

1 **Raw materials and components:** These will have been purchased from outside suppliers. They will be held in

storage until they are used in the production process. These inventories can be drawn upon at any time and allow the firm to meet increases in demand by increasing the rate of production quickly.

2 **Work in progress:** At any one time the production process will be converting raw materials and components into finished goods. During this process there will be 'work in progress' and for some firms, such as building and construction businesses, this will be the main form of inventories held. The value of work in progress depends not only on the length of time needed to complete production but also on the method of production used. Batch production tends to have high work-in-progress levels.

3 **Finished goods:** Having been through the complete production process, goods may then be held in storage until sold and despatched to the customer. These inventories can be displayed to potential customers and increase the chances of sales. They are also held to cope with sudden, unpredicted increases in demand so that customers can be satisfied without delay. Firms will also stockpile completed goods to meet anticipated increases in demand as with seasonal goods or products, such as toys at festival times.

TOP TIP

Remember to apply your answer to the business in the question of the case study when writing about inventories and inventory-handling systems – for example, if the business sells toys, it is likely to hold high inventories of toys at festival times.

ACTIVITY 24.1

[12 marks, 20 minutes]

1 List the likely products held in inventories by the following businesses:
    a café
    b computer repair shop
    c private college.   [6]

2 For one of these businesses, analyse the factors that might influence the inventory levels held.   [6]

Inventory management

Why do inventories need to be managed effectively? Without effective management several serious problems can arise for firms:

- There might be insufficient inventories to meet unforeseen changes in demand.

- Out-of-date inventories might be held if an appropriate rotation system is not used, for example for fresh foods or for fast-changing technological products, such as tablet computers.

- Inventory wastage might occur due to mishandling or incorrect storage conditions.

- Very high inventory levels may result in excessive storage costs and a high opportunity cost for the capital tied up.

- Poor management of the supplies purchasing function can result in late deliveries, low discounts from suppliers or too large a delivery for the warehouse to cope with.

For all of these reasons, inventory management is a crucial aspect of operations management. In analysing inventory-management systems, it is essential to be aware of the costs of holding inventories – and the costs of running out of them.

Inventory-holding costs

These include:

- **Opportunity cost:** Working capital tied up in goods in storage could be put to another use. It might be used to pay off loans, buy new equipment or pay off suppliers early to gain an early-payment discount. The capital could be left in the bank to earn interest. The most favourable alternative use of the capital tied up in inventories is called its 'opportunity cost'. The higher the value of inventories held and the more capital used to finance them, then the greater will be this opportunity cost. During periods of high interest rates, the opportunity cost of inventory holding increases.

- **Storage costs:** Inventories have to be held in secure warehouses. They often require special conditions, such as refrigeration. Employees will be needed to guard and transport the goods. Insurance of inventories is recommended in case they are stolen or damaged by, for example, fire or flood. If finance has to be borrowed to buy the goods held in storage, then this will incur interest charges. These are all costs that add to the firm's overheads. Lower inventory levels are likely to reduce these costs significantly.

- **Risk of wastage and obsolescence:** If inventories are not used or sold as rapidly as expected, then there is an increasing danger of goods deteriorating or becoming outdated. This will lower the value of such inventories. Goods often become damaged while held in storage or while being moved – they can then be sold only for a much lower price.

Costs of not holding enough inventories

Does the existence of these holding costs mean that firms should carry as few inventories as possible? This may well be the case, if the business is able to successfully operate the just-in-time system that is discussed below. In other situations there are real risks to holding very low inventory levels – and these risks may have financial costs for the firm. These costs are often called 'inventory-out' costs:

- **Lost sales:** If a firm is unable to supply customers from goods held in storage, then sales could be lost to firms that hold higher inventory levels. This might lead to future lost orders too. In purchasing contracts between businesses, it is common for there to be a penalty-payment clause requiring the supplier to pay compensation if delivery dates cannot be met on time.
- **Idle production resources:** If inventories of raw materials and components run out, then production will have to stop. This will leave expensive equipment idle and labour with nothing to do. The costs of lost output and wasted resources could be considerable.
- **Special orders could be expensive:** If an urgent order is given to a supplier to deliver additional materials due to shortages, then extra costs might be incurred in administration of the order and in special delivery charges.
- **Small order quantities:** Keeping low inventory levels may mean only ordering goods and supplies in small quantities. The larger the size of each delivery, the higher will be the average level of inventories held. By ordering in small quantities, the firm may lose out on bulk discounts, and transport costs could be higher as so many more deliveries have to be made.

The optimum inventory level will be at the lowest point of the total inventory cost graph (see Figure 24.1).

Optimum order size

Purchasing inventories is not as easy as it sounds. The purchasing manager must ensure that supplies of the right quality are delivered at the right time in sufficient quantities to allow smooth and unbroken production.

The temptation might be to order huge quantities in order to gain economies of scale and to ensure that the firm never runs out. Ordering and administration costs will be low as few orders will need to be placed. Continuous production should be ensured and special order costs for out-of-stock materials should be unnecessary.

However, this policy carries real costs too. Inventory-holding costs will be higher as the large orders will have to be stored until they are needed. Opportunity costs will be higher due to more capital being tied up. The danger of goods held in storage becoming obsolete and out-of-date is increased. What, then, is the optimum order size? It will differ for every firm and every kind of inventory. The '**economic order quantity**' (EOQ) can be calculated for each product but at AS/A Level it is sufficient to just know the forces that influence the size of this optimum order size. These can be summarised in Figure 24.2.

KEY TERM

Economic order quantity: the optimum or least-cost quantity of stock to re-order taking into account delivery costs and stock-holding costs.

TOP TIP

You will not be asked to calculate the optimum order size but it is advised that you remember the costs of holding inventories and the costs of running out of them – and apply these to the business in the question.

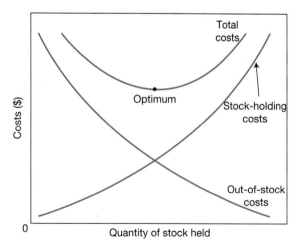

Figure 24.1 Total inventory-holding costs

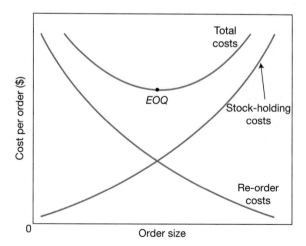

Figure 24.2 Factors influencing the economic order quantity

Controlling inventory levels – a graphical approach

Inventory-control charts or graphs are widely used to monitor a firm's inventory position. These charts record, over time, the numbers of goods held, inventory deliveries, buffer levels and maximum inventory. They aid an inventory manager to determine the appropriate order time and order quantity as well as allowing an analysis of what would happen to inventory levels if an unusual event occurred, such as a competitor operating a really successful promotion campaign (see Figure 24.3).

Figure 24.3 has certain key features:

- **Buffer inventories:** The greater the degree of uncertainty about delivery times or production levels, then the higher this buffer level will have to be. Also, the greater the cost involved in shutting production down and restarting, the greater the potential cost savings from holding high buffer levels of inventories.

> **KEY TERM**
>
> **Buffer inventories:** the minimum inventory level that should be held to ensure that production could still take place should a delay in delivery occur or should production rates increase.

- **Maximum inventory level:** This may be limited by space or by the financial costs of holding even higher inventories. One way to calculate this maximum level is to add the EOQ of each component to the 'buffer' level for that item.

- **Re-order quantity:** This will be influenced by the economic order quantity concept.

> **KEY TERM**
>
> **Re-order quantity:** the number of units ordered each time.

- **Lead time:** The longer this period of time, then the higher will have to be the reorder stock level. The less reliable suppliers are, the greater the buffer stock level might have to be.

> **KEY TERM**
>
> **Lead time:** the normal time taken between ordering new stocks and their delivery.

- **Re-order stock level:** This is the level of stocks that will trigger a new order to be sent to the supplier. In practice, it is very common for computers to be used to keep a record of every sale and every delivery of stock. The reorder quantity and reorder stock level can be programmed into the computer and it can then reorder automatically from the supplier when stocks fall to the reorder stock level. The stock-control chart can also be prepared by the computer. Figure 24.4 shows the stock level of Popsquash soft drinks held by one retailer over a ten-week period.

369

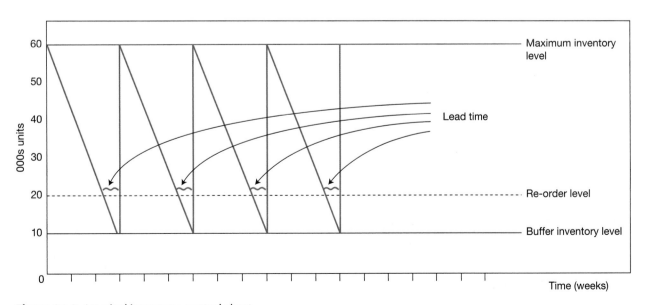

Figure 24.3 A typical inventory-control chart

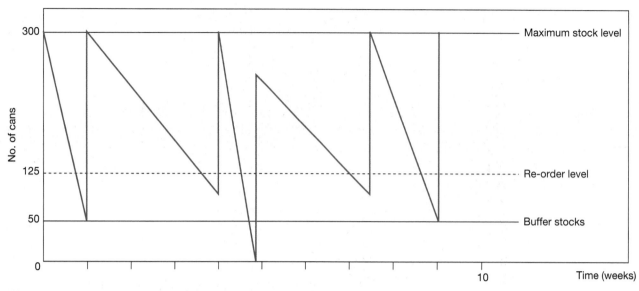

Figure 24.4 Inventory-control chart for Popsquash soft drinks

As can be seen from Figure 24.4, the stock level does not follow the regular and consistent pattern of the previous chart. The sales have been affected by two important factors, shown by the more steeply sloping lines, and deliveries were delayed one week. This is a more realistic situation and helps to illustrate the usefulness of this type of chart for future decision-making regarding stocks.

Just-in-time (JIT) inventory control

Originating in Japan, this approach to stock control is now influencing inventory-holding decisions in businesses all over the world. JIT requires that no buffer inventories are held, components arrive just as they are needed on the production line and finished goods are delivered to customers as soon as they are completed. The principle is easy to understand, but much less easy to put into practice. For JIT principles to be successfully introduced, there are certain very important requirements that a business must ensure are met:

- **Relationships with suppliers have to be excellent:** Suppliers must be prepared and able to supply fresh supplies at very short notice – short lead

time. Suppliers have to see that being reliable and consistent is of great long-term benefit to them as well as the business adopting JIT. This often means that a firm will have only one, or at most two, suppliers for each component, so that a relationship of mutual benefit can be built up.

- **Production staff must be multiskilled and prepared to change jobs at short notice:** There is no point in a worker continuing to produce the same item all the time if this leads to inventories building up. Each worker must be able to switch to making different items at very short notice so that no excess supplies of any one product are made. For example, if a worker in a clothing factory usually makes men's denim jeans, but demand is falling, then the worker should be able to switch to making other garments that are still in demand.

- **Equipment and machinery must be flexible:** Old-fashioned manufacturing equipment tended to be designed to produce one range of very similar products. It might have taken days to adapt it to making other types of products. This equipment would be most unsuitable for JIT-based systems. The machinery would have to produce large batches of one type of component before being converted to making another item. Large inventories of each item produced would be needed to cope with demand while it was producing other goods. Modern, computer-controlled equipment is much more flexible and adaptable – often able to be changed with no more than a different software program. In this way, very small batches of each item can be produced, which keeps stock levels to an absolute minimum. However, such equipment is expensive and, as a result, JIT may not be so appropriate for small or under-financed firms.

- **Accurate demand forecasts will make JIT a much more successful policy:** If it is very difficult for a firm to predict likely future sales levels, then keeping zero inventories of materials, parts and finished goods could be a very risky strategy. Demand forecasts can be converted into production schedules that allow calculation of the precise number of components of each type needed over a certain time period.
- **The latest IT equipment will allow JIT to be more successful:** Accurate data-based records of sales, sales trends, reorder levels and so on will allow very low or zero inventories to be held. Similarly, if contact with suppliers can be set up with the latest electronic data exchanges, then automatic and immediate ordering can take place, when it is recorded that more components will shortly be required.

- **Excellent employee–employer relationships are essential for JIT to operate smoothly:** Any industrial-relations problem could lead to a break in supplies and the entire production system could grind to a halt. It is no coincidence that many of the businesses that have adopted JIT in Japan and in Europe have a no-strike deal with the major trade unions.
- **Quality must be everyone's priority:** As there are no spare inventories to fall back on, it is essential that each component and product must be right first time. Any poor-quality goods that cannot be used will mean that a customer will not receive goods on time. The advantages and disadvantages of JIT are summarised in Table 24.1.

ACTIVITY 24.2

Inventory management at Sportswize Equipment plc

'It's impossible to move in this warehouse. Every single shelf is full of stock, yet the factory is still operating at full capacity. The sooner the economy picks up, the better.' Jack Richards, head of purchasing and stock control at Sportswize, had a good point. He was responsible for controlling purchases of materials and stock management at Sportswize. He was always boasting that 'We have never run out of any item while I've been in charge of stocks' – and it was true. He insisted on ordering large quantities of materials and holding stocks of leather, football studs, metal frames for tennis rackets and so on to allow the production of sports equipment at Sportswize never to be held up.

However, Jack was beginning to worry about the huge stocks of football equipment being held by the firm. The marketing manager had insisted that the combined effects of an economic upturn and the football World Cup would greatly increase the demand for boots, footballs and players' shirts. 'If demand

suddenly increases, then we want to be in the market with stock to sell,' he declared one day. The decision had therefore been taken to increase total finished stocks by $3 million to $7 million. Although this was exceptional, it was quite common for the business to hold high stocks of those items that had just been produced by the batch-production methods in use in the factory. This helped to explain the high levels of work in progress at any one time. The equipment used, for cutting and stitching of materials, for stringing rackets and so on, was rather old-fashioned, so workers took ages to switch from making specialist gear for one sport to equipment for another sport. The finance director was most concerned about this stock-management policy as it greatly increased the capital needed to finance stocks held. He knew also that the sporting public could easily turn against one team or player and then football shirts in that colour or with that name on could hardly be given away, let alone sold.

[31 marks, 40 minutes]

1   Explain why, according to Jack, this business needs to hold stocks of raw materials and components.   [6]

2   Explain the **two** other types of stock held by Sportswize.   [4]

3   Using your knowledge of batch-production methods, explain why stocks of certain goods are likely to be high at particular times.   [6]

4   Assume current interest rates are at 10% per year and capital not used for holding stocks would be left in the bank. Calculate the opportunity cost of increasing stocks from $3 million to $7 million in one year. Explain your result.   [5]

5   Do you think Sportswize has taken the correct decision to increase stocks of finished goods at this time – especially of football equipment and clothing?   [10]

Advantages	Disadvantages
■ Capital invested in inventory is reduced and the opportunity cost of inventory holding is reduced.	■ Any failure to receive supplies of materials or components in time caused by, for example, a strike at the supplier's factory, transport problems or IT failure will lead to expensive production delays.
■ Costs of storage and inventory holding are reduced. Space released from holding of inventories can be used for a more productive purpose.	■ Delivery costs will increase as frequent small deliveries are an essential feature of JIT.
■ Much less chance of inventories becoming outdated or obsolescent. Fewer goods held in storage also reduces the risk of damage or wastage.	■ Order-administration costs may rise because so many small orders need to be processed.
■ The greater flexibility that the system demands leads to quicker response times to changes in consumer demand or tastes.	■ There could a reduction in the bulk discounts offered by suppliers because each order is likely to be very small.
■ The multiskilled and adaptable staff required for JIT to work may gain from improved motivation.	■ The reputation of the business depends significantly on outside factors such as the reliability of supplying firms.

Table 24.1 The advantages and disadvantages of JIT inventory control

ACTIVITY 24.3

Stock control at Saiko

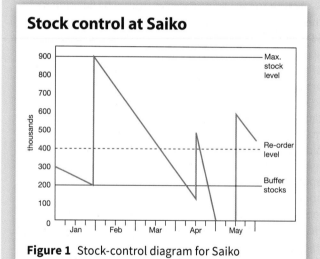

Figure 1 Stock-control diagram for Saiko Trading Ltd

[20 marks, 30 minutes]

1 What factors may have determined the size of the maximum inventory level? **[4]**

2 What size of order was received at the end of January? **[2]**

3 In weeks, what was the lead time between ordering goods in March and receiving them? **[2]**

4 Suggest why inventories fell to zero in April. **[4]**

5 Discuss the problems Saiko Trading Ltd might experience from the pattern of inventory usage shown by the chart. **[8]**

TOP TIP

Any question about JIT that involves discussing how appropriate it is in different business cases should lead to an answer that considers the potential drawbacks of the approach as well as its more obvious benefits.

JIT evaluation

JIT requires a very different organisational culture to that of other inventory-control systems that are often referred to as 'JIC' – holding inventories 'just in case' they might be needed. This change in culture towards not accepting waste or poorly used resources can be of great benefit to business. It requires employees to be much more accountable for their performance and suppliers to be very reliable as any failure to meet targets will lead to production stopping.

There is no surplus or buffer in the JIT system to cover up for inefficient workers, inflexible people and equipment, unreliable suppliers or poor production planning.

JIT may not be suitable for all firms at all times:

■ There may be limits to the application of JIT if the costs resulting from production being halted when supplies do not arrive far exceed the costs of holding buffer inventories of key components.

■ Small firms could argue that the expensive IT systems needed to operate JIT effectively cannot be justified by the potential cost savings.

- In addition, rising global inflation makes holding inventories of raw materials more beneficial as it may be cheaper to buy a large quantity now than smaller quantities in the future when prices have risen. Similarly, higher oil prices will make frequent and small deliveries of materials and components more expensive.

Table 24.1 summarises the advantages and disadvantages of JIT inventory control.

However, as we shall see in following chapters, JIT is an important aspect of the move towards lean production and is definitely a principle that has been so widely adopted that most of the world's manufacturing industry will never return to 'old ways' of inventory control.

KEY CONCEPT LINK

Efficient **management** of inventories can help to reduce waste levels and this can create added **value** for a business

---

ACTIVITY 24.4

Toyota production is halted

A fire at a major supplier of parts to Toyota's Japanese factories has brought all car production to a stop. Toyota's JIT production system relies on suppliers delivering only the necessary volume of vehicle parts to the assembly line at precisely the point in the manufacturing process at which they are required. The problem is that when things go wrong at just one supplier – Aisin Seiki's fire, for example – the lack of spare parts inventory can lead to serious problems. Toyota always relies on one supplier for all major parts, because it believes that this brings huge economies of scale. These suppliers not only have to agree to be 100% reliable – excluding events such as fires or earthquakes – but also accept that they must design parts for Toyota's cars themselves. This special relationship with suppliers has helped Toyota reduce its costs by $820 million in each of the past three years.

Nissan cuts stock to almost zero

Nissan's car factories now operate on an average of just 1.6 days' worth of component and raw-material stocks. This is one of the lowest in the entire motor industry. Computer links with suppliers, which are often located in the same area as the Nissan factories, allow special coded messages to be sent from the Nissan production line. These contain details of the models and colours of cars being assembled. The supplier, for example of car carpets, then knows that it must supply particular colours of carpets directly to the factory. In fact, some suppliers will make up to 120 deliveries in a day. The parts are taken straight to the assembly line – they do not pass through a traditional warehouse first. Nissan production control directors claim that this method brings huge savings in inventory holding and internal inventory handling as well as great space-saving advantages.

[24 marks, 30 minutes]

1 Examine the benefits to both Nissan and Toyota of:
   a the JIT system of inventory control that both use
   b their reliance on just one supplier for each major component. [12]

2 Using evidence drawn from the articles and from your own knowledge, examine the potential drawbacks to the adoption of the JIT concept for manufacturing businesses. [12]

SUMMARY POINTS

- Businesses hold inventories for several reasons but there are holding costs.
- There are also costs of having inadequate inventories.
- There are advantages and disadvantages of traditional inventory-management systems.
- The just-in-time inventory-management concept is widely adopted by businesses in all industrial sectors. However, it does involve risks and it might not be suitable for all businesses.

RESEARCH TASK

- Ask your teacher to help you contact the managers of local shops and supermarkets.
- Find out how often they receive deliveries of the main items they sell.
- Visit the shops/supermarkets. Attempt to identify whether the business holds high or low inventories of main items.
- Discuss with at least one shop/supermarket manager the factors they take in to account when deciding what level of inventories to hold.
- Write up your findings.

AS Level exam practice questions

Short answer questions

[54 marks, 75 minutes]

Knowledge and understanding

1 Explain what is meant by the following terms:
 a 'buffer inventory level' [2]
 b 're-order level' [2]
 c 'lead time' [2]

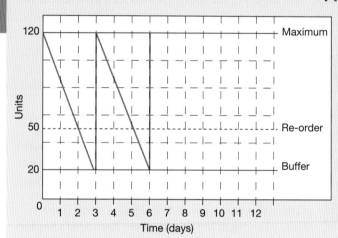

2 From the diagram above identify:
 a buffer inventory level
 b re-order quantity
 c lead time. [6]
3 Explain why most manufacturers will hold inventories in the form of 'work in progress'. [3]
4 Outline **two** costs associated with holding inventories. [4]
6 Explain the factors that influence the economic order quantity of inventories. [4]
7 Explain **two** conditions that must exist for JIT inventory control to work effectively. [6]
8 Explain **two** risks to a business from operating a JIT system. [6]
9 Why might JIT not be appropriate for all businesses? [4]

Application

10 State **three** types of inventory that are likely to be held by a chocolate manufacturer. [3]
11 Explain **two** factors that would determine the maximum inventory level held by a food-processing business. [6]
12 Analyse **two** potential disadvantages to a hospital of adopting a JIT system for essential medical supplies. [6]

Data response

MFLEX to expand operations in Malaysia

MFLEX, the leading global maker of high-quality advanced circuit boards to the electronics industry, has leased a 35,000-square-metre factory in Johor Darul Takzim, Malaysia. It has purchased new manufacturing equipment for the plant and employed 125 workers, so this will mean a considerable increase in capacity and scale of operation for the company.

This factory will allow the business to respond more rapidly and flexibly to just-in-time demands from its customers. The company will also expect its suppliers to be able to deliver materials and components on a JIT basis and it has signed exclusive deals with certain suppliers and is connected to them by computer link to speed up ordering.

Rapid inflation in Malaysia, as in other countries, is forcing some businesses to rethink their use of JIT manufacturing systems. With constantly rising costs of industrial materials and components and higher charges for transport, some operations managers are looking again at whether the 'no buffer inventory' policy of the JIT method with frequent small orders being delivered is actually costing more than a large inventory-order policy.

[30 marks, 45 minutes]

1 a Define the term 'increase in scale of operation'. [2]

   b Briefly explain the term 'no buffer inventory policy'. [3]

2 Analyse the benefits to MFLEX of being able to respond quickly to its customers' demands for JIT supplies of printed circuits and other products. [6]

3 Analyse the factors that MFLEX must put in place before its JIT strategy will work effectively. [8]

4 Assess why JIT is not necessarily appropriate for all businesses in all situations. [11]

AS Level essay questions

[20 marks, 40 minutes each]

1 a Explain why manufacturing businesses need to manage inventories efficiently. [8]

   b Discuss whether a JIT inventory-control system should be used by a soft drink manufacturer that purchases fruit and other supplies from many businesses. [12]

2 a Analyse the costs of holding inventories. [8]

   b Should all businesses aim to minimise their inventory levels at all times? [12]

25 Capacity utilisation

On completion of this chapter, you will be able to:

- understand the meaning and calculation of capacity utilisation
- analyse the problems of excess capacity and capacity shortages
- evaluate the different approaches to overcoming these problems
- assess the reasons for the rapid growth of outsourcing
- evaluate the benefits and limitations of outsourcing.

Introducing the topic

CAPACITY UTILISATION

US car-makers are producing cars round the clock from existing factories to avoid big investments in new capacity. After years of redundancies and plant closures, Ford, General Motors and Chrysler are pushing factories to their limits. More flexible labour contracts allow these companies to operate shift systems and build cars for 120 hours a week while paying less overtime. Capacity utilisation in US car factories has never been higher. Productivity has increased, too. In 2005 the industry produced 17.5 million cars with a workforce of 925,700. In 2012, the numbers employed had dropped to 647,600 but output had only fallen to 15.8 million. The high capacity utilisation has helped the companies increase profitability. Ford USA made US$4.7 billion in the first six months of 2013. The US car-makers do not want to finance new investment in factories and machines because profits would be hit if demand fell. Volkswagen recently made 500 workers redundant from its new US$1 billion plant in Chattanooga after demand for its big saloon cars fell.

High capacity utilisation has its problems too. There are supply shortages of some models – the Jeep Wrangler, for example. One US car worker, James Spizzireo, stated that ten-hour shifts meant that: 'You make great money but the toll it takes on the body and the time away from family is hard to deal with.'

OUTSOURCING

Deutsche Bank has outsourced the design and operation of its IT system that deals with customer relations to a Russian company, Luxoft. The bank does not employ its own IT software developers, preferring to use other specialist companies. Luxoft has 100 developers working on the Deutsche Bank customer system, which covers details such as dates of meetings with customers, amount lent and copies of all documents. Getting the details right is essential, so quality checks on the Luxoft system are essential.

Points to think about:

- Why are US car-makers keen to operate at very high levels of capacity utilisation?
- What potential problems could result from the lack of investment in additional car manufacturing capacity?
- What might be the benefits and risks to Deutsche Bank of outsourcing some of its important operations to another business?

Introduction

Capacity utilisation is calculated by the formula:

$$\frac{\text{current output level}}{\text{maximum output level}} \times 100 = \text{rate of capacity utilisation}$$

KEY TERM

Capacity utilisation: the proportion of maximum output capacity currently being achieved.

The degree of total capacity being used is a major factor in determining the operational efficiency of a business. Maximum capacity is the total level of output that a business can achieve in a certain time period. So, for a hotel, monthly total capacity will be the number of room nights available during this period. For a factory, it will be the total level of output that all of the existing resources – land, capital equipment and labour – can produce. If a firm is working at full capacity, it is achieving 100% capacity utilisation. There is no spare capacity.

Data on capacity utilisation are widely used by analysts and industry experts to compare how one firm is performing compared to the average or how capacity utilisation differs from previous periods.

Capacity utilisation – impact on average fixed costs

This is the most important aspect of the concept of capacity utilisation. It helps to explain why the rate at which capacity is used is of such significance to operational efficiency. When utilisation is at a high rate, average fixed costs will be spread out over a large number of units – unit fixed costs will be relatively low. When utilisation is low, fixed costs will have to be borne by fewer units and unit fixed costs will rise (see Table 25.1).

It might be assumed that all firms will be aiming to produce at 100% capacity at all times. In theory, the cost advantages of this would appear to be great. Unit fixed costs will be at their lowest possible level and this should help to lift profits. The business will be able to claim how successful it is as it has no spare capacity. For example, hotels will put up 'No vacancy' signs and airlines will not have any unsold seats. This situation will also give employees a sense of security for their jobs and, possibly, a sense of pride that the firm they work for is so popular.

There are also potential drawbacks to operating at full capacity for a considerable period of time:

- Staff may feel under pressure due to the workload and this could raise stress levels. Operations managers cannot afford to make any production scheduling mistakes, as there is no slack time to make up for lost output.
- Regular customers who wish to increase their orders will have to be turned away or kept waiting for long periods. This could encourage them to use other suppliers, with the danger that they might be lost as long-term clients.
- Machinery will be working flat out and there may be insufficient time for maintenance and preventative repairs. This lack of servicing may store up trouble in the form of increased unreliability in the future. For these reasons, many firms attempt to maintain a very high level of capacity utilisation, while also keeping some spare capacity for the unforeseen eventualities that can always occur in business.

100-bed hotel	All bedrooms occupied (100% of capacity)	50 bedrooms occupied (50% of capacity)
Hotel fixed costs per day, e.g. rent and salaries	$2,500	$2,500
Average fixed costs per room per day	$25	$50

Table 25.1 How unit fixed costs vary with capacity utilisation

ACTIVITY 25.1

[12 marks, 20 minutes]

1. Explain with a numerical example how unit (average) fixed costs decline as output rises. **[4]**

2. If a business currently has an annual production capacity of 50,000 units, what will be its rate of capacity utilisation if its annual production is:

   - 20,000 units
   - 30,000 units
   - 45,000 units
   - 50,000 units. **[8]**

Excess capacity – what are the options?

Low levels of capacity utilisation lead to high unit fixed costs – so what options do firms have when attempting to reduce **excess capacity**? Before this question can be answered, the time factor needs to be considered.

1. Is spare capacity just a short-term, seasonal problem such as might exist for ice creams in the colder months? The main options for businesses in this case would be to:
   - Maintain high output levels but add to stocks. However, this could be expensive and risky if sales do not recover.
   - Adopt a more flexible production system allowing other goods to be made that might be sold at other times of the year. However, this will require staff, machines and other resources to be flexible enough to produce other goods or services.
   - Offer only flexible employment contracts to staff so that during periods of low demand and excess capacity, staff may be laid off and costs saved. However, this may have a negative impact on staff morale and motivation.

KEY TERM

Excess capacity: exists when the current levels of demand are less than the full capacity output of a business – also known as spare capacity.

2 Is spare capacity a long-term problem resulting from a fashion change, technological development of rival products or an economic recession? In these situations, if demand cannot be revived by means of promotion, a cut in production capacity should be considered. This is often referred to as **rationalisation** and will have both cost and industrial-relations implications.

KEY TERM

Rationalisation: reducing capacity by cutting overheads to increase efficiency of operations, such as closing a factory or office department, often involving redundancies.

The main drawbacks of rationalisation are that if capacity is cut back too much, an unexpected upturn in demand may leave the firm with too little capacity and disappointed customers. In addition, staff redundancies will lead to lost job security and low worker motivation – and bad publicity in the media.

Excess capacity – evaluating the options

1 Excess capacity in the short term

Table 25.2 examines the options available to operations managers. The business may also consider marketing solutions to the problem, such as cutting prices or entering overseas markets in an effort to increase sales.

2 Excess capacity in the longer term

This might be caused by an economic recession, technological changes that make existing products less competitive, or by promotional campaigns by rivals. The precise cause of the excess capacity will be important to identify as it could indicate a range of products that require updating rather than a general recession in demand. Table 25.3 examines the operations-management options that could be considered.

TOP TIP

When making decisions about how to deal with excess capacity it is important to consider both the length of time that the spare capacity might exist for and the causes of the problem.

Working at full capacity

The potential problems connected with operating at **full capacity** have been referred to. When business is operating at close to or at full capacity, then other decisions have to be taken.

KEY TERM

Full capacity: when a business produces at maximum output.

ACTIVITY 25.2

Hotels' excess capacity

The following data apply to the hotel industry. Capacity utilisation in the hotel industry is often referred to as 'room occupancy rates'.

	2012	2013
London hotels – capacity utilisation	85%	75%
Average room price	$135	$145
Istanbul hotels – capacity utilisation	70%	80%
Average room price	$90	$95

[15 marks, 20 minutes]

1 What could account for the falling rates of capacity utilisation in London hotels between 2012 and 2013? [4]

2 Does lower capacity utilisation help to explain the higher prices being charged by London hotels in 2013? Justify your answer. [4]

3 Assume that in 2014 there are a total of 2 million room nights available in London hotels. The number of room nights actually booked was 1.4 million. Calculate the capacity utilisation of London hotels in 2014. [3]

4 What might explain the differences between the 2013–2014 trend in capacity utilisation of hotels in Istanbul and that of London hotels? [4]

ACTIVITY 25.3

GSK announces new strategic investments in Africa

GSK has announced new investments in sub-Saharan Africa designed to address pressing health needs and contribute to long-term business growth. These will help stimulate more research into serious diseases and increase production capacity by localising medicine supply.

GSK will make targeted investments of up to £130 million in Africa over the next five years, creating at least 500 jobs and contributing to the development of localised skills in Africa. The investment builds on GSK's existing business base in sub-Saharan Africa, which currently employs around 1,500 people in over 40 countries, including manufacturing sites in Kenya, Nigeria and South Africa.

Andrew Witty, CEO of GSK, said: "GSK's long-term goal is to equip Africa to discover, develop and produce the medicines required for Africa."

It is hoped that localised pharmaceutical research will improve prevention and treatment strategies and will enable researchers in universities and industry to discover and develop new medicines to address the specific needs of African patients.

Aluminium production capacity to be reduced

Two of the world's biggest producers of aluminium have announced production capacity cuts. Alcoa currently has 13% of its capacity unused and is planning to reduce total annual capacity by 460,000 tons or 11%. It could do this by closing some of its least efficient and highest cost plants in the USA. United Co Rusal, the Russian aluminium producer, plans to cut 7% of its capacity permanently by 2015. Both companies expect to make substantial redundancies. Both decisions are in response to falling global prices for the metal. Cutting idle capacity will reduce costs for both companies and improve cash flow and profitability.

An aluminium production plant

[34 marks, 50 minutes]

1 Explain, with reference to the two texts, what is meant by the terms 'to increase production capacity' and 'to cut production capacity'. **[6]**

2 Analyse the benefits to GSK from its decision to increase medicine production in Africa. **[10]**

3 Using the data provided, calculate Alcoa's current production capacity. **[4]**

4 Evaluate the decision by Alcoa and Unit Co. Rusal to cut capacity permanently rather than to maintain idle production capacity. **[14]**

	SHORT-TERM PROBLEM – e.g. seasonal downturn	
	Advantages	**Disadvantages**
Option 1: Maintain output and produce for stocks	■ no part-time working for staff ■ job security for staff ■ no need to change production schedules or orders from suppliers ■ stocks may be sold at times of rising demand	■ unsuitable for perishable stocks or those that go out-of-date quickly ■ stock-holding costs can be very substantial ■ demand may not increase as expected – the goods may have to be sold at a substantial discount
Option 2: Introduce greater flexibility into the production process: ■ part-time or temporary labour contracts ■ flexible equipment that can be switched to making other products ■ short-term working, e.g. all staff on three-day week	■ production can be reduced during slack periods and increased when demand is high ■ other products can be produced that may follow a different demand pattern ■ avoids stock build-up	■ staff may be demotivated by not having full-time, permanent contracts ■ fully flexible and adaptable equipment can be expensive ■ staff may need to be trained in more than one product – may add to costs

Table 25.2 Dealing with short-term excess capacity

	LONG-TERM PROBLEM – e.g. economic recession or technological changes	
	Advantages	**Disadvantages**
Option 1: Rationalise existing operations and cut capacity, e.g. by closing factory/offices	■ reduces overheads ■ higher capacity utilisation	■ redundancy costs for staff payments ■ staff uncertainty over job security ■ possible threats of industrial action ■ capacity may be needed later if economy picks up or if firm develops new products ■ business may be criticised for not fulfilling social responsibilities
Option 2: Research and development into new products	■ will replace existing products and make business more competitive ■ if introduced quickly enough, might prevent rationalisation and the problems associated with this	■ may prove to be expensive ■ may take too long to prevent cutbacks in capacity and rationalisation ■ requires long-term planning as new products introduced in haste, without a clear market strategy, may be unsuccessful

Table 25.3 Dealing with long-term excess capacity

■ Should the firm increase its scale of operation by acquiring more production resources?

■ Should it keep existing capacity but outsource or subcontract more work to other firms?

■ Could the quality of products obtained from subcontractors be assured?

■ Should it keep working at full capacity and not expand, perhaps because of the danger that demand might fall back in the near future?

The final decision will depend on many factors – not least the cost of expanding the scale of operations. The time factor is once again important – it may prove to be quicker to put work contracts with outside firms, which could produce components that used to be made within the factory, than to actually build a brand new production facility, which could take years to complete. By the time it is completed, demand may have fallen anyway, perhaps because of an economic downturn.

Capacity shortage

What options is a firm faced with if the demand for its products exceeds current output capacity? As with the

> **KEY TERM**
>
> **Capacity shortage:** when the demand for a business's products exceeds production capacity.

> **KEY TERMS**
>
> **Outsourcing:** using another business (a 'third party') to undertake a part of the production process rather than doing it within the business using the firm's own employees.
>
> **Business-process outsourcing (BPO):** a form of outsourcing that uses a third party to take responsibility for certain business functions, such as HR and finance.

opposite situation of excess supply capacity, it is essential to analyse the cause of the excess demand and the time period it is likely to last. For instance, if it results from a reduction in output caused by a faulty machine that will be repaired next month, then drastic action to raise capacity is unlikely. If, however, the firm has been producing at 100% capacity for some time and there seems to be no sign of demand falling, then two options need to be weighed up (see Table 25.4).

These decisions should not be taken lightly as the success of an expansion decision could determine the future profitability of a business. Failure to expand capacity in a growing market could leave the business with a shrinking market share or becoming increasingly dependent on external contractors. Rapid expansion that takes place before demand trends are clear could lead to excess capacity problems if demand trends change.

Outsourcing

The growth of **outsourcing** in recent years by many businesses is not just driven by shortage of capacity. These are the other major reasons for outsourcing:

- **Reduction and control of operating costs:** Instead of employing expensive specialists that might not be fully used at all times by the business it could be cheaper to

'buy in' specialist services as and when they are needed. These specialist firms may be cheaper because they benefit from economies of scale, as they may provide similar services to a large number of other businesses. Much outsourcing involves offshoring – buying in services, components or completed products from low-wage economies.

- **Increased flexibility:** By removing departments from the staff payroll and buying in services when needed, fixed costs are converted into variable costs. Additional capacity can be obtained from outsourcing only when needed and contracts can be cancelled if demand falls much more quickly than closing down whole factories owned by the business. The advantages of using subcontractors to 'take the strain' during periods of full capacity have already been discussed.

- **Improved company focus:** By outsourcing 'peripheral' activities, the management of a business can concentrate on the main aims and tasks of the business. These are called the 'core' parts of the business. So a small hotel might use management time to improve customer service and outsource the accounting function completely.

	LONG-TERM CAPACITY SHORTAGE	
	Advantages	**Disadvantages**
Option 1: Use subcontractors or outsourcing of supplies, components or even finished goods	■ no major capital investment is required ■ should be quite quick to arrange ■ offers much greater flexibility than expansion of facilities – if demand falls back, then the contracts with other firms can be ended	■ less control over quality of output ■ may add to administration and transport costs ■ may be uncertainty over delivery times and reliability of delivery ■ unit cost may be higher than 'in-house' production due to the supplier's profit margin
Option 2: Capital investment in expansion of production facilities	■ long-term increase in capacity ■ firm is in control of quality and final delivery times ■ new facilities should be able to use latest equipment and methods ■ other economies of scale should be possible too	■ capital cost may be high ■ problems with raising capital ■ increases total capacity, but problems could occur if demand should fall for a long period ■ takes time to build and equip a new facility – customers may not wait

Table 25.4 How to overcome long-term capacity shortage problems

- **Access to quality service or resources** that are not available internally. Many outsourcing firms employ quality specialists that small to medium-sized businesses could not afford to employ directly.
- **Freed-up internal resources** for use in other areas. If the HR department of an insurance company is closed and the functions bought in, then the office space and computer facilities could be made available to improve customer service.

There are potential drawbacks to outsourcing too:

- **Loss of jobs within the business:** This can have a negative impact on staff motivation. Workers who remain directly employed by the organisation may experience a loss of job security. Bad publicity may result from redundancies too, especially if the business is accused of employing very low-wage employees in other countries in place of the jobs lost. This could lead to the firm's ethical standards being questioned.
- **Quality issues:** Internal processes will be monitored by the firm's own quality-assurance system. This will not be so easy when outside contractors are performing important functions. A clear contract with minimum service-level agreements will be needed. The company contracting out the functions may have to send quality-assurance staff out to the business undertaking the tasks to ensure that product quality and customer-service standards are being met.
- **Customer resistance:** This could take several forms. Overseas telephone call centres have led to criticism about inability to understand foreign operators. Customers may object to dealing with overseas outsourced operations. Bought-in components and functions may raise doubts in the customers' minds over quality and reliability.
- **Security:** Using outside businesses to perform important IT functions may be a security risk – if important data were lost by the business, who would take responsibility for this?

TOP TIP

You may be asked for your advice on outsourcing an activity. Generally, the more important an activity is to the overall aims and reputation of the business, the less likely it is that outsourcing will be appropriate.

ACTIVITY 25.4

[16 marks, 25 minutes]

1   Refer to the GSK article on page 379. Explain possible reasons why GSK decided to invest in sub-Sarahan Africa.   [6]

2   Explain **two** benefits to an insurance company of outsourcing its customer-service telephone answering system to an overseas call centre.   [4]

3   Are there some functions that you believe a large international hotel business should *not* consider outsourcing? Explain your answer.   [6]

Outsourcing evaluation

The global trend towards outsourcing will continue as firms seek further ways of improving operational effectiveness and as more opportunities arise due to globalisation. The process is not without its risks, however. Before any substantial business-process outsourcing of complete functions is undertaken or before any stage of the production process is outsourced, the company must undertake a substantial cost–benefit analysis of the decision. Having closed or run down a whole department to outsource its functions, it would be time-consuming and expensive to reopen and re-establish it if it was found that the outsourcing had failed.

One of the key factors in any business decision on outsourcing is to decide what is a truly core activity that must be kept within the direct control of the business. The nature of these core activities will vary from business to business.

KEY CONCEPT LINK

Outsourcing ('offshoring' if undertaken overseas) can increase the **value** created by a business as it can reduce cost of bought in components and materials – but management has to consider carefully if the reliability of supplies and quality are likely to be sufficient to satisfy customer expectations. Even operational decisions need to be **customer-focused**.

- Capacity utilisation is measured as the proportion of maximum output that is currently being produced.
- There are both problems and benefits of full- or high-capacity working.
- The business solutions to both excess capacity and capacity shortages have advantages and drawbacks.
- The process of outsourcing is growing in significance and the advantages and potential drawbacks of it need to be considered in context before a decision is taken.

RESEARCH TASK

- Investigate businesses that are cutting or increasing production capacity. Newspaper websites are a good starting point – two articles in this chapter have been taken from the *Wall Street Journal* (http://online.wsj.com/public/page/news-business-us.html).
- Analyse reasons why these capacity decisions were made.
- Evaluate the other options that these businesses had: increasing production through outsourcing or maintaining production capacity and attempting to increase sales.
- Do you think that the companies made the most appropriate decisions? Justify your view.

A Level Exam practice questions
Case study

1 Improving efficiency at Nassau Textile Manufacturing

The problems at NTM began several years ago when the previous chief executive took the decision to double production capacity. He could not have foreseen the worldwide recession and how this would reduce the demand for the textiles made in the factory. The following figures tell their own story and the cost impact on the business was now serious:

	2011	2012	2013
Maximum capacity (metres)	5m	5m	5m
Actual annual output (metres)	4m	3.7m	3.0m
Selling price per metre	$3	$3	$2.7
Annual fixed costs	$3 million	$3 million	$3 million
Variable costs per metre	$2	$2	$2.2

The new board of directors had one key objective – to cut production costs to restore company profitability. They realised that this would mean cutting both overhead costs – possibly moving to a smaller factory – and variable labour costs per unit. Labour costs per unit depended on labour productivity and wage costs. Wage rates had been increased in 2013 but productivity had not increased.

The directors were considering three options:

- Close part of the factory and sell it to another business – this might raise $5 million in capital and would reduce annual fixed costs by $1 million. Fifty jobs would be cut.
- Keep the whole factory open but cut the number of workers (by 100) and managers to increase productivity.
- Keep the factory open and keep all existing workers but offer part-time and temporary contracts to all workers and some managers.

[33 marks, 40 minutes]

1. Calculate the capacity-utilisation rates in each of the three years. [3]
2. Calculate the level of profits made in each of the three years. Comment on your results. [6]
3. Analyse the disadvantages to NTM of operating at a low rate of capacity utilisation. [10]
4. Evaluate the advantages and disadvantages of all three options being considered by the directors. Recommend which option the directors should decide on, justifying your answer fully. [14]

2 World's airlines increase outsourcing

There is one area where major national airlines and their cut-price competitors agree – aircraft maintenance is a lot cheaper when it's performed by low-paid mechanics working for outsourcing companies. JetBlue, Southwest, Qantas, America West and United are among the big airlines that outsource all major maintenance of their aircraft to contractors in other countries. JetBlue's A320 Airbus planes are sent to El Salvador for maintenance, for example. US Airways recently cut 2,000 skilled mechanics' jobs as it outsourced most of its maintenance and repair work.

It wasn't long ago that all global airlines employed their own teams of highly qualified and highly paid aircraft engineers. They were all licensed by their own country's civil aviation authority and could earn at least $60 an hour.

Mechanics working for outsourcers do not have to be licensed – only their supervisors must be fully qualified. In El Salvador the mechanics earn between $10 and $20 an hour.

Most airlines have also outsourced customer-enquiry call centres, baggage handling and in-flight catering and merchandising. Malaysia Airlines recently denied rumours that it was about to outsource its in-flight retail operation called Golden Boutique. The airline has made clear its desire to 'mutually separate' non-core operations. The company described its in-flight business as 'non-core but good value', so it may want to remain in complete control of this with its own employees.

Aircraft mechanics – should aircraft maintenance be outsourced?

[32 marks, 50 minutes]

1 Analyse the potential benefits to major airlines from outsourcing the maintenance of their aircraft. [10]

2 Explain **two** reasons why Malaysia Airlines may not want to outsource in-flight retailing. [8]

3 As a business consultant, write a report to the chief executive of your own national airline discussing the process of outsourcing and recommending whether all non-core activities should be outsourced. [14]

A Level essay question

[20 marks, 45 minutes]

An airline is currently operating at nearly 100% of capacity during the peak of the tourist season. Evaluate the steps management might take in response to this situation. [20]

26 Lean production and quality management

This chapter covers syllabus section A Level 4.5.

In this chapter, you will learn how to:

- analyse the importance of lean production to competitive businesses
- evaluate the main lean production techniques
- explain the concept of quality
- understand the difference between quality control and quality assurance
- explain the importance of businesses establishing quality-assurance systems
- evaluate the effectiveness of total quality management
- assess the costs and benefits of managing quality
- explain how managing quality effectively can improve the competitiveness of business.

Introducing the topic

THE TRIUMPH OF LEAN PRODUCTION

On the assembly line at Toyota's giant assembly plant in Kentucky, USA, Laura Wilshire is not happy. There is something wrong with the seat-belt fitting on the car she is working on. She pulls a cord, stopping production – and her five fellow workers on that production line crowd round. They soon see that the belt is not screwed in properly and fix the problem. 'I don't like to let something like that go,' she says. 'Quality's really important for people who buy our cars.'

Workers pull the cord 2,000 times a week at this car plant. They then become involved in solving quality problems and reducing waste. This is what makes Toyota one of the most reliable and most desired brands in the USA. In contrast, in a typical Ford factory, workers pull the cord only twice a week – a legacy of troubled worker–manager relations in the past. Using workers to solve work problems is part of Toyota's lean production system – which is now being copied around the world. It means that the company can produce cars more cheaply and to a higher quality than its US rivals. Just-in-time deliveries are insisted on from suppliers. Production

changes are now so flexible that consumer needs can be met much more closely than decades ago. The average lifespan of a new model, before it is revised or replaced, is just 25 months. Twenty years ago it was over 60 months.

Jim Press, Toyota's boss in the USA, says: 'Being customer-focused is really important. We can react to changes so quickly.' Toyota claims that with simultaneous engineering and flexible production systems, it can develop a brand new model in just 18 months – it takes General Motors three years. The company's president has said that he did not care if Toyota remained the largest car-maker in the world: 'What is important is to be number one for quality.'

Points to think about:

- Explain the benefits of involving staff in solving work-related problems.
- What does being 'lean' seem to mean within Toyota?
- Do you think it is an advantage to be able to develop new products more quickly than competitors? Explain your answer.

Introduction

In competitive markets, businesses usually focus on improving operational efficiency and productivity. This emphasis is particularly crucial for firms when global economic conditions are depressed. Product quality is another important operational management issue that plays a very significant part in determining the competitiveness of a business. There is no point in

increasing output and efficiency if the product is not of a suitable standard. Low unit costs and low market prices will prove to be inadequate benefits for a business if the consumers receive poor quality and unreliable products. How is quality defined and measured? How can firms attempt to ensure that quality standards are met and maintained? These questions are answered in the second part of this chapter.

Lean production

Lean production is closely associated with Japanese production methods that are now widely adopted throughout much of the industrialised world. This concept is closely linked with some of the practices that we have already considered – such as quality circles, empowerment of workers, efficient use of capacity and JIT. There are also links with the objective of achieving quality output – being lean should involve 'getting it right first time' to reduce wastage of resources.

> **KEY TERM**
>
> **Lean production:** producing goods and services with the minimum of wasted resources while maintaining high quality.

The overall objective of this production method is to produce quality output with fewer resources – that is, less waste, less duplication and elimination of non-added-value activities. Lean means cutting out anything in the production process that adds complexity, cost and time, and does not add value to the customer.

The seven main sources of waste in industry are:

1. Excessive transportation of components and products.
2. Excessive inventory holding.
3. Too much movement by working people, e.g. to get supplies of components.
4. Waiting time – delays in the production process.
5. Overproduction – producing ahead of demand.
6. Over-processing – making goods that are too complex as they could have been designed more simply.
7. Defects – products that do not come up to quality standards and have to be rejected or corrected.

How can the aim of reduced waste be achieved?

The answer lies in the adoption of the following features of lean production.

Simultaneous engineering

This is a method of developing new products by ensuring that essential design, market research, costing and engineering tasks are done at the same time as each other (simultaneously) – not one after the other (sequentially). As most products become more advanced

Toyota factory in the Czech Republic: Toyota was the first major manufacturer to adopt lean production methods; the fact that it is now one of the world's most successful car-makers is no coincidence

and complicated, it could take longer and longer to develop new designs. The problems with this are that during this period, competitors might launch their new products earlier and technology might advance during the design stage, rendering the new product 'obsolete' as soon as it is launched on the market. The advantage of **simultaneous engineering** is that new products can be in the marketplace months or even years earlier than would have been the case with sequential methods. This benefit is illustrated in Figure 26.1 for new car models. Chapter 27 covers a planning technique known as network analysis, which assists with the application of simultaneous engineering.

> **KEY TERM**
>
> **Simultaneous engineering:** product development is organised so that different stages are done at the same time instead of in sequence.

Cell production

Cell production is a form of flow production, but instead of each individual worker performing a single task, the production line is split into several self-contained mini production units – known as cells. Each individual cell produces a complete unit of work, e.g. a complete

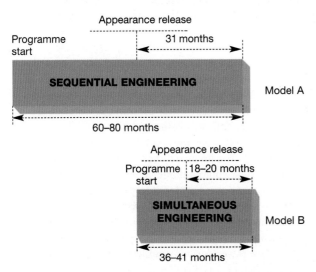

Programme start

Appearance release

31 months

SEQUENTIAL ENGINEERING

Model A

60–80 months

Appearance release

Programme start | 18–20 months

SIMULTANEOUS ENGINEERING

Model B

36–41 months

Figure 26.1 The benefits of simultaneous engineering

washing-machine motor, not just one small part of it. Each cell has a team leader and below that a single level of hierarchy made up of multiskilled workers. The performance of each cell is measured against pre-set targets. These targets will include output levels, quality and lead times. Cells are responsible for the quality of their own complete units of work – this links in with total quality management (TQM), discussed below.

> **KEY TERM**
>
> **Cell production:** splitting flow production into self-contained groups that are responsible for whole work units.

The cell production system has led to:

- significant improvements in worker commitment and motivation because there is teamwork and a sense of 'ownership' of the complete unit of work
- job rotation within the cell
- increased productivity.

Success of cell production depends on a well-trained and multiskilled workforce prepared and able to be flexible and accept a more responsible style of working (see Figure 26.2).

Flexible specialisms

Instead of making the same unchanged product for several years, as was the case with old-fashioned mass-production techniques, lean production recognises that both technological advances and changing consumer tastes can lead to very short production runs. Nowhere is this truer than in the market for electronics products, such as mobile (cell) phones or computer games consoles. Changing from one design of product to another requires flexible working in three main areas:

1. Flexible employment contracts that allow non-core workers to be called in or not employed as demand conditions change.
2. Flexible and adaptable machinery – often computer-controlled – that can be quickly switched from one design to another.
3. Flexible and multiskilled workers able to perform different jobs on different product ranges.

Bought-in components → Machining of components and quality checks ✕ Major sub-assemblies and quality checks ✕ Final assembly, checking and packaging → Finished goods

Figure 26.2 How cell production might be organised in an assembly plant

The great benefits of this flexible approach will be seen in quicker responses to consumer demand changes, wider ranges of products offered to customers, reduced stock holdings as goods can be made to order, and higher productivity. This approach to production is sometimes referred to as 'time-based management' because it aims to cut out all wasted time during the development and production process.

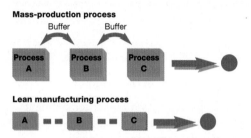

Figure 26.3 Eliminating buffers, reducing transfer distance and streamlining processes will mean products will be delivered to customers more quickly and will be of a higher quality

TOP TIP

This principle of flexible specialisms is obviously linked to mass customisation in Chapter 23.

ACTIVITY 26.1

[12 marks, 20 minutes]

1 Explain how a flexible and multiskilled workforce could contribute to a business achieving 'lean production'. [6]

2 Explain how a business that develops and produces computer games could adopt simultaneous engineering. [6]

Just-in-time inventory-control principle

This has already been discussed in Chapter 24 – it clearly is part of the lean production concept because it involves fewer resources being tied up in buffer inventories. Figure 26.3

ACTIVITY 26.2

Haisho Electronics – is lean production the answer?

Haisho specialises in equipment for construction firms. It has established a reputation for good-quality, reliable products. Sales have not risen for several years due to increased competition from cheaper imports. Many of these imports are low-quality, but one Japanese manufacturer sells high-quality products at prices below those of Haisho. The last board meeting at Haisho discussed this problem.

'What surprises me is how quickly they put new ideas into production. They only announced the remote-controlled crane project last year, but it is already in full production. Our last new idea took us three years to develop for sale,' said the marketing director. The finance director agreed and added: 'Apparently the Japanese firm operates on inventory levels around 10% of ours, yet they are always able to supply their customers' needs.'

'We have a real problem here – I know what the solution is but it will not be cheap or painless,' said the operations director. 'Our equipment is old-fashioned but

would cost millions to update. It takes my workers 24 hours to change tools to make a different component, yet the latest computer-controlled machines can do the same job in five minutes. Our design team lacks coordination with marketing and product development – they operate in offices the other side of town and do not work together closely. Finally, the employees spend too much time getting inventories from the warehouse and sending the half-completed machines to the next production stage. Time is wasted and too much inventory held.' The finance director immediately said that the business could not afford new equipment. The human resources manager leapt to the defence of the workers by stating that they were working hard and were all trained in their own specialist area. The operations director was unimpressed: 'Either we take steps *now* to cut out waste and reduce production times and new product launch times or our employees won't have any jobs in a few months' time!'

[30 marks, 50 minutes]

1 Analyse the problems that Haisho Electronics seems to be facing at the present time. [10]

2 Analyse how the adoption of simultaneous engineering might help this business become more competitive. [6]

3 Considering all of the potential advantages and disadvantages, assess whether the company should adopt lean production methods. [14]

illustrates the differences between a production system based on buffer inventories and one that is JIT-based.

Kaizen – continuous improvement

The philosophy behind this idea is that all workers have something to contribute to improving the way their business operates and the way the product is made. Traditional styles of management – possibly based on a Theory X approach – never give workers the opportunity to suggest improvements to the way things are done because the assumption is that trained managers 'know best'. The objective of managers adopting this approach is to keep production up to the mark and then look for one-off improvements in the form of inventions or to make investments in machines to increase productivity.

> ### KEY TERM
>
> **Kaizen:** Japanese term meaning continuous improvement.

The **kaizen** philosophy suggests that, in many cases, workers actually know more than managers about how a job should be done or how productivity might be improved. Someone who works at a task every day is actually much more likely to know how to change it to improve either quality or productivity than a manager with, perhaps, no hands-on experience of production at all. Another key feature of this idea is that improvements in productivity do not just result from massive one-off investments in new technology. A series of small improvements, suggested by staff teams, can, over time, amount to as big an improvement in efficiency as a major new investment. This idea is illustrated in Figure 26.4.

The following conditions are necessary for kaizen to operate:

- Management culture must be directed towards involving staff and giving their views and ideas importance – managers must accept that, in many areas of the business, work experience will count for as much as theoretical knowledge.
- Team-working – suggesting and discussing new ideas to improve quality or productivity is best done in groups. These kaizen groups are likely to be drawn from the work team – or cell – operating in the place of work. Each kaizen group should meet regularly – and this requires management to provide the time and necessary training – to discuss problems that they have identified. Recommendations for change could then be put forward to managers, or each group may be empowered to put their own ideas into practice.
- Empowerment – by giving each kaizen group the power to take decisions regarding workplace improvements, this will allow speedier introduction of new ideas and motivate employees to come up with even more ideas. You should be

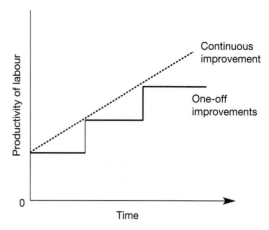

Figure 26.4 Kaizen compared to 'one-off' changes

able to link this suggestion with the work of Herzberg and the concept of job enrichment. If every idea and suggestion made by a kaizen group had to be put to managers – who could then either ignore it or accept it after consideration – staff would become quickly fed up with the process.

- All employees should be involved.

Many firms now use the kaizen approach, but it needs to be adopted throughout an organisation – indeed, problems can occur if some work groups within the business do not make small improvements in this way. The kaizen process has a knock-on effect and improvements in one part of the production system will require improvements further down the line. For example, if a worker on a production line that assembles cars finds a way to save five seconds from the time it takes to weld the roof panels on to the support struts, then the workers who are responsible for the next process must also find a way to save five seconds or there will be a bottleneck and an increase in work in progress. There would be no overall increase in production levels. This example highlights the need for all workers to be involved in a kaizen programme, if the firm is to fully benefit from success.

> **TOP TIP**
> It would be good analysis to link the kaizen principle to the work of Herzberg on job enrichment.

Continuous improvement (kaizen) – an evaluation

Although now a very widely used practice, there are some limitations to the kaizen approach:

- Some changes cannot be introduced gradually and may need a radical and expensive solution, e.g. the need for Kodak to invest heavily in the manufacture of digital cameras rather than 'paper-film'-based cameras when the new technology was introduced.

- There may be very real resistance from senior managers to such a programme due to their existing culture. Kaizen will only work effectively if there is genuine empowerment of the groups involved – authoritarian managers would find this impossible to accept.
- At least in the short term there may be tangible costs to the business of such a scheme, such as staff training to organise meetings and lost output as a result of meeting time.
- The most important advances tend to be made early on during the kaizen programme – later changes can be less significant and this has led some observers to believe that there could be 'diminishing returns' from such an approach.

Main advantages of lean production

- Waste of time and resources is substantially reduced or eliminated.

- Unit costs are reduced, leading to higher profits.
- Working area is less crowded and easier to operate in.
- There is less risk of damage to stocks and equipment.
- New products launched more quickly.

Are lean production and JIT appropriate in all business situations?

Lean production concepts cannot be introduced into a business overnight. The following conditions are necessary for successfully adapting a business towards lean production.

Finance

The purchase of new and advanced capital equipment is expensive. Without machinery that can be quickly

---

ACTIVITY 26.3

Kaizen thinking fires productivity

Mike Brookes, founder and co-owner of Ambi-Rad, when asked why he failed for many years to introduce new ideas aimed at increasing competitiveness, gives a simple answer: he was too busy expanding. His engineering company – based in the Midlands, UK – is a European leader in warm air heating systems. But Mike found little time to think about how to increase quality and productivity in the factory. 'We were a top-down company with all the new ideas coming from the directors,' he explains.

At Ambi-Rad, Mike decided two years ago that it was time to take action. He introduced kaizen thinking, under which employees throughout the company hierarchy are given more control over decisions and encouraged to come up with suggestions for quality and efficiency improvements. Most of the 150 workers at Ambi-Rad's main plant in the UK are divided into eight groups that are each responsible for specific aspects of making the company's heaters. Team leaders encourage new ideas and act as a link between the shop floor and senior managers. One recent idea came from Jean Cox, an assembly worker at Ambi-Rad for 13 years. She suggested punching holes in a piece of metal in a different place so as to shorten the overall production

process. The proposal was implemented, leading to a small but worthwhile productivity improvement. 'I feel I am much more involved,' says Jean. 'As a problem occurs, rather than carry on regardless, we are now encouraged to think of a way round it.'

Suggestions from people like Jean have taken £600,000 a year off the company's costs. The kaizen scheme has enabled Ambi-Rad to maintain profits at a time of severe difficulties in the engineering business. In the past two years, many comparable UK companies have seen sales and profits hit by the economic recession.

'Because of the new manufacturing ideas we have kept pre-tax profits at 10% of sales, which is really excellent by the standards of other engineering companies,' Mike Brookes says. This year Ambi-Rad expects to have sales of £18 million, more than twice the figure five years ago, and exports roughly a quarter of its turnover. Mike wants savings from kaizen-based ideas to reach £1 million annually over the next few years. From a combination of improved competitiveness resulting from this thinking, new products and a stronger export effort, he reckons Ambi-Rad can increase sales by 25% in the next three years, while keeping the profit ratio roughly similar.

[36 marks, 50 minutes]

1 Explain how kaizen groups can help reduce costs for businesses such as Ambi-Rad. [6]

2 Identify and evaluate the benefits for **three** stakeholder groups in Ambi-Rad from the firm adopting kaizen. [12]

3 Examine the conditions that are necessary for the kaizen philosophy to be successful at businesses such as Ambi-Rad. [8]

4 Using the case study as a starting point assess the possible relationship between the use of kaizen groups and the leadership style of an organisation. [10]

adapted to different products, lean production will be impossible. Small production runs and fast switch-over times are essential to make waste and stock reduction a real possibility. This technology does not come cheaply and some firms – particularly smaller manufacturers with limited resources – may decide not to take up this option. By specialising in niche-market products, which are less price-sensitive, firms may still be able to maintain competitiveness without adopting lean production. In addition, the retraining of staff in the multiskills needed to produce a range of different products will be expensive.

Management of change

If lean production is being introduced into a traditional business, then the existing workforce and management team will need to be prepared to accept the necessary changes in working conditions and levels of empowerment. The new culture will need to accept much more worker involvement, for example through kaizen groups and more worker empowerment. Staff need to realise the crucial importance of their reliability and dedication – as so few stocks are held and no buffers exist, the commitment of the workers to the success of lean production is essential. Real lean production depends just as much upon flexible and cooperative staff as it does upon machines.

Lean production might not be suitable when:

■ Businesses have real difficulty in forecasting demand and so are running on virtually zero stocks. This would be a major problem if demand rose unexpectedly.

■ Production processes are very expensive to start up after a break in production. If a steel works ran out of stocks of coke or iron ore, the resulting cool-down in the blast furnace could lead to a huge repair bill because cooling causes cracking of the internal linings.

■ Firms use it as a device for making extensive redundancies. Lean production can result in job losses – this is one aspect of increased efficiency. However, a faltering business that attempts to adopt lean production merely as an attempt to cut job numbers will be unlikely to gain the much-needed support of the workforce.

■ Businesses depend on customer service as their unique selling proposition. In these situations, a less 'lean' approach might give customers more choice of finished product and more certain delivery dates.

■ The costs of new technology and retraining might be so substantial that some businesses might have to survive on making existing systems more efficient rather than fully embracing lean production principles.

These are quite rare situations where lean production might not be applicable, and this suggests that, for most businesses, in most market situations, there remains considerable scope for taking forward the lean production concept in order to improve efficiency and to drive down that all-important statistic – unit costs of production.

ACTIVITY 26.4

Lean production is for service businesses, too

Yukai Resort in the famous Gero Onsen hot spring area of Japan is part of a luxury Japanese hotel chain that performs lean hotel operations. Lean production helps the hotel offer great value to its customers, reduce cost and remain competitive in the competitive hospitality industry. The standard hotel rate in the Gero Onsen hot spring area is US$180 per person, per night including all meals. At Yukai Resort, the price for the same offering is US$91 – every day of the year; regardless of high/low season.

What's the secret?

All hotel duties are shared by all employees. They are all trained to be multiskilled. This has allowed the resort to operate with minimal staff and reduce costs overall while maintaining high quality. For example, the receptionists, in their free time, will go to areas needing assistance – perhaps the kitchen or laundry. Dinner and breakfast are buffet style, which reduces staffing requirements. Employees are also active in lean management or lean kaizen efforts. The manager leads weekly kaizen circles.

Employee engagement is key. Cost minimisation is an obvious benefit. For workers, this system allows them to gain experience in all aspects of hotel operations and gives them direct input in improvement activities. It's not only empowering and motivating but also excellent in terms of career development.

[24 marks, 40 minutes]

1 Analyse the benefits to both Yukai Resort and its employees of the use of lean production methods within the hotel. [10]

2 Evaluate whether lean production methods could be applied effectively to a service business of your choice, from another industry. [14]

Managing operations – quality

What is meant by 'quality'?

A **quality product** does not necessarily have to be the 'best possible'.

ACTIVITY 26.5

Are expensive products always the best quality?

The operations manager at Athletic Shoes was proud of the quality standards his business achieved. 'Our sports shoes sell for a retail price of $25, so they are not the best or most stylish on the market. However, only four customers returned shoes because of serious problems over the past year, when we sold 50,000 pairs. All workers are accountable for the products reaching minimum standards of quality at each stage of production. Of course, there are better shoes available, but our customers know what they are getting.'

The customer service manager at the Exclusive Footwear shoe shop was about to return a pair of 'handmade leather fashion shoes' to Ital Fashion Shoe producers. 'We retail these for $400 a pair and customers paying such high prices expect, reasonably in my view, a near-perfect product. Even the smallest scratch or imperfection means the customers reject them. Even though Ital check every shoe made at each stage of production, a few very minor blemishes are sometimes missed.'

[14 marks, 20 minutes]

1   The consumers of these different types of shoes seem to have different product expectations. Explain why this is.   [4]

2   Using just this case study, how would you attempt to explain what 'quality' means?   [4]

3   Briefly explain how the two different methods used for achieving quality seem to operate.   [6]

KEY TERM

Quality product: a good or service that meets customers' expectations and is therefore 'fit for purpose'.

As Activity 26.5 shows, consumer expectations will be very different for goods and services sold at different prices. So we have to make clear from the outset that a quality product does not *have* to be made with the highest-quality materials to the most exacting standards – but it must meet consumer requirements for it.

In certain cases, a product must meet the highest quality standards and the high cost of it becomes almost insignificant. Internal parts for a jet engine used on a passenger plane will be expected to have a failure rate of less than one in one million. However, if fashion clothing was made to the same exacting standards – with regards to stitching, buttons, zips and so on – how much would a pair of jeans cost then? Designing too much quality into a product that consumers do not expect to last for many years can make the product very expensive and uncompetitive.

A quality product does not have to be expensive. If low-cost light bulbs and clothes pegs last for several years in normal use, then they have still met consumer expectations and have been of the required quality. So a highly priced good may still be of low quality if it fails to come up to consumer requirements. A cheap good can be considered of good quality if it performs as expected. It should now be clear that quality is a relative concept and not an absolute one – it depends on the product's price and the expectations of consumers.

How can consumer 'expectations' or 'requirements' be established by a business? The most common methods would be using market research and analysing results of consumer feedback data. This research can establish the **quality standards** that customers expect.

KEY TERM

Quality standards: the expectations of customers expressed in terms of the minimum acceptable production or service standards.

It is easy to think of quality standards in terms of manufactured goods – the reliability of cars or the wear rate of clothes, for example. However, quality is a crucial issue for service providers too. For example, the quality of service offered by UK banks is claimed to be inferior to those in other countries in terms of:

- time taken to answer the telephone
- no indication of waiting time on the telephone
- queuing time in branches
- contact with the same person on each occasion
- number of accounts errors made
- quality of financial advice given.

The advantages of producing quality products and services are:

- easier to create customer loyalty
- saves on the costs associated with customer complaints, for example compensation, replacing defective products and loss of consumer goodwill
- longer life cycles
- less advertising may be necessary as the brand will establish a quality image through the performance of the products
- a higher price – a price premium – could be charged for such goods and services. Quality can, therefore, be profitable.

TOP TIP

Quality is often viewed by students as an absolute concept and not a relative one. Quality must be explained in reference to the expectations of the target market consumers. The level of quality selected by any business must be based on the resources available to it, the needs of the target market and the quality standards of competitors.

Quality – how can it be achieved?

There are two distinct approaches that a business can take when attempting to achieve quality output. In practice, this distinction can become blurred as elements of both principles can often be adopted. The two approaches are called **quality control** and **quality assurance**.

KEY TERMS

Quality control: this is based on inspection of the product or a sample of products.

Quality assurance: a system of agreeing and meeting quality standards at each stage of production to ensure consumer satisfaction.

What are the differences between quality control and quality assurance?

These two terms are used to classify two very different approaches to managing and achieving quality in any business.

Quality control is based on inspection or checking, usually of the completed product or of the service as it is being provided to a consumer. For example:

- an iPod player being tested at the end of the production line for battery-charging capability
- a telephone-banking adviser having a call to a customer listened to and recorded.

Quality-control techniques

There are three stages to effective quality control:

1. **Prevention:** This is the most effective way of improving quality. If the design of the product follows the requirements of the customer and allows for accurate production, then the other two stages will be less significant. Quality should be 'designed into' a product.
2. **Inspection:** Traditionally this has been the most important stage – but it has high costs and these could be reduced by 'zero-defect' manufacturing that is the aim of total quality management.
3. **Correction and improvement:** This is not just about correcting faulty products, but is also concerned with correcting the process that caused the fault in the first place. This will improve quality in the future.

Inspecting for quality

Traditionally, quality has been checked by inspecting products at the end of the production process. Some checking might take place at different stages of the process, but the emphasis was on the quality of the finished article. Quality inspection is expensive – qualified engineers have to be used – and such checks can involve damaging the product, for example dropping computers to see if they still work. As a result, a sampling process must be used and this cannot guarantee that every product is of the appropriate quality. When quality checks are used during the production process, then statistical techniques are used to record and respond to results. A typical quality-control chart is shown in Figure 26.5 for the recording of weights of loaves of bread. If the recorded weight falls outside the warning limits, then action needs to be taken to improve the accuracy of the production process.

Weaknesses of inspecting for quality

The key point about inspected quality is that it involves a group of quality-control inspectors who check the work of workers. There are several problems related to this approach to quality:

- It is looking for problems and is, therefore, negative in its culture. It can cause resentment among workers, as the inspector believes that they have been 'successful' when they find faults. In addition the workers are likely to look upon the inspectors as management employees who are there just to check on output and to find problems with the work. Workers may consider it satisfying to get a faulty product passed by this team of inspectors. This level of mistrust cannot be good for working relationships and the overall levels of morale in the firm.
- The job of inspection can be tedious, so inspectors become demotivated and may not carry out their tasks efficiently.

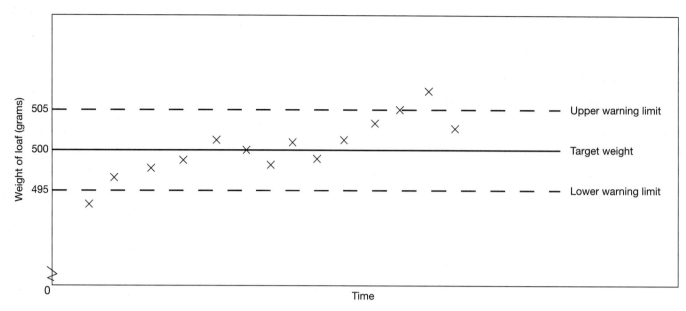

Figure 26.5 Inspecting for quality – a quality-control chart

- If checking takes place only at specific points in the production process, then faulty products may pass through several production stages before being picked up. This could lead to a lot of time being spent finding the source of the fault between the quality checkpoints.
- The main drawback is that it takes away from the workers the responsibility for quality. As the inspectors have full authority for checking products, the workers will not see quality as their responsibility and will not feel that it is part of their task to ensure that it is maintained. Ultimately, this lack of responsibility is demotivating and will result in lower-quality output.

Inspecting for quality, therefore, has many weaknesses. It is hardly surprising that there has been a move away from this approach in recent years.

Quality assurance

Quality assurance is based on setting agreed quality standards at all stages in the production of a good or service in order to ensure that customers' satisfaction is achieved. It does not just focus on the finished product. This approach often involves self-checking by workers of their own output against these agreed quality standards. The key differences between the two methods are that quality assurance:

- puts much more emphasis on prevention of poor quality by designing products for easy fault-free manufacture, rather than inspecting for poor-quality products – 'getting it right first time'

- stresses the need for workers to get it right the first time and reduces the chances of faulty products occurring or expensive reworking of faulty goods
- establishes quality standards and targets for each stage of the production process – for both goods and services
- checks components, materials and services bought into the business at the point of arrival or delivery – not at the end of the production process, by which stage much time and many resources may have been wasted.

The quality-assurance department will need to consider all areas of the firm. Agreed standards must be established at all stages of the process from initial product idea to it finally reaching the consumer. These stages include:

- **Product design:** Will the product meet the expectations of consumers?
- **Quality of inputs:** Quality must not be let down by bought-in components. Suppliers will have to accept and keep to strict quality standards.
- **Production quality:** This can be assured by total quality management (TQM) and emphasising with workers that quality levels must not drop below pre-set standards.
- **Delivery systems:** Customers need goods and services delivered at times that are convenient to them. The punctuality and reliability of delivery systems must be monitored.
- **Customer service including after-sales service:** Continued customer satisfaction will depend on the quality of contact with consumers after purchase.

Some retail companies record staff telephone conversations with customers to help with after-sales training and customer-care quality assurance

Examples:

- Nissan car factories have predetermined quality standards set and checked at each stage of the assembly of vehicles – by the workers accountable for them.
- First Direct, a European telephone-banking organisation, sets limits on waiting times for calls to be answered, average times to be taken for meeting each customer's requests and assurance standards to monitor that customer requests have been acted on correctly.

Quality assurance has the following claimed advantages over quality-control systems based on final inspection:

- It makes everyone responsible for quality – this can be a form of job enrichment.
- Self-checking and making efforts to improve quality increase motivation.
- The system can be used to 'trace back' quality problems to the stage of the production process where a problem might have been occurring.
- It reduces the need for expensive final inspection and correction or reworking of faulty products.

TOP TIP

Quality is not just an issue for large businesses. Small and medium-sized firms also need to give consideration to this vital operations-management area. They must ensure that the quality level selected and the quality-assurance methods used are within their resources. In fact, by using quality assurance with the emphasis on reducing wasted faulty products and on staff self-checking quality levels, these businesses can save money in the long term.

Why is it important for businesses to establish quality-assurance systems?

There are several reasons for this:

- To involve all staff, and this can promote teamwork and a sense of belonging, which aids motivation.
- To set quality standards for all stages of production so that all materials and all production phases are checked before it is too late and the whole product has been completed.
- To reduce costs of final inspection as this should become less necessary as all stages and subsections of the process have been judged against quality standards.
- To reduce total quality costs – by instilling in the whole organisation a culture of quality, it is possible for quality assurance to lead to reduced costs of wastage and faulty products.
- To gain accreditation for quality awards – these can give a business real status or kudos. The most widely recognised quality award within the European Union is ISO 9000.

ISO 9000

This award is given to firms that can demonstrate that they have a quality-assurance system in place that allows for quality to be regularly measured and for corrective action to be taken if quality falls below these levels. This award does not prove that every good produced or service provided by the business is of good quality. It is an indication that a business has a system of quality in place that has relevant targets set and activities ready to deal with a quality problem.

 KEY TERM

ISO 9000: this is an internationally recognised certificate that acknowledges the existence of a quality procedure that meets certain conditions.

To obtain the **ISO 9000** certificate the firm has to demonstrate that it has:

- staff training and appraisal methods
- methods for checking on suppliers
- quality standards in all areas of the business
- procedures for dealing with defective products and quality failures
- after-sales service.

The benefits for a firm of being forced to establish a quality-assurance framework and to have this externally monitored are clear. There are, however, drawbacks such as the costs of preparing for inspection and the bureaucratic form-filling required to gain the certificate.

Total quality management (TQM)

This approach to quality requires the involvement of all employees in an organisation. It is based on the principle that everyone within a business has a contribution to make to the overall quality of the finished product or service.

KEY TERM

Total quality management: an approach to quality that aims to involve all employees in quality-improvement.

TQM often involves a significant change in the culture of an organisation. Employees can no longer think that quality is someone else's responsibility – instead, the search for quality must affect the attitudes and actions of every employee. When adopting this concept, every worker should think about the quality of the work they are performing because another employee is, in effect, their **internal customer**. Every department is obliged to meet the standards expected by its customer(s). These departmental relationships are sometimes known as quality chains. All businesses can, therefore, be described as a series of supplier and customer relationships. Examples include:

- A truck driver who drops off supplies to retailers is the internal customer of the team loading the vehicle – goods must be handled carefully and loaded in the right order. The truck driver has to face the retailer if goods are damaged or the wrong ones delivered.
- A computer assembly team is the internal customer of the teams producing the individual components – a fault with any of these means the assembled computer will not meet quality standards.

The TQM concept has revolutionised the way all workers are asked to consider quality. To be effective the concept must be fully explained and training given to all staff. TQM is not a technique; it is a philosophy of quality being everyone's responsibility. The aim is to make all workers at all levels accept that the quality of the work they perform is important. In addition, they should be empowered with the responsibility of checking this quality level before passing their work on to the next production stage.

This approach fits in well with the Herzberg principles of job enrichment. TQM should almost eliminate the need for a separate quality-control department with inspectors divorced from the production line itself.

TQM aims to cut the costs of faulty or defective products by encouraging all staff to get it right first time and to achieve '**zero defects**'. This is in contrast to traditional inspected quality methods that considered quality control as being a cost centre of the business. Under TQM, if quality is improved and guaranteed, then reject costs should fall and the demand for the products rises over time. TQM will only work effectively if everyone in the firm is committed to the idea. It cannot be introduced into one section of a business if defective products coming from other sections are not reduced. The philosophy requires a commitment from senior management to allow the workforce authority and empowerment, as TQM will not operate well in a rigid and authoritarian structure.

KEY TERMS

Internal customers: people within the organisation who depend upon the quality of work being done by others.
Zero defects: achieving perfect products every time.

What are the costs and benefits of introducing and managing quality systems?

All quality checks and quality-assurance systems involve incurring costs. In a business that is effectively managed, these costs will be covered by the expected revenue gains from producing products of the expected quality. In addition, other costs may be reduced, such as wastage costs and promotion costs to overcome a poor quality image.

The costs of quality are often obvious yet the benefits can be long-term and difficult to measure or quantify (see Table 26.1). This does not mean that they do not exist – in fact, long-term survival in competitive markets can be based upon a good quality image.

How can the competitiveness of a business be improved by managing quality?

- Most markets are now more open to competition than ever before. Globalisation has increased this trend and so has consumer access to the internet. Lowering prices is not the only method of increasing competitiveness and, indeed, it may not be the wisest way if a business is unable to reduce its costs to the same extent. Achieving consistent quality is often a more effective method of competing in both domestic and international markets.
- Consistent high quality can lead to such a well-known brand image that higher prices can be justified for this USP.
- As consumer incomes rise with world economic growth, the average consumer buying decision will become more influenced by quality and fitness for purpose. Excess capacity exists in most of the world's manufacturing industries. It is vital for businesses to differentiate themselves with a quality brand image. Remember, this does not mean 'quality at any price' but regularly and consistently meeting consumers' (rising) expectations. Cost factors involved in improving quality must always be weighed against the expected gains in competitiveness.

The potential costs of quality systems	The potential benefits of quality systems
■ market research to establish expected customer requirements ■ staff training costs to ensure that standards are understood and the operations needed to check them can be undertaken – this will be especially important with TQM ■ material costs – rejecting below-standard materials and components before they are used in the production process will almost certainly lead to higher expectations from suppliers ■ equipment costs for checking standards at each stage, e.g. laser measuring machines for accuracy of panel fit on a vehicle ■ inspection and checking costs ■ reworking of faulty products or rejection wastage costs – the aim of quality assurance is to reduce these to an absolute minimum – 'right first time' ■ stopping production to trace and correct quality problems will disrupt output	■ consumer satisfaction and repeat custom as there is nothing like a good experience with the quality of a product to encourage consumers to buy more – and to tell their friends about it ■ good publicity, e.g. from consumer pressure groups and consumer-oriented articles in the media ■ reputation for quality encourages retailers to stock the firm's products, so this will increase the distribution outlets for a product ■ easier to establish new products in the market as consumers will associate the business's good reputation with the new product ■ allows the brand to be built around a quality image, and branding is an important form of non-price differentiation for businesses ■ may allow a price premium to be charged over other similar products in that market segment – quality can be used as a USP or unique selling point and this would be a clear demonstration that 'quality pays', as the extra revenue gained should cover the quality costs explained above

Table 26.1 The potential costs and benefits of quality systems

ACTIVITY 26.6

Quality assurance at the hairdressers

The Kuala Lumpur branch of FatBoyTrims had the worst record of all of the company's branches for customer satisfaction. The number of complaints received at head office about this branch and the quality of its haircutting and styling services had been much greater than for any other location. Revenue had fallen in recent months and the number of repeat customers had fallen to 15% of total custom. A rival business nearby, that charged at least 30% more, was always full. As a consequence, this FatBoyTrims branch had spent more on advertising for new business than any other. The revenue per customer was also low as high-value services – such as colouring and tinting – were avoided by customers. A new manager had just been appointed to the branch and she immediately set about establishing quality targets for each stage of the 'customer experience'. These included:

■ maximum time for phone to ring
■ maximum waiting time for appointment

■ maximum times between hair wash and when cutting begins
■ all customers to be offered refreshments
■ minimum time spent by stylists with each customer
■ feedback forms completed by 20% of clients, with stylists discussing answers with client.

Each employee was given responsibility for at least one of these targets. A record had to be kept of the branch's success at meeting these targets. At first, branch costs increased as an additional worker was recruited to help meet the quality standards. After two months, the number of repeat clients had reached 36% and the branch reduced its advertising expenditure. After four months, revenue had risen by 38%. The branch reached third place in the company league table for customer satisfaction. The competing hairdressing business had reduced many prices by 15%.

[32 marks, 50 minutes]

1 a Define the term 'quality'. [2]

   b 'quality assurance' [3]

2 Outline **two** drawbacks to this business of not meeting customer expectations. [6]

3 Analyse the benefits to this service business of improving quality. [10]

4 Discuss whether the manager was right to introduce these quality targets. Assess issues in introducing and managing a quality system in your answer. [11]

ACTIVITY 26.7

Trinidad Tractor Factory Ltd (TTF) – quality becomes an issue

The last meeting between the marketing and operations directors of TTF was very heated. They each blamed the other for the disappointing rise in customer complaints and the fall in unit sales. The marketing director had complained: 'The number of faulty tractors leaving our factory has increased. Our reputation is being damaged by these faults and many former customers are now buying imported tractors. We have just lost a government order for 15 tractors as our competitor was able to boast about their ISO 9000 certificate.' The operations director had replied by saying that customers were becoming much more demanding and it was up to the marketing department to provide good after-sales service. 'I have increased the number of quality-control engineers from five to eight and we are correcting more faults in finished products than ever before.'

	TTF customer complaints	TTF sales in units
2012	53	2,345
2013	78	2,124

[34 marks, 50 minutes]

1. Analyse the problems that TTF has because of low-quality products. [10]

2. Assess whether the increase in the number of quality-control inspectors was the best way to try to improve quality. [8]

3. Explain the difference between quality control and quality assurance. [4]

4. Do you think that TTF should establish a quality-assurance system and apply for an ISO award? Justify your answer. [12]

Benchmarking

The full title for **benchmarking** is 'best practice benchmarking'.

This comparison will identify areas of the business that need to be improved to meet the standards of quality and productivity of the best firms.

KEY TERM

Benchmarking: involves management identifying the best firms in the industry and then comparing the performance standards – including quality – of these businesses with those of their own business.

Stages in the benchmarking process:

1. **Identify the aspects of the business to be benchmarked:** This could be decided by interviewing customers and finding out what they consider to be most important. For example, research may reveal that the most important factors are reliability of the product, speed of delivery and after-sales service. These are the areas that the firm would first benchmark.

2. **Measure performance in these areas:** For example reliability records, delivery records and the number of customer complaints.

3. **Identify the firms in the industry that are considered to be the best:** This process might be assessed by management consultants or by benchmarking schemes operated by government or industry organisations.

4. **Use comparative data from the best firms to establish the main weaknesses in the business:** These data might be obtained from firms by mutual agreement, from published accounts, specialist industry publications and contact with customers/suppliers.

5. **Set standards for improvement:** These might be the standards set by the best firms or they could be set even higher to create a competitive advantage.

6. **Change processes to achieve the standards set:** This may require nothing more than a different way of performing one task, but more substantial changes may be necessary.

7. **Re-measurement:** The changes to the process need to be checked to see if the new, higher standards are being reached. Benchmarking is not a one-off exercise and to be effective it should become a continuous process to achieve long-term improvements in productivity and quality.

Benchmarking – an evaluation

Benefits include:

- Benchmarking is a faster and cheaper way of solving problems than firms attempting to solve production or quality problems without external comparisons.

- The areas of greatest significance for customers are identified and action can be directed to improving these.

- It is a process that can assist the firm to increase international competitiveness.

- Comparisons between firms in different industries, for example customer service departments in a retailer compared with a bank, can encourage a useful crossover of ideas.

■ If the workforce is involved in the comparison exercise, then their participation can lead to better ideas for improvement and increased motivation.

Limitations include:

■ The process depends on obtaining relevant and up-to-date information from other firms in the industry. If this is difficult to obtain, then the benchmarking exercise will be limited.

■ Merely copying the ideas and practices of other firms may discourage initiative and original ideas.

■ The costs of the comparison exercise may not be recovered by the improvements obtained from benchmarking.

Quality circles

This is a Japanese-originated approach to quality. It is based on staff involvement in improving quality, using small groups of employees to discuss quality issues. Using team-working and participation can – as well as leading to quality improvements – result in greatly increased worker participation. The overall aim of the groups is to investigate quality problems and present solutions to management – or, if a group is fully empowered, to put the improvements into effect itself (see Table 26.2).

Quality issues – an evaluation

Quality is not an option. It is a fundamental aspect of all successful businesses. Quality is an issue for all firms, not just those in the secondary sector or service-sector firms, such as those in tourism and insurance, for whom it is important to put the quality of their products and customer service at the top of their priorities to survive in competitive markets. Improving quality has obvious cost advantages if the rate of defective products is reduced. The marketing and 'people' benefits should not be overlooked

Main benefits	Main conditions determining success
■ Improves quality through joint discussion of ideas and solutions. ■ Improves motivation through participation. ■ Makes full use of the knowledge and experience of the staff.	■ Circle members must be committed to improving quality. ■ Training given in holding meetings and problem-solving. ■ Full support from management. ■ Team should be empowered to implement the recommendations.

Table 26.2 Quality circles – main benefits and necessary conditions

either. Satisfying customers will give clear advantages when seeking further sales. Involving staff in quality-improvement programmes can lead to a more motivated workforce. Improving quality needs to be the driving force throughout an organisation – it is not just an issue for the factory floor or the bank clerk. At the same time, the meaning of quality must not be forgotten – it is not necessary to produce the best product or service at all costs, but to achieve the quality of product or service that the customer expects and that will encourage them to return in the future.

🔗 KEY CONCEPT LINK

Creating value is not just about cheaper inputs. If a business can establish a reputation for quality products and brand its products successfully, then customers will often be prepared to pay higher prices than for competitors' products. This also creates value.

ACTIVITY 26.8

Benchmarking is key to efficiency

Lord Simon is former chief executive of British Petroleum. He introduced benchmarking at BP. 'Knowing the opposition and where it is making better profits is one of the most crucial bits of information you can get in business,' says Simon. 'In BP we faced the fact that American companies always achieved a higher return on capital than UK equivalents. We set ourselves a target to equal or exceed Exxon, at that time the best performer, within five years. It was a great way of focusing the mind.' Simon now promotes the benefits of benchmarking to small and medium-sized enterprises. 'They need clear data on where competitors are extracting greater profit margins, whether in production, marketing or distribution.'

Benchmarking also offers a powerful tool for improving the focus and motivation of everybody in the company. 'When managers talk to staff about the need for change it can seem like just another demand,' says Simon. 'But if staff look at a benchmark and see the competition is doing better, they say, "if they can do that, so can we".'

'Closing the Gap', a DTI (Department of Trade and Industry) report, indicates big variations in performance. The top 25% of companies achieve profit margins five times greater than those in the bottom quartile. They achieve 98% supplier accuracy and delivery reliability against 60% accuracy and 85% reliability for bottom-quartile companies. Spending on training is ten times greater and employee absenteeism rates up to 75% lower than in the bottom quartile.

[15 marks, 20 minutes]

1   Explain what is meant by 'benchmarking'.   [3]

2   Analyse **three** benefits to small and medium-sized enterprises of adopting benchmarking.   [12]

ACTIVITY 26.9

CaribSugar plc – low price fails to keep customer 'sweet'

CaribSugar's rapid growth was based on the principle of 'pile it high and sell it cheap'. As the region's largest sugar refiner and treacle maker it supplied all of the leading food-processing plants and supermarket chains. Economies of scale helped to keep unit costs very low and 40% of its output was exported. Rising consumer incomes and greater choice in the high street were changing people's taste in foods and their expectations of product and service quality. The number of complaints received by CaribSugar – from both business customers and individual consumers – was increasing rapidly. Broken packs, dirt in the sugar, variable thickness of treacle and late delivery to shops were not new problems, but the arrival of more efficient competitors was leading to substantial reductions in orders. Quality inspectors were now being offered special bonuses at CaribSugar if they detected any of these problems before the products were despatched. The continuous process of sugar refining is difficult to halt to make quality improvements. It is, therefore, important for all supplies of materials to be of first-class quality and for the staff to be aware of the need for zero defects in production and packaging. Workers at CaribSugar were constantly told of the need for improvements in quality and suffered a loss of pay if defects were found in one particular shift. Swift action was needed in many areas of the business if market leadership was not to be lost to imports and domestic producers whose reputation for quality enabled them to charge higher prices than CaribSugar.

[39 marks, 60 minutes]

1   Explain **three** economies of scale that CaribSugar might benefit from.   [6]

2   Outline the benefits that CaribSugar's competitors seemed to be gaining from higher quality standards.   [6]

3   Does CaribSugar seem to be applying quality-control systems or quality-assurance systems in its sugar refinery? Explain your answer.   [5]

4   Explain the potential benefits to CaribSugar from introducing the following approaches into the business:

   a   total quality management

   b   quality circles.   [10]

5   Should the company introduce benchmarking? Justify your answer with explanations of the business areas to be compared in the exercise and the potential benefits and drawbacks.   [12]

SUMMARY POINTS

- Lean production is an important concept that is now widely used in industry –and not just in manufacturing.
- JIT is just one aspect of the lean production concepts that aims to minimise waste in production methods – others are simultaneous engineering and flexible specialisms.
- Kaizen groups of workers can discuss and suggest solutions to work-related problems.
- Continuous improvement in this way can be just as effective as the productivity gains from large-scale investments.
- Quality is an important consideration for all businesses and quality products are those that meet customer expectations.
- There are important differences between traditional quality control and quality assurance.
- Total quality management is a concept that aims to make all workers accountable for quality.
- Quality is a factor in determining the competitiveness of a business.
- The best way to achieve quality output is to design it into new products.
- Inspecting for quality is expensive and takes responsibility for quality away from the workforce.
- Benchmarking allows a business to compare their performance with the best in the industry.
- Quality assurance creates a quality system that can be more effective than statistical quality control.

RESEARCH TASK

Lean production in your school/college

- Write a report to the head teacher on the level of waste within your school or college. Remember, waste can apply to time (e.g. travelling from one class to another) as well as physical waste such as paper. Try to estimate the level of time waste and resource waste.
- Perhaps you should be careful not to mention any teachers by name!
- Recommend to the head teacher the best ways for the school/college to achieve lean production.

A Level exam practice questions
Case studies

1 Wiping out defects at Wheeler's

Wheeler's manufactures pumps, cables, controls and drums used by washing-machine producers. The company is a major supplier to most of the leading firms in the industry. The firm buys in a huge range of materials and components to make up the products it sells to the washing-machine makers. Wheeler's makes more than 2,000 different items. Today's consumers have high expectations for their new washing machines. They look for value for money and reliability. Manufacturers expect suppliers such as Wheeler's to turn out parts to a high quality at the lowest possible cost. To satisfy these demands and to maintain an edge over cheaper foreign imports, Wheeler's follows a strict quality-assurance system. It has been awarded ISO 9000 – a certificate now demanded by many of its customers. There is a world of difference between setting targets for zero defects and low costs and actually achieving them. The growing demand for Wheeler's products is due in no small part to its reputation for quality, which is based on workers checking their own work using statistical control charts and recording the results of quality checks at regular intervals. Wheeler's operations manager believes that the company's success depends on four key features of its production system:

- The recent adoption of a lean production system has made 'just-in-time' a priority. They now produce what is wanted when it is wanted. This requires Wheeler's own suppliers to be reliable and to be involved in the design and quality of each component so that it is perfect for the task it has to perform.

- They have a well-trained, multiskilled and flexible workforce. Workers have to be prepared to operate different machines and produce different items. They work in cells or teams of between six and ten. Each cell is empowered to implement its own quality improvements established through regular kaizen-type meetings. The workers have been successful in achieving very high productivity levels. Staff turnover is low.

- They use different production methods for different types of products. Batch production is used to make a certain number of specialist machine controls for just one manufacturer. However, flow production is used to make pumps that are needed by all manufacturers in great numbers. Technical economies of scale are gained on the flow lines with the use of the latest automated equipment.

- Wheeler's has a quality-assurance system that puts the emphasis on 'prevention, not detection'. Employees share responsibility for making defect-free products. For example, staff making electrical switches check, in their team, the quality of output at each assembly stage. They will not pass any item on to the final assembly and packing stage unless it is defect-free. This approach helped the company gain the ISO 9000 award.

[43 marks, 50 minutes]

1   Explain what is meant by the following terms:

   a 'batch production'   **[3]**

   b 'flow production'   **[3]**

   c 'ISO 9000'   **[3]**

   d 'just-in-time'   **[3]**

   e 'kaizen groups'   **[3]**

   f 'quality assurance'   **[3]**

   g 'technical economies of scale'   **[3]**

   h 'total quality management'   **[3]**

   i 'zero defects'   **[3]**

2   An objective of the company is to achieve 'quality output at low costs'. Evaluate the importance of the **four** factors listed in the case study in helping to achieve this objective.   **[16]**

2   Lack of competitiveness threatens AVCO's survival

AVCO, the leading European manufacturer of toys, is struggling to survive increasing competition from Chinese rivals. These other firms have invested heavily in advanced technology and have adopted the latest management techniques, such as lean production and kaizen. AVCO directors realise that they have some important decisions to make. Do they aim for the higher-income market segments with products such as handmade wooden toys and advanced robot-controlled cars and aircraft, or do they fight the main rivals at their own game and aim to introduce lean production methods? The directors' views are:

Finance: 'We might be able to afford the training and investment programmes demanded by lean production techniques if we can permanently reduce our very high stock levels through just-in-time – these carry an enormous opportunity cost.'

Human resources: 'Our workers realise the seriousness of the current situation and they might be prepared to accept the major changes to working practices required by lean production.'

Design: 'I recognise the need to work more closely and simultaneously with other departments to make sure that our new ideas hit the market first.'

Operations: 'We will need a completely new culture on the factory floor. Staff will need to be flexible and will have to help us make changes – kaizen groups could be really useful for this.'

Marketing: 'Lean production could give us a real competitive advantage if unit costs come down. Also, if we can quickly adapt to market changes in toy demand, then we will meet consumers' needs more quickly.'

The board of directors agreed that the best strategy was to improve efficiency and reduce waste, rather than aim for upmarket niche marketing, which would reduce the overall size of the business.

[43 marks, 60 minutes]

1   Explain what is meant by the following terms:

   a 'lean production'   **[3]**

   b 'JIT'   **[3]**

   c 'kaizen'   **[3]**

2   Consider all five reactions of the directors to the move to lean production techniques. Explain, in detail, what you think each of the directors meant.   **[10]**

3   Analyse the problems this firm might experience in introducing lean production methods.   **[10]**

4   Discuss whether just-in-time inventory control would be appropriate for a toy manufacturer such as AVCO.   **[14]**

A Level essay questions

[20 marks, 45 minutes each]

1   Discuss the issues that should be considered by a small manufacturing firm specialising in quality dining tables before adopting lean production techniques.   **[20]**

2   Evaluate how a business that owns and operates ten hotels might attempt to ensure a high quality of customer service.   **[20]**

Project management

This chapter covers
syllabus section
A Level 4.6.

On completion of this chapter, you will be able to:

- understand the purpose of project management
- analyse the key elements of project planning
- analyse how critical path analysis (CPA) and network diagrams can be used to help with project management
- apply CPA to different projects
- evaluate the usefulness of the technique.

Introducing the topic

BUILDING A NEW BRIDGE

The Eastern Construction Company has just received its first major bridge-building contract from a foreign government. The company managers have been keen to sign this contract as it means that they will be able to add to the range of building projects that they have worked on. Jimmy Chen has been appointed project manager for this key contract. He has seen government officials on several occasions to obtain agreement on:

- the exact size and specifications of the bridge
- the expected completion date
- the value of the contract – the price the government has agreed to pay for the completed bridge. Jimmy has a team of managers to help him calculate the exact materials and equipment needs of this building project – they will take responsibility for seeing the project through to the finish. IT specialists have been asked to draw up a diagram showing all of the different tasks of the project, the estimated time for each task and the resources needed for each. This diagram has shown that some tasks can be done

together – such as laying the tarmac on the road and painting the steel structure, and other tasks must be completed before any other work can start – such as building an access road and laying foundations for the bridge.

After six months, building work has started and the project is on time – so far. Some costs have exceeded estimates – but others are lower than expected. Both Jimmy and his senior managers hope that if the project is seen as a success, other bridge contracts will be awarded to the company.

Points to think about:

- Why is careful management of this project particularly important to this company?
- Why do you think a project team was created with their only task being the successful completion of the bridge?
- Why would a diagram of activities be useful to Jimmy and his team?
- What problems might there be in making sure this diagram was as accurate as possible?

Introduction

Projects are specific tasks that result from the need for an organisation to change. The need for change might be relatively minor – such as the opening of a new shop for a retail company that has 200 outlets already – or it could be major – such as a car manufacturer developing a hybrid vehicle for the first time in response to environmental pressures.

 KEY TERMS

Project: a specific and temporary activity with a start and end date, clear goals, defined responsibilities and a budget.

Project management: using modern management techniques to carry out and complete a project from start to finish in order to achieve pre-set targets of quality, time and cost.

Other examples of business projects include:

- setting up a new IT system
- relocating company operations
- installing new machinery
- marketing products in another country
- building a factory.

Very often, a project team of people, usually adopting the matrix structure, is set up to control and manage the complete task. Such teams will have an overall project manager. This leader must simultaneously manage the four basic elements of any project:

1 **Resources:** The people, equipment and materials needed.
2 **Time:** Each activity will need to be timed so that an overall project duration can be worked out.
3 **Money:** The project must be kept to budget and the expected profit from it should be aimed for.
4 **Scope:** The overall size and scale of the project must be established and the specific objectives for it set.

So, to be completed successfully, a project needs to be planned and managed, costs determined and times allocated, problems dealt with and, eventually, concluded. Formal methods of managing a project offer clear guidelines and deadlines. The key elements of project management include:

- defining the project carefully, including the setting of clear objectives
- dividing the project up into manageable tasks and activities
- controlling the project at every stage to check that time limits are being kept to
- giving each team member a clear role
- providing controls over quality issues and risks.

Impact of project failure

Failure to manage projects successfully can have serious consequences for any organisation. In the case study above, any failure to complete the building of the bridge on time and within budget could result in:

- penalty payments having to be paid to the customer
- bad publicity in the construction industry
- loss of future contracts.

Projects can fail for a number of reasons. The French IT company Bull reports that IT projects in the finance industry often fail for three main reasons: poor planning; poor management; poor communication.

The Standish Report on project management suggested that major projects failed because:

- customers were not involved in the planning and development process

- the project had inadequate or no resources that were vital for its completion
- senior management just did not seem interested in seeing the project through
- project specification kept changing during the course of the project;
- planning was poor
- the scope of the project had become outdated due to change in business environment
- the project team was technically incompetent.

Examples of recent projects: 1 Failure of DMI at the BBC

The British Broadcasting Corporation (BBC) is one of the world's oldest and most respected media production and broadcasting organisations. To improve efficiency when creating new materials, and to allow for better management and integration of archive materials, the BBC initiated the 'Digital Media Initiative' (DMI) in 2008. DMI was intended to provide a single tool that would enable video and radio production from raw materials through to final edit.

The failure to deliver a working system resulted in the project being abandoned in May 2013. The UK Public Accounts Committee described the project as 'a terrible shock and clearly completely shambolic… We were told that there were bits of this system that were working, that you were using them. That wasn't true. That just wasn't true.' The BBC's chief technology officer was suspended pending an enquiry and £100 million was written off.

Causes of project failure:

- Underestimation of project complexity by senior management.
- Hierarchical organisation structure in which accurate flows of information to senior management were blocked.
- Failure to conduct an effective tendering process when selecting the original supplier – the contract was given to Siemens, the BBC's existing technology supplier.
- Lack of supervision of contractors.
- Overstating the benefits of the project.
- The use of a fixed-price contract discouraged the BBC from getting too deeply involved in the design stages for fear of triggering demands to raise the fixed price.

2 Serious project problems overcome at Airbus

The Airbus A380 is the world's largest passenger airliner and the most complex aircraft flying today. The aircraft's entry into service was delayed by almost two years and the project went several billion dollars over budget.

At the heart of the project's problems were difficulties integrating the complex wiring system needed to operate

A380 production line: 'Lack of planning delayed this project by two years, and cost millions of euro'

BBC HQ: 'A hierarchical structure was one of the causes of the DMI project failure'

the aircraft: 530km of wires, cables and wiring harnesses weave their way throughout the airframe. With more than 100,000 wires and 40,300 connectors performing 1,150 separate functions, the Airbus A380 has a very complex electrical system. As the first A380 was being built, wires had been manufactured to specification, but during installation the wires turned out to be too short! Airbus management slowly came to realise that the issue was not an isolated problem and that short wires were a problem throughout the design.

Internal reviews identified what was at the heart of the problem: the different design groups working on the project had used different computer-aided design (CAD) software to create the engineering drawings. German and Spanish designers working on the A380 had used one version of the software (CATIA version 4), while British and French teams had upgraded to version 5. Stripping out the wiring from the prototype, redesigning the wiring and then rethreading it into the airframe was a monumental

task. The project was delayed many times as hundreds of engineers tried to overcome the problems. At one point more than 1,100 German engineers were camped out at the Toulouse production facility trying to rectify the problems.

The root of the problem can be traced back to a single decision: the decision to proceed with the project despite the fact that two CAD systems were in use. That decision resulted in design inconsistencies, mismatched calculations and huge cost over-runs. The A380 is now flying successfully with many international airlines.

The rest of this chapter focuses on one project-planning technique that, when used effectively, can help to reduce the risk of project failure.

Planning operations

We have explained that operations management involves the use of resources. Labour, buildings, machines, management time and factory or office space will all, to varying degrees, need to be used for a new project. Resources are expensive and the most expensive resource is that which is unused or underused – unused stocks take up space and working capital, machinery left idle wastes capital and can require protective maintenance, labour waiting for supplies to arrive will add unnecessarily to the wages bill.

Efficient firms will always aim to use their resources as intensively as possible and avoid wasted time and idle assets. Keeping assets busy is not always as easy as it sounds, especially when the project being worked on is a complex one.

Consider the construction of a house:

- The builder only wants to employ specialist staff on a subcontract basis when the job is ready for their particular skills.

405

He also wants to order bricks and other materials to arrive just as they are needed, not weeks before, blocking up the site, wasting working capital and inviting theft. He certainly does not want them to arrive three days late, with bricklayers kept waiting.

Specialist equipment is often hired and to keep this a day more than necessary will raise costs and hit cash flow.

How can all of the different tasks involved in building a house be put into order so that the right goods and labour can be employed just at the right time? The answer for many businesses is to use a technique known as network analysis (also known as **critical path analysis** or CPA).

KEY TERM

Critical path analysis: a planning technique that identifies all tasks in a project, puts them in the correct sequence and allows for the identification of the critical path.

Critical path analysis — an introduction

CPA or network analysis indicates the shortest possible time in which a project can be completed. The activities that must be completed to achieve this shortest time make up what is known as the **critical path**. The process of using critical path analysis involves the following steps:

1 Identify the objective of the project, e.g. building a factory in six weeks.
2 Put the tasks that make up the project into the right sequence and draw a network diagram.
3 Add the durations of each of the activities.
4 Identify the critical path – those activities that must be finished on time for the project to be finished in the shortest time.
5 Use the network as a control tool when problems occur during the project.

Network diagrams

A **network diagram** can be drawn to help identify the critical path.

KEY TERMS

Critical path: the sequence of activities that must be completed on time for the whole project to be completed by the agreed date.

Network diagram: the diagram used in critical path analysis that shows the logical sequence of activities and the logical dependencies between them – so the critical path can be identified.

The objective is to see if a new machine can be installed and the staff trained to operate it within three weeks (assume a five-day working week) (see Figure 27.1). A network diagram uses the following notation:

An arrow indicates each activity.
An activity takes up time and resources.
A node (circle) indicates the end of each activity.

The activities involved in this project and the estimated time for each activity (duration) are:

Strip out old machine (A) – three days.
Order new machine and await arrival (B) – one day.
Prepare site for new machine (C) – two days.
Assemble new machine (D) – two days.
Install new machine (E) – one week.
Demonstrate to workers (F) – two days.
Obtain necessary raw materials (G) – one day.
Trial test run (H) – three days.

You will notice from the diagram that from the first node, two activities can start. This is because stripping out the old machine and ordering the new one are independent activities. They can be done simultaneously and do not have to be done in sequence.

Clearly, this is a relatively simple project and, if these durations are added to the network diagram (Figure 27.2), it is possible to determine visually:

which is the critical path of activities – these activities are indicated with pairs of short parallel lines
that the project can be completed within three weeks.

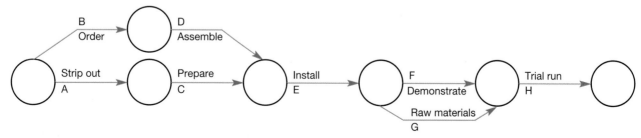

Figure 27.1 Installing a new machine – the network

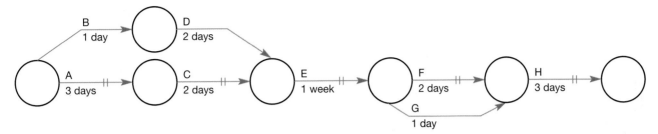

Figure 27.2 Adding durations to find the critical path

It is clear that the 'critical' activities are A, C, E, F and H. If these should be delayed in any way, for example if the preparation of the site takes more than two days, then the whole task will take longer than three weeks. It can be seen that the other activities are not critical – these, in fact, may have some spare time. This is termed float time. In more complex projects, this can be useful for achieving an even more efficient use of resources.

ACTIVITY 27.1

Project management for new IT program

Josh is head of a team that has been given the responsibility for managing the introduction of a new IT project within his company. The new system will allow all employees to be linked to the main ERP software. Customer service should be improved and internal communication speeded up. The project team has been given a budget of $10 million and a time limit of six months. The CEO told Josh: 'Project management will be very important in this case. Our competitors are already ahead of us in the adoption of IT programs.' Josh knew that his first task was to identify the critical path activities.

[22 marks, 30 minutes]

1 What is meant by 'project management'? [3]

2 Analyse the likely consequences for the company if this project failed. [6]

3 What are the **four** key factors in project management? [4]

4 What is meant by the 'critical path' in network analysis? [3]

5 Explain why it important for Josh, as project team leader, to monitor carefully the critical activities on a network diagram. [6]

How the critical path is determined: a more complex example

The objective is to construct a house in 42 days. To create the network diagram, the tasks to be performed in order to build the house have been broken down into ten main activities, such as digging foundations and tiling the roof. These activities must be done in a certain order – the roof cannot be tiled before the walls are built, for instance – and this order of tasks is as shown in Table 27.1. The network diagram for these activities is shown in Figure 27.3.

You will notice that each of the nodes has been numbered for ease of reference. The duration times for each activity (Table 27.2) can now be added to the network diagram (Figure 27.4).

Activity	Preceding activities
A	–
B	–
C	A
D	B and C
E	A
F	E
G	F and D
H	B and C
I	G and H
J	I

Table 27.1 The order of tasks in building a house – the objective is to build a house in 42 days

Activity	Duration (days)
A	8
B	6
C	12
D	6
E	14
F	10
G	3
H	14
I	3
J	4

Table 27.2 Duration times of the tasks in building a house

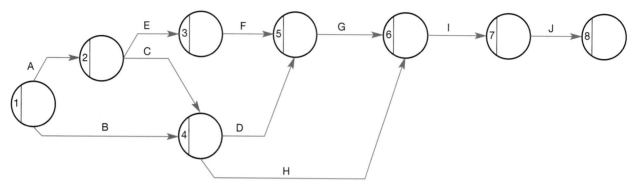

Figure 27.3 The main stages of building a house

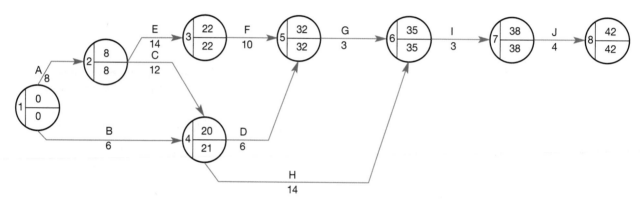

Figure 27.4 Adding in the activities and durations

These durations are very important. They allow us to calculate both the critical path and the spare time – or float time – for the non-critical activities. The critical path is indicated by calculating, at each node, the earliest start time (EST) and the latest finish time (LFT). These have already been added to the nodes in Figure 27.4.

What is the earliest start time and how is it calculated?

It is the earliest time each activity can begin, taking into account all of the preceding activities. So activity E cannot start before day 8 because A will not be finished before then. And D cannot start before day 20 because both A and C have to be completed first.

ACTIVITY 27.2

Verify the ESTs above by working through the diagram from left to right, taking the longest route, in days, to each node.

What is the latest finish time and how is it calculated?

It is the latest time an activity can finish without delaying the whole project. So I (and all preceding activities) must be finished by day 38 or the entire project will take longer than 42 days (because four days must be allowed to finish J itself). Task F (and all preceding activities) must finish by day 32 or the time taken to complete G, I and J will take the total project time over 42 days.

The easiest way to calculate the LFTs is to work from right to left. The LFT at node 8 must be 42 – the total project time. The duration of activity J is now subtracted from this to give 38. This is the LFT at node 7. Where there is a choice of routes back to a node, the aim is to achieve the lowest number for LFT. The LFT for node 4 is therefore 21, achieved by working back through J, I and H, even though a higher number could be reached by working through J, I, G and D. Remember, the lowest number at each node is what is required for the LFT.

Calculating float times for non-critical activities

Look at the network diagram for building a home (Figure 27.4). Non-critical activities B, C, D and H will have 'float' time. All of the non-critical activities, those not on the critical path, will have a certain amount of spare time. This spare time is called float. There are two types of float.

1 Total float

The amount of time an activity can be delayed without delaying the whole project duration. This is calculated by the formula:

Total float = LFT – duration – EST.
Take task D as an example:
The LFT of D is 32.
The duration is 6.
The EST of D is 20 and therefore:
Total float for D = 32 – 6 – 20 = 6 days.

D could be delayed by up to six days without extending the total project duration or changing the critical path.

2 Free float

The length of time an activity can be delayed without delaying the start of the following activities. This is calculated by the formula:

Free float = EST (next activity) – duration – EST (this activity).
Take task B as an example:
The EST of the next activity after B is 20.
The duration of B is 6.
The EST at the start of B is 0 and, therefore:
Free float for B = 20 – 6 – 0 = 14.

B could be delayed by 14 days without delaying the start of either H or D, the following activities (see Table 27.3)

Activity	Total float	Free float
B	15	14
C	1	0
D	6	6
H	1	1

Table 27.3 Float time for all non-critical activities

What is the critical path for this project?

Those activities that have no spare time are the critical ones. These activities are shown by those nodes where EST and LFT are equal. Take node 3 as an example. The EST of F is 22. This is the same as the LFT of E. Therefore no delay is possible – F must start on time or the whole project will overrun. Therefore, the critical path is made up of activities A, E, F, G, I and J. These will take 42 days to complete, so this becomes the project duration. Float times have very significant applications in managing resources: see advantages of critical path analysis below.

Dummy activities

A dummy activity is not strictly an activity at all. It is shown by a dotted line on a network diagram. It does not consume either time or resources. What it shows is a 'logical dependency' between other activities that must be included in certain networks to prevent an illogical path from being created. Consider these activities and the relationships between them:

- The activities A and B are the start of the project. They have no preceding activities.
- C follows A.
- D follows A and B.

How can the network be drawn? Figure 27.5 shows one attempt – but it is wrong. Can you see why? The network shows that both C and D require A and B to be finished, whereas only C requires A to finish before it can start.

The correct network is shown in Figure 27.6, which shows the correct logical dependencies – C starts when A is finished, but D has to wait until both A and B are finished. The dummy activity shows the relationship between B and D – with the arrow indicating the direction of the dependency.

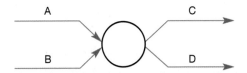

Figure 27.5 First attempt at drawing a network

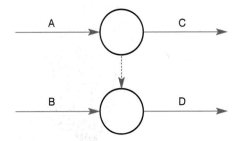

Figure 27.6 The correct network

ACTIVITY 27.4

Activity	Preceding activities	Duration
A	–	4
B	A	6
C	A	7
D	B	12
E	C	9
F	D and E	3
G	A	16
H	G and F	3

Activities and durations for Project X

[20 marks, 30 minutes]

1   Draw the network for Project X.   [6]

2   Use the duration times to calculate the EST and
    LFT of each activity.   [6]

3   Identify the critical path.   [2]

4   Explain the importance of this critical path to the
    operations manager.   [6]

The advantages of critical path analysis (CPA)

It has already been stated that network analysis can be used to assist the planning and management of complex projects. The following are some of the advantages that result from using the technique:

- Using the diagram to calculate the total project duration allows businesses to give accurate delivery dates. Customers may insist on a particular completion date and the critical time shows whether the firm can make this date or not.
- Calculating an EST for each activity allows the operations manager to order special equipment or materials needed for that task at the correct time. This ties the use of network analysis in with JIT strategies and assists in the control of cash flow and working capital.
- Calculating the LFT of each activity provides a useful control tool for the operations manager. The manager will be able to see whether the project is up to schedule by checking the actual completion times of activities against the network LFT.
- Knowing the critical path can be very useful. If there is a delay on a critical activity, there is no float because it is critical and the delay will, unless quick action is taken, put back the whole project. This could lead to expensive damage claims from the customer. By knowing the

critical path, the operations manager can see which other activities need to be speeded up if one has been delayed. For instance, in the network above, if E was delayed by two days due to bad weather or non-arrival of equipment, the operations manager would know that one of the following critical activities needs to be accelerated to catch up on time lost.

- The additional resources for speeding up a critical activity could come from the non-critical ones. To use the house-building example above, if F is to be reduced to eight days to counter the delay on E, the resources of labour, materials and machinery could be taken from D or H, as they both have spare time. This will allow a better and more efficient use of the firm's resources. This shows how the existence of float times on D and H allows resources to be allocated more efficiently.
- The sequential and logical structure of the diagram lends itself well to computer applications and nearly all business applications of network analysis will now be run on computer.
- The need to put all activities into sequence in order to structure the diagram forces managers to plan each project carefully by putting activities in the correct order.
- The need for rapid development of new products has never been greater in the fast-changing consumer markets of today. Network analysis gives design and engineering departments a positive advantage by showing them the tasks that can be undertaken simultaneously in developing a new product. This will help to reduce the total time taken by the new project and supports the principle of simultaneous engineering.

TOP TIP

No planning technique, however good, can ensure that a project will reach a successful conclusion – refer to all of the reasons mentioned at the start of this chapter that can cause a project to fail.

Critical path analysis – evaluation

CPA or network analysis is a planning and control technique to assist with project management. It cannot guarantee a successful project by itself and, as with any plan, requires skilled and motivated staff to put it into effect. In addition, a plan is only as good as the management behind it – if management of the project is poor, then even a good CP network diagram will not ensure success.

This is particularly true when attempting to make up for lost time on a critical activity – experienced managers will need to identify the cheapest option for using and switching resources from non-critical activities.

Staff will feel more committed to the plan of operation if they have been consulted during its construction, for example over likely duration times for each activity.

When using CPA for a completely new project, there may be considerable guesswork involved in estimating the durations for each activity – as there will be no previous experience to go on. Although the manipulation of the network and of duration and float times is likely to be aided by computer, it can take skilled labour hours to put a complex project on to a computer. This time and the related expense must be justified by the subsequent cost and efficiency savings of applying the technique.

KEY CONCEPT LINK

Project planning is an excellent example of the importance of good **management** to business success. A poorly planned project will lead to delays and waste and failure to meet customers' expectations. These problems could all be blamed on poor management.

ACTIVITY 27.5

The launch of a new product

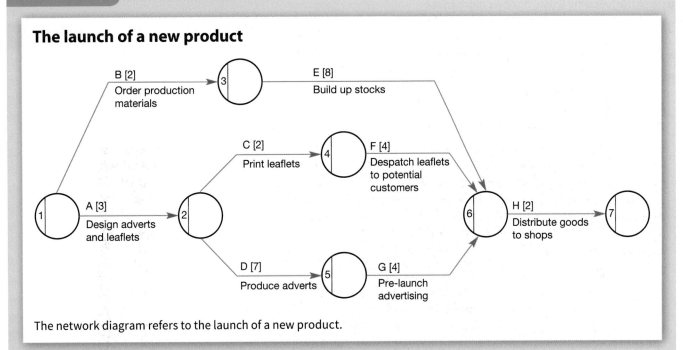

The network diagram refers to the launch of a new product.

[25 marks, 35 minutes]

1. Calculate the EST and LFT at each node (all durations in weeks). **[6]**

2. Identify the critical path. **[1]**

3. Calculate the total floats and free floats for each non-critical activity. **[6]**

4. If D is delayed by an overrun in the production of the advertisements, suggest how the marketing manager might still be able to complete the launch in the original project time. **[4]**

5. Explain how the use of critical path analysis might have assisted the marketing manager during this project. **[8]**

411

SUMMARY POINTS

- Project management is required when a specific task has to be undertaken and completed.
- Network diagrams using critical path analysis are a frequently used technique for coordinating and planning resources.
- Network diagrams can be analysed to identify critical path, ESTs and LFTs and float times.
- The usefulness of critical path analysis needs to be evaluated carefully.

RESEARCH TASK

- Use the following link to discover more about one recent project failure: http://calleam.com/WTPF/?tag=examples-of-failed-projects
- Explain the most likely causes for this project's failure.
- Analyse whether more effective use of critical path analysis/network diagrams might have reduced the chances of the project failing.

A Level exam practice questions
Case studies

1   Jamaica Photos Ltd

Jamaica Photos is a medium-sized photographic processing firm. It operates on two sites in Jamaica. After considerable consultation with employees, it is planning to close one of these sites, at Montego Bay, and to concentrate film-processing at its Kingston branch. The managers of the company want to make sure that the closure is carefully planned to reduce the adverse effects on production and customer delivery times. A project team has been drawn from all levels in the company to carry out this plan. The team has been offered a bonus if it can complete the task in 15 working days.

Closing the factory involves a number of activities as shown below:

Activity	Description	Duration
A	End processing in Montego Bay; run down stocks of materials	2 days
B	Dismantle machinery	4
C	Knock out doorway to allow machinery to be moved	2
D	Pack office equipment	2
E	Transportation	3
F	Suspend processing at Kingston	8
G	Assemble machinery transported from Montego Bay	3
H	Reorganise production facilities in Kingston	2
I	Test new integrated processing system	2

[44 marks, 60 minutes]

1   Construct a CP network diagram for this project based on the following information:
- A is the start of the project
- B, C and D cannot start until A is complete
- E follows B, C and D
- F has no preceding activity
- F must be completed before I can commence
- G and H follow E
- I follows G and H.   [6]

2   Identify the critical path by inserting all ESTs and LFTs.   [4]

3   Explain why this critical path must be supervised carefully.   [4]

4   Calculate all free and total floats for the non-critical activities.   [6]

5   Analyse the usefulness of this technique to the project team, considering the possibility of delays occurring on any of the activities.   [10]

6   To what extent will critical path analysis guarantee that this project will be successfully completed?   [14]

2 Network diagram

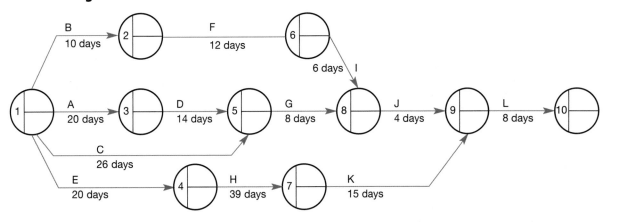

[18 marks, 25 minutes]

1 Calculate all ESTs and LFTs for the network shown in the above figure. [6]

2 Calculate the duration of the critical path. [2]

3 Calculate total floats on all of the non-critical activities. [6]

4 Explain the disadvantages to the operations manager of ordering goods needed for task D to arrive on:

■ day 25

■ day 15. [4]

A Level essay questions

[20 marks, 45 minutes each]

1 a Explain why efficient project management is important for a business operating in a competitive market. [8]

   b Evaluate the usefulness of critical path analysis to a construction business building a new sports complex to a completely new design. [12]

2 Evaluate the usefulness of critical path analysis to an operations manager when planning the relocation of production facilities to another country. [20]

End of Unit 4: Exam-style case study questions

Asia Resort Hotel (ARH)

ARH is a large hotel with 200 bedrooms. It can accommodate 325 guests at full capacity. The facilities of the hotel include three restaurants, a pool and gymnasium and a conference centre with rooms suitable for groups of between 10 and 280 people. Located near the beach in an area popular with tourists, the hotel has a reputation for being quite expensive and exclusive – but offering a high level of customer service.

Directors keen to improve ARH's competitiveness

Since ARH was built six years ago, 30 more hotels have been constructed in the region. Several of them compete in the same market segments as ARH. Although total tourist numbers are rising, ARH's directors understand the importance of improving competitiveness by cutting non-essential costs. If they are successful in doing this, room prices could either be lowered or, if they are kept at the same level, profits could be increased to allow for further investment in the hotel.

The hotel's operations director is planning to outsource some operations. He believes that website design, laundry services, cleaning and the customer telephone call-centre are all activities that could be contracted out to other businesses. He suggested to the CEO, Chas Singh: 'ARH could cut its fixed and operating costs substantially if these services were outsourced to other businesses. We could then focus on what we do best – looking after our guests.'

Lean production – could ARH adopt this principle?

Chas recently attended a hotel managers' conference where the productivity levels of different hotels were compared and benchmarked against industry leaders. On his return to ARH, he was concerned to discover that his hotel's productivity was in the lowest third of all large Asian hotels. When he spoke at the next board meeting it was to issue this warning: 'ARH prides itself on the quality of guests experience with us but our guest-to-employee ratio – one measure of our hotel's efficiency – is one of the lowest in the region. In addition, our food waste levels and energy consumption per guest are some of the highest. We need to involve our employees in improving these efficiency indicators or our profitability will decline rapidly.' The human resource (HR) and operations directors agreed at the meeting to look into the possibility of adopting some lean production principles such as greater employee flexibility and quality improvement groups to suggest ways to cut waste. 'Our employees have been at ARH for an average of five years. Many are skilled in the jobs they were appointed to do and they do not like change. They are not used to being asked for their opinions either,' commented the HR director.

Off-peak season leads to low capacity utilisation

Table 1 shows average guest numbers per night for ARH in 2014.

Forecasts for 2015 suggest that demand in the off-peak season will fall by 15% compared to 2014 owing to the appreciation of Asian currencies making the region expensive for many tourists. Chas has asked his fellow directors to come up with proposals to manage the problem of the projected low rate of capacity utilisation in the 2015 off-peak season. Their proposals are:

	2014	Capacity utilisation (325 maximum guests)
Peak season	315	97%
Off-peak season	180	55%

Table 1

Marketing director: Reduce prices substantially in the off-peak season to attract different market segments and allow the hotel to be kept fully open.

HR director: Issue new employment contracts to 50% of ARH's employees offering only part-time and temporary employment during the off-peak season.

Operations director: Reduce the hotel's room capacity permanently by converting 15 double bedrooms (for two guests each) to small conference rooms. The demand for small rooms for business meetings is growing.

Renovation of swimming pool has fixed time limit

The swimming pool is going to be renovated during the off-peak season. This project must be completed in 18 weeks or guests arriving during the main holiday season will complain about the closure of this major facility. ARH has awarded the contract to a small, local pool construction company that offered the lowest price. ARH's operations director insisted on the company following the network diagram that he had constructed.

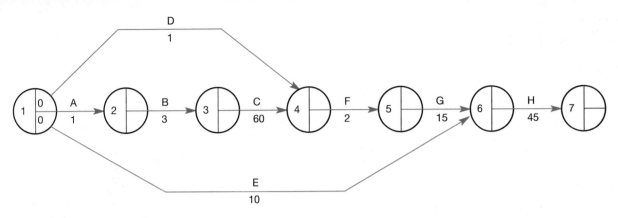

Network diagram

KEY CONCEPTS REVIEW

The management of ARH are keen to improve **efficiency** and **effectiveness** of the business. If these measures are successful, then the business will reduce its unit costs and create additional value. Changes in the external environment such as economic conditions or legal requirements imposed on hotels will also require management action. Can you think of ways in which a hotel could introduce innovations to become more **customer-focused**?

A Level *50 marks 90 minutes*

1 Analyse the potential benefits and risks to ARH from outsourcing some of its operations. [10]

2 a Calculate the forecast rate of capacity utilisation in the 2015 off-peak season. [4]

  b Recommend to ARH how it might manage the problem of low capacity utilisation during the off-peak season. [10]

3 Assess how the management of ARH could introduce lean production principles effectively within the hotel. [12]

4 a Using the network diagram calculate:

    i the length of the critical path (days) [2]

    ii the total float on activity D [2]

  b Evaluate the usefulness of critical path analysis to the successful scheduled completion of the pool renovation project. [10]

Unit 5:
Finance and accounting

Introduction

This section introduces the importance of the management of finance, the keeping of accounts and the analysis of them, and the assessment of business financial performance. The key issues of financial management, the value of financial statements and the measurement of financial performance are all explained and developed. Central to the role of finance and accounting is an understanding of how information produced, analysed and applied can be used by businesses to create value and measure whether financial objectives have been met.

28 Business finance

This chapter covers syllabus sections AS Level 5.1 and 5.2.

On completion of this chapter, you will be able to:

- understand why business activity requires finance
- recognise the difference between capital and revenue expenditure and the different needs for finance these create
- understand the importance of working capital to a business and how this can be managed
- analyse the different sources of long-, medium- and short-term finance, both internal and external
- understand the role played by the main financial institutions
- select and justify appropriate sources of finance for different business needs
- analyse the factors that managers consider when taking a finance decision.

Introducing the topic

TWO BUSINESSES – BOTH NEED FINANCE

There are many differences between Haldia Petrochemicals Ltd (HPL) and the six Khadki villagers who plan to build private water wells. However, there are two similarities – they are both situated in India and they both have a need for finance. HPL is a large company that has operated at a loss for several years. It is in desperate need for finance to prevent the business from collapsing. Finance proposals include converting loans into shares (reducing interest payments) and selling more shares to existing shareholders (a rights issue). The latter option was chosen and 520 million shares were issued at 25.10 Rupees each.

The six Khadki villagers needed finance to dig water wells. These would have a social benefit as well as being potentially profitable. Although poor, they each saved 100 Rupees per month for a year. Although their request for a loan of 25,000 Rupees was rejected by a commercial bank as the villagers had no collateral (they had no property of value themselves), they were successful in obtaining the loan from a microfinance bank. The interest rate was 6% per year. They repaid the loan within two years and they have since returned to borrow bigger amounts to finance even deeper wells. Without this microfinance their business would not have been started.

Points to think about:

- Explain the different financial needs in these two cases.
- Why might commercial banks have been to lend money in both cases?
- Explain the two different sources of finance used.

Introduction

Business activity cannot take place without finance – or the means of purchasing the materials and assets before the production of a good or service can take place. Finance decisions are some of the most important that managers have to take. Inadequate or inappropriate finance can lead to business failure – in fact, shortage of liquid funds is the main reason for businesses failing. The range and choice of finance sources are extensive and skilled managers will be able to match accurately the needs of their business for particular types of finance with the sources available. Selecting an inappropriate source of finance can prove to be expensive for a business or could even lead to a loss of control by the original owners.

Why business activity requires finance

Finance is required for many business activities. Here is a list of just some of the main situations in which businesses will require finance:

- Setting up a business will require cash injections from the owner(s) to purchase essential capital equipment and, possibly, premises. This is called **start-up capital**.
- All businesses need to finance their **working capital** – the day-to-day finance needed to pay bills and expenses and to build up stocks.

KEY TERMS

Start-up capital: the capital needed by an entrepreneur to set up a business.

Working capital: the capital needed to pay for raw materials, day-to-day running costs and credit offered to customers. In accounting terms working capital = current assets – current liabilities.

417

- When businesses expand, further finance will be needed to increase the capital assets held by the firm – and, often, expansion will involve higher working capital needs.
- Expansion can be achieved by taking over other businesses. Finance is then needed to buy out the owners of the other firm.
- Special situations will often lead to a need for greater finance. For example, a decline in sales, possibly as a result of economic recession, could lead to cash needs to keep the business stable; or a large customer could fail to pay for goods, and finance is quickly needed to pay for essential expenses.
- Apart from purchasing fixed assets, finance is often used to pay for research and development into new products or to invest in new marketing strategies, such as opening up overseas markets.

Some of these situations will need investment in the business for many years – or even permanently. Other cases will need only short-term funding – this is usually defined as being for around one year or less. Some finance requirements of the business are for between one and five years and this is referred to as medium-term finance. The list given above of reasons why businesses need finance is not complete – you could probably add to it yourself. The important point to note about this list is that all of these situations are rather different. In practice, this means that no one source or type of finance is likely to be suitable in all cases. Managers will have to decide which type and source of finance are best in each case. Before making finance decisions, it is necessary to be aware of all of the many sources of finance available to businesses.

Capital and revenue expenditure

These two types of spending will almost certainly be financed in different ways and the length of time that the money is 'tied up' will be a major factor influencing the final finance choice.

KEY TERMS

Capital expenditure: the purchase of assets that are expected to last for more than one year, such as building and machinery.

Revenue expenditure: spending on all costs and assets other than fixed assets and includes wages and salaries and materials bought for stock.

Working capital – meaning and significance

Working capital is often described as the 'lifeblood' of a business. Finance is needed by every business to pay for everyday expenses, such as the payment of wages and buying of stock. Without sufficient working capital a business will be illiquid – unable to pay its immediate or short-term debts. What happens in cases such as this? Either the business raises finance quickly – such as a bank loan – or it may be forced into '**liquidation**' by its creditors, the firms it owes money to.

KEY TERMS

Liquidity: the ability of a firm to be able to pay its short-term debts.

Liquidation: when a firm ceases trading and its assets are sold for cash to pay suppliers and other creditors.

The simple calculation for working capital is: current assets less current liabilities. You will see from the section on the Statement of financial position in Chapter 30 that current assets are inventories, accounts receivable and cash in the bank and the tills. Virtually no business could survive without these three assets, although some business owners refuse to sell any products on credit so there will be no trade receivables. This is very rare for businesses beyond a certain size.

Where does the capital come from to purchase and hold these current assets? Most businesses will obtain some of this finance in the form of current liabilities – overdrafts and creditors are the main forms. However, it would be unwise to obtain all of the funds needed from these sources. First, they may have to be repaid at very short notice, meaning the firm is again left with a liquidity problem. Second, it will leave no working capital for buying additional stocks or extending further credit to customers when required.

How much working capital is needed?

Sufficient working capital is essential to prevent a business from becoming illiquid and unable to pay its debts. Too high a level of working capital is a disadvantage; the opportunity cost of too much capital tied up in inventories, accounts receivable and idle cash is the return that money could earn elsewhere in the business – invested in fixed assets, perhaps.

The working capital requirement for any business will depend upon the length of this 'working capital cycle'. The longer the time period from buying materials to receiving payment from customers, the greater will be the working capital needs of the business. Figure 28.1 shows the simple cycle of a business that produces goods, but neither asks for nor offers credit. Credit to customers given by the business will lengthen the time before a sale is turned into cash. Credit received by the business will lengthen the time before stock bought has to be paid for. To give more credit than is received is to increase the need for working capital. To receive more credit than is given is to reduce the need for working capital.

Managing working capital efficiently is vital for all businesses and this is discussed in Chapter 31.

ACTIVITY 28.1

[10 marks, 15 minutes]

1 Using the list of reasons why businesses require finance on pages 417–418, identify:

   a **two** business situations that are likely to need long-term finance (more than five years) [2]

   b **two** business situations that might require only short-term finance. [2]

2 For each case, explain your answer. [6]

ACTIVITY 28.2

Directphone Ltd

Directphone Ltd operates a direct insurance service to motorists. As part of a recent expansion programme, the finance director calculated that stocks of stationery, such as insurance certificates, would have to rise by 10% from $10,000. More motorists would be encouraged to use the company by being offered extended credit terms. This would increase trade receivables to an estimated $50,000 from the existing $40,000. Cash reserves to pay out for accidents would rise to $35,000 from $30,000. The only current liability was creditors (garages that had not yet been paid for accident work). This amounted to $40,000 and the director hoped to be allowed to increase this to $50,000.

[10 marks, 15 minutes]

1 Calculate the proposed increase in the working capital requirements of the business resulting from the expansion. [6]

2 Outline **two** ways in which this increase in working capital might be financed. [4]

Where does finance come from?

This section deals initially with sources of finance for limited companies – and then considers sole traders and

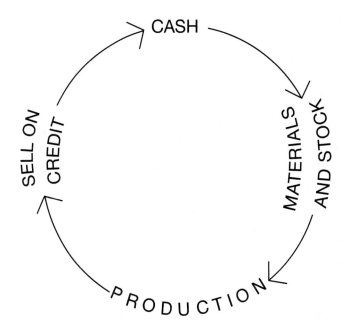

Figure 28.1 The simple working capital cycle – the longer this cycle takes to complete, the more working capital will be needed

partnerships. Companies are able to raise finance from a wide range of sources. It is useful to classify these into:

■ internal money raised from the business's own assets or from profits left in the business (ploughed-back or retained earnings)
■ external money raised from sources outside the business.

Another classification is also often made, that of short-, medium- and long-term finance; this distinction is made clearer by considering Figure 28.2.

Internal sources of finance

Profits retained in the business

If a company is trading profitably, some of these profits will be taken in tax by the government (corporation tax) and some is nearly always paid out to the owners or shareholders (dividends). If any profit remains, this is kept (retained) in the business and becomes a source of finance for future activities. Clearly, a newly formed company or one trading at a loss will not have access to this source of finance. For other companies, retained earnings – if in a liquid form – are a very significant source of funds for expansion. Once invested back into the business, these retained earnings will not be paid out to shareholders, so they represent a permanent source of finance.

Sale of assets

Established companies often find that they have assets that are no longer fully employed. These could be sold to raise cash. In addition, some businesses will sell assets that they still intend to use, but which they do not need to own.

419

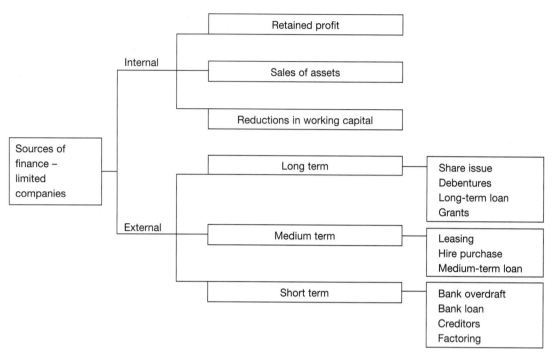

Figure 28.2 Sources of finance for limited companies

In these cases, the assets might be sold to a leasing specialist and leased back by the company. This will raise capital – but there will be an additional fixed cost in the leasing and rental payment.

In 2014 the struggling cell phone manufacturer BlackBerry considered the sale of property assets to raise finance to help the business over a difficult trading period caused by its loss of market share to iPhones and Android phones.

The Coca-Cola Company and its bottling partner, COFCO Coca-Cola Beverages Ltd, have continued their expansion in China with the opening of two bottling facilities in less-developed central and western China – Coca-Cola finances most of its expansion from retained earnings

HSBC, a large international bank, recently sold its huge London headquarters for $2 billion, but will stay in the building and lease it back from the new owners – at an annual rent of $80 million.

Reductions in working capital

When businesses increase stock levels or sell goods on credit to customers (trade receivables), they use a source of finance. When companies reduce these assets – by reducing their working capital – capital is released, which acts as a source of finance for other uses. There are risks in cutting down on working capital, however. As will be seen in Chapter 31, cutting back on current assets by selling inventories or reducing debts owed to the business may reduce the firm's liquidity – its ability to pay short-term debts – to risky levels.

Internal sources of finance – an evaluation

This type of capital has no direct cost to the business, although if assets are leased back once sold there will be leasing charges. Internal finance does not increase the liabilities or debts of the business, and there is no risk of loss of control by the original owners as no shares are sold. However, it is not available for all companies, for example newly formed ones or unprofitable ones with few 'spare' assets. Solely depending on internal sources of finance for expansion can slow down business growth, as the pace of development will be limited by the annual profits or the value of assets to be sold. Thus, rapidly expanding companies are often dependent on external sources for much of their finance.

TOP TIP

Do not make the mistake of suggesting that selling shares is a form of internal finance for companies. Although the shareholders own the business, the company is a separate legal unit and, therefore, the shareholders are 'outside' it.

External sources of finance

Short-term sources

There are three main sources of short-term external finance:

- bank **overdrafts**
- trade credit
- debt **factoring**.

KEY TERMS

Overdraft: bank agrees to a business borrowing up to an agreed limit as and when required.

Factoring: selling of claims over trade receivables to a debt factor in exchange for immediate liquidity – only a proportion of the value of the debts will be received as cash.

Bank overdrafts

A bank overdraft is the most flexible of all sources of finance. This means that the amount raised can vary from day to day, depending on the particular needs of the business. The bank allows the business to 'overdraw' on its account at the bank by writing cheques or making payments to a greater value than the balance in the account. This overdrawn amount should always be agreed in advance and always has a limit beyond which the firm should not go. Businesses may need to increase the overdraft for short periods of time if customers do not pay as quickly as expected or if a large delivery of stocks has to be paid for. This form of finance often carries high interest charges. In addition, if a bank becomes concerned about the stability of one of its customers, it can 'call in' the overdraft and force the firm to pay it back. This, in extreme cases, can lead to business failure.

Trade credit

By delaying the payment of bills for goods or services received, a business is, in effect, obtaining finance. Its suppliers, or creditors, are providing goods and services without receiving immediate payment and this is as good as 'lending money'. The downside to these periods of credit is that they are not free – discounts for quick payment and supplier confidence are often lost if the business takes too long to pay its suppliers.

Debt factoring

When a business sells goods on credit, it creates trade receivables. The longer the time allowed to pay up, the more finance the business has to find to carry on trading. One option, if it is commercially unwise to insist on cash payments, is to sell these claims on trade receivables to a debt factor. In this way immediate cash is obtained, but not for the full amount of the debt. This is because the debt-factoring company's profits are made by discounting the debts and not paying their full value. When full payment is received from the original customer, the debt factor makes a profit. Smaller firms who sell goods on hire purchase often sell the debt to credit-loan firms, so that the credit agreement is never with the firm but with the specialist provider.

Sources of medium-term finance

There are two main sources of medium-term external finance:

- hire purchase and leasing
- medium-term bank loan.

Hire purchase and leasing

These methods are often used to obtain fixed assets with a medium lifespan – one to five years. **Hire purchase** is a form of credit for purchasing an asset over a period of time. This avoids making a large initial cash payment to buy the asset.

Leasing involves a contract with a leasing or finance company to acquire, but not necessarily to purchase, assets over the medium term. A periodic payment is made over the life of the agreement, but the business does not have to purchase the asset at the end. This agreement allows the firm to avoid cash purchase of the asset. The risk of using

KEY TERMS

Hire purchase: an asset is sold to a company that agrees to pay fixed repayments over an agreed time period – the asset belongs to the company.

Leasing: obtaining the use of equipment or vehicles and paying a rental or leasing charge over a fixed period, this avoids the need for the business to raise long-term capital to buy the asset; ownership remains with the leasing company.

unreliable or outdated equipment is reduced as the leasing company will repair and update the asset as part of the agreement. Neither hire purchase nor leasing is a cheap option, but they do improve the short-term cash-flow position of a company compared to outright purchase of an asset for cash.

Long-term finance

The two main choices here are debt or **equity finance**. Debt finance increases the liabilities of a company. Debt finance can be raised in two main ways:

- **long-term loans** from banks
- debentures (also known as loan stock or corporate bonds).

KEY TERMS

Equity finance: permanent finance raised by companies through the sale of shares.

Long-term loans: loans that do not have to be repaid for at least one year.

Long-term loans from banks

These may be offered at either a variable or a fixed interest rate. Fixed rates provide more certainty, but they can turn out to be expensive if the loan is agreed at a time of high interest rates. Companies borrowing from banks will often have to provide security or collateral for the loan; this means the right to sell an asset is given to the bank if the company cannot repay the debt. Businesses with few assets to act as security may find it difficult to obtain loans – or may be asked to pay higher rates of interest.

Alternatively, in the UK, a small business can apply to the Department of Trade and Industry for the loan to

be part of the 'guaranteed loan scheme'. Banks will be more willing to lend if a company has been successful in this application because it gives the bank security of repayment. Merchant banks are specialist lending institutions. They provide advice as well as finance to firms engaging in expansion or merger/takeover plans.

Long-term bonds or debentures

A company wishing to raise funds will issue or sell such bonds to interested investors. The company agrees to pay a fixed rate of interest each year for the life of the bond, which can be up to 25 years. The buyers may resell to other investors if they do not wish to wait until maturity before getting their original investment back. Long-term loans or debentures are usually not secured on a particular asset. When they are secured, which means that the investors have the right if the company ceases trading to sell that

KEY TERM

Long-term bonds or debentures: bonds issued by companies to raise debt finance, often with a fixed rate of interest.

particular asset to gain repayment, the debentures are known as mortgage debentures. Debentures can be a very important source of long-term finance – in BT's recent accounts, the total value of issued loan stock amounted to £3,000 million. Convertible debentures can (if the borrower requests it) be converted into shares after a certain period of time, and this means that the company issuing them will never have to pay the debenture back.

Sale of shares – equity finance

All limited companies issue shares when they are first formed. The capital raised will be used to purchase essential assets. Chapter 2 explained the essential differences between private and public limited companies. Both of these organisations are able to sell further shares – up to the limit of their authorised share capital – in order to raise additional permanent finance. This capital never has to be repaid unless the company is completely wound up as a result of ceasing to trade. Private limited companies can sell further shares to existing shareholders. This has the advantage of not changing the control or ownership of the company – as long as all shareholders buy shares in the same proportion to those already owned. Owners of a private limited company can also decide to 'go public' and obtain the necessary authority to sell shares to the wider public. This would obviously have the potential to raise much more capital than from just the existing shareholders – but with the risk of some loss of control to the new shareholders.

In the UK, this can be done in two ways and these are quite typical for many countries:

1 Obtain a listing on the Alternative Investment Market (AIM), which is that part of the Stock Exchange concerned with smaller companies that want to raise only limited amounts of additional capital. The strict requirements for a full Stock Exchange listing are relaxed.

2 Apply for a full listing on the Stock Exchange by satisfying the criteria of (a) selling at least £50,000 worth of shares and (b) having a satisfactory trading record to give investors some confidence in the security of their investment. This sale of shares can be undertaken in two main ways:
   - **Public issue by prospectus:** This advertises the company and its share sale to the public and invites them to apply for the new shares. This is expensive, as the prospectus has to be prepared and issued. The share issue is often underwritten or guaranteed by a merchant bank, which charges for its services.
   - **Arranging a placing of shares with institutional investors without the expense of a full public issue:** Once a company has gained plc status, it is still possible for it to raise further capital by selling additional shares. This is often done by means of a **rights issue** of shares.

 KEY TERM

Rights issue: existing shareholders are given the right to buy additional shares at a discounted price.

By not introducing new shareholders, the ownership of the business does not change and the company raises capital relatively cheaply as no public promotion or advertising of the share offer is necessary. However, as the rights issue increases the supply of shares to the stock exchange, the short-term effect is often to reduce the existing share price, which is unlikely to give existing shareholders too much confidence in the business if the share price falls too sharply.

Debt or equity capital – an evaluation

Which method of long-term finance should a company choose? There is no easy answer to this question. And, as seen above, some businesses will use both debt and equity finance for very large projects.

Debt finance has the following advantages:

- As no shares are sold, the ownership of the company does not change or is not 'diluted' by the issue of additional shares.
- Loans will be repaid eventually (apart from convertible debentures), so there is no permanent increase in the liabilities of the business.
- Lenders have no voting rights at the annual general meetings.
- Interest charges are an expense of the business and are paid out before corporation tax is deducted, while dividends on shares have to be paid from profits after tax.
- The gearing of the company increases and this gives shareholders the chance of higher returns in the future. This point is dealt with more fully in Chapter 35.

Equity capital has the following advantages:

- It never has to be repaid; it is permanent capital.
- Dividends do not have to be paid every year; in contrast, interest on loans must be paid when demanded by the lender.

Other sources of long-term finance
Grants

There are many agencies that are prepared, under certain circumstances, to grant funds to businesses. The two major sources in most European countries are the central government and the European Union. Usually grants from these two bodies are given to small businesses or those expanding in developing regions of the country. Grants often come with conditions attached, such as location and the number of jobs to be created, but if these conditions are met, grants do not have to be repaid.

423

ACTIVITY 28.5

KOOVS lists on AIM

Online fashion retailer Koovs has been listed on London Stock Exchange AIM. Koovs successfully raised £22 million at the initial public offer (IPO), valuing the business at £36 million. Koovs is the first Indian business to list on London Stock Exchange since Nandan Cleantech, which debuted in November 2011. There are 62 Indian businesses, with a combined value of £90 billion listed in London across AIM and the main stock exchange market. Ibukun Adebayo, Head of Primary Markets, India at the London Stock Exchange Group said "We welcome Koovs to our market.

This is an important listing, not just for the company, but for Indian companies overall."

It will focus on affordable Western fashion rather than Indian ethnic clothing, copying celebrity fashions to appeal to middle-class working men and women aged 18–30 years, exactly like the London-based company. The owners plan to float about 35% of the company with 44% owned by the Nahata family, 11% by Lord Alli and the remainder with management.

Peacocks to go public

Peacocks, the discount clothing and houseware retailer, has issued its prospectus to the public. The company is going public to raise £42 million (after expenses) to fund further expansion and to repay outstanding debt. The managing director believes that there are great benefits in replacing debt finance with equity or share finance.

Rights issue from Australian company

Australian fertiliser-maker Incitec Pivot Ltd plans to raise A$1.17 billion through a rights issue of shares. Some of the capital will be used to repay loans and the rest will be used for long-term investment and research. The rights issue is being offered at A$2.50 per share, a 40% discount to the company's latest traded share price. The share issue is likely to reduce the market share price, at least in the short term. The company has also announced a tripling of annual profits, reflecting gains from a recent takeover and high fertiliser prices.

[28 marks, 40 minutes]

1 Why have Indian companies such as Koovs decided to join AIM rather than the main Stock Exchange? [4]

2 Why has the management of Koovs decided not to sell more than 50% of the shares in the company? [2]

3 Peacocks decided to issue shares by prospectus to the general public. Why do you think this method of selling shares was selected? [4]

4 What did the managing director of Peacocks mean when he said that there were advantages in selling shares to repay debt? What are the advantages of repaying debts? [6]

5 Why do you think Incitec Pivot decided to use a rights issue of shares to raise capital? [4]

6 Evaluate whether a shareholder in Incitec Pivot should buy the rights issue of shares being offered. [8]

Venture capital

Small companies that are not listed on the Stock Exchange – 'unquoted companies' – can gain long-term investment funds from venture capitalists. These are specialist organisations, or sometimes wealthy individuals, who are prepared to lend risk capital to, or purchase shares in, business start-ups or small to medium-sized businesses that might find it difficult to raise capital from other sources. This could be because of risks to the business. These risks could come from the new technology that the company is dealing in or the complex research it is planning, in which other providers of finance are not prepared to get involved. Venture capitalists take great risks and could lose all of their money – but the rewards can be great. The value of certain 'high-tech' businesses has grown rapidly and many were financed, at least in part, by venture capitalists. Venture capitalists generally expect a share of the future profits or a sizeable stake in the business in return for their investment.

KEY TERM

Venture capital: risk capital invested in business start-ups or expanding small businesses that have good profit potential but do not find it easy to gain finance from other sources.

Finance for unincorporated businesses

Sole traders and partnerships were referred to in Chapter 2, so only the main distinctions between company finance and unincorporated business finance will be made now.

Unincorporated businesses – sole traders and partnerships – cannot raise finance from the sale of shares and are most unlikely to be successful in selling debentures as they are likely to be relatively unknown firms. Owners of these businesses will have access to bank overdrafts, loans and credit from suppliers. They may borrow from family and friends, use the savings and profits made by the owners and, if a sole trader wishes to do this, take on partners to inject further capital.

As has been made clear earlier in the book, any owner or partner in an unincorporated business runs the risk of losing all property owned if the firm fails. Lenders are often reluctant to lend to smaller businesses, which is what sole traders and partnerships tend to be, unless the owners give personal guarantees, supported by their own assets, should the business fail.

Grants are available to small and newly formed businesses as part of most governments' assistance to small businesses.

TOP TIP

When answering case study questions, you should analyse what type of legal structure the business has and what sources of finance are available to it.

Microfinance

This approach to providing small capital sums to entrepreneurs is now a very important source of finance in developing, relatively low-income countries. In 1974, Muhammad Yunus, an economics lecturer at the University of Chittagong, Bangladesh, lent US$27 to a group of very poor villagers. Not only did they repay this loan in full after their business ideas had been successful, but it led eventually to Yunus winning the Nobel Peace prize. He founded the Grameen Bank in 1983 to make very small loans – perhaps $20 a time – to poor people with no bank accounts and no chance of obtaining finance through traditional means. Since its foundation, the Grameen Bank has lent $6 billion to more than six million Asian people, many of whom have set up their own very small enterprises with the capital.

KEY TERM

Microfinance: providing financial services for poor and low-income customers who do not have access to banking services, such as loans and overdrafts offered by traditional commercial banks.

Many business entrepreneurs in Bangladesh and other Asian countries have received microfinance to help start their business. In some of these countries, more than 75% of successful applicants for microfinance are women. Females have, in some traditional societies, always found it very difficult to obtain loans or banking services from traditional banks. There is evidence that entrepreneurship is greater in regions with microfinance schemes in operation – and that average incomes are rising because of more successful businesses.

However, interest rates can be quite high as the administration costs of many very small loans is considerable. Some economists also suggest that if a small business start-up financed by microfinance fails, then the scheme has encouraged very poor people to take on debts that they cannot repay.

Crowd funding

This is becoming an increasingly significant source of finance for new business start-ups. The basic idea behind

KEY TERM

Crowd funding: the use of small amounts of capital from a large number of individuals to finance a new business venture.

Muhammad Yunus, founder of the Grameen Bank

it is that entrepreneurs rarely have sufficient finance to set up their own business. Banks may be unwilling to lend or may charge very high interest rates, especially if the entrepreneur has no proven business track record. Crowd funding websites allow an individual to promote their new business idea to many thousands – perhaps millions – of people who may be willing to each invest a small sum, $10 for example. There are many established websites such as Kickstarter and Crowdcube that allow entrepreneurs to publicise their new ideas. Through these websites, the entrepreneur will explain – perhaps with the aid of a video and graphics – what the business is about, what its objectives are and why finance is needed. Investors can commit small sums of money to the new venture until the 'target sum' is reached. The publicity generated can also be an effective form of promotion for the new business and its product.

Some schemes – such as social enterprises – may not aim to make a large profit, or any return at all. In these cases, the investors are, in effect, just making a donation. In all other situations, investors will hope to make a return on their investment – although the failure rate of newly created businesses is high and investors may not receive any returns at all. In business ventures that *are* successful, the crowd funding investors will receive either:

- their initial capital back plus interest – this is sometimes known as peer-to-peer lending, or
- an equity stake in the business and a share in profits – when these are eventually made!

Small businesses using crowd finance benefit from the capital that would otherwise have been difficult to obtain. However, they must keep accurate records of thousands of investors to either pay back interest and capital or a share of the profits. Also, exposing a new project idea on the Internet means that it could be copied by others before the entrepreneur has had a chance to start the business up.

Finance and stakeholders

Providing finance to a business creates a stakeholder relationship with that business. All stakeholders have certain rights, responsibilities and objectives, but these will differ between the various sources of finance. This is made clear in Table 28.1, which looks at the three main providers of company finance.

Raising external finance – the importance of a business plan

Without some evidence that the business managers have thought about and planned for the future it is most unlikely that bankers, venture capitalists or potential shareholders will invest money in the business. The main content sections of a typical **business plan** are explained in Chapter 40.

 KEY TERM

> **Business plan:** a detailed document giving evidence about a new or existing business, and that aims to convince external lenders and investors to extend finance to the business.

If the business plan lacks important details or sections of it are not sufficiently well supported by background research, such as market analysis, then the prospective creditors and investors can delay taking a finance decision until the plan is brought up to the desired standard.

ACTIVITY 28.6

Financing small business start-ups

Nelson is a very good car mechanic. He wants to set up his own business repairing cars. He has some tools and he will work from the shed in his garden. He needs $50 to buy a small stock of oil and other materials needed so that he can get started.

Serena has an idea for a new business – making exclusive luggage cases from a new ultralight material her brother has helped to develop. She has made a video of the design of the new cases she plans to make. She estimates she needs around $50,000 to buy the machines she will need.

[24 marks, 35 minutes]

1 Explain why traditional banks might be unlikely to provide loan finance to these two new businesses. **[8]**

2 Evaluate the usefulness of microfinance for Nelson's business. **[8]**

3 Evaluate the use of crowd funding for Serena's business. **[8]**

	Rights	Responsibilities	Objectives
Shareholders	■ part ownership of the company in proportion to the number of shares owned ■ to attend the AGM and vote, e.g. on election of directors ■ to receive dividend as recommended by the board ■ to receive a share of the capital if the business is wound up after all debts have been paid	■ capital invested cannot be claimed back from the company except when it ceases trading	■ to receive an annual return on investment in shares – the dividend ■ to receive capital growth through an increase in share price ■ possibly, to influence company policy through pressure at the AGM
Banks	■ to receive interest payments as laid down in the loan or overdraft agreement ■ to be repaid before shareholders if the company is wound up	■ to check on business viability before loan or overdraft is agreed; this is both a responsibility to the bank's shareholders and to the business – advice to customers is an important responsibility	■ to make a profit from the loan ■ to receive repayment of capital at the end of the loan term ■ to establish a long-term relationship, of mutual benefit, with the business
Creditors	■ to receive payment as agreed ■ to be paid before shareholders in the event of the business being wound up ■ to attend creditors' meetings if the business is put into liquidation	■ to provide regular statements of amount owing and terms of repayment	■ to provide credit to encourage the business to purchase stock ■ to establish a relationship built on trust so that credit can be offered with confidence

Table 28.1 Main financial stakeholders

ACTIVITY 28.7

Sources of finance

[9 marks, 9 minutes]

Copy the following table and complete it by ticking the appropriate boxes alongside each source of finance.

Sources of finance	Long-term finance	Medium-term finance	Short-term finance	Available to unincorporated businesses	Available to private limited companies	Available to public limited companies
Sale of shares to the public						
Sale of debentures						
Leasing						
Debt factoring						
Loans from family						
Take on partners						
Rights issue of shares						
Ten-year bank loan						
Bank overdraft						

Business plans do not guarantee the success of a new business proposal, but they are likely to increase the chances of avoiding failure. The business-planning process not only provides essential evidence to investors and lenders and makes the finance application more likely to be successful, but it also:

- forces the owners to think long and hard about the proposal, its strengths and potential weaknesses – it might actually dissuade some people from progressing with their proposal, thus avoiding a near-certain business flop
- gives the owners and managers a clear plan of action to guide their actions and decisions, at least in the early months and years of the business.

TOP TIP

You should be able to recommend appropriate sources of finance for businesses needing capital for different reasons.

Making the financing decision

Equity finance is only one option for a business engaged in strategic change. Loan capital is another source of funds. In addition, internal long-term sources can be gained either by releasing finance tied up in current assets, for example permanent reductions in inventory levels, or by retaining more profits. This latter objective could be achieved by reducing dividends to shareholders. The size and the profitability of the business are clearly key considerations when managers make a financing choice. Small businesses are unlikely to be able to justify the costs of converting to plc status. They might also have limited internal funds available if the existing profit levels are low. These and other factors that are considered before making the financing choice are analysed in Table 28.2.

KEY CONCEPT LINK

The sources of finance strategy adopted by **management** can have a very significant impact not just on the future growth and profitability of a business and its ability to **create value** but also on the control over the business exercised by the existing owners.

428

Factor influencing finance choice	Why significant
Use to which finance is to be put – which affects the time period for which finance is required	<ul><li>It is very risky to borrow long-term finance to pay for short-term needs. Businesses should match the sources of finance to the need for it.</li><li>Permanent capital may be needed for long-term business expansion.</li><li>Short-term finance would be advisable to finance a short-term need to increase stocks or pay creditors.</li></ul>
Cost	<ul><li>Obtaining finance is never free – even internal finance may have an opportunity cost.</li><li>Loans may become very expensive during a period of rising interest rates.</li><li>A Stock Exchange flotation can cost millions of dollars in fees and promotion of the share sale.</li></ul>
Amount required	<ul><li>Share issues and sales of debentures, because of the administration and other costs, would generally be used only for large capital sums.</li><li>Small bank loans or reducing trade receivables' payment period could be used to raise small sums.</li></ul>
Legal structure and desire to retain control	<ul><li>Share issues can only be used by limited companies – and only public limited companies can sell shares directly to the public. Doing this runs the risk of the current owners losing some control – except if a rights issue is used.</li><li>If the owners want to retain control of the business at all costs, then a sale of shares might be unwise.</li></ul>
Size of existing borrowing	<ul><li>This is a key issue – the higher the existing debts of a business (compared with its size), the greater the risk of lending more. Banks and other lenders will become anxious about lending more finance.</li><li>This concept is referred to as gearing and is fully covered in Chapter 35.</li></ul>
Flexibility	<ul><li>When a firm has a variable need for finance – for example, it has a seasonal pattern of sales and cash receipts – a flexible form of finance is better than a long-term and inflexible source.</li></ul>

Table 28.2 Factors to be considered in making the 'source of finance' decision

Going exclusive with ice cream

Omah and Sara were convinced that their idea of an exclusive ice cream bar in the city centre would be a success. There were already high-class cafés and restaurants, but there was not yet an establishment that specialised in luxury ice creams. They had considered buying a Häagen-Dazs franchise. This would have provided them with a ready-made business plan to present to bankers and investors. However, the cost seemed excessive and so they decided to 'do their own thing'. They had worked in retailing, but not in catering. They could invest $20,000 each, but the projected cost of the shop, stock and initial promotion was $80,000. The couple had no property themselves apart from cash in the bank. They had seen how successful similar ice cream bars were in America, so they thought that it would be a success in their own country too. Further research had been undertaken among their own friends and work colleagues, who all seemed enthusiastic about the idea. There seemed to be some resistance to the proposed prices of $2 for a standard cone of ice cream, though.

Omah and Sara were keen to have control over their business and be independent of other firms. However, they did not agree entirely about their future motivation for setting the bar up. Omah wanted this to be 'the start of global domination of the ice cream market' – but he was always keen on exaggeration. Sara just wanted to be her own boss and to be in control of her life. This difference of opinion between them was probably reflected in some sections of their business plan. They were both enthusiastic and hard-working, and these qualities impressed both their bank manager and a venture capitalist who was interested in supporting the idea. However, once they had read the rather hurriedly produced business plan, they refused finance. Omah and Sara had been hoping to raise 'about $50,000'. The bank manager said, 'There are many positive points about your proposal, but I want you to put further work into your business plan before agreeing to your loan request.'

[37 marks, 50 minutes]

1 What is meant by a 'venture capitalist'? [3]

2 Outline the benefits for Omah and Sara in preparing a detailed business plan for their new proposal. [8]

3 Discuss what 'further work' on the business plan the bank manager might have been requesting Omah and Sara to undertake. [8]

4 To what extent would a bank loan be preferable to venture capital to finance this new business start-up? [10]

5 Evaluate **two** factors that might determine the success of this new venture. [8]

Tata rights issue leads to fall in share price

Shares in India's Tata Motors fell as much as 6.6% as volatile markets raised concerns that investors may reject its huge $885 million rights issue. Shares in India's top vehicle-maker have taken a hit on the company's fundraising plans and the grim outlook for the car and commercial vehicles market where demand has slowed right down due to high fuel prices and the global economic slowdown. Some shareholders seem keen to take up the rights issue, but others are wary. They are worried about future share prices if the company's expansion plans are not successful.

Tata Motors has also said that it was looking at selling assets in some subsidiaries to raise capital, and independent investment analysts say that this is preferable to diluting ownership equity by the rights-issue method. The company is offering one new ordinary share for 340 Rupees for every six currently held by shareholders. The capital raised will be used to pay off the loans taken out by Tata when it bought some of Ford's car factories.

[20 marks, 30 minutes]

1 What was the strategic decision that required the capital Tata raised from the rights issue? [2]

2 Using evidence from the text and your own knowledge, explain why you think that Tata used a rights issue of shares rather than continuing to use long-term loans. [6]

3 Evaluate the likely reaction of shareholders to this financing decision in:

  a the short term [6]

  b the longer term. [6]

Telkonet raises $3.5 million by sale of debentures

Telkonet Inc. the provider of energy-management systems, has arranged to sell $3.5 million of 13% three-year debentures. The company plans to use the finance to cover working capital needs and to invest in expansion of its range of products. The announcement was made as world share prices recorded another bad day with further falls in most of the major indices.

CuraGen raises $125 million from the sale of convertible debentures

This drug research and development company has issued $125 million of convertible debentures. The capital raised will be used to finance further long-term research into genomics-based drugs for medical purposes. The debentures offer a fixed 6% per year and are convertible into CuraGen's shares in seven years' time at a conversion price of $127 per share.

[16 marks, 20 minutes]

1 a Define the term 'convertible debentures'. [2]

  b Briefly explain the term 'working capital'. [3]

2 Explain the benefits to both companies of raising finance through the sale of debentures rather than either selling shares or taking a long-term bank loan with variable interest rates. [11]

SUMMARY POINTS

- Finance is needed at all stages in the setting up and development of a business.
- No single source of finance is suitable for all business needs – careful choice is essential if the source of finance used is to be appropriate.
- Distinctions can be made between both internal and external finance and short- and long-term finance.
- Working capital is often referred to as the 'lifeblood' of a business, as without adequate working capital a business will not thrive and may not survive.
- There are advantages and disadvantages of the main forms of internal and external finance.
- Many factors influence financing choice made by business managers, including the purpose to which the funds will be used, the amount needed, the time period and the size of the businesses existing debts.

RESEARCH TASK

- Use the Internet to research into the availability of microfinance and crowd funding schemes in your country.
- Are there any microfinance institutions in your country?
- Are there any examples of entrepreneurs in your own country that have used crowd funding?
- Use financial newspapers or the Internet to follow the share price movements of a well-known public limited company in your country.
- Discover reasons why the share price fluctuates and whether the company has used or plans to use a rights issue of shares to raise more capital. Research the published accounts of this company (available online) and identify its level of long-term loans and the size of any overdraft. Have these figures changed in recent years?
- Write a report about the financing of the company you have investigated.

AS Level exam practice questions

Short answer questions

[62 marks, 80 minutes]

Knowledge and understanding

1   State **three** examples of business situations that require additional finance. **[3]**
2   Outline **two** ways in which businesses can raise finance from internal sources. **[4]**
3   Explain the difference between long- and short-term finance. **[2]**
4   Why might a new business find it difficult to raise external finance? **[3]**
5   Explain **two** benefits to a business start-up of using a crowd funding website to raise finance. **[4]**
6   Explain one possible limitation from crowd funding for each of the following:
    a   the entrepreneur using crowd funding
    b   potential investors **[4]**
7   What is trade credit and why is it a source of finance? **[3]**
8   Discuss whether a business would find debt factoring a suitable form of finance. **[3]**
9   State **two** drawbacks to long-term loan finance. **[2]**
10   Why is microfinance particularly important for new business in developing (low-income) countries? **[3]**
11   Why is increasing the long-term loans of a business beyond a certain level often described as being 'risky'? **[4]**
12   State **two** factors that a manager should consider before deciding between loan and share capital to raise additional finance. **[2]**
13   Discuss the importance of the two factors identified in question 10 in detail. **[6]**
14   What information is a bank manager likely to request before granting additional loan capital to a business? **[4]**

Application

15   An entrepreneur plans to set up a business producing a new type of electric plug that he has invented. Consider **two** benefits of him using crowd funding to finance the business start-up. **[4]**
16   Why might the managers of a private limited company be reluctant to apply for public limited company status for the business, despite the prospect of additional finance? **[4]**
17   Why might a business that manufactures electrical components for mobile (cell) phone companies decide to lease new equipment rather than to purchase it outright? **[3]**
18   Explain why a company might use a rights issue of shares rather than increasing loans if the managers plan to take over another business. **[4]**

Data response

1 Sharma Taxis needs finance as it expands

Joe Sharma started his taxi business with just one vehicle. He purchased this vehicle out of his own savings. Initially, he ran his business as a sole trader, but after two years of operation he took on a partner, who injected further capital into the firm. This was used to purchase other vehicles and a small garage where maintenance was carried out. The business continued to expand. Joe and his partner decided to convert into a private limited company and shares were sold to business associates, family and employees of the firm. The capital raised from this conversion was used to start a small road-haulage department with two vans. As the fleet of vehicles was growing, substantial stocks of spare parts were held to avoid cars and vans being off the road for any longer than necessary following a breakdown. Regular business clients of the firm were offered credit terms of up to two months.

Joe has heard of another taxi business being sold by the owners. It has a fleet of prestige cars and substantial premises. The board of Joe's limited company agreed to put a bid in for this business. They agreed that it should be partly financed by floating the company on the Alternative Investment Market (AIM) with a view to obtaining a full Stock Exchange listing if further expansion was planned. The alternative had been to obtain a substantial long-term loan, but the directors were concerned about the chances of an increase in interest rates and preferred the share issue plus the use of finance from retained earnings to buy out the other business. The bid for this firm was successful. The most recent development has been the decision to completely update the computer facilities at the head office. This should lead to efficient scheduling of vehicle use and an update of the accounting and invoicing system. This will allow much speedier sending out of bills to customers.

[30 marks, 45 minutes]

1 Identify the stages of this business's development where additional finance was required. **[4]**

2 At each of the stages you have identified, explain what type of finance was needed. **[4]**

3 In your opinion, how could the increase in spare parts and trade receivables of the business have been financed? **[4]**

4 Examine the decision by the directors to float the company on the AIM. **[7]**

5 If the company were to expand further, evaluate the case for and against financing this expansion with a long-term loan. **[11]**

2 StarJet takes off to $3.42 share price

Shares in StarJet, the region's second-largest low-cost airline, performed strongly on its first day of trading as a public limited company yesterday, rising 10% to $3.42. The offering was priced at $3.10 a share with the issue of 63 million shares raising $195 million. The public issue of shares represented about 25% of the enlarged share capital. The stake held by Stavros, the founder and chairman of the company, is now valued at about $328 million. Stavros and his brother and sister still control a stake of about 75% in StarJet.

Investment bankers said the issue attracted strong interest. The performance of the shares has been helped by the strong rise in the share price of other 'low-cost' airlines and this has encouraged investors to buy into StarJet. Capital raised from the share issue will mainly be used to purchase new aircraft as part of the airline's plans for a rapid expansion during the next four years, which includes the addition of 32 new Boeing 787s, more than doubling the size of the fleet. Some of the capital raised will be used to pay back some of StarJet's substantial debts.

[30 marks, 45 minutes]

1 a Define the terms 'public limited company'. **[2]**
  b Briefly explain the term 'share price'. **[3]**

2 a Calculate the share price on the second day of trading if it's increased by a further 15% **[2]**
  b Explain why the share prices of StarJet might continue to increase in future. **[4]**

3 Analyse why Stavros might be reluctant to sell a further 63 million shares in StarJet to raise additional capital. **[8]**

4 If StarJet planned to take over another airline in several years' time, evaluate the most appropriate sources of finance that the business could use. **[11]**

432

AS Level essay questions

[25 marks, 45 minutes each]

1 a Outline the main sources of finance available to an entrepreneur planning a new business start-up. [10]

   b Explain why the managers of a business might be reluctant to finance long-term expansion plans with a long-term loan. [15]

2 Evaluate the factors that the chief executive and major shareholder in a private limited company should consider before deciding on the most appropriate method of financing:
   - a short-term increase in working capital and
   - a takeover of another similar business. [25]

29 Costs

This chapter covers syllabus section AS Level 5.3.

On completing this chapter, you will be able to:

- explain the different classifications given to production costs
- understand the uses to which cost data can be put
- analyse which costs of production are likely to vary with output and which will not
- use costs of production in break-even analysis
- apply break-even analysis in simple business decision-making situations
- evaluate the usefulness of break-even analysis.

Introducing the topic

COSTS AND BREAK-EVEN

Three important international businesses have announced cost reductions that are likely to lead to higher profits. The clothing store Gap has reported an increase in quarterly operating profit. This is the result not only of higher sales but also of cost cuts – it is holding less stock, so variable costs are lower and fixed operational expenses such as management salaries have also been cut back.

Vodafone aims to save nearly $2 billion in costs. Jobs will be cut in the company. It will also spend less on promotion chasing new customers – it will instead focus on trying to get existing customers to use their phones more. This is a cheaper method of promotion.

AirAsia India is determined to be the lowest cost airline in India. It aims to break-even on its flights within India – no loss and no profit – with a flight occupancy rate of 57%, which is lower than most airlines. A low break-even point suggests low costs and efficient operations – two keys to a profitable future.

Points to think about:

- Why is it important for a business to be able to identify and calculate its costs?
- Why do you think it is important for a company to cut costs during periods of low sales?
- Why is it important for a company to know the output level at which it will 'break-even'?
- If fuel prices increased for airlines, would you advise AirAsia India to increase ticket prices?

Introduction

Management decisions can cover a wide range of issues and they require much information before effective strategies can be adopted. These business decisions include location of the operations, which method of production to use, which products to continue to make and whether to buy in components or make them within the business. Such decisions would not be possible without cost data. Here are some of the major uses of cost data:

- Business costs are a key factor in the 'profit equation'. Profits or losses cannot be calculated without accurate cost data. If businesses do not keep a record of their costs, then they will be unable to take effective and profitable decisions, such as where to locate.
- Cost data are also of great importance to other departments, such as marketing. Marketing managers will use cost data to help inform their pricing decisions.
- Keeping cost records also allows comparisons to be made with past periods of time. In this way, the efficiency of a department or the profitability of a product may be measured and assessed over time.
- Past cost data can help to set budgets for the future. These will act as targets to work towards for the departments concerned. Actual cost levels can then be compared with budgets.
- Comparing cost data can help a manager make decisions about resource use. For example, if wage rates are very low, then labour-intensive methods of production may be preferred over capital-intensive ones.
- Calculating the costs of different options can assist managers in their decision-making and help improve business performance. For example, comparing the costs of different production methods or alternative locations can increase the chances of the most profitable option being decided on.

What are the costs of production?

The financial costs incurred in making a product or providing a service can be classified in several ways. Cost classification is not always as clear-cut as it seems

434

and allocating costs to each product is not usually very straightforward in a business with more than one product. Some costing methods require this allocation to be made, some do not.

Before we can begin to use cost data to assist in making important decisions, it is important to understand the different cost classifications. The most important categories are:

- **direct costs**
- **indirect costs**
- **fixed costs**
- **variable costs**
- **marginal costs**.

Direct costs

- One of the direct costs of a hamburger in a fast-food restaurant is the cost of the meat.
- One of the direct costs for a garage in servicing a car is the labour cost of the mechanic.
- One of the direct costs of the Business Studies department is the salary of the Business Studies teacher.

> **KEY TERM**
>
> **Direct costs:** these costs can be clearly identified with each unit of production and can be allocated to a cost centre.

The two most common direct costs in a manufacturing business are labour and materials. The most important direct cost in a service business, such as retailing, is the cost of the goods being sold.

Indirect costs

Indirect costs are often referred to as overheads. Examples are:

- One indirect cost to a farm is the purchase of a tractor.
- One indirect cost to a supermarket is its promotional expenditure.
- One indirect cost to a garage is the rent.
- One indirect cost of running a school is the cost of cleaning it.

> **KEY TERM**
>
> **Indirect costs:** costs that cannot be identified with a unit of production or allocated accurately to a cost centre.

How are costs affected by the level of output?

It is important for management to understand that not all costs will vary directly in line with production increases or decreases. In the short run – the period in which no

changes to capacity can be made – costs may be classified as follows:

- **Fixed costs:** These remain fixed no matter what the level of output, such as rent of premises.
- **Variable costs:** These vary as output changes, such as the direct cost of materials used in making a washing machine or the electricity used to cook a fast-food meal. Semi-variable costs include both a fixed and a variable element, for example the electricity standing charge plus cost per unit used, salesperson's fixed basic wage plus a commission that varies with sales.
- **Marginal costs:** These are the additional costs of producing one more unit of output, and will be the extra variable costs needed to make this extra unit. So the marginal costs involved in making one more wooden table are the additional costs of wood, glue and screws plus the labour costs incurred.

> **KEY TERMS**
>
> **Fixed costs:** costs that do not vary with output in the short run.
> **Variable costs:** costs that vary with output.
> **Marginal costs:** the extra cost of producing one more unit of output.

> **ACTIVITY 29.1**
>
> ## Types of costs
> *[18 marks, 20 minutes]*
>
> 1 Identify **one** indirect cost for each of these businesses:
>   a a construction company
>   b a high-street bank
>   c a TV repairing business
>   d an oil-fired power station. [4]
>
> 2 Explain why the cost is indirect in each case. [4]
>
> 3 Identify **one** direct cost for each of these business activities:
>   a a carpenter making a wardrobe
>   b an insurance company issuing a new motor-insurance policy
>   c a drinks manufacturer delivering soda drinks to a hotel
>   d a bank agreeing an overdraft
>   e an oil-fired power station. [5]
>
> 4 Why do you think it is important to identify the direct costs of producing a product? [5]

Oil-fired power station in Cyprus – indirect costs are a very high proportion of total costs in electricity generation

Problems in classifying costs

Do you find it easy to classify all of the costs in Activities 29.1 and 29.2? In practice, it may not be very easy or even worthwhile to classify every cost into the categories explained above:

- Are labour costs necessarily variable, direct costs? Certainly not, because when labour is unoccupied because of a lack of orders, most businesses will continue to employ and pay workers in the short run. Wages then become an overhead cost, which cannot be directly allocated to any particular output. Similarly a television presenter may be employed on a fixed-contract salary, which will not be related to the amount of work done. In addition, the salaries of administration, selling and other staff are always considered to be an indirect cost, probably fixed in the short run, because these costs cannot be identified with any one of the firm's products or services.
- Telephone charges in a busy factory could be directly allocated to each range of products made, as long as an accurate and reliable record was kept of the purpose of each call. In practice, this may not be worthwhile and telephone charges would normally be considered as an indirect overhead expense.

TOP TIP
Not all direct costs are variable costs. For example, if a hotel buys a new juicing machine for the bar department, this is a direct cost to that department – but the cost of the machine will not vary with the number of orange juices being served.

Break-even analysis

This form of analysis is widely used in business as it provides useful information for decision-making.

KEY TERM

Break-even point of production: the level of output at which total costs equal total revenue, neither a profit nor a loss is made.

Break-even analysis can be undertaken in two ways:

1 the graphical method
2 the equation method.

The graphical method – the break-even chart

The break-even chart requires a graph with the axes shown in Figure 29.1. The chart itself is usually drawn showing three pieces of information:

1 **Fixed costs**, which, in the short term, will not vary with the level of output and which must be paid whether the firm produces anything or not.
2 **Total costs**, which are the addition of fixed and variable costs; we will assume, initially at least, that variable costs vary in direct proportion to output.
3 **Sales revenue**, obtained by multiplying selling price by output level.

Figure 29.2 shows a typical break-even chart. Note carefully the following points:

- The fixed-cost line is horizontal, showing that fixed costs are constant at all output levels.
- Sales revenue starts at the origin (0) because if no sales are made, there can be no revenue.
- The variable-cost line starts from the origin (0) because if no goods are produced, there will be no variable costs. It is drawn to aid your understanding of how the chart is constructed. It is not necessary to interpret the chart and is often omitted.
- The total-cost line begins at the level of fixed costs, the difference between total and fixed costs being accounted for by variable costs.

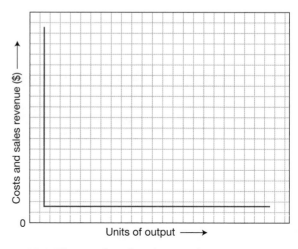

Figure 29.1 The axes for a break-even chart

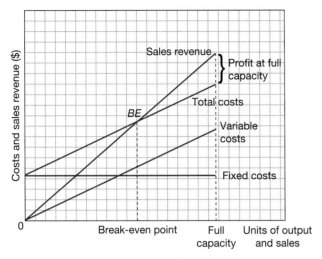

Figure 29.2 A typical break-even chart

The point at which the total-cost and sales-revenue lines cross (BE) is the break-even point. At production levels below the break-even point, the business is making a loss; at production levels above the break-even point, the business is making a profit.

Margin of safety

This is a useful indication of how much sales could fall without the firm falling into loss. For example, if the break-even output is 400 units and current production is 600 units, the **margin of safety** is 200 units. This can be expressed as a percentage of the break-even point. For example:

$$\text{Production over break-even point} = \frac{200}{400} = 50.0\%$$

If a firm is producing below the break-even point, it is in danger. This is sometimes expressed as a negative margin of safety. Hence, if break-even output is 400 and the firm is producing at 350 units, it has a margin of safety of –50. The minus sign simply tells us that the production level is below break-even. See Figure 29.3.

 KEY TERM

Margin of safety: the amount by which the sales level exceeds the break-even level of output.

437

Classifying costs

The management of a furniture manufacturing firm is trying to classify the costs of the business to help in future decision-making. It makes a range of wooden tables and chairs. You have been asked to assist in this exercise.

[16 marks, 20 minutes]

1 Classify these costs by ticking the appropriate boxes in the following table. **[8]**

2 Explain why you have classified these costs in the way you have. **[8]**

Cost	Direct	Indirect	Fixed	Variable
Rent of factory				
Management salaries				
Electricity				
Piece-rate labour wages of production staff				
Depreciation of equipment				
Lease of company cars				
Wood and other materials used in production				
Maintenance cost of special machine used to make one type of wooden chair				

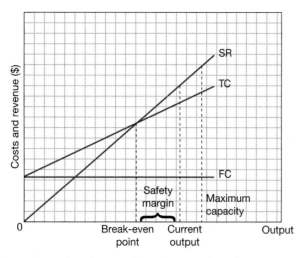

Figure 29.3 A break-even chart showing the safety margin

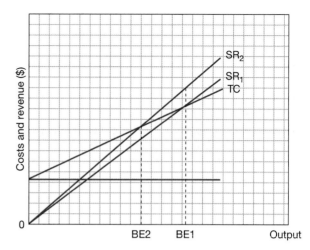

Figure 29.4 A break-even chart showing the effect on the break-even point and maximum total profit of a price rise (BE2)

The break-even equation

A formula can be used to calculate break-even:

$$\text{break-even level of output} = \frac{\text{fixed cost}}{\textbf{contribution per unit}}$$

Contribution per unit: selling price less variable cost per unit.

If fixed costs are $200,000 and the contribution per unit of output is $50, then the break-even level of production is:

$$\frac{200,000}{50} = 4,000 \text{ units}$$

This is an exact answer and, therefore, likely to be more accurate than many break-even graphs. The same method can be used if a manager wants to determine a target profit level and establish the level of output required to achieve it. Suppose the target profit is $25,000. This is treated as if it was an extra fixed cost and the calculation is:

$$\frac{200,000 + \$25,000}{50} = \frac{225,000}{50} = 4,500 \text{ units}$$

Break-even analysis – further uses

In addition to obtaining break-even levels of production and margins of safety, the break-even techniques can also be used to assist managers in making key decisions.

The charts can be redrawn showing a potential new situation and this can then be compared with the existing

position of the business. Care must be taken in making these comparisons, as forecasts and predictions are usually necessary. Here are three examples of further uses of the break-even technique:

1 A marketing decision – the impact of a price increase (Figure 29.4). The assumption made in this example is that maximum sales will still be made. With a higher price level, this may well be unlikely.

2 An operations-management decision – the purchase of new equipment with lower variable costs (Figure 29.5).

3 Choosing between two locations for a new factory.

438

The usefulness of break-even analysis can be summarised as follows:

- Charts are relatively easy to construct and interpret.
- Analysis provides useful guidelines to management on break-even points, safety margins and profit/loss levels at different rates of output.
- Comparisons can be made between different options by constructing new charts to show changed circumstances. In the case study above, charts could be amended to show the possible impact on profit and break-even point of a change in the product's selling price.
- The equation produces a precise break-even result.
- Break-even analysis can be used to assist managers when taking important decisions, such as location decisions, whether to buy new equipment and which project to invest in.

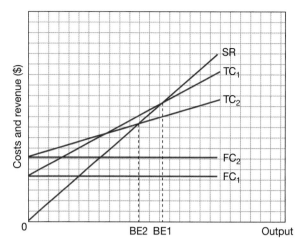

Figure 29.5 A break-even chart showing the possible impact of new equipment (raising fixed costs), but offering lower variable costs (BE2)

439

ACTIVITY 29.4

Location decisions and break-even

The following data have been collected about two possible locations:

	Fixed costs	Direct costs per unit	Forecast selling price per unit	Maximum capacity due to space limits
Site A	$60,000	$3	$6	40,000 units
Site B	$80,000	$2.50	$6	50,000 units

[24 marks, 35 minutes]

1 Use the data above to calculate, for each site:
   a break-even level of output   [3]
   b margin of safety   [3]
   c total maximum profit assuming all units sold [3]

2 Advise the business on which location to choose. Explain your break-even results in your answer.   [10]

3 List **five** other factors that the business should consider before making this location decision.   [5]

Evaluation of break-even analysis

The advantages of this technique were examined above. It is important now to recognise the limitations that this model has in practice:

- The assumption that costs and revenues are always represented by straight lines is unrealistic. Not all variable costs change directly or 'smoothly' with output. For example, labour costs may increase as output reaches maximum due to higher shift payments or overtime rates. The revenue line could be influenced by price reductions

made necessary to sell all units produced at high output levels. The combined effects of these assumptions could be to create two break-even points in practice (Figure 29.6).

- Not all costs can be conveniently classified into fixed and variable costs. The introduction of semi-variable costs will make the technique much more complicated.
- There is no allowance made for inventory levels on the break-even chart. It is assumed that all units produced are sold. This is unlikely to always be the case in practice.
- It is also unlikely that fixed costs will remain unchanged at different output levels up to maximum capacity.

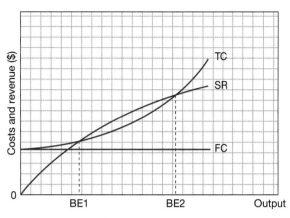

Figure 29.6 A break-even chart showing how non-linear assumptions can lead to two break-even points

KEY CONCEPT LINK

Understanding the classification of costs and being able to interpret break-even analysis are important skills that **management** will need to use to be able to adopt appropriate **strategies** to add to the **value** being created by the business.

ACTIVITY 29.5

Windcheater Car Roofracks

The sole owner of Windcheater Car Roofracks needs to expand output as a result of increasing demand from motor-accessory shops. Current output capacity has been reached at 5,000 units per year. Each rack is sold to the retailers for $40. Production costs are:

- direct labour $10
- direct materials $12
- fixed costs $54,000

The owner is considering two options for expansion:

Option 1: Extend the existing premises, but keep the same method of production. This would increase fixed costs by $27,000 per year, but direct costs would remain unchanged. Capacity would be doubled.

Option 2: Purchase new machinery, which will speed up the production process and cut down on wasted materials. Fixed costs would rise by $6,000 per year, but direct costs would be reduced by $2 per unit. Output capacity would increase by 50%.

[35 marks, 50 minutes]

1 Drawing the two break-even charts for these options would assist the owner in making this decision, but other issues may have to be considered as well.

- Construct break-even charts for these two options. Identify the break-even point for each.
- What is the maximum profit obtainable in each case?
- If demand next year is expected to be 7,000 units, what would be the margin of safety in both cases?
- Which option would you advise the owner to choose? Give both numerical and non-numerical reasons for your decision. [16]

2 The owner of Windcheater Car Roofracks discovers that the fixed costs for Option 1 will in fact be 20% greater than planned. Use a break-even chart to determine the new break-even point and then use the equation to verify it. [10]

3 In Option 2 the increase in fixed costs is now planned to be $8,000 and the direct costs fall by $2.50 per unit:

- explain why the direct costs might fall
- determine the new break-even point. [9]

440

RESEARCH TASK

- Investigate the costs of opening and operating a small café in your town/city.
- Consider the main fixed costs and variable costs of this café.
- Use research into other cafés to investigate the price of a main product – such as a standard cup of coffee.
- Attempt to calculate (or show on a graph) the break-even number of customers per week needed.
- Think about the limitations of your research and the analysis you have undertaken.

AS Level exam practice questions

Short answer questions

[52 marks, 60 minutes]

Knowledge and understanding

1 Explain **two** reasons why cost data would be useful for operations managers. [4]

2 Explain **two** reasons why cost data would be useful for marketing managers. [4]

3 Distinguish, with examples, between direct costs and indirect costs. [3]

4 Distinguish, with examples, between fixed costs and variable costs. [3]

5 Explain why it would be useful to an operations manager to know the break-even level of production for his factory. [3]

6 From the following graph identify:
- the break-even point; the safety margin at output level of 15,000 units; the level of fixed costs [3]

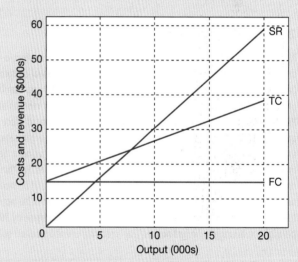

7 Explain two business decisions that would be assisted by using break-even analysis – use sketches of graphs to aid your explanation. [4]

8 Discuss, using graph sketches if necessary, **two** limitations of the break-even technique. [6]

Application

9 Explain why the manager of a café would find it useful to understand the difference between variable costs and fixed costs. [4]

10 Explain **two** ways in which the manager of a hairdressing salon could attempt to reduce the daily number of customers required to break even. [4]

11 An aircraft can carry 120 passengers. Over the last year the average occupancy rate has been 60% and the break-even occupancy rate is 55%. What has been the safety margin (in numbers of passengers) this year? [4]

12 Explain **two** possible limitations of break-even analysis for a newly established shop selling sports clothing. [4]

441

Data response

1 Decision time at the pottery

A pottery business sells clay pots for $3 each. It expects to produce and sell 5,000 pots this year, although there is a total production capacity of 7,500. Fixed costs are $4,000 per year. The variable costs of production are $1.50 per pot.

[30 marks, 45 minutes]

1   a   Define the term 'fixed costs'. [2]

    b   Briefly explain the term 'variable costs'. [3]

2   Draw a break-even graph to represent these data, identifying the break-even level of production and the margin of safety. [6]

3   The manager is considering two options in an effort to increase profits:

    ■   Purchase a new energy-efficient kiln. This would raise fixed costs by $1,000 per year but reduce variable costs to $1.20 per pot. Output would remain unchanged.

    ■   Reduce price by 10%. Market research indicates that this could raise sales by 20%.

    By drawing two new graphs, compare the break-even points of all three situations (including the original), the total levels of profit and the safety margins. [8]

3   Advise the firm, on the basis of your results, whether to remain as it is or to adopt one of the two options above. Justify your answer. [10]

2 Abbey Restaurant

Abbey Restaurant has a good local reputation for first-class meals at first-class prices. It has a weekly capacity for 1,000 customers. It has a loyal customer base, but the manager, Phil, is concerned about the disappointing number of new customers. Total revenue has fallen over the past few months and Phil believes that this is partly due to the closure of the local head office of an insurance company. Job losses occurred at all levels of the organisation, especially among middle managers. Phil is considering introducing a new menu that would offer less variety and less-complicated dishes. He thinks that the new items on the menu would be cheaper to produce and he would not have to replace one of the skilled chefs, who has just given in his notice to leave. Phil estimates that the number of customers could increase by 20% per night on average as he had noticed that a recently opened medium-price café/bar was full every night. Phil has shown the following financial data to the restaurant's accountant, who started to do some calculations. 'I need to calculate the break-even level of output and the margin of safety before I can advise you on what to do,' he told Phil.

Current menu option:
    Revenue per week (600 customers @ average of $20) $12,000
    Average variable cost per meal $5
    Overhead costs per week (including salaries of kitchen staff) $7,000

Proposed new menu:
    Average meal price $14
    Average variable cost per meal $4
    Overheads per week (including salaries of kitchen staff) $6,000

[30 marks, 45 minutes]

1   a   Define the term 'break-even level of output'. [2]

    b   Briefly explain the term 'margin of safety'. [3]

2   Calculate the forecast average monthly profit figures for the two menu options. [6]

3   Calculate the:

    a   break-even level of output of both options (show your workings) [4]

    b   margin of safety of both options (show working) [4]

4   On the basis of your results to question 1 and question 2 and any other information, would you advise Phil to adopt the new menu? Justify your answer. [11]

AS Level essay questions

[20 marks, 40 minutes]

1   a   Explain the construction of a break-even chart. [5]

    b   Discuss the view that break-even analysis is of limited value to retail businesses as it ignores changes in market conditions. [15]

2   a   Explain, with examples, the differences between direct costs, variable costs and fixed costs. [8]

    b   Evaluate the usefulness of break-even analysis to an entrepreneur planning a new business start-up. [12]

30 Accounting fundamentals

This chapter covers syllabus section AS Level 5.4.

On completing this chapter, you will be able to:

- understand why keeping business accounts is so important
- analyse the main users and uses of business-accounting records
- identify and understand the main components of an income statement
- identify and understand the main components of a Statement of financial position
- analyse business accounts by using ratio analysis – liquidity and profit-margin ratios
- evaluate the limitations of ratio analysis and of published accounts.

Introducing the topic

SKY'S THE LIMIT FOR SATELLITE DISHES

Rashid was pleased with himself. In his first month of trading he had sold and fitted ten TV satellite-dish receivers, two more than originally forecast in his business plan. Rashid's electrical skills and his friendly personality had impressed his customers.

He had purchased the first 50 TV satellite dishes from a website specialising in stock sell-offs from failed businesses. He had paid $100 each. This had swallowed up most of his start-up capital. He rented a small truck for $120 a month. The large sign he paid to have painted on the doors had cost him $120 but attracted lots of attention. Other advertising costs in his first month had been more than expected. The local newspaper had just increased its classified rates – $150 was $30 more than planned. He sold the satellite dishes for $275 fully fitted. Rashid could have just sold the dishes themselves but he wanted to add value to them by doing the fitting too. Each fitting kit cost Rashid $10. Other costs – such as road tax and insurance on the truck – had been paid

and totalled £200 per month, just as predicted. He had already paid an accountant for help with setting up the business and writing the business plan.

Rashid started to work out his profit for the first month. His only real worry was that two of his customers – whom he had known from schooldays – had asked if they could delay paying him. He had agreed as he wanted to make the sale. But when would they pay? Should he include these two satellite dishes when working out his first monthly profits?

Points to think about:

- Why do you think it is important for Rashid to keep accurate financial records?
- Do you think he made a profit in his first month of trading? How would you try to work this out?
- Why would profit be important to Rashid?
- If you were Rashid, would you have offered the two customers credit, i.e. time to pay him back?

Introduction

Most people know that accounts are 'monetary records' of transactions. You probably keep simple records of your own income and expenditures – these would be basic accounts. Why do you do this? Probably because you want to know whether you are spending more than you are earning or to find out if you can afford to take that holiday you promised yourself once the A Levels are over.

All businesses have to keep detailed records of purchases, sales and other financial transactions. Why is this? The easiest way to answer this question is to ask another one – what would happen if businesses did not keep accounting records? Table 30.1 lists some problems that would immediately arise and the reasons why stakeholder groups need accounting information. None of these questions could be answered without detailed and up-to-date accounts being kept. We can, therefore, say that accounts are financial records of business transactions, which are needed to provide essential information to groups both within and outside the organisation.

Management and financial accounting

There are several different branches of accounting. Two of the most important types of accountants are financial and management accountants. In general terms, the work of financial accountants is to prepare the published accounts of a business in keeping with legal requirements. The work of management accountants is to prepare detailed and frequent information for internal use by the managers of the business who need financial data to control the firm and take decisions for future success. The different responsibilities of these two types of accountant are summarised in Table 30.2.

Foundations of accounting – accounting concepts and conventions

It is important for accountants all over the world to base business accounts on the same basic principles. If they did not do this, it would never be possible to compare accounts from companies based in different countries. It would also cause huge problems for multinational companies if some of their accounts based on activities in foreign countries were recorded using different concepts and conventions to those in the home country. The following brief explanation of these concepts and principles helps to make key accounting points clearer for you – there will be no AS or A Level Business Studies questions based directly on them.

The double-entry principle

Every time a business engages in a transaction, for example buying materials or selling goods to a customer, there are two sides to the transaction. This means that the accounts of the business must include it twice to ensure that the accounts balance.

Accruals

Accruals arise when services have been supplied to a business but have not yet been paid for at the time the

Problem	Groups affected
How much did we buy from our suppliers and have they been paid yet?	Managers and suppliers (creditors)
How much profit did the business make last year?	Managers, shareholders and the tax authorities
Is the business able to repay the loan to the bank?	Managers and the bank
Did we pay wages to the workers last week?	Managers and workers
What is the value of the profit after all expenses, which is available for payment of dividends?	Managers and shareholders

Table 30.1 Why stakeholders need accounting information

Financial accounting	Management accounting
Collection of data on daily transactions.	Preparation of information for managers on any financial aspect of a business, its departments and products.
Preparation of the published report and accounts of a business – Statement of financial position, income statement and cash statement.	Analysing internal accounts such as departmental budgets.
Information is used by external groups.	Information is only made available to managers of the business – internal users.
Accounts usually prepared once or twice a year.	Accounting reports and data prepared as and when required by managers and owners.
Accountants are bound by the rules and concepts of the accounting profession. Company accounts must observe the requirements of the Companies Acts.	No set rules – accountants will produce information in the form requested.
Covers past periods of time.	Can cover past time periods, but can also be concerned with the present or projections into the future.

Table 30.2 The different work of financial and management accountants

accounts are drawn up, such as an electricity bill. If no adjustment was made for this accrued expense, then the profits in the current accounting period will be overstated.

The accruals adjustment adds the unpaid costs to the total costs of the current accounting period.

The money-measurement principle

Accountants need a common form of measuring the wealth and performance of the businesses they work for. All accounting data are converted into money – hence the principle of money measurement. Only items and transactions that can be measured in monetary terms are recorded in a business's account books and not, for example, the skills and experience of the company's directors.

Conservatism – also known as the prudence concept

Accountants are trained to be realistic about the values used in accounts. The conservatism principle states that accountants should provide for and record losses as soon as they are anticipated. Profits, on the other hand, should not be recorded until they have been 'realised' – that is, until it is certain that goods or services have been sold at a profit.

The realisation concept

The realisation concept states that all revenues and profits should be recorded in the accounts 'when the legal title to the goods is transferred'. This means when the customer is legally bound to pay for them, unless they can be proven to be faulty. So sales are not recorded when an order is taken or when payment is actually made – but when the goods or services have been provided to the customer.

The main business accounts – introduction

At the end of each accounting period, usually one year, accountants will draw up the financial statements of the business. For limited companies, these will be included in the annual report and accounts, which are sent to every shareholder. Table 30.3 gives details of the financial statements of limited companies, as these are the accounts you are most likely to be encounter in your studies.

Recent changes – International Financial Reporting Standards (IFRS)

The IFRS aims to ensure that accounts produced by companies all over the world conform to similar terminology and layout. This is to try to avoid confusion when analysing accounts from companies based in different countries. Recently, many changes to the names of the main accounts, the layout of them and the terminology to be used in them have been made by IFRS. The use of these new terms can be confusing for teachers and students who may either be used to the old names and forms of presentation or who have been taught using older textbooks.

This textbook follows the main changes adopted by IFRS, except where it is necessary to simplify material or slightly adapt account layout to aid student understanding.

> **TOP TIP**
>
> It is important to learn the new terms and forms of layout as these will be the one used by the company accounts that you will study during the course. Where it aids understanding, both the old terms and the new ones are introduced in this chapter – and then the new terms are used for the remainder of Unit 5 chapters.

The income statement – what it shows about a business

This account used to be known as the profit and loss account. In old examination papers or company accounts drawn up some years ago, this term may be used.

KEY TERM

Income statement: records the revenue, costs and profit (or loss) of a business over a given period of time.

The account	What it shows
Income statement (formerly known as profit and loss account)	The gross and operating profit of the company. Details of how the operating profit is split up (or appropriated) between dividends to shareholders and retained earnings (profit).
Statement of financial position (formerly known as the balance sheet)	The net worth or equity of the company. This is the difference between the value of what a company owns (assets) and what it owes (liabilities).
Cash-flow statement	Where cash was received from and what it was spent on.

Table 30.3 Final accounts of limited companies – what they contain

- A detailed income statement is usually produced for internal use because managers will need as much information as possible. It may be produced as frequently as managers need the information – perhaps once a month.
- A less-detailed summary will appear in the published accounts of companies for external users. It will be produced less frequently, but at least once a year. The content of this is laid down by the Companies Acts and provides a minimum of information. This is because, although the shareholders would use additional information to assess the performance of their investment, the published accounts are also available to competitors and detailed data could give them a real insight into their rivals' strengths and weaknesses.

The version used in this chapter is one based on the published accounts of public limited companies, but with additional information where this aids understanding. An example is given in Table 30.4

The sections of an income statement

Income statements have three sections. Each one gives a different total profit figure.

The trading account

This shows how **gross profit** (or loss) has been made from the trading activities of the business.

It is most important to understand that, as not all sales are for cash in most businesses, the **revenue** figure is not the same as cash received by the business. This point is covered in more detail later. The formula for calculating total revenue is: selling price × quantity sold. Therefore, if 120 items are sold at $2 each, the revenue is $240.

	Revenue	3,060	
(minus)	Cost of sales	(1,840)	Trading account
(equals)	Gross profit	1,220	
(minus)	Overheads/expenses	(580)	
(equals)	Operating profit (formerly net profit)	640	
(minus)	Interest	(80)	Profit and loss section
(equals)	Profit before tax	560	
(minus)	Tax @ 20%	(112)	
(equals)	Profit for the year	448	
(minus)	Dividends to shareholders	200	Appropriation account
(equals)	Retained earnings	248	

Table 30.4 Income statement for Energen plc for the year ended 29 March 2013

This figure is unlikely to be the same as the total value of goods purchased by the company during this period as items may have been added to stocks or taken from them. Only the goods used and sold during the year will be recorded in **cost of sales**.

The formula used is:

cost of sales = opening stocks plus purchases minus closing stocks

This can be laid out as:

Opening stocks (at the start of the year)	$500
Purchases during the year	$2,500
Total stock (available for sale)	$3,000
Closing stocks (at the end of the year)	($750)
Cost of goods sold	$2,250

ACTIVITY 30.1

Calculating gross profit

[16 marks, 16 minutes]

1 Calculate gross profit for Cosy Corner Retailers Ltd for the financial year ending 31 October 2013. Show all of your workings.

- 1,500 items sold for $5 each
- opening stocks were valued at $500
- purchases totalled $3,000
- closing stocks were $1,000. [5]

2 Explain **two** reasons why you think it is important for any business to make a profit. [6]

3 Cambridge Boxes Ltd sold 3,500 units in the last financial year ending 31 December 2013. The selling price was $4. Opening stocks were 200 boxes. The business purchased 4,000 boxes during the year. All boxes cost the company $2 each. Calculate the value of closing stocks and the company's gross profit in 2013. [5]

Profit and loss account section

This section of the income statement calculates both the **operating profit** (or profit before interest and tax) and the **profit for the year** (profit after tax) of the business.

KEY TERMS

Operating profit (formerly referred to as net profit): gross profit minus overhead expenses.

Profit for the year (profit after tax): operating profit minus interest costs and corporation tax.

You will recall from Chapter 29 that overheads are costs or expenses of the business that are not directly related to the number of items made or sold. These can include rent and business rates, management salaries, lighting costs and depreciation. Operating profit (sometimes referred to as net profit) is the profit made before tax and interest have been subtracted, but after all costs of sales and overheads have been deducted from revenue. Limited companies pay corporation tax on their profits before they pay dividends or keep profits within the business.

Appropriation account

This final section of the income statement (which is contained in the IFRS 'statement of comprehensive income') shows how the profit for the year of the company is distributed between the owners – in the form of **dividends** to company shareholders – and as **retained earnings** or profit.

KEY TERMS

Dividends: the share of the profits paid to shareholders as a return for investing in the company.

Retained earnings (profit): the profit left after all deductions, including dividends, have been made, this is 'ploughed back' into the company as a source of finance.

The uses of income statements

The information contained in income statements can be used in a number of ways:

- It can be used to measure and compare the performance of a business over time or with other firms – and ratios can be used to help with this form of analysis (see pages 452–456).
- The actual profit data can be compared with the expected profit levels of the business.
- Bankers and creditors of the business will need the information to help decide whether to lend money to the business.
- Prospective investors may assess the value of putting money into a business from the level of profit being made.

All of these users of profit data need to be aware of the limitations of accounting data referred to in the final section of this chapter. In addition, they should also consider the quality of the profit being recorded. For example, a high profit figure resulting from the sale of a valuable asset for more than its expected value might not be repeatable and is, therefore, said to be **low-quality profit**. Profits made from developing, producing and selling exclusive product designs, however, are **high-quality profits** because these are likely to be a continuous source of profit for some time to come.

ACTIVITY 30.2

Calculating profit

Rodrigues buys second-hand computers, updates and cleans them and then sells them in his small shop, Rodrigues Traders. He has many customers who are keen to buy computers at prices below those charged for new machines. Rodrigues took out a bank loan to buy his shop – he has since repaid half of this loan. He employs three electricians to help him with the computer work. He is the main shareholder in the business – three of his friends also invested in the company when it was first set up.

	$
Revenue (4,000 items @ $3 each)	12,000
Cost of goods sold (@ $1 per item)	4,000
Gross profit	U
Overhead expenses	3,000
Operating profit	V
Interest	1,000
Profit before tax	X
Corporation tax @ 20%	800
Profit for the year	Y
Dividends paid	1,200
Retained earnings (profit)	Z

Income statement for Rodrigues Traders plc for the year ending 31 October 2013

[17 marks, 25 minutes]

1. Calculate the missing values *U–Z* for the different types of profit for Rodrigues Traders.   [5]

2. State **three** stakeholders in this business who would be interested in these profit figures.   [3]

3. For each stakeholder group identified, explain why the profits of this business are important.   [9]

Low-quality profit: one-off profit that cannot easily be repeated or sustained.

High-quality profit: profit that can be repeated and sustained.

The Statement of financial position – what it shows about a business

The **Statement of financial position** is still sometimes referred to as the balance sheet but IFRS rules led to a name-change for this important account. It records the net wealth or shareholders' equity of a business at one moment in time. In a company this net wealth belongs to the shareholders. The aim of most businesses is to increase the **shareholders' equity** by raising the value of the businesses **assets** more than any increase in the value of **liabilities**. Shareholders' equity comes from two main sources:

■ The first and original source was the capital originally invested in the company through the purchase of shares. This is called **share capital**.

■ The second source is the retained earnings of the company accumulated over time through its operations. These are sometimes referred to as reserves, which is rather misleading as they do not represent reserves of cash.

In this book the emphasis is on the content and structure of the Statements of financial position of limited companies, not those of sole traders or partnerships.

Statement of financial position (balance sheet): an accounting statement that records the values of a business's assets, liabilities and shareholders' equity at one point in time.

Shareholders' equity: total value of assets – total value of liabilities.

Asset: an item of monetary value that is owned by a business.

Liability: a financial obligation of a business that it is required to pay in the future.

Share capital: the total value of capital raised from shareholders by the issue of shares.

Table 30.5 shows an example of a Statement of financial position with some explanatory notes, which do not appear in companies' published accounts. The figures have been presented in three columns to help understanding of how subtotals are arrived at. In published accounts, all figures will be presented in one column.

Non-current assets: assets to be kept and used by the business for more than one year. Used to be referred to as 'fixed assets'.

Intangible assets: items of value that do not have a physical presence, such as patents, trademarks and current assets.

Current assets: assets that are likely to be turned into cash before the next balance-sheet date.

Inventories: stocks held by the business in the form of materials, work in progress and finished goods.

Trade receivables (debtors): the value of payments to be received from customers who have bought goods on credit.

Current liabilities: debts of the business that will usually have to be paid within one year.

Accounts payable (creditors): value of debts for goods bought on credit payable to suppliers; also known as 'trade payables'.

Non-current liabilities: value of debts of the business that will be payable after more than one year.

Points to note:

■ Companies have to publish the income statement and the Statement of financial position for the previous financial year as well in order to allow easy comparison. These have not been included in the above examples for reasons of clarity.

■ The titles of both accounts are very important as they identify both the account and the company.

■ Whereas the income statement covers the whole financial year, the Statement of financial position is a statement of the estimated value of the company at one moment in time – the end of the financial year.

TOP TIP

Questions that involve the interpretation or analysis of accounts will use the Statement of financial position format used in this book or a very similar one. The horizontal format will not be used.

Non-current or fixed assets

The most common examples of fixed assets are land, buildings, vehicles and machinery. These are all tangible assets as they have a physical existence. Businesses can also own intangible assets – these cannot be seen but still have value in the business. Examples are:

■ patents
■ trademarks
■ copyrights
■ goodwill.

	$m	$m	Notes
ASSETS			
Non-current (fixed) assets:			
Property	300		
Vehicles	45		
Equipment	67		
Intangible assets	30		
	442		
Current assets:			
Inventories	34		
Trade receivables (formerly debtors)	28		
Cash	4		Also called 'cash and cash equivalents'.
	66		
TOTAL ASSETS		508	This total will balance with equity and liabilities – hence the original term 'balance sheet'.
EQUITY AND LIABILITIES			
Current liabilities:			
Accounts payable (or creditors)	42		
Short-term loans	31		These loans will include the company's overdraft with the bank. Other current liabilities might include provisions to pay tax and dividends.
	73		
Non-current liabilities:			These used to be referred to as 'long-term liabilities'.
Long-term loans	125		Other non-current liabilities might include debentures issued by the company.
	125		
TOTAL LIABILITIES	198		If these actually equalled total assets, there would be no shareholders' equity in the company at all.
Shareholders' equity:			
Share capital	200		
Retained earnings reserve	110		The cumulative value of the company's annual 'retained earnings/profits'.
	310		
TOTAL EQUITY AND LIABILITIES		508	This does balance with total assets!

Table 30.5 Example of a Statement of financial position with some explanatory notes

These items make up what is known as the '**intellectual property**' of the business. They can give a business a greater market value than the total value of its tangible assets less its liabilities. These intangible assets can be very important for an IT-based or knowledge-based business. The reputation and prestige of a business that has been operating for some time also give value to the business over and above the value of its physical assets. This is called the **goodwill** of a business and should normally only feature on a Statement of financial position just after it has been purchased for more than its assets are worth, or when the business is being prepared for sale. At other times, goodwill will not appear on company accounts – it is 'written off' as soon as possible if it has been included in the purchase of another company. This is because business reputation and good name can disappear very rapidly, for example with a scare over products that risk consumers' health.

Disputes can arise between accountants about the valuation of intangible assets and there is a current debate regarding the asset value of well-known brand names. There is scope for varying the value of these and other intangibles on the Statement of financial position in order to give a better picture of the company's position. This is one aspect of window-dressing of accounts that can reduce the objectivity of published accounts.

Current assets

These are very important to a business, as will be seen when liquidity is assessed later in this chapter. The most common examples are inventories, trade receivables (debtors who have bought goods on credit) and cash/bank balance.

Current liabilities

Typical current liabilities include accounts payable (suppliers who have allowed the business credit), bank overdraft and unpaid dividends and tax.

ACTIVITY 30.3

Understanding Statements of financial position (balance sheets)

[10 marks, 10 minutes]

Copy this table and indicate in which category the following items would appear on a company Statement of financial position.

[10]

	Non-current (fixed) tangible assets	Non-current (fixed) intangible assets	Current assets	Current liabilities	Non-current liabilities	Shareholders' equity
Company car						
Work in progress						
Four-year bank loan						
Accounts payable						
Issued share capital						
Dividends owed to shareholders						
Value of patents						
Trade receivables						
Retained earnings						
Cash in bank						

Working capital

You will recall this concept from Chapter 28 and it can be calculated from the Statement of financial position by the formula: current assets – current liabilities. It can also be referred to as net current assets.

Shareholders' equity

This is sometimes referred to as shareholders' funds. It represents the capital originally paid into the business when the shareholders bought shares (share capital) or the retained earnings/profits of the business that the shareholders have accepted should be kept in the business. These are also known as reserves. Other reserves can also appear on the Statement of financial position if a company believes that its fixed assets have increased in value (revaluation reserve) or if it sells additional shares for more than their 'nominal' value (share premium reserve). Shareholders' equity is the permanent capital of the business – it will not be repaid to shareholders (unless the company ceases trading altogether), unlike loans that are repaid to creditors.

The most common misunderstanding regarding reserves is to believe that they are 'cash reserves' that can be called upon as a source of finance. They are not. Retained earnings arise due to profits being made that are not paid out in tax or dividends, but they have nearly always been invested back into the business by being used to purchase additional assets. They are, therefore, no longer available as a source of liquid funds. The only cash funds available in the business are those indicated under 'cash' in the current assets section.

Non-current liabilities (long-term liabilities)

These are the long-term loans owed by the business. These are due to be paid over a period of time greater than one year and include loans, commercial mortgages and debentures. As will be seen in the next chapter, the value of non-current assets compared to the total capital employed by the business is a very important measure of the degree of risk being taken by the company's management.

Other information in published accounts

Apart from the three main accounting statements, other information is required by law to be included in company published accounts. Some of the most important sections are:

1 The cash-flow statement

This is the third and final main account published in the annual report and accounts. As its name suggests, it focuses not on profit or net worth but on how the company's cash position has changed over the past year.

KEY TERM

Cash-flow statement: record of the cash received by a business over a period of time and the cash outflows from the business.

These statements, therefore, indicate where the company's cash has come from during the year – and how it has been spent. By focusing on cash – or liquidity – these statements help managers realise why a profitable business might be running out of cash. Perhaps a substantial capital investment has been undertaken or goods have been sold but trade receivables are being given much longer to pay for them. These statements indicate why a loss-making business could be 'cash rich'. Perhaps a loan has recently been taken out, trade receivables have paid back more quickly than usual or investors have made new capital injections. The following worked example helps understanding:

Worked example – cash-flow statement: M and G Taxis Ltd made a profit of $200,000 last year. Mike and Gina LaRochelle were, therefore, surprised to find that, at the end of the year, their business had a bank overdraft. The company's accountant explained to them that they had bought new taxis during the year costing $50,000. In addition, the company had repaid a long-term loan and several major business clients had delayed the payment of their accounts. The accountant showed them the following simplified cash-flow statement to indicate the difference between the profit made and the cash position of the business:

Operating profit	200
less increase in trade receivables	(60)
less purchase of new fixed assets	(50)
less repayment of loan	(100)
Net change in cash	[10]

M and G cash-flow statement for year ending 31 December 2013 ($000)

This example of a cash-flow statement is shown in order to increase understanding. No questions will be set in AS/A Level Business Studies that require a worked example of this statement.

2 The Chairman's Statement

This is a general report on the major achievements of the company over the past year, the future prospects of the business and how the political and economic environment might affect the company's prospects.

3 The Chief Executive's Report

This is a more detailed analysis of the last financial year, often broken down by area of main product divisions. Major new projects will be explained and any closures or rationalisation that occurred will also be briefly referred to.

4 The Auditors' Report

This is the report by an independent firm of accountants on the accuracy of the accounts and the validity of the accounting methods used. If there are no problems with the accounts, the auditors will state that the accounts give a 'true and fair view' of the business's performance and current position. If there are real concerns, then the auditors will 'qualify' their report with details of points of disagreement between themselves and the business management over how the accounts were drawn up.

5 Notes to the accounts

The main accounts contain only the basic information needed to assess the position of the company. They do not contain precise details, such as the types of individual fixed assets, the main long-term loans or the depreciation methods used. These and other details are contained at the end of the annual report and accounts in the 'notes to the accounts'.

Introduction to accounting ratio analysis

How much can we tell about a company's performance by studying the published accounts? It is easy to compare one

---

ACTIVITY 30.4

Mauritius Telecom

Study the simplified version of the 2012 Statement of financial position for Mauritius Telecom as at 31 December 2012 (millions Mauritian Rupees).

	2012	2011
Non-current assets	8,868	8,649
Current assets:		
Inventories	372	321
Trade receivables and other receivables	1,779	1,795
Cash and cash equivalents	4,786	5,261
Total current assets	6,937	7,379
TOTAL ASSETS	**15,805**	**16,028**
Total non-current liabilities	1,020	2,083
Total current liabilities	5,974	4,678
Shareholders' capital and reserves (shareholders' equity)	8,811	9,267
TOTAL EQUITY AND LIABILITIES	**15,805**	**16,028**

[30 marks, 45 minutes, plus research time]

1 Explain what is meant by the following terms:
   a 'trade receivables' [3]
   b 'inventories' [3]
   c 'current assets' [3]
   d 'shareholders equity' [3]

2 Explain why it is important to stakeholders of Mauritius Telecom to be provided with two years of Statement of financial position values in the published accounts. Try to make references to some of the major changes in the data in your answer. [10]

Research task: Use the Internet to research the latest year's accounts from Mauritius Telecom, www.mauritiustelecom.com (or another plc of your choice). Read the Chairman's Statement, the Report of Directors, and the Auditors' Report. How useful do you think these reports would be to:

■ shareholders
■ workers in the company
■ any other stakeholder group?

Explain your answers. [12]

year's profit figure with the previous year. Changes in sales revenue can also be identified – so too can differences from one year to the next in current assets, current liabilities and shareholders' equity. Similar comparisons can be made between different companies too. However, in making these comparisons, one essential problem arises. Look, for example, at these company results from two printing firms:

	2013 Operating profit ($000)
Nairobi Press Ltd	50
Port Louis Press Ltd	500

How much can we tell about the performance of these two companies from these results? Is Port Louis Press more successful than Nairobi Press? Are the managers of Nairobi Press less effective? Are the companies becoming more profitable? Would they make good investments for future shareholders? Are the strategies adopted by Port Louis Press much more successful than those of Nairobi Press?

The answer to all of these questions is the same – we cannot tell from the information given. The only correct statement that can be made is that one company (Port Louis Press) made an operating profit ten times greater than that of the other company.

Now look at other information about these two businesses:

	2013 Revenue ($000)
Nairobi Press Ltd	250
Port Louis Press Ltd	3,200

These additional data begin to give us a more detailed picture of the performance of these two businesses in 2013 especially if we compare the data above with the earlier profit results. Which management team has been more effective at converting sales revenue into profit? Accountants make this assessment by relating two accounting results to each other in the form of a ratio. These ratios are grouped into five main groups, but at AS Level only two of these groups of ratios are studied:

1 **Profitability ratios:** These include the profit margin ratios, which compare the profits of the business with revenue (AS Level), and the return on capital employed ratio, which compares operating profit with capital employed in the business (A Level).
2 **Liquidity ratios:** These give a measure of how easily a business could meet its short-term debts or liabilities.

All other ratios are studied at A Level and are explained in Chapter 35.

Profit margin ratios

These are used to assess how successful the management of a business has been at converting sales revenue into both gross profit and operating profit. They are widely used to measure the performance of a company – and, therefore, by implication, the performance of the management team too.

Using the two businesses referred to above (all figures for 2013):

	Gross profit $000	Revenue $000	Gross profit margin
Nairobi Press Ltd	125	250	$\frac{125}{250} \times 100 = 50\%$
Port Louis Press Ltd	800	3,200	$\frac{800}{3,200} \times 100 = 25\%$

Points to note:
Port Louis Press's gross profit margin could be lower because it is adopting a low-price strategy to increase sales or because it has higher cost of sales. This could be the result of higher material costs or higher direct labour costs compared with Nairobi Press. Perhaps the management of this company is less effective in controlling costs than that at Port Louis.

Port Louis Press's gross profit margin could be increased by reducing the cost of sales, while maintaining revenue – say, by using a cheaper supplier – or by increasing revenue without increasing cost of sales – say, by raising prices but offering a better service.

The **gross profit margin** is a good indicator of how effectively managers have 'added value' to the cost of sales.

> **KEY TERM**
>
> **Gross profit margin:** This ratio compares gross profit (profit before deduction of overheads) with revenue.
> $$\text{gross profit margin } \% = \frac{\text{gross profit}}{\text{revenue}} \times 100$$

It is misleading to compare the ratios of firms in different industries because the level of risk and gross profit margin will differ greatly.

Using the same two businesses (all figures for 2013):

	Operating profit $000	Revenue $000	Operating profit margin
Nairobi Press Ltd	50	250	$\frac{50}{250} \times 100 = 20\%$
Port Louis Press Ltd	500	3,200	$\frac{500}{3,200} \times 100 - 15.6\%$

Points to note:

The profitability gap between these two businesses has narrowed. Whereas the difference in gross profit margins was substantial, the **operating profit margins** are much more alike. This suggests that Nairobi has relatively high overheads (impacting on lower net or operating profit) compared with sales, when contrasted with Port Louis.

Port Louis could narrow the gap further by reducing overhead expenses while maintaining sales or by increasing sales without increasing overhead expenses.

As with all ratios, a comparison of results with those of previous years would indicate whether the performance and profitability of a company were improving or worsening. This would give a more complete analysis of the level of management performance.

The operating profit margin – and the trend in this ratio over time – is a good indicator of management effectiveness at converting revenue into profit after all costs and expenses, other than finance costs, before tax and dividends.

TOP TIP

Many students state that to 'increase profit margins the business should increase sales'. This is a poor answer **unless** sales revenue can be increased at a greater rate than the costs of the business.

KEY CONCEPT LINK

The profitability ratios are a very important way for **management** and shareholders to measure the value created by a business. A declining trend in these profitability ratios over time would suggest that the business is becoming less effective in '**creating value**'. Management will always attempt to introduce **strategies** that increase 'created value' – but will also have to consider the objectives of the stakeholder groups.

See Table 30.6 for an evaluation of ways to increase profit margins.

TOP TIP

Many questions will ask for methods of increasing profitability of a business. If the question needs an evaluative answer, it is very important that you consider at least **one** reason why your suggestion might not be effective.

Liquidity ratios

These ratios assess the ability of the firm to pay its short-term debts. They are an important measure of the short-term financial health of a business. They are not concerned with profits, but with the working capital of the business. If there is too little working capital, then the business could become illiquid and be unable to settle short-term debts. If it has too much money tied up in working capital, then this could be used more effectively and profitably by investing in other assets.

KEY TERM

Liquidity: the ability of a firm to pay its short-term debts.

Current ratio

This compares the current assets with the current liabilities of the business.

KEY TERM

$$\text{Current ratio} = \frac{\text{current assets}}{\text{current liabilities}}$$

The result can either be expressed as a ratio (2:1, for example) or just as a number (for example, 2). There is no particular result that can be considered a universal and reliable guide to a firm's liquidity. Many accountants recommend a result of around 1.5–2, but much depends on the industry the firm operates in and the recent trend in the current ratio. For instance, a result of around 1.5 could be a cause of concern if, last year, the current ratio had been much higher than this.

All figures as at 31 December 2013 ($000)			
	Current assets	Current liabilities	Current ratio
Nairobi Press Ltd	60	30	$\frac{60}{30} = 2$
Port Louis Press Ltd	240	240	$\frac{240}{240} = 1$

Method to increase profit margins	Examples	Evaluation of method
Increase gross and operating profit margin by reducing direct costs	1 Using cheaper materials, e.g. rubber not leather soles on shoes. 2 Cutting labour costs, e.g. relocating production to low-labour-cost countries, such as Dyson making vacuum cleaners in Malaysia. 3 Cutting labour costs by increasing productivity through automation, e.g. Hyundai's production line uses some of the most labour-saving robots in the world. 4 Cutting wage costs by reducing workers' pay.	1 Consumers' perception of quality may be damaged and this could hit the product's reputation. Consumers may expect lower prices, which may cut the gross profit margin. 2 Quality may be at risk; communication problems with distant factories. 3 Purchasing machinery will increase overhead costs (gross profit could rise but operating profit fall), remaining staff will need retraining – short-term profits may be cut. 4 Motivation levels might fall, which could reduce productivity and quality.
Increase gross and operating profit margin by increasing price	1 Raising the price of the product with no significant increase in variable costs, e.g. Mauritius Telecom raising the price of its broadband connections. 2 Petrol companies increasing prices by more than the price of oil has risen.	1 Total profit could fall if too many consumers switch to competitors – this links to price elasticity. 2 Consumers may consider this to be a 'profiteering' decision and the long-term image of the business may be damaged.
Increase operating profit margin by reducing overhead costs	Cutting overhead costs, such as rent, promotion costs or management costs but maintaining sales levels, for example: 1 Moving to a cheaper head office location. 2 Reducing promotion costs. 3 Delayering the organisation.	1 Lower rental costs could mean moving to a cheaper area, which could damage image. 2 Cutting promotion costs could lead to sales falling by more than fixed costs. 3 Fewer managers – or lower salaries – could reduce the efficient operation of the business.

Table 30.6 Evaluation of ways to increase profit margins

Points to note:
From these results it is clear that Nairobi Press is in a more liquid position than Port Louis Press. Nairobi Press has twice as many current assets as current liabilities. For every $1 of short-term debts it has $2 of current assets to pay for them. This is a relatively 'safe' position – indeed, many accountants advise firms to aim for current ratios between 1.5 and 2.0.

The current ratio of Port Louis Press is more worrying. It only has $1 of current assets to pay for each $1 of short-term debt. It could be in trouble in the (unlikely) event that all of its short-term creditors demanded repayment at the same time, especially if some of its current assets could not be converted into cash quickly. For this reason, the next ratio, the acid-test, is often more widely used.

Very low current ratios might not be unusual for businesses, such as food retailers, that have regular inflows of cash that they can rely on to pay short-term debts.

Current ratio results over 2 might suggest that too many funds are tied up in unprofitable inventories, trade receivables and cash and would be better placed in more profitable assets, such as equipment to increase efficiency.

A low ratio might lead to corrective management action to increase cash held by the business. Measures might include: sale of redundant assets, cancelling capital spending plans, share issue, taking a long-term loan.

Acid-test ratio

Also known as the quick ratio, this is a stricter test of a firm's liquidity. It ignores the least liquid of the firm's current assets – inventories (stocks). Inventories, by definition, have not yet been sold and there can be no certainty that they will be sold in the short term. By eliminating the value of inventories from the acid-test ratio, the users of accounts are given a clearer picture of the firm's ability to pay short-term debts.

All figures as at 31/12/13 ($000)	Liquid assets	Current liabilities	Acid-test ratio
Nairobi Press Ltd	30	30	1
Port Louis Press Ltd	180	240	0.75

Points to note:

- Results below 1 are often viewed with caution by accountants as they mean that the business has less than $1 of liquid assets to pay each $1 of short-term debt. Therefore, Port Louis Press may well have a liquidity problem.
- The full picture needs to be gained by looking at previous years' results. For example, if last year Port Louis Press had an acid-test of 0.5, this means that over the past 12 months its liquidity has actually improved and this is more favourable than if its results last year had been 1, showing a decline in liquidity in the current year.
- Firms with very high inventory levels will record very different current and acid-test ratios. This is not a problem if inventory levels are always high for this type of business, such as a furniture retailer. It would be a cause for concern for other types of businesses, such as computer manufacturers, where stocks lose value rapidly due to technological changes.
- Whereas selling inventories for cash will not improve the current ratio – both items are included in current assets – this policy will improve the acid-test ratio as cash is a liquid asset but inventories are not.

See Table 30.7 for an evaluation of ways to improve liquidity.

Limitations of ratio analysis

The benefits of using ratio analysis for investigating firms' profitability and liquidity have been explained. There are some limitations to using these ratios – especially if not combined with other data – to assess business performance in these important areas, however:

1 The four ratios studied give an incomplete analysis of a company's financial position.

2 One ratio result on its own is of very limited value – it needs to be compared with results from other similar businesses and with results from previous years to be more informative.

3 Comparing results with those of other businesses should be done with caution. Different businesses may have slightly different ways of valuing assets and some accounts may have been window-dressed.

4 Poor ratio results only highlight a potential business problem – they cannot by themselves analyse the cause of it or suggest potential solutions to the problem.

5 As noted earlier in the chapter, financial statements can only measure quantitative performance and this is true of the ratios based on them. Other information of a qualitative nature is necessary before the full picture of a company's position and performance can be fully judged.

ACTIVITY 30.5

Is the liquidity of Air Mauritius sufficient?

The following information is taken from Air Mauritius Limited accounts for the year ending 30 September 2013.

- **Current assets:** inventories 15,468; trade and other receivables 65,793; cash and cash equivalents 17,214.
- **Current liabilities:** trade payables 135,921; short-term loans 40,523.

Using this simplified information:

[20 marks, 30 minutes]

1 Calculate the Air Mauritius current ratio. [3]

2 Calculate the Air Mauritius acid-test ratio. [3]

3 Comment on Air Mauritius' liquidity. [6]

4 Why would it be useful to Air Mautitius' stakeholders to have liquidity ratio results for the previous year and for other airline operating companies? [8]

TOP TIP
When commenting on ratio results, it is often advisable to question the accuracy of the data used and the limitations of using just a limited number of ratio results in your analysis.

Internal and external users of accounting information

It is usual to divide the users of accounting information into internal and external users. The managers of a business

Method to increase liquidity	Examples	Evaluation of method
Sell off fixed assets for cash – could lease these back if still needed by the business	■ Land and property could be sold to a leasing company.	■ If assets are sold quickly, they might not raise their true value. ■ If assets are still needed by the business, then leasing charges will add to overheads and reduce operating profit margin.
Sell off inventories for cash (note: this will improve the acid-test ratio, but not the current ratio)	■ Stocks of finished goods could be sold off at a discount to raise cash. ■ JIT stock management will achieve this objective.	■ This will reduce the gross profit margin if inventories are sold at a discount. ■ Consumers may doubt the image of the brand if inventories are sold off cheaply. ■ Inventories might be needed to meet changing customer demand levels – JIT might be difficult to adopt in some industries.
Increase loans to inject cash into the business and increase working capital	■ Long-term loans could be taken out if the bank is confident of the company's prospects.	■ These will increase the gearing ratio (see Chapter 35). ■ These will increase interest costs.

Table 30.7 Evaluation of ways to increase liquidity

ACTIVITY 30.6

How is my business doing?

Mohammed Ahmed is the chief executive of Ahmed Builders plc. The company specialises in the quality fitting out of shops for internationally famous retailers. These customers demand that work is finished to very tight time limits, so it is important for Ahmed Builders to keep stocks of important materials. Mohammed is keen to compare the performance and liquidity of his company with that of another building company that does similar work. He obtained a set of published accounts for Flash Builders plc and used ratios to help him in the comparison. These were the figures he used from both companies.

(All figs $000)	Ahmed	Flash
Gross profit (213)	100	150
Operating profit (2013)	20	60
Revenue (2013)	350	600
Current assets (as at 31/12/13)	100	150
Inventories (as at 31/12/13)	50	60
Current liabilities (as at 31/12/13)	45	120

[46 marks, 1 hour]

1. Calculate **two** profit margin ratios for both companies. Show all working. [6]

2. Comment on the profitability of both businesses. Should Ahmed be pleased about the performance of his business compared to Flash Builders? Explain your answer. [10]

3. Explain and evaluate **two** ways in which Ahmed might attempt to increase the operating profit margin ratio for his business. [10]

4. Calculate two liquidity ratios for both businesses. Show all working. [6]

5. Comment on your results. [6]

6. Explain and evaluate **two** ways in which Flash Builders plc might be able to improve its liquidity position. [8]

---

are termed internal users and they will have access to much more detailed and up-to-date data than other groups. External users include the banks, government, employees and shareholders and other stakeholders of the business. The following lists give details of all users of accounts and the reasons why they need accounting data:

Business managers:

■ to measure the performance of the business to compare against targets, previous time periods and competitors

■ to help them take decisions, such as new investments, closing branches and launching new products

- to control and monitor the operation of each department and division of the business
- to set targets or budgets for the future and review these against actual performance.

Banks:
- to decide whether to lend money to the business
- to assess whether to allow an increase in overdraft facilities
- to decide whether to continue an overdraft facility or a loan.

Creditors, such as suppliers:
- to see if the business is secure and liquid enough to pay off its debts
- to assess whether the business is a good credit risk
- to decide whether to press for early repayment of outstanding debts.

Customers:
- to assess whether the business is secure
- to determine whether they will be assured of future supplies of the goods they are purchasing
- to establish whether there will be security of spare parts and service facilities.

Government and tax authorities:
- to calculate how much tax is due from the business
- to determine whether the business is likely to expand and create more jobs and be of increasing importance to the country's economy
- to assess whether the business is in danger of closing down, creating economic problems
- to confirm that the business is staying within the law in terms of accounting regulations.

Investors, such as shareholders in the company:
- to assess the value of the business and their investment in it
- to establish whether the business is becoming more or less profitable
- to determine what share of the profits investors are receiving
- to decide whether the business has potential for growth
- if they are potential investors, to compare these details with those from other businesses before making a decision to buy shares in a company
- if they are actual investors, to decide whether to consider selling all or part of their holding.

Workforce:
- to assess whether the business is secure enough to pay wages and salaries
- to determine whether the business is likely to expand or be reduced in size
- to determine whether jobs are secure
- to find out whether, if profits are rising, a wage increase can be afforded

- to find out how the average wage in the business compares with the salaries of directors.

Local community:
- to see if the business is profitable and likely to expand, which could be good for the local economy
- to determine whether the business is making losses and whether this could lead to closure.

Shivani's first Statement of financial position

Shivani has been in business for just one year. She is a qualified beauty therapist. Despite lacking experience in accounting, she is determined to save money by trying to draw up her end-of-year accounts herself. The initial attempt to construct a Statement of financial position is shown below.

Assets	
Non-current assets:	
Inventories	15
Equipment	25
Current assets:	
Cash	1
Accounts payable	5
Overdraft	3
Total assets	49

Current liabilities:	
Trade receivables	3
Non-current liabilities:	
Loan	20
Share capital	10
Shareholders' equity:	
Retained earnings	6
Total equity and liabilities	39

Shivani Beauty Salon Ltd, year ending 31 March 2013 ($000)

As you can see, she has not made a very good first attempt. Some assets and liabilities are incorrectly placed and total assets do not equal total equity and liabilities.

[22 marks, 30 minutes]

1   Draw up a correct version of Shivani's Statement of financial position with correct headings, making sure that it finally balances.   [10]

2   Identify **four** stakeholder groups that would be interested in Shivani's Statement of financial position and explain why each would be interested.   [12]

458

Limitations of published accounts

What they do not contain

So all stakeholders in a business have a use for the published accounts of the business, but how effective are these in giving the stakeholders the information they require? It must be remembered that companies will only release the absolute minimum of accounting information, as laid down by company law. Other types of businesses, such as sole traders, do not have to disclose any information at all to the public, but may be asked to provide accounts to their bankers and the tax authorities. Company directors obviously wish to avoid sensitive information falling into the hands of competitors or even pressure groups that could take action against the interests of the business. Obtaining a copy of the published accounts of a public limited company will allow you to see how much disclosure is required by law – and, just as importantly, what is not. Information that does not have to be published in a company's annual report and accounts includes:

- details of the sales and profitability of each good or service produced by the company and of each division or department
- the research and development plans of the business and proposed new products
- the precise future plans for expansion or rationalisation of the business
- the performance of each department or division
- evidence of the company's impact on the environment and the local community – although this social and environmental audit is sometimes included voluntarily by companies
- future budgets or financial plans.

In addition, the data given are all past data for the last financial year and this information could be several months old by the time the accounts are published. Only the internal management of the business will have access to all past accounting records and future plans, presented to them in as much detail as they request, by management accountants.

Are the published accounts really accurate?

Stakeholders are often concerned about the accuracy of the published accounts. This may seem surprising – surely numerical accounting data must be accurate, as it can be checked over and over again? Unfortunately, accounting is not quite as objective as some observers seem to believe. No company can publish accounts that it knows to be deliberately and illegally misleading – they are checked by an independent firm of accountants known as auditors. There is an auditor's report in every published account. However, accounting decisions are not always based on exact science and there are many instances when in compiling accounts it is necessary to use judgement and estimations.

These judgements can often lead to a difference of opinion between accountants, for example over the precise value of unsold goods (stocks) or the value of other assets, especially intangible ones. Where companies attempt to make judgements that present their accounts in a very favourable way, then the accountants could be accused of 'window-dressing' the accounts. This might be done to influence a bank to lend more money to the business or to encourage prospective investors to buy shares in the business. There are several ways in which accountants might boost the short-term performance of a business without actually breaking the law regarding accounting disclosure. Common ways of window-dressing accounts include:

- selling assets, such as buildings, at the end of the financial year, to give the business more cash and improve the liquidity position – these assets could then be leased or rented back by the business
- reducing the amount of depreciation of fixed assets, such as machines or vehicles, in order to increase declared profit and increase asset values
- ignoring the fact that some customers (trade receivables) who have not paid for goods delivered may, in fact, never pay – they are 'bad debts'
- giving stock levels a higher value than they are probably worth
- delaying paying bills or incurring expenses until after the accounts have been published.

For these reasons, published accounts of companies need to be used with considerable caution by stakeholders. They are a useful starting point for investigating the performance of a business, but one set of accounts, on its own, is by no means going to deal with all of the questions that stakeholders want answers to.

 KEY TERM

Window-dressing: presenting the company accounts in a favourable light – to flatter the business performance.

459

Malaysia Tourist Flights Ltd

Leroy is a recently qualified pilot. He has his own small, single-engine aircraft. Having just received his certificate for small-scale, commercial flying he decided to set up his own company offering small groups of tourists one-hour sightseeing flights over Malaysia. He decided to advertise this service by using small leaflets left in hotel reception areas. In his first three months of operation, he had taken 15 groups on air trips. He was surprised to discover, at the end of this period, that he had less money in the bank than at the beginning. Leroy wondered why this was. Was he charging too little? Had he received some unexpected bills or were his running costs higher than expected? He had decided that, after a month of trying to keep his own financial records, he really needed the services of a trained accountant.

Operating from the same tiny airport as Leroy was his best friend, Elvis. He operated a larger aircraft than Leroy and, as well as tourist trips, he ran two scheduled flights a week to Singapore. He has decided to sell his business as he had been offered a job as a commercial-airline pilot with an international airline. Leroy was interested in the business but was surprised by the price Elvis was asking. 'How can you ask that much for your old plane and the limited customer contacts you have?' complained Leroy. He had asked to see Elvis's latest accounts and was surprised to find that there was no allowance made for bad debts, the plane seemed to be overvalued and the profit figure seemed to be based on revenue that had not yet been earned.

Leroy appointed an accountant who was able to advise him on a number of matters:

- Do not buy Elvis's business at the inflated price being asked for it.
- Record petrol costs in the month the fuel is used – not two months later when it is paid for.
- Keep a record of every financial transaction and record each one in the accounting books twice.

These records should enable Leroy to fix an appropriate price for his tourist flights so that he makes a reasonable profit. Leroy is really pleased that he decided to ask for professional help, especially as the company accounts will need to be presented to the government and the other stakeholders.

[27 marks, 40 minutes]

1. Explain to Leroy **three** reasons why it is important for him to keep accurate accounting records for his business. [9]

2. Elvis seems to be window-dressing the accounts for his own business in order to make it seem more successful than it is:
   a. Why is he doing this? [2]
   b. Examine briefly the ways in which he is doing this. [6]

3. In future, how important do you consider Leroy's published accounts will be to stakeholders in the business? Explain your answer. [10]

SUMMARY POINTS

- The contents of the published final accounts of companies are laid down by the Companies Acts of each country.
- Income statements record the trading performance of a business over the previous time period (usually one year), the expenses of the business, corporation tax payable and the appropriation of profits.
- The term 'profit' can have several different meanings, and students must make it quite clear which type of profit calculation is being referred to in answers to questions.
- A Statement of financial position (balance sheet) records the worth of a business at one moment in time – usually the end of the financial year when the accounts are drawn up.
- Assets are items of value that belong to a business – they can either be fixed or current in nature.
- Liabilities are items of value that are owed by the business.
- Shareholders' equity is capital from shareholders including reserves – it is only paid back to them in the event of the business ceasing operations.
- There is an important difference between income statements and cash-flow statements. The latter concentrate on the liquidity of a business – and can explain why the profit or loss of the business will rarely be the same as its current cash-flow position.
- The current ratio and acid-test ratio are used to analyse liquidity and the profit margin ratios are used to analyse the profitability of a business.

RESEARCH TASK

- Obtain the income statements and statements of financial position of **two** well-known public limited companies. Search for them online. If you can, choose two businesses in the same industry.
- Make a table of the two companies' annual revenue, gross profit, operating profit and profit for the latest year.
- Calculate the gross profit margin and the operating profit margin.

AS Level exam practice questions

Short answer questions

[65 marks, 80 minutes]

Knowledge and understanding

1   Explain **two** reasons why an entrepreneur who has just set up a new business should keep a set of accounts.   [2]
2   Explain why it might be even more important for a multinational company to keep accurate accounts.   [2]
3   Outline why managers need more detailed accounts than the external users.   [4]
4   List **three** differences between the work of management accountants and financial accountants.   [3]
5   What is meant by 'window-dressing' accounts?   [3]
6   Explain **two** possible reasons why managers might attempt to window-dress the accounts of a business.   [6]
7   Give **two** reasons, other than window-dressing, why published accounts might not give a full picture of the performance of a business.   [2]
8   Distinguish between an income statement and a cash-flow statement.   [3]
9   What is the difference between gross profit and operating profit?   [2]
10 What are the **two** ways in which profit after tax may be appropriated?   [2]
11 What does a Statement of financial position (balance sheet) show about a business?   [2]
12 What is meant by the 'retained earnings' on a company's accounts?   [2]
13 What is meant by goodwill and why should it be written off the accounts of a business buying another firm, as quickly as possible?   [4]
14 Explain why it is useful to measure a company's liquidity with ratio analysis.   [3]
15 Explain **two** problems associated with accounting ratio analysis.   [4]

Application

16 List **four** likely external users of the accounts of a large plc, such as Microsoft.   [2]
17 Explain why each of these users would find Microsoft's accounts useful.   [8]
18 Explain, with examples, the difference between non-current and current assets for a business such as a restaurant.   [4]
19 Explain how it might be possible for a supermarket's gross profit margin to fall, yet its operating profit margin to increase.   [4]
20 Suggest **three** other pieces of information that an individual considering investing in a limited company in your country might consider important, other than the published annual accounts of that company.   [3]

Data response

1 Highfield Leisure Ltd

The following accounts refer to Highfield Leisure Ltd, which owns and operates several leisure and sports centres. This is a very competitive industry. New competitors have recently been set up and Highfield managers are considering how best to improve company performance during this difficult period.

Income statement	Year ending 31 March 2014 $m	Year ending 31 March 2013 $m
Revenue	320	T
less cost of sales	120	100
Gross profit	U	230
Overhead expenses	150	145
Operating profit	50	85
Interest	10	5
Pre-tax profits	40	V
Tax @ 50%	20	40
Profit for the year	20	40
Dividends	15	15
Retained earnings/ profit	5	25

Key Statement of financial position totals	As at 31 March 2014	As at 31 March 13
Non-current assets	80	75
Current assets		
Inventories	10	15
Trade receivables	25	20
Cash	0.5	2
Total assets	X	112
Current liabilities	30	25
Non-current liabilities	40	46.5
Share capital	30	Y
Retained earnings reserves	15.5	10.5
Total equity and liabilities	Z	112

[30 marks, 45 minutes]

1 a Define the term 'cost of sales'. [2]
  b Briefly explain the term 'operating profit'. [3]

2 Calculate the missing values: *T, U, V, X, Y, Z*. [6]

3 Using the data in any way you consider appropriate, including the use of ratios, analyse *either* the changing profitability *or* liquidity of this business. [8]

4 Evaluate how managers might improve *either* the profitability *or* the liquidity of this business. [11]

2 ADG plc

ADG plc is a large bicycle manufacturing business. It was converted to a public limited company four years ago. Recent expansion has been financed from retained earnings. The business has increased sales of bicycles by 25% over the past two years but revenue has not increased at the same rate. The chief executive officer (CEO) wanted ADG to focus on increasing sales volume to increase market share but prices had to be cut to achieve his ambitious targets. In addition, advertising and promotion were cut back to reduce expenses and this has had a negative impact on the brand image of the company's products. Other expenses such as administration costs and directors' salaries have increased substantially in the past two years. Most of the components for the bicycles are imported.

The CEO has been studying the following summary of ADG's latest accounts:

	2013	2012
Revenue	$32 million	$30 million
Operating profit	$1.6 million	$3 million
Gross profit margin	25%	15%
Non-current liabilities	$45 million	$36 million

[30 marks, 45 minutes]

1 a Define the term 'retained earnings'. [2]

  b Briefly explain the term 'non-current liabilities'. [3]

2 a Calculate the operating profit margin for 2012 and 2013. [3]

  b Comment on the trend in the profit margin ratios. [3]

3 Analyse why and two of ADG's stakeholder groups would find the company's accounts useful. [8]

4 Discuss **two** ways in which this business could become more profitable. [11]

AS Level essay questions

[20 marks, 40 minutes each]

1 a Explain the main purposes of:
   - income statements
   - Statements of financial position. [8]

  b 'The published accounts of a company contain useful information, but they do not give a complete picture of the performance or wealth of the business.' To what extent do you agree with this statement? [12]

2 a Explain the distinction between gross profit, operating (net) profit and retained earnings. [8]

  b The owner of a chain of sports-equipment shops is worried about her business's declining gross profit margin and operating profit margin. Evaluate **three** decisions the owner could take to attempt to increase these profit margin ratios. [12]

31 Forecasting and managing cash flows

This chapter covers syllabus section AS Level 5.5.

On completing this chapter, you will be able to:

- understand the importance of cash to business
- explain the difference between a firm's cash flow and its profit
- structure a cash-flow forecast and understand the sources of information needed for this
- evaluate the problems of cash-flow forecasting
- analyse the different causes of cash-flow problems
- evaluate different methods of solving cash-flow problems.

Introducing the topic

Africa Glasses had been making spectacles for years. The business was in a rut with no sales growth and low profits. The owners recruited a qualified managing director to give new leadership. Jerry Xue did not take long to make changes. He aimed to raise the annual sales revenue from $1 million to $4 million in two years by specialising in fashion sunglasses. New designs were developed. Jerry's contacts within the industry helped him gain big orders from some of the leading retailers. The sunglasses sold for high prices. These large orders were profitable but there was a big problem: the biggest firms were the slowest payers. The big retailers expected several months of credit. They also demanded such high standards that some production had to be scrapped.

Jerry started to worry about the firm's cash position. Suppliers were demanding payment. The bank overdraft had reached record levels. Overtime working by staff to complete orders on time took cash out of the business. Then Jerry discovered that his bookkeeper had not included tax or transport costs in the monthly cash-flow forecast – the business had even less money than he thought.

Friday the 13th was a bad day for Jerry. A department-store buyer was visiting in the morning and the bank manager was due in the afternoon. Midway through the day, he learnt that the main glass-lens machine had broken down and a major supplier had refused the latest order for materials. Within weeks, the assets of the business had been sold off and the people and firms owed money by Africa Glasses received a fraction of what they were owed.

Points to think about:

- As the business is profitable, how could Africa Glasses run out of cash?
- How useful would an accurate forecast of cash flows have been to Jerry?
- What could Jerry have done to improve the cash position of Africa Glasses?
- Do you think it is possible for a business to expand too quickly?

Introduction

The Africa Glasses case study allows us to see the importance of **cash flow** to all businesses – even those that claim to be making a profit. Profit does not pay the bills and expenses of running a business – but cash does. Of course, profit is important – especially in the long term when investors expect rewards and the business needs additional finance for investment. Cash is always important – short and long term. Cash flow relates to the timing of payments to workers and suppliers and receipts from customers. If a business does not plan the timing of these payments and receipts carefully it may run out of cash even though it is operating profitably. If suppliers and creditors are not paid in time they can force business owners into **liquidation** of the business's assets if it appears to be **insolvent**.

 KEY TERMS

Cash flow: the sum of cash payments to a business (inflows) less the sum of cash payments (outflows).

Liquidation: when a firm ceases trading and its assets are sold for cash to pay suppliers and other creditors.

Insolvent: when a business cannot meet its short-term debts.

464

So cash flow is certainly important – especially to small business start-ups. Cash-flow planning is vital for entrepreneurs because:

- new business start-ups are often offered much less time to pay suppliers than larger, well-established firms – they are given shorter credit periods
- banks and other lenders may not believe the promises of new business owners as they have no trading record, they will expect payment at the agreed time
- finance is often very tight at start-up, so not planning accurately is of even more significance for new businesses.

Clearly, the consequences of not having a suitable level of cash in the business can be very serious – or even life-threatening for that business.

Cash and profit – what's the difference?

For many failed business owners there was no difference between cash and profit – which is why their business collapsed. All successful entrepreneurs and business managers, in contrast, understand that these two financial concepts do not have the same meaning or significance for a business – especially a newly formed one. It is very common for profitable businesses to run short of cash. On the other hand, loss-making businesses can have high **cash inflows** in the short term. The essential difference between cash and profit can be explained with three simple examples:

Example 1: Jhumpa buys fresh fish from a market every day. She pays cash to the traders and gets a good deal because of this. She sells all of her stock on a high-street stall to shoppers who also pay her cash.

- In a typical week Jhumpa buys fish costing $1,000 and sells it for $2,000.
- How much profit does she make in a typical week (ignore other costs)? $1,000.
- What was the difference between her cash inflows and **outflows** in a typical week? $1,000 too – as all purchases and sales were in cash.
- In this very simplified example, cash = profit at the end of the week (but we have ignored other expenses too).

KEY TERMS

Cash inflows: payments in cash received by a business, such as those from customers (trade receivables) or from the bank, e.g. receiving a loan.

Cash outflows: payments in cash made by a business, such as those to suppliers and workers.

Example 2: Shula owns Fine Foods, a specialist delicatessen. Last month she bought $500 of fresh goods from a supplier who offers her one month's credit.

The goods sold very slowly during the month and she was forced to cut her prices several times. Eventually she sold them all for only $300, paid in cash by her customers.

- What was her profit or loss (ignoring all other costs)? A loss of $200 – because even though she has not yet paid for the goods they are still recorded as a cost.
- What was the difference between her cash outflow and inflow? A positive inflow $300 – because she has not paid the supplier yet. So Shula has a positive cash flow from these goods this month even though she made a loss on them.
- Cash was not the same as profit for this business.

Example 3: Sanjit is concerned about competition for his jewellery shop. He buys most of his stock over the Internet for cash – but has decided to increase the credit terms he gives to his customers to two months. Last month he bought some rings for $3,000 and paid in cash. He sold them all in the same month for $7,000– yet will not receive payment until two months' time.

- How much profit did he make on these rings? $4,000 – the rings have been sold and revenue recorded from the sale even though no cash payment has been made.
- What was Sanjit's cash-flow position from these deals? A negative outflow of $3,000 – he may be very short of cash until he receives payment from his customers.
- Cash was not the same as profit for this business – and there is a real danger that it could run out of cash to pay its everyday costs, such as wages and rent.

TOP TIP
When given the opportunity, emphasise the importance of having enough cash in the short term. Profit can wait to be earned in the long term – but cash payments are always being made.

How to forecast cash flow

Forecasting cash flow means trying to estimate future cash inflows and cash outflows, usually on a month-by-month basis. Let's take the case of Mohammed, an entrepreneur planning to open a car-valeting service aiming to offer car cleaning to individual customers and owners of car fleets, such as taxi firms.

Forecasting cash inflows

Where to start? The business owner will probably attempt to forecast cash inflows first. Some of these will be easier to forecast than others. Here are some example cash inflows and how they might be forecast:

- **Owner's own capital injection:** This will be easy to forecast as this is under Mohammed's direct control.

- **Bank loan payments:** These will be easy to forecast if they have been agreed with the bank in advance, both in terms of amount and timing.
- **Customers' cash purchases:** These will be difficult to forecast as they depend on sales, so a sales forecast will be necessary – but how accurate might this be?
- **Trade receivables payments:** These will be difficult to forecast as these depend on two unknowns. First, what is the likely level of sales on credit and, second, when will trade receivables actually pay? One month's credit may have been agreed with them, but payment after this period can never be guaranteed.

Forecasting cash outflows

Again, some of these will be much easier to forecast than others. Here are some example cash outflows and how they might be forecast:

- Lease payment for premises – easy to forecast as this will be in the estate agent's details of the property.
- Annual rent payment – easy to forecast as this will be fixed and agreed for a certain time period. The landlord may increase the rent after this period, however.
- Electricity, gas, water and telephone bills – difficult to forecast as these will vary with so many factors, such as the number of customers, seasonal weather conditions and energy prices.
- Labour-cost payments – these forecasts will be based largely on demand forecasts and the hourly wage rate that is to be paid. These payments could vary from week to week if demand fluctuates and if staff are on flexible contracts.
- Variable cost payments such as cleaning materials – the cost of these should vary consistently with demand, so revenue forecasts could be used to assess variable costs too. How much credit will be offered by suppliers? The longer the period of credit offered, the lower the start-up cash needs of the business will be.

TOP TIP

Never fall into the trap of referring to forecasts as actual accounts – they are financial planning estimates that are dealing with the future. There is always considerable uncertainty over the accuracy of **cash flow forecasts** because of this.

The structure of cash-flow forecasts

Due to the crucial importance of cash as the lifeblood of any successful business, all firms should engage in cash-flow forecasting. This helps to identify cash-flow problems – before it is too late. A simplified cash-flow forecast is shown in Table 31.1. It is based on Mohammed's car-valeting service. Although there are different styles of

presenting this information, all cash-flow forecasts have three basic sections:

Section 1 – Cash inflows: This section records the cash payments to the business, including cash sales, payments for credit sales and capital inflows.

Section 2 – Cash outflows: This section records the cash payments made by the business, including wages, materials, rent and other costs.

Section 3 – Net monthly cash flow and opening and closing balance: This shows the net cash flow for the period and the cash balances at the start and end of the period – the opening cash balance and the closing cash balance. If the closing balance is negative (shown by a figure in brackets), then a bank overdraft will almost certainly be necessary to finance this.

TOP TIP

The layout of actual cash flow forecasts can vary slightly so be prepared for the main classifications to be in a different order. Essentially, all cash flow forecasts record the same basic predictions.

KEY TERMS

Cash-flow forecast: estimate of a firm's future cash inflows and outflows.

Net monthly cash flow: estimated difference between monthly cash inflows and cash outflows.

Opening cash balance: cash held by the business at the start of the month.

Closing cash balance: cash held at the end of the month becomes next month's opening balance.

ACTIVITY 31.1

Think of another likely cash payment that could be received by a business and one more cash payment made by a business.

What does the forecast in Table 31.1 tell Mohammed about the prospects for his business? In cash terms, the business appears to be in a good position at the end of four months. This is because:

- in April the closing cash balance is positive, so the bank overdraft has been fully repaid
- there was only one month – the first month of operation – in which the monthly net cash flow was negative
- the monthly net cash flow is increasing each month.

CASH INFLOWS	All figures in $000	JAN	FEB	MAR	APR
	Owner's capital injection	6	0	0	0
	Cash sales	3	4	6	6
	Payments by trade receivables	0	2	2	3
	Total cash in	9	6	8	9
CASH OUTFLOWS					
	Lease	8	0	0	0
	Rent	1	1	1	1
	Materials	0.5	1	3	2
	Labour	1	2	3	3
	Other costs	0.5	1	0.5	1.5
	Total cash out	11	5	7.5	7.5
NET CASH FLOW	**Net monthly cash flow**	(2)	1	0.5	1.5
	Opening balance	0	(2)	(1)	(0.5)
	Closing balance	(2)	(1)	(0.5)	1

Table 31.1 Mohammed's cash-flow forecast for the first four months (figures in brackets are negative)

However, never forget that these are only forecasts and the accuracy of the cash-flow forecast will depend greatly on how accurate Mohammed was in his demand, revenue and material-cost forecasts.

467

ACTIVITY 31.2

April cash flow

[8 marks, 8 minutes]

Draw up a revised cash-flow forecast for April assuming:
- cash sales are forecast to be $1,000 higher
- materials are forecast to be $500 higher
- other costs are forecast to be $1,000 higher. **[8]**

What uses does this type of financial planning have?

There are several important advantages to cash-flow forecasting, especially for new businesses: by showing periods of negative cash flow, plans can be put in place to provide additional finance, for example arranging a bank overdraft or preparing to inject more owner's capital.

If negative cash flows appear to be too great, then plans can be made for reducing these – for example, by cutting down on purchase of materials or machinery or by not making sales on credit, only for cash.

A new business proposal will never progress beyond the initial planning stage unless investors and bankers have access to a cash-flow forecast – and the assumptions that lie behind it.

Cash-flow forecasting – what are the limitations?

Although an entrepreneur should take every reasonable step to increase the accuracy of the business cash-flow forecast – by using relevant market research, for example – it would be foolish indeed to assume that it will always be accurate. So many factors, either internal to the business or in the external environment, can change to blow a cash-flow forecast off course. This does not make forecasts useless – but, as with any business forecast, they must be used with caution and the ways in which the cash flows have been estimated should be understood. Here are the most common limitations of them:

- Mistakes can be made in preparing the revenue and cost forecasts or they may be drawn up by inexperienced entrepreneurs or staff.
- Unexpected cost increases can lead to major inaccuracies in forecasts. Fluctuations in oil prices can lead to the cash-flow forecasts of even major airlines being misleading.
- Wrong assumptions can be made in estimating the sales of the business, perhaps based on poor market research, and this will make the cash inflow forecasts inaccurate.

Fashion-shop forecasts look good

'I have stood outside some of these fashion shops for hours counting the number of people coming out with their carrier bags and I am convinced my sales forecasts are OK,' announced Sayuri to her business partner, Korede. They were both putting the finishing touches to their business plan for an exclusive 'top brands only' fashion store in the city. Sayuri's primary research was not the only evidence they had used in arriving at the sales forecasts and the cash inflow forecasts. Some desk research on the Internet had also revealed the rapid growth of high-income consumer numbers spending increasing amounts on expensive clothing.

Cash-outflow forecasts had been based on estimates of electricity and telephone usage. Korede had found what he thought was a suitable shop, so they knew how much the rent would be. They would pay themselves a salary of $2,000 a month each initially. Other labour costs were less certain. Should they employ full-time salaried staff or part-time hourly wage employees? The cost of buying the clothes was also uncertain. There would be no problem if they sold all the suits and dresses that they bought in – but how likely was that? And what would happen to cash-flow forecasts if stock was left unsold and huge price reductions had to be advertised? Whatever the uncertainties, both Sayuri and Korede realised why they had to construct a cash-flow forecast for their business plan. The almost completed forecast is shown below:

CASH INFLOWS	All figures in $000	APRIL	MAY	JUNE	JULY
	Owners' capital injection	28	0	0	0
	Cash sales	6	8	12	9
	Payments by trade receivables (e.g. credit card companies)	0	2	2	3
	Total cash in	34	10	14	12
CASH OUTFLOWS					
	Lease	18	0	0	0
	Rent	2	2	2	2
	Clothes purchases	6	4	3	4
	Labour	3	3	4	3
	Other costs	6.5	2	2.5	1.5
	Total cash out	35.5	11	11.5	y
NET CASH FLOW	Net monthly cash flow	x	(1)	2.5	z
	Opening balance	0	(1.5)	(2.5)	0
	Closing balance	(1.5)	(2.5)	0	1.5

[30 marks, 45 minutes]

1 Complete the cash-flow forecast by inserting values for x, y and z. [3]

2 Analyse **two** problems of drawing up a cash-flow forecast, which Sayuri and Korede may have experienced. [6]

3 The first three months' actual trading was poor and cash sales were 20% below forecast. Draw up a new cash-flow forecast for July assuming 20% lower cash sales, 20% lower clothes purchases, an opening cash balance of ($2,000) and all other factors remaining unchanged. [7]

4 To what extent would drawing up a cash-flow forecast increase the chances of this business being successful? [14]

The causes of cash-flow problems

Lack of planning

Cash-flow forecasts help greatly in predicting future cash problems for a business. This form of financial planning can be used to predict potential cash-flow problems so that business managers can take action to overcome them in plenty of time. What might happen without cash-flow forecasts?

> **TOP TIP**
>
> Cash-flow forecasts do not solve cash-flow problems by themselves – but they are an essential part of financial planning and can help prevent cash-flow problems from developing.

Poor credit control

The credit-control department of a business keeps a check on all customers' accounts – who has paid, who is keeping to agreed credit terms and which customers are not paying on time. If this credit control is inefficient and badly managed, then trade receivables will not be 'chased up' for payment and potential **bad debts** will not be identified.

KEY TERMS

Credit control: monitoring of debts to ensure that credit periods are not exceeded.

Bad debt: unpaid customers' bills that are now very unlikely to ever be paid.

Allowing customers too long to pay debts

In many trading situations, businesses will have to offer trade credit to customers in order to be competitive. Assume a customer has a choice between two suppliers selling very similar products. If one insists on cash payment 'on delivery' and the other allows two months' trade credit, then customers will go for credit terms because it improves their cash flow. However, allowing customers too long to pay means reducing short-term cash inflows, which could lead to cash-flow problems.

Expanding too rapidly

When a business expands rapidly, it has to pay for the expansion and for increased wages and materials months before it receives cash from additional sales. This **overtrading** can lead to serious cash-flow shortages – even though the business is successful and expanding.

KEY TERM

Overtrading: expanding a business rapidly without obtaining all of the necessary finance so that a cash-flow shortage develops.

ACTIVITY 31.4

[6 marks, 8 minutes]

Using your knowledge of finance from Chapter 28, what sources of finance could a small business with ambitious expansion plans use to prevent cash-flow problems arising? [6]

Every day this truck is off the road reduces the cash inflows for the transport company

Unexpected events

A cash-flow forecast can never be guaranteed to be 100% accurate. Unforeseen increases in costs – a breakdown of a delivery van that needs to be replaced, or a dip in predicted sales income, or a competitor lowering prices unexpectedly – could lead to negative net monthly cash flows.

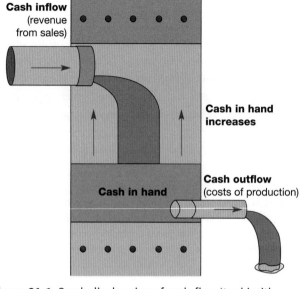

Figure 31.1 Symbolic drawing of cash-flow 'tank' with leakages and injections of cash

ACTIVITY 31.5

Taxi firm's cash flow

[8 marks, 8 minutes]

How would the following events be likely to affect the cash flow of a taxi-operating company:

- increase in oil prices
- increased unemployment
- lower train fares [8]

KEY CONCEPT LINK

Although 'cash flow' is not a key concept, maintaining an adequate cash flow to avoid liquidation of the business is an important objective for any **management** team. External changes can be a major cause of cash-flow problems for a business. For example, an economic recession or a new competitor with innovative technology could both lead to reduce demand and poor cash inflows.

TOP TIP

If you suggest 'cutting staff and using cheaper materials', this may reduce cash outflows, but what will be the negative impact on output, sales and future cash inflows? This suggestion will nearly always be inappropriate for a question on improving cash flow.

Ways to improve cash flow

There are two main ways to improve net cash flow:

1. increase cash inflows
2. reduce cash outflows (see Figure 31.1).

Care needs to be taken here – the aim is to improve the cash position of the business, not sales revenue or profits. These are different concepts. For example, a decision to advertise more in order to increase sales, which will eventually lead to increased cash flows, will make the short-term cash position worse as the advertising has to be paid for.

See Tables 31.2 and 31.3 for methods of increasing cash inflows and reducing cash outflows.

TOP TIP

Remember: just writing 'the firm should increase sales' does not demonstrate true understanding of the difference between sales revenue and cash flow.

Trade receivables

Trade receivables can be managed in many different ways:

- **Not extending credit to customers – or extending it for shorter time periods:** Will they still buy from this business? Will a major aspect of this business's marketing mix have been removed?

  Evaluation of this approach: Many customers now expect credit and will go elsewhere if it is not offered. So the marketing department might argue for an increase in credit terms to customers at the same time as the finance department is trying to cut down on them.

- **Selling claims on trade receivables to specialist financial institutions acting as debt factors:** These businesses will 'buy' debts from other concerns that have an immediate need for cash.

  Evaluation of this approach: This will involve a cost, however, as the factors will not pay 100% of the value – they must make a profit for themselves.

- **By being careful to discover whether new customers are creditworthy:** This can be done by requiring references – from traders or from the bank is common, or by using the services of a credit enquiry agency.

- **By offering a discount to clients who pay promptly:** Although cash might be paid quickly, discounts reduce the profit margin on a sale.

Method	How it works	Possible drawbacks
Overdraft	Flexible loans on which the business can draw as necessary up to an agreed limit.	■ Interest rates can be high – there may be an overdraft arrangement fee. ■ Overdrafts can be withdrawn by the bank and this often causes insolvency.
Short-term loan	A fixed amount can be borrowed for an agreed length of time.	■ The interest costs have to be paid. ■ The loan must be repaid by the due date.
Sale of assets	Cash receipts can be obtained from selling off redundant assets, which will boost cash inflow.	■ Selling assets quickly can result in a low price. ■ The assets might be required at a later date for expansion. ■ The assets could have been used as collateral for future loans.
Sale and leaseback	Assets can be sold, e.g. to a finance company, but the asset can be leased back from the new owner.	■ The leasing costs add to annual overheads. ■ There could be loss of potential profit if the asset rises in price. ■ The assets could have been used as collateral for future loans.
Reduce credit terms to customers	Cash flow can be brought forward by reducing credit terms from, say, two months to one month.	■ Customers may purchase products from firms that offer extended credit terms.
Debt factoring	Debt-factoring companies can buy the customers' bills from a business and offer immediate cash – this reduces risk of bad debts too.	■ Only about 90–95% of the debt will now be paid by the debt-factoring company – this reduces profit. ■ The customer has the debt collected by the finance company – this could suggest that the business is in trouble.

Table 31.2 Ways to increase cash inflows and their possible drawbacks

Method	How it works	Possible drawbacks
Delay payments to suppliers (creditors)	Cash outflows will fall in the short term if bills are paid after, say, three months instead of two months.	■ Suppliers may reduce any discount offered with the purchase. ■ Suppliers can either demand cash on delivery or refuse to supply at all if they believe the risk of not being paid is too great.
Delay spending on capital equipment	By not buying equipment, vehicles, etc. cash will not have to be paid to suppliers.	■ The efficiency of the business may fall if outdated and inefficient equipment is not replaced. ■ Expansion becomes very difficult.
Use leasing, not outright purchase, of capital equipment	The leasing company owns the asset and no large cash outlay is required.	■ The asset is not owned by the business. ■ Leasing charges include an interest cost and add to annual overheads.
Cut overhead spending that does not directly affect output, e.g. promotion costs	These costs will not reduce production capacity and cash payments will be reduced.	■ Future demand may be reduced by failing to promote the products effectively.

Table 31.3 Ways to reduce cash outflows and their possible drawbacks

Creditors or trade payables

Credit from suppliers can be managed in two main ways:

1 **Increasing the range of goods and services bought on credit:** If a business has a good credit rating, this may be easy, but in other circumstances it is difficult.

   Evaluation of this approach: The danger is that an unpaid creditor may refuse to supply and this will cause production hold-ups. In addition, discounts from suppliers for quick cash payment might be given up.

2 **Extend the period of time taken to pay:** The larger a business is, the easier it is to extend the credit taken. This will improve the larger firm's working capital.

   Evaluation of this approach: Slow payment by larger businesses is often a great burden for small businesses that supply them. Suppliers may be reluctant to supply products or to offer good service if they consider that a business is a 'late payer'.

> **KEY TERM**
>
> **Creditors:** suppliers who have agreed to supply products on credit and who have not yet been paid.

Inventory

Inventory can be managed in the following ways:

- keeping smaller inventory levels
- using computer systems to record sales – and, therefore, inventory levels – and ordering as required
- efficient inventory control, inventory use and inventory handling so as to reduce losses through damage, wastage and shrinkage
- just-in-time inventory ordering – by producing only when orders have been received, working capital tied up in inventories will be minimised. Getting goods to customers as quickly as possible will speed up the receipt of payment. The evaluation of this approach was given in Chapter 24.

Cash

Cash can be managed by:

- use of cash-flow forecasts – as identified above, these can help the management of cash flows and working capital needs
- wise use or investment of excess cash
- planning for periods when there might be too little cash and arranging for overdraft facilities from the bank to avoid a liquidity crisis.

A permanent increase in working capital

When businesses expand, they generally need higher inventory levels and will sell a higher value of products on credit. This increase in working capital (see Chapter 28) is likely to be permanent, so long-term or permanent sources of finance will be needed, such as long-term loans or even share capital.

Working capital conclusions

- There is no 'correct' level of working capital for all businesses. Business requirements for working capital will depend on a number of factors, especially the length of the working capital cycle. For example, supermarkets can manage on a much lower level of working capital than a shipbuilding business.
- Too much liquidity is wasteful.
- Too little liquidity can lead to business failure.
- Managing working capital is not just about looking after cash. Clearly the timings of cash received and spent are important but other features of management are important too – efficient operations management will reduce wastage of resources (and money) and cut inventory levels. Efficient marketing will help to speed up the sale of goods – and, therefore, the cash inflows from this.

ACTIVITY 31.6

Cash flow drying up for Indian small firms

Madhu Gupta has a problem. His company, Mojj Engineering Systems, makes large-scale equipment for food and chemical plants. His customers keep ringing up and saying: 'We don't need the equipment yet – hold it in stock,' 'Can we have an extra discount?' or even 'We will only buy it if you give us credit.'

'Three months back we had no idea things could happen as quickly as this,' said Madhu. 'It was too sudden to prepare for it.' He was, of course, complaining about the global recession and the speed with which it has hit many businesses.

Madhu has already paid cash for all of his raw materials. Completed machines are filling up the yard in his factory. He will not get the money back for materials bought, or for labour costs, until he delivers these machines and is paid for them. The finance the business was planning to use for expansion to a new factory is now being used to pay for the increase in working capital.

[24 marks, 30 minutes]

1 Explain the term 'working capital'. [3]

2 Explain why Madhu is finding it so difficult to control his working capital. [9]

3 Evaluate three ways in which Madhu could try to reduce the finance tied up in working capital. [12]

472

SUMMARY POINTS

- The difference between cash and profit is very important.
- A profitable business can run out of cash.
- It is important to know the sources of data for cash-flow forecasts.
- The structure of a typical cash-flow forecast includes cash inflows, cash outflows, net cash flows and opening and closing balances.
- Cash-flow forecasts can be amended on the basis of the new information.
- The usefulness and accuracy of cash-flow forecasts can be evaluated.
- Cash-flow problems arise when businesses have insufficient net cash flow.
- There are several causes of business cash-flow problems.
- A business attempt to overcome cash-flow problems in different ways and these can be evaluated.

RESEARCH TASK

- Investigate the causes for recent business failures in your country and investigate businesses that seem to be 'in trouble' – use newspapers and Internet searches.
- Most of these failures of business problems are likely to be caused by poor cash flow.
- How did the businesses attempt to solve the problem of too little cash?
- Why did you think they were unable to solve the problem?

AS Level exam practice questions

Short answer questions

[39 marks, 50 minutes]

Knowledge and application

1 Outline **two** reasons why businesses should prepare cash-flow forecasts. [4]

2 State **two** factors that could make a cash-flow forecast inaccurate. [2]

3 What is meant by 'monthly net cash flow'? [2]

4 What is meant by 'closing cash balance'? [2]

5 How can sale and leaseback of fixed assets improve business cash flow? [3]

6 If cash-flow forecasts can be made inaccurate by actual events, is there any purpose to them? [4]

7 How could a business vary its trade receivables/ creditor policy to improve its cash-flow position? [4]

8 How does a cash-flow forecast assist a business in planning its finance requirements? [3]

Application

9 Explain why a bank manager would be particularly keen to see a cash-flow forecast in the business plan of a new business when it is applying for a loan. [3]

10 What particular problems would a new business have in establishing a cash-flow forecast? [4]

11 Why might a business that operates in a fast changing market – such as consumer electronics – have problems accurately forecasting cash inflows and outflows? [4]

12 Explain why a can manufacturer that operates in a very competitive market experience problems when trying to manage trade receivables more efficiently? [4]

Data response

1 Setting up in business

Asif Iqbal was disappointed to hear the news that the Central Bank had announced an unexpected increase in interest rates. He had just submitted his business plan to the bank manager for approval for the business start-up loan and overdraft arrangement he would need to establish his proposed building business. The business was to specialise in building house extensions. Asif had read that the Central Bank had taken the decision to raise interest rates to prevent further increases in inflation – the rate at which prices were rising. Asif's business plan had contained the following cash-flow forecast for the first six months of trading (all figures in $000):

	March	April	May	June	July	August
Cash receipts						
Capital injection	5,000	0	0	0	0	0
Start-up loan	15,000	0	0	0	0	0
Cash sales	1,000	3,000	5,000	5,000	16,000	19,000
Payments from trade receivables	0	12,000	10,000	10,000	12,000	13,000
Total cash in	21,000	15,000	15,000	15,000	28,000	32,000
Cash payments						
Capital expenditure	10,000	0	0	0	0	0
Labour	2,000	6,000	7,000	7,000	7,000	7,000
Materials	5,000	10,000	8,000	8,000	10,000	12,000
Overheads inc. interest	5,000	7,000	7,000	7,000	9,000	9,000
Total cash out	22,000	23,000	22,000	22,000	26,000	28,000
Net cash flow	(1,000)	(8,000)	(7,000)	(7,000)	2,000	4,000
Opening cash balance	0	(1,000)	(9,000)	(16,000)	(23,000)	(21,000)
Closing cash balance	(1,000)	(9,000)	(16,000)	(23,000)	(21,000)	(17,000)

[30 marks, 45 minutes]

1 a Define the term 'net cash flow'. [2]
   b Briefly explain the term 'closing cash balance'. [3]
2 Explain **two** ways in which the increase in interest rates could have an impact on the cash-flow forecast. [6]
3 Analyse **four** ways in which Asif might reduce the negative cash flows of his business in the first six months. [8]
4 Discuss the usefulness to Asif of constructing the cash-flow forecast as part of the business plan. [11]

2 Gita Fashions Ltd

The bank manager had just been on the telephone to Gita. The bank was not prepared to pay a cheque she had written to her main supplier. 'Did you know that your overdraft has reached its limit of $15,000?' the bank manager had queried. 'We are only prepared to consider continuing with your overdraft arrangement if you come into the office tomorrow with a cash-flow forecast for the next three months.'

Gita had never worried too much about finance because this had always been looked after by her business partner. He had recently left the business, taking his share of the capital with him. Gita had used her savings to help pay him his share of the business. Now she had no idea how the business had reached such a poor cash position and she certainly could not put any more money in herself.

All that evening she looked over the accounting records of the business, including all recent sales invoices and bills for materials and other expenses. She had managed to arrive at some idea of what the business could expect over the next three months in terms of cash payments and receipts. Sales were likely to be $12,000 for the next two months (starting in July) and 50% lower than this in the third month. Half of these sales would be for cash. Half would be on one month's credit. She had sold $8,000 on credit in June.

She estimated all overhead expenses to be $6,000 per month. Labour was likely to be $3,000 per month. Materials, paid for one month after delivery, were always one half of that month's sales. They were delivered in the same month in which the goods they were used to make were sold. Opening cash balance was negative – the overdraft was the opening balance for the three-monthly period.

[30 marks, 45 minutes]

1 a Define the term 'cash flow forecast'. [2]

  b Briefly explain the term 'opening cash balance'. [3]

2 Prepare a three-month cash-flow forecast for Gita's business starting in July. [6]

3 a Would you advise the bank manager to increase the overdraft limit? Explain your answer. [4]

  b What additional information would help you to advise the bank manager? [4]

4 Evaluate whether, if Gita had prepared a cash-flow forecast, her business would have avoided the problem it now faces. [11]

AS Level essay questions

[20 marks, 40 minutes each]

1 a Explain how a profitable business might run out of cash. [8]

  b Evaluate the importance of cash-flow forecasting to a business experiencing rapid expansion. [12]

2 a Explain the importance of cash-flow forecasting to a new entrepreneur. [8]

  b Evaluate **three** ways in which a house-building company, operating in a very competitive market, might try to improve its poor cash-flow position. [12]

32 Costs (A Level)

On completion of this chapter you will be able to:

- understand the differences between full and contribution costing
- apply the technique of contribution costing
- evaluate situations in which contribution costing would and would not be used
- apply contribution costing to 'accept/reject' order decisions
- solve numerical problems involving costing methods.

Introducing the topic

HOW MUCH DOES THE GYM ACTUALLY COST?

The Africa Spa Resort is a popular tourist attraction. It has four main divisions: spa and beauty, hotel and restaurant, pool, gymnasium.

The business is profitable and recorded an operating profit of $4.5 million last year. However, Chris Jordan, the CEO, believes that the gym should be closed because, as he told a recent board meeting: 'According to my estimates, if we closed the gym we would increase the profits of the resort by $0.25 million each year.'

The data he used is shown below:

2013 $m	Spa and beauty	Hotel and restaurant	Pool	Gymnasium
Revenue	5	7	3	4
Direct costs	2.75	4	2	3.25
Share of overhead costs	1	1	0.5	1

Points to think about:

- Why is it important to differentiate between direct and overhead costs?
- Do you agree with Chris Jordan that the profit of the resort would increase if the gym was closed? Justify your reasoning.

Introduction

Managers need to know, as accurately as possible, the cost of each product or service produced by the firm. One reason for this is the need to make pricing decisions. Managers may also need to decide whether production should be stopped, increased or switched to new methods or new materials. It would be foolish to think about any of these decisions unless accurate costings were made first. Managers also need to compare actual costs with original targets or budgets and to compare the current period with past time periods. Therefore, accurate product-cost information is vital and the different approaches to calculating the cost of a product or service will now be considered.

Costing methods – a major problem

In calculating the cost of a product, both direct labour and direct materials should be easy to identify and allocate or charge to each product. For instance, the materials used in making Product X are allocated directly to the cost of that product. These are not the only costs involved, of course. Overheads, or indirect costs, cannot be allocated directly to particular units of production but must be 'shared' between all of the items produced by a business. There is more than one way of sharing or apportioning these costs and, therefore, there may be more than one answer to the question: 'How much does a product cost to produce?' This uncertainty causes potential problems when pricing products, when deciding whether to continue producing it and when deciding whether to accept a new order for the product.

Costing methods: important concepts

Before studying the alternative costing methods, four important concepts need to be understood.

1 Cost centres

Examples of **cost centres** are:

- in a manufacturing business: products, departments, factories, particular processes or stages in the production, such as assembly
- in a hotel: the restaurant, reception, bar, room letting and conference section
- in a school: different subject departments.

Different businesses will use different cost centres that are appropriate to their own needs.

KEY TERM

Cost centre: a section of a business, such as a department, to which costs can be allocated or charged.

2 Profit centres

Examples of **profit centres** are:

- each branch of a chain of shops
- each department of a department store
- in a multi-product firm, each product in the overall portfolio of the business.

KEY TERM

Profit centre: a section of a business to which both costs and revenues can be allocated – so profit can be calculated.

So, why divide operations into cost and profit centres? If an organisation is divided into these centres, certain benefits are likely to be gained:

- Managers and staff will have targets to work towards – if these are reasonable and achievable, this should have a positive impact on motivation.
- These targets can be used to compare with actual performance and help identify those areas performing well and not so well.
- The individual performances of divisions and their managers can be assessed and compared.
- Work can be monitored and decisions made about the future. For example, should a profit centre be kept open or should the price of a product be increased?

There are some problems with using these centres, however. These include:

- Managers and workers may consider their part of the business to be more important than the whole organisation

itself. There could be damaging competition between profit centres to gain new orders.

- Some costs – indirect costs – can be impossible to allocate to cost and profit centres accurately and this can result in arbitrary and inaccurate overhead-cost allocations.
- Reasons for good or bad performance of one particular profit centre may be due to external factors not under its control.

TOP TIP

You may be asked to evaluate the usefulness of dividing a business into profit centres.

3 Overheads

They are usually classified into four main groups:

1. **Production overheads:** These include factory rent and rates, depreciation of equipment and power.
2. **Selling and distribution overheads:** These include warehouse, packing and distribution costs and salaries of sales staff.
3. **Administration overheads:** These include office rent and rates, clerical and executive salaries.
4. **Finance overheads:** These include the interest on loans.

4 Unit cost

This is the average cost of producing each unit of output:

$$\text{unit cost} = \frac{\text{total cost of producing this product}}{\text{number of units produced}}$$

A firm produces 20,000 desks at a total cost of \$1,000,000. Unit cost is \$1,000,000 divided by \$20,000 = \$50. Clearly, unit cost is an essential step towards pricing the desks.

Full costing technique

Using this method – also known as absorption costing – accountants calculate the total overheads incurred by the business and share or 'apportion' them on the basis of one or more methods of allocation. For example, total overheads could be divided between products and cost centres on the basis of the proportion of total direct labour costs that each accounts for. Alternatively, factory and administration overheads could be apportioned

KEY TERM

Full costing: a method of costing in which all fixed and variable costs are allocated to products, services or divisions of a business.

477

to products on the basis of the proportion of factory or office space taken up by each product or service. Example: Heath Electronics Ltd (see Activity 32.1) total direct labour amounts to $220,000. The pump accounts for $150,000 (68%) of this total and the fan for $70,000 (32%). Total overheads are $200,000. If these overheads are allocated on the basis of the proportion of total labour costs incurred by both products, then a full costing statement will look like the example in Table 32.1. Full costing therefore means that 'all of the costs' of the business have been allocated to the products, services or divisions of the business.

	Pump ($)	Fan ($)
Direct materials	100,000	150,000
Direct labour (Total = $220,000)	150,000 (68.2% of $220,000)	70,000 (31.8% of $220,000)
Apportioned overheads	68.2% of $200,000	31.8% of $200,000
	136,400	63,600
Total or Full cost	386,400	283,600

Table 32.1 Full costing statement

ACTIVITY 32.1

Heath Electronics Ltd

The firm produces two product ranges, a pump for central-heating systems and an extractor fan. Both products pass through three process cost centres during their manufacture, although different equipment is used for each product. The direct labour and material costs have been identified and allocated to the two products as outlined opposite.

The management accountant has been asked for the full cost of both products. This will allow the unit cost to be calculated. In 2013, 50,000 pumps and 40,000 fans were produced.

	Pump ($000)	Fan ($000)
Machining department:		
Direct materials	100	150
Direct labour	40	10
Assembly department:		
Direct labour	80	40
Testing department:		
Direct labour	30	20
Total direct cost	250	220

The total overheads of the business in 2013 were:

	$000
Rent and rates	60
Power	20
Administration	80
Depreciation	40
Total overheads	200

[26 marks, 35 minutes]

1 Calculate the total direct labour costs for:
   a pump production [3]
   b fan production. [3]

2 Calculate the total direct labour cost for both products. [2]

3 Express, as a proportion of total direct labour costs:
   a the direct labour cost of the pump
   b the direct labour cost of the fan. [4]

4 Divide the total overhead costs between the pump and the fan in proportion to the use of direct labour in producing each product. [6]

5 Calculate total costs for each product. [4]

6 Calculate the unit cost of producing each product, based on this full costing approach. [4]

478

Full costing – an evaluation

- Full costing is relatively easy to calculate and understand – unless each overhead cost is absorbed by using a different basis, which makes the process more complex.
- Full costing is particularly relevant for single-product businesses as there is no uncertainty about what share of overheads should be allocated to which product.
- All costs are allocated (compared with contribution costing) so no costs are 'ignored'.
- Full costing is a good basis for pricing decisions in single-product firms – if the full unit cost is calculated, this could then be used for mark-up pricing.

However:

- There is no attempt to allocate each overhead cost to cost/profit centres on the basis of actual expenditure incurred. For example, a product may take up a large proportion of factory space but use low-cost and easy-to-maintain machinery. Should all overheads be allocated on the basis of factory space?
- Arbitrary methods of overhead allocation can lead to inconsistencies between departments and products.
- It is sometimes dangerous to use this cost method for making decisions, because the cost figures arrived at can be misleading. See the section on 'Contribution costing and decision-making'.
- If full costing is used, it is essential to allocate on the same basis over time; otherwise sensible year-on-year comparisons cannot be made.
- The full unit cost will only be accurate if the actual level of output is equal to that used in the calculation. A fall in output will push up the allocated overhead costs per unit.

Contribution or marginal costing

> **KEY TERM**
>
> **Contribution or marginal costing:** costing method that allocates only direct costs to cost/profit centres, not overhead costs.

This approach to costing solves the problem of deciding on the most appropriate way to apportion or share out overhead costs – it does not apportion them at all. Instead, the method concentrates on two very important accounting concepts.

1 Marginal cost which, as we have seen, is the cost of producing an extra unit. This extra cost will clearly be a variable direct cost. For example, if the total cost of producing 100 units is $400,000 and the total cost of producing 101 units is $400,050, the marginal – or extra – cost is $50.

2 The contribution of a product is the revenue gained from selling a product less its marginal (variable direct) costs. This is not the same as profit, which can only be calculated after overheads have also been deducted. For example, if that 101st unit with a marginal cost of $50 is sold for $70,

it has made a contribution towards fixed costs of $20. The unit contribution is found as the difference between the sale price ($70) and the marginal cost ($50), i.e. $20.

ACTIVITY 32.2

[17 marks, 25 minutes]

The direct cost of each hotel guest at the Seaview hotel is $15 per night. The hotel manager has estimated that the average overhead cost per guest is $10 per night, based on 100 guest nights per week. The room price is $50 per night.

1 What is the total unit cost per guest per night? [1]

2 What is the contribution per guest per night? [2]

3 Calculate the total overhead costs per week. [2]

4 Calculate the profit made in one week with 100 guest nights. [2]

5 A large group of 50 people have asked to spend one night at the hotel during a week when only 30 other guests are booked. The group of 50 has offered to pay a price of $20 each. Discuss whether the manager should accept this offer. [10]

ACTIVITY 32.3

479

Cost centres at school

[12 marks, 15 minutes]

1 Identify and list **four** possible cost centres within your own school or college. Discuss with the managers or heads of these cost centres the benefits and drawbacks of using this form of organisation. Check with your bursar/college accountant the accuracy of your answer. [4]

2 Explain the difference between a cost centre and a profit centre. [4]

3 Explain whether any of the cost centres identified in question 1 above are, in fact, profit centres. Explain your answer. [4]

Contribution costing and decision-making

Contribution costing has very important advantages over full costing when management plans to take important decisions based on cost data. An example contribution-costing statement is shown in Table 32.2.

As can be seen, this statement avoids apportioning overhead costs between these two products. Overheads cannot be ignored altogether, however. They are needed to calculate the profit or loss of the business:

- Total contribution for Cambridge Printers Ltd = $15,000
- If total overheads amounted to $12,000, then: profit = contribution less overheads.
- Therefore, the business has made a profit of $3,000.

This link between contribution to overheads and profit is a crucial one and you can see the role of contribution costing in pricing decisions if you read the pricing section in Chapter 18.

Should a firm stop making a product?

If a business makes more than one product or provides more than one service, marginal costing shows managers which product or service is making the greatest or least contribution to overheads and profit. If full costing were used instead, a manager could decide to stop producing a good that seemed to be making a loss, even though it might still be making a positive contribution. In cases such as this, ending the production of a good making a positive contribution will reduce the overall profits of the business. This is because the fixed overhead costs will still have to be paid – but there will be reduced contribution to pay them. Activity 32.4 – some of which has been worked out for you – illustrates this point.

Should a business accept a contract or a purchase offer at below full cost?

If a firm has spare capacity or if it is trying to enter a new market segment, marginal or contribution costing assists managers in deciding whether to accept an order at below the full cost of the product or service. Hotels often offer very low rates to customers in off-peak seasons, arguing that it is better to earn a contribution from additional guests than to leave rooms empty.

 KEY CONCEPT LINK

It might appear to be unwise to accept an order or contract that does not immediately create additional **value** for the business, but as long as additional **contribution** can be earned then this could be the best decision – especially if it leads to further future orders that create further value.

ACTIVITY 32.4

Should Product Z be dropped?

An electrical assembly firm produces three products. The following data (in $) are available:

Products	X	Y	Z
Different labour costs	5	7	9
Different materials costs	4	12	10
Selling price	20	30	21
Current annual output (units)	500	1,000	400

Total overhead costs are $10,000. The company currently uses full costing and each product is apportioned a proportion of overheads on the basis of floor space taken up: X–30% Y–50% Z–20%

[20 marks, 35 minutes]

1. Calculate the unit contribution of each product:

   Answer: X = $20 – $9 = $11
   Calculate the unit contribution of Y and Z. **[4]**

2. If annual output is all sold, calculate the total contribution of each product.

   Answer: X = 500 × $11 = $5,500
   Calculate the total contribution of Y and Z. **[4]**

3. Calculate the profit or loss made by each product using full costing at the current output level.

   Answer: X: Total contribution = $5,500. Allocated overheads = 30% of $10,000 = $3,000
   Total profit on Product X is $5,500 – $3,000 = $2,500

   Calculate the profit or loss made by Y and Z. **[6]**

4. Calculate the impact on the total profit of the business if production of Product Z is stopped. (Do not forget that the overhead costs allocated to product Z will still have to be paid.) **[6]**

	Novel	Textbook
$000		
Sales revenue	50	100
Direct materials	15	35
Direct labour	20	50
Other direct costs	10	5
Total direct costs	45	90
Contribution	5	10

Table 32.2 Marginal-costing/contribution statement for Cambridge Printers Ltd

If contracts are accepted or customers gained by using prices below full unit cost, this can, in certain circumstances, lead to an increase in the total profits of the business. This is because the fixed overhead costs are being paid anyway and if an extra contribution can be earned, profits will increase. There are dangers in this policy, however:

■ Existing customers may learn of the lower prices being offered and demand similar treatment. If all goods or services being sold by a business are sold at just above marginal cost, then this could make earning a profit very unlikely.

■ When high prices are a key feature in establishing the exclusivity of a brand, then to offer some customers lower prices could destroy a hard-won image.

■ Where there is no excess capacity, sales at contribution cost may be losing sales based on the full cost price.

■ In some circumstances, lower-priced goods or services may be resold into the higher-priced market.

In fact, many businesses do use contribution-cost pricing, but try to make sure that there is no leak into the higher-priced market. For example, railway companies sell Saver and Supersaver tickets, but make the offers exclusive by banning their use for certain days, times or journeys. Gas and electricity companies use time bands for cheaper-priced use of energy.

The following example illustrates this principle of using marginal costing in accepting new business.

Example: Yelena is a dressmaker who pays $45 a day to use a workshop. This covers all the fixed costs of her small business. She makes three dresses a day and sells them for $30 each. Materials cost her $8 a dress. So unit costs per dress using full costing are:

Fixed costs per dress	$15
Material cost	$8
Unit cost	$23

ACTIVITY 32.5

Bureau Office Supplies Ltd

The marketing director was determined to gain a large order for computer desks from a major local authority. There was spare capacity on the production line as a recent contract had just been cancelled. The buyer wanted to purchase 1,000 desks at a price of $70 each. Bureau's marketing director knew this was a price lower than that offered to most of their customers. The order was being discussed at a board meeting and the production manager presented the following cost data:

Computer desks full unit cost statement	
Direct labour	$25
Direct materials	$30
Apportioned overheads	$30
Full unit cost	$85

The production manager was amazed at the willingness of the marketing department to sell the desks for $70

each. 'How can you possibly justify selling these desks at a total loss of $15,000?' he asked. Who has the better case? Is the marketing director justified in his attempt to capture this order? Is the production manager right to be concerned at the apparent loss the order will make? The appropriate answer depends on the following factors:

■ Does the order make a contribution to overheads by the price exceeding direct costs?

■ Is there spare capacity?

■ Can the order be accepted without further overhead expenditure – e.g. a special machine needed just to make goods for this order?

■ Are other orders likely?

■ Is there another customer who is prepared to pay a higher price for these goods?

■ Will the price of the order become known to other customers?

[25 marks, 35 minutes]

1 Use the contribution/marginal-costing approach to calculate whether the new order will add to the profits of the business or not. **[10]**

2 Prepare a brief report, containing your marginal-costing statement, to the board, together with a recommendation on whether to accept the order or not. Consider both quantitative and qualitative factors in coming to your recommendation. **[15]**

ACTIVITY 32.6

Onyx Garages

The managing director of Onyx Garages Ltd is concerned about the profitability of the business. She asked for cost details of the three divisions of the business – repairs, petrol sales and spare parts – together with a breakdown of sales revenue. Unaware of the differences between costing approaches, she asked for overheads to be apportioned on full-cost principles according to labour cost. The following data were provided. When the managing director saw these details, she said, 'If we close down our repair division, then total annual profits will rise – they would have been $15,000 higher last year if we had shut down repairs in 2008.'

Overall profit made by the business in 2009 = (55,000 + 6,000) – 15,000 = $46,000.

As a trainee accountant working with this company, you have been asked for your opinion on the figures.

2013 ($000s)	Repairs	Petrol	Parts
Revenue (A)	27	300	68
Direct labour cost	15	25	10
Direct materials	5	180	35
Other direct costs	4	10	5
Apportioned overheads (total $60,000)	18	30	12
Total cost (B)	42	245	62
Profit/(Loss) (A–B)	(15)	55	6

[20 marks, 35 minutes]

1 Use the contribution- or marginal-costing method and produce a new costing statement. **[10]**

2 Do you agree with the managing director that the repairs division should be closed in order to increase overall garage profits? Justify your answer with both quantitative and qualitative reasons. **[10]**

One day she has orders for only two dresses. Today a new customer telephoned and wants to buy a dress but will only pay $20. Should she accept this order? Surely she will make a loss on this dress?

If she does *not* accept the order, she will make a loss of $1 today: $(2 \times \$30) - (2 \times \$8 + \$45)$

If she *does* accept the order, she will make a profit of $11: $(2 \times \$30 + \$20) - (3 \times \$8 + \$45)$

TOP TIP
Fixed costs have to be paid whether the factory or workshop is busy or not.

TOP TIP
Even though a positive contribution can be made by accepting an order, there are real dangers that other customers will find out that a lower price is being offered on a particular contract. Qualitative factors are important too.

Contribution costing – a summary

- Overhead costs are not allocated to cost centres, so contribution costing avoids inaccuracies and arbitrary allocations of these costs.
- Decisions about a product or department are made on the basis of contribution to overheads – not 'profit or loss' based on what may be an inaccurate full-cost calculation.
- Excess capacity is more likely to be effectively used, as orders or contracts that make a positive contribution will be accepted.

However:

- By ignoring overhead costs until the final calculation of the business's profit or loss, contribution costing does not consider that some products and departments may actually incur much higher fixed costs than others. In addition, single-product firms have to cover the fixed costs with revenue from this single product, so using contribution costing is unlikely to be so appropriate.
- It emphasises contribution in decision-making. It may lead managers to choose to maintain the production of goods just because of a positive contribution – perhaps a brand new product should be launched instead that could, in time, make an even greater contribution.

■ As in all areas of decision-making, qualitative factors may be important too, such as the image a product gives the business. In addition, products with a low contribution may be part of a range of goods produced by the firm and to cease producing one would reduce the appeal of the whole range.

Evaluation of the costing approaches

Full costing

Full costing can be useful for single-product firms and as a quick guideline to the costs of products. However, it does have serious flaws for multi-product businesses because the approach does not apportion overheads on a real basis. The final costing figure may, in fact, be inaccurate or misleading. Thus, full-costing data could be used to make comparisons of costs calculated on the same basis over time, but it should not be widely used for decision-making.

Contribution or marginal costing

Contribution or marginal costing is now the most widely used method for decision-making, because it accepts that fixed overhead costs must be paid during a particular time period, regardless of the level of production. This should help management take appropriate decisions when faced with the option, for example, of accepting a new contract or scrapping a product altogether. Marginal costing does have one potential drawback, however.

If overheads are set aside for costing purposes, there is a danger that they could be overlooked altogether. This could mean that contribution is confused with profit, and pricing decisions for products could ignore the fixed-cost element. Eventually overheads have to be paid for and this important fact must not be forgotten when applying the marginal-costing approach.

Final evaluation of costs and costing methods

Operations management and marketing decisions often require accurate and up-to-date cost data. Managers need to be aware of the different types and classifications of costs in making their decisions. The importance of cost and profit centres cannot be overemphasised. The need to consider more than one method of costing in making crucial decisions is also vital – to depend solely on fixed costing would lead to poor decisions in many instances. The need to address qualitative factors has been referred to more than once and you are advised to incorporate a discussion of these into answers to questions that demand that a choice between different options be made. Costs are significant but the successful operations manager will also consider other data from a wide range of sources before making decisions on issues such as location, 'make or buy' and purchasing of new capital equipment.

SUMMARY POINTS

- Cost centres are sections of a business to which costs can be allocated.
- Profit centres are sections of a business to which both costs and revenue can be allocated.
- Costing methods are techniques used to calculate the cost of producing products or services or the cost of operating a department/division.
- Full costing attempts to allocate or apportion all costs – direct and overhead – to cost centres.
- Contribution costing focuses on allocating only direct costs – and if products or services make a contribution, this can be used to help pay for overhead costs.

RESEARCH TASK

1   Use the Internet to find out more about the difference between full (or absorption) costing and contribution (or marginal) costing. Here is a good starting point: www. gilbertfinance.co.uk/marginal-and-full-costing.htm

2   Look up ticket airline ticket prices for a popular local air route.

- How many different prices can you find?
- Do you think the lowest cost airline is using contribution/marginal costing to calculate the price of air tickets or full cost pricing? Explain your answer.

484

A Level exam practice questions
Case studies

1   Midtown Imperial Hotel

'We would be mad to accept this special request at $1,850 below our normal price and $500 below the cost of providing the conference facilities and equipment hire.'

The hotel manager, Rajesh, was annoyed that Sheila Burns, the conference manager of the Imperial Hotel, had even bothered to consult him about the enquiry from the Friends of General Hospital for the use of the conference suite for their annual general meeting involving 100 people. Sheila had been asked for a price to organise the Friends AGM and had used the normal hotel practice of adding 50% to the total cost of the facility. This had been too much for the charity, so they had requested a reduction and had suggested a lower figure of $2,200. As the AGM was planned for the end of February, a very slack time for all hotels, Sheila had been tempted to take up the offer and had put it to Rajesh for his approval. She knew that many of the Friends were quite influential people with business interests and she believed that this could be to the hotel's long-term advantage.

The costing statement for the conference suite was as follows:

- Variable cost per delegate including food, three drinks each and waiting staff $15.
- Hotel overhead allocation per conference $1,000.
- In addition, the Friends had requested some special audio-visual equipment, which the hotel would have to hire in for the day at a cost of $200.

[22 marks, 35 minutes]

1   Calculate:
   a   the full cost of the conference for the Friends of the General Hospital (including the equipment hire)   **[4]**
   b   the price that the hotel would normally charge for a conference of this size with the equipment requested   **[4]**
   c   the contribution to the hotel's overheads and profit if the conference suite were let out for $2,200.   **[2]**

2   Advise the hotel manager on the advisability of accepting this special request for the use of the conference facilities. Include both quantitative and qualitative data in your answer.   **[12]**

2 Cosmic Cases

Cosmic Cases manufactures a range of suitcases. There are four sizes of case, ranging from a small vanity case to a large luggage case with wheels for mobility. The cases are sold mainly through department stores, either as a complete set or, more frequently, as individual items. The latest six-monthly costing statement (see below) had just been prepared, together with the sales figures for the same period. Jill Grealey, the managing director, was concerned about the performance of the medium-sized case and wanted to discuss the data with the finance director.

Costing statement for six months ending 31 September 2013				
	Vanity case	Small suitcase	Medium suitcase	Large suitcase
Total direct costs	$30,000	$35,000	$12,000	$20,000
Allocated overheads	$15,000	$12,500	$10,000	$10,000
Total costs	$45,000	$47,500	$22,000	$30,000
Total output	5,000	4,000	1,000	1,500

The selling prices to the department stores were: Vanity case $15, Small case $18, Medium case $20, Large case $25.

[26 marks, 40 minutes]

1 Calculate the total revenue (price × quantity sold) for each size of case. **[4]**

2 Calculate the total profit/loss made by each size of case. **[2]**

3 Calculate the total contribution made by each size of case. **[4]**

4 Jill Grealey wanted to stop production of the medium-sized case. She said to the finance director, 'If we stop making this case, then our total profits will rise.' The finance director was convinced that this would be the wrong decision to make. As a management consultant, write a report to the managing director giving your recommendation for the action to be taken with the medium-sized case. You should justify your recommendation with both numerical and non-numerical factors. **[16]**

A Level essay questions

[20 marks, 45 minutes]

1 Evaluate the usefulness of contribution costing to the management of a multi-product sports shoe manufacturing business that has operations in more than one country. **[20]**

2 Discuss whether a service sector business should ever accept an order from a new customer for a price below the estimated full unit price. **[20]**

33 Budgets

On completing this chapter, you will be able to:

- understand why financial planning is important
- analyse the advantages of setting budgets – or financial plans
- examine the importance of a system of delegated budgeting
- analyse the potential limitations of budgeting
- use variance analysis to assess adverse and favourable variances from budgets.

Introducing the topic

BILLIONS OVER BUDGET, ANGLO AMERICAN KEEPS GOING IN BRAZIL

Anglo American plc – the mining giant – is spending US$8.8 billion on a massive iron ore mine in Conceicao do Mato Dentro, Brazil. This sum is more than three times the originally budgeted – or planned – figure. The project is also three years behind schedule. The senior management of Anglo American did not foresee the planning problems with the Brazilian government, which have added to costs and slowed the opening of the new mine down. Neither did they accurately budget for the construction costs of the mine in very difficult terrain with poor transport connections.

The former CEO, Cynthi Carrol, is convinced the mine will still be profitable when it finally opens, despite the price of iron ore falling from $159 per tonne to $111 a tonne in recent months. The slowdown in the Chinese economy has hit demand for iron ore so prices have fallen below the level that Anglo American used in their original financial plans for the mine. However, once the purchase price of $4.6 billion and the construction costs of $8.8 billion have been paid for, the mine is expected to yield strong cash flows for the next 45 years.

Points to think about:

- Why was it important for Anglo American to have a financial plan or budget for a project this size?
- Explain as many reasons as you can why the budgeted costs and revenues for this site proved to be so unrealistic.
- What are the problems in trying to set financial plans for a project such as this mine, which could last for 45 years?

Figure 33.1 Delays at Anglo American's massive Minas Rio iron-ore mine have led to cost budgets being exceeded by billions of dollars

Introduction

We should all plan for our future finances to some degree. We might plan for the long term – such as possible career choices, the incomes we could earn and the cost of the training courses to gain the qualifications needed. We should also plan for the short term – such as how much to spend over the weekend. This type of financial planning should apply to business organisations too. This process is known as budgeting and a budget is a detailed, financial plan for a future time period. Planning for the future is important for all organisations. If no plans are made, an organisation drifts without real direction and purpose. Managers will not be able to allocate the scarce resources of the business effectively without a plan to work towards. Employees working in an organisation that has no plans or targets for future action are likely to feel demotivated, as they have no goals to work towards – and no objective to be praised for achieving. If no targets are set, then an organisation cannot review its progress because it has no set objective against which actual performance can be compared.

Advantages of setting budgets – measuring performance

Planning for the future must take into account the financial needs and likely consequences of these plans. This is the budgeting process. Setting and agreeing financial targets for each section of a business will have many benefits. The primary benefit is the ability to measure the performance of each part of the organisation that has been allocated budgets.

> **KEY TERM**
>
> **Budget:** a detailed financial plan for the future.

Budgets are set for both sales revenue and costs and it is usual for each cost centre and profit centre to have budgets set for the next 12 months, broken down on a month-by-month basis. Setting budgets and establishing financial plans for the future have seven main purposes:

1 **Planning:** The budgetary process makes managers consider future plans carefully so that realistic targets can be set.

2 **Effective allocation of resources:** Budgets can be an effective way of making sure that the business does not spend more resources than it has access to. There will be priorities to discuss and to agree on, since what can be done is always likely to be greater than resources will permit.

3 **Setting targets to be achieved:** Research shows that most people work better if they have a realisable target at which to aim. This motivation will be greater if the **budget holder** or the cost-profit-centre manager has been given some delegated accountability for setting and reaching budget levels. These then become delegated budgets.

4 **Coordination:** Discussion over the allocation of resources to different departments and divisions requires coordination between these departments. Once budgets have been set, people will have to work effectively together if targets set are to be achieved.

5 **Monitoring and controlling:** Plans cannot be ignored once in place. There is a need to check regularly that the financial objective is still within reach. All kinds of conditions may change and businesses cannot afford to assume that everything is fine.

6 **Modifying:** If there is evidence to suggest that the objective cannot be reached and that the budget is unrealistic, then either the plan or the way of working towards it must be changed.

7 **Measuring and assessing performance:** Once the budgeted period has ended, **variance analysis** will be used to compare actual performance with the original budgets. This is an important way of assessing managers' performance.

> **KEY TERMS**
>
> **Budget holder:** individual responsible for the initial setting and achievement of a budget.
>
> **Variance analysis:** calculating differences between budgets and actual performance, and analysing reasons for such differences.

Key features of budgeting

A budget is not a forecast, although much of the data on which it is based will come from forecasts, since we are looking into the future. Budgets are plans that organisations aim to fulfil. A forecast is a prediction of what could occur in the future given certain conditions.

Budgets may be established for any part of an organisation as long as the outcome of its operation is measurable. This means most cost centres and profit centres will have budgets set including budgets for sales, capital expenditure, labour costs, profit and so on.

Coordination between departments when establishing budgets is essential. This should avoid departments making conflicting plans. For example, the marketing department may be planning to increase sales by lowering prices, yet the production department may be planning to reduce output and lower the direct-labour-cost budget. These targets will conflict and need to be reconciled. Setting of budgets should be an exercise in participation. Decisions regarding budgets should be made with the subordinate managers who will be involved in putting them into effect. Those who are to be held responsible for fulfilling a budget should be involved in setting it. This sense of 'ownership' not only helps to motivate the department concerned to achieve the targets but also leads to the establishment of more realistic targets. This approach to budgeting is called **delegated budgets**.

KEY TERM

Delegated budgets: giving some delegated authority over the setting and achievement of budgets to junior managers.

The budget will be used to review the performance of the managers controlling the cost or profit centre such as department or division of a business. The managers of the department will be appraised on their effectiveness in reaching targets. Successful and unsuccessful managers can therefore be identified.

These stages of involvement in constructing the budget, taking responsibility for its operation and being appraised in terms of success, are the human aspects of the process. They have a very important role to play in the motivation of staff.

TOP TIP

Delegated budgeting ties in with the motivational approach of Herzberg – making work more challenging and rewarding.

The stages in preparing budgets

Stage 1: The most important organisational objectives for the coming year are established – these will be based on:

- the previous performance of the business
- external changes likely to affect the organisation
- sales forecasts based on research and past sales data.

Stage 2: The key or limiting factor that is most likely to influence the growth or success of the organisation must be identified. For most businesses this is likely to be sales. Therefore, the sales budget will be the first to be prepared. Care and accuracy are essential at this stage, because an error in the key-factor budget will distort all other budgets as well. For example, if the sales budget proves to be inaccurate – e.g. set at a level that proves to be too high – then cash, production, labour budgets and so on will become inaccurate too.

Stage 3: The sales budget is prepared after discussion with sales managers in all branches and divisions of the business.

Stage 4: The subsidiary budgets are prepared, which will now be based on the plans contained in the sales budget. These will include cash budget, administration budget, labour-cost budget, materials-cost budget, selling and distribution budget. The budget holders, e.g. cost- and profit-centre managers, should be involved in this process if the aim of delegated responsibility for budgets is to be achieved.

Stage 5: These budgets are coordinated to ensure consistency. This may be undertaken by a budgetary committee with special responsibility for ensuring that budgets do not conflict with each other and that the spending level planned does not exceed the resources of the business.

Stage 6: A master budget is prepared that contains the main details of all other budgets and concludes with a budgeted income statement and Statement of financial position.

Stage 7: The master budget is then presented to the board – hopefully for the directors' approval.

Once approved, the budgets will become the basis of the operational plans of each department and cost centre within the organisation. However, the overall plan is usually over too long a time period to be a motivating target and will be broken down into short periods like a month or even a week. See Figure 33.2.

Setting budgets

There are several ways in which the budget level can be set. The most widely used are:

- incremental budgeting
- zero budgeting
- flexible budgeting.

Incremental budgeting

In many businesses that operate in highly competitive markets there may be plans to lower the cost budget for departments each year, but to raise the sales budgets. This puts increased pressure on many staff to achieve higher productivity. **Incremental budgeting** does not allow for unforeseen events. Using last year's figure as a basis means that each department does not have to justify its whole budget for the coming year – only the change or 'increment'.

KEY TERM

Incremental budgeting: uses last year's budget as a basis and an adjustment is made for the coming year.

How budgets are commonly prepared

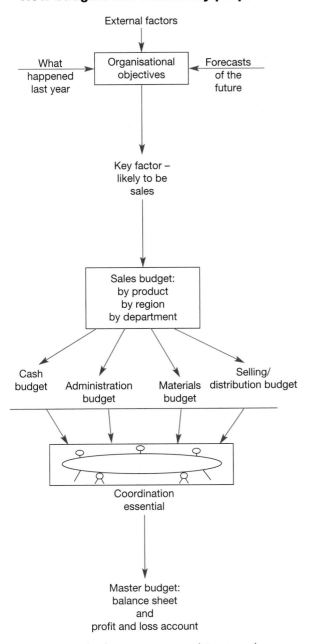

Figure 33.2 How budgets are commonly prepared

Zero budgeting

This is an approach to setting budgets that requires all departments and budget holders to justify their whole budget each year. This is time-consuming, as a fundamental review of the work and importance

of each budget-holding section is needed each year. However, it does provide added incentive for managers to defend the work of their own section. Also, changing situations can be reflected in very different budget levels each year.

Flexible budgeting

So far we have referred to a system of budgeting known as 'fixed' budgeting. This is based on the assumption that the level of output remains at the predicted or budgeted level. If actual output fell or rose above this level, then this could lead to obvious variances – but these will not necessarily indicate real efficiency problems. See below:

	Budgeted level	Actual level
Output Direct materials	100 units $20,000	80 units $18,000

489

This shows a favourable variance of $2,000 because direct materials are lower than budgeted and lower costs should increase profit. However, this ignores the fact that output is 20% below budget – and this should lead to lower material use anyway. A more realistic direct materials budget would be to adjust for the lower output figure. This is called flexible budgeting – it sets new budgets depending on the actual output level achieved.

	Fixed budget	Flexible budget*	Actual
Output Direct materials	100 $20,000	$16,000	80 $18,000

Note: *down 20% as output has fallen by this percentage.

This now gives an adverse direct material variance of $2,000, reflecting the fact that materials seem to be used less efficiently or are costing more per unit than originally budgeted.

Flexible budgets are more motivating for middle and lower-level managers as they will not be criticised for adverse variances that might occur just because output was lower than budgeted. The flexed targets they are given are more realistic. Also, flexible budgets make it easier to produce valid and accurate variance analyses as they will now highlight changes in efficiency, not changes in output.

TOP TIP

Remember that budgets are not forecasts although they may be based on, for example, sales forecasts. Budgets are targets for departments and people in the organisation to reach.

ACTIVITY 33.1

'I have been told that the shop that I have managed for the last four years is underperforming yet I was never told what level of sales I should be aiming for,' complained a manager of a food and drink shop. The shop is owned by a large company with many outlets. 'If I had been asked I would have forecast lower sales for this year anyway,' he continued when he met with the area manager to discuss the future of the shop.

[18 marks, 30 minutes]

1   Explain the difference between a budget and a forecast.   [4]

2   What evidence is there that a system of budgets does not operate in this business?   [4]

3   Analyse the benefits to this business of adopting a system of delegated budgeting.   [10]

Potential limitations of budgeting

Lack of flexibility: If budgets are set with no flexibility built into them, then sudden and unexpected changes in the external environment can make them very unrealistic. See the 'Introducing the topic' case study on page 486. These external changes often come in the form of unplanned-for increases in world materials- and energy-cost inflation.

Focused on the short term: Budgets tend to be set for the relatively short term – for example, the next 12 months. Managers may take a short-term decision to stay within budget that may not be in the best long-term interests of the business. For example, a decision to reduce the size of the workforce to stay within the labour budget may limit the firm's ability to increase output if sales were to rise unexpectedly quickly in the future.

May lead to unnecessary spending: When the end of the budgeting period approaches and managers realise that they have under-spent their budgets, unnecessary spending decisions might be made so that the same level of budget can be justified next year. If a large surplus exists at the end of the budget period, how could managers justify the same level of resources next year?

Training needs must be met: Setting and keeping to budgets is not easy and all managers with delegated responsibility for budgets will need extensive training in this role.

Setting budgets for new projects: When a major new project is being undertaken, perhaps a one-off building scheme such as a large bridge or tunnel, setting realistic budgets may be difficult and frequent revisions in the budgets might be necessary.

Budgetary control – variance analysis

During the period covered by the budget and at the end of it the actual performance of the organisation needs to be compared with the original targets, and reasons for differences must be investigated. This process is known as variance analysis. A variance is the difference between budgeted and actual figures. Analysing these variances is an essential part of budgeting for a number of reasons:

- It measures differences from the planned performance of each department both month by month and at the end of the year.
- It assists in analysing the causes of deviations from budget. For example, if actual profit is below budget, was this due to lower sales revenue or higher costs?
- An understanding of the reasons for the deviations from the original planned levels can be used to change future budgets in order to make them more accurate. For example, if sales revenue is lower than planned as a result of market resistance to higher prices, then this knowledge could be used to help prepare future budgets.

The performance of each individual budget-holding section may be appraised in an accurate and objective way.

If the variance has had the effect of increasing profit, e.g. sales revenue higher than budgeted, then it is termed a favourable variance. If the variance has had the effect of reducing profit, for example direct material costs higher than budget, then it is termed an unfavourable or adverse variance (see Table 33.1).

Variance analysis – worked example

West Indian Computers Ltd

Financial variable	Budget $	Actual result $	Variance $	Favourable or adverse
Revenue	15,000	12,000	3,000	Adverse – this reduces profit
Direct costs	5,000	4,000	1,000	Favourable – this increases profit
Overhead costs	3,000	3,500	500	Adverse – this reduces profit
Operating profit	7,000	4,500	2,500	Adverse – profit is below forecast

Adverse variances	Favourable variances
Causes:	**Causes:**
■ Sales revenue is below budget *either* because units sold were less than planned for *or* the selling price had to be lowered due to competition.	■ Sales revenue is above budget due to higher-than-expected economic growth *or* problems with one of the competitor's products.
■ Actual raw material costs are higher than planned for *either* because output was higher than budgeted *or* the cost per unit of materials increased.	■ Raw material costs are lower *either* because output was less than planned *or* the cost per unit of materials was lower than budget.
■ Labour costs are above budget *either* because wage rates had to be raised due to shortages of workers *or* the labour time taken to complete the work was longer than expected.	■ Labour costs are lower than planned for *either* because of lower wage rates *or* quicker completion of the work.
■ Overhead costs are higher than budgeted, perhaps because the annual rent rise was above forecast.	■ Overhead costs are lower than budgeted, perhaps because advertising rates from TV companies were reduced.

Table 33.1 Possible causes of adverse and favourable variances

 KEY TERM

Adverse variance: exists when the difference between the budgeted and actual figure leads to a lower-than-expected profit.

 KEY TERM

Favourable variance: exists when the difference between the budgeted and actual figure leads to a higher-than-expected profit.

491

Indian computer shop – budgets can be set for each shop in the chain

The variance calculations for West Indian Computers Ltd can be verified by checking the operating profit variance ($2,500 adverse) against the net sum of the other variances ($3,500 adverse – $1,000 favourable = $2,500 adverse). The benefits to be gained from regular variance analysis include:

■ Identifying potential problems early so that remedial action can be taken. Perhaps, in this case, a new competing carpet retailer has opened up and West Indian Carpets will have to quickly introduce strategies to combat this competition.
■ Allowing managers to concentrate their time and efforts on the major, or exceptional, problem areas – this is known as management by exception. In this case it seems that managers should investigate quickly the likely causes of the lower-than-expected sales figures.

Responding to variance analysis results

Managers may need to respond quickly to both adverse and favourable variances. Clearly, adverse variances will need to be looked at in some detail to see if cheaper supplies or working methods could be adopted. However, an adverse variance caused by an increase in output leading to higher raw material costs is of much less concern.

Favourable variances cannot be ignored either. They may reflect a poor and inaccurate budgeting process where cost budgets were set too high. A favourable direct cost variance caused by output being much less than planned for is not very promising – why were sales and output lower than planned for?

Budgets and budgetary control – an evaluation

Setting, agreeing and controlling budgets is time-consuming. Budgets can fail to reflect changing circumstances and become inflexible. Budget-holders can look upon a budget as a limit up to which they can spend, whether their department needs all of the resources or not. Therefore, is the budgetary process worthwhile?

Try to think of the alternative:

■ Without a detailed and coordinated set of plans for allocating money and resources of the business, who would decide 'who gets what'?

■ Without a clear sales budget as the cornerstone of the budgetary process, how would departments know how much to produce or to spend on sales promotion or how many people to employ?

■ Would it be possible to assess how the business had done or how well individual departments had performed without a clear series of targets with which to compare performance?

■ Without figures to monitor progress during the budgetary period, how would it be possible to know where the business is or to suggest changes that might be made?

■ Budgets have to be agreed and controlled. This gives responsibility and a sense of direction to those delegated to work with them. These human advantages are difficult to ensure without planned money values to work with.

Based on these arguments in favour of budget setting and budgetary control, all businesses are likely to undertake some form of financial planning and control.

KEY CONCEPT LINK

Setting **budgets** and measuring performance against budgets is an important **management** function. External **changes** can make long-term budgets very inaccurate, which is why flexible budgeting is often used as a means of helping to 'manage change'.

ACTIVITY 33.2

Variance analysis at Oasis Cookers Ltd

Oasis Cookers Ltd makes gas and electric ovens. The business has a good reputation for quality products. These are sold through a number of selected retailers who have agreed to display and market the ovens in ways that differentiate them from cheaper models. The national economy is experiencing a downturn with no economic growth. The government has been forced to increase interest rates to control cost inflation and this has contributed to an appreciation of the currency's exchange rate. Foreign oven imports are falling in price because of this. The management of Oasis Cookers Ltd are studying the latest variance analysis results:

$000	Budgeted figures	Actual figures	Variance
Revenue	165	150	
Cost of materials	80	70	
Labour costs	22	23	
Gross profit	63	57	
Overheads	40	43	
Operating profit	23	14	

[42 marks, 1 hour]

1 Calculate the variances and indicate whether they are favourable or adverse variances. [6]

2 Explain **two** possible reasons for the variances in:
 a sales revenue [4]
 b labour cost. [4]

3 Evaluate **two** ways in which the management of Oasis Cookers could respond to these variance-analysis results to improve performance of the business. [10]

4 The managers of Oasis Cookers asked for additional information from the management accountants. In particular, they asked for a breakdown of the overhead cost variances:

Overhead costs $000	Budgeted figures	Actual figures	Variance
Promotion and distribution	8	6	
Administration	9	8	
Production	22	27	
Personnel	1	2	

Calculate the variances for each type of overhead cost and indicate whether they are favourable or adverse. [4]

5 Evaluate the benefits of setting budgets and using variance analysis to manufacturing businesses such as Oasis Cookers Ltd. [14]

SUMMARY POINTS

- Budgets are financial plans for the future – when set at appropriate levels and when managers are involved in establishing them, they can prove to be powerful motivational tools.
- Budgets can provide direction, encourage business planning, give a sense of purpose and allow for a review procedure of actual results against original targets.
- Budgeted and actual figures can be compared by using variance analysis.
- Likely causes of both adverse variances and favourable variances should be investigated as this could help improve business performance in future.

RESEARCH TASK

- Your country's government will set an annual budget of expenditure. Find out how much your government spent this year and whether it was above or below budget.
- Which government departments had the highest annual expenditure budgets?
- Government budgets are often inaccurate – does this mean that they should not be set each year?

A Level exam practice questions

Case studies

1 Kinibali Timber Ltd

	Budgeted figures ($000)	Actual figures ($000)
Sales revenue	66	70
Direct labour	15	18
Direct materials	12	17
Fixed costs	6	5
Profit	–	–

Budgeted and actual figures for the year ending 31 December 2013

[24 marks, 40 minutes]

1 Calculate the budgeted profit and actual profit figures. [2]

2 Using variance analysis, discuss whether the management of Kinibali Timber Ltd should be satisfied with the performance of the business over the past 12 months. [12]

3 Outline **two** other pieces of information that would have helped you in your answer to question 2. [4]

4 If the volume of timber sold had actually increased by 10% above budget over this period, explain briefly the benefits to the business of using a system of flexible budgeting. [6]

2 Karmali Carpets plc

The managing director of Karmali Carpets was angry. The profits of the business had fallen for the third year running and he was determined to put all the blame on the sales manager, Sarah Fellows. He called her into his office to discuss the latest company results. 'The company's profits have worsened again this year and your department must take the blame – sales revenue was down from what I had expected it to be,' he grumbled. 'Why can't you manage to increase sales each year?'

Sarah expressed real surprise at this complaint. 'What do you mean, sales are down? We sold more carpets this year than ever before. I know we had to increase our discounts towards the end of the year, but you are always telling us "If they come through that door, then they go home with a carpet" and we acted on that.'

'But you failed to reach your annual targets that I decided on and sent you last month,' said the managing director.

Sarah defended herself by saying, 'Those targets were received after most of the year had gone and I never thought they were realistic anyway. I wanted to increase advertising, but you rejected my new campaign because you used the money to buy new computers for the accounts office. How can I be expected to reach your targets, when I don't believe in them myself?'

[22 marks, 40 minutes]

1   Evaluate the managing director's approach to budgeting. **[10]**

2   Write a report to the managing director explaining the likely advantages to his business from a delegated budgetary control system using the stages of the budgeting process as outlined in this chapter. **[12]**

A Level essay questions

[20 marks, 45 minutes each]

1   Currently, the senior managers of a multinational retailing company allocate annual budgets, decided at head office, to each shop manager. Discuss whether the managers should establish a system of delegated budgeting. **[20]**

2   Evaluate the view that a budgetary system is a waste of time and effort for a travel business that organises holidays for tourists owing to the problems of forecasting demand. **[20]**

On completing this chapter you should be able to:

- make simple amendments to Statements of financial position and income statements from given data
- understand the importance of accounting for the depreciation of fixed assets and apply the straight-line method to simple problems

- analyse the impact on the Statement of financial position of a change in valuing non-current assets or inventories
- explain the significance of goodwill, net realisable value of stocks and depreciation to the final accounts of a business.

Introducing the topic

TAKEOVER LEADS TO SOME ACCOUNTING PROBLEMS

The takeover of SASCo by WESCo seemed to be a good idea to WESCo's chief executive. His hotel and catering company was gaining access to SASCo's excellent reputation for supplying fresh and frozen food to catering businesses and its good customer relationships. In addition, he thought that SASCo's inventory was undervalued and he believed that he had made a good decision. The $2 million paid for SASCo seemed to be a bargain.

WESCo's accountant was not as keen on the takeover as he was, though. 'We are paying about $0.5 million more for this company than I think its net assets are worth. Reputation and customer links are important – but is it worth paying so much for these?'

The accountant was also worried about two other factors. Firstly, SASCo's inventories included some stocks of frozen food that had been held for many months. These would now be difficult to sell unless they were offered to customers at large discounts. Surely these should be revalued on the Statement of financial position? Secondly, SASCo's method of depreciating its assets assumed that most of them would last for many years. WESCo assumed its equipment would last for only four years – its finance director had always adopted a conservative approach.

Points to think about:

- What difference would it make to profits if WESCo made the same assumption as SASCo about its equipment?
- Why are some companies prepared to pay more for another business than its net assets are worth?
- How do you think a business should value its inventories on its Statement of financial position?
- Do you think that when assets fall in value over time, this lower value should be recorded on the company's accounts? Explain your answer.

Introduction

In Chapter 30, the basic structure of the final accounts of a limited company was explained. The two most important accounting statements were the income statement and the Statement of financial position (balance sheet). This chapter is based on extended A Level work and takes this basic understanding and develops the skill of accounts amendment.

Being able to amend company accounts following a change in a key variable, increases understanding of the fundamental concepts underlying the final accounts of a business. This chapter also considers four important issues that must be considered by accountants when preparing final accounts.

Amending income statements

Accountants often have to make adjustments to the accounts they are preparing when new financial data become available or when one of the key variables used in the final accounts changes. As an A Level Business student, it is important to remember these few basic rules when adapting existing accounts:

- Use the same format of presenting the income statement as shown in the case study.

- If a change to the number of units produced and sold occurs, this is most likely to lead to changes in sales revenue and variable costs.
- Some overheads might change with a variation in the level of sales; for example, annual promotion or transport costs might be affected by variations in the number of units produced and sold.

Amending Statements of financial position

When calculating the Statement of financial position for the end of the current financial year it is common to start with the statement for the end of the previous financial year. Relevant amendments can then be made to it. Table 34.1 shows some of the amendments that are possible – with the possible double entry needed to keep the account balanced.

Further amendments to the published accounts

Goodwill

The reputation and prestige of a business that has been operating for some time also give value to the business over and above the worth of its physical assets. This is called the goodwill of a business. This should normally only feature on a Statement of financial position just after the business has been purchased for more than its assets are worth, or when the business is being prepared for sale. At other times, goodwill will not appear on company accounts – it is 'written off' as soon as possible if it has been included in the purchase of another company. This is because business reputation and good name can disappear very rapidly – for example, with a scare over products that risk consumers' health.

Goodwill example: If business A buys out business B for $2 million, yet the net asset value of B is only $1.5 million, then A has paid $0.5 million for the 'goodwill' of business B. Why might business A have been prepared to pay this extra $0.5 million?

Goodwill has value when the business being sold is well-known, well-established and has good trading links with both customers and suppliers. A newly formed business does not yet have goodwill, but an existing business is said to be a 'going concern' with the intangible

496

ACTIVITY 34.1

Estimated income statement for Karachi Traders Ltd

Year ending 31 December 2013.

	$
Revenue (5,000 units @ $3.00)	15,000
Cost of goods sold (@ $1.00 per unit)	5,000
Gross profit	10,000
Overhead expenses	4,000
Operating profit (profit before tax and interest)	6,000
Finance costs (interest)	2,000
Profit before tax	4,000
Corporation tax @ 20%	800
Profit for the year	3,200
Dividends paid	1,200
Retained earnings	2,000

[25 marks, 30 minutes]

1 By amending this income statement, calculate the new level of retained earnings if the following changes actually occurred:
   - each unit had been sold for $4.00
   - the cost of each unit sold rose to $1.60
   - overhead expenses rose by 25%
   - interest costs were reduced by 50%
   - corporation tax rate rose to 25%.

   Assume dividends remain unchanged. **[15]**

2 Amend the same income statement but now:
   - the number of units increased by 20%, but the selling price remained unchanged
   - cost of goods sold per unit falls to $0.90
   - transport costs (included in Overheads) increased by $500.

   Calculate the new level of retained earnings assuming no other change to overheads, interest, corporation tax and dividends. **[10]**

Cause of change	Impact on Statement of financial position	Double entry
Sale of inventories for cash (sold for same price as valued in accounts)	Value of inventories will fall	Cash balance will increase
Sale of inventories for cash – sold at higher price than valued in accounts	Value of inventories will fall	Cash balance will increase Shareholders' equity will increase by the value of the profit recorded
Depreciation of equipment	Value of non-current assets will fall	Shareholders' equity will fall – the company is now 'worth less' than before
Intangible assets – such as intellectual property – are revalued	Value of non-current asset increases	Value of shareholders' equity increases
Accounts payable (creditors) ask for much speedier payment	Value of accounts payable falls	Cash balance will decline
Additional shares sold and share capital raised is used to buy property	Value of share capital will increase	Value of property in non-current assets will increase

Table 34.1 Some common amendments to the Statement of financial position

advantages listed above. Hence, other firms are prepared to pay a price exceeding net asset value in order to purchase this goodwill.

There are two accounting conventions regarding goodwill:

- It should not appear as an asset of an existing business because it is so difficult to value and can disappear rapidly, for example with an accident that damages the environment and destroys a firm's reputation.
- It will appear on the Statement of financial position of a business that has bought another firm and has paid for goodwill. It will appear as a non-current intangible asset. However, this should be taken off the Statement of financial position (written off) as soon as possible for the same reason as above – it is not necessarily permanent and just because it was worth $0.5 million last year does not mean that the reputation and customer contacts are still worth that amount this year.

Valuing intangible assets

Goodwill is an example of an intangible asset, but it is not the only one. Patents, copyrights, well-established brand names and capital spent on research and development into new products – these are all assets that do not exist in a physical sense, yet they add value to a company. They are often referred to as '**intellectual property**'. The two main problems are how to value them and whether they should be included on the company Statement of financial

position. These are very technical accounting areas and it is not necessary for an A Level Business student to be aware of the details. However, we need to recognise that:

- intangible assets are difficult to put a value on
- Statements of financial position prepared under normally accepted accounting rules do not usually record these assets unless acquired through takeover or merger
- for many companies, they are their main source of future earnings, especially in a world increasingly dominated by the knowledge-based economy – for example, scientific research companies, publishing and music companies, companies with famous brand names and so on
- the **market value** of companies with considerable intangible assets will be much greater than the net asset value or book value.

497

KEY TERM

Market value: the estimated total value of a company if it were taken over.

Capital expenditure and revenue expenditure

What is the difference, in accounting terms, between a business purchasing a van and purchasing the fuel

KEY TERMS

Capital expenditure: any item bought by a business and retained for more than one year, that is the purchase of fixed or non-current assets.

Revenue expenditure: any expenditure on costs other than non-current asset expenditure.

KEY TERM

Intellectual property: the amount by which the market value of a firm exceeds its tangible assets less liabilities – an intangible asset.

ACTIVITY 34.2

Estimated Statement of financial position for Energen plc as at 31 December 2013

ASSETS	$m	
Non-current assets:		
Property	2,000	
Equipment	500	
	2,500	
Current assets:		
Inventories	120	
Accounts receivable	650	
Cash	20	
	790	
TOTAL ASSETS		3,290
EQUITY and LIABILITIES		
Current liabilities:		
Accounts payable	450	
Overdraft	30	
	480	
Non-current liabilities:		
Long-term loans	250	
	250	
TOTAL LIABILITIES	730	
Shareholders' equity:		
Share capital	2,000	
Retained earnings	560	
	2,560	
TOTAL EQUITY and LIABILITIES		3,290

[16 marks, 30 minutes]

1 Make the following amendments to this Statement of financial position:

   a The property assets of the business have been increased by purchasing a new building for $800 million. This was paid for by an increase in share capital and a further long-term loan (50% of cost each).

   b Some of the inventories have remained unsold for several months, so their value should be reduced by 20%.

   c $50 million worth of debts are now believed to be irrecoverable – that is, it is most unlikely that these trade receivables will pay, so they should be written off from the Statement of financial position.

   d It has been discovered that accounts payable (trade creditors) have been under-recorded by $30 million due to poor accounting procedures.

   e Annual retained earnings of $100 million were earned, but half of this figure was used to finance an increase in debts receivable – the other half is in cash.

   f The retained earnings figure – part of shareholders' equity – has to be adjusted to ensure that the Statement of financial position still balances.

   Recalculate the totals for total assets and total equity and liabilities. [16]

to fill the tank? There is expenditure involved in both cases, but one purchase is of an asset that will be kept and used by the business for several years. The petrol will be used up in the process of using the van in the day-to-day activities of the business. The purchase of the van is called capital expenditure; the purchase of the petrol is an example of revenue expenditure.

How do accountants record these two types of spending in the accounts? Revenue expenditure is easy to deal with. All revenue expenditure is on assets and expenses that give short-term benefit to the business – within one year. They will all be recorded in full on each year's income statement and will, therefore, reduce that year's profits – with the exception of the unsold inventories, which will be entered under 'closing inventories'.

Capital expenditure is more complicated. Consider this situation. A removal business purchases two new trucks, which are expected to last for ten years. This is obviously capital expenditure on fixed assets. If the cost of these trucks was recorded as an expense immediately

---

ACTIVITY 34.3

Revenue expenditure or capital expenditure?

[10 marks, 15 minutes]

Copy this table and complete it by writing either 'revenue expenditure' or 'capital expenditure' in the second column, and a brief explanation of your decision in the third column.   [10]

Expenditure	Capital or revenue expenditure	Reason
Purchase of computers for administration department		
Salaries of the administration staff		
Purchase of supplies added to inventories for resale		
Maintenance costs of the building		
Extension to the existing building		

---

and recorded in the income statement, there would be two serious disadvantages for the business:

- The trucks would not appear as fixed assets on the Statement of financial position because they had been recorded as an annual expense. This would lower the value of the business below its true worth – after all, the trucks will have value many years from now.
- This year's profits will be low as a result of the entire cost of the trucks being recorded straight away – and profits in later years will be higher because they do not bear any of the charge of this purchase.

How, then, is capital expenditure recorded on the accounts? By a process called **depreciation**.

 KEY TERM

Depreciation: the decline in the estimated value of a non-current asset over time
Assets decline in value for two main reasons:
1. normal wear and tear through usage
2. technological change, making either the asset, or the product it is used to make, obsolete.

Depreciation of assets

Nearly all fixed/non-current assets will **depreciate** or decline in value over time. It seems reasonable, therefore, to record only the value of each year's depreciation as a cost on each year's income statement. This will overcome both of the problems referred to above:

- The assets will retain some value on the Statement of financial position each year until fully depreciated or sold off. This is the **net book value**.

- The profits will be reduced by the amount of that year's depreciation and will not be under- or over-recorded.

 KEY TERM

Net book value: the current Statement of financial position value of a non-current asset = original cost – accumulated depreciation.

How depreciation is calculated: the straight-line method of depreciation

There are a number of different methods accountants can use to calculate depreciation – but you only need to understand the straight-line method for the Cambridge syllabus. The title of this method indicates the way in which depreciation is calculated.

 KEY TERM

Straight-line depreciation: a constant amount of depreciation is subtracted from the value of the asset each year.

$$= \frac{\text{original cost of asset-expected residual value}}{\text{expected useful life of asset (years)}}$$

To calculate the annual amount of depreciation, the following information will be needed:

- the original or historical cost of the asset
- the expected useful life of the asset
- an estimation of the value of the asset at the end of its useful life – this is known as the residual value of the asset.

The formula given above is then used to calculate the annual depreciation charge.

Example: A firm of lawyers purchases three new computers costing $3,000 each. Experience with previous computers suggests that they will need to be updated after four years. At the end of this period the second-hand value of each machine is estimated to be just $200. Using straight-line depreciation, the annual depreciation charge will be:

$$\$9,000-\$600 = \frac{\$8,400}{4} = \$2,100$$

For each of the four years of the useful life of these computers a depreciation charge of $2,100 will be made. This will be included in the firm's overhead expenses on the income statement. On the Statement of financial position, the annual depreciation charge will be subtracted from the value of the computers. At the end of four years, each computer will be valued at $200 on the Statement of financial position. Table 34.2 shows how the value of these computers falls over the four-year period.

Suppose that at the end of the fourth year, the computers are sold for more than their expected residual value. If they are sold for a total of $900, then the firm has made a surplus of $300. If, however, the computers were scrapped, because they had become so out-of-date compared with more recent models, the firm would have to record a loss, in the fourth year, on the disposal of these assets.

Straight-line depreciation – an evaluation

Compared to other methods of depreciation, this is easy to calculate and understand. It is widely used by limited companies. You can check this for yourself. Look in the annual accounts of any plc and you will find a statement about the depreciation methods it has used – more often than not, it will have used this method.

However, as with most other methods, it does require estimates to be made regarding both life expectancy and residual value. Mistakes at this stage will lead to inaccurate depreciation charges being calculated.

Year	Annual depreciation charge	Net book value of the three computers
Present	0	$9,000
1	$2,100	$6,900
2	$2,100	$4,800
3	$2,100	$2,700
4	$2,100	$600

Table 34.2 Net book value declines with each annual depreciation

In addition, cars, trucks and computers are examples of assets that tend to depreciate much more quickly in the first and second years than in subsequent years. This is not reflected in the straight-line method calculation – all annual depreciation charges are the same. An alternative method – the diminishing balance method of depreciation – depreciates assets by a greater amount in the first few years of life than in later years.

There is also no recognition of the very rapid pace at which advances in modern technology tend to make existing assets redundant.

Finally, the repairs and the maintenance costs of an asset usually increase with age and this will reduce the profitability of the asset. This is not adjusted for by the fixed depreciation charge of the straight-line method.

Depreciation and cash flow

This is important – the amount of the annual charge for depreciation does not affect the cash flow out of the business. If a machine is purchased for $5,000, the cash outflow occurs when payment is made to the suppliers of the machine. All that depreciation does is to spread the cost of this asset over its useful life – it is not a cash payment. Depreciation, therefore, is classified as a non-cash expense on the income statement.

Valuation of inventories

Inventories are unsold goods. They might also be in the form of raw materials and components that have not yet been made into completed units. Some goods are in the process of being made and have clearly not yet been sold – and these are referred to as work in progress. How should these unsold goods and materials be valued on the business Statement of financial position? Accountants are quite clear on this – inventories should be recorded at their purchase price (historical cost) or their '**net realisable value**', whichever is the lower. Net realisable value sounds very complicated, but actually it is easy to understand. Consider these examples:

Example 1: A shoe shop buys in ten pairs of shoes from a supplier for $10 a pair. At the end of the financial year, it has three pairs remaining unsold. They have now gone out of fashion. The shopkeeper believes that they could only be sold at a reduced price, below the price he paid for them – $8 a pair.

KEY TERM

Net realisable value: the amount for which an asset (usually an inventory) can be sold minus the cost of selling it – it is only used on Statements of financial position when NRV is estimated to be below historical cost.

Therefore, the realisable value of the three pairs of shoes is only $24. It is this value – not $30 – that should appear on the Statement of financial position as the conservatism principle states that losses should be recorded as soon as they are believed to occur.

Example 2: A furniture retailer has a dining table that has been in stock for six months. It was bought from the manufacturer for $60. It has been damaged in the shop and needs a repair costing $20. The shopkeeper believes that after the repair the table could be sold for $70. The table should not be valued on the Statement of financial position at $70 as this assumes that a profit will be made and this is against conservatism. It should not be valued at $60 as this ignores the fact that it is damaged. The net realisable value is $70 – $20 = $50, and as this is less than the historical cost of the asset, this becomes its value on the Statement of financial position.

ACTIVITY 34.4

Depreciation exercises
[20 marks, 25 minutes]

1 A machine is purchased for $20,000. It is expected to last for six years and have a residual value of $2,000.

   a Calculate the annual depreciation charge using straight-line depreciation. [3]

   b How much will the asset be worth after one, two, three, four, five years? [5]

   c If the machine is sold off at the end of year 3 for $13,000, as it is no longer required, how much profit or loss on disposal has the firm made? [2]

2 A vehicle is purchased for $12,000. It is expected to have a useful life of four years. Using straight-line depreciation, it is depreciated by $2,500 per year.

   a What is the expected residual value of the vehicle? [3]

   b Using this residual value, calculate the new annual depreciation charge if the life expectancy had been three years. [3]

   c Explain what happens to annual operating profit when the depreciation charge is raised, as in the example above. [4]

ACTIVITY 34.5

An inventory valuation problem

The Thai leather company is still recovering from a disastrous flood that had damaged much of the stocks of leather coats and skirts that it manufactured. The company accountant was working out the new balance-sheet valuation of some of the damaged stock. Ten coats, that had cost $30 each to make, had slight water marks. These marks could be repaired at a cost of $10 per jacket. It was estimated that they could then be sold for $35 each. Without the repairs they would have to be sold as scrap for $5 each. Before the fire the coats would have been sold to shops for $50 each.

[10 marks, 12 minutes]

1 Should the firm go ahead with the repair of the coats? Explain your answer. [3]

2 Assuming that the coats are repaired, what should be the correct valuation recorded on the Statement of financial position? Justify your answer. [7]

Drawing up new accounts

You will not be asked to draw up income statements and statements of financial position from original data without an example to help you. You may be asked to amend existing accounts – so the structure of the income statement or Statement of financial position will always be given to you.

However, it is good practice to try to recall the basic structure of both accounts and how items are classified under each heading. Activities 34.7 and 34.8 are for revision purposes only. They require students to remember the basic structure and headings of both accounts. Each item of data must then be correctly identified and placed in the correct section of the accounts.

ACTIVITY 34.6

Tesco and BlackBerry revise asset values

Tesco, the major supermarket group, has reduced the asset value of its global operations by £2.3 billion. This is due to the ending of its venture in the USA market. It has also reduced the value of its UK property by £804 million as it has decided not to develop some of the sites it owns into supermarkets. Goodwill has also been reduced on its accounts by £495 million to take account of much lower demand in countries such as Turkey and the Czech Republic.

RIM – the makers of BlackBerry phones and tablets – has reduced the value of inventories on its Statement of financial position by US$360 million. This is a result of the disappointing sales of its Playbook tablet computer, which means that the expected realisable value of remaining stock is lower than expected.

[16 marks, 25 minutes]

1 Explain the impact on the shareholders equity of both companies as a result of these valuation changes. [6]

2 Explain why the accounts of these two companies would be misleading to stakeholders if these asset revaluations were not made. [10]

ACTIVITY 34.7

Income statement

[10 marks, 20 minutes]

Using the layout used in Chapter 30, construct an income statement for Lancashire Traders Ltd from the following data for the year ending 31/3/10.

- Units sold – 5,000 items @ $11.00
- Opening inventories $3,000
- Corporation tax rate 20%
- Interest paid $1,000
- Purchases of materials $40,000
- Closing inventories $8,000
- Overhead expenses $12,000
- Dividends $4,000. [10]

ACTIVITY 34.8

Statement of financial position

[10 marks, 20 minutes]

Using the layout on page 498 for Energen plc, construct a Statement of financial position for Namibia Logistics Ltd as at 31 September 2013 from the following data:

- Long-term loans $5 million
- Vehicles $10 million
- Offices $2 million
- Equipment $1 million
- Inventories $1 million
- Cash $0.2 million
- Accounts payable $1 million
- Overdraft $2.5 million
- Trade receivables $3 million
- Share capital $6 million
- Retained earnings $2.7 million. [10]

SUMMARY POINTS

- Amendments need to be made to income statements and Statements of financial position when new accounting transactions are recorded or decisions to change asset values are made.

  Capital expenditure can be differentiated from revenue expenditure by being identified as spending on an asset with a useful life of more than one year.

- Capital spending is not recorded as a cost on the income statement in the year the asset is bought, but is charged to profit in each year of the asset's useful life by a process known as depreciation.

- Valuing assets is not an exact science, as it is rare for assets to retain historical or original cost. Valuing inventories and goodwill can cause particular problems, but there are some important accounting conventions that deal with these cases.

RESEARCH TASK

- Use the Internet to view the accounts of at least one well known public limited company.

- Compare the latest income statement and the Statement of financial position with those of the previous year.

- Make a note of the major changes, e.g. changes in the revenue, profit for the year, value of non-current assets etc.

- Read the 'notes to the accounts', which usually appear after the financial statements, to discover the reasons for these major changes.

A Level exam practice questions
Case study

Midas Toys Ltd

Midas Toys Ltd was established ten years ago as a private limited company. It assembles cheap, mass-produced toys and games. The company's sales and profits have grown rapidly over the last five years, due largely to competitive prices and unusual toy designs. The major threat to the business is the risk of cheaper imports from countries with much lower wage levels. The directors of Midas are planning two strategies to defend the business against this threat.

- Take over a toy-making business – SouthAm Toys – based in a low-wage economy in South America. The purchase price has been agreed – $4 million.
- Purchase computer-controlled assembly machines for the existing factory that will make toys more quickly and with fewer workers. These machines will cost $1 million and are expected to last for five years.

	$000
Revenue	5
Cost of sales	2.4
Gross profit	3.6
Expenses	0.6
Operating profit	3.0
Tax	0.6
Profit for the year	2.4
Dividends	0.6
Retained earnings	1.8

The income statement for the year ending 31 September 2013

In the financial year ending 31 September 2014 the business recorded the following transactions and costs:

- Items sold: 3,000,000 at average price of $2.00
- Average material cost per toy: $0.85
- Overhead costs: $750,000
- Corporation tax rate: 20%
- Dividends paid: $500,000.

The company's Statement of financial position just before the takeover of SouthAm Toys and the arrival of the new machinery is shown below:

ASSETS	$000	
Non-current assets:		
Property	7,000	
Equipment	2,000	
Intangible assets	50	
	9,050	
Current assets:		
Inventories	240	
Trade receivables	640	
Cash	80	
	960	
TOTAL ASSETS		**10,010**
EQUITY and LIABILITIES		
Current liabilities:		
Accounts payable	525	
Overdraft	320	
	845	
Non-current liabilities:		
Long-term loans	3,500	
	3,500	
TOTAL LIABILITIES	**4,345**	
Shareholders' equity:		
Share capital	2,000	
Retained earnings	3,665	
Other reserves	0	
	5,665	
TOTAL EQUITY and LIABILITIES		**10,010**

[27 marks, 50 minutes]

1 Amend the income statement shown by calculating and substituting in the values for the year ending 31 September 2014,from the information provided. **[10]**

2 Calculate the annual depreciation charge for the new computer-controlled machines if, after five years, they are expected to have a residual value of $100,000. **[4]**

3 What would be the net book value of these machines at the end of the second year? **[3]**

4 Amend the Midas Statement of financial position to show the situation just after the takeover of SouthAm Toys and the arrival of the new machinery, based on the following assumptions:

   - Midas paid $300,000 more for SouthAm than the value of its net assets.
   - The net value of SouthAm is added to the non-current assets of Midas under property and intangible assets.
   - Assume that if goodwill briefly appears on the Statement of financial position, it will be included in intangible assets.
   - The takeover was financed by the issue of additional shares bought by the family owning Midas.
   - The machinery was financed by increasing long-term loans.
   - 25% of existing inventories are of old designs of toys that have been in stock for over six months. The company accountants believe that they are now worth only 50% of their original value. **[10]**

A Level essay questions

[20 marks, 45 minutes each]

1 Discuss the view that the valuation of a company's assets can never be accurate so the published Statement of financial position is of limited use to shareholders and other stakeholder. **[20]**

2 a Explain how the depreciation of non-current assets affects both a company's income statement and its Statement of financial position. **[8]**

   b Assess the reasons why accurate valuations of a company's non-current and current assets are important. **[12]**

35 Analysis of published accounts

This chapter covers syllabus section A Level 5.8.

On completing this chapter, you will be able to:

- calculate the return on capital employed ratio
- calculate the gearing ratio, the financial efficiency ratios and investment ratios
- analyse ratio results and evaluate ways in which these results could be improved
- assess the practical use of ratio analysis.

Introducing the topic

COMPARING THE ACCOUNTS OF THE COLA GIANTS

How can stakeholders in PepsiCo and Coca-Cola, the world's two best-known soft drink businesses, compare their performance? One way is to analyse their accounting results. Ratio analysis is widely used by shareholders, banks and creditors – as well as the management of the business – to assess and compare company performance.

Here are extracts from both companies' 2012 (end of December, in $ million) published accounts:

	Sales revenue	Cost of goods sold	Operating profit	Current assets	Current liabilities	Inventories	Trade accounts receivable	Capital employed
PepsiCo	65492	31291	9112	18720	17089	3581	7041	57549
Coca-Cola	48017	19053	10779	30328	27821	3264	4759	58353

trade receivables more efficiently? If a potential shareholder was planning to buy shares in just one of these companies, which one might be the better investment?

These and other questions can be answered by further analysis of published accounts.

The liquidity of both companies can be assessed by using the current ratio and acid-test ratio. The gross and operating profit margin ratios can be calculated from using the data above. This would be a good starting point in comparing the performance of these two businesses. But these ratios do not give us the complete picture. Which company is making more profitable use of the capital invested in it? Which one seems to handle inventories more effectively? Does Coca-Cola or PepsiCo manage its

Points to think about:

- Would it be sensible to compare these two companies' accounts with those of a construction company? Explain your answer.
- Do you think a high level of inventories compared with the total cost of sales is a sign of good management or not? Explain your answer.
- Why would it be useful for stakeholders to make a comparison between profit and capital invested into a business?

Introduction

The main accounting statements contained in the published accounts of a company have been explained. In Chapter 30, these accounts were analysed by using liquidity and profit margin ratios – understanding how these are measured, what the results mean and how business liquidity and profitability can be improved are important considerations for both AS and A Level

students. Further analysis of published accounts is for A Level students only.

How can the published accounts of companies be further analysed for the benefit of the account users and stakeholder groups? There are several other groups of accounting ratios and the way in which these ratios are calculated is important and has to be remembered. Just as important is what the results mean and how disappointing company performance, indicated by the results, might be improved. These are the issues focused on in this chapter.

TOP TIP

The Cambridge Business syllabus only requires you to calculate some of the ratios that follow. Other ratio results have been included to aid your understanding of the analysis of accounts and to provide a more complete assessment of ratio analysis.

Interpreting company performance

Accounting ratios are grouped into five main classifications:

1 **Profitability ratios:** These compare the gross and operating profits of the business with sales revenue. These were examined on pages 453 and 454. In addition, the return on capital employed ratio is examined below and is an important measure of the profit performance of a business.

2 **Liquidity ratios:** These give a measure of how easily a business could meet its short-term debts or liabilities. These are required for AS and A Level and were examined on page 454.

3 **Financial efficiency ratios:** These give an indication of how efficiently a business is using its resources and collecting its debts.

4 **Shareholder ratios:** These can be used by existing or potential shareholders to assess the rate of return on shares and the prospects for their investment.

5 **Gearing ratios:** These examine the degree to which the business is relying on long-term loans to finance its operations. It is a reflection of a business's financial strategy.

Profitability ratios

These are used to assess how successful the management of a business has been at earning profits for the business from sales and from capital employed. They are widely used to measure the performance of a company – and, therefore, by implication the performance of the management team too.

ACTIVITY 35.1

[16 marks, 25 minutes]

Use the extracts from the accounts of Coca-Cola and PepsiCo on page 505 to calculate, for 2012:

1 Gross profit margin for both companies. [4]

2 Operating profit margin for both companies. [4]

3 Comment on your results. [8]

TOP TIP

You are advised to remind yourself of how to calculate the gross profit margin and operating profit margin ratios.

Return on capital employed (RoCE)

This is the most commonly used means of assessing the profitability of a business – indeed, it is often referred to as the primary efficiency ratio. It compares profit with the capital that has been invested in the business. Both 'profit' and '**capital employed**' can be calculated in several ways – pity the poor A Level student! However, for the Cambridge syllabus, the following definitions and formula will be used and the profit figure will always be operating profit. You should be aware, however, that in some business situations, other ways of calculating this ratio do exist – but they do not concern us here.

 KEY TERMS

Return on capital employed (%):

$$\frac{\text{operating profit}}{\text{capital employed}} \times 100$$

Capital employed: the total value of all long-term finance invested in the business: it is equal to (non-current assets + current assets) – current liabilities *or* non-current liabilities + shareholders' equity.

	Operating profit $m	Capital employed $m	Return on capital employed RoCE
Nairobi Press Ltd	50	400	$\frac{50 \times 100}{400} \times 12.5\%$
Port Louis Press Ltd	500	5,000	$\frac{500 \times 100}{5000} \times 10\%$

From these results it is clear that the management of Nairobi Press is more effective at making the capital invested in the business earn profit.

Points to note:

- The higher the value of this ratio, the greater the return on the capital invested in the business.
- The return can be compared both with other companies and the RoCE of the previous year's performance. Making comparisons over time allows the trend of profitability in the company to be identified.
- The result can also be compared with the return from interest accounts – could the capital be invested in a bank at a higher rate of interest with no risk?

- Crucially, the RoCE result should be compared with the interest cost of borrowing finance – if it is less than this interest rate then any increase in borrowings will reduce returns to shareholders.
- The RoCE of a business can be raised by increasing the profitable, efficient use of the assets owned by the business, which were purchased by the capital employed.
- The method used for the calculation of capital employed is not universally agreed and this causes problems for comparisons between companies.
- RoCE is not related to the risks involved in the business. A high return may be the result of a successful undertaking with high risk rather than true business or managerial 'efficiency'.

See Table 35.1 for an evaluation of ways to increase RoCE.

Liquidity ratios

TOP TIP
Refer back to Chapter 30 to remind yourself how these were calculated and how to interpret the results.

ACTIVITY 35.2

[16 marks, 25 minutes]
Use the extracts from the accounts of Coca-Cola and PepsiCo on page 505 to calculate for 2012:

1 Current ratio for both companies. [4]
2 Acid-test ratio for both companies. [4]
3 Comment on your results. [8]

Financial efficiency ratios

There are many efficiency or activity ratios that can be used to assess how efficiently the assets or resources of a business are being used by management. The two most frequently used are inventory turnover ratio and days' sales in trade receivables ratio.

Inventory turnover ratio

KEY TERM

$$\text{Inventory turnover ratio} = \frac{\text{cost of goods sold}}{\text{value of inventories}}$$

In principle, the lower the amount of capital used in holding inventories, the better. Modern inventory-control theory focuses on minimising investment in inventories. This ratio records the number of times the inventory of a business is bought in and resold in a period of time. In general terms, the higher this ratio is, the lower the investment in inventories will be. If a business bought inventory just once each year, enough to see it through the whole year, its inventory turnover would be 1 and investment in inventories would be high.

This ratio can be calculated in three other ways (these will not be examined):

1 using average inventory holding – that is, the average value of inventories at the start of the year and at the end
2 using revenue, not cost of sales – this would give a very different result, but could be used if cost of sales data were not available
3 using an alternative formula that measures the average number of days that money is tied up in inventories:

$$\text{Inventory turnover ratio (days)} = \frac{\text{value of inventories}}{\text{cost of sales}/365}$$

	Cost of goods sold $m (2013)	Inventory level $m (31/12/13)	Inventory turnover ratio
Nairobi Press Ltd	125	25	$\frac{125}{25} = 5$
Port Louis Press Ltd.	2,400	600	$\frac{2,400}{600} = 4$

Possible strategies to increase RoCE	Potential limitations
Increase operating profit without increasing capital employed, for example: ■ raise prices ■ reduce variable costs per unit ■ reduce overheads, such as delayering or reducing promotion costs.	■ demand could be price elastic ■ cheaper materials could cut back on quality ■ may not be effective in increasing profit in the short run and may have drawbacks, e.g. less promotion could reduce sales
Reduce capital employed, for example: ■ sell assets that contribute nothing or little to sales/profit – use the capital raised to reduce debts	■ assets may be needed in the future, e.g. for expansion of business

Table 35.1 Evaluating strategies for increasing RoCE

According to the 2013 stock turnover ratio, Nairobi Press has more effective control over inventory management – it has a lower level of inventories compared to costs of goods sold than Port Louis Press. If Port Louis Press introduced a system of just-in-time stock management, then inventory deliveries would be more frequent but smaller in size and this would increase its inventory turnover ratio.

Points to note:

■ The result is not a percentage but the number of times inventory turns over in the time period – usually one year.

■ The higher the number, the more efficient the managers are in selling inventory rapidly. Very efficient management – such as the use of the JIT system – will give a high inventory turnover ratio.

■ The 'normal' result for a business depends very much on the industry it operates in – for instance, a fresh-fish retailer would (hopefully) have a much higher inventory turnover ratio than a car dealer.

■ For service-sector firms, such as insurance companies, this ratio has little relevance, as they are not selling 'products' held in inventories.

Days' sales in trade receivables ratio

Also known as the trade receivables' collection period, this ratio measures how long, on average, it takes the business to recover payment from customers who have bought goods on credit – the trade receivables. The shorter this time period is, the better the management is at controlling its working capital.

> **KEY TERM**
>
> **Day's sales in receivables ratio =**
> $$\frac{\text{trade accounts receivable} \times 365}{\text{revenue}}$$

It can also be calculated by using total sales on credit, thus excluding sales for cash from the calculation – which could be explained as being more accurate, as cash sales will never lead to trade receivables. A similar ratio – known as the accounts receivable turnover ratio – is calculated by:

$$\frac{\text{revenue}}{\text{trade receivables}}$$

These results shows that both companies give their customers a very long time to pay debts. Perhaps the printing market is very competitive in these cities and to gain business, long credit periods have to be offered. However, days' sales in trade receivables as high as these put a great strain on companies' working capital requirements.

Points to note:

■ There is no right or wrong result – it will vary from business to business and industry to industry. A business selling almost exclusively for cash will have a very low ratio result.

■ A high days' sales in trade receivables ratio may be a deliberate management strategy – customers will be attracted to businesses that give extended credit. Despite this, the results shown above are higher than average for most businesses and could result from poor control of trade receivables and repayment periods.

■ The value of this ratio could be reduced by giving shorter credit terms – say, 30 days instead of 60 days – or by improving credit control. This could involve refusing to offer credit terms to frequent late payers. The impact on sales revenue of such policies must always be borne in mind – perhaps the marketing department wants to increase credit terms for customers to sell more, but the finance department wants all customers to pay for products as soon as possible.

Shareholder or investment ratios

These are of particular interest to prospective investors in a business. Buying shares in a company has the potential for two kinds of financial return. Capital gains can be made by the **share price** rising. In addition, companies pay annual **dividends** to shareholders unless profits are too low or losses are being made. The shareholder ratios give an indication of the prospects for financial gain from both of these sources.

> **KEY TERMS**
>
> **Share price:** the quoted price of one share on the stock exchange.
> **Dividend:** the share of the company profits paid to shareholders.

Dividend yield ratio

This measures the rate of return a shareholder gets at the current share price.

	Trade accounts receivable $m (31 December 2013)	Revenue $m Year ending 31 December 2013	Days' sales in trade receivables
Nairobi Press Ltd	75	250	$\frac{75 \times 365}{250} \times$ 109.5 days
Port Louis Press Ltd	600	3,200	$\frac{600 \times 365}{3,200} \times$ 68.4 days

ACTIVITY 35.3

Pakistan State Oil Company Ltd (PSO)

A sharp fall in the world price of crude oil at the end of 2008 caused PSO to record a large loss in the last three months of the year. However, since then the company has become profitable and the following ratios can be used to measure the performance of the business and its financial efficiency.

	2013	2012
Gross profit margin	2.82%	2.86
Operating profit margin	0.97%	0.75
Current ratio	1.04	1.15
Acid-test ratio	0.55	0.84
Days sales in trade receivables	42	52
Inventory turnover	13.3	13.05

[40 marks, 60 minutes plus research time]

1 Do you think the management of PSO should be pleased with the performance and liquidity of the business in 2013? Justify your answer by analysing the ratio results for both years. **[16]**

   RESEARCH TASK: Use the internet link above to compare the latest ratio results for PSO with those in the table above.

2 Has the performance of PSO improved or worsened since 2013? Justify your answer. **[12]**

   RESEARCH TASK: Use the internet to research the accounting ratios of another oil company – perhaps one that operates in your country.

3 Compare these ratio results with those for PSO in the table above. Evaluate the financial performance of these two businesses. **[12]**

Pakistan State Oil facilities

509

	Dividends (2013) $m	Number of shares (m)	Dividend per share $	Market share price $ (31/12/13)	Dividend yield %
Nairobi Press Ltd	21	140	0.15	$1.50	$\frac{\$0.15 \times 100}{\$1.50} = 10\%$
Port Louis Press Ltd	140	200	0.70	$10.00	$\frac{\$0.70 \times 100}{\$10.00} = 7\%$

Shareholders in Nairobi Press are earning a higher return on their investment than if they had bought shares in Port Louis Press. Before a judgement can be made about which company to invest in, potential shareholders need to consider other ratios as well as the result for the dividend yield over time for both companies.

Points to note:

■ If the share price rises, perhaps due to improved prospects for the business, then with an unchanged dividend the dividend yield will fall.

■ If the directors propose an increased dividend, but the share price does not change, then the dividend yield will increase.

■ This rate of return can be compared with other investments, such as bank interest rates and dividend yields from other companies.

■ The result needs to be compared with previous years and with other companies in a similar industry to allow effective analysis.

■ Potential shareholders might be attracted to buy shares in a company with a high dividend yield as long as the share price is not expected to fall in coming months.

■ Directors may decide to pay a dividend from reserves even when profits are low or a loss has been made in order to keep shareholder loyalty.

■ Directors may decide to reduce the annual dividend even if profits have not fallen in an attempt to increase retained earnings – this could allow further investment into expanding the business.

■ A high dividend yield may not indicate a wise investment – the yield could be high because the share price has recently fallen, possibly because the stock market is concerned about the long-term prospects of the company.

Dividend cover ratio

This is the number of times the ordinary share dividend could be paid out of current profits after tax and interest – the 'profit for the year'. The higher this ratio, the more able the company is to pay the proposed dividends, leaving a considerable margin for reinvesting profits back into the business.

	Dividends (2013) $m	Profit after tax and interest $m	Dividend cover
Nairobi Press Ltd	21	30	$\frac{30}{21} = 1.3$
Port Louis Press Ltd	140	400	$\frac{400}{140} = 2.9$

KEY TERM

$$\text{Dividend cover ratio} = \frac{\text{profit for the year}}{\text{annual dividends}}$$

This ratio indicates to shareholders that, although the dividend yield is currently less on shares in Nairobi Press, the directors of Port Louis Press could have paid out a substantially higher dividend. Perhaps they are retaining a high level of profit to expand the business, from which shareholders could benefit in future.

Points to note:

■ If directors decided to increase dividends to shareholders, with no increase in profits, then this ratio would fall. Potential investors might start to query whether this level of dividend can be sustained in future.

■ A low result means the directors are retaining low profits for future investment and this could raise doubts about the company's future expansion.

Price/earnings ratio (P/E ratio)

This is a vital ratio for shareholders and potential shareholders. It reflects the confidence that investors have in the future prospects of the business. In general, a high P/E ratio suggests that investors are expecting higher earnings growth in the future compared with companies with a low P/E ratio. A ratio result of 1, for example, would mean that investors had very little confidence in the future earnings power of the company.

KEY TERMS

$$\text{Price/earnings ratio} = \frac{\text{current share price}}{\text{earnings per share}}$$

$$\text{Earnings per share} = \frac{\text{profit for the year}}{\text{number of issued shares}}$$

This is the amount of profit (after tax and interest) earned per share.

Points to note:

The ratio should only be compared with other companies in the same industry as investors may have different levels of optimism about the prospects for different industries. It would not be useful for investors using the P/E ratio as a basis for their investment decisions to compare the P/E of a technology company (possibly a high P/E), to

510

a utility company (possibly a low P/E), as each industry has different growth prospects. The result shows how much investors are currently willing to pay for each $1 of earnings. If a company currently has a P/E of 20, investors are willing to pay $20 for $1 of current earnings. Another way of considering the result is that shareholders in this company will wait 20 years at present earnings levels to receive payback on their investment in shares.

Gearing ratio

This measures the degree to which the capital of the business is financed from long-term loans. The greater the reliance of a business on loan capital, the more 'highly geared' it is said to be. There are several different ways of measuring gearing, but this is one of the most widely used ratios.

The same result will be obtained by using the latest terms:

$$\frac{\text{non-current liabilities} \times 100}{\text{shareholders' equity} + \text{non-current liabilities}}$$

	Non-current liabilities	Capital employed (shareholders' equity + non-current liabilities)	Gearing ratio
Nairobi Press Ltd	40	400	$\frac{40}{400} \times 100 = 10\%$
Port Louis Press Ltd	2,000	5,000	$\frac{2{,}000}{5{,}000} \times 100 = 40\%$

Nairobi Press is, clearly, less dependent on long-term loans to finance its assets than is Port Louis Press. This is a safer business strategy – but could the directors of Nairobi Press be missing some potentially profitable investment opportunities by their reluctance to increase debts? On the other hand, if interest rates and company profits fell as a result of a recession, then the directors of Port Louis Press might start to regret their decision to raise finance from debts to this extent.

Points to note:

- The ratio shows the extent to which the company's assets are financed from external long-term borrowing. A result of over 50%, using the ratio above, would indicate a highly geared business.

- The higher this ratio, the greater the risk taken by shareholders when investing in the business. This risk arises for two main reasons:
  1 The higher the borrowings of the business, the more interest must be paid and this will affect the ability of the company to pay dividends and gain retained earnings. This is particularly the case when interest rates are high and company profits are low – such as during an economic downturn.
  2 Interest will still have to be paid – but from declining profits.

- Debts have to be repaid eventually and the strain of paying back high debts compared to capital could leave a business with low liquidity.

- A low gearing ratio is an indication of a safe business strategy. It also suggests, however, that management are not borrowing to invest in, or to expand, the business. This could also be a problem for shareholders if they want rapid and increasing returns on their investment. The returns to shareholders may not increase by as great a proportion as they could for a highly geared business with a vigorous growth strategy. Shareholders in a company following a successful growth strategy financed by high debt will find their returns increasing much faster than in a slower-growth company not prepared to take risks through high borrowings.

- The gearing ratio of a business could be reduced by using non-loan sources of finance to increase capital employed, such as issuing more shares or retaining profits. These increase shareholders' funds and capital employed and lower the gearing ratio.

Alternative gearing ratios

$$\frac{\text{long-term debt}}{\text{shareholders' equity}} \times 100$$

A result of more than 100% with this ratio would indicate high gearing. Another gearing ratio is:

$$\frac{\text{total debt} \times 100}{\text{total assets}}$$

TOP TIP

Only the following gearing ratios are required for the Cambridge syllabus:

$$\frac{\text{long-term loans}}{\text{capital employed}} \times 100$$

or

$$\frac{\text{non-current liabilities}}{\text{shareholders' equity} + \text{non-current liabilities}} \times 100$$

511

ACTIVITY 35.4

Financial efficiency and gearing ratios

$m	Value of inventories (31 December 2013)	Cost of sales 2013	Sales revenue	Capital employed	Non-current liabilities	Trade accounts receivable (31 December 2013)
Company X	73	580	1,120	1,575	500	112
Company Y	150	750	1,460	2,050	1,025	319

Both of these companies operate in the same industry – furniture manufacture.

[28 marks, 50 minutes]

1 Calculate for both companies:
   - days' sales in trade receivables ratio
   - inventory turnover ratio
   - gearing ratio

   Show all workings. [12]

2 Company Y is planning to invest in a new expansion project costing $75 million.
   a Would you advise the business to raise all of this finance by selling good held in inventory and reducing its inventory levels? Explain your answer. [4]
   b Would you recommend Company Y to finance this expansion with a bank loan? Explain your answer. [8]

3 Recalculate the new gearing ratio for Company Y assuming the capital was raised from loans. (Hint: you must increase both non-current liabilities and capital employed by the amount of the increased loan.) [4]

Interest cover ratio

This is frequently used in conjunction with the gearing ratio. It assesses how many times a firm could pay its annual interest charges out of current net or operating (before tax and interest) profit. The higher this figure is, then the less risky the current borrowing levels are for the business. If the result is around 1, however, it means that all of the operating profits are being used to pay back interest costs – bad news for shareholders and for the firm's capital investment plans.

$$\text{interest cover} = \frac{\text{operating profit (before tax and interest)}}{\text{annual interest paid}}$$

Ratio analysis of accounts – an evaluation

All of the external and internal users of accounts could find ratio analysis of great help when studying the degree of success of a company's strategy. The ratios we have considered are widely used by company analysts and prospective investors before making assessments and taking important decisions on:

- whether to invest in the business
- whether to lend it more money
- whether profitability is rising or falling
- whether the management are using resources efficiently.

However, as with any analytical tool, ratio analysis needs to be applied with some caution as there are quite significant limitations to its effectiveness. These will now be considered to allow a full evaluation of this approach to be made.

Limitations of ratio analysis

1 One ratio result is not very helpful – to allow meaningful analysis to be made, a comparison needs to be made between this one result and either:
   - other businesses, called inter-firm comparisons, or
   - other time periods, called trend analysis.
   See Figure 35.1 for an example of trend analysis, showing Tesco's return on capital employed.

2 Inter-firm comparisons need to be used with caution and are most effective when companies in the same industry are being compared. Financial years end at different times for businesses and a rapid change in the economic environment could have an adverse impact on a company publishing its accounts in June compared with a January publication for another company.

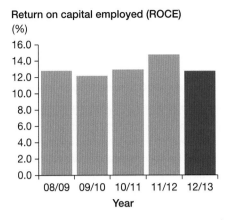

Figure 35.1 Trend analysis – Tesco's return on capital employed

3 Trend analysis needs to take into account changing circumstances over time that could have affected the ratio results. These factors may be outside the company's control, such as an economic recession.

4 As noted above, some ratios can be calculated using slightly different formulae, and care must be taken to only make comparisons with results calculated using the same ratio formula.

5 Companies can value their assets in rather different ways, and different depreciation methods can lead to different capital employed totals, which will affect certain ratio results. Deliberate window-dressing of accounts would obviously make a company's key ratios look more favourable – at least in the short term.

6 Ratios are only concerned with accounting items to which a numerical value can be given. Increasingly, observers of company performance and strategy are becoming more concerned with non-numerical aspects of business performance, such as environmental policies and approaches to human rights in developing countries that the firms may operate in. Indicators other than ratios must be used for these assessments.

7 Ratios are very useful analytical tools, but they do not solve business problems or underperformance. Ratio analysis can highlight issues that need to be tackled – such as falling profitability or liquidity – and these problems can be tracked back over time and compared with other businesses. But ratios alone do not necessarily indicate the true cause of business problems and it is up to good managers to locate these and form effective strategies to overcome them.

TOP TIP
Ratios covered by this chapter include some that are not required for the Cambridge Business syllabus: interest cover; earnings per share.

ACTIVITY 35.5

Ratio analysis

[46 marks, 60 minutes]

1 Make a list of the ratios that would be of most use to the:
   - managers of a company
   - workforce of a company
   - prospective shareholders in a company
   - bankers of a company.

   Justify your selection in each case.   [12]

2 Using the following data taken from the published accounts of two public limited companies, calculate as many of the profitability ratios, financial efficiency ratios and liquidity ratios for 2013 as you have information for. (All figures in $ million.)   [14]

Company	Capital employed	Non-current liabilities	Current assets	Current liabilities	Gross profit	Operating profit	Revenue	Inventories
A	3,000	1,500	1,200	1,400	1,100	750	4,000	400
B	200	50	70	70	75	25	300	35

3 Using your results, compare the performance, efficiency and liquidity of these two businesses, which operate in the same industry.   [8]

4 Assess the limitations of the ratio analysis you have just undertaken.   [8]

5 Explain what additional information would be useful when making this comparison   [4]

SUMMARY POINTS

- At A Level there different categories of ratio analysis in addition to those studied at AS Level.
- The return on capital employed ratio is a key measure of performance and the ways this measure of a company's profitability can be increased can be assessed.
- The financial efficiency ratios indicate manager's performance in managing working capital.
- The financial efficiency ratio results can be improved but there may be drawbacks to the methods used.
- The gearing ratio indicates the dependence of a business on external long-term finance. Finance decisions may have to take into account the likely impact on the gearing.
- The investor/shareholder ratios are important to current and potential shareholders.
- Ratio results can be compared between companies and over time.
- The limitations of ratio analysis need to be evaluated and it must be recognised that ratios do not provide the only way of analysing accounts.

514

RESEARCH TASK

- Use the Internet and newspaper stock exchange prices pages to select **two** companies that you might be interested in investing in.
- Calculate the current P/E ratios, dividend yield and dividend cover ratios – and try to find out what they were one year ago.
- Image you have 1,000 units of your own currency to spend on buying the shares of one of these companies.
- Monitor carefully what happens to the share price of 'your' company over the next three months. Recalculate the three ratios above if more up to date data is available.
- Was your investment in the shares of your company a good one? Explain your answer.

A Level exam practice questions
Case study

1 Is Intel a good shareholder investment?

Intel is the world's largest supplier of microchips and other components to companies such as Lenovo, Hewlett-Packard and Microsoft. It is expected to continue to benefit from the turnaround in demand for PCs and tablet computers since the world financial crisis and other economic problems. Intel took major steps to increase competitiveness – price cuts and substantial redundancies – and these have helped to return the company to profit.

From a shareholder's point of view, it has been a good investment over the past 12 months as the share price has risen by 18% to January 2014. The latest share price is US$24.80.

The price earnings (P/E) ratio is now 13.4 compared with a Stock Exchange average of 15.4. The earnings per share figure was $1.37 last year and this is expected by some economists to rise to $1.50 in January 2015.

The performance of the share price has been helped by management's objective of increasing dividends by over 10% per year.

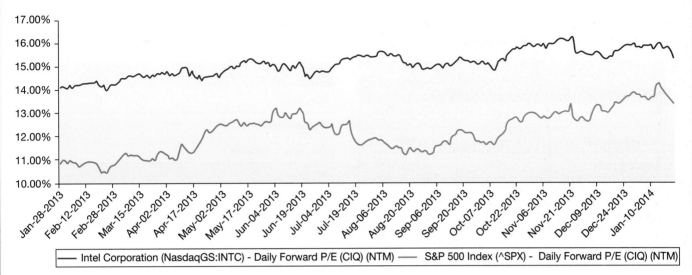

Figure 35.2 Intel's dividend yield over five years

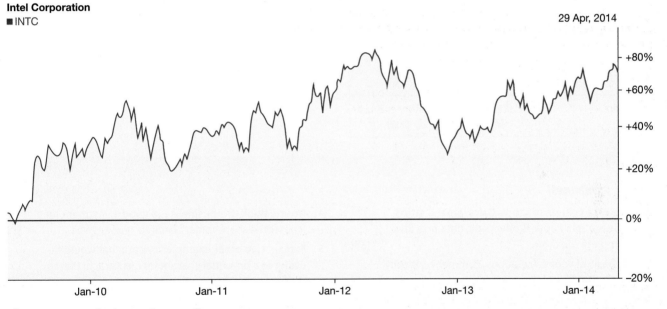

Figure 35.3 Intel's share price over five years

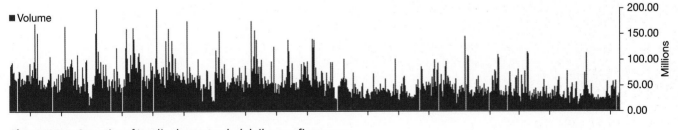

Figure 35.4 Quantity of Intel's shares traded daily over five years

[28 marks, 50 minutes]

1 Calculate the price/earnings ratio for Intel for January 2015 assuming the share price rises by a further 10% and the earnings per share forecast is accurate. [4]

2 Evaluate the usefulness of the data provided for potential shareholders when making a decision about buying Intel shares. [14]

3 Assess the importance of other information that shareholders could analyse before taking a decision to buy Intel's shares. [10]

515

2   Karachi Paper Products plc

Look at the extracts from the published accounts for Karachi Paper Products plc and answer the questions that follow.

$m	Year ending 31 October 2013	Year ending 31 October 2012
Revenue	400	330
Cost of goods sold	120	100
Operating profit	35	33
Profit for the year	30	29
Inventories	58	36
Trade accounts receivable	80	70
Current assets	125	120
Current liabilities	140	120
Dividends	20	15
Non-current liabilities	150	120
Capital employed	300	260
Number of shares issued	80m	80m
Share price	At 31 October 2013 = $4.00	At 31 October 2012 = $3.60

	2013	2012
Current ratio		
Acid-test ratio		
Days' sales in receivables		
P/E ratio		
Gearing ratio		
Gross profit margin		
Operating profit margin		
RoCE		
Dividend yield		

[54 marks, 75 minutes]

1   Copy out the column of ratios. Calculate the ratios from the Karachi Paper Products plc data provided and complete the table.   [16]

2   On the basis of your calculations, comment critically on the profitability of this business.   [8]

3   Assess the sources of finance this business could use for a new long-term expansion project costing $25 million. Use liquidity ratios and gearing ratio calculations in your answer.   [12]

4   Do you think this business is a good investment for a potential shareholder? Explain your answer.   [12]

5   Explain **two** other examples of data that would be useful to a potential shareholder in Karachi Paper Products plc.   [6]

3 Habib Manufacturing Ltd

Habib Manufacturing Ltd produces a range of saucepans and cooking pots. The manufacturing process is noisy and results in waste products that cannot be reused. The saucepans and pots are sold mainly online. Since becoming managing director of the family business four years ago, Asif Habib has taken the following decisions:

■ New machinery has been purchased. This led to higher-than-expected staff-retraining costs. Half of the necessary finance was borrowed. The government recently announced higher interest rates to deal with inflation.

■ Cheaper raw materials and components were bought in, with orders taking place only twice a year. This was designed to maximise scale economies.

■ Advertising and promotional expenses were doubled in efforts to increase sales.

■ Payments to suppliers have been delayed in order to improve cash flow.

	2011	2012	2013
Return on capital employed %	15	9	7
Gross profit margin %	38	42	43
Operating profit margin %	20	15	12
Inventory turnover	5	4	3
Current ratio	2	1.5	1.4
Acid-test ratio	1.5	0.9	0.4

Habib Manufacturing Ltd: Ratio analysis of accounts 2011–2013

Despite these changes, the overall performance of the business is not encouraging. Asif has asked the company accountant to prepare a ratio analysis of key performance indicators for the last three years. The table shows the results.

Asif is determined to take further action to improve the prospects of the business. He is now working on two further strategies. His first idea is to increase the prices of the most popular range of saucepans and pots. This will aim these products at higher-income segments of the market. Asif believes this should help to increase profitability.

His second plan is to relocate the factory away from its expensive site near the city centre. This site could be sold and a new factory on the edge of the city would be built. This should lower production costs in the long term. The new site is about 20 kilometres from the present location. It is near good roads but close to a school and a park. Asif believes that the main stakeholders in the business will benefit from this move. These are the groups in society most interested in the actions and performance of the business, such as workers, shareholders, customers, local residents and the government.

Production methods have not been changed since the business first switched to mass production. Workers have their own workstations on the production line and perform repetitive tasks each day. Communication is difficult on account of the noisy machines. Asif is concerned about reports from his human resources (HR) manager that the staff lack motivation and interest in their jobs. The HR manager has indicated that this problem could be tackled by adopting personnel- and operations-management strategies that enrich the jobs of the production-line workers, such as team-working and quality circles. Asif is confident that a higher level of pay will solve the problem once and for all.

[30 marks, 50 minutes]

1 Refer to the accounting ratio results for Habib Manufacturing Ltd and the information on recent management decisions. Analyse the possible reasons for the changing performance of the business over the last three years. [10]

2 Explain the problems this business might experience from:
 ■ declining liquidity
 ■ declining inventory turnover ratio. [8]

3 Evaluate **two** ways in which Habib might attempt to increase profitability. [12]

A Level essay questions

[20 marks, 45 minutes each]

1 Discuss the usefulness of ratio analysis to the stakeholder groups of a public limited company. [20]

2 a Outline **three** of the main groups of accounting ratios. [8]

 b 'Accounting ratio analysis has so many limitations that it is of limited use in assessing the performance of any company.' To what extent do you agree with this statement? [12]

36 Investment appraisal

On completing this chapter, you will be able to:

- understand what investment means and why appraising investment projects is essential
- recognise the information needed to allow for quantitative investment appraisal
- assess the reasons why forecasting future cash flows contributes a considerable element of uncertainty to investment appraisal
- understand and apply the payback method of investment appraisal and evaluate its usefulness
- understand and apply the average rate of return method of investment appraisal and evaluate its usefulness
- analyse the importance of qualitative or non-numerical factors in many investment decisions
- understand and apply the net present method of investment appraisal and discounted payback and evaluate their usefulness
- understand and apply the internal rate of return method of investment appraisal and evaluate its usefulness.

Introducing the topic

GLASGOW NHS INVESTS IN RFID TO REDUCE COSTS

NHS Greater Glasgow and Clyde has invested in a wireless networking project in one of its hospitals that involves tracking medical equipment with RFID (radio frequency identification) tags. The scheme will cost £70,000 and 1,500 items of equipment used for patient care will eventually be tagged. According to NHS clinical scientist Jason Britton, the hospital loses between £20,000 and £40,000 per year in wasted staff time looking for misplaced equipment such as defibrillators, infusion pumps and blood-pressure monitors. 'Devices can get lost in the system for years before they are discovered,' he said. With RFID a central office will know exactly where each of the tagged items is in the hospital. Doctors will be able to lay their hands on equipment quickly, thereby improving the level of patient care. The investment should pay back within two to three years.

NIGERIAN WATER PRIVATISATION APPEARS TO BE A GOOD INVESTMENT

The privatisation scheme selected by the Nigerian government for water supply involved private firms buying 20-year contracts to build and operate water-supply services to regions of the country. These were quite risky investments for private-sector businesses as it was unclear how much consumers would be prepared to pay for clean water supplies. An analysis of the likely profitability of these potential investments suggested that:

- profit in today's values (net present value) might be around $67 million
- the discounted rate of return (internal rate of return) should be close to 28%
- the discounted payback period would be approximately 3.8 years.

Points to think about:

- Both of these investment projects were expected to earn returns greater than the original cost. Why might it be difficult to forecast future returns from an investment?
- Both articles refer to the time to 'pay back' the investment cost. Why do you think this might be important?

Introduction

All businesses take investment decisions. Investment means purchasing capital goods – such as equipment, vehicles and new buildings – and improving existing fixed assets. Many investment decisions involve significant strategic issues – such as relocation of premises or the adoption of computer-assisted engineering methods. Other investment plans are less important to the overall performance of the business – such as replacing worn-out photocopiers. Relatively minor investment decisions will not be analysed to the same degree of detail as more substantial decisions on capital expenditure.

What is meant by 'investment appraisal'?

Investment appraisal is usually undertaken by using quantitative techniques that assess the financial feasibility of the project. Managers use investment-appraisal techniques to assess whether the likely future returns on projects will be greater than the costs and by how much. Non-financial issues can also be important too and therefore qualitative appraisal of a project might also be very important. It is still the case in some businesses, especially those dominated by the founding entrepreneur, that formal investment appraisal is not applied. Instead, the owner may develop a 'feel' for what is likely to be most successful and go ahead with that project even though no formal analysis has been undertaken. The use of such 'intuitive' or 'hunch' methods of taking investment decisions cannot be easily explained or justified – unless they turn out to be very successful.

> **KEY TERM**
>
> **Investment appraisal:** evaluating the profitability or desirability of an investment project.

In most businesses it is becoming increasingly common to find some or all of the following techniques being applied before new investment projects are given the go-ahead or abandoned. All business investments involve capital expenditure as a cash outflow. Investment projects are undertaken because the business expects there to be a return from them, in the form of cash inflows, received over the useful life of the assets purchased. Quantitative methods of appraisal will make comparisons between the cash outflows or costs of the project and the expected future cash inflows. The five most widely used methods of investment appraisal will be explained and discussed here and an analysis of the importance of qualitative factors will also be given.

We start, however, by considering the information needed to allow for quantitative appraisal of investment projects.

Quantitative investment appraisal – what information is necessary?

In judging the profitability of an investment project by using quantitative techniques the following information will be required:

- The initial capital cost of the investment, including, in the case of equipment and machinery, installation costs.
- The estimated life expectancy – over how many years returns can be expected from the investment.
- The residual value of the investment – at the end of their useful lives, the assets will be sold, earning additional net returns.
- The forecasted net returns or net cash flows from the project – these are the expected returns from the investment less the annual running cost of it.

Very little of this financial data can be said to be certain or definite and it is true to say that the quantitative techniques rely heavily on estimates and forecasts.

The five quantitative methods of investment appraisal are:

1. Payback period.
2. Average rate of return.
3. Discounted payback.
4. Net present value.
5. Internal rate of return.

Forecasting cash flows in an uncertain environment

All of the techniques used to appraise investment projects require forecasts to be made of future cash flows. These figures are referred to as '**net cash flows**'.

> **KEY TERM**
>
> **Annual forecasted net cash flow:** forecast cash inflows minus forecast cash outflows.

We assume at A Level, perhaps rather simplistically, that the cash inflows are the same as the annual revenues earned from the project, and the cash outflows are the annual operating costs. These net cash flow figures can then be compared with those of other projects and with the initial cost of the investment. Forecasting these cash flows is not easy and is rarely likely to be 100% accurate. With long-term investments, forecasts several years ahead have to be made and there will be increased chances of

519

external factors reducing the accuracy of the figures. For instance, when appraising the construction of a new airport, forecasts of cash flows many years ahead are likely to be required. The scope for external factors affecting the revenue forecasts is very great:

- An economic recession could reduce both business and tourist traffic through the airport.
- Increases in oil prices could make air travel more expensive than expected, again reducing revenue totals.
- The construction of a new high-speed rail link within the country might encourage some travellers to switch to this form of transport.

These future uncertainties cannot be removed from investment-appraisal calculations. The possibility of uncertain and unpredicted events making cash-flow forecasts inaccurate must, however, be constantly borne in mind by managers. All investment decisions involve some risk due to this uncertainty – the question is: will the future profits from the project compensate for these risks?

ACTIVITY 36.1

Cash-flow uncertainties
[15 marks, 25 minutes]

For each of the following investment projects, explain **one** reason why there is likely to be some uncertainty about the future net cash-flow forecasts earned by them:

a A project to construct a factory to make large and expensive luxury cars. [3]

b An investment in a new computerised banking system offering customers new services using the latest 'state-of-the-art' equipment that has not yet been thoroughly tested. [3]

c Cash-flow forecasts for a new sports centre that are based on a small market research sample of the local population. [3]

d The building of a new toll motorway between two cities. [3]

e The construction of an oil-fired power station. [3]

Quantitative techniques of investment appraisal

Payback method

If a project costs $2 million and is expected to pay back $500,000 per year, the **payback period** will be four years. This can then be compared with the payback on alternative investments. It is normal to refer to 'Year 0'

Year	Annual net cash flows ($)	Cumulative cash flows ($)
0	(500,000)	(500,000)
1	300,000	(200,000)
2	150,000	(50,000)
3	150,000	100,000
4	100,000 (inc. residual value)	200,000

Table 36.1 Cash flows of an investment

KEY TERM

Payback period: length of time it takes for the net cash inflows to pay back the original capital cost of the investment.

as the time period in which the investment is made. The cash flow at this time is therefore negative – shown by a bracketed amount (see Table 36.1). Table 36.1 shows the forecast annual net cash flows and cumulative cash flows. This latter figure shows the running total of cash flows and becomes less and less negative as further cash inflows are received. Notice that in year 3 it becomes positive – so the initial capital cost has been paid back during this third year. But when during this year? If we assume that the cash flows are received evenly throughout the year (this may not be the case, of course), then payback will be at the end of the fourth month of the third year. How do we know this? At the end of year 2, $50,000 is needed to pay back the remainder of the initial investment. A total of $150,000 is expected during year 3; $50,000 is one-third of $150,000, and one-third of a year is the end of month 4. To find out this exact month, use this formula:

$$\frac{\text{additional net cash inflow needed}}{\text{annual cash flow in year 3}} \times 12 \, \text{months}$$

$$= \frac{\$50,000}{\$150,000} \times 12 \, \text{months} = 4 \, \text{months}$$

So the payback period is two years and four months.

Why is the payback of a project important?

Managers can compare the payback period of a particular project with other alternative projects so as to put them in rank order. Alternatively, the payback period can be compared with a 'cut-off' time period that the business

Virgin Atlantic invested £200,000 in a new technology communication system providing direct contact with potential customers and giving them details about special fare offers: the system earned extra net cash flow of £200,000 in three months – a very rapid payback

may have laid down – for example, they will not accept any project proposal that pays back after five years.

- A business may have borrowed the finance for the investment and a long payback period will increase interest payments.
- Even if the finance was obtained internally, the capital has an opportunity cost of other purposes for which it could be used. The speedier the payback, the quicker the capital is made available for other projects.
- The longer into the future before a project pays back the capital invested in it, the more uncertain the whole investment becomes. The changes in the external environment that could occur to make a project unprofitable are likely to be much greater over ten years than over two.

- Some managers are 'risk averse' – they want to reduce risk to a minimum, so a quick payback reduces uncertainties for these managers.
- Cash flows received in the future have less real value than cash flows today, owing to inflation. The more quickly money is returned to an investing company, the higher will be its real value.

Evaluation of payback method

The payback method is often used as a quick check on the viability of a project or as a means of comparing projects. However, it is rarely used in isolation from the other investment appraisal methods (see Table 36.2).

Accounting rate of return (ARR)

The ARR may also be referred to as the average rate of return. If it can be shown that Project A returns, on average, 8% per year while Project B returns 12% per year, then the decision between the alternative investments will be an easier one to make. For simplicity, at A Level, we assume that the net cash flows equal the annual profitability.

Advantages	Disadvantages
■ It is quick and easy to calculate. ■ The results are easily understood by managers. ■ The emphasis on speed of return of cash flows gives the benefit of concentrating on the more accurate short-term forecasts of the project's profitability. ■ The result can be used to eliminate or 'screen out' projects that give returns too far into the future. ■ It is particularly useful for businesses where liquidity is of greater significance than overall profitability.	■ It does not measure the overall profitability of a project – indeed, it ignores all of the cash flows after the payback period. It may be possible for an investment to give a really rapid return of capital, but then to offer no other cash inflows. ■ This concentration on the short term may lead businesses to reject very profitable investments just because they take some time to repay the capital. ■ It does not consider the timing of the cash flows during the payback period – this will become clearer when the principle of discounting is examined in the final two appraisal methods.

Table 36.2 Payback method: advantages and disadvantages

KEY TERMS

Accounting rate of return: measures the annual profitability of an investment as a percentage of the initial investment.

$$ARR(\%) = \frac{\text{annual profit (net cash flow)}}{\text{initial capital cost}} \times 100$$

An alternative formula is:

$$ARR(\%) = \frac{\text{annual profit (net cash flow)}}{\text{average capital cost}} \times 100$$

where the average capital cost =

$$\frac{\text{initial capital cost} - \text{residual capital value}}{2}$$

TOP TIP

The formula with initial capital cost will be used in this book – but you can use either version in examination.

Table 36.3 shows the expected cash flows from a business investment costing $5 million in a fleet of new fuel-efficient vehicles. The inflows for years 1 to 3 are the annual cost savings made. In year 4, the expected proceeds from selling the vehicles are included.

The four stages in calculating ARR are shown in Table 36.4.

What does this result mean? It indicates to the business that, on average over the lifespan of the investment, it can expect an annual return of 20% on its investment. This could be compared with:

- the ARR on other projects
- the minimum expected return set by the business – the so-called criterion rate (in the example above, if the business refused to accept any project with a return of less than 15%, the new vehicle fleet would satisfy this criterion)
- the annual interest rate on loans – if the ARR is less than the interest rate, it will not be worthwhile taking a loan to invest in the project.

Evaluation of average rate of return

ARR is a widely used measure for appraising projects, but it is best considered together with payback results. The two results then allow consideration of both profits and cash-flow timings (see Table 36.5).

Year	Net cash flow
0	($5 million)
1	$2 million
2	$2 million
3	$2 million
4	$3 million (including residual value)

Table 36.3 Net cash flows for fleet investment

1	Add up all positive cash flows	= $9 million
2	Subtract cost of investment	= $9 million – $5 million = $4 million (this is total profit or total net cash flow)
3	Divide by life span	= $4 million/4 = $1 million (this is average annual profit or net cash flow)
4	Calculate the % return to find the ARR by dividing by the capital cost and x 100.	$= \dfrac{\$1 \text{ million}}{\$5 \text{ million}} \times 100 = 20\%$

Table 36.4 The four stages in calculating ARR

Advantages	Disadvantages
<ul><li>It uses all of the cash flows – unlike the payback method.</li><li>It focuses on profitability, which is the central objective of many business decisions.</li><li>The result is easily understood and easy to compare with other projects that may be competing for the limited investment funds available.</li><li>The result can be quickly assessed against the predetermined criterion rate of the business.</li></ul>	<ul><li>It ignores the timing of the cash flows. This could result in two projects having similar ARR results, but one could pay back much more quickly than the other.</li><li>As all cash inflows are included, the later cash flows, which are less likely to be accurate, are incorporated into the calculation.</li><li>The time value of money is ignored as the cash flows have not been discounted – this concept is considered later in the chapter.</li></ul>

Table 36.5 Advantages and disadvantages of ARR

Discounting future cash flows

If you have worked through the activities, you will realise that managers may be uncertain which project to invest in if the two methods of investment appraisal used give conflicting results: If project A is estimated to pay back at the end of year 3 at an ARR of 15%, should this be preferred to project B with a payback of four years but an ARR of 17%?

Managers need another investment appraisal method that solves this problem of trying to compare projects with different returns and payback periods. This third method considers both the size of cash flows and the timing of them. It does this by discounting cash flows. If the effects of inflation are ignored, a rational person would rather accept a payment of $1,000 today instead of a payment of $1,000 in one year's time. Ask yourself which you would choose. The payment today is preferred for three reasons:

1 It can be spent immediately and the benefits of this expenditure can be obtained immediately. There is no waiting involved.

2 The $1,000 could be saved at the current rate of interest. The total of cash plus interest will be greater than the offer of $1,000 in one year's time.

3 The cash today is certain, but the future cash offer is always open to uncertainty.

This is called taking the 'time value of money' into consideration. Discounting is the process of reducing the value of future cash flows to give them their value in today's terms. How much less is future cash worth compared to today's money? The answer depends on the rate of interest. If $1,000 received today can be saved at 10%, then it will grow to $1,100 in one year's time. Therefore, $1,100 in one year's time has the same value as $1,000 today at 10% interest. This value of $1,000 is called the present value of $1,100 received in one year's time.

Gezhouba Dam, China – most expensive projects are evaluated using investment appraisal

ACTIVITY 36.3

Textile company plans investment

A textile business is planning an investment programme to overcome a problem of demand exceeding capacity. It is considering two alternative projects involving new machinery. The initial outlays and future cash outflows are given below. Project Y machinery is forecast to have a life expectancy of just four years.

Year	Project X	Project Y
0	($50,000)	($80,000)
1	$25,000	$45,000
2	$20,000	$35,000
3	$20,000	$17,000
4	$15,000	$15,000
5	$10,000	–

[30 marks, 45 minutes]

1 Calculate the payback for both projects. [6]

2 Explain which project should be selected if payback is the only criterion used – and why. [3]

3 Calculate ARR for both projects. [6]

4 The business has a cut-off or criterion rate of 11% for all new projects. Would either project be acceptable with this restriction? [3]

5 Taking both the results of payback and ARR together, which project would you advise the business to invest in and why? [7]

6 What additional information would help you advise the business on the more suitable project? [5]

Discounting calculates the present values of future cash flows so that investment projects can be compared with each other by considering today's value of their returns.

Discounting – how is it done?

The present value of a future sum of money depends on two factors:

1 The higher the interest rate, the less value future cash has in today's money.

2 The longer into the future cash is received, the less value it has today.

These two variables, interest rates and time, are used to calculate discount factors. You do not have to calculate

Years	6%	8%	10%	12%	16%	20%
1	0.94	0.93	0.91	0.89	0.86	0.83
2	0.89	0.86	0.83	0.79	0.74	0.69
3	0.84	0.79	0.75	0.71	0.64	0.58
4	0.79	0.74	0.68	0.64	0.55	0.48
5	0.75	0.68	0.62	0.57	0.48	0.40
6	0.71	0.63	0.56	0.51	0.41	0.33

Table 36.6 Extract from discounted cash flow table

Year	Net cash flow $m	Discount factor	Discounted cash flow $m	Cumulative discounted cash flows
0	(5)	1	(5)	(5)
1	2	0.91	1.82	(3.18)
2	2	0.83	1.66	(1.52)
3	2	0.75	1.50	(0.02)
4	3	0.68	2.04	2.02

Table 36.7 Calculating discounted payback

these – they are available in discount tables and an extract of one is given in Table 36.6. To use the discount factors to obtain present values of future cash flows, multiply the appropriate discount factor by the cash flow. For example, $3,000 is expected in three years' time. The current rate of interest is 10%. The discount factor to be used is 0.75 – this means that $1 received in three years' time is worth the same as 75 cents today. This discount factor is multiplied by $3,000 and the present value is $2,250.

Discounted payback

This method of investment appraisal uses discounted cash flows to calculate the payback period of the capital cost. It has the same advantages and disadvantages as the simple payback period *except* that it does take the time value of money into account.

Example: Refer to Table 36.7. The simple or non-discounted payback period is two years six months. Can you confirm this? What is the discounted payback period if the rate of discount to be used is 10%? The net cash flows must be discounted first.

The discounted payback is just at the start of the fourth year and because the additional cash needed is so little, the discounted payback period would be identified as being three years – this is longer than the simple payback period and this will always be the case.

Net present value

This method again uses discounted cash flows. It is calculated by subtracting the capital cost of the investment from the total discounted cash flows. The three stages in calculating NPV are:

1 Multiply discount factors by the net cash flows. Cash flows in year 0 are never discounted, as they are today's values already.
2 Add the discounted cash flows.
3 Subtract the capital cost to give the NPV.

KEY TERM

Net present value (NPV): today's value of the estimated cash flows resulting from an investment.

The working is clearly displayed in Table 36.8. The initial cost of the investment is a current cost paid out in year 0. Current cash flows are not discounted.

Net present value is now calculated:

total discounted cash flows	= $11,940
original investment	= ($10,000)
net present value	= $1,940

What does this result mean? The project earns $1,940 in today's money values. So if the finance needed can

Year	Cash flow	Discount factors @ 8%	Discounted cash flows (DCF)
0	($10,000)	1	($10,000)
1	$5,000	0.93	$4,650
2	$4,000	0.86	$3,440
3	$3,000	0.79	$2,370
4	$2,000	0.74	$1,480

Table 36.8 Discounted cash flows

be borrowed at an interest rate of less than 8%, the investment will be profitable. What would happen to NPV if the discount rate was raised? If interest rates increased, the business would be advised to discount future cash flows at a higher rate. This will reduce NPV, as future cash flows are worth even less when they are discounted at a higher rate. The choice of discount rate is crucial to the assessment of projects using this method of appraisal.

Usually, businesses will choose a rate of discount that reflects the interest cost of borrowing the capital to finance the investment. Even if finance is raised internally, the rate of interest should be used to discount future returns. This is because of the opportunity cost of internal finance – it could be used to gain interest if left on deposit in a bank. An alternative approach to selecting the discount rate is for a business to adopt a cut-off or criterion rate. The business would use this to discount the returns on a project and, if the net present value is positive, the investment could go ahead.

Internal rate of return

Net present value is a widely used technique of investment appraisal in industry but, as it does not give an actual percentage rate of return, it is often considered together with the **internal rate of return** (see Table 36.9).

KEY TERM

Internal rate of return (IRR): the rate of discount that yields a net present value of zero – the higher the IRR, the more profitable the investment project is.

The final appraisal technique also employs the discounting concept.

This rate of discount is then compared with:

- the IRR of other projects – the highest reflects the most profitable investment
- the expected cost of capital or rate of interest and, if IRR is greater, the project should be profitable, taking the cost of borrowed capital into account
- a cut-off rate or criterion of return pre-set by the business.

The actual calculation of IRR is tedious without a spreadsheet software package. It may, however, be estimated graphically, as described below. You may wish to demonstrate your computer skills by calculating the exact IRR of this project.

The discounted cash flows of an investment project at varying rates of interest are shown in Table 36.10. As the discount rate increases, the net present value declines until a negative value is reached. These results can be plotted on a graph and the IRR estimated (see Figure 36.1).

The line formed on the graph cuts the discount rate axis. The discount rate at which this occurs is the estimated IRR. This percentage can be compared with:

- other projects
- the expected rate of interest over the life of the investment
- the business's criterion or cut-off rate – as shown on the graph; because the firm expects projects to yield at least 16%, the project is just viable according to this criterion.

TOP TIP

When calculating investment-appraisal methods, lay out your working carefully, using the types of table used in this chapter.

525

Advantages	Disadvantages
■ It considers both the timing of cash flows and the size of them in arriving at an appraisal. ■ The rate of discount can be varied to allow for different economic circumstances. For instance, it could be increased if there was a general expectation that interest rates were about to rise. ■ It considers the time value of money and takes the opportunity cost of money into account.	■ It is reasonably complex to calculate and to explain – especially to non-numerate managers. ■ The final result depends on the rate of discount used, and expectations about interest rates may be wrong. ■ Net present values can be compared with other projects, but only if the initial capital cost is the same. This is because the method does not provide a percentage rate of return on the investment.

Table 36.9 Advantages and disadvantages of net present value

ACTIVITY 36.4

Discounting cash flows

[19 marks, 25 minutes]

1 Calculate the present day values of the following cash flows:
   - $10,000 expected in four years' time at prevailing rate of interest of 10% [2]
   - $2,000 expected in six years' time at prevailing rate of interest of 16% [2]
   - $6,000 expected in one year's time at prevailing rate of interest of 20%. [2]

2 The following net cash flows have been forecast by a manufacturer for the purchase of a labour-saving machine:

Year	Net cash flows ($)
0	(15,000)
1	8,000
2	10,000
3	5,000
4	5,000

a Calculate the simple payback period. [3]
b Discount all cash flows at a rate of discount of 10%. [4]
c Calculate the discounted payback period. [3]
d Calculate the net present value. [3]

ACTIVITY 36.5

Net present value

[12 marks, 20 minutes]

Using the data in Table 36.10:
a recalculate the net present value at a discount rate of 20% [4]
b explain why the net present value is negative [2]
c explain why the project would not be viable if the business had to borrow finance at 20% [2]
d if the criterion rate used by the business for new investments is 10%, would this project have a positive net present value, and would it therefore be acceptable? [4]

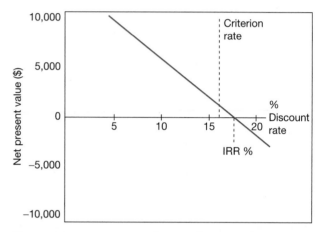

Figure 36.1 Net present value as a function of discount rate

Year	Net cash flows	DCF @ 8%	DCF @ 12%	DCF @ 20%
0	($35,000)	($35,000)	($35,000)	($35,000)
1	$15,000	$13,950	$13,350	$12,450
2	$15,000	$12,900	$11,850	$10,350
3	$10,000	$7,900	$7,100	$5,800
4	$10,000	$7,400	$6,400	$4,800
Net present value		$7,150	$3,700	($1,600)

Table 36.10 Discounted cash flows at varying rates of interest

Evaluation of internal rate of return

This is a widely used method of investment appraisal due to it taking the time value of money into account and also because of the simplicity of comparing IRR results for different investment projects. However, even a project with a very high IRR will require a healthy cash position if the business is to be able to afford a large initial capital

investment that might take several years to pay back (see Table 36.11).

 KEY TERM

Criterion rates or levels: the minimum levels (maximum for payback period) set by management for investment-appraisal results for a project to be accepted.

Advantages	Disadvantages
■ By giving a percentage rate of return, different projects costing different amounts can be compared. ■ The IRR is easily compared with the rate of interest or the **criterion rate** of the business. ■ It avoids the need to choose an actual rate of discount.	■ The calculation is tedious without a computer. ■ By giving an exact result, it can mislead business users into believing that investment appraisal is a precise process without risk and uncertainties.

Table 36.11 Advantages and disadvantages of internal rate of return

Qualitative factors – investment decisions are not just about profit

Investment appraisal techniques provide numerical data, which are important in taking decisions. However, no manager can afford to ignore the other factors that cannot be so easily expressed in a numerical form and may have a crucial bearing on a decision. These are referred to as qualitative factors and may include the following:

■ The impact on the environment and the local community – growing concern about environmental issues is forcing businesses to consider carefully plans for developments in sensitive areas. Bad publicity stemming from the announcement of some proposed investment plans may dissuade managers from going ahead with a project because of the long-run impact on image and sales. An example is the dispute over the building of a third runway at London's Heathrow Airport.

■ Closely related to this is the risk that certain projects may not receive planning permission and this would prevent continuation of the scheme. It is the duty of local planning officers to weigh up the costs and benefits of a planned undertaking and to act in the best interests of the community. Members of that community will often have a direct role through a public enquiry or may set up a pressure group to make their views known and try to achieve a particular outcome.

■ The aims and objectives of the business must be a key consideration. The decision to close bank branches and replace them with internet- and telephone-banking services involves considerable capital expenditure – as well as the potential for long-term savings. Managers may, however, be reluctant to pursue these investment policies if there is concern that the aim of giving excellent and personal customer service is being threatened. Similarly, the decision to replace large numbers of workers with labour-saving machinery may be reversed if the negative impact on human relations within the business appears to be too great.

■ Different managers are prepared to accept different degrees of risk. No amount of positive quantitative data will convince some managers, perhaps as a result of previous experience, to accept a project that involves a considerable chance of failure.

TOP TIP

Unless the question asks **only** for an analysis of numerical or quantitative factors, your answers to investment appraisal questions should include an assessment of qualitative factors too.

KEY CONCEPT LINK

Business investment projects aim to **create value** for shareholders but the impact on other stakeholders is usually considered too. Is it necessarily true that more **innovative** investment projects – such as completely new technology - create more value than less innovative ones?

Investment appraisal – final evaluation

A danger of analysing numerical results is that the user of the information – managers or, in your case, students – may be misled into assuming that the results must be certain and definite. This is very rarely the case and is clearly not true as far as the results of investment appraisal are concerned. Due to the uncertainties over future cash flows, operating costs, movements in interest rates and other variables, the results of the four investment-appraisal techniques can only produce important guides upon which managers may build their final decision.

A further point of evaluation concerns the conflicting nature of the results that are often obtained from investment appraisal calculations. Should a project with a fast payback period be preferred over one with a higher ARR or net present value? Much will depend on the manager's attitude to risk and the balance to be achieved between risk and potential future profits. Investment decisions should not be taken without a detailed consideration of the objectives of the business,

527

ACTIVITY 36.6

Location investment decision

The owner of a shoe shop is planning another branch and has to decide between two new locations that involve large capital investment – the business cannot afford both of them. He has forecast the following annual net cash flows for these two locations. These forecasts are based on market research and cost estimates. The cash flows are as follows:

(All in $000)		
Year	Location A	Location B
0	(12)	(12)
1	3	6
2	4	5
3	5	3
4	6	2
4	5	5

[36 marks, 50minutes]

1 Calculate the simple payback period for both projects and comment on your results. [4]

2 Calculate the ARR for both projects. [4]

3 Explain why the manager might find it difficult, in the light of your results, to make a choice between these two projects. [4]

4 Using the discount factors on page 524, calculate the net present value of both locations at:
   ■ 10% discount
   ■ 20% discount [6]

5 Comment on your results to question 4. [4]

6 Using all of your results, recommend to the manager which location you consider should be selected, on the basis of quantitative data. [8]

7 How reliable are these cash-flow forecasts likely to be? [6]

as sheer profit may be of less importance than a quick and relatively certain return on the investment.

The significance of objectives is again apparent when the impact of qualitative factors is being considered. Increasing weight is being given to these by businesses in many countries as a result of the growing impact of pressure groups and the rising demands for ethical decision-making that considers wider issues than just short-term shareholder returns. Creating value from new investment projects need not just be about shareholder returns but about benefits to other stakeholder too.

Therefore, investment appraisal results are often necessary but not sufficient guidelines for business investment decisions. For example, a clothing manufacturer could decide not to open a new factory in a country with no labour-protection laws for fear of pressure-group action – even though the investment appraisal results could have been very positive.

SUMMARY POINTS

- Business investment is expenditure on capital assets.
- Decisions about which investment project to go ahead with have to be taken because, as resources are always limited, not every project can be financed.
- Decisions about new investment projects could be taken on the basis of a business owner's 'hunch' or belief that such a scheme would be successful, but this is not true investment appraisal.
- Both quantitative and qualitative factors should be considered when analysing an investment project.
- Quantitative techniques require forecasts to be made – most crucially about future net cash returns from the proposed investment, but also about the expected lifespan of the assets, residual value and interest rates.
- The five techniques of investment appraisal that can be divided into two groups: those that do not require future returns to be discounted – payback and average rate of return – and those that do – discounted payback, net present value and internal rate of return.
- Qualitative factors are becoming increasingly important for business when investment decisions are being taken – they include the impact on the environment, the reaction of pressure groups, the attitude of the business to risk and the impact of the change on the workforce.

RESEARCH TASK

- Identify a major investment project that is planned or being undertaken in your country – either in the private sector or in the public sector.
- Analyse how the initial capital cost and future cash flows could be estimated for this project.
- Which technique of investment appraisal is likely to be most significant in the case of this investment? Explain your answer.
- Examine the likely qualitative factors that could have been considered before this investment decision was taken.

A Level exam practice questions
Case studies

1 King and Green Ltd

King and Green Ltd is an old, established soft drinks business. It manufactures and sells a wide range of soft drinks. Since the huge growth of supermarket 'own label' brands, the business has depended for most of its sales on cafés and restaurants – mainly in the south of the country. The company is profitable – but only just – and the return on capital employed is below that of much larger drinks businesses. The directors of King and Green are considering investing in new equipment to update the production line. There are two main options:

Option 1 is to purchase fully automated equipment that would require just one operator per shift. This would allow a very fast switch from one type of soft drink to another. Water-pollution levels are expected to be very low. Two shifts a day will be used.

Option 2 is to invest in less-expensive machines that have an established reliability record but higher pollution levels. Each machine needs its own operator for each shift. Four machines would be needed, each producing one type of soft drink. The firm operates two shifts a day at present. Therefore four production workers are needed for each shift.

The expected life of each option is five years. Excluding labour costs, the net cash flows (cash returns less running costs) anticipated from each option are as shown in the table below. The total initial investment required would be:

- Option 1 $355,000.
- Option 2 $140,000.

Production workers in option 2 will be paid the same rate as currently – $7,000 per year. The operators for option 1 will receive $10,000 because of the higher degree of technical proficiency required. The company can borrow capital at 10%.

Year	Option 1 $	Option 2 $
1	150,000	120,000
2	120,000	100,000
3	100,000	100,000
4	100,000	80,000
5	80,000	80,000

529

[43 marks, 60 minutes]

1   Calculate the total labour costs of option 2 for each year of operation. [3]

2   Recalculate the net cash flows for both options, taking the labour costs into account. [6]

3   Using these cash flows, undertake an investment appraisal of the two options using:
   - payback [6]
   - discounted payback [6]
   - accounting rate of return [6]
   - net present value. [6]

4   Using only the results of your investment appraisal, which option would you advise the directors to accept? [4]

5   Explain **two** other factors that might influence the final investment decision. [6]

2   Investing to stay competitive

Asia Print plc is a large printing firm offering a range of services to industry, such as printed catalogues, leaflets and brochures. It operates in a very competitive market as it is relatively easy for new firms to join using the latest computer software 'page-making' packages. In an effort to maintain market share, the directors of Asia Print plc are considering several new investment projects. The two most promising schemes are:

Project Y: A newly designed highly automated Japanese-built printing press with fast changeover facilities and full-colour capability. Direct internet links with customers would allow for rapid input of new material to be printed. Two highly trained operatives will be required and this would mean six redundancies from existing staff.

Project Z: A semi-automated German-built machine with a more limited range of facilities but with proven reliability. Existing staff could operate this machine but there would be three redundancies. It is very noisy and local residents might complain.

The finance director was asked to undertake an investment appraisal of these two machines. He had gathered the following data. Each additional unit produced would be sold for an average of $1.25 but there would be additional variable costs of $0.5 per unit. In addition, the annual operational cost of the two machines is expected to be $1 million for Y and $0.5 million for Z. The introduction of either machine would involve considerable disruption to existing production. Staff would have to be selected and trained for project Y and the trade union was very worried about potential job cuts. The residual value of Y is expected to be $1 million and of Z, $0.5 million.

	Project Y	Project Z
Purchase price ($m)	20	12
Expected life expectancy	5 years	4 years
Forecast annual sales (m. units)	8	6

[58 marks, 75 minutes]

1   Calculate the forecast annual net cash flows from the information given. [8]

2   Present all relevant data in a table and calculate the simple payback period for both projects. [4]

3   Calculate the ARR for both projects. [4]

4   Calculate the net present value for both projects. The company's existing cost of borrowed capital is 12%. [8]

5   Estimate, using the graphical technique, the internal rate of return for both projects. [12]

6   Using your results for all four methods of investment appraisal, write a report to the directors to advise them which project they should opt for, on the basis of quantitative information. [12]

7   To what extent do you think qualitative factors should influence investment decisions such as this one by Asia Print plc? [10]

....

A Level essay questions

[20 marks, 45 minutes each]

1   a   Explain:

■   the payback method of investment appraisal

■   the average rate of return method.   [8]

b   Discuss the view that as quantitative investment appraisal is based on potentially inaccurate cash-flow forecasts
there is little point in a business such as Apple using these two techniques when making the strategic choice
between investment projects.   [12]

2   Evaluate the relative significance of quantitative investment-appraisal results and qualitative issues in appraising a
proposed new airport development in your country.   [20]

End of Unit 5: Exam-style case study questions

Sports Shoe Traders (SST)

SST is a public limited company that makes a wide range of sports shoes. These are sold to some of the biggest retailers in the country. SST sports shoes are cheap copies of the most popular styles from famous international sport shoe brands. The company owns four factories that manufacture these shoes. At present it is difficult for the finance director to analyse the performance of each factory and each shoe style as costs and revenues are not clearly divided between profit centres. He reported to his fellow directors: 'I propose a new budgetary system that allocates annual financial targets to each factory manager and the marketing managers responsible for each shoe style. These budgets will be agreed in advance with the managers concerned so they will feel that it is their responsibility if there are any adverse variances.'

Sportstar brand

Senior managers in the company have recently conducted a strategic analysis of the business. The results of this convinced the CEO that SST should start developing sports shoe styles for the high income market. These shoes, to be marketed under the Sportstar brand, would be designed and developed by a new team of SST designers and the styles would not be copies of internationally known brands. The new styles of quality sports shoes will be manufactured in a new SST factory.

Factory location

Two potential locations are being studied by the operations director of SST. She has collected the data shown in Appendix 1. Location A is in an area of high unemployment and a government grant is available that would reduce initial capital costs. However, employee training costs would be high.

Location B is close to other shoe-making factories, some of which have closed recently, creating redundancies among skilled shoe-makers. The operations director and the finance director are meeting this afternoon to assess the financial benefits of both sites by analysing the data in Appendix 1.

Raising capital – cut dividends?

The CEO wants to finance the new investment in the Sportstar range of shoes from internal sources. He suggested at a recent board meeting that dividends should be reduced to $40 million this year. 'We need to retain most of the profits in the company to finance this new project and to keep the gearing ratio at an acceptable level. If the shareholders agree to this proposal to cut dividends at the annual general meeting (AGM) then they can look forward to higher profits in future when the Sportstar brand investment starts to yield returns.' Appendix 2 shows a summary of SST's accounts that will be presented to the AGM.

Should SST amend the way it records its accounts?

As a public limited company, SST has to publish its financial statements each year. These are used by many stakeholders to assess the performance and stability of the company. The CEO has been discussing with SST's finance director whether the company's methods used to record the valuation of assets should be changed. The CEO explained: 'If we extended the depreciation period on equipment, the asset values would appear to be greater and the annual depreciation charge against profits lower.' 'Yes, I agree,' replied the finance director, 'and if the Sportstar brand takes off we could include a value for that under intangible assets. However, some stakeholders might be concerned that we will be making it more difficult to assess SST's performance over time if we amend the way we record the accounts.'

A Level 50 marks 90 minutes

1   Analyse the benefits to SST of adopting the budgeting system proposed by the finance director.   [10]

2   a   Refer to Appendix 2. Calculate for 2013 the:
      i   price/earnings ratio   [3]
      ii   dividend yield.   [3]
   b   Recommend to the directors of SST whether to reduce the 2013 dividend payment to shareholders, as proposed by the CEO. Justify your recommendation using your results from question 2a and other information.   [10]

3   Evaluate whether the CEO and SST's finance director should amend the ways in which assets are valued on SST's financial statements.   [10]

4   Refer to Appendix 1. Recommend which of the two locations SST should choose, using the results of appropriate quantitative techniques in your answer.   [14]

Appendix 1: Forecast data for the two proposed locations for the new factory

	Location A	Location B
Cost of site and capital construction costs	$15 million	$25 million
Forecast annual cash inflows	$14 million	$14 million
Forecast annual cash outflows	$8 million	$6 million
Life expectancy of factory and equipment	10 years	10 years
Annual fixed costs	$5 million	$6 million
Forecast unit contribution	$15	$18
Kilometres from SST head office	50	20
Kilometres to nearest motorway	12	34

KEY CONCEPT REVIEW

Innovative new shoe styles could help SST create value for **shareholders**. Might other **stakeholders** benefit too? The management of SST are using a range of techniques to help them determine the best future strategies for the business. Is there any evidence that these options are **customer-focused**? Should they be? Moving to a new location will involve managing change including the impact on the workforce.

Appendix 2: Summary accounting data for SST

	Year ending 31 October 2013	Year ending 31 October 2012
Total dividends	$40 million (proposed by CEO)	$60 million
Total profit after tax	$85 million	$90 million
Total number of issued shares	200 million	200 million
Dividend per share	$0.20	$0.30
Earnings per share	$0.425	$0.45
Share price	$5	$6
Price/earnings ratio	See question 2a	13.3
Dividend yield	See question 2a	5%

Unit 6:
Strategic management

Introduction

Strategy in business refers to the key decisions that are taken to ensure that businesses survive and succeed in the long term. These strategic decisions often involve initiating and managing major change within an organisation. This unit examines models of the strategic management process – such as strategic analysis, strategic choice and strategic implementation – together with the related strategic thinking and analysis tools that help to highlight choices and put resulting strategies into action.

This section brings together the underlying concepts of the subject. In developing and

deciding between appropriate strategies, management must be:

- customer focused – to ensure that the long-term plans meet consumers' needs and generate conditions that will allow the creation of value

- aware of external changes and conscious of the need to manage internal change as a result of new strategies

- innovative – as the pace of external change often requires completely new solutions to business problems.

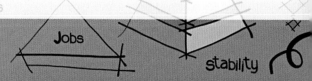

What is strategic management?

On completing this chapter, you will be able to:

- understand the meaning of corporate strategy and strategic management
- differentiate between strategic decisions and tactical decisions
- analyse the need for strategic management
- discuss the link between strategy and organisational structure
- evaluate the importance of business strategy in determining competitive advantage in an increasingly competitive world.

Introducing the topic

SIEMENS STRATEGY FOR HIGHER PROFITABILITY

Poor planning in recent years has been blamed for the current low levels of customer orders and weak share price performance of Siemens.

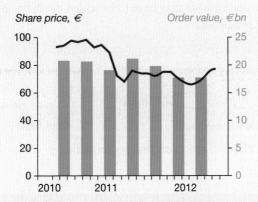

Figure 37.1 Siemens share price and value of customers' orders

Siemens is now targeting a profit margin of at least 12%. To reach this target, the company plans to reduce its costs by €6 billion, increase competitiveness, and reorganise its structure to become less bureaucratic.

Two stages of this new 'Siemens 2014' strategy have already been decided upon and are being implemented. First, it has acquired LMS International for around €680 million. LMS sells simulation software in 15 countries for evaluating mechatronic systems in airplanes and cars. With the acquisition of LMS, Siemens will hold a top position in this software segment and can improve the innovative strength of its customers.

Second, Siemens will restructure its water technology business. In the future, the water business will focus on Siemens' core competencies in automation and advanced equipment, while activities involved in processing and treating water and wastewater will be sold.

Other elements of the new strategy include:

- **Cost reduction:** Cost savings of around €3 billion are expected from the improved integration of the key processes of design, development and production. Around €1 billion is to be saved by increasing global capacity utilisation.
- **Go-to-market:** The sales setup will be more flexibly adapted to regional circumstances.
- **Optimised structure and management:** The company's worldwide structure will be further optimised and redundant functions and duplicate processes will be eliminated.

The complexity of processes and regulations will be reduced in order to give the company's business units greater entrepreneurial freedom and optimise their work with customers.

Points to think about:

- What do you understand by the term 'strategy' from this case study?
- What are likely to be the benefits to Siemens of introducing the plans outlined in the case study? Explain your answer.
- In deciding on long-term strategies, explain why it is important to establish a clear long-term aim.

Introduction

The first five units of this book have all been focused on either external constraints (Unit 1) or decision-making within functional departments (Units 2–5). Unit 6 is different because it deals with those business decisions that determine and influence the long-term direction of the whole business. These decisions have an impact on all functional departments – 'cross-functional decisions'– not just one of them. See Table 37.1 for the stages of **strategic management**.

Corporate strategy

In simple terms a strategy is 'how we get from where we are now to where we want to be in the future'. A successful business will have a vision or ultimate goal. Its strategy will be a clear plan and set of policies that should push it towards achieving this vision. Before we go on to assess the role of **corporate strategy**, it will help to have some clear definitions of the terms we will be using in this unit.

KEY TERMS

Corporate strategy: a long-term plan of action for the whole organisation, designed to achieve a particular goal.

Tactic: short-term policy or decision aimed at resolving a particular problem or meeting a specific part of the overall strategy.

Strategic management: the role of management when setting long-term goals and implementing cross-functional decisions that should enable a business to reach these goals.

A longer explanation of corporate strategy is that it is a future plan, based on an assessment of the company's current position and the external environment, containing key business objectives and the decisions needed to achieve these. Corporate strategy asks the big questions – such as 'which markets and products do we want to be in?' It also makes the big decisions – such as 'can we expand from manufacturing operations into retailing too?' All businesses – indeed all organisations – need a corporate strategy to provide integration, direction and focus.

Establishing corporate strategy

Corporate strategy will be influenced by four main factors (see Figure 37.2).

Resources available

All business resources are finite. Scarce resources will force firms to choose which strategies to proceed with and which to drop or scale back. A strategy of launching a new product nationwide may have to be scaled down because of lack of resources.

Figure 37.2 Influences on strategy formation

Key stages of strategic management	Reasons why important
1 Assessing the current position of the company in relation to its market, competitors and the external environment.	Decisions that do not start from knowledge of 'where the business is now' may be inappropriate and ineffective.
2 Setting the company's mission, vision and objectives – these may be new if the business is undergoing a significant change of direction.	Chapter 4 examined the importance of having clear and well-defined aims and objectives to provide a clear sense of overall direction to the work of the whole organisation.
3 Taking important long-term decisions that will push the business towards the objectives set.	A new direction for a business will require key decisions to be taken about products and markets.
4 Integrating and coordinating the activities of the different functional areas.	As strategic decisions are cross-functional, all departments must work together to implement them successfully. So a decision to enter a new geographical market will need input from finance, marketing, HR and operations management.
5 Allocating sufficient resources to put decisions into effect.	Changing strategy is rarely cheap and resources must be provided at the right time and in sufficient quantities to allow the new policies to work.
6 Evaluating success – evaluating the overall performance of the business and its progress towards objectives.	The outcome of the strategy should be measured against the original objectives set for it. Lessons can be learnt from both failed and successful strategies.

Table 37.1 What strategic management involves

Other strengths of the business

If a business has proven capabilities in certain areas – for example in researching heart-disease drugs or in converting large country houses into apartments – it is often wisest to apply these strengths when devising future strategies. A long-term plan that takes a business away from a proven field of operation may require business skills and experience it does not have. In addition, expansion of the business may be best achieved if some low-performing areas of the business (or non-core businesses) are sold off. In this way, the firm will be concentrating on its current successes to achieve growth. Thus, Pepsi, after it purchased Quaker Oats, sold off the breakfast cereal division, but kept the soft drink division, which sells the highly successful Gatorade drink in the USA.

Competitive environment

Competitors' actions are a major constraint or limit on business strategy. Innovations by competitors may be difficult to copy or to better. An example is Nintendo's Wii gaming system, which was a break from the incremental development of computer games by Nintendo's rivals. Major new promotional campaigns could prove to be very effective. All businesses operate in a competitive environment to a greater or lesser degree. Price reductions by supermarkets selling petrol in the UK forced a change of strategy on to the main petrol retailers. Esso quickly adopted a 'price-watch' strategy, which promised prices as low as local supermarkets. Would this plan have been introduced without competitive pressures?

Objectives

Clearly, the objectives of the business will influence strategy. Increasing shareholder wealth in the short term might not be best served by investing in extensive research and development with a payback many years into the future. In fact, maximising returns to shareholders might not be the central objective of the business – consider the 'triple bottom line' approach to corporate objectives in Unit 1. If a business has a clear social-responsibility objective, it is likely to pursue different strategies from those of a business that is focusing on short-term shareholder returns.

Strategy and tactics

Strategic management is the highest level of managerial activity. It is undertaken by or at least closely supervised by the chief executive officer and approved by the board of directors. In most large organisations there are several layers of management. Under the broad corporate strategy role of the senior directors there are typically

Strategies	Description
Corporate strategy	The overall strategy development for the whole corporation.
Business strategy	Separate business divisions of a large corporation – product or geographical-market business units – must form strategies to achieve and sustain competitive advantage. If successful, the corporate strategy is also likely to succeed.
Functional strategies	These plans are limited to the department's own functional responsibilities such as product development strategies, marketing strategies and human resource strategies.

Table 37.2 The strategy hierarchy

Figure 37.3 Functional strategy (formed after corporate and business strategy)

business-level competitive strategies and functional department strategies. These must be coordinated with the overall corporate strategy to increase the chances of achieving the organisation's long-term aims (see Table 37.2 and Figure 37.3).

Tactics, on the other hand, are concerned with making smaller-scale decisions aimed at reaching more limited and measurable goals, which themselves are part of the longer-term strategic aim. It is important to be clear about the distinction between tactics and strategies (see Table 37.3 and Activity 37.1).

The need for strategic management

The process of strategic management has three key stages (see Figure 37.4):

1 strategic analysis – where is the business now?
2 strategic choice – identifying, choosing and deciding between options
3 strategic implementation – planning for and managing change

These three stages are the focus of the final three chapters of this book. If a business did not engage in strategic management it would fail to:

- plan for the future
- respond logically to the changing business environment
- make effective long-term decisions based on clear objectives.

Strategic decisions, e.g. to develop new markets abroad	Tactical decisions, e.g. to sell a product in different-sized packaging
long-term	short- to medium-term
difficult to reverse once made – departments will have committed resources to it	reversible, but there may still be costs involved
taken by directors and/or senior managers	taken by less senior managers and subordinates with delegated authority
cross-functional – will involve all major departments of the business	impact of tactical decisions is often only on one department

Table 37.3 Key differences between tactical decisions and strategic decisions

ACTIVITY 37.1

Business strategy or business tactics?

Business context	Decision	Strategic or tactical – and explanation
Multinational drinks company	switch from cans to plastic bottles	
Supermarket business	start selling non-food items, such as clothes, for the first time	
Steel-making company	recruit production supervisors internally, not externally	
Holiday tour operator	increase prices of holidays to a popular destination	
Major computer manufacturer	develop a range of advanced mobile (cell) phones with Internet capability	

[15 marks, 15 minutes]

Copy the following table. Are the decisions strategic or tactical? Explain your answer in each case.   **[15]**

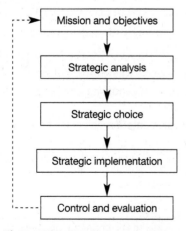

Figure 37.4 Strategic management

 KEY CONCEPT LINK

Strategic decisions need to be **customer-focused** to increase the probability that the new long-term plans will **create value**.

Corporate strategy and organisational structure

Is there a link between the strategies that businesses decide on and the internal organisational structure? The famous business historian Alfred Chandler certainly thought so. His thesis that 'structure follows strategy' was based on detailed case studies of four giants of US industry – DuPont (chemicals), General Motors (vehicles), Sears Roebuck (retailing) and Standard Oil. Over time all four of these organisations had:

- acquired labour and raw materials to allow for growth that required the build-up of marketing and distribution channels
- established a functional or departmental structure to improve specialisation and efficiency
- adopted growth-and-diversification strategies – new markets and new products to overcome the limits of the original home market
- developed divisional organisational structures that allowed geographical regions or product groups to be created with considerable independence but controlled, ultimately, from a centralised headquarters – Chandler called this the M-form organisational structure.

Chandler's central conclusion was that companies are driven by market growth and technological change to develop greater diversity in the markets they operate in and the products they sell. This strategy of diversity could only be managed effectively, according to Chandler, if they changed their internal management structure to a multi-divisional one (see Figure 37.5).

Example 1: Merger with the strategic objective of creating product-focused profit centres

The 1988 merger of Asea and Brown Boveri was, at the time, Europe's biggest-ever cross-border merger. The organisational structure of the merged Asea Brown Boveri (ABB) was changed radically by a young new chief executive, Percy Barnevik. He adopted the strategy of global market penetration in key product areas such as power systems and robotics. The functionally oriented groups at head office were replaced by a cross-functional team of top executives. Product divisions were made increasingly independent of head office so that they could

operate flexibly within the markets they traded in. There was a strong principle of decentralisation of responsibility. ABB's mission, values and policies stated: 'Our guiding principle is to decentralise the group into distinctive profit centres and give individual accountability to each.'

Crucially, this new structure was only made operationally possible by the development of electronic forms of communication and management-information systems that allowed the business to delayer its traditional hierarchical structures. The fully automated ABACUS system (**A**sea **B**rown Boveri **A**ccounting and **C**omm**U**nication **S**ystem) allowed accurate and speedy information flows between the decentralised product divisions and the executives at head office.

Example 2: Strategy of developing new markets leading to new structure

The strategy of operating in new geographical markets usually means that a business creates a 'division' or section that takes responsibility for key decisions and overall performance. This is the classic M-form as analysed by Chandler.

As the global spread of Coca-Cola increased, the company decentralised its organisational structure by cutting half of its Atlanta headquarters and moving regional managers closer to the countries they were responsible for. In India, decision-making has been moved further down the chain of command to different geographical areas of that vast and diverse country – with different market requirements in different regions.

Example 3: Strategy of a conglomerate to cut costs and increase flexibility

The Tata group of companies has embarked on a programme of delayering the organisational structures of all of its business units. The intention is to reduce the average number of management layers from ten to six. A spokesman said that, from an organisational point of view, layers one to six will have clearly defined job descriptions to equate jobs of a similar nature across the Tata group of companies. This will ensure mobility across the organisation. Managers will get the opportunity to work in different departments within each business division, as well as the opportunity to work in different group companies.

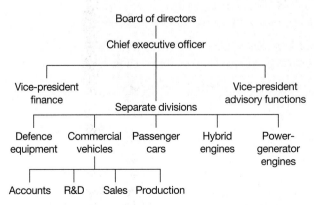

Figure 37.5 A typical multi-divisional structure (vehicle manufacturer)

TOP TIP
When answering questions about strategic decisions, try to analyse the external and internal changes that are making strategic change inevitable.

539

Strategic management at Johnson & Johnson

Johnson & Johnson is a broadly based health care company. Across its pharmaceutical and consumer businesses, it has the know-how to bring completely new health care solutions to market.

The senior management team set the company's fundamental strategic direction centrally with the advice and support of the board of directors. Strategies are implemented locally at more than 275 operating companies located in 60 countries worldwide.

The company operates a decentralised management system. Senior management groups at each operating company are responsible for their own strategic plans within the strategic outline set by the board. In developing these plans, employees worldwide are guided by the ethical principles and responsibilities outlined in the company's 'Our Credo'.

The senior management team meets throughout the year with board members to discuss strategic direction and major developments of the company's businesses. This interactive, ongoing dialogue provides the directors with insight into the activities and direction of the company's business and highlights the need for any changes in strategy.

[28 marks, 40 minutes]

1 Assess the advantages and potential risks to a multinational business of setting 'the company's fundamental strategic direction **centrally**' but implementing strategies **locally**. [14]

2 Evaluate the importance to effective strategic management of frequent discussions to evaluate and possibly amend the strategic direction of a business. [14]

Business strategy and competitive advantage

World trade is growing faster than world GDP – this is a key consequence of globalisation. Trade barriers are being reduced and protectionist policies are no longer acceptable to the many countries that believe in the free-trade concept. This means that companies must compete not only with domestic rivals but with competitors from across the globe. Many of these competitors will have either:

1 lower costs, or
2 differentiated products.

These, according to Michael Porter, are the two main factors that can lead to a significant **competitive advantage**. Business managers must decide whether they want the business to focus on competitiveness gained through low costs (and prices) or differentiated products that would allow higher prices to be charged (see Figure 37.6).

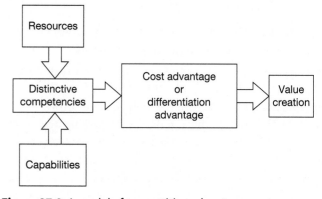

Figure 37.6 A model of competitive advantage

What strategies can be adopted to increase a business's competitive advantage when faced with a globalised marketplace? Here are some examples:

Automation: BMW has increased its investment by £400 million in the Mini production line to buy 230 new robots at its UK factory. These offer some of the most advanced and productive manufacturing production facilities in the world. This helps to reduce the costs of manufacture, but it also allows a flexible production system that can make all three types of Mini body shell on the same production line. So, in effect, both lower costs and differentiated products are achieved by this automation strategy.

Rationalisation: The merger of two of Europe's main travel companies, Thomas Cook and MyTravel aimed to cut costs to increase competitiveness. It seemed to achieve its aims because, within two years, cost savings of more than US$300 million had been achieved by a combination of redundancies – especially when job titles were unnecessarily duplicated after the merger – and bulk purchasing of holiday accommodation.

Research and development (R&D): Shell, the oil giant, spends more than US$1.3 billion on R&D each year but plans to increase this substantially. The company has a strategy of technological developments to allow diversification away from its original oil and gas business. This strategy is partly driven by the fact that it has relatively low reserves of oil and gas compared with other big firms in the industry. Product differentiation by means of R&D at Shell is focusing on biotechnology, carbon-emission storage and alternative fuels.

All three of these strategies will, if successful, allow these businesses to gain or sustain their competitive advantages in an increasingly tough competitive world. These examples also illustrate the fundamental importance of businesses having a clear corporate strategy that focuses on plans that should allow the achievement of long-term goals. The next three chapters give details of the strategic management process.

 KEY CONCEPT LINK

To be competitive in some industries it is not enough to achieve low costs if customers are looking for unique products. **Innovation** will be the important competitive feature of successful businesses in such cases.

SUMMARY POINTS

- Corporate strategy is a long-term plan of action to achieve a business aim.
- Successful businesses need a corporate strategy and effective strategic management.
- There are clear links between corporate strategy and business/functional structure.
- The difference between strategic decisions and tactical decisions is important.
- According to Chandler, there are links between business strategy and business structure.
- Corporate strategy can have a major impact on a company's competitive advantage and on its ability to create value in the future.

RESEARCH TASK

Select a well-known business that you have studied. Undertake research into this businesses current plans and strategies using its published accounts, newspaper articles and the internet.

- Is the company's long term aim clear?
- Do the strategies being followed seem to match this long term aim?
- Write a report on the businesses aims, current strategies and assess whether the aims are likely to be achieved.

A Level exam practice questions
Case study

GlaxoSmithKline (GSK) – strategy influenced by competition

GSK is a large multinational pharmaceutical business. It spends billions of dollars each year researching for new medicines – at any one time it has more than 150 projects in clinical development. The company's mission statement is to 'improve the quality of human life by enabling people to do more, feel better and live longer'. It aims to launch several new drugs for medical purposes each year. Last year five important new medicines were marketed, including cancer drugs and one for reducing risk of heart failure. However, sales of existing products are being increasingly affected by the rise of 'generic drugs' made by companies that copy the successful GSK formula when the patent period has ended.

The company strategy for the next few years is to:

- maximise sales performance of existing key products
- improve R&D productivity
- ensure patients have access to new medicines.

The internal business structure has been adapted to deliver these strategies. R&D groups are given much more independence from central control and are encouraged to deliver novel solutions to important medical problems. In addition, an 'emerging markets' unit has been created to increase sales from the growing markets of Brazil, Russia, India and China (BRIC). The chief executive said in a statement: 'Making the changes required to develop our business for the next decade needs a rigorous and disciplined focus on corporate strategy. A key element of the organisational changes is to proactively seek new business opportunities to expand our global reach and drive sales growth.'

[26 marks, 40 minutes]

1. Do you think GSK's strategies reflect the company's mission statement? Explain your answer. [10]
2. Explain how competition is affecting GSK's strategies. [6]
3. Discuss the importance of the link between business strategy and business structure by references to GSK and other business examples. [10]

A Level essay questions

[20 marks, 45 minutes each]

1. Discuss, with reference to businesses you have studied, the view that long-term corporate strategies have little relevance in an uncertain and rapidly changing global business environment. [20]
2. Evaluate, with examples, the links between corporate strategy and organisational structure for at least **two** businesses that you have studied. [20]

38 Strategic analysis

This chapter covers syllabus section A Level 6.2.

On completing this chapter, you will be able to:

- understand the meaning and importance of strategic analysis
- undertake and interpret a SWOT analysis
- undertake and interpret a PEST analysis
- evaluate the role of business vision and mission statements in strategic analysis
- undertake and interpret Boston Matrix analysis of the product portfolio of a business
- assess the significance of Porter's Five Forces analysis as a framework for business strategy
- assess the significance of core competencies analysis as a framework for business strategy.

Introducing the topic

THE GREAT WALMART OF CHINA

Before moving into China, America's biggest and most successful retailer had to learn its business all over again. 'China will be as big and as successful a market for Walmart as the United States,' said a retail-industry analyst for Deutsche Bank. However, this will not be easy, as China's retail market is dominated by domestic retailers and other foreign retailers have gained ground quickly. For example, the French group Carrefour has sales in China nearly 50% bigger than Walmart's. Success is not guaranteed, despite the careful analysis that Walmart's management did before taking the big strategic move into China.

They identified the company's own strengths – such as great economies of scale – and possible weaknesses – such as being seen mainly as a US retailer. Management also identified the huge opportunities offered by the retail market in China – with the world's largest population and fastest-growing economy. There were obvious threats to success too – such as Carrefour's expansion plans.

Attention was then focused on the wider issues that would be important in China. These included political and legal differences with the USA, economic factors such as the Yuan exchange rate, social and cultural factors that could determine demand for certain goods and the impact of technological change on retailing practices and consumer-buying habits.

Despite all of this strategic analysis, according to a senior consultant with Strategic Resource Group, 'Walmart is being outmanoeuvred by Carrefour because its executives have taken too long to understand the Chinese market and add stores.' Perhaps one of the

A Walmart store in Beijing

problems for retailers, even giant ones such as Walmart, is the possible lack of a core competence, other than substantial economies of scale that could allow them to differentiate what they offer to retail consumers.

Points to think about:

- Why do you think it is important to analyse the existing strengths and weaknesses of a business before taking a major strategic decision?
- Explain, from Walmart's point of view, additional strengths, weaknesses, opportunities and threats in this case.
- Explain why it would have been important to consider the major differences between China and the USA before going ahead with this expansion.
- Identify one business that you think has a 'core competence' that helps to set it apart from other businesses in the same industry. Explain your answer.

Introduction

If you try to plan your own future career – perhaps applying to study at university and then seeking an employment post with promotion prospects – without considering what is happening in the world around you and how this could affect your future, how realistic will your plans be? Do your early dreams to be an astronaut or pop star seem so reasonable now you are older and realise the external constraints that limit you achieving these ambitions? **Strategic analysis** is about looking in detail at your current position and what is happening to you now and what might happen to you in the future – and then making sure that your long-term plans or strategy fit in with this external analysis.

KEY TERM

> **Strategic analysis:** the process of conducting research into the business environment within which an organisation operates, and into the organisation itself, to help form future strategies.

This chapter explains the key role of strategic analysis to senior managers when strategically managing business organisations.

Strategic analysis tries to find answers to three key questions:

1 Where is the business now?
2 How might the business be affected by what is happening or likely to happen?
3 How could the business respond to these likely changes?

Effective strategic analysis will lead to clearer and more relevant business goals, better-quality strategic decisions and a less risky future for a business, as it should be better prepared for the future. Strategic analysis is aided by a number of different techniques and the rest of this chapter focuses on these.

SWOT analysis

A **SWOT analysis** provides information that can be helpful in matching the firm's resources and strengths to the competitive environment in which it operates.

KEY TERM

> **SWOT analysis:** a form of strategic analysis that identifies and analyses the main internal strengths and weaknesses and external opportunities and threats that will influence the future direction and success of a business.

It is, therefore, useful in strategy formulation and selection. It comprises:

Strengths: These are the internal factors about a business that can be looked upon as real advantages. These could be used as a basis for developing a competitive advantage. They might include: experienced management, product patents, loyal workforce and good product range. These factors are identified by undertaking an internal audit of the firm. This is often undertaken by specialist management consultants who analyse the effectiveness of the business and the effectiveness of each of its departments and major product ranges.

Weaknesses: These are the internal factors about a business that can be seen as negative factors. In some cases, these can be the flip side of strengths. For example, whereas a large amount of spare manufacturing capacity might be a strength in times of a rapid economic upturn, if it continues to be unused then it could add substantially to a firm's average costs of production. Weaknesses might include: poorly trained workforce, limited production capacity and ageing equipment. This information would also have been obtained from an internal audit.

Opportunities: These are the potential areas for expansion of the business and future profits. These factors are identified by an external audit of the market the firm operates in and its major competitors. Examples include: new technologies, export markets expanding faster than domestic markets, and lower rates of interest increasing consumer demand.

Threats: These are also external factors gained from an external audit. This audit analyses the business and economic environment, market conditions and the strength of competitors. Examples of threats are: new competitors entering the market, globalisation driving down prices, changes in the law regarding the sale of the firm's products, and changes in government economic policy.

This information is usually presented in the form of a four-box grid as shown in Table 38.1.

SWOT and strategic objectives

The SWOT diagram focuses on the key issues under each heading. A brief outline of each of these could then accompany the grid to make it more useful to the managers responsible for strategic planning. This approach helps managers assess the most likely successful future strategies and the constraints on them. A business should not necessarily pursue the most profitable opportunities. It may stand a better chance of developing a competitive advantage by identifying a good 'fit' between the firm's strengths and potential opportunities. In many cases, a business may need to overcome a perceived weakness in order to take advantage of a potential opportunity. SWOT is a common starting point for developing new corporate strategies, but it is rarely sufficient. Further analysis and planning are usually needed before strategic choices can be made.

	Strengths	Weaknesses
Internal	■ specialist marketing expertise ■ a new, innovative product or service ■ location of your business ■ quality products and processes ■ any other aspect of your business that adds value to your product or service	■ lack of marketing expertise ■ undifferentiated products or services (i.e. in relation to your competitors) ■ location of your business ■ poor-quality goods or services ■ damaged reputation
	Opportunities	**Threats**
External	■ a developing market such as the internet ■ mergers, joint ventures or strategic alliances ■ moving into new market segments that offer improved profits ■ a new international market. ■ a market vacated by an ineffective competitor	■ a new competitor in your home market ■ price wars with competitors ■ a competitor has a new, innovative product or service ■ competitors have superior access to channels of distribution ■ taxation of your product or service

Table 38.1 SWOT analysis – some common issues

SWOT evaluation

Subjectivity is often a limitation of a SWOT analysis as no two managers would necessarily arrive at the same assessment of the company they work for. It is not a quantitative form of assessment so the cost of correcting a weakness cannot be compared with the potential profit from pursuing an opportunity. SWOT should be used as a management guide for future strategies, not a prescription. Part of the value of the process of SWOT analysis is the clarification and mutual understanding that senior managers gain by the focus that SWOT analysis provides.

TOP TIP

Some questions may ask you to undertake a SWOT analysis while others will ask you to evaluate the technique for a particular business – read the question carefully to grasp the key requirements of it.

PEST analysis

This is another form of strategic analysis. It focuses on analysing the macro-environment in which a business operates. The macro-environment means the wide-ranging and 'big-picture' factors that could influence a firm's future strategies as opposed to micro-environmental factors, such as customers and suppliers. **PEST analysis** is an acronym for:

P = political (and legal) factors

E = economic factors

S = social factors

T = technological factors.

KEY TERM

PEST analysis: the strategic analysis of a firm's macro-environment, including political, economic, social and technological factors.

545

PEST analysis plays an important role in assessing the likely chances of a business strategy being successful. The four key areas covered by it are clearly external to the business and beyond its control. They are considered as either being opportunities or threats. PEST is complementary to SWOT, not an alternative.

TOP TIP

You should be able to make a clear distinction between SWOT and PEST analysis.

PEST evaluation

Any significant new business strategy should be preceded by a detailed analysis of the wider environment in which the strategy has to operate and be successful. The use of PEST analysis formalises this process and the results of the analysis should be an important part of strategic decision-making. Once completed, PEST analysis cannot just stop. It may need to be constantly updated and reviewed, especially in a rapidly changing wider environment. For multinational businesses – or for a firm considering foreign expansion for the first time – it will be important to undertake PEST analysis for each

ACTIVITY 38.1

Strategic analysis of LVM Ltd

LVM owns a major assembly plant for laptop computers. It supplies products to some of the major brand names in the computer industry but, at present, it does not sell any under its own name. Every six months the managers hold a key strategic review meeting to consider the current position of the business and the long-term plans. The following are extracts from the most recent of these meetings:

Imran Khan – marketing director: 'Sales of our latest TFT screen models have exceeded expectations and the switch towards laptops from desktop PCs is expected to continue. The chance for computer companies to break into the expanding Asian market when trade barriers are lifted should lead to increased orders too. We need to undertake some market research in Asia as this market has higher growth potential than Europe, where most of our computers are marketed. The uncertainty over the newest mobile phone technology and links with the internet remain a concern for us. We decided two years ago not to develop this technology, and, if our competitors succeed in getting a major breakthrough, then sales of laptops will dive in some markets.'

Liz Collins – operations manager: 'The automation of the screen-assembly section is now complete.

We managed to push this through while maintaining excellent staff relationships. This was helped by our continued expansion, which meant that no jobs were lost. We had to turn down a big order from a big-name brand last month due to too little factory capacity and shortages of skilled labour. I do urge you to agree to my plan to extend the factory space by 35% and to train more new recruits. Research into the lighter, faster computer model that was agreed on last year is making excellent progress and we will soon have to decide whether to proceed into the production stage.'

Lukas Klimas – finance director: 'Our profits are holding steady, but cash flow remains a concern due to the expenditure on automated machines and research costs. We would need to borrow substantially to finance a factory extension. We would be in trouble if interest rates increased – there is already some government concern about inflation rising. There is a new range of grants available for businesses relocating into areas of high unemployment. We must constantly be aware of exchange rate movements too – the recent depreciation helped our international competitiveness.'

[32 marks, 50 minutes]

1 Prepare a SWOT analysis based on your assessment of the internal and external factors that influence LVM's success. [10]

2 Evaluate the usefulness of SWOT to a business such as LVM. [10]

3 Identify and evaluate **two** potential strategic options available for LVM Ltd by using the SWOT analysis prepared in question 1. [12]

country being operated in. It is clear from Table 38.2 that many of the factors listed will have a different outcome in different countries.

KEY CONCEPT LINK

Do not forget that 'change is the only constant' in business and strategic analysis attempts to identify how changes are affecting the business.

Business vision/mission statements and strategic analysis

In Chapter 4, the importance of **mission statements** in setting out what a business stand for was explained.

Now that the main functions of business have been studied in other chapters of this book, we can add some further insight into both mission statements and a business's **vision statement**.

KEY TERMS

Mission statement: a statement of the business's core purpose and focus, phrased in a way to motivate employees and to stimulate interest by outside groups.

Vision statement: a statement of what the organisation would like to achieve or accomplish in the long term.

Political and legal	Economic	Social	Technological
Stability of the government	Rate of economic growth (or recession)	Demographic changes, e.g. ageing or more youthful population	Rapidly changing technology allowing products to be made more cheaply
Are changes in the law likely to impact on a particular industry?	Exchange rate stability	Dominant religion and impact this could have, e.g. on marketing strategies	Government support for R&D spending
Environmental regulations	Country's membership of free-trade areas	Education standards, e.g. skilled labour force	Internet access, speed of broadband and its impact on marketing and other strategies
Employment law	Membership or likely membership of a common-currency scheme, such as the euro	Roles of men and women in society	Renewable energies and the cost of these compared to fossil fuels
Competition regulations	Tax rates and likely changes	Social and environmental issues could be of increasing concern to the population	Speed of technological obsolescence
Consumer protection laws	Interest rates and likely changes	Labour and social mobility, such as migration between countries or from rural areas to cities as in China and India	New product inventions and the importance of these to consumers
Government attitude to free market or controls over business	Inflation rates and stage of the business cycle	One or many languages spoken	Changes in IT speed and range of applications

Table 38.2 Examples of PEST factors analysed by a business planning to sell products to another country

ACTIVITY 38.2

PEST for a foreign retailer in your country

A large retailing company, Tasco, is looking into opening a chain of stores in your country for the first time. Tasco already has shops in several different countries as well as its own domestic market where it holds a 33% market share in food and drink retailing.

[24 marks, 40 minutes]

1 Undertake a PEST analysis for Tasco of the macro-environment in your own country. **[12]**

2 On the basis of this analysis, would you advise Tasco to go ahead with this expansion in your country at this time? Justify your answer. **[12]**

The distinction between these two statements may seem quite small. Basically a vision statement is what the organisation wants to become (future) but a mission statement concerns what an organisation is all about (present). An effective mission statement should answer three key questions:

1 What do we do?
2 For whom do we do it?
3 What is the benefit?

Mission statements outline the overall purpose of the organisation. A vision statement, on the other hand, describes a picture of the 'preferred future' and outlines how the future will look if the organisation achieves its mission. It is a clear statement of the future position that offers the ideal of what owners and directors want their business organisation to become (see Table 38.3).

Vision statement, mission statement and strategic analysis

So what is the link between these concepts? It is simple. Without the direction and focus brought to an organisation by vision and mission statements, planning new strategies will be like trying to steer a ship with no idea of where it is or the direction it is meant to be heading in. Vision and mission statements give the sense of purpose to an organisation, such as a business, that can prevent it from

	Vision statement	Mission statement
Nokia	Our vision is a world where everyone is connected.	Nokia exists to connect people with each other and the information that is important to them with easy-to-use and innovative products. Nokia aims to provide equipment, solutions and services for consumers, network operators and corporations.
Minnesota Health Department (USA)	The vision is to keep all residents healthy.	This health department aims to protect, maintain and improve the health of all residents.
McDonald's	McDonald's has a vision where the world buys more McDonald's than any other fast-food.	McDonald's aims to be the world's best quick-service restaurant experience. Being the best means providing outstanding quality, service, cleanliness and value so that we make every customer in every restaurant smile.

Table 38.3 Examples of vision and mission statements

drifting between the tides and currents of powerful events. There is little point in undertaking strategic analysis – asking: where is the business now? – unless senior management have a clear idea of where they want the business to be in the future.

Evaluation

In your research (see Activity 38.3), you may find some vision and mission statements that are so general and ill-defined that they could prove to be of little direct benefit to directors of the organisation when making strategic decisions. It is really important that both vision and mission statements are not 'works of art' to be framed so that they impress visitors to head office. They need to be applicable to the business, understood by employees and convertible into genuine strategic actions.

548

ACTIVITY 38.3

Researching mission statements

Use the Internet site www.samples-help.org.uk/mission-statements to look up more mission statements for well-known corporations. Evaluate the usefulness of any one of these mission statements for the planning of future strategies for this business.

Boston Matrix – product portfolio analysis

This method of analysing the market standing of a firm's products and the firm's overall product portfolio was developed by the Boston Consulting Group (see Figure 38.1)

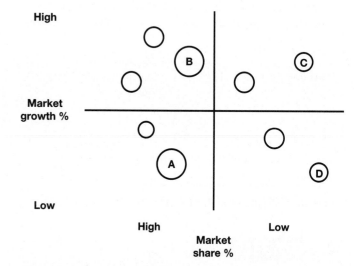

Figure 38.1 The Boston Matrix

KEY TERM

Boston Matrix: a method of analysing the product portfolio of a business in terms of market share and market growth.

It highlights the position of each of a firm's products when measured by market share and market growth. This allows not only an analysis of the existing product portfolio, but also what future strategies the firm could take next. The size of each circle represents the total revenue earned by each product. The four sectors created by the matrix can be analysed in the following way:

Low market growth – high market share: product A: 'cash cow'

This is a well-established product in a mature market. Typically, this type of product creates a high positive cash flow and is profitable. Sales are high relative to the market and promotional costs are likely to be low, as a result of high consumer awareness. The cash from this product can be 'milked' and injected into some of the other products in the portfolio – hence, this product is often referred to as a 'cash cow'. The business will want to maintain cash cows for as long as possible.

High market growth – high market share: product B: 'star'

This is clearly a successful product as it is performing well in an expanding market – because of this it is often called a 'star'. The firm will be keen to maintain the market position of this product in what may be a fast-changing market – therefore, promotion costs will be high to help differentiate the product and reinforce its brand image. Despite these costs, a 'star' is likely to generate high amounts of income.

High market growth – low market share: product C: 'problem child'

The 'problem child' consumes resources but generates little return. If it is a newly launched product, it is going to need heavy promotion costs to help become established – this finance could come from the 'cash cow'. The future of the product may be uncertain, so quick decisions may need to be taken if sales do not improve, such as revised design, relaunch or even withdrawal from the market. It should, however, have potential as it is selling in a market sector that is growing fast.

Low market growth – low market share: product D: 'dog'

The 'dog' seems to offer little to the business either in terms of existing sales and cash flow or future prospects, because the market is not growing. It may need to be replaced shortly, or the firm could decide to withdraw from this market sector altogether and position itself into faster-growing sectors.

Boston Matrix and strategic analysis

By identifying the position of all of the firm's products, a full analysis of the portfolio is possible. This should help focus on which products need support or which need corrective action. This action could include the following strategies:

- **Building** – supporting 'problem child' products with additional advertising or further distribution outlets. The finance for this could be obtained from the established 'cash cow' products.
- **Holding** – continuing support for 'star' products so that they can maintain their good market position.

Work may be needed to 'freshen' the product in the eyes of the consumers so that high sales growth can be sustained.
- **Milking** – taking the positive cash flow from established products and investing in other products in the portfolio.
- **Divesting** – identifying the worst performing 'dogs' and stopping the production and supply of these. This strategic decision should not be taken lightly as it will involve other issues, such as the impact on the workforce and whether the spare capacity freed up by stopping production can be used profitably for another product.

These strategies can only be undertaken if the business has a balanced portfolio of products. If there are too many 'dogs' or 'problem children', then the overall shortage of cash may not allow the firm to take appropriate action.

Evaluation of the Boston Matrix

This analytical tool has relevance when:

- analysing the performance and current position of existing product portfolios
- planning action to be taken with existing products
- planning the introduction of new products.

No technique can guarantee business success – this will depend on the accuracy of the analysis by the marketing managers and the skills they possess in employing appropriate marketing strategies. The Boston Matrix helps to establish the current situation in which the firm's products find themselves – but it is of little use in 'predicting' future success or failure.

- On its own it cannot tell a manager what will happen next with any product. Detailed and continuous market research will help – but at all times, decision-makers must be conscious of the potentially dramatic effects of competitors' decisions, technological changes and the fluctuating economic environment.
- It is only a planning tool and it has been criticised as simplifying a complex set of factors determining product success.
- The assumption is made that higher rates of profit are directly related to high market shares – this is not necessarily the case when sales are being gained by reducing prices and profit margins.

TOP TIP
The Boston Matrix does not provide strategic choices for a business – but it analyses a business's product portfolio and highlights those products that might need action to be taken at a strategic level.

ACTIVITY 38.4

Applying the Boston Matrix

Undertake detailed research into the product portfolio of one well-known business in your country that sells a range of different products. For example, this might be a chocolate manufacturer, soft drinks producer, car manufacturer and so on. Try to discover the market share of the different products sold and the rate of growth of the market segment the products are sold in. Answer the following questions once your research is complete.

[24 marks, 35 minutes]

1   Analyse the firm's product portfolio, using the Boston Matrix. [12]

2   Evaluate **two** strategies that the business could adopt for any one of its products. [12]

Porter's Five Forces analysis

Michael Porter provided a framework that models an industry as being influenced by five forces. It has been suggested that the strategic business manager, attempting to establish a competitive advantage over rivals, can use this model to understand the industry context in which the business operates. It has similarities with other tools for external environmental audit, such as PEST analysis, but it focuses on single or stand-alone business units rather than a single product or range of products. For example, Dell would analyse the market for business computers as being one of its strategic business units (SBUs).

Figure 38.2 shows these five forces with the key one – competitive rivalry – at the centre.

1 Barriers to entry

This means the ease with which other firms can join the industry and compete with existing businesses.

This threat of entry is greatest when:

■   economies of scale are low in the industry
■   the technology needed to enter the industry is relatively cheap
■   distribution channels are easy to access, e.g. retail shops are not owned by existing manufacturers in the industry
■   there are no legal or patent restrictions on entry
■   the importance of product differentiation is low, so extensive advertising may not be required to get established.

2 The power of buyers

This refers to the power that customers have on the producing industry. For example, if there are four major supermarket groups that dominate this sector of retailing,

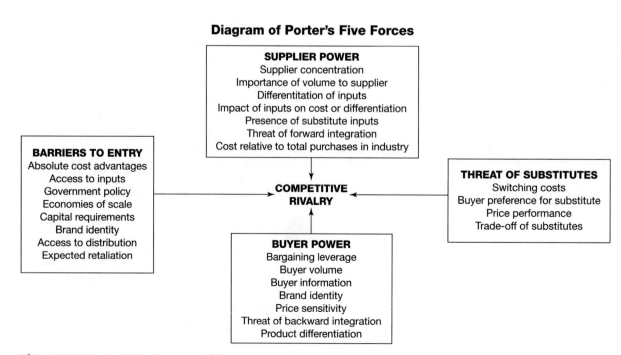

Figure 38.2 Porter's Five Forces model

their buyer power over food and other producers will be great. Buyer power will also be increased when:

- there are many undifferentiated small supplying firms, e.g. many small farmers supplying milk or chickens to large supermarket businesses
- the cost of switching suppliers is low
- buyers can realistically and easily buy from other suppliers.

3 The power of suppliers

Suppliers will be relatively powerful compared with buyers when:

- the cost of switching is high, e.g. from PC computers to Macs
- when the brand being sold is very powerful and well-known, e.g. Cadbury's chocolate or Nike shoes
- suppliers could realistically threaten to open their own forward-integration operations, e.g. coffee suppliers open their own cafés
- customers have little bargaining power as they are small firms and fragmented, e.g. dispersed around the country as with independent petrol stations.

4 The threat of substitutes

In Porter's model, 'substitute products' does not mean alternatives in the same industry, such as Toyota for Honda cars. It refers to substitute products in other industries. For instance, the demand for aluminium for cans is partly affected by the price of glass for bottling and of plastic for containers. These are substitutes for aluminium, but they are not rivals in the same industry. Threats of substitution will exist when:

- new technology makes other options available, such as satellite TV instead of traditional antenna reception
- price competition forces customers to consider alternatives – for example, lower bus fares might make some travellers switch from rail transport
- any significant new product leads to consumer spending that results in less being spent on other goods – for example, increasing spending on mobile (cell) phones by young people reduces the available cash they have to spend on clothes.

5 Competitive rivalry

This is the key part of this analysis – it sums up the most important factors that determine the level of competition or rivalry in an industry. It is based on the other four forces, which is why it is often illustrated in the centre of the Five Forces diagram. Competitive rivalry is most likely to be high where:

- it is cheap and easy for new firms to enter an industry
- there is a threat from substitute products
- suppliers have much power
- buyers have much power.

There will also be great rivalry between competing firms in an industry when:

- there are a large number of firms with similar market share
- high fixed costs force firms to try to obtain economies of scale
- there is slow market growth that forces firms to take a share from rivals if they wish to increase sales.

Porter's Five Forces as a framework for business strategy

How does this analysis of the competitive situation in an industry help a business take important strategic decisions?

- By analysing new markets in this way, it helps firms decide whether to enter or not. It provides an insight into the potential profitability of markets. Is it better to enter a highly competitive market or not?
- By analysing the existing markets a business operates in, decisions may be taken regarding: 'Do we stay in these markets in future if they are becoming more competitive?' and 'How could we reduce the level of competitive rivalry in these markets – and thus increase potential profitability?'
- With the knowledge gained and the power of competitive forces, businesses can develop strategies that might improve their own competitive position. These could include the following:
  1 Product differentiation, e.g. Honda hybrid cars with a distinctive appearance.
  2 Buying out some competitors, e.g. Exxon taking over Shell to reduce rivalry.
  3 Focus on different segments that might be less competitive, e.g. Nestlé entering niche confectionery markets such as vegan chocolates.
  4 Communicate and collude with rivals to reduce competition, e.g. the major cement producers in the European Union have been accused of this.

Having completed the first five units of the course, you should now be able to evaluate the chances of success of the four strategies identified above.

> **🔗 KEY CONCEPT LINK**
>
> **Strategy** is a key concept in Business and Michael Porter's work on strategy is highly regarded.

> **ACTIVITY 38.5**
>
> **Evaluating four strategies**
> *[20 marks, 30 minutes]*
>
> Evaluate the **four** strategies referred to above and discuss the most important factors that will influence their success. **[20]**

Evaluating the Five Forces model

It is argued that the benefit of Porter's model is that it enables managers to think about the current competitive structure of their industry in a structured and logical way. It is usually regarded as a good starting point for further analysis.

However, it is sometimes criticised because:

- it analyses an industry at just one moment in time – static analysis – and many industries are changing very rapidly due to, for example, globalisation and technological changes
- the model can become very complex when trying to use it to analyse many modern industries with joint ventures, multiple product groups and different market segments within the same industry – which have their own competitive forces.

Core competencies

The concept of **core competencies** was first analysed in the work of Hamel and Prahalad. They argued that

if a business develops core competencies, then it may gain competitive advantage over other firms in the same industry.

To be of commercial and profitable benefit to a business, a core competence should:

- provide recognisable benefits to consumers
- not be easy for other firms to copy, e.g. a patented design
- be applicable to a range of different products and markets.

According to Prahalad and Hamel, core competencies lead to the development of **core products**. Core products are not necessarily sold to final consumers. Instead they are used to produce a large number of end-user products. For example, Black and Decker, it is claimed, has a core competence in the design and manufacture of small electric motors. These core products are used in a huge variety of different applications from power tools, such as drills, to lawnmowers and food processors.

KEY TERM

Core competence: an important business capability that gives a firm competitive advantage.

KEY TERM

Core product: product based on a business's core competences, but not necessarily for final consumer or end user.

552

ACTIVITY 38.6

Which industry is more competitive?

It is interesting to compare two completely different industries in terms of competitive rivalry. The world fashion industry has many famous names that compete for our attention and for our 'consumer dollar'. The images of these businesses, such as Versace, Armani and Chanel, have been carefully built up with celebrity endorsements and expensive advertising. It would be difficult for new firms trying to break into the industry to compete with these businesses. Certainly, using low prices to attract consumers to buy an 'exclusive' new brand of clothing is unlikely to be successful. Exclusive shops often have agreements with fashion companies to be their exclusive outlets – again making it difficult for new firms to get established. However, the rapid growth of technology could make traditional retailers appear old-fashioned and consumers may be happy in future to buy even top fashion names through e-commerce.

The world car industry has huge excess capacity. Industry specialists estimate that total car sales in 2013 were 67 million, yet the production capacity of the world's car factories is around 80 million. The only new mass-market producers in recent years have come from Korea – such as Hyundai – and China, and the cost advantages they enjoy have reduced output in the USA and Europe, which has reduced the economies of scale of producers in these countries. The technological expertise and capital needed to build a new mass-market car factory make it very unlikely that new firms will now join the world car industry. There is likely to be a number of mergers and takeovers. However, small niche-market producers – such as makers of electric cars or super-fast sports cars – are still launching new products in a desperate attempt to create product differentiation.

[20 marks, 30 minutes]

Using Porter's Five Forces model, the information above and any other information you have researched, compare the likely competitive rivalry of these two industries.

[20]

Developing core competencies

It is important to realise that a business might be particularly good at a certain activity – it might have competence in this activity – but this does not necessarily make it a core competence if it is not exceptional or is easy to copy. So a computer-assembly business might be very efficient and produce computers at low cost, but if it depends on easily available and cheap bought-in components from suppliers, this is not a core competence. It does not make the business very different from many other computer-assembly firms.

Developing a core competence, according to Prahalad and Hamel, depends on integrating multiple technologies and different product skills that probably already exist in the business. It does not necessarily mean spending huge amounts on R&D – although patented production processes, such as Pilkington's float-glass process, may give a core competence. If a management team can effectively bring together and coordinate designers, production specialists, IT experts and so on into a team to develop new and different competences, then these may become differentiated and core competences. Two excellent business examples are the development of Philips's expertise in optical media and Sony's ability to miniaturise electronic components that has led to many core products.

Core competencies and strategy

Once a core competence has been established, it opens up strategic opportunities for developing core products and then new 'end' products and new markets.

The business units in Figure 38.3 are the divisions of a business that will use the core products. So they might be 'consumer products business' and 'industrial products business' but they would both use the core competencies of the business, e.g. a new very fast microchip or a new design of electric motor. By building up new products for new markets in this way, there will now be a greater opportunity to gain economies of scale in the manufacture of the core products.

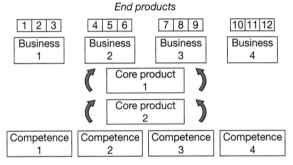

Figure 38.3 Core competencies can lead to a large number of end products

SUMMARY POINTS

- Points Strategic analysis is the first stage of strategic management and asks the question 'where is the business now?'
- SWOT analysis is a form of strategic analysis and its usefulness can be evaluated.
- PEST analysis focuses on identifying and explaining the main macro-environmental issues impacting on a business.
- Boston Matrix analysis can be used to assess the existing product portfolio of a business.
- Porter's Five Forces concept analyses the degree of competitive rivalry in an industry.
- The concept of core competencies can be used to help form successful business strategies.

RESEARCH TASKS

1. Honda is often claimed to have a core competence in building powerful and efficient petrol engines. Black and Decker is recognised as having a core competence in making small electric motors.

   Research the range of products offered either by Honda or Black and Decker. Write a report discussing the benefits to either of these businesses of having the core competence outlined above.

2. Assess the competitive rivalry that exists for any well-known business in your country. Consider buyer power, supplier power, ease of entry and threat of substitutes.

A Level exam practice questions
Case studies

1   Cash cow at the dairy

Salman Gasim is looking at the latest sales data for FarmGate dairies. As usual, there is some good news and bad news. The four main products are organised into business units. They record very different sales performances, and marketing decisions have to be made concerning the company's product portfolio. Here are the sales data:

% share of the market segment each product is sold in			
	2011	2012	2013
Gold Seal milk	25	26	24
Lo Fat yoghurts	–	7	6
Churn butter	8	6	5
Hi Energy spread	30	28	31

Gold Seal milk is the oldest-established product. Sales have not risen greatly over the last few years, but it is in a mature market. FarmGate has not promoted the brand for the last three years.

Lo Fat yoghurts were launched two years ago with a substantial marketing campaign. Although there is great competition in this 'health segment' of the market – it is becoming one of the fastest-growing segments in the high-profit-margin yoghurt market – FarmGate's Lo Fat product initially caught the public's imagination. Product developments might be needed to sustain consumer interest.

Churn butter had for many years been a weak brand in its sector. Frequent promotional campaigns and special offers had failed to create much consumer loyalty. Butter sales in general were suffering because of increasing health concerns.

Hi Energy spread was introduced to the market only five years ago. Sales took off immediately – partly due to very competitive pricing. Healthy eating habits were driving the market forward, but new brands are now making their presence felt. Should a further advertising campaign be introduced? Should the product be developed with a wider range of flavours?

[40 marks, 60 minutes]

1. Classify each of these products according to the Boston Matrix. Justify your classification.   [8]

2. Explain the benefits to managers of using this analysis when deciding on future marketing strategy.   [10]

3. Assess what strategies the business could adopt for **either** Lo Fat yoghurts **or** Hi Energy spread.   [10]

4. FarmGate dairies' small research department has discovered a new way of preserving and adding flavours to fresh milk. This production method will be patented. It could be used to develop a basic core product, which could be used in different consumer products, such as flavoured milk drinks, yoghurts and spreads. Evaluate the likely importance of this core competence to the business.   [12]

2   Games consoles

Nintendo, Sony and Microsoft dominate the console gaming industry. The threat of substitutes is high as many smartphones and tablets now offer a wide range of entertainment apps. The three established companies have spent millions of dollars developing new games and more advanced consoles. They have well-established brand identities supported by extensive advertising. There are many components suppliers in the electronics industry. Buyer power is limited as there are few supplying firms in the market and once one brand of games console has been purchased it would be expensive to switch to another manufacturer. Some gamers are extremely loyal to a particular brand of games console.

[24 marks, 40 minutes]

1   Assess the level of competitive rivalry in the games console market using the data above and your own knowledge.   [12]

2   Evaluate any **two** strategies that one of the existing businesses in the market could adopt to increase market share.   [12]

A Level essay questions

[20 marks, 45 minutes each]

1   Select a multinational company that operates in your country. Evaluate the importance to this company of undertaking SWOT and PEST analysis before it substantially expands its operations.   [20]

2   Assess the view that strategic analysis is of little value to businesses that operate in a fast changing and competitive environment. Support your answer by references to businesses you have studied.   [20]

39 Strategic choice

On completing this chapter, you will be able to:

- understand the importance of strategic choice
- analyse strategic choices, using the Ansoff matrix model, and evaluate its usefulness
- analyse strategic choices using force-field analysis and evaluate its usefulness
- apply the decision tree technique to strategic choices in different business contexts and evaluate its usefulness.

Introducing the topic

WHERE TO NOW FOR ABCA POWER PLC?

Privatised in 2003, this profitable gas and electric power company has expanded rapidly since being freed of government controls. It has now reached a crossroads in its development as the energy market it operates in is becoming saturated and ceasing to grow. The directors are considering four growth strategies after undertaking an extensive strategic analysis. The four options are to:

1 increase market share in gas and electricity in the existing countries where the firm operates – by using marketing tactics or taking over a rival firm

2 enter other countries' markets for gas and electricity supply

3 develop renewable forms of energy, e.g. solar and wind power, for sale in existing markets; but technological differences between renewable and non-renewable energy supplies are considerable

4 develop a range of non-energy-related products, such as office equipment, for sale in new markets.

One of the directors of ABCA had formerly been a senior manager for a US-based office-equipment company.

The directors had asked management consultants to estimate the potential costs and likely future revenues from these four options. The consultants had attempted this, but also reported that, as some of the options were riskier than others, the forecasts were likely to be open to a wide margin of error. The directors understood this point – but they would still have to make a decision based on as much data as possible.

Points to think about:

- What forms of strategic analysis do you think the directors might have undertaken?
- Which of the four options listed is: (a) the safest option and (b) the riskiest option? Explain your answer.
- Explain why a bad strategic choice could put the future of the whole business at risk.

Introduction

Strategic choice is the next logical element in the strategic decision-making process. Choice is at the centre of strategy formulation. If there are no important choices to be made, there is no point in giving much consideration to the decision-making process at all. Strategic choice is concerned with the identification of different strategic options and deciding between them. Good strategic choices have to be challenging enough to gain competitive advantage, but also achievable and within the resource capabilities of the organisation. There are logical techniques available to assist managers in making strategic choices, but judgement and skill are also very important.

Ansoff's matrix

This analytical tool is one of the most widely used means of portraying alternative corporate growth strategies.

KEY TERM

Ansoff's matrix: a model used to show the degree of risk associated with the four growth strategies of market penetration, market development, product development and diversification.

Ansoff popularised the idea that long-term business success was dependent upon establishing business strategies and planning for their introduction. His best-known contribution to strategic planning was the development of the Ansoff matrix, which represented the different options open to a marketing manager when considering new opportunities for sales growth.

He considered that the two main variables in a strategic marketing decision are:

1 the market in which the firm was going to operate
2 the product(s) intended for sale.

In terms of the market, managers have two options:

1 to remain in the existing market
2 to enter new ones.

In terms of the product, the two options are:

1 selling existing products
2 developing new ones.

When put on a matrix, these options can be presented as shown in Figure 39.1.

As there are two options each for markets and for products, this gives a total of four distinct strategies that businesses can adopt when planning to increase sales. These are shown on the matrix and can be summarised as follows.

Market penetration

In 2013 Samsung reduced the European prices of its range of 4k TVs by up to €1,200. This was in response to price cuts by other manufacturers – but Samsung's reductions were larger in an attempt to increase market share. **Market penetration** is the least risky of all the four possible strategies in that there are fewer 'unknowns' – the market and product parameters remain the same. However, it is not risk-free as, if low prices are the method used to penetrate the market, they could lead to a potentially damaging price war that reduces the profit margins of all firms in the industry.

KEY TERM

Market penetration: achieving higher market shares in existing markets with existing products.

Product development

The launch of Diet Pepsi took an existing product, developed it into a slightly different version and sold it in the soft drinks market where Pepsi was already available. **Product development** often involves innovation – as with 4G mobile (cell) phones – and these brand new products can offer a distinctive identity to the business.

KEY TERM

Product development: the development and sale of new products or new developments of existing products in existing markets.

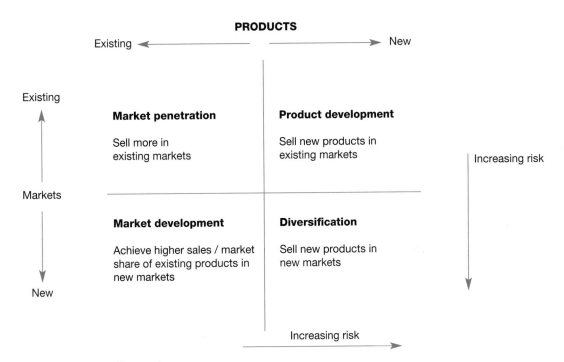

Figure 39.1 Ansoff's matrix

Market development

This could include exporting goods to overseas markets or selling to a new market segment. Lucozade used to be promoted as a health tonic for people with colds and influenza. It was successfully repositioned into the sports-drink market, appealing to a new, younger range of consumers. Dell or HP can use existing business-computer systems and repackage them for sale to consumer markets.

> **KEY TERM**
>
> **Market development:** the strategy of selling existing products in new markets.

Diversification

The Virgin Group is constantly seeking new areas for growth; the expansion from a media empire to an airline and then a train operator, then into finance, is a classic example of **diversification**, which was continued with the bid for the National Lottery in the UK. Tata Industries in India is another classic example of a very diversified business, making a huge range of products – from steel to tea bags. Related diversification, e.g. backward and forward vertical integration in the existing industry, can be less risky than unrelated diversification, which takes the business into a completely different industry.

> **KEY TERM**
>
> **Diversification:** the process of selling different, unrelated goods or services in new markets.

As the diversification strategy involves new challenges in both markets and products, it is the most risky of the four strategies. It may also be a strategy that is outside the core competences of the firm. However, diversification may be a possible option if the high risk is balanced out by the chance of a high profit. Other advantages of diversification include the potential to gain a foothold in an expanding industry and the reduction of overall business-portfolio risk.

Evaluation of Ansoff's matrix

Clearly, the risks involved in these four strategies differ substantially. By opening up these options, Ansoff's matrix does not direct a business towards one particular future strategy. However, by identifying the different strategic areas in which a business could expand, the matrix allows managers to analyse the degree of risk associated with each one. Managers can then apply decision-making techniques to assess the costs, potential gains and risks associated with all options. In practice, it is common for

large businesses, in today's fiercely competitive world, to adopt multiple strategies for growth at the same time.

While Ansoff's analysis helps to map the strategic business options, it has limitations too. It only considers two main factors in the strategic analysis of a business's options – it is important to consider SWOT and PEST analysis too in order to give a more complete picture. Recommendations based purely on Ansoff would tend to lack depth and hard environmental evidence.

Management judgement, especially based on experience of the risks and returns from the four options, may be just as important as any one analytical tool for making the final choice.

The matrix does not suggest – and to be fair to Ansoff, it was never intended to – actual detailed marketing options. For instance, market development may seem to be the best option but which market/country and with which of the existing products produced by the business? Further research and analysis will be needed to supply answers to these questions.

> **ACTIVITY 39.1**
>
> **ABCA and Ansoff's matrix**
> *[12 marks, 20 minutes]*
>
> Reread the 'Introducing the topic' case study at the start of this chapter. Analyse the four strategic options by using the Ansoff matrix. [12]

Force-field analysis

This technique, first developed by Kurt Lewin, involves looking at all of the forces for and against a decision. In effect, it weighs up the 'pros and cons' of a decision before a choice is made. The main purpose of the technique is to allow managers the insight that will allow them to strengthen the forces supporting a decision and reduce the forces that oppose it. In business, decisions such as introducing a new product or service, or implementing a major internal change, e.g. new IT systems, could be analysed using this approach.

> **KEY TERM**
>
> **Force-field analysis:** technique for identifying and analysing the positive factors that support a decision ('driving forces') and negative factors that constrain it ('restraining forces').

The technique uses the force-field diagram. This is used to represent the forces that work in favour of a major

ACTIVITY 39.2

Caffè Nero and Asda – contrasting strategies to achieve growth

Although both companies have similar objectives – sales growth, leading to profitability – Asda and Caffè Nero present an interesting contrast in business strategy. The coffee-bar operator is going for market development. Gerry Ford, Caffè Nero's chairman, has set a target of 100 branches to be opened in Turkey. He said that he was 'also looking around Europe and scouting out China'. He is confident of success in Turkey. He has appointed Isik Asur, a Harvard Business School graduate, who used to run the Starbucks operation in Turkey, so knows all about the changing consumer tastes in the country as well as the political, social and economic environment there.

Asda – the number-two supermarket chain in the UK – has decided on the strategies of market penetration and product development to build sales growth. New food stores will be opened in the next few years in an attempt to gain ground on Tesco. It aims to be the lowest-price supermarket to increase food sales further. In addition, it is expanding rapidly into non-food retailing. It plans to open ten new Asda Living stores, selling a huge range of items for the home – but not food.

Different businesses in different markets will often decide on different strategies for the future – even though overall objectives may be similar.

[46 marks, 60 minutes]

1 Analyse why companies like these need long-term plans to help achieve their objectives. **[10]**

2 Suggest **six** facts about the Turkish consumer market and economy that Caffè Nero would have found useful before taking this strategic decision. Briefly explain why each one is important. **[12]**

3 Using Ansoff's matrix, compare and contrast the different strategies being adopted by these two companies and comment on possible reasons why these were decided upon. **[12]**

4 Discuss the factors that might influence the long-term plans or strategies adopted by a business. **[12]**

change and those that work against it. Figure 39.2 shows such a diagram for the decision to introduce a big new IT system for the administration department of a business.

Conducting a force-field analysis

- Analyse the **current situation** and the **desired situation**.
- List all of the **factors driving** change towards the desired situation.
- List all of the **constraining factors** against change towards the desired situation.
- Allocate a **numerical score** to each force, indicating the scale or significance of each force: 1 = extremely weak and 10 = extremely strong.
- Chart the forces on the **diagram** with driving forces on the left and restraining forces on the right.
- Total the scores and establish from this whether the change is really **viable** – is it worth going ahead? If yes, then the next stage is important.
- Discuss how the success of the change or proposed decision can be affected by **decreasing the strength** of the restraining forces and **increasing the strength** of the driving forces.

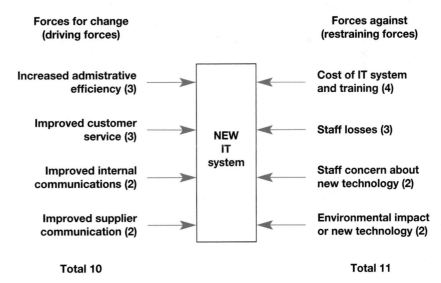

Forces for change (driving forces)		Forces against (restraining forces)
Increased admistrative efficiency (3)	NEW IT system	Cost of IT system and training (4)
Improved customer service (3)		Staff losses (3)
Improved internal communications (2)		Staff concern about new technology (2)
Improved supplier communication (2)		Environmental impact or new technology (2)
Total 10		Total 11

Figure 39.2 A force-field diagram

At present it can be seen that the forces against the new IT system are greater than those that are positive towards it (11:10). Forcing through this decision without responding to this analysis could be very unwise – people may be uncooperative and resistant if change is forced through with no attempt to reduce the forces against change.

Possible management strategies include:

- Staff could be trained (increase cost by 1) to help eliminate fear of technology (reduce staff concern about new technology, −2).
- It would be important to show staff that change is necessary for business survival (add a new force in favour, +2).
- Staff could be shown that new IT equipment would introduce new skills and interest to their jobs (add a new force in favour, +1).
- Managers could raise wages to reward staff for higher productivity (increase cost, +1, but reduce cost by loss of staff, −2).
- IT machines could be selected that are more energy efficient (environmental impact of new technology, −1).

These changes would swing the balance of the force-field analysis from the original 11:10 against to 13:8 in favour of the decision.

Evaluation of force-field analysis

This technique is widely used in 'change situations' for the reasons given, yet it has two main limitations as a strategic-choice method:

- Unskilled or inexperienced managers could fail to identify all of the relevant forces involved in the change process.
- The allocation of numerical values to the driving and constraining forces is rather subjective – two managers independently undertaking the same force-field analysis could arrive at rather different values for the forces and, consequently, propose very different decisions based on their assessments.

Decision trees

No decision-making technique can eliminate the risks involved in choosing between options, but managers can help themselves greatly if they adopt a logical approach to decision-making. One method of considering all the options available and the chances of them occurring is known as **decision trees**.

KEY TERM

Decision tree: a diagram that sets out the options connected with a decision and the outcomes and economic returns that may result.

ACTIVITY 39.3

Major change proposed at Buildit Construction plc

The economic recession had not been kind to construction companies. The fall in demand for houses and apartments occurred at the same time as government cutbacks on the building of schools and hospitals. The directors of Buildit Construction had achieved successful and profitable growth of the company during the good times. The question now was, would the business survive the downturn?

The directors' survival plan for the company was in two parts:

1 Use existing building sites owned by the company to construct small homes for rent and not for sale – this would mean operating in a new market segment of the property market, dealing with tenants renting property and not prospective house owners.

2 Make major cutbacks in administration overheads.

The second part of the plan would involve delayering of the management structure and increased multiskilling of the administration staff to increase flexibility and productivity. The 120 administration staff were consulted, but the directors made it clear that cost savings must be made to ensure the company survived. There would be an opportunity for older staff to retire early – the managers wanted to avoid redundancies if at all possible. Staff remaining would be expected to take on more financial and accounting work as well as decision-making tasks.

[26 marks, 45 minutes]

1 Analyse part 1 of the directors' survival plan, according to Ansoff's matrix. [4]

2 Using a force-field analysis diagram identify and assess the relative strength of the forces that will drive the change in part 2 of the plan and those that will constrain it. [12]

3 Recommend to the directors ways in which they could increase the chances of this strategic choice being successful. [10]

This technique is based on a diagram that is drawn to represent four main features of a business decision:

1 all of the options open to a manager
2 the different possible outcomes resulting from these options
3 the chances of these outcomes occurring
4 the economic returns from these outcomes.

By comparing the likely financial results from each option, the manager can minimise the risks involved.

Decision trees – how they are constructed

The tree is a diagram, which has the following features:

- It is constructed from left to right.
- Each branch of the tree represents an option together with a range of consequences or outcomes and the chances of these occurring.
- Decision points are denoted by a square – these are decision nodes.
- A circle shows that a range of outcomes may result from a decision – a chance node.
- Probabilities are shown alongside each of these possible outcomes. These probabilities are the numerical values of an event occurring – they measure the chance of an outcome occurring.
- The economic returns are the expected financial gains or losses of a particular outcome.

Decision trees – working out the expected values

Therefore, the **expected value** of tossing a coin and winning $5 if it comes down heads is 0.5 × $5 = $2.50. In effect, the average return, if you repeated this a number of times, would be to win $2.50. The purpose of a decision

tree is to show that option that gives the most beneficial expected value.

Example: The manager of an events-organising business has to decide between holding a fundraising auction indoors or outdoors. The financial success of the event depends not only on the weather, but also on the decision to hold it indoors or outdoors.

Table 39.1 shows the expected net financial returns or 'economic returns' from the event for each of these different circumstances. From past weather records for August, there is a 60% chance of fine weather and a 40% chance of it being poor. The indoor event will cost $2,000 to arrange and the outdoor event will cost $3,000.

The decision tree of the event is shown in Figure 39.3.

This diagram demonstrates the main advantages of decision trees:

- They force the decision-maker to consider all of the options and variables related to a decision.
- They put these on an easy-to-follow diagram, which allows for numerical considerations of risk and economic returns to be included.
- The approach encourages logical thinking and discussion among managers.

Using our tree diagram above, which option would give the highest expected value – holding the event indoors or outdoors? The answer is gained by calculating the expected value at each of the chance nodes. This is done by multiplying the probability by the economic return of both

Weather	Indoors	Outdoors
Fine	$5,000	$10,000
Poor	$7,000	$4,000

Table 39.1 The possible economic returns from the alternative options

KEY TERM

Expected value: the likely financial result of an outcome obtained by multiplying the probability of an event occurring by the forecast economic return if it does occur.

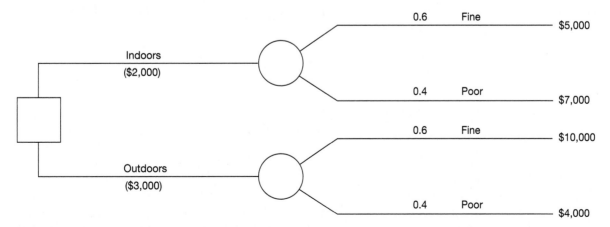

Figure 39.3 Decision tree for the fundraising auction

outcomes and adding the results. The cost of each option is then subtracted from this expected value to find the net return. This is done by working through the tree from right to left, as follows (see Figure 39.4).

- The expected value at node 1 is $5,800.
- The expected value at node 2 is $7,600.

- Subtract the cost of holding the event either indoors or outdoors.
- Indoors = $5,800 – $2,000 = $3,800
- Outdoors = $7,600 – $3,000 = $4,600.

Therefore, the events manager would be advised to hold the event outdoors as, on average, this will give the highest

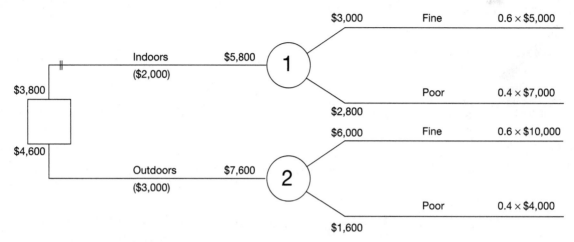

Figure 39.4 Calculating expected values – working from right to left

ACTIVITY 39.4

Location decision tree

The decision tree shown below has been produced to assist a manager with a decision to open a store either in Town A or in Town B. The annual cost of running the store in A is $50,000 and in B is $75,000. The annual economic results depend upon the state of the national economy, which could be either in recession or expanding.

Based on past data, the chance of an expanding economy is 0.7 and the chance of a recession is 0.3.

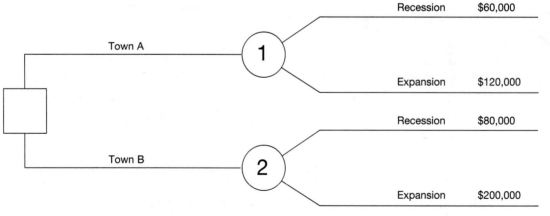

Figure 1 The decision tree of opening a new store

[14 marks, 20 minutes]

1 Calculate the expected values at both nodes 1 and 2. [4]

2 Which option is more desirable from an economic viewpoint? [2]

3 Explain the factors that should be taken into account in estimating the economic returns. [8]

ACTIVITY 39.5

Expansion decision

The owner of a car-repair garage is planning to expand the business. The two options are to build a forecourt to sell petrol or to construct a showroom to sell cars. The cost of the petrol forecourt is estimated at $100,000 and that of the showroom at $150,000. The expected economic consequences or payoffs during the expected lives of these investments will depend on the level of demand in the economy, as shown in the table below. The probability of demand being low during the lifespan of these investments is 0.2 and the probability of high demand is 0.8.

Demand	Petrol forecourt	Car showroom
High	$500,000	$800,000
Low	$400,000	$200,000

The economic returns from these two options

[15 marks, 20 minutes]

1 Show these options on a decision tree, adding the payoffs and probabilities. [6]

2 Calculate the expected value of both investments and recommend which option should be taken. [6]

3 State **three** other factors that you consider might influence the business owner's final decision. [3]

expected value. The other option is 'blocked off' with a double line in the figure to indicate that this decision will not be taken.

More complex decision trees

The examples used above have been based on fairly straightforward decisions where only one choice had to be made. Life is rarely that easy and a more complex decision tree, which concerns a construction company's options over a derelict building that it has owned for some time, is shown in Figure 39.5. There are two options facing the business initially:

1 The building could either be sold now for $1 million or improved and updated at a cost of $0.5 million. After renovation, the building could be sold as one house.

2 However, after renovation, another option is to split the building into three flats, which will cost a further $0.25 million.

The payoffs from these options will depend on interest rates at the time of sale. High rates will reduce the

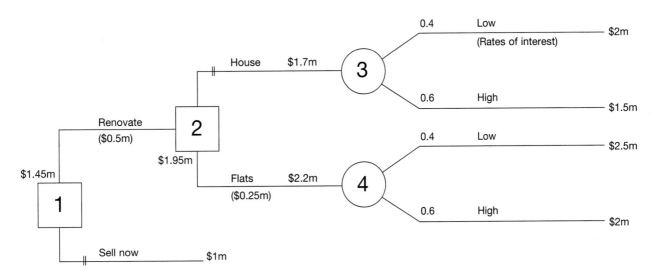

Figure 39.5 The decision tree for the construction company's options

Interest rates	Revenue: sale of house	Revenue: sale of flats
Low	$2m	$2.5m
High	$1.5m	$2m

Table 39.2 Interest rates and the revenue outcomes

returns in both cases, as seen in Table 39.2. Based on past economic records, the chance of interest rates being high during the sale period for the house or flats is 60% and the chance of low rates is 40%. The decision tree for these options is shown in Figure 39.5. The important rule of working from right to left in calculating expected values is still relevant with these more complex examples. The calculations must now be divided into two stages:

1   First, the expected values of selling either the house or the flats must be worked out, taking the additional conversion cost of the flats into account.
2   Second, the values of the two initial options can be compared, that is the immediate sale or the investment in the building, using the higher of the two outcomes from the second decision.

Thus, at node 3, the expected value is $1.7 million. At node 4, the expected value is $2.2 million. From this must be subtracted the additional flat conversion costs of $0.25 million to leave $1.95 million. Verify these results with your own calculations. The flat option is preferred to selling as one house. This is the return that is taken back to node 2.

Now we subtract the renovation costs of the building from this return to give the overall net return of not selling the building immediately. This is compared with the $1 million from the sale of the building now and it is clear, based on quantitative issues alone, that the business would be advised to both develop the building and convert it into flats. Therefore, working from right to left, the highest expected value at node 1 becomes $1.45 million, obtained from the 'flats' option.

Decision trees – an evaluation

The benefits to be gained by applying this technique have already been assessed. The potential limitations of it also need to be analysed because business decision-makers may not always wish to be dictated to by the results of the approach.

■   The primary limitation concerns the accuracy of the data used. Estimated economic returns may be quite accurate when they concern projects where experience has been gained from similar decisions. In other cases, they may be based on forecasts of market demand or estimates of the most likely financial outcome. In these cases, the scope for inaccuracy of the data makes the results of decision-tree analysis a useful guide, but no more.

■   In addition, the probabilities of events occurring may be based on past data, but circumstances may change. What was a successful launch of a new store last year may not be repeated in another location if the competition has opened a shop there first.

■   The conclusion must be that decision trees aid the decision-making process, but they cannot replace either the consideration of risk or the impact of non-numerical, qualitative factors on a decision. The latter could include the impact on the environment, the attitude of the workforce and the approach to risk taken by the managers and owners of the business. There may well be a preference for fairly certain but low returns, rather than taking risks to earn much greater rewards.

■   Finally, it must not be forgotten that the expected values are average returns, assuming that the outcomes occur more than once. With any single, one-off decision, the average will not, in fact, be the final result. Decision trees allow a quantitative consideration of future risks to be made – they do not eliminate those risks.

 KEY CONCEPT LINK

Choosing the most appropriate **strategy** in any given situation is of vital importance if a business is to maximise created **value**.

Which market?

Joe Keenan has an important decision to take. He operates a mobile market stall selling cooking pans and kitchen equipment. He has to decide which market to visit next Saturday. There are four options but, of course, he can only go to one town. He has estimated the revenues he could earn from each location by using past records and by consulting with other stallholders. His estimates, together with the chances of earning them, are given below:

Town A		Town B		Town C		Town D	
Probability	Revenue ($)	Probability	Revenue ($)	Probability	Revenue ($)	Probability	Revenue ($)
0.4	5,000	0.3	3,000	0.4	3,000	0.3	5,000
0.6	8,000	0.5	4,000	0.5	6,000	0.3	6,000
		0.2	8,000	0.1	10,000	0.4	9,000

[26 marks, 45 minutes]

1 Using the data above draw a decision tree of the options Joe has and add the probabilities and forecast economic returns. [6]

2 Calculate the expected values of Joe's **four** options. Which town should Joe visit on Saturday on the basis of quantitative data alone? [10]

3 Assess the value of decision tree analysis to Joe when taking this decision. [10]

SUMMARY POINTS

- Strategic choice means selecting the strategy – often from a range of options – which will best assist the company towards its long-term aim.
- Ansoff's matrix can be used to analyse business strategies and its effectiveness can be evaluated.
- Force-field analysis is a method of establishing the main driving and constraining factors when making strategic choices.
- Decision trees are a quantitative technique that blend the probability of outcomes occurring with the economic pay-offs of them.
- The usefulness of force-field analysis and decision trees can be evaluated.

RESEARCH TASK

Identify a recent major strategic decision made by a well-known business. It could be the launch of a new product, selling in a country for the first time, a takeover or merger.

- Research, using company reports, newspapers and the internet:
  a the reasons given for this strategic decision
  b the factors used by the company, e.g. quantitative forecasts or qualitative issues, to help make this decision.
- Assess how the company will determine whether the strategic decision is successful or not.

A Level exam practice questions
Case studies

1 Hairdressers' dilemma

Mark and Stella are qualified hairdressers who own their own salon. It is popular and profitable. They only employ two junior assistants, as they take pride in the fact that they deal with each customer themselves. This close personal service has worked well up until now. Mark and Stella's daughter is planning to marry in Argentina next April and this is a very busy period for the salon. Mark and Stella both want to go to the wedding, but they realise that this will mean being absent from the business for two weeks. They have considered three alternative options:

- Close the salon for the entire period and give up the $6,000 profit it would have made over the two weeks.
- Employ a professional hair stylist to take over the running of the salon for two weeks. She would cost $2,000 to employ but Mark believes that there is a 50% chance of her making a $3,000 profit and a 50% chance of a $4,000 profit (before her salary is subtracted).
- Ask two relatives to manage the business in their absence. They would receive a payment of $500 each. They know most of the customers personally, but their experience of hairdressing is limited to taking a course at college several years ago. Mark believes that the two relatives have a 60% chance of making a profit (before payment) of $3,000 and a 40% chance of making $5,000.

[28 marks, 45 minutes]

1 Draw a decision tree of the options available to Mark and Stella and add to it the probabilities and economic returns of each option. [6]

2 Calculate the expected values of the three options. [6]

3 Explain which option is best on financial grounds alone. [4]

4 Evaluate the other factors you would advise Mark and Stella to consider before taking the final decision. [12]

2 Restaurant owner considers her options

June Wong is the owner and manager of a popular restaurant. It is so busy at lunchtimes that June is considering an expansion of the premises. She has asked builders for estimates of the costs and they produced two possible plans.

One would be to double the size of the restaurant and to fit it out with high-quality fittings. This might then allow June to charge higher prices and try to appeal to a higher-income market segment. This would be an expensive option costing $200,000.

The other option suggested by the builders is a smaller extension with the same fittings as now. This would only cost $75,000. However, June estimates that this would not have such a high economic return, partly due to its smaller size, but also because there would be no opportunity to raise prices. June also realises that she has a third option, which would not cost a cent – to keep her restaurant as it is. The danger is that customers might become tired of waiting for a table and go to another restaurant. June usually avoids risks, but she now wonders if it is time to take a chance and raise capital to go ahead with expansion.

June has constructed the following decision tree to help her make this decision.

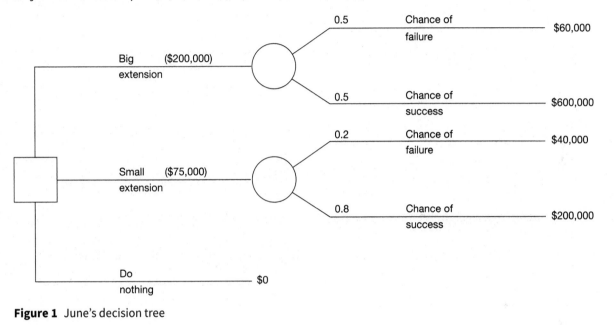

Figure 1 June's decision tree

[22 marks, 35 minutes]

1 Calculate the expected values of June's options. [8]

2 Advise June on which option she should take. Your answer should consider the results from question 1 and any other information that you consider to be important. [14]

A Level essay questions

[20 marks, 45 minutes each]

1 Assess the usefulness of strategic choice techniques to managers of a large manufacturing or hotel business in your country that is considering different growth strategies. [20]

2 The directors of a cosmetics company plan to double profits within five years. An aggressive expansion plan will be necessary. Two options for growth are:

   a Develop a new range of ecofriendly cosmetics made from natural ingredients.

   b Set up marketing operations in three developing countries for the first time.

   Discuss whether decision tree results should be the main consideration when making this strategic choice. [20]

40 Strategic implementation

By the end of this chapter, you will be able to:

- understand what strategic implementation means
- evaluate the importance of business plans and corporate planning to strategic implementation
- analyse different types of corporate culture and assess the impact culture can have on strategic implementation

- understand how businesses can establish a 'change culture'
- assess how businesses can manage and control strategic change
- evaluate the importance of contingency planning and crisis management.

Introducing the topic

MANAGING BUSINESS CHANGE

Constant change is a business reality, and organisations must continually adapt to their environments to stay competitive or risk becoming obsolete. That is why the ability to incorporate big changes into the culture of a business while still achieving good operating results is a much-sought-after competency. Five key questions are helpful in determining the likelihood that a major business change will succeed or fail:

1 How is the new vision different, better and more compelling?
2 Are the business leaders personally committed to the change?
3 Does the organisation have the resources to make the change?
4 How ingrained is the current culture?
5 Will the employees accept that change is necessary?

Organisations that fail to manage change effectively often experience internal disputes and increased costs. Consider Lufthansa Airlines; since it announced the details of an aggressive cost-cutting programme in February 2012, the airline has not demonstrated the skill or culture to execute its plan effectively. Alienated employees have taken part in ongoing strikes that have inconvenienced customers and increased costs.

Figure 40.1 Organisational change

What organisations get the thumbs up on their ability to change? Based on these five key questions, Cisco Systems, Citrix Systems and eBay are some companies that have reacted well. Citrix, a multinational software business, is building a change-management system in which leaders' and team members' confidence and ability to lead change are increased by real-world case studies, coaching and employee-designed workspaces.

As the pace of change continues to increase, an organisation's change capability will become a greater requirement for sustainable performance. The organisations that are investing in these capabilities are more likely to benefit from future opportunities.

Introduction

This is the final section of the strategic management process. Implementation means 'putting into effect or carrying out an idea'. So this stage of strategic management involves putting the strategic plans that have been analysed and chosen 'into effect'.

KEY TERM

Strategic implementation: the process of planning, allocating and controlling resources to support the chosen strategies.

Without successful strategic implementation, there can be no effective change within the organisation. Implementing a major strategic change is a very important cross-functional management task. It involves ensuring that all of the following factors are in place:

- an appropriate organisational structure to deal with the change
- adequate resources to make the change happen
- well-motivated staff who want the change to happen successfully
- a leadership style and organisational culture that allow change to be implemented with wide-ranging support
- control and review systems to monitor the firm's progress towards the desired final objectives.

This chapter assesses some of these key factors and it starts with the overall planning document that should be prepared before a new strategy can be implemented.

Business plans

KEY TERM

Business plan: a written document that describes a business, its objectives and its strategies, the market it is in and its financial forecasts.

The contents of a typical **business plan** for a new business are:

- the executive summary – an overview of the new business and its strategies

- description of the business opportunity – details of the entrepreneur; what is going to be sold, why and to whom
- marketing and sales strategy – details of why the entrepreneur thinks customers will buy what the business plans to sell and how the business plans to sell to them
- management team and personnel – the skills and experience of the entrepreneur and the people he/she intends to recruit to work with
- operations – premises to be used, production facilities, IT systems
- financial forecasts – the future projections of sales, profit and cash flow – for at least one year ahead.

Importance of business plans

Business plans are most important when setting up a new business, but they should be referred to and updated when important strategic choices are being made too. The main purpose of a business plan for a new business is to obtain finance for the start-up. Potential investors or creditors will not provide finance unless clear details about the business proposal have been written down clearly.

The planning process is very important too. If an entrepreneur went into a new business – even if no external finance was required – without a clear sense of purpose, direction, marketing strategies and what employees to recruit, the chances of success would be much reduced.

The financial and other forecasts contained in the plan can be used as the targets that the business should aim for. The benefits of SMART objectives were explained in Chapter 4.

Existing business – uses for the business plan

- Rewrite and adapt it to accommodate new or revised strategies, such as expansion plans.
- The original financial forecasts can act as budgets and control benchmarks.
- Updated versions can be used to apply for additional funding or to attract additional partners or to supply data for the experts if 'going public' becomes an option.

Some existing organisations, rather than new start-ups, refer to business plans as being short-term plans – say for one year – while longer-term planning documents are referred to as corporate plans.

Corporate plans – what do they contain?

A typical **corporate plan** will include:

1 The overall objectives of the organisation within a given time frame – perhaps three to four years. These could be:
   - profit target
   - sales growth
   - market share target.

KEY TERM

Corporate plan: this is a methodical plan containing details of the organisation's central objectives and the strategies to be followed to achieve them.

TOP TIP

Refer back to Chapter 4 to remind yourself of the importance of corporate aims and objectives. It should now be clear that these form the basis and focus of strategic decisions.

2 The strategy or strategies to be used to attempt to meet these objectives (see Figure 40.2). For instance, to achieve sales growth the business could consider the choices as analysed by Ansoff's matrix:
   - increase sales of existing products – market penetration
   - develop new markets for existing products – market development
   - research and develop new products for existing markets – product development
   - diversify – new products for new markets.

3 The main objectives for the key departments of the business derived from the overall objective.

Figure 40.2 The corporate planning process – linking objectives and strategies

Corporate plans – what are they for?

Potential benefits

- The value of corporate planning for several years ahead is that senior managers have a clear focus and sense of purpose for what they are trying to achieve and the means they should use to reach these aims.
- Hopefully, they will communicate this sense of purpose and focus to all managers and staff below them in the organisation – and this is an important requirement for corporate plans to be effective. This advantage is important to any business organisation – a start-up firm or an established one, small firms or large corporations.
- An important benefit of any corporate plan is the 'control and review' process. The original objectives can be compared with actual outcomes to see how well the business's performance matched its aims. An example of this is given in Activity 40.1.
- The actual planning process is a very useful exercise as well. When effectively done, actually preparing for and producing the corporate plan can have the benefits of forcing senior managers to consider the organisation's strengths and weaknesses in relation to its environment and to think about how all of the different functional departments of the firm inter-relate.

Potential limitations

Plans are great if nothing else changes. The best-laid plans of any business can be made obsolete by rapid and unexpected internal or external changes. This does not mean that planning is useless – far from it, as part of the planning process may well be looking ahead to consider how to respond to unforeseen events – see the section on contingency planning on page 579. What change does mean, however, is that if a business puts, say, a five-year plan into effect and then refuses to make any variations or adaptations to it no matter how much external environmental factors might change, then this inflexibility will be punished. The planning process and the plans that result from it should be as adaptable and flexible as possible to allow plans to continue to be relevant and useful during periods of change.

The value of corporate plans

The fact that there are very few businesses without a formal planning process for the future suggests that corporate planning is very important. The plan is not just for senior management consumption, it will be essential to share the contents of such a document with:

- potential investors when a share sale is considered
- major lenders to the organisation
- other stakeholder groups, e.g. the government if requesting development grants for expanding into an area of high unemployment

all staff – in the form of specific and tangible objectives for all departments, sections and individuals that will be based on the original objectives and strategies contained in the corporate plan.

The main influences on a corporate plan

Internal

- Financial resources – can the new proposed strategies be afforded?
- Operating capacity – will this be sufficient if expansion plans are approved by directors?
- Managerial skills and experience – this may be a major constraint on the plan's success, especially if the diversification strategy is chosen.
- Staff numbers and skills – workforce planning is a key factor in the success of any corporate plan.
- Culture of the organisation – this is discussed in detail below.

External

- Macro-economic conditions – expansion may have to be put on hold during a recession.
- Central bank and government economic policy changes.
- Likely technological changes – these could make even the best-laid plans appear very outdated quite rapidly.
- Competitors' actions – the competitive nature of the market was explained in Chapter 38.

TOP TIP

The relative importance of these factors will vary from business to business. A company producing income-elastic luxury products may find its corporate plan is most influenced by macro-economic forecasts. The directors of a small company may consider that the plan for their business is most constrained by internal financial limits.

Corporate culture – what is meant by this?

A commonly used definition of **corporate culture** is 'the way we do things around here'. This means how the people within the organisation look at the world and how they respond to it in trying to achieve certain goals.

KEY TERM

Corporate culture: the values, attitudes and beliefs of the people working in an organisation that control the way they interact with each other and with external stakeholder groups.

It is widely understood that different organisations have distinctive cultures. This is very true of businesses as well as other organisations, such as schools and colleges. The culture of a steel company will be very different from that of a nursing home. Similarly, in some schools, culture is driven by the need for better examination results, while others view that educating the 'complete person' is more important. The culture of an organisation gives it a sense of identity and is based on the values, attitudes and beliefs of the people who work in it – especially senior management.

ACTIVITY 40.1

PepsiCo Announces Strategic Investments to Drive Growth

- PepsiCo plans to increase annual advertising and marketing support behind its global brands by US$500–600 million.
- Multi-year productivity programme expected to generate $1.5 billion of cost savings rationalisation of operating practices and organisation structure, including a reduction in force of about 8,700 employees, about 3% of global workforce.
- Company targets high-single-digit earnings per share (EPS) growth to increase returns for shareholders.
- A plan to further increase returns to shareholders in the form of higher dividends has been announced.

These decisions are part of PepsiCo's corporate plan and are based on a comprehensive review by the company's management of its portfolio, brands, costs and organisation.

'In a volatile global environment over the past five years, PepsiCo has delivered double-digit compound annual growth in net revenue, 8% compound annual growth in core EPS, and returned about $30 billion to shareholders in the form of dividends and share repurchases,' said PepsiCo chairman and CEO Indra Nooyi. 'Our goal is to continue on that earnings trajectory over the next five to ten years, fully recognising that we need to make changes in how we operate to address the challenges the company faces.'

1 Analyse the benefits to PepsiCo of having a corporate plan. [10]

2 Analyse **two** factors that might lead to PepsiCo having to revise its corporate plan. [10]

3 Evaluate the importance to corporate planning of having clear financial targets – as in this case. [12]

Values, attitudes and beliefs have a very powerful influence on the way staff in a business will act, take decisions and relate to others in the organisation. They define what is 'normal' in an organisation. So it is possible for the same person to act in different ways in different organisations. What we do and how we behave – in society in general and in business in particular – are largely determined by our culture.

TOP TIP

Culture is such a powerful force in any organisation that you should take every opportunity in your answers to questions to make reference to it as a factor that helps explain managers' decisions and behaviour.

The main types of corporate culture

Many management writers have used different ways to identify and classify different types of organisational culture. These are the most widely used culture types.

Power culture

This is associated with autocratic leadership. Power is concentrated at the centre of the organisation. Swift decisions can be made as so few people are involved in making them.

KEY TERM

Power culture: concentrating power among just a few people.

Role culture

This is most associated with bureaucratic organisations. People in an organisation with this culture operate within the rules and show little creativity. The structure of the organisation is well-defined and each individual has clear delegated authority. Power and influence come from a person's position within the organisation.

KEY TERM

Role culture: each member of staff has a clearly defined job title and role.

Task culture

Groups are formed to solve particular problems and there will be lines of communication similar to a matrix

structure. Such teams often develop a distinctive culture because they have been empowered to take decisions. Team members are encouraged to be creative.

KEY TERM

Task culture: based on cooperation and teamwork.

Person culture

There may be some conflict between individual goals and those of the whole organisation, but this is the most creative type of culture.

KEY TERM

Person culture: when individuals are given the freedom to express themselves fully and make decisions for themselves.

Entrepreneurial culture

Success is rewarded in an organisation with this culture, but failure is not necessarily criticised as it is considered an inevitable consequence of showing enterprise and risk-taking.

KEY TERM

Entrepreneurial culture: this encourages management and workers to take risks, to come up with new ideas and test out new business ventures.

ACTIVITY 40.2

Corporate culture

Suggest, for each of these different types of culture, one business situation in which it would be the most appropriate culture to adopt.

TOP TIP

As with leadership styles, there is no one right or wrong culture for a business. The appropriate culture will depend on the firm's objectives, the type of market it operates in and the values and expectations of managers and employees.

TOP TIP

Do not expect all departments in a business to have the same culture. It can be very different. Would you expect the IT team to have the same jargon, patterns of behaviour, values and beliefs as HR staff or marketing teams?

KEY CONCEPT LINK

Business culture will influence the style of **management**/leadership used. An autocratic style will lead to difficulty in managing and leading **change** in ways that will convince the workforce that it is a change for the good.

Changing organisational culture – possible reasons for change

Many businesses have turned themselves around, converting potential bankruptcy into commercial success. Very often this transformation has been achieved by changing the culture of the business. The existing culture of a business can become a real problem when it seems to stand in the way of growth, development and success. Here are some examples of situations when changing culture would seem to be essential:

- A traditional family firm, which has favoured members of the family for promotion into senior posts, converts to a public limited company. New investors demand more transparency and recognition of natural talent from recruited employees.
- A product-led business needs to respond to changing market conditions by encouraging more staff involvement. A team- or task-based culture may need to be adopted.
- A recently privatised business formerly run on bureaucratic principles needs to become more profit-oriented and customer-focused. An entrepreneurial culture may need to be introduced for the first time.
- A merger or takeover may result in one of the businesses involved having to adapt its culture to ensure consistency within the newly created larger business unit.
- Declining profits and market share may be the consequences of poorly motivated staff and a lack of interest in quality and customer service. A person-based culture might help to transform the prospects of this business.

573

ACTIVITY 40.3

'Uncomfortable reading': key extracts from the Salz Review into Barclays' culture

The Salz Review – a report into Barclays Bank's cultural shortcomings after well-publicised financial scandals at the bank – makes for 'uncomfortable reading', according to the bank's current CEO. The report suggests that if there were company values at Barclays, no one knew about them:

- There was no sense of common purpose in a group that had grown and diversified significantly in 20 years.
- There were no clear and understood shared values.
- Pay was emphasised above any other aspect of people management.
- People management was considered mainly as a tool to increase business profits.
- Barclays attracted senior employees who measured their personal success principally in levels of pay.

The new CEO says it could take up to a decade to fully revise the culture at the bank. He has made a start by introducing the 'Barclays Way' – a code of how employees should do business in future. It contains statements such as:

- Helping people achieve their ambitions – in the right way.
- We act fairly, ethically and openly in all we do.
- We put our clients and customers at the centre of what we do.
- We are passionate about leaving things better than we found them.

[24 marks, 40 minutes]

1 Analyse the problems Barclays had as a result of not having 'shared values'. [10]

2 Evaluate the most significant steps that the new CEO might have to take in order to change culture effectively at the bank. [14]

ACTIVITY 40.4

Porsche culture contributes to success

Perhaps one of the reasons for the astonishing success of the Porsche motor-manufacturing business was the culture embodied by the views of its boss, Wendelin Wiedeking. 'The Porsche philosophy is that first comes the client, then come the workers, then the suppliers and finally the shareholders. When the first three are happy, then so are the shareholders.' Compare this with the typical view in US- and UK-based businesses that often promote 'shareholder culture' as being most important. These differences in outlook and culture help to explain why high-profile integrations between BMW and Rover Cars and then Chrysler and Mercedes-Benz were such disasters.

[10 marks, 15 minutes]

Explain how the merger of two businesses with different cultures can make success of the expansion less likely. **[10]**

The collapse of the merger between Chrysler and Mercedes-Benz was largely due to differences in corporate culture

The problems of changing organisational culture

Changing the value system of a business and attitudes of all staff who work for it is never going to be an easy task. The process could take several years before all staff and processes have been fully 'converted'. It means changing the way people think and react to problem situations. It can mean directly challenging the way things have been done for years. It can also involve substantial changes of personnel, job descriptions, communication methods and working practices.

Much work has been done on analysing the 'best way' to bring about change to an organisation's culture. The key common elements to these different approaches are:

- Concentrate on the positive aspects of the business and how it currently operates, and enlarge on these. This will be much easier and more popular with staff than focusing on, and trying to change, negative aspects.
- Obtain the full commitment of people at the top of the business and all key personnel. If they cannot or will not change, it might be easier to replace them altogether. Unless the key personnel model the behaviour they expect to see in others, change will be very difficult to achieve.
- Establish new objectives and a mission statement that accurately reflect the new values and attitudes that are to be adopted – and these need to be communicated to all staff.
- Encourage 'bottom-up' participation of workers when defining existing problems or when devising new solutions. The biggest mistake could be to try to impose a 'new culture' on workers without explaining the need for change or without giving them the opportunity to propose alternative ways of working.
- Train staff in new procedures and new ways of working to reflect the changed value system of the business. If people believe in the change and understand the benefits of it, then it will become more acceptable to them.
- Change the staff reward system to avoid rewarding success in the 'old ways' and ensure that appropriate behaviour that should be encouraged receives recognition. People need to be reassured that if they adjust to the new approach, then they will gain from it.

Corporate culture and strategic implementation

How does a corporation's culture affect strategic implementation?

One way is to consider how different organisations with different cultures would introduce important changes. For example, a business that has a power culture will not consult or communicate with staff affected by major strategic changes. These changes will be imposed on them – possibly with a 'take it or leave it' attitude. This approach may stir up resentment and resistance to change and the cooperation of the workforce is most unlikely to be obtained in future. In contrast, businesses that operate with task- or people-based cultures are more likely to encourage active participation in implementing major strategic change. Consultation and participation through two-way communication could lead to staff willingly accepting change – and contributing to a successful change process.

The other link between culture and strategic implementation occurs when culture is either strong or weak. Strong culture promotes and facilitates successful strategy implementation while weak culture does not. By strong culture is meant that there is very widespread sharing of common beliefs, practices and norms within the business. Everyone – or nearly everyone – in the business has accepted what the business stands for and the 'way things are done around here'. This energises people to promote successful strategy implementation – people want the new strategy to be successful. For example, if the culture of an organisation is built around people – listening to customers and empowering staff – then this promotes the implementation of a strategy that leads to an improvement in customer service. In organisations with weak cultures, employees may have no agreed set of beliefs and there is no pride in ownership of work. People may form their own groups within this type of organisation that are based around cultures that conflict with the weakly expressed business culture. Such situations provide little or no assistance to strategic implementation.

Evaluating the importance of corporate culture

The significance and power of an organisation's culture to drive people's behaviour and attitudes should not be underestimated – especially during a period of strategic change. Most of us do not want to be seen to 'do the wrong thing' within any group of people that we work with, and this feeling is particularly strong within a business environment. However, the impact of culture goes beyond the desire of most people to conform to accepted values. It can, as has been seen above, have a significant impact on how new strategies are implemented.

The following examples help to reinforce the importance of organisational culture:

- The values of a business establish the norms of behaviour of staff – what is and what is not acceptable in certain situations. For example, is it acceptable for an organisation to offer bribes to attract a large contract 'as long as we are not found out'?
- Culture determines the way in which company managers and workers treat each other. For example, if the chief executive is open and receptive to new ideas and proposals from senior managers, then this approach is likely to filter through the whole organisation – to its potential long-term benefit.
- A distinctive organisational culture can support a business's brand image and relationships with customers. For example, The Body Shop almost invented the 'ethical

trading' culture. Will this approach to business change after its takeover by L'Oréal?
- Culture determines not just how strategic decisions are made and implemented – with the participation of staff or by top managers alone – but also the type of strategic decisions that are taken. For example, the culture of a European state health service in target setting and rewards for meeting short waiting times within accident and emergency departments is, it is claimed, encouraging hospital managers to decide to leave patients in ambulances for up to two hours. How different would it be if doctors were actually taking these decisions?
- Organisational culture has been clearly linked to the economic performance and long-term success of organisations. Businesses dedicated to continuous improvement with staff involvement have been shown to be more profitable in the long term. For example, Toyota is the prime example of success based on this principle.

Change – techniques for implementing, managing and controlling change

1 Understand what change means

Change is the continuous adoption of business strategies and structures in response to changing internal pressures or external forces. Change happens whether we encourage and welcome it or not. To take control of it and to ensure that it is a positive and not a negative process, businesses must have a vision, a strategy and a proven and adaptable process for **managing change**.

> **KEY TERM**
>
> **Change management:** planning, implementing, controlling and reviewing the movement of an organisation from its current state to a new one.

Today, change in business is not the exception but the rule – it has become an accelerating and ongoing process. Table 40.1 gives some common causes of change. 'Business as usual' will become increasingly rare as global, economic and technological upheavals necessitate a business response. Change management requires firms to be able to cope with dramatic one-off changes as well as more gradual evolutionary change:

- Evolutionary or incremental change occurs quite slowly over time, e.g. the swing towards more fuel-efficient cars has been happening for several years. These changes can be anticipated or unexpected – the decision to increase the London congestion charge was announced months in advance, but a sudden oil-price increase may not have been expected. Obviously, incremental changes that are easy to anticipate tend to be the easiest to manage.

575

ACTIVITY 40.5

President Supermarkets – a case study in cultural change

As one of Europe's largest family-owned chain of supermarket stores, President Supermarkets had established a culture among employees that had contributed to its many years of growth. Loyalty to the family managers was high. In fact, workers often commented on the whole business being like a 'big family'. Employees were promoted for long service. Relationships with suppliers had been built up over many years and long-term supply contracts were in place. Customer service was a priority and was especially important as President never planned to be the cheapest shop in the towns it operated in. However, profits were not high and the younger members of the owning family lacked the skills to take over.

Some industry experts believed that some of these values and attitudes had to change once the business was sold by the family and converted into a public limited company. The new chief executive, Sally Harte, had experience in the USA as Walmart's chief food buyer. She announced on the first day of her appointment: 'This business is like a sleeping giant. There is great shareholder value that I can unlock to allow for higher dividends and to underpin a higher share price.' Within five weeks, 50% of the directors and key managers had been replaced. Suppliers' terms were changed, on Sally's insistence, to '5% below the cheapest or we drop you' and the staff salary and pension scheme was replaced for new recruits with flexible pay and conditions contracts. Labour turnover increased sharply. Sally had not predicted the adverse media coverage of these changes. 'I am only trying to adapt the organisational culture of this business to one that allows us to be successful in a highly competitive national marketplace where consumers want low prices and fresh goods.'

[30 marks, 50 minutes]

1 Explain **one** possible reason why Sally thought it necessary to change the organisational culture of President Supermarkets. [4]

2 Outline the type of culture that Sally seems to be introducing at President Supermarkets. [6]

3 Analyse the key steps that Sally should have taken to manage cultural change more effectively. [8]

4 To what extent will the change in culture guarantee future success for this business? [12]

■ Dramatic or revolutionary change, especially if unanticipated, causes many more problems. Civil conflict in Egypt in 2011 forced many holiday companies to re-establish themselves in other countries or markets. In extreme cases, these dramatic changes might lead to totally rethinking the operation of an organisation using a 'clean slate'. This is called **business process re-engineering**.

KEY TERM

Business process re-engineering: fundamentally rethinking and redesigning the processes of a business to achieve a dramatic improvement in performance.

TOP TIP

When discussing how change will affect a business and its strategies, try to analyse whether the change is incremental or dramatic, anticipated or unanticipated.

Trouble in Cairo in 2011: civil conflict in Egypt forced holiday companies to implement rapid changes

[12 marks, 20 minutes]

1 Identify and explain **three** recent changes in the external business environment that have occurred that have an **incremental** impact on businesses. [6]

2 Identify and explain **three** other recent changes that have occurred that have had a **dramatic** impact on business. [6]

2 Recognise the major causes of change
See Table 40.1.

3 Understand the stages of the change process
Here is a checklist of essential points that managers should consider before attempting to introduce significant changes in an organisation:

- **Where are we now and why is change necessary?** It is important to recognise why a business needs to introduce change from its current situation.
- **New vision and objectives:** For substantial changes, a new vision for the business may be needed – and this must be communicated to those affected by the change.

- **Ensure resources are in place to enable change to happen:** Starting a change and then finding that there is too little finance to complete it could be disastrous.
- **Give maximum warning of the change:** Staff in particular should not be taken by surprise by change – this will increase their resistance to it. See section below on 'Resistance to strategic change'.
- **Involve staff in the plan for change and its implementation:** This will encourage them to accept change and lead to proposals from them to improve the change process.
- **Communicate:** The vital importance of communication with the workforce runs through all of these other stages.
- **Introduce initial changes that bring quick results:** This will help all involved in the change to see the point of it.
- **Focus on training:** This will allow staff to feel that they are able to make a real contribution to the changed organisation.
- **Sell the benefits:** Staff and other stakeholders may benefit directly from changes – these need to be explained to them.
- **Always remember the effects on individuals:** A soft human resource approach will often bring future rewards in terms of staff loyalty when they have been supported and communicated with during the change process.
- **Check on how individuals are coping and remember to support them:** Some people will need more support

577

Nature of change	Examples of change	Managing change
Technological advances – leading to new products and new processes	■ products – new computer games, iPads and iPhones, hybrid-powered cars ■ processes – robots in production; CAD in design offices and computer systems for stock control.	■ need for staff retraining ■ purchase of new equipment ■ additions to product portfolio – other products to be dropped ■ need for quicker product development, which may need new organisational structures and teams.
Macro-economic changes – fiscal policy, interest rates, fluctuations in the business cycle	■ changes in consumers' disposable incomes – and demand patterns that result from this ■ boom or recession conditions – need for extra capacity or rationalisation.	■ need for flexible production systems – including staff flexibility – to cope with demand changes ■ explain need for extra capacity or the need to rationalise ■ deal with staff cutbacks in a way that encourages staff who remain to accept change.
Legal changes	■ changes to what can be sold (raising age for buying cigarettes) or when (24-hour licences for restaurants).	■ staff training on company policy on sale of cigarettes and alcohol ■ flexible working hours and practices.
Competitors' actions	■ new products ■ lower prices – based on higher competitiveness/lower costs ■ higher promotion budgets.	■ encourage new ideas from staff ■ increase efficiency by staff accepting the need to change production methods ■ ensure resources are available to meet the challenge.

Table 40.1 Types of change

than others – a 'sink or swim' philosophy will damage the business if it leads to low-quality output or poor customer service because staff were poorly supported during the change period.

TOP TIP

Use your understanding of communication gained from Chapter 15 to assess the importance of two-way communication in motivating staff to accept change.

4 Lead change, not just manage it

All strategic change must be managed. This means that:

- new objectives need to be established that recognise the need for change
- resources – finance and staff – need to be made available for the change to be implemented
- appropriate action needs to be taken – and checked on – to ensure that the planned changes are introduced.

Managing change effectively is important to successful implementation. But managing change is not the same as leading change. Leading strategic change is much more than just managing resources. Change leadership involves having a much greater vision than just making sure the right resources are available to deal with change. Leading change means:

- dynamic leaders who will shake an organisation out of its complacency and away from resistance to change ('corporate inertia')
- motivation of staff at all levels of the organisation so that change is looked upon as a positive force that could improve people's lives – this motivation will lead to significant changes in the behaviour of workers
- ensuring that acceptance of change is part of the culture of the organisation
- visible support of all senior managers who will help the change process to be accepted at all levels and within all departments of the business.

KEY CONCEPT LINK

An effective **manager** will be able to lead **change** in a positive way and this will encourage the employees to accept the consequences of change.

5 Project champions

A **project champion** is often appointed by senior management to help drive a programme of change though a business.

A project champion will come from within the organisation and be appointed from middle to senior management – they need to have enough influence within the organisation to make sure that 'things get done'. They are like cheerleaders for the project, but they will not necessarily be involved in the day-to-day planning and implementation of the new scheme. They will smooth the path of the project team investigating and planning the change and they will remove as many obstacles as possible. For example, they will speak up for the changes being suggested at board or other meetings of senior managers, they will try to ensure that sufficient resources are put in place and they will try to make sure that everyone understands the project's goals and objectives.

ACTIVITY 40.7

Project champions

Jane Moger is HR director within the restaurant business Compass Group. She has acted as project champion for the implementation of an e-recruitment system within the organisation. 'Being a project champion in HR gives you an opportunity to get involved in complex, long-term and high-value-added activities. Project champions get a new project off the ground and give the team momentum to see the change through,' she said.

A business is planning to adopt a new IT system that will allow many staff to work from home several days a week. Some senior managers are against this as it will 'reduce control over workers'. The IT manager in charge of implementing this strategy decides to appoint a project champion to smooth the changeover.

[10 marks, 15 minutes]

What are likely to be the key qualities needed by this project champion? Explain your answer. **[10]**

6 Project groups or teams

'Problem solving through team-building' is a structured way of making a breakthrough on a difficult change situation by using the power of a team.

> **KEY TERM**
>
> **Project groups:** these are created by an organisation to address a problem that requires input from different specialists.

When a difficult problem arises regarding a major change in a business's strategy or structure, one of the most common ways to analyse it and suggest solutions is to organise a project group. Project groups should work with the manager responsible for introducing the change. A team meeting of experts should provide a rigorous exchange of views that may well lead to an appropriate action plan being developed and agreed. The responsibility for carrying the plan out still lies with the original manager. Now, however, he or she will be better equipped to solve the problem that was preventing change from being effectively implemented.

Promoting change

Promoting change is an important function of management. Gaining acceptance of it – by both the workforce and other stakeholders – will be much more likely to lead to a positive outcome than imposing change on unwilling groups. According to John Kotter, a leading writer on organisational change, the best way to promote it in any organisation is to adopt the following eight-stage process:

1 establish a sense of urgency
2 create an effective project team to lead the change
3 develop a vision and a strategy for change
4 communicate this change vision
5 empower people to take action
6 generate short-term gains from change that benefit as many people as possible
7 consolidate these gains and produce even more change
8 build change into the culture of the organisation so that it becomes a natural process.

If change is not 'sold' or promoted to the people most affected by it, then it is almost certainly going to build up damaging resistance that could increase the chances of failure.

> **TOP TIP**
>
> Effective management of change should, where possible, focus on the positive benefits of change to the stakeholders most affected by it.

Resistance to strategic change

This is one of the biggest problems any organisation will face when it attempts to introduce changes. The managers and workforce of a business may resent and resist strategic change for any of the following reasons:

- **Fear of the unknown:** Change means uncertainty and this is uncomfortable for some people. Not knowing what may happen to one's job or the future of the business leads to increased anxiety – this results in resistance.
- **Fear of failure:** The changes may require new skills and abilities that, despite training, may be beyond a worker's capabilities. People know how the current system works – but will they be able to cope with the new one?
- **Losing something of value:** Workers could lose status or job security as a result of change and they want to know precisely how the change will affect them.
- **False beliefs about the need for change:** To put themselves at ease and to avoid the risks of change, some people fool themselves into believing that the existing system will 'work out some day' without the need for radical change.
- **Lack of trust:** Perhaps because of past experiences there may be a lack of trust between workers and the managers who are introducing the change. Workers may not believe the reasons given to them for change or the reassurances from managers about the impact of it.
- **Inertia:** Many people suffer from inertia or reluctance to change and try to maintain the status quo. Change often requires considerable effort, so the fear of having to work harder to introduce it may cause resistance.

The importance of the 'resistance factors' will vary from business to business. In those firms where previous change has gone well, where workers are kept informed and even consulted about change and where managers offer support and training to the staff involved, resistance to change is likely to be low. In contrast to this is the likely resistance to change in businesses where there is a lack of trust and little communication.

> **TOP TIP**
>
> When discussing the possible resistance to changes proposed by management, try to think of the leadership style being used to implement the change. This could be a major contributory factor in determining the degree of resistance.

Contingency planning and crisis management

This is also known as 'business continuity planning' or 'disaster-recovery planning', which perhaps gives a better idea of what it is for. Unplanned events can have a devastating effect on businesses of any size. Crises such as fire, floods, damage to stock, illness of key staff, IT system failure or accidents on the business's premises or involving its vehicles could all make it difficult or impossible to carry out normal everyday activities. At worst, important customers could be lost or the firm could go out of business altogether.

However, effective **contingency planning** allows a business to take steps to minimise the potential impact of a disaster – and ideally prevent it from happening in the first place.

 KEY TERM

Contingency plan: preparing an organisation's resources for unlikely events.

The key steps in contingency planning are:

1 Identify the potential disasters that could affect the business

Some of these are common to all businesses, but others will be specific to certain industries. For example, the oil industry must plan for oil tankers sinking, explosions at refineries and leakages in oil and gas pipelines.

2 Assess the likelihood of these occurring

Some incidents are more likely to occur than others and the degree of impact on business operations varies too. It seems obvious to plan for the most common disasters, but the most unlikely occurrences can have the greatest total risk to a business's future. These issues need to be balanced carefully by managers when choosing which disaster events to prepare for most thoroughly.

3 Minimise the potential impact of crises

Effective planning can sometimes cut out a potential risk altogether. When this is not possible, the key is to minimise the damage a disaster can do. This does not just mean protecting fixed assets and people, but also the company's reputation and public goodwill, as far as possible. This is often best done by the publicity department telling the truth, indicating the causes when known and giving full details of how to contact the business and the actions being taken to minimise the impact on the public. Staff training and practice drills with mock incidents are often the most effective ways of preparing to minimise negative impact.

580

ACTIVITY 40.8

Constant change a feature of modern industry

Britax has undergone many changes in recent years. The business grew out of a diverse group of companies. The Britax name and brand were adopted at the end of the 1990s when the business decided to concentrate its efforts and sold off some of its activities. It now focuses on child safety seats and designing and building aircraft interiors. The sales of the child safety seats have been boosted by recent changes in the law. Aircraft interiors are a niche market with four international competitors. Overall turnover of Britax's aerospace division has grown from £20 million to £150 million in six years, despite intense competition and an aircraft-building industry that fears a fall in aircraft orders.

Britax has just introduced a new, complex and expensive computer system to manage its production-resource planning. Stock levels have fallen dramatically and productivity has improved. However, the change involved changes in many people's work practices and skills. As with all changes of this nature, the crucial key to success lies not with the product but with those who have to use it. 'People react in different ways to change,' said Graham Leake, the business systems manager. 'How people approach change is a critical factor. A big factor in managing this is to build a strong project team. The right people need to be involved from the start. The next step is training and communicating the need for change. We spent a great deal of time and effort in this area and it was well worth it.'

[36 marks, 60 minutes]

1 Why is almost constant change likely to occur within businesses such as Britax? [6]

2 Outline **two** ways in which Britax reduced resistance to change. [6]

3 Analyse how force-field analysis *and* a project champion could have helped during this change. [10]

4 Evaluate the most important stages in the process of implementing and managing large-scale changes within a business. [14]

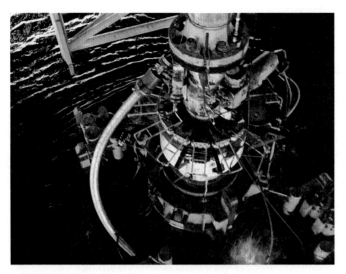

It is claimed that BP failed to make adequate contingency plans for the Deepwater Horizon oil rig disaster

4 Plan for continued operations of the business

As in Activity 40.10, prior planning can help with alternative accommodation and IT data – the sooner the business can begin trading again, the less the impact is likely to be on customer relationships.

TOP TIP

Contingency planning does not guarantee that disasters will not occur – but it could reduce the chances of them occurring and, just as importantly, it prepares the business for them so they should have a less damaging impact.

Cadbury had a plan ready

The risk of salmonella contaminating millions of chocolate bars put Cadbury's corporate plan in doubt. The problem was caused by a leaking pipe in Cadbury's UK factory but the company's contingency plan swung into action. More than a million chocolate bars were recalled by the company, they were disposed of in a completely safe way and the Food Standards Agency was informed. Retailers were fully compensated for stock that was destroyed. Cadbury apologised to all customers. Business consultants doubted whether the incident would cause any long-term damage to the company's image or brand names because of the detailed contingency plan that was put into operation.

[20 marks, 25 minutes]

1   Outline **two** other incidents or 'disasters' that could have a major impact on Cadbury's sales and reputation.   [8]

2   Evaluate the importance of contingency planning in this case.   [12]

See Table 40.2 for the benefits and limitations of contingency planning.

Benefits	Limitations
■ reassures staff, customers and local residents that concerns for safety are a priority ■ minimises negative impact on customers and suppliers in the event of a major disaster ■ public relations response is much more likely to be speedy and appropriate, with senior managers being used to promote what the company intends to do, by when and how.	■ costly and time-consuming – not just the planning process but the need to train staff and have practice dry runs of what to do in the event of: fire, IT failure, terrorist attack, accident involving company vehicles and so on ■ needs to be constantly updated as the number and range of potential disasters can change over time ■ staff training needs increase if labour turnover is high ■ avoiding disasters is still better than planning for what to do if they occur.

Table 40.2 Benefits and limitations of contingency planning

Setting the scene: planning for the worst pays off

When arsonists destroyed the head office of Kent-based marketing agency, FDS Group, chairwoman Allison Williams ensured her 75 employees were relocated and the business fully operational within three working days. 'Having a disaster recovery plan as part of our corporate plan helped to rehouse the entire business in days and sent out a strong positive signal to our customers,' said Allison. 'Our contingency-planning routines meant that our data were backed up off-site. We made use of our contacts in the local business community and had two temporary offices to view within 24 hours. The company secretary made sure the insurance company's loss adjustor was on site by noon of the day after the fire. I've never been so proud of my staff, and suppliers fell over themselves to help us too. There was no time to dwell on the situation – most of our customers are blue-chip businesses and they wanted the reassurance that we could be operational again as soon as possible.'

Managers from FDS held several informal meetings with customers within days of the fire to reassure them that it was 'business as usual'. This was also part of the firm's contingency plan. This demonstration of the firm's commitment to its customers paid off as it showed that customers' needs were valued above everything else.

[38 marks, 60 minutes]

1 Explain whether you think the time spent by this business in planning for disasters was worthwhile or not. [12]

2 Analyse the problem this business could have experienced if it had not 'prepared for the worst' [10]

3 Do you think that even very small businesses should engage in some form of contingency planning? Justify your answer. [16]

SUMMARY POINTS

- Business plans and corporate plans provide the focus for implementing strategic change.
- A business's corporate plan will be influenced by several factors and there are many reasons why plans may not be implemented effectively.
- Corporate culture is often ingrained within a business and it may be difficult to change unless key steps are followed.
- There are several types of corporate culture and they can influence strategic implementation.
- The need for change resulting from strategic implementation is ever-present in business organisations.
- Strategic change can be most effectively implemented within organisations when everyone 'buys into it'.
- It is important to promote change positively and communicate the benefits of it.
- Resistance to change is common but this can often be overcome.
- The process of contingency planning is recognised as being of great significance but its effectiveness can be evaluated.

RESEARCH TASK

Investigate a recent 'business disaster' that has been well publicised.

- What was the cause of the 'disaster' and exactly how did it affect the ability of the business to continue its operations?
- Examine how the business dealt with the disaster and the problems that resulted from it. Is there evidence that contingency planning was not undertaken – or was inadequate?

A Level exam practice questions
Case studies

1   New goals for Choclite

Choclite is a major multinational confectionery and drinks business. Four years ago the directors published details of their new corporate plan, which set specific goals for the company to be achieved over the next three years. Last year, it reported that these had been achieved. For example, one objective was to: 'Profitably and significantly increase global confectionery market share.' The success was measured by 'a 30% increase in global market share' and an '11% increase in emerging markets' revenue growth per year'.

Encouraged by this success, the directors set out new company goals and strategies for the next three years. These included:

- **goal:** 'Deliver superior shareholder returns'
- **strategy:** Focus on cost reduction and efficiency improvement'
- **goal:** 'Be the best regional confectionery business'
- **strategy:** 'Further product innovation and expand consolidation of chocolate making plants'.

[28 marks, 50 minutes]

1   Explain how Choclite might measure its success in achieving the two goals outlined in the case study.   [6]

2   Analyse factors that might make it difficult for Choclite to achieve the two goals contained in the case study.   [10]

3   Evaluate the usefulness of corporate planning to a multinational confectionery business such as Choclite.   [12]

2 Culture change to meet increased competition

DLM is a European airline that underwent a spectacular turnaround. Under a new chief executive the company switched from a product- and technology-focused business to a market- and customer-service-oriented one. Under the old organisational culture, the pilots, technicians and autocratic managers were the company's heroes. Planning and sales were based on maximising flight hours with the most modern aircraft possible. Worsening profits forced a change of approach. The new CEO understood the changing and increasingly competitive air-travel market and the need to cater for the needs of current and potential customers.

Those needs were best known by the employees with face-to-face contact with the customers – cabin crew and ground staff. These people had never been asked for their opinions. They had just been a disciplined group of uniformed 'soldiers' trained to follow clear rules and procedures. The CEO changed all this. These staff were now considered to be 'on the firing line' and the organisation has been completely restructured to support them, not to order them around. Superiors are now advisors, much simulation training is given in customer relations and the staff are given considerable independence in dealing with customers' problems on the spot. They only check with their senior managers after the event – which involves much confidence in employees' judgement with all the risks this entails. Customer numbers and profits have been on a steady upward flight path since these changes in culture were introduced.

[30 marks, 50 minutes]

1 What do you understand by the term 'organisational culture' from this case study? [6]

2 Analyse why the new CEO thought that he had to make changes to this culture. [10]

3 Do you think that the changes made by the CEO have been introduced successfully? Justify your answer. [14]

A Level essay questions

[20 marks, 45 minutes each]

1 The effective management of strategic change in today's world will be the main factor determining the success or failure of businesses. To what extent do you agree with this view? Refer to business examples in your answer. [20]

2 Evaluate the view that: 'Contingency planning is a waste of resources, as major accidents are often unavoidable but, in any case, they rarely occur.' [20]

3 A housing development for disabled workers has been owned and operated by a profit-making private company for many years. A charity has just been successful in buying the development from the company. Evaluate the most important steps the new management might have to take to change the culture of the organisation. [20]

End of Unit 6: Exam-style case study questions

LeFranc Kitchen Machines (LKM)

Sachin was only 21 when he became managing director and majority shareholder of the family business, LKM, after his father died three years ago. The business makes electrical kitchen equipment such as ovens, mixers and coffee machines for use in home and restaurant cooking. The demand for these products is increasing from high-income consumers. LKM distributes its products through wholesalers but also sells directly online through its website. LKM products have a good brand image and prices are usually higher than those of competitors. LKM currently only sells products within country X.

LKM's factory is currently operating at 90% capacity. The operations manager wants to introduce some of the latest technology to increase operational efficiency. The leaders of the three trade unions, who have members among LKM's workforce, have asked for urgent discussions with the operations manager. They want to review the impact new technology will have on employment contracts and job numbers within LKM. When Sachin heard of this request he urged the operations manager to ignore it: 'The introduction of new technology will be a management decision and we will only consider the impact on the future profitability of LKM. The final decision will depend on which strategic growth option I decide on.'

Globalisation – threat or opportunity for LKM?

Country X recently joined a large international free-trade area. Sachin thinks this will increase competition in country X from imported kitchen machinery. However, he also believes that it will give his business the chance to export for the first time. Sachin has been encouraged by a management consultant to use an agent or distributor based in country Y if he decides to start exporting LKM products there. However, Sachin is keen to retain full control over the marketing of LKM products. He wants to directly employ selling staff within country Y. He also believes that if the marketing department translates existing LKM advertising and promotional material into the language most widely used in country Y, then his business could enter this market successfully.

Which strategic option for growth?

Apart from exporting products to country Y, Sachin has other plans for expanding LKM. The business has three competitors in country X and LKM has only the third largest market share. The economies of scale experienced by two of the other companies give them a competitive cost advantage. However, the LKM brand is well recognised and the quality of its products is a differentiating factor, even though it has a limited budget for research and development. The two growth options are:

Option A – take over LKM's smallest rival: CPS is the smallest of LKM's competitors in country X. The owner of CPS, Kath, is retiring and she has advertised her business for sale for $18 million. She is well known in the industry for her laissez-faire style of leadership. Employee performance within CPS is among the highest in the industry, but the business lacks finance for investment and research and development. The existing CPS factory is small but uses highly automated machinery. The combined LKM and CPS market share would be 32%. LKM is a private limited company. Sachin would have to sell shares in LKM to business contacts and members of his family to finance this option.

Option B – new LKM factory: This option involves selling the existing factory site, near the city centre, which is worth $5 million. LKM would then relocate to a region with much lower land prices and build a larger factory that would allow LKM to expand its product range. Sachin is keen to start producing complete kitchen furniture units that would allow LKM's electrical machines to be fully integrated into them. He estimates that around 40% of existing workers would be prepared to relocate. This plan would also include adopting lean production techniques including kaizen groups.

To help Sachin make a strategic decision between these two growth options, he asks the finance manager and operations manager to gather the data contained in Table 1 on the next page.

585

KEY CONCEPT LINK

The implementation of strategic decisions completes the 'strategic cycle'. The result of these decisions should be measured and monitored to ensure that they achieve the original objectives set for them. If they do not, further changes might be needed. Perhaps the most important function of **management** is to set the strategic direction of the business, based on **market research** (customer-focused) and incorporating effective new ideas (**innovation**).

	Option A	Option B
Estimated capital cost	$18 million	$12 million – before allowing for sale of existing factory
Estimated ARR % for first ten years	10%	8%
Decision tree: Estimated expected monetary values	$15 million	$8 million
Ansoff's Matrix	Market penetration – so low risk, but the takeover needs to be managed well	Product development – medium risk, but new products complement existing ones
Force field analysis: Forces for change: driving forces	15	13
Forces against change: constraining forces	12	12
Major constraining force:	Culture clash	Employee/trade union resistance

Table 1 Data to be used by Sachin to help make the strategic choice between Option A and Option B

A Level 50 marks 90 minutes

1 Analyse the benefits to LKM of undertaking strategic analysis before deciding on market development in country Y. [10]

Essays

2 Recommend which of the two strategic options, A or B, Sachin should decide between. Your answer should include analysis of the data in Table 1 and other relevant information. [20]

3 Evaluate how Sachin could effectively manage the changes that will be necessary as a result of the strategic decisions he proposes. [20]

Preparing for your examinations

On completing this chapter, you will be able to:

- understand the key differences between the two Cambridge International Examinations AS Level examination papers 1 and 2
- understand the differences between these two AS papers and the Cambridge A Level paper
- appreciate what you need to do to revise effectively
- understand what the 'assessment objectives' are and how you can demonstrate these clearly.

Introduction

You can help yourself greatly in preparing for your final examinations by following some important steps. No one likes examinations but there is no need to be afraid of them if you prepare yourself well and apply straightforward examination techniques. Revision is, of course, one of the keys to success but just learning facts and figures is insufficient at AS and A Level. The need to apply your knowledge to the business context given in the question or the case study, analyse the question set and, where necessary, show judgement are often overlooked by students who focus too much on the content of the subject.

The aims of this guide to help you prepare for your examinations are to:

- inform you about the examination papers and their requirements
- tell you about the key skills that will help you to write effective answers
- alert you to the important 'trigger' words contained in all questions
- help you with some simple revision tips.

The Cambridge examination papers

Cambridge Advanced Subsidiary (AS) Level

- There are two AS Level papers.
- They may be taken halfway through an A-Level course and then resat, if required, at the end of the A Level course.
- Alternatively, they may be taken at the end of an A Level course during the same examination session as the two A Level papers.
- Paper 1 is worth 40% of the AS qualification (20% of the full A Level).

- Paper 2 is worth 60% of the AS qualification (30% of the full A Level).
- The two papers contain different types of questions.
- Paper 1 has two sections. Section A contains five compulsory short answer questions. Section B has a choice of three essay questions – only one must be answered.
- Paper 2 has two compulsory data response questions.
- AS Level papers form part of the full A Level examination.

Advanced (A) Level

- There is one A Level paper.
- It is taken at the end of your A Level course.
- Paper 3 is worth 50% of the A Level qualification.
- The paper contains different types of questions.
- It is a case study paper with five compulsory questions in section A. Some of these will be structured into more than one part.
- Section B has a choice of two essays – only one must be answered.

These details are summarised in Table 41.1.

Preparing for the examinations, step 1 – getting organised

- Ask your teacher for a copy of the syllabus – use the guidance notes as a check list when you are revising. You may find it useful to tick off each topic as you revise and understand it.
- Your teacher may show you the mark scheme for these papers. Looking at the mark scheme can help you to understand how credit is given to answers in examination. Ask your teacher about any parts you don't understand.
- Put your class notes in order with a clear set of dividers so that each topic is easy to refer to – you should use the same subject headings as the syllabus.
- Plan your revision time carefully. A revision timetable is always a good idea as it will allow you to allocate a certain amount of time to each important topic area. Be as detailed as possible in your timetable; for example: *'Thursday – revise operations management'* is not detailed enough, it is better to lay out your timetable like this:

Thursday: 9am to 9.30am – costs and costing methods
Break – 10 minutes
    9.40am to 10am – special-order decisions using contribution costing

SCHEME OF ASSESSMENT ADVANCED SUBSIDIARY QUALIFICATION (Core syllabus)					
Paper	Type	Duration	Number of questions	Maximum mark	% of total marks for the syllabus
1	Short answer	1h 15 mins	5	20	20
2	Essay (Core)	1h 30 mins	1 from choice of 3	20	20
	Data response		2	60	60
ADVANCED LEVEL (Core syllabus plus Extension topics)					
Paper	Type	Duration	Number of questions	Maximum marks	% of total marks for the syllabus
1	Short answer	1h 15 mins	5	20	10
2	Essay (Core)	1h 30 mins	1 from choice of 3	20	10
3	Data response	3 hours	2	60	30
	Case study		5 + 1 essay from choice of 2	100	50

Table 41.1 The A Level syllabus will include the core AS syllabus as well as the additional A Level material

Step 2 – revision techniques

Everybody has their own favoured methods of revision. This section is not aiming to make you change these methods if you are happy with them and if they work. However, you may like to consider trying some of these approaches, especially if you are not very satisfied with how you currently prepare for examinations:

1 Short sessions, but lots of them. Psychological studies have shown that our learning abilities decline sharply after around 30 minutes of intensive study. Arrange your timetable so that in each day you have several 30-minute sessions with breaks in between – not just one session of several hours.

2 Use active-revision techniques. Reading notes and sections of this textbook has a place in revision – but it is a passive form of revision. Active methods have been shown to be more effective. These include:

■ rewriting notes in a different style

■ making new notes, e.g. from this textbook

■ making spider diagrams or 'mind maps' with key words and terms (see Figure 41.1 and the examples given on the Student's CD-ROM)

■ testing yourself with simple written tests that you can mark yourself, e.g. lists of definitions

■ revising with a friend and testing each other, e.g. working through the multiple-choice questions on the Student's CD-ROM

■ making easy-to-refer-to revision cards containing a few key facts, figures or diagrams – an example is shown in Table 41.2.

Step 3 – understand the assessment objectives

Examination papers test a range of knowledge and skills and are designed around specific assessment objectives. The key skills the Cambridge examinations will test are:

1 **Knowledge and understanding** of the content of the syllabus.

2 **Application** of this knowledge to problems and issues that will be from both familiar and unfamiliar situations, e.g. business information given in the data response paper 2 and the case study around which paper 3 is based.

3 **Analysis** of problems, issues and situations – this will involve the use of subject theory and techniques to explain in detail and with reasoned arguments these problems, issues and situations.

4 **Evaluation** of data, drawing and supporting conclusions and showing judgement when making decisions as in discriminating between alternatives – will also involve assessing the relevance of the subject's main concepts and models in analysing problems, issues and business situations.

Each of the different papers will test your skills in a different way. Table 41.2 shows how many marks are available for each of the skills in each of the papers.

The most important point about the explanations given above is that AS and A Level examinations are not simply testing your subject knowledge. You will be expected to *apply* this knowledge, especially to data response and case study situations, but also to the business situation referred to in an essay question. You will be expected to use the theories and techniques of the subject to analyse and explain situations. Finally, you will be expected to show judgement.

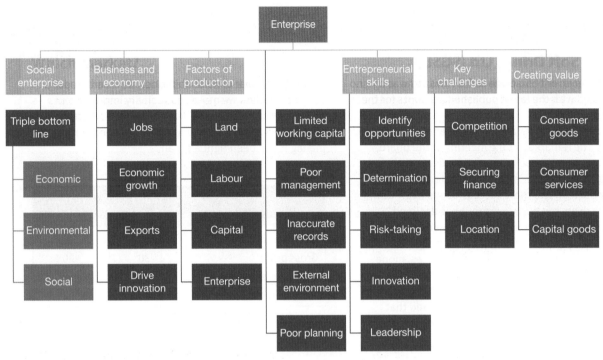

Figure 41.1 A sample mind map to help revision

	Knowledge	Application	Analysis	Evaluation	Total marks available
Paper 1	20	6	8	6	40
Paper 2	18	18	12	12	60
Paper 3	20	20	30	30	100
Total	58	44	50	48	200

Table 41.2 Syllabus grid

So how important is your revision of subject knowledge? It is vital because without accurate and detailed subject knowledge you will not be able to demonstrate the other skills effectively. For example, you will not be able to apply, analyse or evaluate a break-even chart unless you know how it is constructed and unless you know the assumptions behind it.

Step 4 – understand what makes an effective answer

This is best considered by looking at a sample exam question and mark scheme. The question and mark scheme that follow are in the style of a Cambridge paper 2 question.

Sample mark scheme

1 *a* *Define the term 'gross profit'.*   *[2]*

    b *Briefly explain the term 'batch production'.* *[3]*

    a Gross profit – sales revenue less cost of sales (before overheads are deducted). SGSD made a gross profit in both years.

    b Batch production – manufacture of a number of identical products with each item in the batch proceeding through each stage of production together – currently used by SGSD

Mark scheme:

Level two: Complete understanding of the concept is demonstrated – in context (3 marks).

Level one: Some understanding of the concept is shown (1–2 marks).

2a *Calculate, for both years, the gross profit margin of the business.*   *[3]*

  a gross profit/sales turnover. × 100 = gross profit margin%

Mark scheme:

1 mark for correct formula if all other working is incorrect.

One correct result (2 marks)

Two correct results (3 marks)

Year 1 = 20%, Year 2 = 11.1%.

So Good Soft Drinks Ltd (SGSD)

The chief executive of So Good Soft Drinks Ltd was most disappointed with the latest published accounts for the company.

'In one year our profitability has fallen to very low levels,' he remarked at the meeting of the board of directors. 'If only I had rejected the advice of my marketing manager when she said that lowering our prices would lead to a more successful business. Our sales have risen, but our gross profit has declined.'

The operations manager was very angry too. Last year, he had suggested that instead of an expensive marketing campaign to advertise lower prices, money should be spent in the production department. He had suggested replacing the current batch-production methods with flow production. He had argued that this could lead to lean production, including the use of just-in-time stock-control methods. 'We cannot reduce our prices unless we make productivity improvements first,' he had said last year. The chief executive looked at the latest results and wondered if the operations manager had been right after all.

	Year 1 ($000)	Year 2 ($000)
Revenue	150	180
Gross profit	30	20
Overhead expenses	15	18
Net (operating) profit	15	2

Extract from 'So Good' Soft Drinks Ltd accounts

1 a Define the term 'gross profit'. [2]
   b Briefly explain the term 'batch production'. [3]
2 a Calculate, for both years, the gross profit margin of the business. [3]
   b Explain how a reduction in prices might have led to an increase in sales revenue yet lower profits. [5]
3 Analyse the factors this business should consider before changing to a method of flow production. [6]
4 Discuss and recommend a marketing mix that a soft drink manufacturer could use to increase sales profitably in your own country. [11]

b *Explain how a reduction in prices might have led to an increase in sales revenue yet lower profits.* [5]

b Content: Lower prices can lead to higher sales – and if sales rise by a higher percentage than the percentage reduction in prices, sales revenue will increase. However, by reducing gross profit margin so much, despite higher sales, total gross profit falls. This can be seen in this case where the gross profit margin falls and lower profits result from the lower-price strategy.

Mark scheme:

Knowledge and application	Analysis and evaluation
Level one: Explains the relationship in general terms. (1–2 marks)	Level one: Analyses how the results of gross profit margin ratio support this explanation. (1–3 marks)

3 *Analyse the factors this business should consider before changing to a method of flow production.* [6]

3 Content: Cost of new equipment – is capital available, especially with falling profits? Is space available? Impact on workforce? Is demand for a standardised product high and consistent enough? Will the costs of flow-production methods be regained from increased sales of soft drinks?

Mark scheme:

Knowledge and application	Analysis and evaluation
Level two: Explains clearly why these factors are important to this business (2–3 marks).	
Level one: Identifies relevant factors but not developed or explained (1 mark).	Level one: Analyses factors, using appropriate theory (1–3 marks).

4 *Discuss and recommend a marketing mix that a soft-drink manufacturer could use to increase sales profitably in your own country.* [11]

4 Content: Definition of marketing mix: the four factors that can be varied to achieve a marketing objective: promotion, product, price and place (distribution changes). Any reasonable points allowable. For higher marks the answer must refer to the nature of this

product and the likely market segment aimed at and 'own country' conditions, e.g. high- or low-income country, level of competition in this market.

Mark scheme:

Knowledge and application	Analysis and evaluation
Level two: Explains clearly how these might operate to increase sales for soft within own country (3–4 marks).	Level two: Justified recommendation for an appropriate marketing mix in this case (3–7 marks).
Level one: Identifies two marketing-mix factors, but not applied to soft drinks or own country (1–2 marks).	Level one: Analyses how factors identified will influence sales (1–2 marks).

You should also notice that the skills are not evenly examined in every paper. Knowledge and application are relatively more important at AS Level. The higher-order skills of analysis and evaluation are relatively more important at A Level. This means that you will be asked for more detailed analytical explanations and much more judgement in paper 3 than in papers 1 and 2.

Points to note:

■ The questions are of graded difficulty.
■ Question 1 is based on knowledge with some application to the business in the case.
■ Question 2a requires some knowledge (the appropriate ratio) and then application to the data.
■ Question 2b has just two marks for knowledge and three marks for analysis.
■ Question 3 has just one mark for knowledge, two for application and three marks for analysis.
■ Question 4 is the most challenging part to this question. Two marks are awarded for knowledge, two for application, two for analysis, but four marks for evaluation – showing judgement in the recommendation of the marketing mix to be adopted. So a really good answer would explain *why* the marketing mix selected is, in the opinion of the student, the best one and the one most likely to succeed in selling soft drinks in the student's own country.

Common errors in answering data response questions

■ Ignoring the data altogether and writing answers that make no application to the business in the data at all: to gain application marks answers should be applied to the data given.
■ Failing to use appropriate theory – such as the marketing mix and important parts of it – to explain answers. This is often caused by students failing to recognise the key trigger words for analysis such as **analyse, examine, explain why.**

■ Not recognising that trigger words such as **discuss, recommend, evaluate, to what extent** require students to show judgement.
■ Not allocating time effectively – if there are two questions of equal length you should allow equal time for each.

Common errors in answering short answer/essay questions

1 Allocate time for each question carefully using the number of marks available as a guide. You need to allow enough time for the longer essay questions with more marks for analysis and evaluation available. Do not be tempted to write long answers for the short answer questions – they require short but adequate answers. An example question might be:

*Outline **two** benefits of democratic leadership.* [4].
A four-mark answer would be:

Democratic leadership would allow the workers of a business to have a role in decision-making. This could help to motivate staff to work harder as they are being given responsibility.

Another benefit of democratic leadership is that it could lead to better decisions being made. If workers are involved in decisions about working methods, the practical 'hands-on' experience they have could lead to a more efficient work method being decided on.

2 Failing to apply Business theory to the essay answer and concentrating only on descriptive content.
3 Not applying an essay answer to the business context given. For example: *Discuss how a manufacturing business could motivate production workers.* If the essay answer does not analyse how financial and non-financial methods of motivation could be introduced into a manufacturing business such as car or TV production, then no marks will be gained for 'application'. For example, would piece-rate pay be an appropriate method to use if the quality of TVs was essential to gain consumer loyalty?
4 Failing to evaluate in an essay. There is no such thing as a 'one-sided essay'. You should aim to consider at least two viewpoints or two approaches and then show judgement in discussing them. An example question might be:

Evaluate the factors that a mobile (cell) telephone manufacturer would consider before deciding on the price for a new mobile phone.

Knowledge: Costs of production, market conditions, market segment being aimed at, competitors' prices, marketing objective, strategy, e.g. skimming or penetration, price elasticity.
Application: Applying these – or at least three or four of them – to mobile telephones and the mobile telephone market.
Analysis: Using theory to explain the significance of these points, for example simple case of price elasticity or analysis of the concept of niche market.

Evaluation: Showing judgement in considering which might be the most important factors, for example if the mobile phone market is very competitive, then competitors' prices will need to be watched carefully or else consumers will not buy this new phone unless it has a genuine unique selling proposition.

Common errors in answering case study questions

1 As with the other types of question, failure to apply answers to the business referred to in a case-study question is a common weakness. All answers should contain a relevant observation about the business that students could not have known about before they read the case study. This does not mean just using the name of the business or the manager's name on every line of each answer.
2 In addition, it is important to realise that analysis and evaluation are even more important skills when responding to case study questions.
3 It is equally important to manage your time carefully in a case-study based examination paper and to allocate enough time to each question guided by the marks available.
4 With case study essay answers, the same points apply as with the essay comments above – especially the need to apply the answer to the case study business (or other businesses if asked for in the question) and the importance of evaluating fully throughout the answer and in the final conclusion.
5 Where there is a choice of questions make sure you select one and only answer that question. This is the only way to use the time effectively.

Step 5 – Final advice – during examination

1 Read the question paper very carefully. For data response and case study questions it is essential to read the business context carefully. You are advised to underline or highlight the information that you consider to be particularly important. Read the data/case study twice – once before reading the questions and again after looking at the questions to see how they are directed to the context material.
2 Where there is a choice of essay questions, you must make your choice carefully. A few minutes deciding definitely which questions you are going to tackle could save much wasted time.
3 Plan your answers to the longer questions in particular. A little forward planning can avoid irrelevant material and maximise your potential for success.
4 Timing is an essential ingredient of success. You should calculate how much time is available for each mark on the paper. For example, Cambridge Paper 2 is worth 60 marks and must be completed in 90 minutes. Allowing 20 minutes' reading and planning time, this leaves just over one minute per mark. So do not spend ten minutes on a question worth just five marks!
5 Layout and clarity are important. If your answer is illegible, you will gain no credit. If you do not lay out numerical solutions clearly, spacing out each stage and showing your workings, then marks may be lost, especially if, finally, you do not arrive at the correct answer. Remember, marks are awarded for calculations as well as correct solutions.

Good luck in your examinations – we hope that you obtain the results you deserve!

Index

599

Acknowledgements

The author and publishers acknowledge the following sources of copyright material and are grateful for the permissions granted. While every effort has been made, it has not always been possible to identify the sources of all the material used, or to trace all copyright holders. If any omissions are brought to our notice, we will be happy to include the appropriate acknowledgements on reprinting.

Text permissions

p 72 The Times, 15 May 2007; p 51 The Times, 11 January 2008; p 81 The Times, 9 April 2008; p 89 Source: Office for National Statistics licensed under the Open Government Licence v.2.0.; p 127 Entrepreneur Media, Inc; p 138 Manimala, M. J., & Wasdani, K. P. "Distributed Leadership at Google: Lessons From the Billion-Dollar Brand". Ivey Business Journal May/June 2013; p 146 Susan Heathfield, Management Consultant and writer at humanresources.about.com.; p 167 https://bdaily.co.uk/opinion/12-06-2013/starbucks-3-inspirational-ways-it-develops-its-staff/; p 225 Thaindian News; p 256 Labbrand, a leading China-originated global brand consultancy. http://www.labbrand.com/brand-source/branding-segment-pepsi-next-step; p 376 by Christina Rogers; p 379 By John W. Miller, Matt Day and Alex MacDonald; p 391 Process Improvement Japan; p 404 Robert Calleam; p 405 Robert Calleam; p 535 Siemens

Photography and illustration permissions

Cover Badahos/Shutterstock; p2 Caiaimage/Paul Bradbury; p 4tl © dbimages / Alamy; p 4tr © Image Source / Alamy; p 6tl pressureUA / Thinkstock; p 4b Monkey Business Images / Shutterstock; p 6tr istockphoto/Olivier Blondeau; p 6b MSRPhoto; p 12 Rex Features/David Fisher; p 13 © photomaniauk / Alamy; p 16t © Christine Osborne Pictures / Alamy; p 16c © SCPhotos / Alamy; p 16b © wendy connett / Alamy; p 24 © incamerastock / Alamy; p 25 Daj / Thinkstock; p 29 AFP/Getty Images; p 32 © dpa picture alliance archive / Alamy; p 40 Getty Images; p 47 © Jose Fuste Raga/Corbis; p 47 Still Pictures/© Ron Giling; p 49 © Randy Duchaine / Alamy; p 51 Tata; p 55 AFP/Getty Images; p 57 Shell Foundation; p 60 AFP/Getty Images; p 59 jui248 / Thinkstock; p 66 Siri Stafford / Thinkstock; p 78 Greg Pease / Getty; p 90 Sean Gallup / Thinkstock; p 124 © Tetra Images / Alamy; p 131bl © Ozimages / Alamy; p 131t Ryan McVay / Thinkstock; p 131br Fuse / Thinkstock; p 134 Still Pictures/© Ron Giling; p 140 Ford Motor Company; p 150l Purestock / Thinkstock; p 150r kpatyhka / Shutterstock; p 157 © Radius Images / Alamy; p 179 © imageBROKER / Alamy; p 181 © david pearson / Alamy; p 183 AFP/Getty Images; p 185 Padmayogini / Shutterstock; p 190 © [apply pictures] / Alamy; p 197 Still Pictures/Joerg Boethling; p210 aodaodaod / Thinkstock; p 212 © JLImages / Alamy; p 217 © Mark Boulton / Alamy; p 218 © Nick Turner / Alamy; p 222 © Dan Vincent / Alamy; p 227 © Iain Masterton / Alamy; p 252 Anantara.com; p 255 Bloomberg via Getty Images; p 259 Hulton Archive / Getty; p 273 Brian Balster / Thinkstock; p 279 JaysonPhotography / Thinkstock; p 279 trekandshoot / Thinkstock; p 279 © Alex Hinds / Alamy; p 279 Maria Dryfhout / Shutterstock; p 279 chrisdorney / Shutterstock; p 279 © Art Directors & TRIP / Alamy; p 280 Razvan / Thinkstock; p 282l © Art Directors & TRIP / Alamy; p 282r Tissot; p 285 Rex; p 291 © ZUMA Press, Inc. / Alamy; p 297 Cameron Spencer / Thinkstock; p 324 © Stuwdamdorp / Alamy; p 329 Matthew Lloyd / Thinkstock; p 330 digital vision / Thinkstock; p 333l istockphoto/Mario Hornik; p 333r Edward Rozzo/Fuse / Thinkstock; p 336 © craft images / Alamy; p 341l © Cyberstock / Alamy; p 341r Photodisc / Thinkstock; p 342 Pilkington Group Ltd; p 343 © Oleksiy Maksymenko / Alamy; p 344 © Michael Rosenfeld/Science Faction/Corbis; p 344 AFP/Getty Images; p 348 Bloomberg via Getty Images; p 352 © Xie Guang Hui/Redlink/Corbis; p 355 paul prescott / Shutterstock; p 359 © Franz Bishof/VISUM; p 373 digital vision / Thinkstock; p 379 © Aerial Archives / Alamy; p 384 © xPACIFICA/Corbis; p 386 Getty Images; p 395 Fuse / Thinkstock; p 405l Getty Images; p 405r Bloomberg via Getty Images; p415 XiXinXing / Thinkstock; p 416 © Reuters/CORBIS; p 420 © Eye Ubiquitous / Alamy; p 425 PA Photos/AP; p 436 © Radharc Images / Alamy; p 469 KrivosheevV /istock; p 475 Maria Teijeiro / Thinkstock; p 478 hxdyl / Thinkstock; p 479 AFP/Getty Images; p 486 © SIPHIWE SIBEKO/Reuters/Corbis; p 491 Bloomberg via Getty Images; p 502 Getty Images; p 509 Drimi / Shutterstock; p 514 © imageBROKER / Alamy; p 521 © Anthony Kay/Flight / Alamy; p 523 © Zhai Dong Feng / Redlink/Redlink/Corbis; p 534 everythingpossible / Thinkstock; p 543 AFP/Getty Images; p 574 U. Baumgarten via Getty Images; p 576 AFP/Getty Images; p 581 Bloomberg via Getty Images.